The Emergence of Modern Architecture

LIANE LEFAIVRE AND ALEXANDER TZONIS

The Emergence of Modern Architecture

A documentary history from 1000 to 1810

Routledge
Taylor & Francis Group

LONDON AND NEW YORK

Uses material from L. Lefaivre and A. Tzonis, *De Oonsprong van de moderne architectuu*, Niemegen, SUN, 1984 and 1990. The cover is based on a design concept by Leo de Bruin

First published 2004 by Routledge
11 New Fetter Lane, London EC4P 4EE

Simultaneously published in the USA and Canada
by Routledge
29 West 35th Street, New York, NY 10001

Routledge is an imprint of the Taylor & Francis Group

Typeset in Dante and News Gothic by Wearset Ltd, Boldon, Tyne and Wear
Printed and bound in Great Britain by TJ International Ltd, Padstow, Cornwall

British Library Cataloguing in Publication Data
A catalogue record for this book is available from the British Library

Library of Congress Cataloging in Publication Data
The emergence of modern architecture : a documentary history from 1000 to 1810 / edited by Liane Lefaivre and Alexander Tzonis. Includes introductory essay, short introductions, illustrations, bibliographies and index.
    p. cm.
Index compiled by Rebecca Casó Donadie
    1. Architecture–History. 2. Architecture–Sources. I. Lefaivre, Liane. II. Tzonis, Alexander.
    NA200 .E65 2003
    720′.9–dc21

2003001192

ISBN 0-415-26025-6 (pbk)
ISBN 0-415-26024-8 (hbk)

to Etienne de Cointet and Mary Otis Stevens

Contents

Contents

Contents

Illustration sources

Illustration sources

Illustration
sources

Preface

The idea of investigating the birth and evolution of modern design thinking out of the archaic began as a Freshman Seminar given by Alexander Tzonis at Harvard College in 1968. Within the freedom and inspiration of this uniquely privileged time and place, conceiving it as a multidisciplinary research, cutting across architectural history, design methodology, anthropology and economics came naturally. Soon the subject also became a course at the Graduate School of Design at Harvard University.

It was great luck that the opportunity to give lectures on this topic as a visitor in the Université de Montreal arose. It permitted Alexander Tzonis to come into contact with French culture and with similar studies carried out by scholars in France. It was during these lectures that Tzonis met with Liane Lefaivre, which marked the beginning of a long collaboration on this subject as well as on other topics in the theory and history of architecture. An invitation to teach in France followed by an award of a major research grant made it possible to deepen the studies in French architectural history, to continue collaborating with French specialists and to bring a number of American researchers into the project. For the last thirty years, many publications have followed from this initial inquiry in the form of articles and books, including a documentary history published in Dutch in 1984 and, second edition 1990, the predecessor of the present book. The research still continues today, not because very few findings were produced but, on the contrary, because each answer mined out of the material yielded even more questions.

If it had not been for the enthusiastic support of students, this work would have stopped by the end of the 1960s. They helped discover not only new answers but also new questions. Some of these students are now prominent academics, some moved onto other endeavours. Here follows a partial list. Margaret Ray spent a semester and a summer at the Bibliothèque Nationale in Paris doing research while an undergraduate at Harvard College. Brigit Williams spent a semester while a student at Harvard College. Other students from Harvard and the Université de Montréal who helped with the research were: Thor Anderson, Daniel Bluestone, Robert Berwick, Denis Bilodeau, Philippe Bourgois, Elinor Charlton, Claude Cohen, Susan Henderson, Kim Ik Jae, Réjean Legault, Naomi Lev, Molly Moran, Sergio Modigliani, Nancy Murdock, Edward Paul, José Salgado, Eve Siu and Jean-Marie Therrien.

We would like also to thank those colleagues who helped us with crucial exchanges at critical moments: James Ackerman, Eugenio Battisti, Anthony Blunt, Antonio Bonnet

Correa, Philippe Boudon, Etienne de Cointet, Joop Doorman, Luis Fernandez-Galiano, Bruno Fortier, Jacques Guillerme, David Herlihy, Wolfgang Herrman, Jacques Le Goff, Michael Müller, Werrner Oechslin, Richard Pommer, Juan Antonio Ramírez, Eduard Sekler, Cesare de Seta and Evon Vogt. Special thanks go to Angela Giral and Mark Jarzombek for their support.

Among the friends who also contributed in sustaining our research were Maurice Kilbridge, Serge Carreau, Jean-Pierre Halévy and Skiddy von Stade. We are also grateful to Giovanni Buzzi, Gavin Borden, Michael Levin, Peter Papademetriou, Mary Otis Stevens, Fritz Schroeder.

Special thanks go to Henk Hoeks, Mayke van Dieten, Leo de Bruyn of SUN, who saw the first, Dutch, editions through with incredible speed, care, efficiency and great graphic design. For the present work we are grateful for the dedicated help of Janneke Arkesteyn and Merel Miedema, along with Jorrit Sipkes, Rebecca Caso Donadei and Michael Woodford, all of the DKS Research Center, TUDelft.

The great libraries we were fortunate enough to be able to use were the Bibliothèque Nationale in Paris, and, especially, the Fogg, Houghton, Loeb, and Widener Libraries at Harvard University, the Avery Library at Columbia University, the Blackader Library at McGill University, the library at the architecture school at the Université de Montréal, and at TUDelft.

Thanks to James Ackerman for permission to use his translation of the *Annals of the Cathedral of Milan* and Ian White for his translation of the *Hypnerotomachia*. All other translations are by Liane Lefaivre or Eurotexte, except for Rudolf Wittkower's translation of Francesco Zorzi, John Spencer's of Alberti's *On Painting*, Patricia Waddy's of Michelangelo the Younger, part of Indra McKewen's of Perrault's *Ordonnance*, Hart and Hicks of Serlio, David Brittle of Camus de Mézières and Wolfgang Herrman of Laugier's *Essai.* The authors would like to thank The Getty Publications, Dover Publications Inc. and Yale University Press for permission to use the translations of Perrault, Le Camus de Mezieres and Galileo under their imprint.

The Graham Foundation provided for the most generous support of this publication.

Our editor, Caroline Mallinder, gave us exceptional support. Rarely does one find intellectual, moral and practical support joined so felicitously. Our debt to her is invaluable. To Helen Ibbotson we are also grateful for her good nature, matched only by her thoroughness.

The Structure of Change

Co-Revolutions, Roots and Emergence of Modern Architecture

by Alexander Tzonis

How did Modern architecture come about as a way of thinking? What was new about it? From where did the desires, beliefs, methods and building types that make up a new conceptual system to guide design originate? And what exactly was the nature of this revolution? These are questions about history. But, based on the experience that the way humans view reality and act upon it at a given moment is constrained by the way they construed and constructed it in the past, these questions are also about the present and the future. Thus, studying the revolution that brought about Modern architecture relates to our appetite of knowledge about events that occurred between the beginning of the second millennium and the end of the *ancien régime*, but it also relates to worries and aspirations about the quality, physical and social, of our contemporary buildings, cities and landscapes.

The first idea was to call this book *The Roots of Modern Architecture*. The title *The Emergence of Modern Architecture* came after. The shift was not casual or arbitrary. The choice had to do with characterising the nature of change of mind, the structure of the conceptual revolution we have been studying. 'Roots' and 'emergence' have many things in common. They both entail a passage. They both imply direction, movement and possibly progress. But there are also significant differences. 'Roots' call to mind a well-articulated object that can be depicted in terms of its shape and structure. 'Emergence' suggests a dynamic process hard to describe in such static terms. The historical change that this book covers was not an unbroken, incrementally growing trunk of well-articulated events. It was a complex process of parallel, interacting events with ruptures, stopgaps, reversals and leaps. 'Emergence' was more appropriate to characterise it.

On the other hand, when one looks at this perplexing process from the vantage point of the beginning of the twentieth-first century, it appears to have continuity and order. It is a cognitive 'co-revolution', a mesh of parallel revolutionary interdependent changes occurring in many places at the same time: courts, monasteries, palaces, villas, academies and workshops. It is the story of a movement that swapped, in a period of eight centuries, an archaic design mentality based on myth and ritual with today's dynamic frame of mind. Marked with contradictions, Modern architecture emerges as multiplicity of a highly differentiated way of conceiving projects making use of rigorous science but also freewheeling fantasy, driven by desire for efficiency as well as for luxury and

[1]

aesthetic delight, for adventure of experiences and for critical reflection, for global universality and for regionalist identity, for totalitarian power and for emancipation of the
deprived and the oppressed.

The 'co-revolution' that brought Modern architecture created a new approach to
designing buildings, landscapes and cities that employed scientific knowledge but also
individualistic fantasies that were driven by a desire for efficiency as well as for aesthetic
delight, for adventure and for critical reflection, for global universality and for regionalist
identity, for totalitarian control and for the emancipation of the deprived and the
oppressed. Most of these beliefs and desires, central to Modern architecture today,
would have appeared strange to people a thousand years ago. Similarly, Adelhard's
praise of the Abbey of Saint-Trond (1057) because it was shaped 'after the image of the
human body', around the end of the first millennium, is alien to Modern architectural
thinking today. On the other hand, Petrarch's 'single motive . . . to see from a great ele-

vation' (1342) the view of the landscape, while familiar in architecture by the end of the
eighteenth century and common today, was unusual in the architecture of the middle of
the fourteenth century. When and how were pre-modern or *archaic* approaches to architecture abandoned, transformed and replaced by those of Modern architecture? When
did this conceptual shift begin? What kind of material should we delve into to find
answers for these questions?

Historiography of the beginnings of Modern architecture

During the second half of the twentieth century, it was common practice to locate the
'sources' of Modern architecture at the end of the Victorian times. Historians such as
Siegfried Giedion and Nicolaus Pevsner came to this conclusion subscribing to a combination of 'vulgar materialist' and 'naïve idealist' views of history. According to this view,
Modern architecture was the outcome of mechanistic 'means of mass production' and
the '*weltanschauung*' associated with industrial technology. It was also the outcome of a
methodological bias in doing history, focusing on the form and materials of buildings and
paying lip service to the processes that generated them. They interpreted buildings, to
quote the great French historian and theoretician of history Marc Bloch, like those
German soldiers in 1914 who 'envisioned . . . as so many loopholes prepared for snipers
. . . the innocent contrivances of the masons . . . on the fronts of a great many Belgian
houses . . .' which were only 'designed to help the plasterers in setting up their scaffolding' (1953). A consequence of this bias was a speculative, limited and anachronistic
understanding of what preceded Modern architecture and how this earlier development
related to Modern architecture.

Most of the historians who wrote about the origins of Modern architecture with such
a technophile bias were very closely associated to architectural practice before the
Second World War and immediately after it. Their views were influenced to a high
degree by professional tendencies and interests. But there was also a smaller number of
historians that were independent of such associations who took a different course in
investigating the origins of Modern architecture. It is no surprise that they arrived at different conclusions. Departing from the premise that Modern architecture was identified
by the meaning of its buildings and not just their form and materials, they searched to
find this meaning in written documents of the times revealing what the architects, clients
and other contemporaries thought in conceiving these buildings. Turning their attention

from the products to the process of design, they located the origins of Modern architecture earlier. As Lewis Mumford (1934) observed, 'before the new industrial processes could take hold on a great scale, a reorientation of wishes, habits, ideas, and goals was necessary'. In other words, the software had to be changed in advance of the changes in the hardware to produce the new environment.

Emil Kaufmann, a Viennese born art historian of the generation of the 1920s followed the approach of his senior colleague Julius Schlosser Magnino (1856, 1924, 1979) and belonged to the 'Quellen' school of art history that employed textual or source-bound documents to interpret products of the past. The Quellen school was not unique in this approach. It was part of a broader movement that included historians as diverse as Aby Warburg, Erwin Panofsky, Jacques Maritain, Rudolf Wittkower and most of the members of the Warburg Institute. Despite their numerous differences, all of these historians shared a common dislike for impressionistic, anachronistic, and formalistic history and a common conviction that authentic meaning could be found in contemporary literary sources. In this way Kaufmann researched the writings of architects of the period of the enlightenment. In two studies referring explicitly to a modern architect and to radical change, the first in 1933, *Von Ledoux bis Le Corbusier*, and the second in 1952, *Three Revolutionary Architects: Boullée, Ledoux, and Lequeu*, he clearly showed that behind the much criticised 'sterile' classical architecture of the eighteenth century buildings, the written documents revealed that a significant number of architects held ideas very close to those of the twentieth century. Kaufmann's conclusion was that there was a 'unity of the period 1750–1950' that 'allows us to treat it as a single architectural age'.

The work of Peter Collins was similar in method and results. But in contrast to Kaufmann, who was a highly trained professional historian, Collins was an autodidact with a degree in architecture and a PhD in law. He was openly critical of linking historical research with professional interests of the time. Inspired by writings of the nineteenth-century theoretician and journalist of architecture César Daly, Collins proposed 'a philosophical history'. He was concerned with 'ideals', 'philosophical and ethical' issues that played a real role in the conception of buildings. To discover these 'ideals' Collins, not unlike Kaufmann, searched inside theoretical texts of the past and came to a conclusion, very close to Kaufmann's, that there was a continuity of architectural ideals starting in the middle of the eighteenth century up until the 1950s; that the years between these two dates should be considered as one period; and that the beginnings of Modern architecture go back to the middle of the eighteenth century.

Conceptual systems and the cognitive history of architecture

The path of the history of ideas that Kaufmann and Collins followed in investigating the origins of Modern architecture was without doubt very fruitful. However, it was not without limitations. They discovered plenty of evidence in support of their conjecture that twentieth-century Modern architecture ideas and ideals went back to the middle of the eighteenth century. But they also claimed that, prior to this time, to quote Collins, ideas and ideals 'differ . . . quite markedly from what they were before'. But this was never established. This is because to draw a rigorous conclusion about changes of mind, one has to look at the mental leaps as well as the bridges, the landmarks that characterise the skyline of ideas of an epoch but also the foundations. In addition, investigations should not be restricted to theoretical texts only, assuming that the predominant theories of a period can be found exclusively in the theoretical discussions. 'Theory', in the sense of the web of desires and beliefs, principles and categories that make architectural thinking possible, as well as communication and ultimately practice, is present everywhere. Every architectural choice and every intentional design action is loaded with this basic theory. To reconstruct therefore this shifting conceptual system, a cognitive history has to look at a wider and more diverse spectrum of records that manifest how people tried to construe and construct the world anew.

Accordingly, one has to examine not only architectural treatises, handbooks and textbooks, where theoretical statements are explicit, but also documents where desires and beliefs operate implicitly. One has to research letters, articles from the press of the times, scientific memoirs, maxims, poems, plays and novels where a wider spectrum of people – who can be patrons, politicians, artists, poets, scientists, priests, philosophers or journalists – dispute, explain, narrate, envision, or try to persuade, to identify not only continuities but also gaps. Backtracking and using such a wide spectrum of material, one discovers that the Modern Architecture Revolution coincides with the Scientific and Commercial Revolutions and has its beginnings somewhere 'around the year 1000'.

The year 1000

The 'year 1000' is a convenient label with signpost characteristics – a date easy to remember giving a dramatic echo to the date of the beginning of our era. In reality the beginnings of the process we are discussing take place during a period of time extending, approximately, over a century. It is a kind of ridge zone rather than thin line of history that divides, to quote Petrarch, the epoch of *tenebrae* from the epoch of the *nova*. Looking back from that dividing ridge there is a long stretch of 'dark' Middle Ages extending roughly 600 years up to the border of another epoch that again Petrarch called '*antiqua*'. During this dark stretch of time, the institutional and cultural constructs set up by the Hellenistic kingdoms, the Roman Republic and the Roman Empire continued – in the words of Edward Gibbon – to 'decline and fall' in Western Europe. The city of Rome, the heart of the empire, sacked and plundered by 'barbarians' repeatedly, became a 'wretched' city of ruins and memories (Fig. 1). Lands that were previously productive were turned into marshes and wasteland. Slave resources were depleted, reducing productivity. Stocks of coins drained away and gold coinage was abandoned, starving commercial exchanges. The schism between a Hellenised East and a Latinised West, the result in part of the invasion of the 'northern barbarians', was widened by the Mohammedan incursion. The Arabs disrupted the unity of 'mare nostrum'. Among the consequences was the termination of the trading of Nile papyrus with disastrous effects on communication and exchange of knowledge. The whole terrain of Western Europe was fragmented into self-sufficient homesteads, castles, abbeys, villae and manors (Fig. 2). Within these units and between them social mobility and circulation of knowledge came to a standstill. Building construction activity was minimal and undistinguished by volume, quantity or quality of craftsmanship. In fact, as much as it is appropriate to characterise this period as 'dark' because of lack of knowledge, goods and money, it is equally fit to call it 'frozen' because of the deficiency of movement, mechanisms of exchange and networks of interaction.

It is no surprise, then, that around the year 1000, with such unpromising conditions worsened by the periodic return of famines – in 970, in 1000, in 1033 and in 1040 –

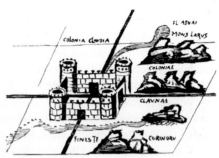

1. Anonymous. *Liber Historiarum Romanorum*. Twelfth century. Plan of Rome shaped as a lion.

2. Huginus Gromaticus. *Corpus Agrimensorum Romanum*. Castle built at the intersection of Roman roads.

there is a widespread conviction that 'the ruins multiply' and that the 'end of the world' is nigh: *'mundi terminum ruinis crescentibus'* (Focillon, 1969).

However, it appears that not all people in Western Europe shared the conviction that the 'end of a history' was around the corner and some not only expected an alternative future but also worked towards it. Thus, on Pentecost Sunday of the year 1000, the young Emperor of the north, Otto III, succeeded in being crowned in Rome. Whatever the precise motivations of this rather pathetic event, in the context of the harsh realities of the times and the powerlessness of Otto, more than a 'nostalgia' for the past *'imperium mundi'*, it was an act of faith in a world to come. In his documentary sketch of the year 1000, Georges Duby (1980) cites the Benedictine chronicler Raoul Glaber recording that in the third year after the celebration of the millennium, 'almost all over the earth', people 'renovated their basilicas and churches'. It was as if the whole world 'divested their clothes to put on the white robe of the church'. The 'white robe' referred to the brighter surface of the walls of the churches that were scrubbed, mended or built anew. In addition, it was, as Duby remarked, Glaber's 'admirable metaphor' to suggest that an ideological and institutional renovation was nascent at this moment.

The consciousness that there had been a Middle Ages was expressed by Giorgio Vasari (1550) the first Modern historian of art and architecture, himself part of the emergence of the new times, in his *Le Vite de' più eccellenti Architetti, Pittori, et Scultori* (*Lives of the Painters, Sculptors and Architects*). Vasari observed that during this period, 'the arts declined by the day to the point that they lost entirely design perfection' and 'only formless and inept things' were produced and only buildings of 'rude', 'inferior', 'sad design' quality and 'devoid of arrangement' were erected as opposed to the present.

The conceptual framework of archaic architecture

It can easily be seen how far architectural thinking of 'dark' Middle Ages is from that of Modern architecture in particular from the architecture discussed in Richard Krautheimer's classic essay, *'Introduction to an "Iconography of Mediaeval Architecture"'* (1942–1943). Krautheimer discusses a large number of documents that demonstrate that the conception of ecclesiastical architecture during the medieval period was dominated by the objective to resemble the configuration of the Anastasis or Holy Sepulchrum in Jerusalem. Securing the fidelity of such architectural reproduction was so important that trustworthy informers were sent to inspect *in situ* the prototype and bring back data to assist its faithful replication. Surprisingly, despite expense and effort, the various buildings that were replicas of the same prototype did not resemble each other; neither did they resemble the prototype. Certainly, one can blame medieval architects of having a very low sense of 'exactness' in making copies of an original building or of being geometrically 'illiterate'. Yet, there is another explanation that does not pass judgement on medieval people. It is possible that the architects of the Dark Ages were not inferior in intelligence or ignorant, but that they simply used a different set of spatial categories to identify similarity and design. While Renaissance or Modern architects would have used shape and size to make a building resemble a prototype, medieval architects applied

number, topology and orientation. This is supported by the fact that even educated people like Gregory of Nissen appeared to pay little attention to Euclidean terminology, calling an octagon a 'circle' or 'a circle with eight corners'. Thus informers, responding to requests from clients or architects, brought data back from Jerusalem related to ciphers and contiguity and not to contour and dimensions. Most medieval people, architects and clients included, shared a common conceptual system that guided their behaviour. They had reasons to design '*ad similitudinem*' that were neither technological nor aesthetic. Their reasoning appears to have related to contemporary desires and beliefs. They were grounding their beliefs with reference to some normative authority and they did not employ scientific, empirical methods. They thought artefacts ought to obey the norm of harmony whereby all objects of the universe, natural or human made, the astral macro-cosm, the human body microcosm, prototypical buildings like the Holy Sepulchre and the Temple of Salomon in Jerusalem – as imagined in ways far removed from Mai-monides' studies (Herrman, 1967) (Fig. 3a, b) – were in correspondence with each other and obeyed the Divine Model. In other words, their thinking was theocratic or archaic (Tzonis, 1972).

The same conceptual system was employed in Byzantium. The Justinian (527–565) text about St Sophia, the Cathedral of Edessa (modern Urfa in Turkey), talks about the architects Asaph and Addain and their client, the bishop Amidonius, using the taber-nacle 'that Bezaleel erected instructed by Moses' as their 'model' for the 'glorious' square Temple covered with a windowless dome, which 'in its smallness should resemble the great world'. 'Its ceiling like the heavens because it was stretched without columns'. Its four 'splendid arches' 'represented the four sides of the world', its marble details in their perfection like the divine universe appearing not to have been made by human hand, '*acheiropoietos*'. Here we have the theory of designing in analogy to divine prototype structures grounded on the Bible, combined with the analogy between microcosm and macrocosm. As the Oriental, Byzantine narrator made clear, this analogy was 'not in size, but in type'. And as in the Western texts referred to above, it was expressed reduc-tively through the use of abstract attributes such as normative numbers, proportion, and geometric shapes.

As one can see in the treatises of Francesco di Giorgio (1474–1482) and Filarete (1451–1464) elements of the conceptual framework of theocratic archaic design such as astrology, numerology, anthropomorphism, the analogy between macrocosm and micro-cosm can be found surviving within the period of change covered here. Some continued to

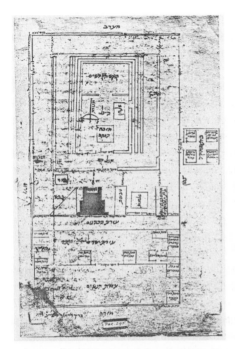

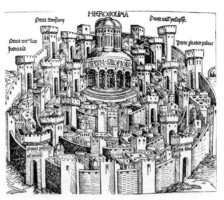

3b. Wilhelm Pleydentwurff. *Liber Chronacorum*. Woodcut by Wilhelm Pleydenwurff of an imaginary view of Jerusalem with the Temple of Salomon.

3a. Maimonides. *Commentary of Middoth.* Late twelfth century. The plan of the Temple of Herod. Sanctuary with cult implements, courtyard and altar. The manuscript containing several drawings probably by the hand of Maimonides. It was obtained in Aleppo from decendents of Maimonides by the antiquarian Edward Pococke.

exist intact, as in the Annals of the Milan Cathedral (1400, 1401) (Ackerman, 1949) in Cesariano (1521) or in Francesco Giorgi (1535). But in other cases, being present in a text, for example in Alberti (1440–1472, 1485) or Palladio (1570), does not necessarily mean, as Wittkower assumed in *Architecture in the Age of Humanism*, that the role they play is the same as in archaic design. The presence of elements of archaic origin do not demonstrate the robustness of archaic methods of thinking, the absence of a real division between 'Renaissance' from the 'Middle Ages', and do not manifest 'continuity' and 'variation' at the expense of change in the history of culture. Neither was the 'Antirinascimento' to borrow from Eugenio Battisti (1962), inside the Renaissance the result of the resistance to the new or of temporal reversals that existed at the time of the counter-reformation. The presence of archaic elements of design thinking was, most of the time, the result of their recruitment, reinterpretation, recombination and reuse as foundations or building blocks within a new conceptual structure and in response to new problems. And this is, to a great extent, the case of the appearance of preferred proportions and geometrical figures in Alberti, da Vinci and Palladio. The search for the discovery of the perfect proportions still plays a most important role as late as the second part of the seventeenth century as one can see in the debates related to the Académie d'Architecture in France and the writings of François Blondel, 'royal professor' of 'mathematics and architecture' and the first head of the Académie of Architecture in Paris. What occurred in this case was what Fritz Saxl observed about Renaissance astrology, that it 'enabled mankind to overcome the . . . heritage of demonology and fatalism'. In a kind of historical paradox, if not cruel irony, they play the role of preconditions contributing to new, previously unintended, tasks.

Vasari, who did not find relevance in the values of 'congruentia' or 'concordia', thought that the path of the Dark Ages was 'steadily going from bad to worse . . . until the point the lowest depths of baseness were reached . . . at around the year 1000', when a process of 'general improvement in the arts begun'. He does suggest that 'architecture started to improve slightly' earlier with Charlemagne's 'small but beautiful' St Apostolo in Florence. Improvements continue steadily but slowly, leading to the middle of the thirteenth century when 'some rising spirits . . . purged themselves of that crude style' of the Dark Ages.

Luxury

What were the conditions that contributed to the shift that marks the beginning of what Vasari called 'improvements'? What were the changes in modern thinking?

Was it the introduction of the stirrup, the horseshoe, the plough and the water-mill? To a great extent the very bad conditions of the dark Middle Ages in Western Europe, much worse than those in Byzantium, were important preconditions for this transformation in architectural thinking. They contributed to the development of a new value system, in a paradoxical way. The scarcity of slaves and the high cost of a workforce brought about a unique appreciation of labour and the discovery of the idea of efficiency, an unprecedented lust for energy sources, a 'power-consciousness (Fig. 10a, b) to the point of fantasy' (White, 1962) and a search for labour-saving devices, mechanical or organisational. This, in turn, boosted the belief in science as a means for achieving technological innovation. These conditions, together with the decentralised structure of Western Europe, were conducive to the rise of the guilds and corporations that will play a most significant role in the revolution of building. It also elevated the appreciation of trade, which was regarded as a low occupation in Rome (White, 1962, Lopez, 1976), and of communications. In the end, these new developments enhanced productivity, increased protein input in the diet, which probably made people more energetic, physically and mentally, and generated surplus. In architecture, they led to a new attitude towards artefacts and buildings seen as objects of pleasure, to be consumed and possessed. Thus, Abbot Suger (1144, 1144–1149) measured the gold and the precious gems built into his cathedral. He accompanied these statements with the declaration that he was 'transferring what is material to that which is immaterial'. In this 'anagogical way' the archaic divine model was compromised but not disposed. Three centuries later, however, Filarete (1451–1464) declared categorically that 'building is a wholly voluptuous pleasure', and, to quote Frederick Hart (1958), Gonzaga developed a mania 'to collect buildings' as others collected jewellery or paintings.

Byzantine documents show that during the time of 'decline and fall' of the West, Byzantium possessed, in addition to higher standards of theoretical architectural knowledge and building technology, an attitude towards buildings dominated by sensual pleasure, luxury and a fascination with spatial effects that is hard to pigeonhole as belonging to the archaic theocratic conceptual system. Characteristic is the description of St Sophia of Constantinople by Procopius: its 'enormous spherical dome . . . [as if] suspended from

4. Hartmann Schedell. *Nuremberg Chronicle*. 1493. View of Constantinople with St Sophia.

heaven by a golden chain' has such an impact on the spectator that he cannot 'rest his gaze', his 'vision constantly shifting around'. Equally representative is the hymn by Paulus Silentiarius on St Sophia, who describes the glow of the gold of the top of its columns 'brilliant . . . like the high peaks which . . . the sun strikes with its arrows' and its marble base 'like a white cloud' and of its Ambo like a 'wave-washed' 'island rising in the middle of the . . . sea'. Many references to these descriptions may be interpreted as corresponding in a subtle way to divine cosmological ideas. On the other hand, it is very hard to reject the idea that the core of the text is not a celebration of the hedonistic impact and the aesthetic wonder – a sublime sense of hovering, floating and flight – aroused by the building's materials, colours, light and iconological metaphors.

These texts were probably not read in the West; still, as Cyril Mango has remarked (1986), the image of the St Sofia 'grew to legendary proportions . . . across the Middle Ages, well beyond the confines of the Byzantine Empire' (Fig. 4). It was carried over by merchants, diplomats, and returning crusaders, and it contributed to the construction of a new architecture. It becomes, next to the Temple of Salomon or the Holy Sepulchrum, a prototype. However, this time, the intention in using precedent monuments as a prototype is not to practice *'commensuratam congruentiam'* architecture, to bring about cosmic harmony. As can be seen in the texts by Leo of Naples (tenth century), Baudri (*c.*1110), Albrecht (*c.*1270) and later by Alberti (1440–1472) or Colonna (1467), it is supportive of the movement towards a culture of luxury, a new artificial environment: sensual, hedonistic and aesthetic. Colonna's book has a special place among these writings (Lefaivre, 1977). Partly a novel, partly a collection of antiquarian facts and partly a set of design instructions, it assumed a role similar to the Hollywood movies immediately after the Second World War, documenting as well as promoting a new world view and a new 'ancient–modern' lifestyle.

Anti-luxury

The Church appears split about this new phenomenon. On one hand it enthusiastically embraces it – to the degree of claiming its singular design expression – with the justification that the worth embodied in the materials, the craftsmanship and the design had a symbolic, *per analogiam* significance. On the other hand, it is polemically opposed to it, as this is expressed in reoccurrences of iconoclastic and ascetic pronouncements – of the same type that had already appeared in the East – and especially in the Cistercian critique of precious materials, gold, gems, textiles and architecture as the passionate text of Bernard of Clairveaux (1125) manifests. The dichotomy will continue up to the seventeenth century. To the grandiose spectacles of Bernini, one can juxtapose the stern text of Fénelon (1699). Fénelon's text is a precursor of the eighteenth-century anti-luxury but also anti-ornament critique of 'rigorism' that I will refer to later. Interestingly, the critique was not initiated by the architects. It was the work of amateurs of architecture who were mostly priests such as Lòdoli, de Cordemoy (1706, 1710) and Laugier (1753). Their anti-luxury arguments, however, were moralistic and secular and did not make any references to religion.

Libraries and voyagers

A significant factor contributing to the innovative developments in architectural thinking around the year 1000 was the availability of Greek and Roman writings. Some of these texts supplied factual information, some would be reused as building blocks for totally different kinds of intellectual edifices from the one intended by their original authors, and some would simply serve as desire stimulants for action. Despite the closed, 'frozen' and 'dark' character of the period before the end of the first millennium, and the serious rupture of the traffic between East and West that Mohammedans created, as the great medieval historian Henri Pirenne (1925) claimed, some commercial and cultural links across the Mediterranean remained unbroken (Dennett, 1948). Goods and information from the East reached the West, thanks to the Jews who took over the trade from the Christians. Goods and, most importantly, information continued to flow modestly not only from Byzantium and Islam but also from India and China. In addition to the migration and immigration of Christian scholars and artists from the East to the West, Arabs and Jews saved, translated and transported manuscripts. Aristotle's *Poetics*, translated in the ninth century by the Syrian Ishaq ibn Husain and retranslated into Arabic in the tenth century, found its way to Western Europe and was translated into Latin by Averroes in the thirteenth century. The same Arab as well as Jewish sources made some of the work of Plato and the Platonists available to the West. Plato's *Timaeus*, a most important text for the development of a theory of Modern architecture – and not Neoplatonic texts, as Klibansky has stressed – was studied in Western Europe even during the Carolingian period. Hero of Alexandria's manuscript, which was very significant for the development of architectural engineering, as well as copies of Pliny's *Natural History*, which contained more practical information about architecture, were available. Certainly, the most important text was *De Architectura* by Vitruvius. Seventy-eight manuscripts were in existence in medieval centres such as the libraries of Reichenau, Murbach, Melk, Cluny and the celebrated St Gallen (Fig. 5) (Krinsky, 1967). The discovery by Poggio Bracciolini and Cencio Rustici of a copy of a Vitruvius manuscript in this library, about 1416, has been considered as one of the most significant events marking the new beginnings of the Renaissance. Many of these manuscripts were in the hands of important thinkers. Hugo of St Victor (late 1120s) made use of Vitruvius, as did Isidore, Archbishop of Seville in his Summa *Etymologiae*, in Book fifteen, *On Buildings and Lands*, and in Book eighteen, *On Wars and Games*. Petrarch made annotations on the manuscript he owned, as did Boccaccio.

In his Introduction to the Second Part of his *Vitae*, Vasari emphasises that he was not only interested in the products of artists but also in their 'methods, manners, processes, behaviour, and ideas' and that he was 'investigating . . . the roots of things', the causes of decline or rise of an era. And although, like most of the humanists, he often refers to miracles and ingenuity and describes Brunelleschi – whom he considered a major figure in the 'progress of the renaissance' – as a 'divine spirit', 'given by heaven' – he is a true believer in the effectiveness of education. Thus, he presents the barbarians as ignorant and the ancients as learned. For learning, the best vehicle has been writings, because writings, Vasari comments in his text on Alberti, 'enjoy the greatest power and vitality . . . and easily penetrate everywhere and inspire confidence'. His *Vitae*, a collection of biographies, was a book for teaching, 'to be of service to the artists of [his] own age'. As a kind of 'textbook', it was like Plutarch's *Parallel Lives*. It taught mostly a way of life – an artist's life – by individual example and not by the general rules of art.

Search for rules in the authority of antiquity

Such rules were to be found in a different type of writing, the treatise, which Vasari obviously thought were not enough to make the case for the change that was occurring in his time.

Search for rules
and the authority
of antiquity

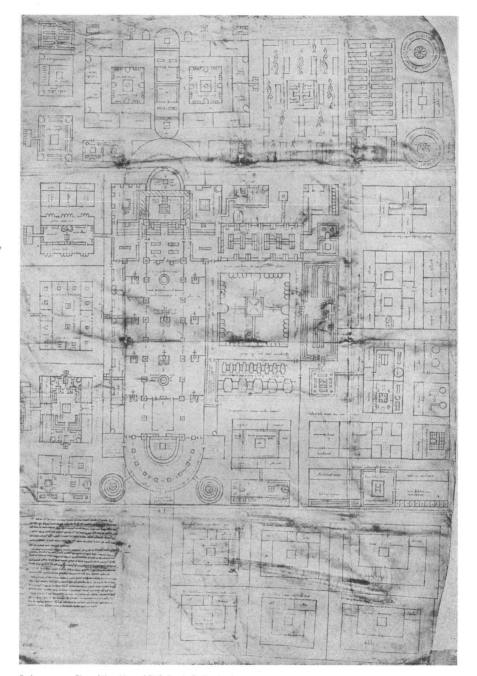

5. Anonymous. Plan of the abbey of St Gallen in Switzerland.

Medieval treatises, such as Hugo of St Victor (late 1120s) and Isidore of Seville, as mentioned earlier, included partial references to architecture and only as one of their numerous topics. By contrast, the text of Vitruvius, in its formidable encyclopaedic content and organisation, appeared to be a treasurehouse and a mine containing everything one needed to design buildings. Up to the eighteenth century, many of the writings on architecture appear to be simply commentaries, positive or negative, on Vitruvius. The attachment to Vitruvius resulted from its abundance of useful information clearly superior to anything available at the time. This was the case with most areas of inquiry of the Renaissance. Thus, Petrarch collected antiquity manuscripts. As did Poggio Bracciolini (1380–1459) who travelled to France, Germany and England in pursuit of them. The chancellor of Florence, Coluccio Salutati (1331–1406), invited the Byzantine scholar and diplomat Chrysoloras to Florence in 1396; a later chancellor, Leonardo Bruni (c.1370–1444), translated Aristotle's *Ethics* and *Politics* and six dialogues of Plato into Latin. Flavio Biondo (Flavius Blondus; 1392–1463) and later Pomponius Laetus (1428–1497) began to study the ancient monuments of Italy and, at the same time, collect coins, inscriptions and works of art. One should not forget that the vision of the revolution since the beginning of the new millennium was very much seen as a literal revolution, a turning around, a process in the circuit of time, the coming back of a past period of achievement (Fig. 9).

Thus, rescuing knowledge from the ruins of antiquity was advancing the solution of current problems and enhancing innovation. On the other hand, it was perpetuating a key 'habit of thought', a component of the archaic conceptual system, dependence on the authority of the text and disregard for empirical observation. In this context, the Vitruvian text played a dual role: conformist, especially as it appeared to be in agreement with a number of other authors of antiquity as well as with the religious doctrines – and innovative.

The making of the classical canon

The illustrated pages by Villard de Honnecourt, containing notes on almost every subject related to architecture, from how to measure buildings in a site to machines and plans of cathedrals, suggest that there were attempts during the Middle Ages to produce a treatise entirely devoted to architecture. (Fig. 10a, b, Fig. 11a, b). However, it was Alberti (1440–1472 composed; 1485 published) who first, since antiquity, undertook the writing of a complete treatise. He stated that he had identified as sources of knowledge of architectural rules 'all the most . . . useful observations left to us' in several writings by the ancients. But he also stated that he included his own 'observations' of the surviving buildings of antiquity, which, together with the ancient texts, ought to be considered as a source. That antique buildings can be a guide for the design of future ones had already been demonstrated by Brunelleschi a generation earlier through his legendary study sojourn to Rome (Fig. 6). There, he is supposed to have studied in depth the precedent of the Pantheon and, through that, achieve the unprecedented feat of the dome of Florence (Fig. 8). In Rome, the idea of 'renovation' had already been put into architectural practice (Fig. 7) much earlier, motivated apparently by politics rather than thinking about architectural problems (Heckscher, 1937–1938). Other authors of treatises that followed Alberti, Filarete (1451–1464), di Giorgio (1474–1482), Cesariano (1521) – and one might add here Colonna's strange hybrid book (1467, 1499), whose author might be Alberti himself – appear to have tried a similar compromise. They struggled to devise rules that balanced respect for the authority of the texts and for the active absorption of data from actual buildings.

The immediate educational impact of the writings we have already mentioned was

6. Pietro Bertelli. *Theatrum Urbium Italicarum*. 1599. Reconstruction of ancient Rome, the ancient monuments standing out within the city fabric.

7. Anonymous drawing. Roman house of the Crescenzi family. Seventeenth century. Illustration showing the curious colonnade erected in 1143, in imitation of Roman architecture, combined with antique friezes. An inscription pronounces that: 'the owner of this house, Nicolaus (probably a revolutionary member of the local autonomist party) 'built it out of vain love of glory but also with the aim to incite a campaign for the regeneration of the city (*Romae veterem renovarem decorem*). The campaign did not succeed but the building is a first precedent of the use of architecture to satisfy regionalist aspirations for emancipation.

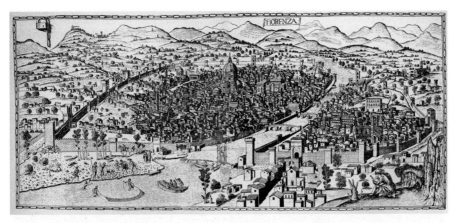

8. Florence. End of the fifteenth century, print. View of the city dominated by Brunellesci's dome of the cathedral of Santa Maria del Fiore, a project that transformed equally architectural formal vocabulary, technology and practice.

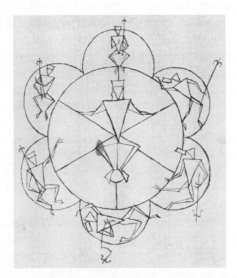

9. Villard de Honnecourt. *Sketchbook*. 1225–1250. The wheel of fortune. Allegory of the decline, fall and reawakening of cultures.

modest. Filarete's and di Giorgio's remained manuscripts; Cesariano's and Colonna's, although printed and illustrated, because of the obscure and bizarre language style were not easy reading. The first book that succeeded in instructing and influencing on a large scale was Serlio's (1537–1575). Serlio's was the first original architectural treatise written in a modern language to be published. Like Vesalius, in the field of medicine, he is the first to exploit the didactic possibilities that the new techniques of representation of objects were offering and the first to recognise the significance of illustrations in explaining the three-dimensional organisation, structure and details of buildings (Fig. 35, Fig. 36, Fig. 37, Fig. 38). Together with Dürer – who in a characteristic drawing, makes fun of the bulk fabrication of books, likening it to the mass production of loaves of bread – is the first to understand the technical potentials of the printing medium and occupies in history the place of the first illustrator of the canonical five kinds, or orders, of classical architecture. His theoretical approach in identifying general rules of architecture was less modern, or, to be fairer, more involved in identifying specific problems of his time, as we will see in the next sections.

A generation later, Palladio (1570), in the introduction of his *Quattro Libri* stressed the importance of empirical observation – even outside of Italy – to observe, draw and measure real buildings of antiquity rather than conform with Vitruvius's text. His follower, Scamozzi, stated even more explicitly his preference for deriving the rules of architecture from empirical observations of existing buildings rather than from authors. In France, a newcomer to the debate by the middle of the seventeenth century, Fréart de Chambray (1650), critical of Serlio's lack of independence from Vitruvius's authority and following the example of Palladio and Scamozzi, openly confronted and contradicted the rules drawn from the text of Vitruvius. His book documenting Roman works demanded a return to the 'source of the Orders': the original buildings which he called epigrammatically 'the best book available on the subject'.

It may be difficult for the reader of this book today to understand how the dispute about such a major problem, the rules of architecture, focused on such as limited aspect, proportions, and how proportions became such a central paradigmatic issue around which decisive epistemological battles were fought. In the context of the Western European archaic conceptual system of architecture, and the transition period of the sixteenth and seventeenth centuries, though, proportions, despite their narrow area of application, played a central role. Originally an Aristotelian belief, interwoven with other Hellenistic and Jewish ideas, they were thought to constitute, together with geometry, the 'form' of any body distinct from 'matter', that is material or metric, and were embraced by the scholastic philosophers in their 'Scientia'. As part of Scientia they were incorporated in the archaic conceptual system of architecture inside which, together with geometry, were considered comprising the 'form' of a building. One can see this illustrated in the Annals of the Cathedral of Milan (1400, 1401), the concise text by Francesco Giorgi (1535) and later in the apologetic writings of Philibert De l'Orme (1561, 1567–1648) where, together with a family of regular geometrical shapes, proportions occupy the position of constituent elements of the Divine Model linking the astral macrocosm, the human body microcosm and the human products, buildings, artefacts and even music. Of course, as the luxury revolution advanced, they lost their magical cosmological significance and assumed a sensual, hedonistic value. This is clear in Alberti's Treatise, which explains the reason that certain proportions are 'pleasurable' is because they are 'inborn', 'implanted in the mind'.

As within the archaic conceptual system of architecture, inside Alberti's system, proportions, together with geometry, played an even broader role than being 'pleasurable'. They were linked with a building or a part of a building being firm or fragile, operational or ineffective. Perfect proportions or geometrical shapes were associated with beauty as well as structural and functional performance.

Building as an optimising machine

The rise of the culture of luxury was possible because of improvements in productivity around the year 1000. At the same time, the awakening of the desire for luxury goods stimulated the expansion of commerce and the need to advance industry to produce these goods. Given constraints of labour resources, which continued to rule over Western Europe, this meant being increasingly under pressure to enhance efficiency.

Yet, the adoption of efficiency as a design norm and the development of new knowledge to achieve it did not occur first in the construction of spacious, glittering and crafty buildings but in military architecture, specifically in the design of fortifications. This new development challenged archaic beliefs about perfect proportions and geometrical shapes. It also confronted the archaic reliance on the role of authority to ground facts with the modern approach that trusted only facts obtained by observation or logic. The importance of military architecture is clear from the place it occupies in scholastic summae, such as Hugo of St Victor's (late 1120s) or Isidore's of Seville and certainly in Vitruvius who, together with Vegetius, the Roman author of *De Re militari*, is regarded once more as the authority on this subject. The first modern challenge to the authority of Vitruvius came from a woman, Christine de Pisan, in her book which is also the first modern treatise (c.1410) on architecture. In her treatise, which was repeatedly copied without her name later, Christine challenged the practice of her time, preferring 'regular outline' for fortifications as opposed to the 'crooked'. It is not clear if, by 'crooked', she meant irregular as opposed to angular. However, Christine initiated a controversy that became increasingly important during the fifteenth century, focusing on the preferred shape of the bastions. Alberti's text in his treatise went one step further, pointing out the weaknesses of 'round or square or . . . any regular forms' and opting for forms adapted to the specifics of the site. Furthermore he systematised the problem of defence, identifying the elements of a fortification, recognising their hierarchical interdependence and defining the problem of designing as a problem of optimisation whereby the maximum of control is achieved with the minimum of spending resources. In his treatise, Francesco di Giorgio (1474–1482) struggled further with the problem, introducing the method of examination of alternative cases – casually rather than systematically selected – and the technique of graphic representation. Bernard Palissy, a professor at the Royal College in Paris and inventor, tried to conceive the form of a fortified town through more holistic, intuitive means by developing an analogy to the form of a natural creature, the shell of the purple whelk (1563). Analogy played a very important role in solving the optimisation problem – in a qualitative sense, rather than quantitative – by a contemporary of di Giorgio, Leonardo da Vinci. Like di Giorgio, da Vinci applied graphic representation but he did so in combination with an analogy between visual and ballistic rays (Fig. 22, Fig. 23). This permitted him to recruit and exploit recent developments in perspective and his own studies in the representation of shadows, sciagraphia (Tzonis, 1989, 1993, 1994).

The new optimizing method soon found its place in the growing stream of published treatises. Pietro Cataneo's (1554, Fig. 45) being the first and, with the exception of Scammozi's, the last to include military architecture with the other kinds of architecture (Fig. 46). From that moment on, military architecture became a subject of its own even if it included regular buildings such as residences and warehouses. The division, presented and defended forcefully by Giovan Battista Bellucci (c.1554, 1598) was not only related to publications. It reflected a new development in architectural thinking involving a split in the kind of norms adopted – the military being dominated by the economy, ignoring hedonistic and aesthetic norms – as well as the kinds of techniques and facts admitted to achieve this norm – the military engineers espousing novel quantitative, quasi-optimisation–analytical techniques combined with empirically collected data detesting vague arguments grounded in authority. It also reflected an institutional split of specialisation of knowledge and professional activity.

An even more significant assault against the archaic theocretic thinking as a dogma to guide the design of buildings was carried out by Galileo (1638). He focused on the problem of firmness and stability of structures and the identification of the form that would provide the maximum performance for the minimum material (Fig. 73, Fig. 74). He disregarded authorities of ancient texts and, like Palladio and Scamozzi, replaced them with empirical observation and analytical calculations. Galileo confronted archaic design thinking with the way technicians in his time designed support machines. His revolution in structures put an end to beliefs about macrocosm–microcosm correspondences, the prototype of the harmonious human body, and invariant properties of proportions and geometry, replacing them with the model of the machine, the norm of efficiency, grounding by empirical observation and calculation, and determining form through matter and metric.

Positive and
arbitrary beauties Galileo's approach, like that of the military engineers, concerned only part of architecture, that which related to the norm of efficiency and optimisation. It did not touch on aspects of visual gratification. Thus it split architecture further into two specialised domains, one dealing with the question of firmness and stability of buildings using empirical analytical methods; the other with what makes a building an object of pleasure and beauty, methodology that had to be developed.

Positive and arbitrary beauties

Less than a century after Galileo's discoveries, a new series of debates and investigations began on this new problem in France, the upcoming military and economic power of the moment. In the framework of the new economy of luxury of the late medieval society and of absolutist mercantilism that followed, such questions affected the flow of money and economic dependence. Parallel to the engineer, he who knew how to design beautiful buildings, as well as the other objects of voluptuousness, water fountains (Fig. 13b, Fig. 76a, b, Fig. 77a, b) and gardens, could decide on their form, and thus control their production. In addition, objects of luxury were not only for consumption. Their possession had symbolic meaning, signifying power and legitimacy to rule, especially if, through their form – 'all'antica' – an analogy could be made between the new ruler and one of established reputation from antiquity.

For all of these reasons, the government programme of Monseigneur Colbert, 'surintendant des baiment' of Louis XIV had to be seriously involved with architecture. Colbert, a firm believer in the mercantilist, zero sum model of the economy, worried about the 'bleeding' of exporting gold to buy luxury artefacts for the court of the king and the nobility. His priority was to arrest, if not to reverse, this haemorrhage by securing the production of such goods inside France. He believed that, in order to achieve that goal and enable sustainable production of sophisticated cultural commodities, initiating a number of workshops and inviting foreign artists – which he did anyway – was not enough. He had to establish and secure a long-term, solid mechanism to acquire, control, advance and further develop fundamental knowledge about these products and their fabrication. This knowledge, rather than being purely technical, was related to what made artefacts, paintings, dresses or buildings so pleasing and sought after. He also realised, as Italian courts realised before, that the existing guilds and corporations, due to their protectionist and conservative character, were not encouraging innovation. A new kind of institution was necessary for this purpose. The solution the Italians had already supplied was the academy. Vasari, a great advocate of the modernisation of the arts and vehement enemy of medieval traditions, imitating the example of two Byzantine scholars who started two decades before the Platonic Academy focusing on humanistic and linguistic Greek studies, founded the Academia del Disegno in Florence in 1563. His example was followed in Rome and, in 1593, the Academy of St Luke was founded with Zuccarro (1608) its first president.

Colbert founded the Académie d' Architecture (Lemonnier, 1911–1929) with the intention of producing concrete results for a number of practical problems for which archaic architecture had no answers. Thus, on the 12 July 1678, the Académie was asked to examine the condition of the stones used for the buildings in and around Paris to discern the degree of their damage by the rain, the sun, humidity and the moon. Numerous inspections of monuments and quarries by academicians followed that lasted until November of that year. The resulting report was a major step in the development of the modern science of materials but did not arrive at general rules, which were the main goal of Colbert.

In addition, Colbert was concerned with another very urgent problem: what makes a building beautiful? This was a preoccupation from the day of the opening of the Académie (Lemonnier, 1911–1929) on 'Thursday, the last day of December 1671' in his presence. Blondel, 'professeur royal' in 'mathematics and architecture', also occupying a chair at the Academy of Science as well as in the College Royale, opened the first day discussion with a lecture 'on the excellence of architecture'. He continued his lecture for the next three sessions. The topic was 'le bon gout', the subject Colbert was mainly interested in. Are proportions based on nature or are they the result of custom? Are there any first principles of beauty in architecture, 'real' and 'positive', similar to those that Galileo established concerning the firmness of the structure of buildings? Blondel's lessons were later published in book form (1675).

In addition to lectures and discussions, Colbert established a series of what we would call today research projects. They included the definitive translation, with critical commentaries, of the text of Vitruvius which was undertaken by Claude Perrault, a physician, a member of the l'Académie des Sciences, with a special status in the l'Académie d' Architecture (1673, Fig. 79, Fig. 80a, Fig. 80b).

In his commentaries, Perrault posed the problem of the authority of Vitruvius. Superficially the problem appeared to be one of 'ancients' opposed to 'moderns'. More profoundly, the dispute was not about a model of architecture, ancient or modern, but about a model of thinking in architecture. Should one adopt the rules from the authority of the books of antiquity or derive them from concrete successful precedents?

To put an end to the endless disputes about this problem, Colbert turned to empirical observation and documentation of the buildings of the 'ancients' to confirm the existence of universal attributes that could lead to general rules. He arranged for Antoine Desgodetz (Herrmann, 1958), a young architect, and student of François Blondel, to travel to Rome with the assignment of taking exact measurements of key antique monuments. Applying the most advanced techniques and instruments for this purpose, Desgodetz returned to Paris in 1677, his task accomplished in sixteen months. The work was presented to the Académie, where it was received with muted praise, despite the fact that he introduced to the study of architecture new, modern standards of accuracy and a new attitude towards authority both in concert with Colbert's programme. The reasons for the rejection were clear. The measurements of the Pantheon (Fig. 92) negated the numerical, harmonic, speculative calculations of Blondel. In addition, as

Desgodetz himself wrote, his documentation contradicted data claimed by Vitruvius and earlier authorities – an opinion voiced already by Fréart in his comparative study of Roman and contemporary buildings (1650). In addition, Desgodet's findings weakened the claim that there were general, invariant rules, and based on the natural law rules of proportions, taken for granted by Blondel. It is interesting that, despite the fact that Blondel was a scientist more than an architect, he behaved dogmatically and subjectively and, more than anything else, was eager to assure his audience that the authority of Vitruvius was not debased. He did not hesitate to dismiss observations made by Degodet, even ridiculing them as insignificant, too tediously concerned with 'details'.

The origins of the techniques used by Desgodet are to be found in the major revolutionary achievements of the Renaissance: Alberti's egocentric perspective system of representation (1435–1436) and Raphael's (1519) later development of an orthogonal projection system. Insightful as always, Vasari celebrated Alberti's 'invention' of this 'instrument' for 'representing landscapes and diminishing and enlarging figures' as equivalent in importance to Gutenberg's discovery of 'the most useful art of printing books'. Almost a century later, Raphael replaced the Albertian visual pyramid for painters interested in developing virtual pictures of reality with a system of projection of parallel lines in order to produce more reliable descriptions of objects on paper, more adapted to the new needs for documentation of the antique buildings of Rome and the reproduction and recombination of their parts in new buildings.

The origins of these methods of representation go even further back into the past, into the Hellenistic developments in optics and geometry that, combined, produced variants of the Albertian system for realist pictorial descriptions. The same studies, however, led in the opposite direction to realism – optical illusions. Once more, Vitruvius refers to this problem and discusses the need to alter sizes and proportions to compensate for optical distortions. The theme was investigated by numerous commentators of Vitruvius. As one can see in the illustrations of Cesariano (Fig. 26) and Serlio (Fig. 34), according to this theory the viewer perceives apparent sizes and proportions and not the real ones. The diagrams suggest that to have a viewer perceive the right proportions, the architect must correct the real dimensions of the various parts of a building and, using the new opticogeometrical tool to adapt them, according to the viewer's position. Among these commentators of Vitruvius was Blondel who found in the theory of optical illusions the explanation of Desgodetz's documented absence of concordance of proportions in antique buildings, thus a means to save the doctrine of universality and invariance of proportions. Perrault, however, in his commentary, refused the claim by putting forth a new cognitive theory of vision: that the sizes of parts and objects we see are not the result of retinal passive reception. What people see also involves the active interpretation of the viewer. Thus, for Perrault, the visual illusions that Blondel spoke of were not enough to explain why the buildings of antiquity did not have common proportions. The only explanation was that the taste for certain proportions was acquired, 'arbitrary' was the term Perrault used. Perrault went a step further, to link positive attitudes to architectural beauties with manners in the court establishing a linkage between aesthetic preferences fashion, persuasion and power.

Interestingly, neither Desgodet's findings nor Perrault's had an impact in the Académie, despite the fact that Desgodet became a member of the institution later. In 1681, Blondel, representing the official view of the Académie, compromised, accepting that Vitruvius's rules do not always agree with those of Palladio, without commenting or

Positive and arbitrary beauties

explaining the conflict. Finally, in 1683, Blondel stated that the built examples of the ancients, rather than the text of Vitruvius, should be the source of authority. He refused to recognise the more theoretical repercussions of these remarks. Thus Desgodet did not manage to have a fair hearing. He did not win the battle. Time and developments closed the debate by making it irrelevant. Julien David Le Roy's documentation of the antiquities of Athens, the *Ruins of the most Beautiful Monuments of Greece* (1758), almost a century later, followed the steps of Desgodet's study. Like Desgodet, Le Roy did not confirm the existence of any universal norms or the authority of Vitruvius. Unlike Desgodet, however, Le Roy's study was greeted with admiration and he soon joined the Académie as a leading member. The question of perfect proportions was a dead issue by then, despite the fact that the Académie continued to worship Vitruvius until the day of its forceful closure by the French Revolution (Lemonnier, 1911–1929).

Anticlassicism, informalism and the unmaking of the canon

The discovery of mathematical techniques that could transform rule-based proportions and shapes through rule-based geometrical manipulations found enthusiastic followers among artists and architects.

Already in Dürer's writings and in the treatise of Serlio (1537–1575) the issue of optical corrections as well as rule-based transformation of regular shapes had been discussed and illustrated. Serlio went one step further. Concerned not only with the making of the classical canon but also its pragmatic implementation, it dealt with the conflict created when a regular shape cannot be inscribed within the constraints of an irregular context as this applied to problems of classical elements, ornamental details and site. The proposed solution was the introduction of a new family of shapes, trapezoids or, more generally, 'oblique' shapes (Fig. 34), irregular but derived from a 'legal formal operation' of 'cutting corners' (Fig. 41, Fig. 42).

By the middle of the sixteenth century, these techniques were recruited in the domain of stone cutting in construction, as noted by Philibert De l'Orme (1567–1648), and expanded into what we would today call 'shape stretching' deformation (Fig. 51, Fig. 52). And, by the beginning of the seventeenth century, techniques of geometric distortion of forms which became increasingly more potent and easier to use attracted many architects. Juan Caramuel de Lobkowitz (1678) proposed a new kind of architecture, the 'oblique' (Fig. 83, Fig. 84, Fig. 85, Fig. 86, Fig. 87). Guarino Guarini's interest in these methods, like De l'Orme's, was related to construction (Fig. 90) but also with aesthetic aspects (1678) (Fig. 88, Fig. 89). While some found in these new methods of representation and manipulation of form tools for serving the need to save the classical canon by adapting regular, perfect shapes and proportions inside wicked spatial frameworks, others saw in them the opportunity to develop an anticlassical architecture.

But other architects mobilised these methods to unleash creative potentials by exploring new and unprecedented abstract spatial formal arrangements, as the illustrations by Andrea Pozzo (Fig. 97, Fig. 98) and Juste-Aurèle Meissonnier (Fig. 108, Fig. 109) suggest, and as the reactions against this development by Charles Nicolas Cochin (1754, 1755) and T.N. Loyer (1762) reveal. All of these developments manifest an increasing tendency towards subjective variability of individual forms and a decline in the belief in universal, objective norms. They are forerunners of current computer-based experiments in architecture such as those by Renzo Piano, Frank Gerhy and the generator of the CAD 'blobs'. Finally, these opticogeometrical experiments will be applied to display an 'antirennaissance' – to use Eugenio Battisti's (*L'Antirinanscimento*, 1962) term – counter-reformation message: the impossibility of a perfect world on earth and the rejection of the humanistic promise of perfection on earth one might find implied in the classical canon.

More extreme anticlassical, informalist proposals beyond any rigorous method of transformation by arresting the process of shaping, leaving the form 'unfinished', loosely configured, rough, broken (Michelangelo Buonarroti, The Younger, 1625) between nature and artifice is introduced by Vasari in reference to the sculptures of Michelangelo Buonarroti and to the architecture of Giulio Romano (1550). Serlio (1537–1575, Fig. 43, Fig. 44) and later Palladio (1570) try to compromise, incorporating what they call the 'rustic', as one of the kinds of architecture (1537–1575).

Designs for narration, and as emotion- and mood-machines

The theory that proportions and shapes were apparent, egocentric, that they were subjectively perceived, generated by optical illusions, and not real and objective, found enthusiastic followers among the designers of theatre sets, interested more in the temporary world of simulacra and illusion rather than reality and permanence. But there were also architects who began to find in buildings the potential not only to generate an abstract gratification but also, as in literature, through narrative representations, strong emotions. One of the earliest examples discussed by Vasari (1550) was the Palazzo del Tè by Giulio Romano where icons of disorder and destruction, carried out in a mixed strategy of painting and architecture, aroused terror. The movement moved further, exploring and developing means of narration and rhetoric, trying to exploit techniques from literature (Count Emanuele Tesauro, 1654, Gabriel Germain Boffrand, 1745). It also delved into associative techniques using shapes, size and colour abstractly and iconically, to represent 'character' (Jacques François Blondel, 1752–1757 and 1771, Fig. 125) and bring forth feelings of surprise (Chambers, 1793–1799), ambiguity and discovery as pointed out by Montesquieu (1748) and especially by Denis Diderot (1766), and, also of strong emotions, as analysed by Edmund Burke in his treatise *On the sublime* (1757). More variant feelings (Alexander Gerard's, 1759, de Montesquieu, 1748) were also sought after.

In his famous *Reveries of a Solitary Walker* (1776–1778), Jean Jacques Rousseau manifests the possibility of an almost therapeutic use of an environment, characterised by a highly informal and fluid geometry determining sentiments (Tzonis and Lefaivre, 1977). Several of the writings on landscape architecture began to discuss design in purely environmental, psychological terms with no reference to the rules of spatial ordering of the classical canon (Watelet, 1774, Morel, 1776). An equally behaviourally deterministic approach, seeing buildings as mood generators, was suggested by Nicolas Le Camus de Mézières, *The Genius of Architecture* (1780), and by Etienne Louis Boullée in his *Treatise on Architecture* (1793–1799). These are developmental predecessors of contemporary uses of architecture as a mood-generating art, struggling, as demonstrated today by Jean Nouvel, for a place next to cinema. But it is also a forerunner of contemporary environmental design techniques applied in commercial buildings and work facilities.

Rigorism

The most important kind of architecture that carried meaning and a message came, ironically, out of a movement whose origins were against everything that was not essential in a building, which was seen to be its structure. 'Rigorism', as the tendency was called, probably first by Algarotti, a follower of Lòdoli, who was the founder of the movement in Italy, appeared at around the end of the seventeenth century. Rigorism in the broadest sense censured everything arbitrary, applied without rule and reason in the design of a building. One can consider Teofilo Gallaccini's writings (1621, Fig. 70) as part of this critique. In a more narrow sense, however, rigorists were the ones who attacked everything that did not serve a utilitarian purpose as we can see in the vitriolic and highly intelligent definitions in the 1797 *Dictionary* by Francesco Milizia. This was not a new idea. Military engineers had made this point a century earlier and patrons like Colbert would not hesitate to humiliate architects of the status of Bernini for not serving the real operational needs of the palace. The point the rigorists made was that buildings, in addition to being efficient in terms of cost and effective in terms of operation, had something equally important to do. Contrary to Piranesi's fears and accusations that they were condemning architecture to silence, rigorists wanted buildings to signify (Frémin, 1702), but signify 'the essential', the rational and the structurally potent; in other words, the new values of an industrial society in its genesis. Neither were the rigorists against beauty. Beauty, for them, however, was a synonym of the essential and the useful (William Hogarth, 1753). In France the most important writings were authored by people who were not members of the Académie and, as in the case of Frémin (1702), Cordemoy (1739) and Laugier (1753, 1765, Fig. 114), not even architects. Most of these writings played an important role in shaping architecture in their time but also functionalism, the grand movement of twentieth-century architecture.

Before the Gothic assumed its regionalist, nationalist significance, discussed in the following section, it became an object of admiration and imitation because of its rigorist qualities. And although Laugier and Milizia were more attached to classical prototypes because of their direct way of showing their structural organisation and the relative simplicity of ornament, most rigorists saw in the Gothic cathedrals, in their feats of construction and the vegetal configuration of their construction members, an illustration of what a rigorist architecture could be like (Vincent Sablon, 1671, Jean François Félibien des Avaux, 1699, Abbé Jean-Louis de Cordemoy, 1706, Jacques Germain Soufflot, 1741).

Regionalism

The unmaking of the classical canon was also the result of the new political movements of emancipation of groups whose sense of identity came into conflict with the universalistic values of the classical canon. Once more, it was Vitruvius who touched upon the issue of difference in architecture as opposed to global standards. After identifying diverse kinds of architecture associated with different regions, he tried to relate their architecture with behavioural attributes of the residents. However, the idea of a conscious regionalist–nationalist and not simply regional architecture came much later. A kind of regionalist architectural stance can perhaps be detected in the case of the curious colonnade erected in 1143, in imitation of Roman architecture, in the Roman House of the Crescenzi family (Heckscher, 1937–1938) (Fig. 7). An embryonic form of regionalist-

'proto-nationalist' architecture can also be seen in the efforts to invent a new 'French' order by De l'Orme (Fig. 47, 1561), later by Colbert and the French architects and the Académie, and in the eighteenth century by the Ribart de Chamoust, arguing in an opportunist compromise for the 'French order found in nature' (1783).

However, the idea of using architecture as a means of confronting the illegitimacy and 'unnaturalness' of an external power imposing an alien rule on an endogenous group of a region sprung from Britain. The argument for the values of the particular, the individual, the uncorrupted 'natural' and free were interwoven with the 'genius of the place' and concretely formulated informality design strategies that became clearer as the century progresses (Addison, 1712, Castell, 1728, Langley, 1728, Gilpin, 1792) (Fig. 105, Fig. 106, Fig. 107). Pro-parliamentary Whig party ideas (Pevsner, 1944) were combined with imperial ambitions, the rise of utilitarianism and scienticism encompassed what Pope epigrammatically (1731, Fig. 110), recalling Roman precedents, branded the 'spirit of the place' (Fig. 128). Regionalist architecture was not only used for nationalist patriotic political purposes in Britain. Social conflicts, together with environmental dysfunctionalities, generated a reaction against urban living. The debate of country versus city is at least as old as the Renaissance (Alberti, c.1428). Adapting to nature, integrated into the shapes and materials of an existing landscape, regionalist architecture suggested not only an environmental alternative but also a way of living which, even if it was not as extreme as that envisaged by Rousseau, was an improvement over the urban conditions at that time (James Malton, *Essay*, 1798, Fig. 130, Richard Elsam, *Essay on Rural*, 1803).

Part of the search for an architecture that would overcome the straitjacket effect of the classical canon was the interest in documenting, analysing and reproducing Chinese buildings. Already in 1711, M. de Cotte, the first Royal architect, honoured the Académie with his visit and suggested that it should study the architecture of other countries, drawing on the descriptions by voyagers, such as the buildings of China, including the Great Wall; and Félibien had suggested, for Versailles, a small palace out of jojoba wood in the Chinese manner. But it was through Chambers' publications (1759, 1772) that Chinese architecture became really popular (Fig. 116, Fig. 117).

Whatever the geographical national origins of the regionalist concepts, the text that confronted the classical canon, framing it as what we will call today 'imperialist', while at the same time setting up a new approach to design with an emancipative nationalist–regionalist programme was Johann Wolfgang von Goethe, *On German Architecture* (1772), using the case of the Cathedral of Strasbourg.

Architecture of control

As a result of the increase of differentiation and specialisation of services and social functions, the plan rather than the façade, and the notion of distribution rather than compositional ordering of space, became key issues in architecture during the first part of the eighteenth century (Jacques François Blondel, 1752–1757). Despite that, there were no widespread conflicts with the classical canon inherited from the Renaissance. However, serious conflicts appeared in specialised buildings and announce the dethronement of classical architecture in the next century. The most interesting example of such conflict is the one between Claude Perrault, himself a scientist, and Cassini (1669) the new director of the Royal Observatory of Paris. Like Galileo, Cassini looked at a building as he looked at the celestial universe. He saw both as machines. Tersely, he stated – to my knowledge for the first time in history – that even a building is an 'instrument'. Thus it should obey, primarily, requirements of function rather than rules of *ordonnance* or to signify the French monarchy, i.e. the way Perrault had designed it (Fig. 80). Similar statements were echoed a century later in hospital design, in studies carried out in the French Academy of Science by medical doctors as well as physicists and mathematicians, and not in the Académie d'Architecture by architects. The studies did produce prototypes that would be diffused and used in the nineteenth century in utilitarian and welfare buildings (Jean Baptiste Le Roy, 1777, Fig. 126, 127, Jaques René Tenon, 1788) but also concepts and procedures that would go on to rationalise the design process. 'Jeremy Bentham (1787, Fig. 129), in his notorious proposal for the building-machine Panopticon, placed his hopes for the solution to all socioeconomic problems and reforms in an architecture that was not capable yet of being conceived by architects.

Social architecture

The first steps towards a new approach of conceiving cities occurred during the first phase of the revolution of Modern architecture in the works of Christine de Pisan (c.1410), Leon Battista Alberti (1440–1472, 1485), Filarete (1451–1464) and Francesco di Giorgio Martini (1474–1482) as we have seen. In most cases their approach was taxonomic, identifying a list of repertories for residences and public buildings, streets and squares. Their beliefs were still dependent on the authority of the 'ancients' and not on empirical observation, analysis and calculation. They carried on with archaic dogmas of perfect shapes, anthropomorphism and macro–microcosmic analogies, and the system of norms driving their designs still did not articulate the new desire for economic efficiency and pleasure in consumption. There were also few visionary, exploratory, even revolutionary 'utopian' Modernists around this time. Two most interesting ones were French Protestants, Bernard Palissy (1563) and Jacques Perret (Fig. 65, Fig. 66). Their impact was small. The more pragmatic writings of Sebastiano Serlio's (1537–1575), that addressed the new conditions of living in towns were influential. They involved not only new typologies of residences but also aspects of urban change and adaptation. It was Serlio, together with his contemporary Cornaro (1567–1575), who introduced the problem of housing for all the classes, including the poor, and tried to establish minimal standards for living.

With the unprecedented expansion of urbanisation, the increase of division of labour inside the city and the explosion in quantity and complexity of the services during the second part of the eighteenth century, there was a wave of critiques against existing practices as well as new proposals for ways to relate buildings and city, city and its constituent components, public spaces, circulation and servicing conduits. Pierre Patte's study for Paris (1769, Fig. 122, Fig. 123, Fig. 124) was pioneering. He introduced a comparative approach to the study of urban problems that ranged from technical problems to what is called 'urban renewal' today. Indicative of the crisis and the newness of the problem was Sir James Steuart's commentary on the condition of London (1771). Parallel with these pragmatic works are visionary texts such as Morelly's *The Code of Nature* (1755) and Louis Sébastien Mercier, *The Year 2440* (1770). More architectural, taking an intermediate position between utopia and professionalism, but still critical and revolutionary is Claude Nicolas Ledoux, *Architecture Considered under the Relation of Art, Morals and Legislation* (1804).

The parts put together

Alberti's writings about the relationship of the parts and the whole of a building were fundamental for the development of classical theory of composition. Cesariano's system of partitioning and labelling the parts of a façade or a plan went a step further formalising the classical system. However, it was Durand's system (1802–1805, Fig. 131, Fig. 132, Fig. 133), using a procedure of overlays of axes together with a combinatorial procedure to produce complex plans from elementary components of space and structure that made the system operationally possible. Durand referred to his method as a 'méchanisme de la composition', an elementarist, rule-based, combinatorial approach, opening the way to the efforts of Modern architecture to generate, through computers, efficient and effective schemes today that, in terms of arrangement, may have nothing to do with the classical canon.

Following Durand's texts and illustrations, the series of documents presented here ends with a drawing by Gaspard Monge (Fig. 138). Monge was one of the founders of the Ecole Polytechnique. He was a revolutionary in his politics, and in his ideas about technology and education. His greatest contribution was the system of descriptive geometry. Its value is not so much mathematical as technological, offering an efficient and effective way to represent the most complicated relations of solids in space and solve problems related to them. It contributed enormously to the economy but also to deference. Monge's association with military matters becomes clear through another important book he authored, entitled *Description de l'art de fabriquer les canons*, published in 1794. However his system of descriptive geometry plays an equally important role in solving problems of representation of space in the dream world of virtual reality and the media.

The text by Milizia (*c.*1810) with which this panorama of a period of revolution ends, addresses very consciously the problem of achieving an architecture that might be truly revolutionary. Written for the post-Revolutionary French audience, it deals with central cultural issues that a new, post-Revolutionary, Modern regime ought to be concerned with: education and the role of the artist of a new era, destruction versus preservation of the achievements of a pre-Revolutionary culture. Of all the rigorists, Milizia was the most revolutionary in the political sense. His declaration that the architect should be freed from the 'yoke' of authority and have only one master – 'his own reason' – was referring equally to architectural culture and to politics. Through Horatio Greenhough, they became part of the American democratic Modern architecture ethos that led to Sullivan and Mumford. The issues that the document raises introduce themes that became standard in the burning and bitter political polemics of Modern architecture and art for the coming two centuries. Milizia touches upon another typically twentieth-century preoccupation, media. It is discussed not as technology but as a means to instruct in politics and morality. He criticises the authorities of the young French republic, that places engraving below painting. In contrast to Walter Benjamin, Milizia, more militant and pragmatic, sees in the mechanically reproduced, low-cost print the 'best way' to 'influence opinion and public instruction'. It is interesting that, despite the fact that Milizia is a typical radical internationalist, and despite his adherence to functionalism that we have seen before, he raises the issue of regionalist culture, censuring the Republic for its centralist tendencies.

The alternative to a top-down, centralist, narrow-minded approach to planning is a central concern in Nicolas Caritat Condorcet's *Report on Hospitals* (1786), perhaps the most radical conceptually, institutionally and politically, document of the eighteenth century (Tzonis, 1977). Taking part of the debate on the future of hospital facilities in Paris, referred to earlier (p. 25), Condorcet recommended decentralising the health services, allocating a unit to each neighbourhood. He also proposed a collaborative, participatory – the first time in history, to my knowledge – multidisciplinary design process combining experts as well as users living in the neighbourhood. However, it was René Descartes in his *Discourse on Method* (1637), writing at a time of great political upheavals and the great take off of the French absolutist state, who presented the first explicit critique of top-down total plans, proposing as an alternative an incremental process.

As a result of these multiple, parallel, distributed in space and time innovations, architectural thinking at the end of the eighteenth century appears to have grown into a much more complex, highly differentiated and specialised system than it was at the end of the first millennium.

Coda

The documents assembled here did present the emergence of Modern Architecture over a period of eight centuries, from the earliest stirrings of the Renaissance in the tenth century to the Enlightenment and collapse of the Ancien Regime. Before this period, Modernism did not exist. From it, it emerged fully formed.

Was the outcome of the process documented here 'progressive'? An immediate expectation one has is that in the eight centuries of evolution or rather co-evolution of architectural thinking, the subjects that were very hotly discussed should have produced some important theory. As the case of the great debate about proportions shows, the discussion dissolves into the horizon leaving no trace of such theory however. But what they may have left behind is a way of thinking that did not exist before, which was a necessary condition for later developments to occur.

Another expectation one might have is that certain conclusions arrived at in the past that could be beneficial would have been selected and passed on. Instead, as in the case of the conclusions drawn by Perrault about positive and arbitrary beauties, they were ignored and forgotten because they failed to combine with other promising traits at that time and, as a result, they had to be reinvented later. Resembling in many respects natural evolution, the change that occurred between the end of the Dark Ages and the end of the Ancien Regime occurred at an enormous cost of intellectual effort and waste. It appears that redundancy and not efficiency was the name of the game of history. The emergence of modern architectural thinking was a long and tangled affair, with fits and starts, major studies and reversals.

The fact is that, by the end of the eighteenth century, some sub-domains of architecture, such as climatic control, economic management and construction safety became more objective, rational and empirical. In other cases, such as decisions about the general configuration of prestige buildings, things became more subjective, *je ne sais quoi*, and defied reason. This trend continues today. There are practices employing ways of conceiving buildings that are completely computerised, next to others that rely on manual, naïve habits that are no more sophisticated than the most astrology-based practices of the year 1000.

The new way of thinking, Modern architecture, made people at the end of the Ancien Regime more competent to represent, compare and discuss design products from multiple points of view. Awareness of 'other' architectures, 'oriental' or of the past, offered a culturally broader and historically deeper awareness, not only of the differences but also of the universality of humans. Indeed, there was a remarkable development from the time of the schematic taxonomy of building plans by Montfaucon (Fig. 99, Fig. 100) and the speculative fantasies by von Erlach (Fig. 101, Fig. 102, Fig. 103, Fig. 104) to the almost evolutionary thinking by Julien-David Le Roy (1758, Fig. 119) and de Quincy (1785). Through such studies, people became more conscious of multiple realities and pluralism of the world than they were at the end of the first millennium involving values of identity, objectivity, equity and the role they play in the design of buildings, landscapes or cities. On the other hand, it is not certain that the constructed world today satisfies these values more than it did a thousand years ago. At its best, this mixed pattern suggests, to paraphrase Ernst Mayr (2001), the 'bizarre diversity' of the world of variations of architecture. There is no doubt that, as long as a culture maintains and prolongs creativity and diversity, its chances of surviving abrupt, unexpected crises are high. And that is something the revolution, or co-revolution, of Modern architecture achieved.

The documents assembled here did not just express or reflect the reality that surrounded them, they were not just passive recorders of events, but an active force in changing the world, in modernizing it. Because of the multiple paths this process of modernization took, the order in which they appear is chronological. This order is meant to convey the many ways they interacted in the web of people who constructed the new thinking in order to construct the new world.

Coda

Leo of Naples (late tenth century)

'Letter of Alexander the Great to Aristotle', *Alexander Romance* (late tenth century)

This description of the sumptuous palace of the Indian monarch, Porus, is part of a larger fictional letter supposedly sent by Alexander the Great while on military campaign in the East to his childhood teacher, Aristotle, on the wonders to be found there. Widely known in antiquity, this description was forgotten during the early Middle Ages, then rediscovered in the wake of the crusades with the re-opening of trade routes with the East, where antique culture had survived. Leo of Naples based his version of the palace on a Greek text that he found while visiting Constantinople. The text is one of the earliest examples of a genre that has come to be known as *'Mirabilia'*, in this instance describing the marvels of domestic luxury, to reach renascent Europe, just starting to emerge from the period of extreme poverty that characterised the Middle Ages (Le Goff, 1985; Lefaivre, 1997). Like the many other writings which belong to the extensive corpus of *Mirabilia* tales grouped under the title of the *Alexander Romance*, it enjoyed great popularity in emerging court circles well into the Renaissance (Pfister, 1910), no doubt serving as a seductive prototype for the newly emerging luxurious building projects. This fabulistic, dream-like description of India can be read as the first awakening of an envious, covetous 'orientalism' on the part of the 'West' which will also fuel future attempts of impoverished, post-medieval Europe to conquer and dominate the far richer and more civilised East (Lefaivre, 1997). Modern architecture begins as orientalism.
Further reading Said, 1978; Sombart, 1967.

... And we learnt of this city of Porus's and of his palace in which there were four hundred golden columns with golden capitals and the walls of this house were clad with gold panels that were as thick as the finger of a man; and I saw other such golden panels gleam in many places. Vines of gold, with golden leaves, hung between the columns, and bunches of grapes were of crystal interspersed with glowing gems and emeralds. All the rooms were also ornamented with gems that are called pearls and bigger pearls called onion pearls and carbuncles. The regal chambers were of white ivory with ceilings covered with a kind of wood called ebony, that is a wood that comes from India and Ethiopia, and the rooms were made of cypress wood. And outside this palace were statues covered with gold and there were trees of gold and among their branches there were many different kinds of birds of various colours and their claws and beaks were gilded and from their ears hung pearls and onion pearls. We drank from glasses covered with gems and crystal and gold and a bit of silver.

luxury • hedonism • consumption • orientalism

Adelhard (1055–1082)

Account of the Abbey of Saint-Trond (1057)

Baudri, Bishop of Dol

This description of the church of Saint-Trond near Liège, Belgium, is thought to be the first to suggest an allegorical interpretation for ecclesiastical architecture (de Bruyne, 1946, II, 81–84 and 362–363). It is also seen as an example of the pre-humanist revival of the Vitruvian analogy between the temple and the human body (Conant, 1968). Interestingly, the reference to the breast and uterus of the church indicates that the sex of the body is female, an indication perhaps of the growing erotic attachment to architecture in medieval Europe (Lefaivre, 1997).

Further reading Harvey, 1972, 26; Mortet, 1929, 157; Schlosser, 1979, 241; Tatarkiewicz, 1970–1974, II.

At this time the fabric of this church was so much enlarged that one might say of it, as the learned doctors do of well-fashioned churches, that it was formed after the image of the human body. For it had, as can still be seen, a chancel which, with the sanctuary, is like the head and neck; the choir with its stalls the breast; the transept projecting as two sleeves or wings on each side of the choir, the arms and hands; the crossing of the bell tower the uterus; and the lower arm of the cross, displaying symmetrically two aisles to the north and south, the thighs and shins.

archaic beliefs • body model

Baudri, Bishop of Dol (unknown)

Description of Fécamp (c.1110)

Baudri wrote the following as Archbishop of the Breton province of Dol on a trip to the great Romanesque abbey church of Fécamp in Normandy reconstructed towards the end of the tenth century and enlarged between 1080 and 1108 (Harvey, 1972, 26). The source of legitimisation for this luxurious earthly building, which went against the traditional *contemptus mundi* mentality of the medieval church, represented by Bernard of Clairvaux (c.1125), is its supposed orientalising similarity to 'the Heavenly Jerusalem', the same as in descriptions of Gothic churches by later authors (Simson, 1962, II).

Further reading Frugoni, 1991; Mortet, 1911, 343–347; Said, 1978.

The monastery is endowed with high and beautiful walls and covered all over with lead: it is said to resemble the gates of heaven and the palace of God there and to be like the Heavenly Jerusalem. It is resplendent with gold and silver, covered with beautiful silk, holy relics that shine in the honour of the Holy Trinity. Pilgrims gather to see them in great number and with solemnity.

archaic beliefs • body model • luxury • hedonism • consumption • orientalism

Hugh of Saint-Victor (1096–1141)

Didascalicon (late 1120s)

From the twelfth century onwards, interest in the secular sciences increased in the cathedral schools. The church had taught, since Augustine, that whatever man learned outside the Scripture was harmful and worthy of condemnation. Hugh, Saxon born and abbot of the school of Saint Victor in Paris, widened the limits of knowledge within the framework of scholastic method and systems. The importance of this encyclopaedic work was that it includes mechanical engineering, including the building arts, within the boundaries of acceptable knowledge for the first time (Taylor, 1961) since antiquity. The modernisation of school curricula in this way no doubt goes a long way in explaining the spread of the structurally complex Gothic, as opposed to the far simpler Romanesque, churches that was to follow.

Further reading Mortet, 1929, 21–23; Tatarkiewicz, 1970–1974, II, 190.

Chapter Twenty: The Division of Mechanical Sciences into Seven

Mechanical science contains seven sciences: fabric making, armament, commerce, agriculture, hunting, medicine and theatrics. Of these, three pertain to external cover for nature, by which she protects herself from harm and four to internal, by which she feeds and nourishes herself. . . .

These sciences are called mechanical, that is adulterate, because their concern is with the artificer's product, which borrows its form from nature. Similarly, the other seven are called liberal either because they require minds which are liberal, that is, liberated and practised (for these sciences pursue subtle inquiries into the causes of things), or because in antiquity only free and noble men are accustomed to study them, while the populace and the sons of men not free sought operative skill in things mechanical. In all this appears the great diligence of the ancients, who would leave nothing untried, but brought all things under definite rules and precepts. And mechanics is that science to which they declare the manufacture of all articles to belong.

Chapter Twenty-two: Armament

. . . Sometimes any tools whatever are called 'armament', as when we speak of the arms of war, or the arms of a ship, meaning the implements used in war or on a ship. For the rest, the term 'arms' belongs properly to those things that protect us, like the shield, the breastplate and the helmet – or those by which we strike – like the sword, the two-faced axe and the lance . . .

Armament, therefore is called, in a sense, an instrumental science, not so much because it uses instruments in its activity as because, from some material lying shapeless at hand, it makes something into an instrument, if I may so name its product. To this science belong all such materials as stones, woods, metals, sands and clays.

Armament is of two types, the constructional and the finishing. The constructional is divided into the building of walls, which is the business of the wood-worker and carpenter and of other craftsmen of both these sorts, who work with mattocks and hatchets, the file and the beam, the saw and the auger, planes, vises, the trowel and the

[31]

level, smoothing, hewing, cutting, filing, carving, joining, daubing in every sort of material – clay, stone, wood, bone, gravel, lime, gypsum and other materials that may exist of this kind.

systemisation of space distribution • scientification

Bernard of Clairvaux (1090–1153)

Strong Words to William (c.1125)

Bernard of
Clairveaux
1090–1153

Bernard entered the Cistercian monastery of Citeaux and became the first member of the newly founded reformed branch of that order. In his many writings, characterised by a renowned oratorical skill, he called the church back to earlier forms of asceticism, condemning its current propensity towards orientalism and worldly pursuits such as usury and the accumulation of capital. These moral strictures were accompanied by criticism of the new monarchical social order and by political support for the papacy versus the nationalist French dynasty of the Capetians. Part of Bernard's criticism took the form of an invective against excessive architectural indulgence. He was targeting most particularly the royal abbey of Saint-Denis, which was being renovated by his arch-enemy, the abbot Suger. Underlying Bernard's critique of the Capetians and their new-found wealth was his support for the papacy whose dominion extended to France. Eventually he was reconciled with the French monarchy on the matter (Panofsky, 1979, 10). Both Bernard and Suger were extremely influential in their own way. While Suger left his mark on all subsequent Gothic architecture, Bernard did much to initiate the sensitivity towards a stark, unadorned architecture as well as the moralistic condemnation of ornament in the subsequent debate on the issue, still extant today (Bruyne, 1946, vol II, 135–144; Duby, 1976; Lefaivre, 1997; Mortet, 1911).
Further reading Simson, 1962, 43–47; Said, 1978; Tatarkiewicz, 1970–1974, II, 183–190.

I say nothing of the great height of your churches, their inordinate length, their superfluous breadth, their luxurious polish, and their bizarre carvings and paintings that attract the worshipper's gaze and hinder his attention, and seem to me to be nothing but a revival of some sort of ancient Jewish rite. Let this pass and say it is done for the glory of God. But, as a monk, I ask my brother monks in the same way the pagan asked his fellow-pagans: 'Tell me, high priests, what is this gold doing in the sanctuary?' Similarly I say, 'Tell me, poor men, tell me, poor people, what is this gold doing in *your* sanctuary?' Of course, the high priests had an excuse that monks do not have. For we know that they, being debtors both to the wise and the unwise and unable to excite the devotion of carnal folk by spiritual things, did so through bodily adornments. But we, who have now risen from the people, we who are supposed to have left all the precious and beautiful things of the world for Christ's sake, we who count nothing but shit so that we may win Christ, and who have abandoned all things beautiful to see, soothing to hear, sweet to smell, delightful to taste, or pleasant to touch – in a word, all bodily delights – please tell me, why do we get excited by these things? What profit, I say, do we expect from them? The admiration of fools, or the praise of the simple? Or, since we are scattered among the nations, have we perhaps learnt their works and now serve their graven images? To speak plainly, does the root of all this not lie in covetousness, which is idolatry, and do we not seek profit . . . ? If you ask: 'How does this profit come about?' I say: 'In an unnatural way.' For money artfully scattered multiplies, when it is spent it grows, and prodigality gives birth to plenty. At the very sight of these expensive but marvellous vanities, men are more kindled to offer gifts than to pray. Thus wealth is drawn up by ropes of wealth, and money begets money; for I know not how it is that, the more wealth is seen to be abundant, the more freely men contribute to it. Feast their eyes on relics cased in gold, and their purse strings are loosened. Show them a most comely image of some saint, and they will think him all the more saintly if he is more gaudily painted. Men run to kiss him, and are invited to give, and there is more admiration for his beauty than veneration for his sanctity. Hence the church is adorned with gemmed crowns of light – no, with lustres like cart-wheels, girt all round with lamps, but no less brilliant with the precious stones that stud them. Moreover we see candelabra standing like trees of massive bronze, fashioned with marvellous subtlety of art, and glistening no less brightly with gems than with the lights they carry. What do you think the purpose of all this is? The regret of penitents, or the admiration of beholders? O vanity of vanities, no less vain than insane! The church is resplendent in her walls and beggarly in her poor, she adorns her stones with gold and leaves her sons naked; the rich man's eye is fed at the expense of the poor. The curious may find their delight here but the needy find no relief. In short, so numerous and so marvellous are the varieties of diverse shapes left and right that we are more tempted to read the marble than our books, and to spend the whole day marvelling at these things rather than in meditating on the law of God. For the sake of God, if men are not ashamed of these follies, why at least do they not shrink from the expense?

luxury • hedonism • consumption • social reform • democratisation • orientalism

Anonymous

The Marvels of the City of Rome (c.1143)

In 1143, Rome was overtaken by an internal crisis caused by the temporary overthrow of the papal regime. The new popular government, the Senate, sought the revival of the antique republican institutions (Heckscher, 1937–1938). It seems quite possible that this famous pamphlet was composed during these events as propaganda, disseminating the Senate's ideas (ibid.). It consists of three books. One of them, **The Marvels of the City of Rome**, excerpted here, is a catalogue of the luxurious splendour of antique Pagan City. Translated widely and re-edited many times, this, perhaps the most popular of the *Mirabilia*, accompanied the awakening of the spirit of renewal or *renovatio* all over Europe and prefigured the Renaissance cult of conspicuous consumption, private and public (Lefaivre, 1997; Panofsky, 1960, 72, 210).

Further reading Bruyne, 1946, II, 95–96; Chastel, 1969, 216ff.; Frugoni, 1991; Graf, 1915; Pollak, 1971; Schlosser, 1979, 27, 53, 56–57, 209; Schramm, 1929, II, IV, 73–104; Weiss, 1973, 6–10.

Part II, 7. Of the Coliseum, and of Saint Silvester

The Coliseum was the Temple of the Sun, of marvelous greatness and beauty, disposed with many diverse vaulted chambers, and all covered with a heaven of gilded brass, where thunders and lightning and glittering fires were made, and where rain was shed through slender tubes.

[33]

Part III, 1. The Vatican, and the Needle

Within the Palace of Nero is the temple of Apollo, that is called Saint Parnel; Before which is the basilica that is called Vatican, adorned with marvellous mosaic and ceiled with gold and glass. It is therefore called Vatican because in that place the *Vates*, that is to say the priests, sang their offices before Apollo's temple, and therefore all that part of St Peter's church is called Vatican. There is also another temple, that was Nero's Wardrobe, which is now called Saint Andrew; close by is the memorial of Caesar, that is the Needle, where his ashes nobly rest in his sarcophagus. The purpose is that as in his lifetime the whole world was conquered by him, so in death the same may lie beneath him forever. The memorial was adorned in the lower part with tables of gilded brass, and fairly stamped with Latin letters; and above at the ball, where he rests, it is decked with gold and precious stones . . .

Part III The Castle of Crescentius

Moreover there is a castle, that was the temple of Hadrian, as we read in the Sermon of the festival of Saint Peter, where it says that the memorial of the Emperor Hadrian, a temple built up, of marvellous greatness and beauty which was covered all over with stones and adorned with many stories, and fenced with bronze railings all around, with golden peacock. . . . At the four sides of the temple were four horses of gilded brass, and in every face were brazen gates.

Part III The Capital

The capital was the head of the world where the consuls and senators lived and governed the world. Its face was covered with high and strong walls that rose above the top of the hill and was covered all over with glass and gold and marvellous carved work. . . . Within the fortress was a palace all adorned with marvelous works in gold and silver and brass and costly stones, to be a mirror to all nations and which was said to be worth the third part of the world. . . . Many more temples and palaces of emperors, consuls, senators and prefects were in the time of the heathen within this Roman city, even as we have read in old chronicles, and have seen with our eyes and have heard tell of ancient people. And moreover, how great was their beauty in gold and silver and brass and ivory and precious stones, we have tried as well as we could to bring all this back to the remembrance of humankind.

luxury • hedonism • consumption

Abbot Suger (1081–1151)

On the Consecration of the Church of Saint Denis (1144)

Of humble origins (as opposed to his rival, Bernard of Clairveaux, who was from a family of barons), Suger rose to some of the most powerful political positions of his time. He was political adviser to the Capetian monarchs, first Louis VI (c. 1081–1137) and then Louis VII (1120–1180) and his queen, Eleanor of Acquitaine (1122–1204). He was also official historian of the reign of Louis VI, ambassador to the papal court and regent, no less, during the king's journey to the crusades. Attesting to the importance that architecture played in cultural politics of the time, Suger was named as the administrator of the renovations to the royal abbey of Saint Denis in 1121, which for many centuries had been the tomb of French kings. Saint Denis subsequently became an important showcase of Capetian dynastic pride and a powerful means of propaganda in their support (Panofsky, 1979; Simson, 1962, chs III, IV; Viollet-le-Duc, 1858, II, 284ff.). Both of the treatises excerpted here are accounts of the enterprise. Their unrestrained, often ecstatic praise of luxury in buildings, backed up with extremely sophisticated and learned orientalising iconographic references – in particular the writings of the Hellenistic writer, the Pseudo-Dionysius (first century AD), by coincidence the namesake of the patron saint of the church – was in conscious opposition to Bernard's moralistic, populist arguments (Bruyne, 1946; Panofsky, ibid.; Simson, ibid.). It was an astute discursive strategy, aiming at justifying both the pursuit of material wealth and political power in the name of higher spiritual values (Lefaivre, 1997). Suger was innovative not only as a theoretician but also as an architectural patron. His church has gone down in history as the first example of Gothic architecture in Europe.

Further reading Frankl, 1960; Schramm, 1939.

I used to compare the smallest to the greatest. Solomon's riches could not have sufficed for his Temple any more than ours did for this work if the same Author of the same work had not abundantly supplied His attendants. . . . In carrying out such plans, my first thought was for the concordance and harmony of the ancient work with the new. By reflection, by inquiry, and by searching through different regions of remote districts, we attempted to learn where we might obtain marble columns or columns equivalent to them. Since we did not find any, only one solution was left to us, distressed as we were in mind and spirit. And this was that we might obtain them from Rome (for in Rome we had often seen wonderful ones in the Palace of Diocletian and other Baths) by safe ships through the Mediterranean, then through the English Sea and the tortuous windings of the Seine, at great expense to our friends and even by paying passage fare to our enemies, the surrounding Saracens.

aesthetisation of architecture • archaic beliefs • body model • luxury • hedonism • consumption • orientalism

Abbot Suger (1081–1151)

On Matters of Administration (1144–1149)

Chapter XXXI

Into this panel, erected before his most sacred body, we have put, in our estimation, about forty-two marks of gold; [further] a great abundance of precious gems, hyacinths, rubies, sapphires, emeralds and topazes, and also an array of different large pearls – as great as we had ever hoped to find. You could see how kings, princes, and many eminent men, following our example, took the rings off the fingers of their hands and ordered, out of love for the Holy Martyrs, that the gold, stones and precious pearls of the rings be put into that panel. Similarly archbishops and bishops put there the very rings of their investiture as if it were a safe place, and offered them devoutly to God and His Saints. And so great a crowd of dealers in precious gems flocked in on us from diverse dominions and regions that we did not wish to buy any more than they hurried to sell, with everyone contributing donations. [. . .]

[35]

Furthermore we had the actual receptacles of the holy bodies enclosed with gilded panels of cast copper and with polished stones, fixed close to the inner stone vaults, and also with continuous gates to block disturbances by crowds, but in such a manner that religious people, as was fitting, might be able to see them with great devotion and through a flood of tears . . .

Chapter XXXIII

We hastened to adorn the Main Altar of the blessed Denis where there was only one beautiful and precious frontal panel from Charles the Bald, the third Emperor; for this is the altar we had been offered to the monastic life at. We had it all encased, putting up golden panels on either side and adding a fourth, even more precious one so that the whole altar would appear golden all the way round. On either side, we installed the two candlesticks of King Louis, son of Philip, of twenty marks of gold, lest they might be stolen on some occasion. Then we added hyacinths, emeralds and sundry precious gems; and we gave orders carefully to look out for others to be added further. The verses on these panels are these.

On the right side:

'Abbot Suger has set up these altar panels
In addition to that which King Charles has given before.
Make worthy the unworthy through thy indulgence, O Virgin Mary. May the
fountain of mercy cleanse the sins both of the King and the Abbot.'

On the left side:

'If any impious person despoils this excellent altar
May he die, rightfully damned, like Judas.'

But the rear panel, of marvellous workmanship and lavish sumptuousness (for the barbarian artists were even more lavish than ours), we ennobled with chased relief work equally admirable for its form as for its material, so that certain people might be able to say: *The workmanship surpassed the material.* Much of what had been acquired and more of such ornaments of the church as we were afraid of losing – for instance, a golden chalice that was curtailed of its foot and several other things – we ordered to be fastened there. And because the diversity of the materials such as gold, gems and pearls is not easily understood by the mute perception of sight without a description, we have seen to it that this work, which is intelligible only to the literate, which shines with the radiance of delightful allegories, be set down in writing. . . .'

We often contemplate, out of pure affection for our mother the church, these different ornaments both new and old. When we behold how that wonderful cross of St Eloy – in addition to the smaller ones – and that incomparable ornament commonly called 'the Crest' are placed upon the golden altar, I then say, sighing deeply in my heart: *Every precious stone was your covering: the sardius, the topaz, and the jasper, the chrysolite, and the onyx, and the beryl, the sapphire, and the carbuncle and the emerald.* To those who know the properties of precious stones it becomes evident, to their utter surprise, that none is absent from their number here, with the single exception of the carbuncle,

Abbot Suger
1081–1151

and that they abound most copiously. Thus, when – out of my enjoyment of the beauty of the house of God – the loveliness of the many-coloured gems has called me away from external cares, and worthy meditation has induced me to reflect, transferring what is material to that which is immaterial, on the diversity of the sacred virtues, it seems to me that I see myself dwelling, as it were, in some strange part of the universe which neither exists entirely in the slime of the earth nor entirely in the purity of Heaven. And that, by the grace of God, I can be transported from this lower to that higher world in an anagogical way. I used to speak with travellers from Jerusalem and, to my great delight, I learned from those to whom the treasures of Constantinople and the ornaments of Haghia Sophia had been accessible, whether the things here could claim some value in comparison with those there. When they declared that the ones here were the more important, it occurred to us that the marvels of which we had heard before might have been put away, as a matter of precaution, for fear of the Franks, for fear that through the rash greed of a stupid few the partisans of the Greeks and Latins, called upon the scene, might suddenly be moved to sedition and warlike hostilities. After all, quarrelsomeness is a special trait of the Greeks.

Abbot Suger
1081–1151

It might happen, therefore, that the treasures that are not visible here but put in safe keeping amount to more than those that were visible there under conditions unsafe on account of disorders. From very many truthful men, even from Bishop Hugues of Laon, we had heard wonderful and almost incredible reports about the superiority of Haghia Sophia's and other churches' ornaments for the celebration of Mass. If this is so – or rather because we believe it to be so because of their word – then such inestimable and incomparable treasures should be exposed to the judgement of the many. *Let every man abound in his own sense.* To me, I confess, one thing has always seemed fitting above all. This is that every object more costly or most costly should serve, first and foremost, for the administration of the Holy Eucharist. If golden pouring vessels, golden vials, golden little mortars used to serve, by the word of God or the command of the Prophet, to collect the blood of goats or calves or the red heifer, then how much more must golden vessels, precious stones and whatever is most valued among all created things, be laid out, with continual reverence and full devotion, for the reception of the blood of Christ! Surely neither we nor our possessions suffice for this duty. If, by a new creation, our substance were reformed from that of the holy Cherubim and Seraphim, it would still offer inefficient and unworthy means for so great and so ineffable a victim. And still we have such a great price to pay for our sins. The detractors also object that a saintly spirit, a pure heart, a faithful intention ought to suffice for this sacred function. We, too, explicitly and especially affirm that it is these that principally matter. We profess that we must also pay homage through the outward ornaments of sacred vessels to nothing in the world so much as to the service of the Holy Sacrifice, with all inner purity and with all outward splendour.

[...]

aesthetisation of architecture • archaic beliefs • body model • luxury • hedonism • consumption • orientalism

Robert of Clari (c.1170–after 1216)

The Conquest of Constantinople (1216)

Robert of Clari
c.1170–after
1216

Robert was a small vassal from Amiens, France, who followed his lord or 'suzerain' in the Fourth Crusade (1201–1204) and dictated his account of his adventure upon his return. The expedition, which had set out to free the Holy Land from Muslim rule, was diverted by the Venetian contingent to the Dalmatian coast in order to reinforce Venetian holdings there. The crusaders were then re-routed to Constantinople where they engaged in wholesale slaughter, sacking, looting and killing. Thus, in what was to have been the highest Christian enterprise, the crusaders hypocritically brought great profit upon themselves and disastrously weakened the opulent, but no less Christian, city. The first-hand account of the architectural luxury of the East does not differ much from the earlier descriptions in the tradition of the *Mirabilia* by Leo of Naples (late tenth century), for instance, or of **The Voyage of Charlemagne** (c.1150) in its repeated attempts to calculate the worth of luxurious buildings and objects in them. Still, the text retains much of the wide-eyed and breathless state that Robert and his European cohorts must have felt in the discovery of such great Byzantine wealth. Although experienced in reality, the riches inspire such a sense of unreality and wonder that Robert has trouble telling the actual city and marvellous hearsay apart (Lefaivre, 1997). Here we see the effects of the attraction of the Orient as displayed in the *Mirabilia*: the invasion and despoiling of the East by the West.

Further reading Said, 1978; Sombart, 1967.

Once the city had been captured and the pilgrims lodged, as I have told you already, and the palaces were occupied, we found so many riches that it was excessive. How rich and well finished were the palaces of Boukoleon I will now tell you. There was inside this palace that Boniface, the marquis of Montferrat, had occupied, five hundred rooms, all connected one to the other and all covered in gold mosaic. There were also at least thirty chapels, big and small. There was one that was called the Holy Chapel, that was so rich and noble that not one hinge or bolt that was of anything but silver instead of iron, and there was no column that was not of jasper or porphyry or some other expensive precious stone. And the pavement of this chapel was of a white marble so smooth and bright that it seemed to be made of crystal. And this chapel was so rich and noble that no one could describe the great beauty and nobility of this chapel....

And in the palace of Blachernae we found very great treasures. Among them were rich crowns that had belonged to former emperors and the rich ornaments of gold and rich silks and gold and rich imperial robes and rich precious stones and so many other riches that it would not be possible to calculate the worth of the great treasure of gold and silver that was found in the palaces and in many other places in the city.

Afterwards the pilgrims began to notice the great size of the city and of the palaces and the fine abbeys and the rich churches and the great marvels that were in this city, and they marvelled greatly. And they marvelled especially at the church of Haghia Sophia and at the riches that it contained.

Now I will tell you about the church of Haghia Sophia.... It was entirely round, and within the church there were domes, all about, which were carried atop great and very rich columns, and there was no column that was not of jasper or porphyry or some other precious stone, nor was there one of these columns that was not capable of working cures. There was one that cured the sickness of the kidney when it was rubbed against, and another that cured the sickness of the ribs, and others that cured other maladies. And there was no door in this church and no hinges or bolts or other parts that are usually made of iron that were not made of silver. The master altar of the church was so rich that it was impossible to give it a price, for the table for the altar was made of gold and precious stones all crushed and mixed together that a rich emperor had had made. This table was fourteen feet long and around the altar were columns of silver supporting a canopy over the altar. It was made like a church spire and it was all of solid silver and was so rich that no one could tell how much money it was worth... Through the church there hung at least one hundred chandeliers, and not one was worth less than two hundred marks of silver. On the handle of the great door to the church, that was entirely of silver, there hung a tube of a material no one could divine. It was the size of a pipe of the kind that shepherds play. This pipe had the following virtue. When an infirm man who had some illness in his body like diarrhoea that bloats the belly put it in his mouth, however little he put it in, when this tube took hold, it sucked all the illness out and made the poison come out of his mouth. It held the man so fast that it then made his eyes roll and turn in his head and he could not escape until the tube had sucked all the illness out of him.

Robert of Clari
c.1170–after
1216

luxury • hedonism • consumption • orientalism

Villard de Honnecourt

Sketchbook (1225–1250)

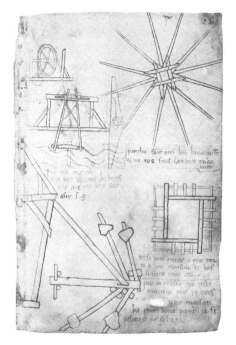

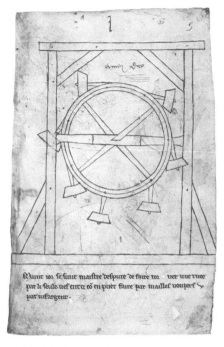

10. Villard de Honnecourt. *Sketchbook*. 1225–1250. Various engines and mechanical devices.

10b. Villard de Honnecourt. *Sketchbook*. 1225–1250. A perpetual-motion machine.

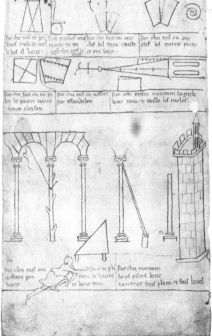

11. Villard de Honnecourt. *Sketchbook*. 1225–1250. Figures drawn 'by the art of geometry'.

Albrecht von Scharfenberg (?–?)

The Young Titurel (c.1270)

This German work is probably the work of several poets or 'trouvères' rather than a solitary figure like 'Albrecht', to whom it is generally attributed. Like others in the cycle of epic poems about the quest for the Holy Grail in the Eastern Mediterranean, for instance the Parsifal and Arthurian versions, this is a legitimising account, under the guise of legend, of the establishment of the first royal dynasties in Europe. In this version, Titurel is elected to become lord and king of the Grail and to build a temple to house it. The Holy Grail falls into the same category as the Indian palace of King Porus in the Alexander Romance, of descriptions of ancient Rome, pre-crusade Constantinople and China, that is of orientalist architectural *Mirabilia*. The importance of the temple was considerable. Around it a new order was founded, both religious and chivalric, whose role it was to ensure the hereditary transmission of the royal title (van den Berghe, 1857). The description of the temple makes luxury desirable in a fashion similar to that in Robert of Clari's account (1216). The precious materials it is made of have magical powers, also as in Robert of Clari's report.

Albrecht von Scharfenberg c.1270

Further reading Bruyne, 1946, III, 131ff.; Frankl, 1960, 176–184; Sombart, 1967; Zarncke, 1879.

5 They began work on the temple with great enthusiasm. Tradition reports that it was in the form of a rotonda. Seventy-two octagonal chapels projected from it. Such great magnificence would have driven a pauper to vexation.

6 On columns of brass rested vaults that had been worked with great art. Joy rendered my heart imperishable. If only I could see them again. Everything was decorated with great luxury: gold and fine stones shone and sparkled greatly.

7 There the vaults curved following the inclination of the arches, seemed to fly from their columns. And over there, were works of enamel, chased with coral and precious pearls [. . .], precious in their material and in the work that went into them, placed there, according to the wishes of the King, in order to move hearts. We wept with joy. [. . .]

10 The altars were richly decorated and laden in honour of God, with masterful art. To describe such magnificence would be a task beyond my capacity, even if I were more capable than I am now.

11 The sapphire has the sublime property of erasing from the book of life the sins of man and to help him turn again towards God in making him weep tears that scatter right up to the tops of mountains. Its power grants the grace to weep away sins. [. . .]

14 And as it purifies man, Titutel took upon himself to insure that the altars were covered with sapphires. In all things the King wanted the best, and he cared little about the price of this magnificence. [. . .]

19 Beryls and crystals took the place of glass [in the windows]. And, indeed, a vivid light came down from them, hurting the audacious eye that dared to gaze upon them at length.

20 Figures were represented in them for reasons doubly positive: to temper the shining brightness and also to increase the richness in God's and the Grail's honour. This decoration, indeed, is most suitable to the temple.

21 The masters sketch on the glass and apply colour by means of crystal, and it throws light rays that are like inflamed sparks. It was a beautiful sight to see the sun come through the windows, coloured by all the stones. [. . .]

[41]

30 For those who are thinking about the roof of the temple, I will say that it was of pure gold, enamelled with blue so that it would not be too bright in the light of day. The wisdom of the master had ornamented it with symbolic figures. [...]

36 The building could have done without windows, so numerous were the precious stones within that shone like fire. Their shine made the gilded parts of the temple sparkle with blinding light. To be honest, such wealth makes me envious.

luxury • hedonism • consumption • orientalism

Marco Polo (1254–1324), Rustichello of Pisa (?–?) and others

The Travels of Marco Polo (late thirteenth century)

Marco Polo
1254–1324

About the year 1260 the Venetian trader, Marco Polo, who had established a business at the Crimean port of Sudak, formed a caravan to China and reached Kahn-Balik (Beijing). Sometime towards the end of the thirteenth century he is reported to have given his account of his travels to Rustichello of Pisa, a writer of some repute. The book, certainly the oldest 'orientalist' pieces of literature still popular in the West, contains a lengthly and enthralled discovery of architectural *Mirabilia*. Remarkably, we find the same commonplaces regarding this architecture – that of the Kubilai Khan in Xanadu (Kemenfu), Manzi (Mangi) and Kahn-balik (Beijing) – as in the other *Mirabilia*: a courtly setting, glittering polychromic surfaces and expensive materials such as gold, silver and gems adorning the columns and walls (Lefaivre, 1997). In some cases the buildings are also feats of engineering or endowed with supernatural, magical powers. His description of the new town of Taidu, outside of Beijing, must also have been read as marvelous.

When the traveller leaves this city and journeys north–north–east for three days, he comes to a city called Xanadu, which was built by the Great Kahn now reigning, whose name of Kubilai. In this city Kubilai Kahn built a huge palace of marble and other ornamental stones. Its halls and chambers are all gilded, and the whole building [...] Let me tell you of a strange thing I had forgotten. You must know that the garden is marvellously embellished and richly adorned. At one end it extends into the middle of the city; at the other it abuts on the city wall. At this end another wall, running out from the city wall in the direction opposite to the palace, encloses and encircles fully sixteen miles of park-land well watered with springs and streams and diversified with lawns. [...]

In the midst of this enclosed park, where there is a beautiful grove, the Great Khan has built another large palace, constructed entirely of canes, but with the interior all gilt and decorated with beasts and birds of very skilful workmanship. It is reared on gilt and varnished pillars, on each of which stands a dragon, entwining the pillar with his tail and supporting the roof on his outstretched limbs. The roof is also made of canes, so well varnished that it is quite waterproof. Let me explain how it is constructed. You must know that these canes are more than three palms in girth and from ten to fifteen paces long. They are sliced down through the middle from one knot to the next, thus making two shingles. These shingles are thick and long enough not only for roofing but for every sort of construction. The palace, then, is built entirely upon such canes. As a protection against the wind each shingle is fastened with nails. And the Great Khan has had it so designed that it can be moved wherever he fancies; for this it is held in place by more than 200 cords of silk.

The Great Khan stays at Xanadu for three months in the year, June, July and August, to escape from the heat and for the sake of recreation it affords. During these three months he keeps the palaces of canes erected; the rest of the year it is dismantled. And he has had it so constructed that he can erect or dismantle it at pleasure.

Great Khan was staying in his palace and the weather was rainy and cloudy, he had wise astrologers and enchanters who by their skill and their enchantments would dispel all the clouds and the bad weather from above the palace so that, while bad weather continued all around, the weather above the palace was fine.

[...]

Within this wall (of Kahn-Balik, or Beijing) is the Great Khan's palace, which I will now describe to you. It is the largest that was ever seen. It has no upper floor, but the basement on which it stands is raised ten palms above the level of the surrounding earth; and all round it there runs a marble wall level with the basement, two paces in thickness. The foundation of the palace lies within this wall, so that as much of the wall as projects beyond it forms a sort of terrace, on which men can walk right round and inspect the outside of the palace. At the outer edge of this wall is a fine gallery of columns, where men can meet and talk. At each face of the palace is a great marble staircase, ascending from ground level to the top of this marble wall, which affords an entry into the palace.

Marco Polo
1254–1324

The palace itself has a very high roof. Inside, the walls of the halls and chambers are all covered with gold and silver and decorated with pictures of dragons and birds and horsemen and similarly adorned, so that there is nothing to be seen anywhere but gold and pictures. The hall is so vast and so wide that a meal might well be served for more than 6,000 men. The number of chambers is quite bewildering. The whole building is at once so immense and so well constructed that no man in the world, granted that he had the power to effect it, could imagine any improvement in design or execution. The roof is all ablaze with scarlet and green and blue and yellow and all the colours there are, so brilliantly varnished that it glitters like crystal and the sparkle of it can be seen from far away. And this roof is so strong and so stoutly built as to last for many a long year.

In the rear of the palace are extensive apartments, both chambers and halls, in which are kept private possessions of the Khan. Here is stored his treasure: gold and silver, precious stones and pearls, and his gold and silver vessels. And here too are his ladies and concubines. In these apartments everything is arranged for his comfort and convenience, and outsiders are not admitted.

Between the inner and outer walls, of which I have told you, are stretches of parkland. The grass grows here in abundance, because all the paths are paved and built up fully two cubits above the level of the ground, so that no mud forms on them and no rainwater collects in puddles. But the moisture trickles over the lawns, enriching the soil and promoting a lush growth of herbage. In these parks there is a great variety of game, such as white harts, musk-deer, roebuck, stags, squirrels and many other beautiful animals. In the area within its walls is full of these graceful creatures, except the paths people walk on.

In the northwestern corner of the grounds is a pit of great size and depth, very neatly made, from which the earth was removed to build the mound on which I shall speak. The pit is filled with water by a fair-sized stream so as to form a sort of pond where animals come to drink. The stream flows out through an aqueduct near the mound and fills another similar pit [...]

On the northern side of the palace, at the distance of a bowshot but still within the walls, the Great Khan has made an earthwork, that is to say a mound fully 100 paces in height and over a mile in circumference. This mound is covered with a dense growth of trees, all evergreens that never shed their leaves. And I assure you that whenever the Great Khan hears tell of a particularly fine tree he has it pulled up, roots and all, and with a quantity of earth, and transported to this mound by elephants. No matter how big the tree may be, he is not deterred from transplanting it. In this way he has assembled here the finest trees in the world. In addition he has had the mound covered with lapis lazuli, which is intensely green, so that trees and rock alike are as green as green can be, and there is no other colour to be seen.

[...] On the banks of a great river in the province of Cathay there stood an ancient city of great size and splendour which was named Khan-Balik, that is to say in our language 'the Lord's City'. Now the Great Khan discovered through his astrologers that this city would rebel and put up a stubborn resistance against the Empire. For this reason he had his new city built next to the old one, with only the river between. And he removed the inhabitants of the old city and settled them in the new one, which is called Taidu, leaving only those whom he did not suspect of any rebellious designs; for the new city was not big enough to house all those who lived in the old. [...]

I assure you that the streets are so broad and straight that from the top of the wall above one gate you can see along the whole length of the road to the gate opposite. The city is full of fine mansions, inns and dwelling houses. All the way down the sides of every main street there are booths and shops of every sort. All the building sites throughout the city are square and measured by the rule; and on every site stand large and spacious mansions with ample courtyards and gardens. These sites are allotted to heads of households, so that none belong to such-and-such a person, representing such-and-such a family, the next to a representative of another family, and so all the way along. Every site or block is surrounded by good public roads; and in this way the whole interior of the city is laid out in squares like a chess-board with such masterly precision that no description can do justice to it.

In this city there is such a multitude of houses and people, both within the walls and without, that no one could count their number. Actually there are more people outside the walls in the suburbs than in the city itself. There is a suburb outside every gate, such that each one touches the neighbouring suburbs on either side. They extend in length for three or four miles. And in every suburb or ward, at about a mile's distance from the city, there are many fine hostels which provide lodging for merchants coming from different parts: a particular hostel is assigned to every nation, so we might say one for the Lombards, another for the Germans, another for the French. Merchants and others come here on business in great numbers, both because it is the Khan's residence and because it affords a profitable market. And the suburbs have as fine houses and mansions as the city, except of course for the Khan's palace.

[...]

In this city (Manzi, or Mangi) also is the palace of the fugitive king, the one-time lord of Manzi, which is the most beautiful and splendid palace in the world. No words of mine could describe its superlative magnificence, but I will briefly relate some of its main features. You must know that the king's predecessors had enclosed a space of land some ten miles in circumference with lofty battlemented walls and divided it into three parts. The middle part was entered through a wide gateway flanked by pavilions of vast dimensions standing at ground level with their roofs supported by columns painted and wrought in fine gold and azure. Ahead was seen the largest and most important of these pavilions, similarly adorned with paintings and with gilded columns, and the ceiling gorgeously embellished with gold. On the inner walls were pictures of beasts and birds, knights and ladies and scenes from the history of past kings, portrayed with consummate artistry. On every wall and every ceiling nothing met the eye but a blaze of gold and brilliant colour. Here every year, on certain days dedicated to his idols, King Facfur used to hold court and offer banquets to the chief lords and magnates and the wealthy industrialists of the city of Kinsai. At one service ample accommodation was found in all the halls of the palace, which numbered no less than twenty, for 10,000 persons. These festivities lasted for ten or twelve days on end and were a truly stupendous affair. It was a sight past all believing to behold the magnificence of the guests, robed in silk and gold and laden with precious stones, because everyone was at pains to make the greatest possible display of opulence.

Behind this chief pavilion, which faced the great gateway, was a wall with one way through, which shut off the other part of the palace. Beyond this was a large court, made in the style of a cloister with pillars supporting a portico, which extended right round it. Here there were various chambers for the king and queen, adorned with the same elaborate workmanship and all the walls likewise. Leading out of this cloister was a long covered corridor six paces wide, which ran right through the lake at the other end. Communicating with this corridor were ten courtyards on one side and ten on the other, constructed in the form of long cloisters with surrounding colonnades. Every cloister or courtyard had fifty chambers with their gardens, and these were occupied in all by 1,000 damsels whom the king kept in his service and some of whom used to accompany him and the queen when he went for recreation on the lake in barges canopied with silk or to visit the temples of the idols.

luxury • hedonism • consumption • orientalism

Dante (Alighieri)

Inferno (c. 1306–1309)

Dante's **Inferno**, written seven centuries ago, is the most enduring horror story in Western culture. The first of Dante's three-part **Divine Comedy**, the **Inferno**, was a runaway popular success compared to the more measured **Purgatorio** and **Paradiso**. Here is a sample description: 'wretches naked and sorely stung by hornets and wasps that were there, their faces streaming with blood, that mingled with their tears and was gathered at their feet by loathsome worms' (Canto III). Short on architectural content, it does contain a description of the abyss and the descent into it by Dante and his fictitious guide, Virgil. For all the laconic tone of the description, the impact of the aesthetics of horror it puts forth marks the beginning of the taste for the grotesque and the sublime.

Canto I The Dark Wood

Half way down the journey of my life, I came upon a dark wood where the straight way had disappeared. Oh, how hard it is to talk about that wood, wild and harsh and

[45]

mirror ⇒ how it shows life

overpowering as it is. The thought of it only renews my fear. So bitter is it that it is very close to being like a death.

Canto XII The Seventh Circle

There was the place we came to for the descent of the ravine and it was as steep as the Alps. And what was to be found there would have caused anyone to avert their eyes. Like the destruction that hit the flank of the Adige of Trento [a mountain chain in the Italian Alps] as a result of the earthquake and inherent instability, the rocks were so shattered from the mountain top all the way to the plain below that it was impossible to get a footing on the way down the ravine. On the edge of the jagged-edged chasm lay, outstretched, the infamy of Crete [the Minotaur] that was conceived by the false cow. And when he saw us, he started to eat away at his own flesh, like one that is consumed by an inward rage.

The sage cried out to him 'Do you think that maybe the Duke of Athens is here, who caused you to die? Be on your way, beast. This man is not here by the workings of your sister [Ariadne]. He is here on way to see your pains.'

Like a bull that thrashes about at the moment it has received the mortal wound, and that, unable to fully turn, heaves this way and that, I saw the Minotaur do the same. Upon which my guide yelled that I take a run to the passage because it was good to descend while he was in such a rage. So we took the path down that heap of debris that often gave away under our feet with the new addition of our weight.

I was pursuing my thoughts when he said 'You are thinking perhaps, of this cliff in ruin that is guarded by that furious beast I tamed just now. I want you to know that the last time I came this way into the hell below this rock had not yet fallen. But, if I am correct, it was a little while before the person who carried off from Dis the great spoil of the highest circle that the deep, foul valley shook all over in such a way that it seemed to me that the entire universe was shuddering in the ecstasy of love, by which, as some believe, the world has been turned into chaos many times.'

emotions • passions • sentiments

(Francesco) Petrarch (1307–1374)

The Ascent of Mount Ventoux (April 26, 1342)

These two texts by Petrarch, taken from his correspondence, contain the first literary description of the landscape of the South of France. They were the first instance of the new Renaissance sensitivity towards what would come to be called the 'picturesque landscape'.

Today I made the ascent of the highest mountain in this region, which is not improperly called Ventosum [breath]. My only motive was to see what so great an elevation had to offer . . .

At the time fixed we left the house, and by evening reached Malaucène, which lies at the foot of the mountain, to the north. Having rested there a day, we finally made the ascent this morning, with no companions except two servants; and a most difficult task it was. The mountain was very steep and an almost inaccessible mass of stony soil. . . . It was a long day and the air fine. We enjoyed the advantages of vigour of mind and strength and agility of body, and everything else essential to those engaged in such an undertaking, and so had no other difficulties to face than those of the region itself. We found an old shepherd in one of the mountain dales, who tried, at great length, to dissuade us from the ascent, saying that some fifty years before he had, in the same ardour of youth, reached the summit, but had gotten for his pains nothing except fatigue and regret, and clothes and body torn by the rocks and briars.... At last I became disgusted with the intricate way I had chosen, and resolved to ascend without more ado. When I reached my brother, who, while waiting for me, had ample opportunity to rest, I was tired and irritated. We walked along together for a time, but hardly had we passed the first spur when I forgot about the circuitous route which I had just tried, and took a lower one again. Once more I followed an easy, roundabout path around winding valleys, only to find myself soon in my old difficulty. I was simply trying to avoid the exertion of the ascent; but no human ingenuity can alter the nature of things, or cause anything to reach a height by going down. Suffice it to say that, much to my vexation and my brother's amusement, I made this same mistake three times or more during a few hours.... (Francesco) Petrarch 1307–1374

One peak of the mountain, the highest of all, the country people call 'Sonny', why, I do not know, unless by antiphasis, as I have sometimes suspected in other instances; for the peak in question would seem to be the father of all the surrounding ones. On its top is a little level place, and here we could at last rest our tired bodies.

... At first, owing to the unaccustomed quality of the air and the effect of the great sweep of view spread out before me, I stood like one dazed. I beheld the clouds under our feet, and what I read of Athos and Olympus seemed less incredible as I myself witnessed the same things from a mountain of less fame. I turned my eyes towards Italy, whither my heart most inclined. The Alps, rugged and snow-capped seemed to rise close by, although they were really at a great distance....

view • movement

Vaucluse (late summer, 1347)

This retreat is fifteen miles distant from that most boisterous of cities and from the left bank of the Rhône. Though the intervening distance is so short, still the two places are so utterly different that, whenever I leave here for that city, I seem to have encircled the globe from the farthest west to the extreme east. The two places have nothing in common but the sky: men have different natures, waters are of a different quality, the land brings forth different vegetation.

... The spot is most suitable to my studies. The hills cast a grateful shadow in the morning and in the evening hours; and at noon, many a nook and cranny of the vale gleams in the sunlight. Round about, the woods lie still and tranquil, woods in which the tracks of wild animals are far more numerous than those of men. Everywhere a deep and unbroken stillness, except for the babbling of running waters, or the singing of birds ...

Hither then, as I was saying, I fled with great longing, both to give my mind and my ears rest from the distracting whirl of the city, and also to put the finishing touches to some work I had in hand, the thought of which, in its unfinished condition, weighed heavily upon me. The very aspect of the forest urged me to compose a poem dealing with the wild woodlands....

view • movement • emotions • passions • sentiments • romanticism

Anonymous

Annals of the Duomo of Milan (1400, 1401)

The Gothic Cathedral of Milan, founded in 1386, was one of the monumental building projects carried out under the reign of Gian Galleazo Visconti (Ackerman, 1949). Over the years, the building council in charge of overseeing the construction of the Cathedral was prompted to consult a number of 'engineers' or master masons. Jean Mignot, a Parisian, was among these. The following excerpts, drawn from the records of these meetings, reveal that the new 'science' of geometry could still be controversial and that in some circles 'art', in the sense of traditional, scientifically unsound notions, was held in greater esteem. In addition, these passages show how unscientifically geometry was applied to construction problems before the advent of modern engineering in the works of humanists like Leon Battista Alberti, over a quarter of a century later (Ackerman, 1949). In particular it gives an idea of what a backward context it was that humanists like Alberti were up against, and how gigantic was the leap in knowledge they managed to make.

Further reading Ackerman, 1949; Frankl, 1945; Harvey, 1969, 1972; Lefaivre, 1997; Shelby, 1976; Simson, 1962, 19–20, 33–34; Tzonis, 1972, 22.

1400. Sunday, 25 January. Master Jean Mignot has stated to the council here present that he has given in writing to the said council a note computing to date all the reasons and every motive that led him to say that the aforesaid work lacks strength, and he does not wish to give other reasons. . . .

Master Jean Mignot points out to you excellent lords of the workshop council of the Milanese church with respect and pure truth that he had demonstrated in writing elsewhere and among other matters, the defects of said church, he reiterates and affirms that all the buttresses around the church are neither strong nor able to sustain the weight which rests upon them, since they ought in every case to be three times the thickness of one pier in the interior of the church. The Masters reply:

Concerning the first statement, they say that all the buttresses of said church are strong and capable of sustaining their weight and many times more, for many reasons, since one braccio of our marble and saritium [a local building stone], whatever its width, is as strong as two braccia of French stone or of the French church which he gives to the aforesaid masters as an example. Therefore they say that if aforesaid buttresses are one-and-a-half times the size – and they are – of the piers in the interior of the church, that they are strong and correctly conceived, and if they were larger they would darken said church because of their projection, as at the church in Paris, which has buttresses of Master Jean's type, and since they can be an obstruction there are other reasons.

Moreover Mignot says that four towers were begun to support the crossing-tower of said church, and there are no piers nor any foundation capable of sustaining said tower, and if the church were to be made with said towers in this position it would infallibly fall. Concerning the claims, however, which were made by certain ignorant people, surely through passion, that pointed vaults are stronger and exert less thrust than round, and moreover concerning other matters, proposals were made in a fashion more wilful than sound; and what is worse, it was objected that the science of geometry should not have a place in these matters since science is one thing and art another. Master Jean said that art without science is nothing and that whether the vaults are pointed or round, they are worthless unless they have a good foundation, and nevertheless, no matter how pointed they are, they have a very great thrust and weight.

Whereupon the Masters say that the towers which they wanted to make are for many reasons and causes desirable. Namely, in the first place, to integrate aforesaid church and transept so that they correspond to a rectangle according to the demands of geometry, but beyond this, for the strength and beauty of the crossing-tower. To be sure, as if as a model for this, the Lord God is seated in paradise in the centre of the throne, and around the throne there are the four Evangelists according to the Apocalypse, and these are the reasons why they were begun. And although two piers of each sacristy are not founded, but begin at ground level, the church is truly strong nevertheless for these reasons, that there are projections upon which the said piers stand, and the said projections are of large stones joined with iron dowels as was said above with other statements, and that the weight on these three [sic] towers falls evenly on their square, and that they will be built properly and strong, and what is vertical cannot fall; therefore they say that they are strong in themselves, and for that reason will give strength to the crossing-tower, which is enclosed in the centre of those towers. Therefore the church is truly strong.

Christine de Pisan c.1363–1431

archaic beliefs • body model • design methodology • precedent • authority • invention

Christine de Pisan (c.1363–1431)

The Book of Military and Chivalric Feats (c.1410)

This military treatise was the first to recognise the importance of the recently invented siege cannon as a factor in military architecture. It revolutionised fortress design by advocating the use of angular bastions rather than the traditional round or square fortifications of the Middle Ages and reveals a wholly new, totally functionalist approach to construction that prefigures modern engineering. Italian born, but settled in France from an early age, Christine was a prolific and celebrated poetess, moral and social philosopher and a champion of the cause of women. This did not protect her from gender discrimination, however. No one championed her cause in this specific case. Her treatise was repeatedly published without her name (de la Croix, 1963).

Book II, chapter 13 ... The Wise ancients did not make the walls of their city or fortress with a regular outline as men do now. They said that walls so made were readier and better disposed to receive the strokes of all manner of engines and to have ladders drawn up on them, and so they made them crooked and some well built doors and steps and the stones strongly bound together with lime and sand. [. . .]

[. . .] Walls may be doubly fortified against all engines, that is to say that two walls of strong stuff must be made with an interval or space that is twenty feet broad between them. And the earth that is dug should be taken out to settle the foundations that ought to be made as deep into the earth as the ditches nearby. Between both the aforesaid walls the twenty-foot space shall be trodden and stamped on as hard as can be. And the walls must be first made up above and so thick and so broad that a passage can be made to fit in between them, and holes and splits must be made so that archers can sit there to shoot and send all manner of stones and all other projectiles outward. And a proper place must be ordained and made at every face of the walls in order to set

[49]

up guns and other engines to shoot with if there be a need to make a defence. And coverings and barbicans of timber should be attached closely to the battlements of the outside walls to act against the shots without.

social control • defence • systemisation of space distribution

Leon Battista Alberti (1404–1472)

Book of The Family (c.1428)

Leon Battista
Alberti
1404–1472

In his **De Re Aedificatoria** (1440s–1450s), Alberti would confer to architecture the scholarship typical of the civic humanist writers. But to the present work, he brought the practical, mercantile and worldly spirit that characterised the new economic order prevalent in the immensely affluent Northern Italian Renaissance towns. Using the device of a dialogue between uncle and nephew, he provided a set of directives about running a country estate as a business for the purpose of attaining the greatest possible profit (Gadol, 1969). His concerns for maximising gain and indulging in luxury are taken for granted as natural facts of life – a far cry from the kind of thinking that characterised, for example, Suger's writings about the same matter some two hundred years earlier.

Book III

Giannozzo: Why say it all, Lionardo? You cannot praise the farm half as much as it deserves to be praised. It is excellent for our health, helps maintain us, and is good for family life. Good men and prudent householders are always interested in the farm, as everyone knows. And indeed the farm is, first of all, profitable, and second, a source of both pleasure and honour. There is no need, as with other occupations, to fear deceit and fraud from debtors or suppliers. Nothing goes on under cover, everything is out in the open and understood by all. You will not be cheated, nor do you need to call in notaries and witnesses, undertake lawsuits, or engage in other irritating and depressing intrigues, most of which are not worth the convulsions of spirit involved in carrying them to a successful conclusion. Consider, too, that you can retire on your farm and live there in peace, nurturing your little family, dealing on your own with your private affairs. On a holiday, you can discuss pleasantly in the shade about oxen and wool or about vines and seeds. You can live undisturbed by rumours and tales, with none of the violent strife that breaks out periodically in the city. You can be free of the suspicions, fears, slanders, injuries, feuds and other miseries that are too ugly to talk about and horrible even to remember. Among all the subjects discussed on the farm, not one can fail to delight you. All are pleasant to talk about and are heard by willing ears. Everyone says what he knows is useful to agriculture. Everyone teaches and corrects you where you erred in some of your planting or in your manner of sowing. The cultivation and management of fields give rise neither to envy, hate, nor malevolence.
Lionardo: In addition, you enjoy on the farm clear and happy days of pure, open air. You have a lovely view when you look at those leafy hills and verdant plains. Clear springs and streams leap through the waving grass, and lose themselves within it.
Giannozzo: Yes, by God, a true paradise. And, moreover, in the enjoyment of your estate you can escape the violence, the riots and the storm of the city, the market-

place and the town hall. On the farm you can hide yourself away and avoid seeing all the stealing and crime, the vast numbers of depraved men who are always flitting past your eyes in the city. There they never cease to chatter in your ears, to scream and bellow in the streets hour after hour, like a dangerous and repulsive kind of beast. What a blessing to live on the farm, what unheard of happiness.

Lionardo: Do you think one should, in fact, live in the countryside instead of the middle of town?

Giannozzo: As far as I am concerned, seeing that it is freer of vice, requires less care and less expense, offers more health and more enjoyment of life, yes, indeed, my children, I do praise the country estate.

Lionardo: Are you convinced of this enough to raise your children there?

Giannozzo: If my children could expect to spend their whole lives never talking to anyone but good persons, I would certainly want to have them grow up in the country. But the number of men who are not of the very worst sort is so small that we fathers, in order to protect ourselves from the wicked and their many devices, must make sure that our children recognise them. A man cannot distinguish who is wicked if he knows nothing of wickedness. If you have never heard the sound of the bagpipe, you cannot judge the quality of the instrument. Let us imitate those who wish to become skilled shieldsmen: first we must learn to wound others so that we know how to nimbly avoid the pointed lance and how to protect our flank from the blade. If vices dwell among men, as they do, I can see the wisdom of raising the young where vices abound no less than men, and that is in the city.

Leon Battista Alberti 1404–1472

Lionardo: Also, Giannozzo, it is in the city one learns to be a citizen. There people acquire valuable knowledge, see many models to teach them the avoidance of evils. As they look around them they notice how handsome honour is, how lovely fame is, how divine a thing glory is. There they taste the sweets of praise, of being named and esteemed and admired. By these wonderful joys the young are awakened to the pursuit of excellence and come to devote themselves to endeavouring to carry out difficult things worthy of immortality. Such great advantages may not, perhaps, be found in the country amid the logs and the clods.

Giannozzo: I have some doubts, in spite of all this, Lionardo, as to which is better, to bring up one's children in the country or the city. But let us evaluate it this way. Every situation has its own natural advantages. In the city there are the workshops of great dreams, for this is what governments, constitutions and fame are. In the country we find peace, contentment and freedom to pursue life and health. As far as I am concerned, I think that if I had the kind of farm that I was describing I would wish to stay there a good part of the year and enjoy myself while cultivating the means to feed my family abundantly and well.

efficiency • economisation • fit • utility • urbanisation of architecture • planning • aesthetisation • luxury • hedonism and consumption

Leon Battista Alberti (1404–1472)

On Painting (1435–1436)

Written before his celebrated *On Building* (1440s–1450s), Alberti's book *On Painting* captures the spirit that accompanied the cognitive revolution of the Renaissance: the attachment to innovation in the name of progress (Smith, 1992; Tafuri, 1992; Lefaivre, 1997). It also contains the first formulation of the rules of perspective (Argan, 1967; Gadol, 1969; Panofsky, 1927; Parronchi, 1964; White, 1967).

Leon Battista
Alberti
1404–1472

I used to marvel and at the same time grieve that so many excellent and superior arts and sciences from our most vigorous and antique past could now seem lacking and almost wholly lost. We know from [remaining] works and through references to them that they were once widespread. Painters, sculptors, architects, musicians, geometricians, rhetoricians, seers and similar noble and amazing intellects are very rarely found today and there are few to praise them. Thus I believed, as many said, that nature, the mistress of things, had grown old and tired. She no longer produced either geniuses or giants that in her more youthful and more glorious days she had produced so marvellously and abundantly.

Since then, I have been brought back here [to Florence] – from long exile in which we Alberti have grown old – into this our city, adorned above all others. I have come to understand that in many men, but especially you Pippo [Filippo Brunelleschi], and in our close friend Donato [Donatello] the sculptor and in others like Nencio [Lorenzo Ghiberti], Luca [della Robbia] and Masaccio [Tommaso di Giovanni di Simone Guidi], there is *ingegno* for accomplishing every praiseworthy thing. For this they should not be slighted in favour of anyone famous or of long-standing in these arts. Therefore, I believe the power of acquiring wide fame in any art or science lies in our industry and diligence more than in the times or in the gifts of nature. It must be admitted that it was less difficult for the ancients – because they had no models to imitate and from which they could learn – to come to acknowledge of those supreme arts that today are most difficult for us.

Our fame ought to be much greater [because] we discover unheard-of and never-before-seen arts and sciences without teachers and without any model whatsoever. Who could ever be hard or envious enough to fail to praise Pippo, the architect, on seeing here such a large structure, rising above the skies, ample enough to cover with its shadow all the Tuscan people, and constructed without the aid of centring or great quantity of wood? Since this work seems impossible of execution in our time, if I judge rightly, it was probably unknown and unthought-of among the ancients. But there will be other places, Pippo, to tell your fame, of the virtues of our Donato, and of the others who are most pleasing to me by their deeds.

As you work from day to day, you persevere in discovering things through which your extraordinary *ingegno* acquires perpetual fame . . .

Book I

I beg you to consider me not as a mathematician but as a painter writing of these things. Mathematicians measure with their minds alone the forms of things separated from all matter. Since we wish the object to be seen, we will use a more sensate wisdom. [. . .] The painter is concerned solely with representing what can be seen. The plane is measured by rays that serve the sight called visual rays which carry the form of the thing seen. We can imagine those rays to be like the finest hairs [...] tightly bound within the eye where the sense of sight has its seat. The rays, gathered together within the eye, are like a stalk; the eye is like a bud, which extends its shoots rapidly, and in a straight line to the plane opposite. [...] The extrinsic rays, thus encircling the plane – [...] like the willow wands of a basket-cage, and make, as is said, this visual pyramid. [...] The base of this pyramid is a plane that is seen. The sides of the pyramid are those rays that I have called extrinsic. The cuspid, that is the point of the pyramid, is located within the eye.

When painters fill the circumscribed places with colours, they should only seek to present the forms of things seen on this plane as if it were of transparent glass. Thus the visual pyramid could pass through it, placed at a definite distance with definite lights and a definite position of centre in space and in a definite place in respect to the observer.

Leon Battista Alberti 1404–1472

He who looks at a picture, done as I have described, will see a certain cross-section of a visual pyramid, artificially represented with lines and colours on a certain plane according to a given distance, centre and lights [...]

First of all about where I draw. I inscribe a quadrangle of right angles, as large as I wish, which is considered to be an open window through which I see what I want to paint. [...]

I doubt if much will be understood by the reader, either because of the newness of the material or because of the brevity of the commentary. [...]

Book II

[...] That veil which among my friends I call an intersection [...] is between the eye and the thing seen, so the visual pyramid penetrates through the thinness of the veil which is considered to be an open window through which I see what I want to paint. [...]

representation • truth • illusion

Leon Battista Alberti (1404–1472)

On Building (written 1440s–1450; published 1485)

This treatise, by a Florentine civic humanist (Baron, 1966; Gadol, 1969), is the first since antiquity to be exclusively devoted to architecture. It succeeds in establishing a daringly innovative, systematic and coherent set of practices and ideas which continue to shape architectural practice today. Like the *Ten Books* of Vitruvius, whose title it echoes (Krautheimer, 1963), it covers matters of construction. But it is equally innovative in dealing with other concerns of a practical nature: town and fortification planning (Tzonis, 1989a, 1993, 1994) new building types, economy in building, ornamentation, model making, as well as with the social status and inner workings of the architectural profession. In addition, Alberti expounds a new aesthetic theory for architecture, which is free of the scholastic conceptions, which had held sway since the twelfth century. Based on classical theories of rhetoric and poetics (Muehlmann, 1981) and especially on Alberti's own new views on the nature of the human mind and cognition, it argues that the formal

[53]

rules which produce beauty in certain buildings are natural – as opposed to divine in origin – and that these natural laws are also implanted in the human mind (Tzonis and Lefaivre, 1984a; Lefaivre, 1997). It was translated into Italian, Spanish, French and English and re-edited many times.

Further reading Baron, 1966; Baxandall, 1972; Blunt, 1940; Borsi, 1975; Briggs, 1927; Brucker, 1977; Chastel, 1959; Choay, 1981; Fraser-Jenkins, 1970; Gadol, 1969; Goldthwaite, 1980; Grayson, 1960; Hersey, 1976; Krautheimer, 1963; Lefaivre, 1997; Lücke, 1975–1976; Muehlmann, 1981; Muratori, 1975; Onians, 1971; Rykwert, 1972; Tafuri, 1978; Tatarkiewicz, 1970–1974; Tzonis and Lefaivre, 1984a; Vagnetti, 1973; Venturi, 1936; Westfall, 1974; Wiebenson, 1982; Wittkower, 1962; Zoubov, 1958, 1960b.

Here begins the *De Re Aedificatoria* by Leon Battista Alberti. I wish you an agreeable read.

Leon Battista
Alberti
1404–1472

Many of the different arts that go into the making of the good life were mastered by our ancestors through great labour and diligence. These arts have finally come down to us. And although all of them seem to vie for the same end, which is to be of the greatest possible use to the greatest number of people, we observe that each is like a distinct fruit that stands out from the rest. Some arts we follow out of necessity, some we approve of for their usefulness, and some we esteem because they are the embodiment of grace. I do not need to enumerate the arts I am referring to. They are obvious. But if you consider them as a whole, you will hardly find one that does not have its particular aims that exclude all the others. And if you do encounter any that you can in no way do without, and which combine utility combined with voluptuous pleasure and dignity, you will, I believe, be convinced that architecture should not be excluded from that number. Indeed – when you think about it – architecture gives inexpressible delight and is of the greatest convenience in all respects, both public and private; and, to be sure, it ranks not with the lowest in dignity. But before I proceed further, it will not be improper to explain what an architect is in my view. He, whom I rank with the greatest masters in the other disciplines, is not a carpenter or a joiner. The manual worker is but an instrument of the architect. An architect is someone who does not merely distribute weights and bind and bring together bodies. By the exercise of sure and admirable *ratio* and method, he knows how to conceive in his mind and spirit and then materialise in built form whatever most beautifully accommodates the worthiest deeds of man. This requires a comprehension and cognition of all the greatest and most noble things. This is what makes someone an architect. But let me return to the matter at hand.

It has been stated by some that it was fire and water that originally brought men together into societies, but it seems to us, given the usefulness and necessity that roofs and walls are for mankind, that they are what drew men together and kept them so. We are indebted to the architect not only for providing that safe and welcome refuge from the heat of the sun and the frosts of winter – though this is no mean consideration – but also for his many other inventions, both of a private and public nature of the highest use and convenience to daily life.

How many good families, reduced by the calamity of the times, in our own cities but also in others throughout the world, would have been utterly destroyed if their paternal homes had not saved and cherished them, as it were, in the bosom of their forebears? Daedalus received much praise from his fellows for having built a vault in

Selinunte where a cloud of vapour provoked a healthy sweat that it cured the body with great ease and pleasure. Do I need mention others? There are many who have contrived similar things conducive to health, such as places for exercise, for swimming, baths and the like. And what of vehicles, mills, timepieces and other smaller inventions, which however small play such a big part in our lives? And why should I insist upon the great abundance of waters brought from the most remote and hidden places and employed in so many different and useful purposes? Upon trophies, shrines, sanctuaries, temples and the like, designed by the architect for a divine cult and for the good of posterity. And lastly, do I have to stress that by cutting through rocks, boring through the mountains, filling in valleys, by protecting against the waters of the sea and lakes, by changing the course and dredging rivers, and through the construction of harbours and bridges, the architect has not only met the temporary needs of man, but also opened up new paths to all the parts of the world? This is how men have been able to furnish one another with provisions, spices, gems, and to communicate their knowledge and whatever else is healthy or pleasurable. Add to these the engines and machines of war, fortresses and the like inventions necessary to the defence of the liberty of our country and to maintaining the honour and increasing the greatness of a city, and to the acquisition and establishment of an empire.

Leon Battista
Alberti
1404–1472

I am really convinced that if we were to inquire of all the cities that, within human memory, have fallen prey by siege to the power of new masters, who was it that subjected and overcame them, that they would tell you 'the architect'. And that they were strong enough to have despised the armed enemy but not withstand the shocks of engines, the violence of the machines, the force of the other instruments of war with which the architect distressed, demolished and ruined them. And the besieged, on the contrary, would inform you that their greatest defence lay in the art and assistance of the architect. And if you were to go and look into the expeditions that have been undertaken, you would go near to finding that most of the victories were the result of the art and skill of architects than the conduct or fortune of generals. And that the enemy was more often overcome and conquered by the architect's wit, and without the captain's arms than by the captain's arms without the architect's ingenuity. It is of great consequence, then, that the architect conquers with a small number of men, and without the loss of troops. Let this suffice as proof of the usefulness of architecture.

It is obvious how pleasurable and inborn the spirit of building is to our *ratio*. Indeed, you shall never find anyone who has the means without the inclination to build. And if a man happens to think of a new thing in architecture, he is fond of communicating and divulging it for the use of others, as is constrained to do so by nature. And how often does it happen that even when we are employed in other activities, we cannot keep our mind and *ratio* from conceiving some building? And when we see each other men's houses, we immediately set about a careful examination of all the proportions and dimensions and, to the best of our ability, consider what might be added, retrenched or altered. And presently give our opinions about how it might be added, retrenched or altered, and then our opinions about how it might be made more complete or beautiful. And if a building is well laid out, and nicely finished, who does not view it with the utmost voluptuous desire and even exhilaration? But why need I mention not only how much benefit and delight but also how much glory architecture has brought to nations that have cultivated it both at home and abroad? [. . .]

The consideration of these things induced me, for my diversion, to look a little further into this art and business and into the principles from which they are derived and the parts they consist of. Finding them to be of various kinds and in number almost infinite, their nature marvellous, their use incredible, I wondered what human condition, and what part of the state, and what social class owed more to the architect as he is responsible for every comfort. This is true whether one considers the prince or the ordinary citizen, a building sacred or profane, one dedicated to leisure or business, the single individual or mankind as a whole. We thus decided for many reasons, too lengthy to deal with here, to collect them inside the following ten books.

These will be broached in the following order: first we observe that the building is a kind of body consisting, like all other bodies, of matter and of *lineamenti*, the one the product of nature and the other the product of *ingenio*. The one dependent on preparation and selection and the other one arising from the mind and cognition. We realised, nevertheless, that without the hand of the skilled workman neither would suffice to fashion matter according to *lineamenti*. Since buildings are suited to different uses, it became necessary to inquire whether the same *lineamenti* was fit for all sorts of buildings. We therefore distinguished several species of buildings and noted the importance of how the many lines came together and related to one another in forming them in determining their beauty. Upon which we began to inquire further into the nature of beauty – of what kind it should be, and in what way it should be made appropriate in each case. And, as we often come across faults in all these respects, I considered how they might be altered or amended. [. . .]

Leon Battista
Alberti
1404–1472

Book I, Chap. 1

Here starts the *First Book on Building* by Leon Battista Alberti. It deals with the *lineamenti*.

In order to deal with the design of edifices, we shall collect and transcribe into this work of ours all the most curious and useful observations left to us by the ancients which they gathered in the actual execution of these works; and to these we shall join whatever we ourselves may have discovered by our study, application and labour that seems likely to be of use. But as we desire, in the handling of this difficult, knotty and commonly obscure subject, to be as clear and intelligible as possible, we shall, according to our custom, explain what the nature of our subject is. This will show the origin of the important matters that we are to write of, at their very fountain-head, and enable us to express the things that flow from it in a more easy and perspicuous style.

We shall therefore first lay down that the whole art of building consists in lineaments and structure. The whole force and rule of the *lineamenti* consists in a right and exact adapting and joining together of the lines and angles that frame and enclose the surfaces of the building. It is the property and business of the *lineamenti* to appoint to the edifice and all its parts their proper places, determinate number, proper scale and beautiful order for whole buildings and for each of their parts. Indeed, the whole form of the building depends on the *lineamenti* alone. Nor do *lineamenti* have anything to do with matter. They are of such a nature that we may recognise that the same design is in a multitude of buildings which have all the same form, and are exactly alike as to the location of their parts and disposition of all of their lines and angles. And we can in our spirit and mind contrive perfect forms of buildings entirely separate from matter by settling and regulating in a certain order the disposition and conjunction of the lines and angles. Accordingly, we shall call the *lineamenti* the precise and correct prescription made up of lines and angles conceived in the spirit and erudite *ingenio*. [...]

Book I, Chap. 9

The whole force of invention and all our skill and knowledge in the art of building is required for partitioning because the distinct parts of the entire building and, to use such a word, the integrity of each of those parts, and the union and agreement of all the lines and angles into a single harmonious work that respects function, dignity and delight. For if a city, as the philosophers, is no more than a great house, then a house is no less than a small city. Why may it not be said that the parts of a house are so many small houses, such as the courtyard, the parlour, the portico and the like? And what is there in any of these which, if omitted by carelessness or negligence will not greatly take from the praise and dignity of the work? [...] Just as the members of the body are correspondent to one another, so it is fit that one part should answer to another in a building. Whence we say that great buildings require great members. [...] To every member therefore ought to be allotted its fit place and proper situation, no less than dignity requires, no more than convenience demands, but in a condition so proper to itself that it could be set nowhere else more fitly. [...] Moreover, in the forming of these members we ought to imitate the modesty of nature. In this as in other cases, the world never commends moderation so much as it condemns extravagant excess in building.

Leon Battista
Alberti
1404–1472

Book II, Chap. 4

> The things to be prepared are lime, timber, sand, stone, and also iron, brass, lead, glass and the like. [...] Pliny relates that Nero the Emperor, having formed a design of dedicating a huge statue in Rome a hundred and twenty feet high in honour of the sun, exceeding anything that had been done before in greatness and magnificence, before giving final orders for the work to be done by Zenodorus, a famous and excellent sculptor in those days, first demanded to see his capacity for such a work by first examining a Colossus of extraordinary weight which he had already made in the country of Auvergne in France.

These things duly considered, we proceed to the others. We intend, then, in treating of the materials necessary for building, to repeat those things which have been taught us by the most learned among the Ancients, and particularly Theophrastus, Aristotle, Cato, Varro, Pliny and Virgil, because they have learned more from long observation than from any quickness of *ingegno*; knowledge is best gathered from those who have observed with the greatest diligence. We shall therefore go on to collect those rules which the most approved ancients have left us in many and various places, and to there, according to our custom, we shall add whatever we ourselves have deduced from antique works, or the instructions of most experienced artificers, if we happen to know anything that may be serviceable to our purpose. And I believe it will be the best method, following nature herself, to begin with those things which were first in use among men in their buildings; which, if we mistake not, were timber trees which they felled in the Woods [...]

> But to return to our subject. The ancients, then, and particularly Theophrastus,

inform us that most trees, and especially the fir, the pitch tree and the pine ought to be cut as soon as they begin to put forth their young shoots, when through their abundance of sap you most easily strip off the bark. But that there are some trees, such as the maple, the elm, the ash and the linden, which are best cut after vintage. The oak if cut in summer, they observe, is apt to breed worms; but if cut in winter, it will keep sound and not split. And it is not foreign to our purpose what they remark that wood which is cut in winter, in a North wind, though it be green, will nevertheless burn extremely well and without smoke; which manifestly shows that their juices are not crude, but well-digested. Vitruvius is for cutting timber from the beginning of autumn, till such time as the soft westerly winds begin to blow. And Hesiod says that when the sun darts his burning rays directly upon our heads, and turns men's complexions to brown, then it is harvest time. But that when the trees drop their leaves, it is the season for cutting timber. Cato moderates the matter thus; let the oak, says he, be felled during the solstice because in winter it is always out of season. Other woods that bear seed may be cut when the seed is mature; those that bear none, when you please. Those that have their seeds green and ripe at the same time should be cut when the seed is fallen, but the elm when the leaves drop. [. . .]

Leon Battista
Alberti
1404–1472

Book IV, Chap. 3

It is certain the form of the city and the distribution of its parts must be various according to the variety of places; since we see it is impossible upon a hill to lay out an area whether round or square, or of any other regular form, with the same ease that you may have on an open plain. The ancient architects in encompassing their towns with walls condemned all angles jutting out from the naked side of the wall, as thinking they help the enemy more in their assault than the inhabitants in their defence; and that they were very weak against the shocks of military engines; and indeed for treacheries, and for the safer throwing of darts they are of some advantage to the enemy, especially where they can run up to the walls, and withdraw again immediately to their camp. But they are also sometimes of very great service in towns seated upon hills, if they are set just answering to the streets. At the famous city, Perugia, which has several little towers placed here and there upon the hills, like the fingers of a man's hand extending out, if the enemy offers to attack one of the angles with a good number of men, he can find no place to begin his assault, and being obliged to march under the towers, is not able to withstand the weapons that will be cast, and the sallies made upon him. [. . .] From what has already been said, we may conclude that of all cities the most capacious one is round one. And the most secure, that which is encompassed with walls broken here and there into angles or bastions jutting out at certain distances, as Tacitus informs us Jerusalem was. Because it is certain the enemy cannot come up to the wall between two angles jutting out without exposing themselves to very great danger.

Book IV, Chap. 4

[. . .] In my opinion, one very good way of building a strong wall, capable of withstanding the shocks of engines, is this: make triangular projections out from the naked wall, with one angle facing the enemy, at the distance of every ten cubits, and turn arches from one projection to the other; then fill in the vacancies between them with straw and earth, well rammed down together. [...] Some think no wall is so safe against battery as those that are built in uneven lines, like the teeth of a saw.

I am very well pleased with those walls in Rome that about half way up to the top have a walk with little private holes out of which the archers may privately annoy the enemy as he moved about the field in security. And at the distance of every fifty cubits are towers adjoining the wall-like buttresses, projecting out in a round figure forwards and somewhat higher than the wall itself. So that whoever tries to approach between those towers is exposed to be taken. And thus the wall is defended by these towers, and the towers by one another.

Book V, Chap. 1

[...] The wall within a city ought to run through a district of the town. And it should be built so strong and thick in all respects and be raised so high, as indeed so ought all the other city walls, that it may overlook all the private houses. It should be fortified with battlements and towers, and a good ditch on both sides would not be remiss, in order that your men may be more capable of defending it on many sides. The towers upon this wall should not be open to the inside but walled right round. Moreover they should be seated so as not only to repel the assaults of a foreign enemy but also, upon occasion, of a domestic one [...] In a word, the whole should be in the power of the prince and it should not be in the power of any person whatsoever to prevent his men from over-running the whole city as he pleases.

Leon Battista
Alberti
1404–1472

Book V, Chap. 4

I find that even men of good experience in military affairs are in doubt about what is the best and strongest manner of building a fortress, either upon a hill or plain. There is scarcely any hill but what may be either attacked or undermined; nor any plain but what may be so well fortified that it shall be impossible to assault it without great anger. But I shall not dispute about this question. Our business is to contrive everything suitably to the nature of the place; and indeed all the rules which we have laid down for the building of a city, should be observed in the building of a fortress. The fortress particularly should be sure to have even and direct streets, by which the garrison may march to attack the enemy, or in case of sedition or treachery, their own citizens and inhabitants, and bring in succour, either out of their own country or from abroad, without impediment, by land, river, lake or sea. One very good form for the area of a fortress, is that of a C joining to all the city as to a round O with bending horns, but not encompassing them quite round; as is also that which is shaped like a star with rays running out to the circumference; and thus the fortress will be, as we before observed it ought, neither within or without the city. If we were to give a brief description of the fortress, or citadel, it might perhaps be not amiss to say that it is the backdoor to the city strongly fortified on all sides. But let it be what it will, whether the crown on the wall, or the key to the city, it ought to look fierce, terrible, rugged, dangerous and unconquerable; and the less it is, the stronger it will be. A small one will require the fidelity only of a few, but a large that of a great many: and, as Euripides says, there was never a multitude without a great many dangerous spirits in it; so that in the case before us, the fewer we have occasion to trust, the safer we will be.

The outward wall, or enclosure of the fortress should be built very strong, of large stone, with a good slope on the outside, so that the ladders set against it may be weakened by their standing too oblique; and that the enemy who assaults it and endeavours to scale it may lie entirely open to the stones thrown down upon him. And that things cast at the wall by the military engines may not strike it full, but be thrown off. The ground or area on the inside should be paved with two or even three layers of very large stones, that the besiegers may not get in upon you by mines run under the wall. All the rest of the walls should be made very high, and very strong and thick quite to the uppermost cornice, that they may stoutly resist all manner of battery, and not easily be mounted by ladders, or commanded by entrenchments cast up on the outside. In other respects the same rules are to be observed that we have given for the walls of the city. [. . .]

Within the fortress ought to be one principle tower, built in the stoutest manner, and fortified as strongly as possible, higher than any other part of the castle, and not accessible by more than one way, to which there should be no other entrance but by a drawbridge.

Leon Battista
Alberti
1404–1472

Book V, Chap. 14

I now come to treat of private edifices. I have already observed elsewhere that a house is a small city. We are therefore in the building of it, to have an eye almost to everything that related to the building of a city. That it be healthy and furnished in all manner of necessities that conduce to the repose, tranquillity or delicacy of life. What those are and how they are to be obtained, I think I have already, to a great degree, shown in the preceding books.

Book VI, Chap. 1

[. . .] Vitruvius is indeed a writer of universal knowledge, but his writings are so maimed by age that in many places there are great chasms, and many things imperfect in others. Besides this, his style is absolutely devoid of any ornament, and he wrote in such a manner that to the Latins he seems to write Greek and to the Greeks, Latin. But, indeed, it is plain from the book itself that he wrote neither Greek nor Latin, and he might almost as well have never written at all, at least with regard to us, since we cannot understand him. There remained many examples of the ancient works, temples and theatres from then, as from the most skilful masters, and a great deal was to be learned from them; but these I saw, and with tears, mouldering away daily. I observed, too, that those who in these days happen to undertake any new structure generally run after the whims of the moderns, instead of being delighted and directed by the justness of more noble works. By this means it was plain, that this part of knowledge, and in a manner of life itself, was likely in a short time to be wholly lost. In this unhappy state of things, I could not help having it long, and often, in my thoughts to write upon this subject myself. At the same time I considered that in the examination of so many noble and useful matters, and so necessary to mankind; it would be a shame to neglect any of those observations which voluntarily offered themselves to me; and I thought of the duty of an honest and studious mind, to endeavour to free this science, for which the most learned among the ancients had always a very great esteem, from its present ruin and oppression. [. . .]

There was not the least remain of any ancient structure that had any merit in it, but what I went and examined, to see if anything was to be learned from it. Thus I was continually searching, considering, measuring and making draughts of everything I could hear of, till such time as I had made myself perfect master of every contrivance or invention that had been used in those ancient remains; and thus I alleviated the fatigue of writing by the thirst and pleasure of gaining information. And indeed the collecting together, rehearsing without meanness, reducing into a just method, writing in an accurate style, and explaining perspicuously so many various matters, so unequal, so dispersed, and so remote from the common use and knowledge of mankind, certainly required a greater genius, and more learning than I can pretend to. But still I shall not repent of my labour, if I have only effected what I chiefly proposed to myself, namely to be clear and intelligible to the reader, rather than eloquent. How difficult a thing it is in handling subjects of this nature is better known to those who have attempted it than is believed by those who never tried it. And I flatter myself with the thought that it will at least be allowed that I have written according to the rules of this language, and in no obscure style. [...]

Leon Battista
Alberti
1404–1472

Book VI, Chap. 2

It is generally allowed that the pleasure and delight which we feel on the view of any building arise from nothing else but beauty and ornament, since there is hardly any man so melancholy or stupid, so rough or unpolished, but that is very much pleased with what is beautiful, and pursues those things which are most adorned, and rejects the unadorned and neglected; and if in anything that he views he perceives any ornament is wanting, he declares that there is something deficient which would make the work more delightful and noble. We should therefore consult beauty as one of the main and principal requisites in anything which we have a mind should please others. How necessary our forefathers, men remarkable for their wisdom, looked upon this to be, it appears, as indeed from almost everything they did, so particularly from their laws, their militia, their sacred and all other public ceremonies. It is almost incredible what pains they took to adorn. So much so that one would almost imagine they had a mind to have it thought, that all these things (so absolutely necessary to the life of mankind) if stripped of their pomp and ornament, would be somewhat stupid and insipid. When we lift up our eyes to heaven, and view the wonderful works of God, we admire him more for the beauties which we see, than for the conveniences which we feel and derive from them. But what occasion is there to insist upon this? When we see that nature consults beauty in a manner to excess, in everything she does, even in painting the flowers of the field.

If beauty therefore is necessary in any thing, it is so particularly in building, which can never be without it, without giving offence both to the skilful and the ignorant. How are we moved by a huge shapeless ill-contrived pile of stones? The greater it is, the more we blame the folly of the expense, and condemn the builder's inconsiderate lust of heaping up stone upon stone without contrivance. Then, having satisfied necessity is a very small matter, and having provided for convenience results in no manner of pleasure, where you are shocked by the deformity of the work. Add to this, that the very thing we speak of is itself no small help to convenience and duration. For who will deny that it is much more convenient to be lodged in a neat handsome structure, than in a nasty ill-contrived whole? Or can any building be made so strong by all the contrivance of art, as to be safe from violence and force? No. Beauty will have such an effect even upon an enraged enemy, that it will disarm his anger, and prevent him from offering it any injury. So much so that I will daresay that there can be no greater security to any work against violence and injury than beauty and dignity. Your whole care, diligence and expense, therefore, should all tend to this, that whatever you build may be not only useful and convenient, but also handsomely adorned, and by that means delightful to the sight, that whoever views may think the expense could not have been better invested.

But what beauty and ornament are themselves, and what difference there is between them, may perhaps be easier for the reader to conceive in his mind than for me to explain by words. In order therefore to be as brief as possible, I shall define beauty to be a *concinnitas* of all the parts within a body, so that nothing can be added, removed or altered but for the worse. A quality so noble and divine, that our whole *ingenio* and art are needed to achieve it. And it is but very rarely granted to any one, or even to nature herself, to produce any thing in every way perfect and complete. How rare, says a person created by Cicero, is a handsome youth in Athens! This critic in beauty found that there was something deficient or superfluous in the person he disliked, which was not compatible with the perfection of beauty which I imagine might have been obtained by means of ornament by painting and concealing anything that was deformed, and trimming and polishing what was handsome; so that the unsightly parts might have given less offence, and the more lovely more delight. If this be granted, we may define ornament to be a kind of an auxiliary brightness and improvement on beauty. So that then beauty is something lovely which is proper and innate, and diffused throughout the whole body, and ornament something added or extra, rather than proper and innate.

Leon Battista
Alberti
1404–1472

Book IX, Chap. 2

[...] There is certainly a vast deal of satisfaction in a convenient retreat near the town where a man is at liberty to do just what he pleases. The great beauties of such a retreat are being near the city upon an open airy road, and on a pleasant spot of ground. The greatest commendation of the house itself is its making a cheerful appearance to those that go a little way out of town to take the air. [...] And for this reason I would have it stand pretty high, but upon so easy an ascent that it should hardly be perceptible to those that go to it till they find themselves at the top and a large prospect opens itself to their view. Nor should there be any want of pleasant landscapes, flowery meadows, open countryside, shady groves or limpid brooks [...].

[...] Lastly, what I have already said conduces extremely to the pleasantness of all buildings, I would have the front and the whole body of the house perfectly well-lit and that it be open to receive a great deal of light and sun and a sufficient quantity of wholesome air. Let nothing be within view that can offend the eye with a melancholy shade. Let all things smile and seem to welcome the arrival of your guests. Let those who are already entered be in doubt whether they shall for pleasure continue where they are, or pass on further to those other beauties which tempt them on. Let them be led from square rooms into round ones, and again from round into square, and so into others of mixed lines, neither all round nor all square; and let the passage into the very innermost apartments be, if possible, without the least ascent or descent, but all be upon one even floor, or at least let the ascents be as easy as may be.

Book IX, Chap. 4

[...] Our minds are delighted in a particular manner with the pictures of pleasant land-scapes, of heavens, of fishing, hunting, swimming, country sports, of flowery fields and thick groves. Neither is it foreign to our present purpose just to mention that Octavian, the emperor, adorned his palace with the huge bones of some extraordinary animals. The ancients used to dress the walls of their grottoes and caverns with all manner of rough work, with little chips of pumice, or soft Tiburtine stone, which Ovid calls the living pumice; and some I have known daub them over with green wax, in imitation of the mossy slime which we always see in moist grottoes. I was extremely pleased with an artificial grotto which I have seen of this sort, with a clear spring of water falling from it; the walls were composed of various sorts of sea-shells, lying roughly together, some reversed, some with their mouths outwards, their colours being so artfully blended as to form a very beautiful variety.

Leon Battista
Alberti
1404–1472

Book IX, Chap. 5

Now come once more to those points that I before promised to enquire into, namely, wherein it is that beauty and ornament, universally considered, consist, or whence they arise. This is an inquiry of the utmost difficulty, for whatever that property be which is so gathered and collected from the whole number and nature of the several parts, or to be imparted to each of them according to a certain and regular *ratio*, or which must be contrived in such a manner as to join and unite a certain number of parts into one body or whole, by an orderly and sure coherence and agreement of all those parts. This property is what we are here to discover. It is certain, such a property must have in itself something of the force and spirit of all the parts with which it is either united or mixed, otherwise they must jar and disagree with each other. And by such discord they destroy the uniformity or beauty of the whole. The discovery of this, as it is far from being easy or obvious in any other case, is particularly difficult and uncertain because the art of building consists of so many various parts, and each of those parts requires so many various ornaments as you have already seen. However, as it is necessary in the prosecution of our design, we shall use the utmost of our abilities in clearing this obscure point, not going so far about as to show how a complete knowledge of a whole is to be gained by examining the several parts distinct. By beginning immediately upon what is to our present purpose, by enquiring what that property is which in its nature makes a thing beautiful.

The most expert artists among the ancients, as we have observed elsewhere, were of opinion that an edifice was like an animal, so that in the formation of it we ought to imitate nature. Let us therefore enquire how it happens that in the bodies produced by nature herself some are valued as more and others valued as less beautiful or even deformed. It is obvious that in those that are esteemed to be beautiful, the parts or members are not constantly all the same so as not to differ in any respect. But we find that even in those parts where they vary most, there is something inherent and implanted which, though they differ extremely from each other, makes each of them beautiful.

I will make use of an example to illustrate my meaning. Some admire a woman for being extremely slender and fine shaped. The young gentleman in Terence preferred a girl that was plump and fleshy. You perhaps are for a medium between these two extremes, and would neither have her so thin as to seem wasted with sickness, nor so strong and robust as a ploughman in disguise and fit for boxing. In short, you would have her such a beauty as might be formed by taking from the first what the second might spare. But then, because one of these pleases you more than the other, would you therefore affirm the other to be not at all handsome or graceful? By no means. But there may be some hidden cause why one should please you more than the other, into which I will not now pretend to enquire.

Leon Battista
Alberti
1404–1472

The judgement which you make that a thing is beautiful, does not proceed from mere opinion, but from the spirit and *ratio* that are innate; which plainly appears to be so from this, that no man beholds any thing ugly or deformed without an immediate hatred and abhorrence. Whence this sensation of the mind arises, and how it is formed, would be a question too subtle for this place. However, let us consider and examine it from those things that are obvious, and make more immediately to the subject at hand. For without question, there is a certain excellence and natural beauty in the figures and forms of buildings which immediately strike the mind with pleasure and admiration. It is my opinion that beauty, majesty, gracefulness and the like charms, consist in those particulars which if you alter or take away cause the whole to become homely and dis-agreeable. If we are convinced of this, it can be no very tedious inquiry to consider those things that may be taken away, increased or altered, especially in figures and forms. For every body consists of certain peculiar parts, of which if you take away any one, or lessen, or enlarge, or remove it to an improper place, causes the beauty and grace of this body to at once be lamed and spoiled.

From hence I may conclude, to avoid prolixity in this research, that there are three things principally in which the whole of what we are looking into consists: number, and that which I have called *finitio*, and collocation. But there is still something else besides, which arises from the conjunction and connection of these other parts, in which beauty shines full face. This we will call *concinnitas*, which we may consider as the origin of all that is graceful and handsome. The business and office of *concinnitas* is to put together members differing from each other in their natures, in such a manner that they may conspire to form a beautiful whole.

This is why whenever our *ratio*, either by sight or by hearing, or any of the other sense, is stimulated, it immediately perceive this *concinnitas*. For it is in our nature to desire perfection and to cling to it with desirous pleasure when they are offered to us. Neither in the whole body nor in its parts does *concinnitas* flourish as much as it does in nature; so that its true seat is in the spirit and in the *ratio*. And, accordingly, it has a very large field to exercise itself and flourish in, and runs through every part and action of man's life, and every production of nature herself, which are all directed by the law of *concinnitas*. Nor does nature study anything more than to make all her works absolute and perfect, which they could never be without this *concinnitas*, since they would lack that consent of parts which is so necessary to perfection.

But we need not say more on this point, and if what we have here laid down appears to be true, we may conclude beauty to be such a consensus and conspiring of the parts into a whole, as to number, *finitio* and collocation, as *concinnitas*, that is to say, the absolute primary *ratio* of nature requires. This is what architecture chiefly aims at, and thus obtains its dignity, grace and authority.

The Ancients knowing from the nature of things, that the matter was in fact as I have here stated it, and being convinced, that if they neglected this main point they should never produce anything great or commendable, did in their works propose to themselves chiefly the imitation of nature, as the greatest artist at all manner of compositions; and for this purpose they laboured, as far as the industry of man could reach, to discover the laws upon which she herself acted in the production of her works, in order to transfer them to the business of architecture. Reflecting therefore upon the practice of nature as well with relation to an entire body, as to its several parts, they found from the very first principles of things, that bodies were not always composed of equal parts or members; whence it happens, that of the bodies produced by nature, some are smaller, some larger; and some middling: and considering that one building differed from another, upon account of the end for which it was raised, and the purpose which it was to serve, as we have shown in the foregoing books, they found it necessary to make them of various kinds. Thus from an imitation of nature they invented three manners of adorning a building, and gave them names drawn from their first inventors. One was better contrived for strength and duration: this they called *Doric*; another was more tapered and beautiful, this they named *Corinthian*; another was a kind of medium composed from the other two, and this they called *Ionic*. Thus much related to the whole body in general. Then observing that those three things which we have already mentioned; namely, the number, finishing and collocation, were what chiefly conduced to make the whole beautiful, they found how they were to make use of this from a thorough examination of the works of nature; and, as I imagine, upon the following principles.

Leon Battista
Alberti
1404–1472

The first thing they observed, as to number, was that it was of two sorts, even and uneven, and they made use of both, but on different occasions. From the limitation of nature, they never made the ribs of their structure, that is to say, the columns, angles and the like, in uneven numbers; as you shall not find any animal that stands or moves upon an odd number of feet. On the contrary, they made their apertures always in uneven numbers, as nature herself has done in some instances, for although in animals she has placed an ear, an eye and a nostril on each side, yet the great aperture, the mouth, she has set singly in the middle. But among their numbers, whether even or uneven, there are some which seem to be greater favourites with nature than others, and more celebrated among learned men; which architects have borrowed for the composition of the members of their edifices, on account of their being imbued with some qualities which make them more valuable than any others.

Thus all the philosophers affirm, that nature herself consists in a ternary principle; and so the number five, when we consider the many things, and those so admirable and various, which either follow this number in themselves, or are derived from those things which do, must be allowed to be divine in its nature, and worthily dedicated to the gods of the arts, and particularly to *Mercury*. It is certain, that Almighty God himself, the creator of all things, takes particular delight in the number seven, having placed seven planets in the skies, and having been pleased to ordain with regard to man, the glory of his creation, that conception, growth, maturity and the like, should all be reducible to this number seven.

Aristotle says that the Ancients never used to give a child a name till it was seven days old, as if not thinking it was destined to life before. Both the seed in the womb, and the child after its birth, is liable to very dangerous accidents till the seventh day is over. Among odd numbers, that of nine is highly celebrated, in which number that great artist, nature, made the spheres of heaven; and the philosophers say, that nature in many, and those the greatest things, is contented with making use of the ninth part of a whole. Thus forty is about the ninth part of all the days of the year, according to the revolution of the sun, and *Hippocrates* tells us, that in forty days the *foetus* is formed in the womb. Moreover we find that in the generality of acute distempers, the patient recovers at the end of forty days. At the end of the same time women that are with a male child, cease their purgations, which, if they are delivered of a boy, after the same term of forty days, begin afresh. They say further that the child itself for forty days is never seen either to laugh or shed tears while it is awake though in its sleep, it will do both.

So much for odd numbers. As to even numbers, some philosophers teach that the number four is dedicated to the deity, and for this reason it was used in taking the most solemn oaths, which were repeated four times; and they tell us, that even among the most excellent numbers, that of six is the most perfect, or consisting of all its own entire parts.

Leon Battista
Alberti
1404–1472

And it is certain, that the number eight has an extraordinary power in the nature of things. Except in *Aegypt*, we never find that any child born in the eighth month, lives long; nay, and even the mother herself who is so delivered in the eighth month, when the child is dead, will certainly, we are told, die soon afterwards. If the father touches his wife in the eighth month, the child will be full of foul humours, and its skin will be leprous and scruffy, and nauseous to the sight. *Aristotle* was of the opinion that the number ten was the most perfect of all, which was probably because its square is composed of four continued cubes put together. Upon these accounts the architects have most frequently made use of the foregoing numbers; but in their apertures they seldom have exceeded that of ten for an even, or nine for an odd number, especially in temples. We are now to treat of the finishing.

By the finishing I understand a certain mutual correspondence of those several lines, by which the proportions are measured, whereof one is the length, the other the breadth, and the other the height.

The rule of these proportions is best gathered from those things in which we find nature herself to be most complete and admirable; and indeed I am every day more and more convinced of the truth of *Pythagoras*'s saying, that nature is sure to act consistently, and with a constant analogy in all her operations. From whence I conclude that the same numbers, by means of which the agreement of sounds affects our ears with delight, are the very same which please our eyes and our mind. We shall therefore borrow all our rules for the finishing our proportions from the musicians, who are the greatest masters of this sort of number, and from those particular things wherein nature shows herself most excellent and complete. Not that I shall look any further into these matters than is necessary for the purpose of the architect. We shall not therefore pretend to say anything of modulation, or the particular rules of any instrument; but only speak of those points that are immediately to our subject which are these. We have already observed that harmony is an agreement of several tones, delightful to the ears. Of tones, some are deep, some more acute. The deeper tones proceed from a longer string; and the more acute, from a shorter: and from the mutual connection of these tones arises all the variety of harmony. This harmony the ancients gathered from interchangeable concords of the tones, by means of certain determinate numbers; the names of which concords are as follows: *Diapente,* or the fifth, which is also called *Sesquialtera: Diatessaron,* or the fourth, called also *Sesquitertia: Diapason,* or the eighth, also called the double tone; *Diapason Diapente,* the twelfth or triple tone, and *Disdiapason,* the fifteenth or *Quadruple.* To these was added the tonus, which was also called the *Sesquialtera.*

These several concords, compared with the strings themselves, bore the following proportions. The *Sesquialtera* was so called because the string which produced it bore the same proportion to that to which it is compared, as one and a half does to one; which was the meaning of the word *Sesqui,* among the ancients. In the *Sesquialtera* therefore the longer string must be allowed three, and the shorter, two. But in that concord which was called *Diapason,* the numbers answer to one another in a double proportion, as two to one, or the whole to the half: and in the *Triple,* they answer as three to one, or as the whole to one-third of itself. In the *Quadruple* the proportions are as four to one, or as the whole to its fourth part.

Lastly, all their musical numbers are as follows: One, two, three, four, and the tone before-mentioned, wherein the long string compared to the shorter, exceeds it one-eighth part of that shorter string.

Of all their numbers the architects made very convenient use, taking them sometimes two by two, as in planning out their squares and open areas, wherein only two proportions were to be considered; namely, length and breadth; and sometimes taking them three by three, as in public halls, council-chambers and the like; wherein as the length was to bear a proportion to the breadth, so they made the height in a certain harmonious proportion to them both.

Antonio Averlino
c.1400–1469

aesthetisation of architecture • classical canon • antiquity • abuses • design methodology • legitimation • representation of power • luxury • hedonism • consumption • precedent • authority • invention • social control • defence • systematisation of space distribution

Antonio Averlino, called Filarete (c.1400–1469)

Treatise on Architecture (1451–1464)

The author was a Florentine sculptor and architect. His treatise, for which he is best known, is written in the form of a dialogue between an architect and his patron – a thin disguise for himself and Duke Francesco Sforza, to whom the text was first dedicated – engaged in the construction of the fictional city of Sforzinda. This literary device serves to pleasurably instruct the reader about a wide variety of topics, including the architect–patron relationship, the organisation of the construction process, beauty and style in buildings, prison design and city planning.

Further reading Blunt, 1940, 43; Dizionario Enciclopedico dell'Architettura e Urbanistica; Fiore, 1973; Firpo, 1954; Garin, 1969; Klein, 1964; Lang, 1972b; Marconi, 1973; Onians, 1971; Panofsky, 1968; Saalman, 1959; Schlosser, 1979, 129, 136, 160, 713; Spencer, 1958; Tigler, 1963; Wiebenson, 1982.

Book II

How it is that the building is conceived like a human body.

In the first book you have seen, as I have demonstrated to you, the origins of the building, its origins in my opinion that is, how it is proportioned to the body of man, how it needs to be fed and governed and how through want it sickens and dies like a man. You have seen briefly the measures, understood their names and sources, and their qualities and forms. I told you they are called by their Greek names, that is Doric, Ionic and Corinthian. The Doric, I told you, is of the greatest quality; the Corinthian is in the middle, and Ionic is the minor one for the reasons alleged by the architect Vitruvius in his book. There he shows how they were in the time of the emperor Octavian. In these modes, the Doric, Ionic and Corinthian correspond in measure and members to the form or, better, to the quality of the form to which they are proportioned. I will explain to you as well as I can, and as far as my poor mind can demonstrate, what we can do with these three modes and orders.

You could say perhaps that 'you have told me that the building is similar to a man. If this is so, then it needs to be conceived and born'. As with man himself, so with a building. First it is conceived, using a kind of simile you can understand, and then it is born. The mother delivers her child at the term of nine months or sometimes seven. By caring and keeping things in good order she makes him grow.

'Tell me, how is this conception achieved?' The building is conceived this way. Since no one can conceive by himself without a woman, by another simile, the building cannot be conceived by a man by himself. The same way it cannot be done without a woman, he who wishes to build needs an architect. He conceives it with him and then the architect carries it. When the architect has given birth, he becomes the mother of the building. Before the architect gives birth, he should dream about his conception, think about it, and turn it over in his mind in many ways for seven to nine months, the same way a woman carries her child in her body for seven to nine months. He should also make various drawings of this conception that he has made with the patron, according to his own desires. As the woman can do nothing without the man, so the architect is the mother to carry this conception. When he has pondered and considered and thought in many ways, he then ought to choose what seems most suitable and most beautiful to him according to the terms of the patron. When this birth is accomplished, that is when he has made, in wood, a small relief of its final form, measured and proportioned to the finished building, then he shows it to the father.

I have compared the architect to the mother, but in addition he also needs to be the nurse. He is in fact both nurse and mother. As the mother is full of love for her son, he will rear the building with love and diligence, cause it to grow, and bring it to completion if it is possible; if it is not possible, he will leave it ordered in such a way that it will not perish on account of its incompleteness. A good mother loves her son and with the aid and knowledge of the father strives to make him good and beautiful, and with a good master to make him good and praiseworthy. In the same way the good architect should strive to make his building good and beautiful. As the mother makes every effort to find good masters for her son, so the architect ought to find good masters, masons and all the others who are needed for the work, if the patron does not prevent him. Without the goodwill of the patron he would be like a woman who cannot go against her husband's will; so with the architect.

[. . .]

Building is a wholly voluptuous pleasure, like that of a man in love. Anyone who has experienced it knows there is so much pleasure and desire in building that no matter how much of it a man does, it can never be enough. Sometimes he is not concerned with the expense. Examples of this are seen every day. When a man is in love,

Antonio Averlino
c.1400–1469

Patron ^ = architect = a love story

he gladly goes to see his beloved. When she is in a place where he can see her, he does not regret the time spent nor is he bored. So it is that he who builds goes gladly to see his building, and the more he sees it, the more he wants to see it and the more his heart swells. Time goes by and he never gets enough of looking at it nor of talking about it, exactly the same way as a man in love when he talks about his beloved. He is pleased when it is praised, and his heart swells even more. When he is absent and someone comes to talk about it to him, he is greatly pleased and desires to go see it. His soul is drawn to it and he always desires the things that he thinks are best for it, exactly the same way a man in love would. There is no halfway for him; he loves it. He makes it useful and honourable for only two reasons. The first is for utility and the second for fame, so that they will say it was he who caused such a beautiful building to arise.

Book IV

Antonio Averlino
c.1400–1469

I firmly believe that such a case will not befall our city, for my lord has already told me that every time everything necessary has been prepared, he wants to hire enough masters to complete it in a week or in ten days at the most. For this reason there will be no reason for plotting. You may say I cannot do this because so many masters and helpers all together would only cause confusion. I reply that orders will be given in such a way that even if there were many more, the work would move towards completion, and would be well done. In order to avoid this inconvenience, he who commands me has ordered me to make arrangements and to give such orders that no time will be wasted. To get to these orders we need first to examine how many masters and labourers we will need for this job.

First we shall see how many masters and labourers are needed for one braccio of wall. Then we will multiply how many will be needed to complete the entire wall according to the terms given above. One braccio of this wall from the ground level up to the top will require per day four masters and seven labourers to serve each master, counting in the production of the mortar and the transporting of the brick. These are necessary to keep the master from wasting time. More importantly, we need someone between every two masters to come to aid them, that is to bridge the distance between them. In order to make our computation from this braccio, since there are 375 braccia in a stadio, we will multiply four times 375; this makes 1,500. Thus in a stadio we need this number of masters.

You have seen the number of masters needed in a stadio. By multiplying eight stadio to the mile you will see how many masters there will be. I get 12,000. Now we have to determine the labourers and fillers-in. In short we want seven labourers to each master; that will be 84,000, and 6,000 fillers-in. According to this reckoning there will be 90,000 labourers and fillers-in, and with the masters there will be 102,000 persons. These masters, served in the above-stated way, will lay 30 million bricks a day. Our city will thus be completed in ten days.

'You have told me about the masters and labourers that will be needed, but there is another thing which is very important for our business and which counts for a lot. It is this: if all are to work together at the same time, the first as well as the last, it will have to be like a dance. The first dances in time with the last if they have a good leader and good music.'

'I hope this is how it will be because first of all we will have music as good as we have for dancing. If the best leader in the world were to lead the dancing and the music were not good, he could never lead in such a way that everyone danced well. This is exactly the same here. He whose business it is to provide it has provided us with such music that the leader can never make a mistake. In other words, he wants the music here to be the same as in his other affairs. He especially wants every man to be well paid, for this is the music that makes everything harmonious. In this way each one will do his duty in the hope of hearing the sweetness of the music. The leader will know what and how every man will do what he has been contracted to do.'

'I would like to know what orders you give him to accomplish this so that I can know if everyone is doing his duty.'

Antonio Averlino
c.1400–1469

'I will tell you. Here you need to make arrangements to have men do what they are told concerning the necessary preparations. I will tell you what I think should be done to make everyone careful and fearful and also know who is responsible when something is lacking. First of all, the masters should be separated. When they are separated there should be men, as I have said above, who guide and correct them so that they work without having cause to make plots or have disagreements among themselves. To this end the masters should be separated in this manner. They should be three braccia apart, and for every ten masters there should be one of the above-named, that is one who can command masters and labourers. These masters are thus spaced every 30 braccia. I do not wish them ever to turn back but always to build as high as they can and always go round and round, encircling this work. There will be about 1,000 of these overseers. All these persons come to 103,200. The overseers should be young and quick-witted but also be discreet. When all these persons and masters are organised and separated as I have stated above, they will cover a space of six miles and build continuously according to this plan. In this space of six miles you will have four miles left over. As the masters finish, they can start building the scaffolding. In this way no time will be lost.'

'So far I like this plan, but there is one question. Do you think that such a number of masters and labourers will respect the overseers, that they will obey them? Even if there were 10,000 instead of 1,000, they would not respect them, although I believe that there is certainly danger in such a multitude.'

'We will take care of this, since your lordship wishes it. It will be necessary at first for your lordship to be present for a week or ten days, because every man will be full of fear and reverence on seeing you present.'

'See here, when there is such a crowd, they neither fear nor reverence anyone, nor do they honour lord or lady.'

'All in good time. We can take care of this if you are dubious. Have the army come and draw them up in a battle line. Then give an order, under pain of the gallows, that everyone stay in his place. For anyone who disobeys, the order will be carried out without mercy or remission.'

[...]

'As you see, each overseer is responsible for guiding his ten men and for assigning them their work. He will say to each master that he has to bring his workers to him so that they will always be there at the same time. This order will be observed; in the morning they will work no more and no less than four hours. Then everyone will go eat with his squad. Every squad will have a standard that they leave on the job. They will have an hour to eat and then, when a trumpet sounds at each mile, they will all go

[70]

back to work. Whatever [time] is lost will be held back from their wages, and double time if it is not a case of necessity. During the four or five hours of work after lunch they can be given a half hour or more, as seems best at the time, to rest a while.'

[. . .]

'I shall give these orders so that no uprising can occur. I shall bring up my men-at-arms to separate the masters from the labourers. So that there will be no cause for words or mistakes I shall give every overseer ten armed horses and fifty infantry. The squads will follow each other in a line and in order; the other men-at-arms will stand a little aside. I want these overseers who have to work with such a multitude for eight to ten days to be reputable persons. Then I want a procession arranged in which will be the bishop, and the lords who recently came here, and my lady together with my sons. The procession will depart from the same place where the things you spoke of were to be put in the foundations and [proceed to] where the first stone is to be laid. Here Monsignore will bless the stone, the place and the site [. . .].'

Antonio Averlino
c.1400–1469

'After the benediction, your lordship will take a shovel and dig the first three shovel fulls. Then your sons, beginning with the eldest and ending with the youngest, will each dig three shovel fulls. When this is done, we will eat with the bishop in an act of charity so that the men who are to inhabit the city will be charitable and loving with each other. In this way enough of the foundation will be dug so your lordship and the bishop can lay the stone and the other things. Then they will fill the foundation of the wall up to the level of the ground. On that day nothing more will be done, except to continue digging the foundations. Everyone can then return except those who are commissioned to do the things stated.' [. . .]

Book VII

'[. . .] the building is derived from the form of man. The building has its members as has man, and thus it should be.'

'My lord, it is true, but you know very well that men are formed and put together differently. The members are brought together in different ways, but even so, in that they are like, they are the same.'

'I beg you, explain it to me.'

'Perhaps it would be better for you to understand first what drawing is.'

[. . .]

The following day I half believed that he would not come, but he came with many drawings on his tablet as he had been told. [They were] drawn in such a way that even though he had no experience, he did much better than one would have expected. He immediately asked me to explain the rules, measures, proportions, qualities and members, as he had asked.

'I will tell you all. I will first speak of qualities. There are many qualities in buildings, just as there are many among men. As I have said before, the major quality is the most worthy. You clearly understand that some men are more dignified than others; buildings are the same, according to the persons who live in them and according to their use. As men should be dressed and adorned according to their dignity, so ought buildings. This [building] is one of the most dignified. It should, therefore, be as nobly decorated as is its owner, because of whom it is used to promote divine offices and sacred things. Since those who administer the rites adorn themselves in exercising their office with different sorts of beautiful vestments decorated with gold, silver, pearls, embroidery and noble and precious things, the building that serves this purpose should be [decorated] in the same degree. For this reason it should be clothed and adorned with beautiful stones. In addition to the beautiful stones, it should be decorated with beautiful and noble carvings, with gold and colours. Paint them and make them as beautiful as possible.

'You have seen the quality and dignity and why it should be beautiful and ornate. You know that it would not be well for a bishop or canons or priests to proceed unceremoniously, especially when they administer the sacred rites. It is equally improper for a bishop to be malformed in his members or person. Therefore, the building should also be well proportioned and have members suitable to its size. As the body of man is arranged with voids, entrances and hollow places for its maintenance, so the building needs them too. As you know a person is recognised by the appearance of the face, breast and all the other parts; the church too should be most beautiful and pleasant in its forward parts. As the major part of the beauty of a man is in his face, so it should be with the building. The entrance to the body of man is the mouth and he sees through the eyes. The building too needs them, that is, a door and windows through which one sees the light. The other members conform to the same likeness; as man lives through eating, so the building should be maintained and regulated as you have already understood.

Antonio Averlino
c.1400–1469

'This is enough for the present on the formation of the building on the analogy to man. The members and proportions of the building should be in harmony with its size. If the building is large, all its members should be large. It would not be well to give a large temple small columns, arches, doors, or other members. They should be proportionate to the body of the building. [. . .]'

'[. . .] The analogy is this. You asked me why churches were made in the form of a cross. I said they are made cruciform as a simile for the cross, and this is the truth. Take into account that there are four men who spread out their arms. Each touches the other with the tip of the longest finger, and all turn their backs to each other. These four will make a square from their own four [members]. If they do not have some support under their arms, they cannot stand this way for very long, but if you should put something [under their arms], they could stand without fatigue and endure a long time. Since this edifice is strong at the corners, it will be more durable. I have put them here for this reason. I do not know if this reason and rule satisfies you.'

[. . .]

Book VIII

'I have understood so far [and] I am pleased. I think that in the execution you will perhaps add some things and also omit [others], as it seems best to you.'

'You are correct; during construction I will rearrange some things for the better, as the need occurs, for greater utility or beauty. You can understand from this little drawing how the façade will be, and from it you can consider how the parts will be.'

'This is true. I am pleased.'

'Then as we have said, in the execution you and your father can add and subtract as you wish. [A building] can be made in many different forms, but in the end one must choose one [form] and hold to it. You have seen one way. There is also another way of making it with a court and with rooms and dwellings on the angles and on every side. You can also make two courts, one in front of the other with living quarters between them, that is, halls and rooms both above and below, as they are needed and as seems best. There is still another way, by making a large court in the fore part with rooms neither on the front nor the sides. As I said, there are so many ways that it would take too long to describe them all; moreover, they would not all be understood. But one thing I will tell you: as you learn more about drawing by yourself, you will understand little by little many kinds and types [of buildings]. You will know more different kinds of buildings than you can tell.'

[...]

'I freely praise anyone who follows the antique practice and style. I bless the soul of Filippo di ser Brunellesci, a Florentine citizen, a famous and most worthy architect, a most subtle follower of Dedalus, who has revived in our city of Florence the antique way of building. As a result no other manner but the antique is used today for churches and for public and private buildings. [...]'

Antonio Averlino
c.1400–1469

'I beg everyone to abandon modern usage. Do not let yourself be advised by masters who hold to such bad practice. Cursed be he who discovered it! I think that only barbaric people could have brought it into Italy. I will give you an example. [There is the same comparison] between ancient and modern architecture [as there is] in literature. That is [there is the same difference] between the speech of Cicero or Virgil and that used thirty or forty years ago. Today it has been brought back to better usage than had prevailed in past times – during at least several hundred years – for today one speaks in prose with ornate language. This has happened solely because they followed the antique manner of Virgil and other worthy men. I give you architecture in the same comparison, for whoever follows antique practice participates precisely in the above comparison, that is, the one on Ciceronian and Virgilian letters.

[...]

'My lord, your lordship begins to have taste and understanding. The pointed [arches] and the doors, with some impediment in the square that you describe, are these poor modern [examples].

'You have understood the derivation of the arch and the rectangular door. You have heard about their origins. Now understand the [reason] why the round ones are most beautiful, how they should be used, and how they should be constructed according to antique usage.

'The reason round [arches] are more beautiful than pointed. It cannot be doubted that anything which impedes the sight in any way is not so beautiful as that which leads the eye and does not restrain it. Such is the round arch. As you have noticed, your eye is not arrested in the least when you look at a half-circle arch. It is the same when you look at a circle. As you look at it, the eye or, better, the sight, quickly encompasses the circumference at the first glance. The sight moves along, for it has no restraint or obstacle whatsoever. It is the same with the half circle, for as you look at it, the eye, or the sight, quickly runs to the other side without any obstacle, impediment, or other restraint. It runs from one end to the other of the half circle. The pointed is not so, for the eye, or sight, pauses a little at the pointed part and does not run along as it does on the half circle.

[...]

'Let us now leave these magnificent cities erected in the past as well as the present;

they are very marvellous, large, and built at great expenditure of time and money. I do not say that this one can be built without great expense. Some buildings that are to be constructed cannot be produced [without] great expense, but magnanimous and great princes, and republics as well, should not hold back from building great and beautiful buildings because of the expense. No country was ever impoverished nor did anyone ever die because of the construction of buildings. [. . .]'

'[. . .] In this respect I can only encourage everyone who has ever been concerned about the expense of building, particularly those who can afford it, such as nobles and governments; still they do not spend. In the end when a large building is completed there is neither more nor less money in the country, but the building does remain in the country or city together with its reputation and honour.'

Book X

Antonio Averlino
c.1400–1469

'The fruitsellers can stand under the portico and on the steps when it rains. In the space left over at either end of the piazza, vegetables will be sold and at the other end other things will be sold, either wood or secondhand goods of any sort.'

'I like it so far. The palace of the Capitano should be near here to strike terror into the people.'

Book XII

'[. . .] A poor man cannot make his house very attractive by himself. He will build it any way he can in order to have shelter. It will not require much measuring or laying out of members, except a square of ten or 12 braccia. He can plan it as he chooses. Because he has little money, he does not need much; only enough for spending. However, he does have to know how to lay it out so it will be most useful: Make his little house in whatever way you can. [. . .]'

'I want to tell you what I want us to build. First I want to make a place for jousting where people can go to watch without disturbing each other. When this is done, I want us to build another where we can have festivals, games with ships and naval battles as they did in Rome. [. . .]'

Book XX

'It says that to this building, Eragastolon, which means prison of slaves, were sent those who had committed an act deserving the death penalty and that they were never allowed to leave. In it there were various places, according to the kind of death that these malefactors deserved.'

Book XXI

'But tell me first how these guilds were separated and ordered.'

'First merchants, bankers and goldsmiths were arranged as your lordship has arranged them around the piazzas. The market square, butcher shops, inns and other public places are exactly as they are in Sforzinda. The other guilds are each completely by themselves. The painters are together; the masters of wood, the tailors, cloth merchants, cobblers; smiths who work in iron, copper and tin and all those who work with fire were on one street, with the exception of those who make brick furnaces and other works done with earth. Those who worked in glass were, appropriately, with the others named above. The barbers were scattered throughout the city in various places for the greater convenience of the people. All the other guilds were together except that certain guilds were granted permission to have representatives live in different places, as for example pharmacists and some guilds that are most necessary to the life of man. Nevertheless there were many pharmacists all together, and they too were separated from the others. All the others as I have said lived apart. The wool merchants' guild and their subordinates all lived in one district, according to the quality of the trade they practised, as for example weavers, dyers and others belonging to that guild. The same for the silk workers and their subordinates, and for all other guilds and their helpers. Each lived apart by itself and away from the others. Those who worked at the grosser trades, as for example the coopers, shipwrights, wheelwrights and others required for the life of man, lived outside the wall of the suburbs. The same for those who made ropes and other such trades.'

Antonio Averlino
c.1400–1469

[...]

'Those who shod horses and other animals were placed near the gates of the city, as were the stonemasons.'

archaic beliefs • body model • efficiency • economisation • fit • utility • luxury • hedonism • consumption • professional practice • education

One interpretation of Filarete.   (point :)
 Orgin of architecture is already in the body. the
    architect is then building the body...
        Architecture is body..

12. Antonio Averlino (known as Filarete). *Trattato di architettura*. 1451–1464. Plan for an ideal city in the landscape circumscribed in the Vitruvian circle and square.

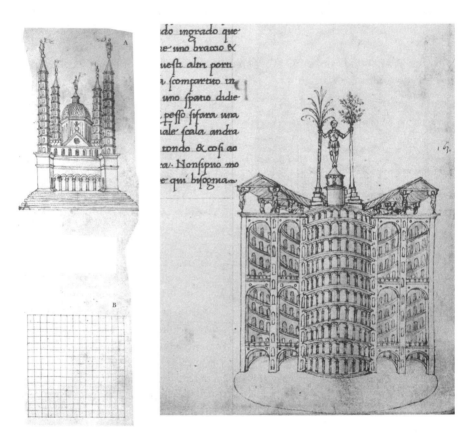

13. and 13b. Antonio Averlino (known as Filarete). *Trattato di architettura*. 1451–1464. Plan and perspective section of multi-storey buildings with mechanical moving figures. Notice the uncoordinated interior section perspectives.

Francesco Colonna (generally attributed)

Hypnerotomachia Poliphili (completed 1467; published 1499)

This allegorical romance recounts Poliphili's quest for his beloved, Polia. It is generally attributed to Francesco Colonna, a man of letters probably belonging to the princely Colonna family, although it was probably written by Leon Battista Alberti (Lefaivre, 1997). The numerous lengthy, detailed, enthusiastic and erudite descriptions of architecture – of its terminology, building types, stylistic features, materials and theory – which the book contains made it one of the most influential in the field, both with the reading public and with the architectural profession until the end of the seventeenth century (Blunt, 1937; Huper, 1956). Among other things, it contains the first description of a swimming pool, and the description of some grotesque architecture and the *terribilità* it inspires. The work was equally important in relation to garden design. It was translated into Spanish, English and French and re-edited many times. In addition, it is one of the first illustrated architectural books, generally thought of as one of the most beautiful books ever produced, which greatly contributed to its success.

Further reading Argan, 1934; Battisti, 1960, 1962; Billanovich and Menegazzo, 1966; Bruschi, 1978a; Casella and Pozzi, 1959; Comito, 1971, 1978; Donati, 1968; Gombrich, 1951; Hersey, 1976; Miller, 1977, 1983; Mitchell, 1960; Painter, 1963; Parronchi, 1963; Popelin, 1883; Pozzi, 1962; Schlosser, 1979; Schmidt, 1978; Sombart, 1967; Tzonis, 1972, 48; Weiss, 1961; White, 2004.

With voluptuous movements, with virginal gestures, with persuasive countenances, with girlish caresses, with lascivious glances, with sweet words – soothing and flattering they led me towards the place. I was happy with everything present, except that my golden-haired Polia was not there to complete my supreme felicity, being a sixth with them to constitute the perfect number. On the other hand, I was ill at ease because my clothing was not appropriate among this delightful company. But having made myself more at home, I began to be amiably jolly with them; and they were laughing sweetly, and I likewise was laughing with them. Finally we arrived at the place.

There I gazed in wonder at a marvellous octagonal bath-house. At every single external angle there was a pair of twinned pillars. Set below them, and rising from the level of the area, were pedestals or areobates, joined together all round. Then followed the pilasters, standing out from the wall by a third of their breadth, with capitals placed beneath a straight beam, and above it a frieze beneath a cornice, going completely around. The frieze was ornamented with exceptional sculpture: there were a number of naked infants, in remarkable modelling, set at equal intervals, with their hands intertwined, in which they were holding thick bundles of leafy branches banded together and bound round with ribbons.

Then, above the cornice just mentioned, there sprang an octagonal cupola, elegantly vaulted, following the plan of what was below. Between one corner and another, this was perforated all over and all through with marvellous open-works, in a thousand noble devices, and filled in with plates of clear crystal, which from a distance I had thought to be lead.

The vane was attached above a pointed apex following the octagonal shape of the cupola, and rose quite high beyond it. Here, immediately on top, was placed a ball. Fixed in the uppermost centre of this, there rose a very firm stem, into whose hollow end was inserted another stem, unfixed and turnable, that played freely. A wing was attached to this, which, when impelled by a wind blowing from any direction, turned with itself both the stem in the socket and a ball at its top one-third of the size of the one below.

On the latter stood a naked boy, supporting himself on his right leg while he held the other leg hanging. The back of his head, right through as far as his mouth, was hollowed out in the form of a funnel with its orifice bored through to the mouth, and to this junction was attached a trumpet, held by one hand of the boy close to the join, while the other hand was extended towards the end of the trumpet, exactly in line with the wing. Everything was cast perfectly in very thin bronze, and brilliantly gilded. This wing easily governed both the ball and the boy, with his expression or face in the act of playing, so that the hollowed-out back of his head turned towards the blowing of the wind, where, when it was breathed into, the trumpet trumpeted. And in this way, while the Egyptian seed-pods were shaking in the wind, here likewise the wind made the trumpet sound. This made me reflect with amusement, on a man who finds himself alone in an unknown place and scared, how easily he terrifies himself with every little noise.

Just then, in the face of the building opposite the beautiful nymph on the fountain, I saw the entrance, with a most finely finished door – all the workmanship of the outstanding sculptor who had carved the sleeping nymph, I thought. On its frieze I saw the following inscription in Greek characters: ΑΣΑΜΙΝΘΟΣ. Well, the munificence of Tacius would not be equal to such a bath! Inside, seats ran all round, in the form of four stone steps, joined together continuously in a circuit. They were all minutely inlaid with jasper and chalcedonies of every colour. The warm water covered the steps, as far as the edge or tread of the third step. From each corner stood out an unengaged and fully rounded corinthian column, of varied colouring, with undulating veins of jasper all the more delightful as being a normal product of artful nature. The columns had appropriate bases, and excellently composed capitals beneath a beam. Above this lay the zophorus, composed of naked cherubs playing in the water with little sea-monsters, with wrestling and children's contests, with the apt efforts and alertness characteristic of their age, and lively movements and games. The frieze went most beautifully all the way round, with a cornice placed on top of it. Above the row of projecting columns, extending perpendicularly from each into the top of the cupola, was a rib with a restrained swelling of oak leaves, laid closely and intricately one upon the other, serrated and curly-edged, in rich green jasper, and bound round with gilded bands. As they rose, they converged in the hollow vault of the cupola, uniting in a roundel, which was occupied by a lion's head with a bristling mane. This held gripped in its jaws a ring, from which were suspended loops of a precious metal, hanging down and ingeniously linked together. They held up a highly polished vessel – wide-mouthed and shallow, and made of the same very shiny material – suspended two cubits above the water. The rest of the vault in between, where it was not filled with crystal, was all covered with the cyan blue colouring of litharmen, sprinkled with gilt studs like acorns, exceptionally brilliant.

Not far off was a fissure in the ground, which continually emitted flaming material. When this had been drawn from the place, to fill the bowl of the vessel, some resins and sweet-smelling woods were placed on top, and they made an incredible scented smoke with a fragrance like that of the very best pastilles. Then, when they were closed, the double doors made of perforated metal glazed with the clearest crystal gave a cheerful light coloured in many places. Through this same perforated work of knot-like apertures, they brightly illuminated the sweet-smelling baths, the fragrance remained trapped and the heat did not evaporate outside. The smooth wall interposed between each column and the next displayed a very black stone of a hardness that would resist metal, and was mirror-like. This was edged with a fascia of exactly fitting breadth going all round the room, made of coral-red jasper, ornamented with an edge of double convex mouldings, or rather little balls. In the middle of each such wall, between one column and the next, an elegant naked nymph stood posing, each with a different attitude and attribute, in shining ivory-white milkstone. All were firmly placed on appropriate pedestals, which were round in plan and which were arranged to coincide with the same circumference as the bases of the columns. I admired these images so exquisitely sculptured that many times I allowed my eyes to wander from the true and real nymphs, and return to the artificial ones! The paved floor below the water, in varied mosaic of hard tesselated stone in marvellous designs, was visible in its diverse colouring. Because the water was very clear, not sulphurous but sweet-smelling and temperately warm without hypocaust or boiler, and very pure beyond belief, there was no obstructing medium between the object and the sense of sight.

Francesco Colonna

And therefore the various little fishes on the facing of the seats and the bottom, visibly modelled with artful mosaic rivalling nature, appeared to be alive and swimming. There were triglie or mullets, mustelle or lampreys, and many other kinds, without regard to nature but only for the beauty of the picture. The deep black stones of the wall were incised and very carefully inlaid with a most remarkable composition of loops or knots of antique-style foliage, of flowers, of shining Cytherean shells, as agreeable to the eyes as any that ever merited description. In the space above the door, in milkstone, I saw a dolphin arching its back among the calm waves, and a youth was sitting on top playing a lyre. On the opposite side, above the jocular fountain, there was another swimming dolphin, and Poseidon astride it with his pointed trident. These subjects had been carved from adjacent pieces of the same stone, and set into the deep black ground. Here I gave well-deserved praise to the excellent architect, and no less to the sculptor. On the other hand I highly appreciatcd the beautiful grace of the shapely and delightful young girls, so that I could not tell by comparison which was greater, my previous terror, or this unforeseen and fortunate solace: but without doubt I was in a state of extreme delight and pleasure. And now that we had entered most joyfully into as fragrant an atmosphere as ever could arise in Arabia, the nymphs, using the stone seats in place of a changing-room or apodyterium, were stripping themselves and laying aside their silk garments, having beautifully wrapped up their blonde tresses under netted caps, woven and most nobly intertwined with threads of gold. And without any concern – though with honour preserved – they allowed their shapely and delicate persons to be freely seen and individually inspected, totally nude – delicate flesh without blemish, infused with the tints of rose and early snow. Ah me, my agitated heart – I felt it leaping up as it opened itself to them and was entirely filled with voluptuous joy.

archaic beliefs • body model • luxury • hedonism • consumption • emotions • passions • sentiments • romanticism

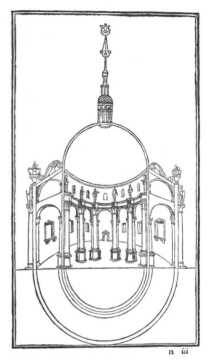

14. Generally attributed to Francesco Colonna. *Hypnerotomachia Poliphili*. 1499. The entrance of the first building the hero encounters, in the form of a triumphal arch.

14b. The circular-plan temple of Venus.

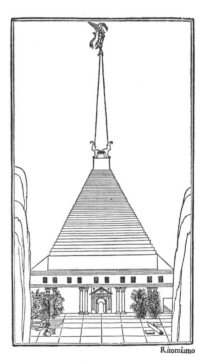

15. Generally attributed to Francesco Colonna. *Hypnerotomachia Poliphili*. 1499. Altar under canopy in the midst of a pagan bacchanalian celebration.

16. Generally attributed to Francesco Colonna. *Hypnerotomachia Poliphili*. 1499. The first building the hero of the novel encounters: part triumphal arch, part peripteral temple, part pyramid, part obelisk.

17. Generally attributed to Francesco Colonna. *Hypnerotomachia Poliphili*. 1499.

18. Generally attributed to Francesco Colonna. *Hypnerotomachia Poliphili*. 1499. Doors carved out of the sheer rock of a cliff, leading to three alternative life choices, the Glory of God, Eros Nurtured, and Worldly Glory inscribed in Arabic, Hebrew, Greek and Latin.

18b. Generally attributed to Francesco Colonna. *Hypnerotomachia Poliphili*. 1499. Depiction of the interior of a grotto.

Francesco di Giorgio Martini (1439–1501)

Treatises on Civil and Military Architecture (written 1474–1482)

Francesco di Giorgio was active as a painter and sculptor before entering the practice of 'military and civil architecture' which encompasses what we know today as architecture, mechanical, civil and naval engineering, fortification design and town planning. In addition, we have by his hand a translation of Vitruvius (Fiore, 1978) and four of five treatises (Betts, 1972) of architecture dealing with such technical innovations as radial town planning, domestic sanitation and the design of bastions capable of withstanding the new use of firearms. The books display an almost universal application of the prototype of the human body to architectonic elements. Among architects well acquainted with his work, although it was never published, were Antonio de Sangallo, Cataneo, Leonardo da Vinci, and later Barbaro and Scamozzi (de la Croix, 1960, 270).

Further reading Betts, 1971, 1972; Borsi, 1967; De la Croix, 1960, 1963, 1972; Fiore, 1973; Hellmann, 1961; Jähns, 1889; Maltese, 1959, 1967; Millon, 1958; Muratori, 1975; Papini, 1946; Parronchi, 1971; Promis, 1841, 1862–1874; Rocchi, 1902; Rotondi, 1970; Venturi, 1901–1938; Weller, 1943.

Francesco di
Giorgio Martini
1439–1501

Treatises on Civil and Military Architecture

[...]

To me it seems that the walls of the fortress, city and stronghold should be sufficiently broad and thick for them to be able to resist bombards, and all the walls low not per se but by virtue of their location and of their ditches, the towers with defences on their flanks and lower sections such that they cannot be attacked by siege engines, with ravelins enclosing filled-in and hollow spaces, with vaults and passageways, and disposed in many various ways in accordance with the aspect and requirements of the place, in such a way that the defences can safely be manned.

And up against the ravelins, wide, broad and deep ditches, and on the other side, on the summit of the banks of the ravelin, tall, thick, sloping sills: extending not towards the fortress but outwards, in this way defending and not offending, because if they had a height or gradient such that they could not be seen or monitored from the defences, they should be very harmful and dangerous, and allow those wishing to attack or engage in hostilities to approach unseen.

[...]

Although the ancients did not have the scourge and the inconvenience of the bombard, from whose angry fury only with great difficulty and exertion is protection to be had, and given that whosoever might have succeeded in protecting themselves against such machines must have had a divine rather than human intelligence, and although the ancients had the battering ram, the catapult, the siege tower, the ballista, the scorpion and many other instruments of offence and defence, never did they manage, nonetheless, to find anything similar to this, notwithstanding the supercilious ravings of those for whom the bombard existed in other times; looking in ancient cities and fortresses we see no example of such; and we are unable to find any authoritative testimony to the existence of such a weapon.

I come now to speak of the new and modern cities, strongholds and castles, and of the orders and methods which should be used in building them. First it should be ensured, as is said below, that the fortresses be compact and self-contained, and their walls of limited circumference, since the smaller their circumference the easier they are to defend and watch over.

And for all that the ancient architects greatly commended the circular form because it is perfect in itself, nonetheless this form does not seem to have been put into practice to any great extent since, for purposes of defending the walls, it would have been necessary to build extremely thick towers with the purpose that one tower should provide cover for another, and being so close together they would hinder more than help one another, since defensive actions from the flanks of one tower would impinge upon the other tower by virtue of the slight distance separating them.

Whence having asked myself which form should be the most convenient, the strongest and of greatest utility, the rhombus and the rhomboid seem to me to be the most perfect. Here the equilateral, isosceles and scalene forms are quite convenient; as are the square, rectangle, pentagon, hexagon: all these forms are suitable for fortresses because their external angles present an oblique, not frontal, surface to aggressors.

Francesco di Giorgio Martini 1439–1501

[...]

Since cities have the proportions, measures and form of the human body, I shall now describe their circumference and subdivisions. First we must consider that if a string is attached to the navel of a human body spread out on the ground, this string will describe the form of a circle around the extremities of the body. Similarly, the body fits inside a square form. We must therefore consider that since all the divisions and members of the body are perfectly proportioned to one another and are disposed in perfect harmony, the same should be observed in the city and in other buildings. And when a stronghold is not to be built in the city, its place shall be taken by the cathedral, with the seignorial palace facing the piazza before the cathedral and in correspondence with it. And the navel shall be the main piazza. At the hands and feet other churches and piazza shall be built. And just as the eyes, ears, nose, mouth, veins, innards and other internal organs are disposed around and within the body in keeping with its needs and requirements, so we should proceed with cities, some instances of which we shall now examine.

Now of the manners in which the sites of the city and castle are to be constituted, whether on a mount or a plain, whether next to rivers or on the coast, each of which requires a different composition, I shall presently examine in turn.

If the city is to occupy a mountainous location, therefore, first it should be seen that the countryside is fertile enough for the sustenance of the inhabitants. It should be near or next to rivers to drive the mills and other necessary buildings. There should be springs and wells of running water, and if not, an abundance of cisterns. It should be divided up such that the lanes, squares and streets are neither steep, tortuous nor irregular in form, but stepped, circular or spiral, following the gradient and declivity of the hillside, with each road converging on the other. And when the roads are stepped, they should facilitate movement in such a way that the inhabitants shall not be inconvenienced when they walk in them. And the piazza should be made to a size which corresponds to the city, with the public roads and thoroughfares set out as straight as possible, and lined by warehouses and the premises of other mercantile crafts. And all the churches should be placed beside the common streets, distributed in such a way that the inhabitants can attend them without accident during bad weather. The palaces and offices of the civic officials and magistrates should be on or near the main piazza.

[83]

The same holds for the city which is located on a plain, whether rectangular, pentagonal or hexagonal in shape, which are the forms I find most suitable for purposes of the defence of the towers. First the walls should be built in such a way that the gates correspond to each other. And in the middle of the city the main piazza, which may be round, faceted, square or any other form that may be desired. And every street should converge on this piazza in a straight line, as from a point to the centre. And whether these streets be eight, six or four in number, halfway along the length of each there should be a piazza, at a point marking half the radius between the gate and the main square. And each of these streets should lead to its own gate. And then all the other streets should intersect with one another, either at right angles or by convergence, just as we see in the human body that one member corresponds to another in equal proportion, as is the case of the head to the bust, one arm to the other, the thighs to the legs, and the legs to the feet, all in proportionately corresponding order and sequence. And just as it is said that all the entrails are arranged and distributed so as to govern and sustenance the body, as are the divisions inside and outside the body, so it is necessary that all the elements of the city be distributed in the manner most suited to its sustenance, beauty and governance.

[...]

[...] But if the architect does not have a keen mind and singular ingenuity, he shall never be able to exercise any aspect of such arts with perfection, and therefore architecture shall be no more than a subtle fancy conceived in the mind and made manifest in the building's execution.

And it should be noted that reason cannot take each and every thing into its embrace, because ingenuity consists more in the mind and the intellect of the architect than in designs and drawings, and many things intervene, of which the architect or builder had never thought. And so the architect needs to be practical and diligent, with a good memory; to have read and seen many things and to be prepared for eventualities. And not like many arrogant and presumptuous architects who are founded in error and who have corrupted the world by demonstrating the false with the force of their language. And I shall now describe in turn each of the fields of learning in which the architect must be conversant.

First it must be known that two things above all are necessary: practice and theory. Practice concerns the use and the intention of the building. Theory is demonstrating things, before they have been built, with the due reasoning. And this said, we must first appreciate how necessary drawing is, without which no form can take shape or be built.

[...]

It should be known that the corona or cornice with their frieze and architrave are derived from the face, neck and chest of the human body. First the face shall be divided into four, from the peak of the brow to the tip of the chin. The first part shall consist of the cymatium with its fillets, the second the dripstone and the third the ovolo [editor's note: a convex moulding, less than a semicircle in profile]. And the fourth and final part, which goes from the nose to the chin, shall be divided into three: the first part, from the nose to the mouth, shall correspond to the dentils, and the other two parts to the cyma reversa with its bed mouldings. And the chin and the junction of the collar bones shall correspond to the frieze. And from the junction of the collar bones to the point where the chest terminates shall correspond to the architrave. And just as the

Francesco di Giorgio Martini 1439–1501

chest has four ribs in close array on either side, so we shall constitute four bands of fillets and astragal. It should be known that the uppermost part of the cornice should be given the same projection as it has height, just as can be illustrated by turning through ninety degrees on the imaginary vertical plane from the tip of the corona the square in which the profile of the head, rendered in modular fashion, is inscribed. The ancients too divided the height of the entablature into three, with the cornice forming one part, the frieze another and the architrave the third, and the three parts of exactly equal height and proportions. Similarly, the ovolo was one-eighth smaller than the dripstone. And they also fleshed out the proportions by adding many ornaments such as astragals, cordons, braids, leaves, paternosters and various other mouldings, in accordance with the imagination of the builders. And the aforementioned cornice, frieze and architrave they made the same height of the capital of the column on top of which they were placed, which column was seven times the height of the cornice from top to base, and the distance from the cornice to the ground was divided into twelve parts.

I shall now describe how the façades and *porti* of churches are set out. And since the façades of churches are based on the human body, and have the same proportions and ratios as the human body, I shall first give an account of these. It should be known that the human body is divided into nine parts, or in nine heads measured from the peak of the brow to the tip of the chin. And by the span of the arms is another nine parts, of which four and a half parts measure from one elbow to the other. And just as the height of the body is nine heads, so the height of the church should be divided into nine parts, and its breadth in four-and-a-half, just as there are four-and-a-half parts from one elbow to the other. The rest, that is to say the length of the forearms, shall be divided between the flanking aisles, which shall be two-and-a-half parts with their due and corresponding heights as described above. And the nave and aisles shall be as high as they are broad. The height and width of the door of the central body shall be two parts and a half of the nine, which is to say the height from the knees to the soles of the feet. The bases of these churches should be as high as the feet are thick, which is to say, half a head.

[...]

... contains, because in his being has something in common with the elements and metals; is similar to plants in that he feeds, grows and reproduces, to the brute animals in his sensory cognition and, finally, to the angels and immaterial substances in his ability to reason, and so in his being the similarities of all creatures are resplendent. Similarly, since from him there must proceed more actions than from any other creature, there are in him more instruments than in other corporeal natures, and therefore his parts correspond to a greater degree than those of the other animals. Whence in anything that he makes the human builder must with great artifice take from those things the form that in some way can be assimilated to the human body, just as we see that columns expressly have almost all the proportions of man, as they will make apparent in their location.

[...]

Since it appears much more necessary that we should satisfy reason instead of any of our sensual appetites, and most of all those parts of reason which by art and intelligence must be governed, so the same holds for the building of any divine and sacred temple, and since there are many varied opinions on where such a subdivision might have had its origin and principle, it should be considered that many diligent and inquiring minds have gone to the trouble of imitating

Francesco di
Giorgio Martini
1439–1501

[85]

nature in every exercise, and from nature have extracted the ratios as well as the subdivisions and members of the human body, from which the perfect number, as Plato describes it, is found to derive, and from which, for Vitruvius, the measures and proportions of temples and columns derive, without whose symmetry, he says, no architect can properly build anything founded on reason. And finding many varied instructions on the schematic representation of the body, I have resolved to demonstrate some briefly. [. . .]

[. . .]

Some, however, the better to defend the walls against the bombard and the greater to offend their enemies, have the walls made thick and with more fortified towers, with points of defence and offence on their flanks. Which more by their thickness than by their ingenuity of remedy offer rather more resistance than those of the ancients, from which, nevertheless, they are separated by an infinite lapse of time. To consider the fortresses built in Italy, in general we can truthfully say that there exists not a single stronghold or fortress that under the cannon fire which tears its walls down, or its offences [and defences] at least, cannot be stormed and subdued, with the exception of the natural fortress, such as any high and rugged mount, or one surrounded by sheer cliffs, where nature more than artifice is to be commended. Whence there arises the need, for the well-being and conservation of [states and] powers, to demonstrate additional manners and different forms [different to the other ingeniously conceived forms] by way of which a limit and curb can be put to such violence, and whereby enemies are stripped of their dastardly schemes and power, and friends and allies gain in vigour and courage.

To my mind we should not scorn, as some undiscerning souls often do, [those methods and] instruments which, in so far as understanding and exercising them is concerned, hold few secrets and are easy to use. Instruments and means are neither useful nor necessary other than for obtaining the ultimate end or effect [of those who wield them]: therefore, the lesser the [moment and] difficulty and the greater the simplicity of that which leads us to our desired end, the more powerful should it be esteemed, in so far as the *simpler and more concise* instrument can achieve everything that other more [and more] complex instruments can. [And although once they are discovered they might be easy to understand and to deploy, the power of invention nevertheless is not easy, and conceded only to rare individuals; such occurs in every science, whose niceties have been uncovered only by extremely skilled and gifted men, and which, once demonstrated, can easily be comprehended by anyone of average intellect. The same applies to this art, whose perfection nevertheless consists in invention, without which one can hardly use the inventions of others.]

archaic beliefs • body model • design methodology • representation • truth • illusion • social control • defence • systematisation of space distribution

Francesco di Giorgio Martini 1439–1501

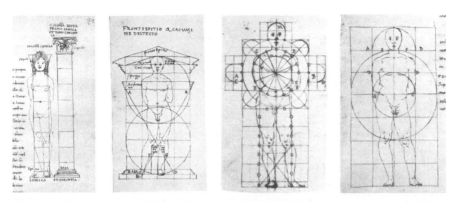

19., 19b., 19c., 19d. Francesco di Giorgio Martini. *Trattati sull'architettura civile e militare*. 1474–1482. Columns, gate and building plans configured and proportioned according to the human body.

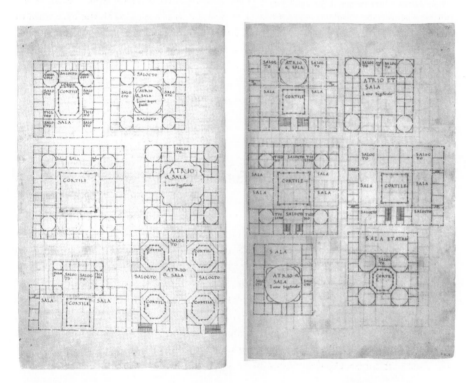

20., 20b. Francesco di Giorgio Martini. *Trattati sull'architettura civile e militare*. 1474–1482. Examples of possible atrium-type building plans.

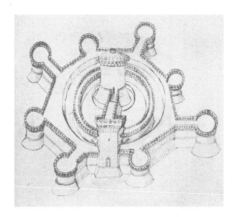

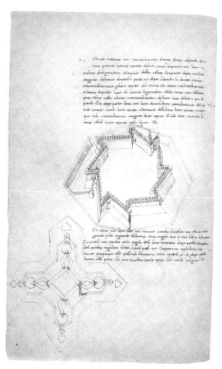

21., 21b. Francesco di Giorgio Martini. *Trattati sull'architettura civile e militare*. 1474–1482. Two examples of possible types of bastions, circular and triangular.

Leonardo da Vinci. 'Studies of Fortification'

Codex Atlanticus, c.1504

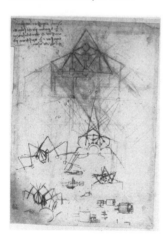

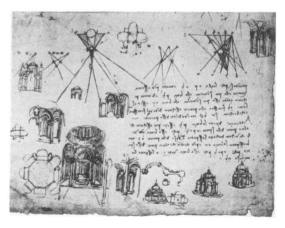

22. Leonardo da Vinci. Studies of Fortification. *Codex Atlanticus*, f.48 v–a. c.1504. Notice the analogy in the representation of visual and ballistic lines revealing the genesis of the idea of the triangular bastion.

22b. Leonardo da Vinci. Studies of shadows and sketches for a centrally-planned church. *Codex Atlanticus*, f.37 v–a. c.1508.

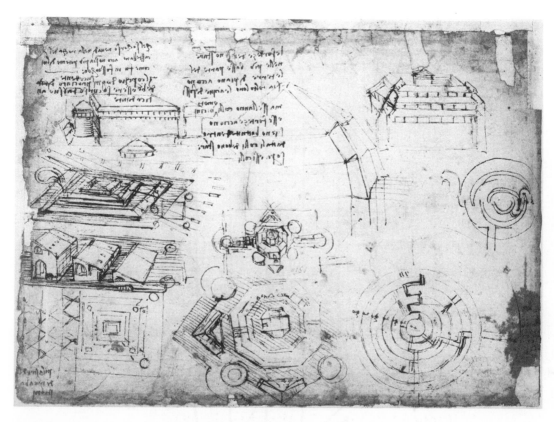

23. Leonardo da Vinci. Studies of the Piombino Fortifications showing ballistic lines shaping the profile of a fortification. *Codex Atlanticus*, f.120 v–a. *c.*1504.

Luca Pacioli

De Divina Proportione, 1509

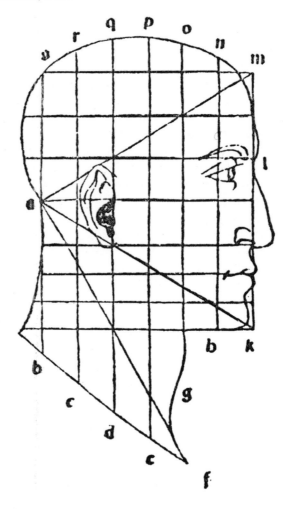

24. Luca Pacioli. *De Divina Proportione*. 1509. Study of the proportions and geometrical structure on the human head.

Raphael (Sanzio) (1482–1520)

Letter to Pope Leo X (1519)

In 1515, the great Renaissance painter and architect Raphael Sanzio was appointed as successor to Bramante [editor's note: Bramante trained as a painter of perspective with Mantegna and was a student of Piero della Francesca. He worked with Leonardo da Vinci in Milan], his relative, as architect of St Peter's and superintendent of Roman antiquities. One of his tasks was to make measured drawings of all the Roman remains and restore a large number of them. The present letter, a report to his patron, Pope Leo X, on the progress of the undertaking is probably the result of collaboration. Raphael headed an architectural and archaeological 'bottega', or workshop (Fontana and Morachiello, 1975; Bonelli, 1978) which brought together many scholars and architects – Giuliano da Sangallo, Baldassare Castiglione, Peruzzi, Fabio Calvo and Donato Bramante to name only a few. Raphael's avowed preference in the text for the rounded arch in classical architecture as 'good' in opposition to the Gothic, that was 'without grace', reveals the typical aesthetic prejudice of the Renaissance. The letter is also significant because it marks the first time an explicit differentiation is made between orthogonal projection and perspective drawing in the graphic representation of architecture. Orthogonal projection, possibly thanks to the introduction of the astrolabe, is applied here in order to render the standard representations of a building – ground plan, façade and section – which were necessary in order to make reliable construction drawings (Lotz, 1972, 27–29). Exactitude was not Rafael's only goal, however. Apparent too is his concern for good presentation drawings. The letter also reveals Raphael employing the painterly and distorting practice of perspective as public relations packaging with the sole aim of conveying the 'gracefulness' of the building in order to seduce the patron.

Further reading Bonelli, 1978; Brizio, 1966; Bruschi, 1977; Carter, 1975; Castagnoli, 1968; Emiliani, 1980; Fontana and Morachiello, 1975; Förster, 1956; Frankl, 1960; Gentili di Guiseppe, 1933; Geymüller, 1884; Huelsen, 1979; Lotz, 1972, 27–29; Müntz, 1878–1882; Panofsky, 1969; Parronchi, 1964; Pastor, 1955; Roscoe, 1816; Shearman, 1967, 1968; Vogel, 1910; White, 1967; Wittkower, 1962.

To some it might seem hard to differentiate the ancient buildings from the modern ones, or the most ancient from the younger ones. To allow no doubt in the minds of those who might wish to gain this knowledge I would say that with a little effort one might succeed in doing it. This is because there are only three styles of building to be found in Rome. The first is the good antique, that lasted from the first Emperors until the time when Rome was ruined and despoiled by the Goths and other barbarians; the second is what lasted from that time until the Gothic domination of Rome and for one hundred years afterwards; and the third is from that age down to our own. The modern buildings are easy to recognise not only because they are new but also because their workmanship is not as good. Moreover they are not built at such great expense as the ancient buildings we see and admire. For although today architecture is active and comes close to the antique style, as may be seen in many beautiful buildings of Bramante, the ornamentation still is not made of such precious material as that used by the men of ancient times who spent a fortune to build what they had imagined, and by their strength of will overcame every difficulty. The buildings of the time of the Goths, however, are so wholly without grace or any style whatsoever that they are different from both ancient and modern. It is therefore not difficult to recognise the buildings of the period of the Emperors, which are more excellent in style and built more perfectly, at greater expense and with more mastery than all the others. It is only the work of this period that I would like to speak of. There is no need for anyone to question whether the less ancient of this era are lesser in beauty, less well conceived or of a different style because they are all built with the same type of beauty. And although many of the buildings were often restored by the men of that age – for example we read that in the same place where the Golden House of Nero stood the Baths of Titus [editor's note: luxurious baths in Rome built under the Roman Emperor Titus Flavius Sabinus Vespasianus, AD c.40–80] and his House and the Amphitheatre were built – still these were constructed in the same style and manner as the other buildings of a period still older than the time of Nero and contemporary with the Golden House. For although literature, sculpture, painting and almost every art were long in declining and deteriorated right up to when the last Emperors, architecture alone observed and maintained the same principles, and building was carried on with the same kind of greatness and dignity as before. Of all the arts, architecture was the last to decline . . .

Raphael (Sanzio)
1482–1520

When Rome was ruined, burned and destroyed by the barbarians, it seems that by the same fire and tragic ruin of the monuments the art of erecting them was also ruined. The fortunes of Rome were then so changed that in the place of limitless victories and triumphs came humiliations and wretchedness of enslavement. It appeared unfitting for those who were conquered and in bondage to live in the grand manner to which they had been accustomed while they were the conquerors of the barbarian. And with the change of fortune came a change in the manner of living and building, as far distant from what they had known as slavery is from freedom. Men were reduced to a life suited to their misery, knew not how to make baked bricks or any other kind of ornament. They stripped the ancient walls to obtain bricks and broke marble into little squares. With a mixture of these squares and bricks they built their walls, as we may see today in the tower called the Tower of the Militia. So, for a goodly space of time, they continued in their ignorance, as is shown by all the work of the age. The cruel and dreadful storm of war and destruction broke not only over Italy but also spread over Greece, where once the inventors and perfect masters of all the arts had prevailed. There also the worst and most worthless style of painting and sculpture arose. Next, in almost every country, the German style of architecture appeared – a style that, as one can see by its ornament, is far removed from the good style of the Romans and the antique. In the Roman period, besides the structure of the building itself, there may be seen the most beautiful cornices, friezes and architraves, columns, capitals and bases, decorations of a perfect and most pure style. German architecture, which in many places still persists, often used cramped and poorly constructed small figures for ornament, and worse still, strange animals, figures and leaves out of all reason, as corbels to support a beam. Nevertheless, this architecture has a certain justification: it originated by the taking of branches of unpruned trees, binding them together and bending them to construct pointed arches. Although this invention is not wholly to be despised, it is weak, because the huts described by Vitruvius in his account of the origin of the Doric order, in which tree trunks chained together serve as columns, and with their tops and roofs, can support a far greater weight than the pointed arch, which has two thrusts. Moreover, a half circle, whose every line presses towards a single centre, can, according to mathematical rules, bear a much greater load. Aside from the weakness of a pointed arch, it lacks the grace of our style, which is pleasing to the eye because of the perfection of a circle. It may be observed that nature herself strives for no other form. But it is unnecessary to compare Roman architecture with that of the barbarians, for the difference is well known; nor it is necessary to speak in detail of the Roman style since it has been so admirably described by Vitruvius. It is enough to know that Roman building, down to the time of the last Emperors, was always constructed in a good way. There is no difficulty in distinguishing the Roman buildings from those of the times of the Goths, or even from those of later times, because the two are the extreme opposite of each other. Nor is it difficult to distinguish them from those of our own modern age, even if it were not for the novelty that makes them noticeable.

I have spoken enough now of the ancient buildings of Rome to show that it was of these that I wished to speak, and also to make plain how easy it is to distinguish them from the others. It remains now for me to teach the method by which we have tried to measure and draw them, so that anyone who himself wishes to devote himself to architecture may learn by this method to execute both processes without error. It is right to know that in the description of this method we have not been governed by chance, or by experience only, but by following a well thought-out plan. Since I have never read or heard that the men of ancient times knew of the method used by us of measuring with the magnetic compass, the manner which I am used to, I therefore believe it to be a modern invention. However, wishing to obey the command of your Holiness in this matter, I will explain in detail how it is to be used, before we go any further.

Raphael (Sanzio)
1482–1520

A round flat instrument, like an astrolabe, should be constructed, about two palms in diameter, more or less, however the user wishes. The circumference of the instrument should be divided into eight equal parts, and in each part should be written the name of one of the eight winds. . . . And since, to my mind, there are many people who are wrong when it comes to representing buildings (for example they believe that what is right for the painter is right for the architect), I will describe the method that I think should be followed in order for all measurements to be correctly described and in order for all the parts of the building to be identified without error.

My method is to divide the drawing of the building into three parts, of which the first is the plan, by which we mean the outlay at ground level; the second is the walls seen from outside with their ornaments; the third is the walls seen from inside, also with their ornaments.

The ground plan indicates the subdivisions of the surface of the ground plan of a building, in other words it is the design of the foundations of the entire building, the way they are at grade level. This surface, if it is on a hill, must be reduced to a plane, so that the base line of the hill is parallel to the base line of the floor of a building. To this end, one should measure the straight line at the foot of the hill, and not the circumference of the real ground level above. In this way all the walls will fall straight and perpendicular to the base line; and this is called the ground plan. Just as the space that is taken up by the sole of the foot forms the base for the whole body, so this plan is the base for the whole building.

After the ground plan has been drawn, subdivided into parts (they can be circular or square or in any other form), one should draw, always measuring everything in scale, a line of the length of the base of the whole building, from the middle of this line, draw another straight line that will form two right angles, left and right, and this will be the vertical middle line of the façade of the building. From the two ends of the base line two perpendicular lines should then be drawn, and these should be as long, in scale, as the building is high. Then, between these two end-lines, that indicate the height, one derives the vertical dimensions of the columns, pilasters, windows and other ornaments indicated upon the front of the entire building, namely upon the front half-part of it, as is the case with the ground plan. And this should be done by drawing lines that are parallel to the two end-lines according to every measurable point in the columns, pilasters and openings, or even window ornaments. One should complete the façade by always drawing lines that are parallel to the two end-lines. Then, horizontally, one should add the breadth of the bases of the columns, of the capitals, of the architraves, of the windows, friezes, cornices and such details. All this should be done with lines parallel to the base line of the building. Dimensions should not grow smaller towards either end of the building, whether it is round or square, to make the building show two façades, as some are wont to do, diminishing the side that recedes farthest from the eye. This is because when buildings do diminish, it means they are formed from the intersection of the pyramidal rays of the eye, and this is a technique belonging to perspective drawing and perspective drawing may belong to the painter, but not to the architect who is unable to obtain any correct measurement from a diminished line and who needs measurements that are all perfect in reality and not, misleadingly, perfect in appearance. An architectural drawing requires measurements that are always drawn with lines parallel in every respect. If, sometimes, architectural members that are round in plan seem to have a tapering form in elevation, they will be correctly represented in the ground plan. And, conversely, in the elevation it will be possible to immediately find the correct representation of the members that appear diminished in the ground plan, for instance the vaults, arches, triangles and other members. To insure this is possible, one must always rely on exact measurements in palms, feet, fingers, grains, down to the smallest increments.

Raphael (Sanzio)
1482–1520

The third kind of drawing (besides the ground plan and the orthogonal projection of the façade), is the one that we call section, with its ornamentation, and this is no less necessary than the other two. It is made in the same way as the façade, from the ground plan up, using parallel lines. It reveals the inner half of the building as if it were sectioned in two parts. It reveals the inner court, the relationship in height of the outer cornices to the inner ones, the height of the windows, of the doors, of arches and vaults, namely barrel-vaults, cross-vaults, or any other kind of vault.

With these three means, one can examine closely all the parts of all buildings, both inside and out. [. . .]

Besides the aforesaid three systems of architectural drawings, and in order to satisfy more completely the desire of those who like to look at and understand all the things that are represented in drawings, we have also drawn a few buildings in perspective. We have decided to represent them in this manner because the eye can see them and appreciate the gracefulness of their appearance, resulting from proportion and symmetry. This is not visible in the kind of architectural drawings that render correct measurements only. The three-dimensionality of objects cannot be conveyed on a picture plan without making the farthest parts of these diminished the way the eye sees them naturally ... Therefore, in our designs we have observed the rules related to perspective, employing the previous three systems of design only for rendering measurements, because with these three systems of design it would be impossible or at least exceedingly hard to present objects the way they appear in proper form even though we may still be able to calculate the proportions of buildings in them. And though the method of drawing in perspective is fitting to the painter, it is also useful to the architect. This is because, the same way the painter needs architectural knowledge in order to paint exact and well proportioned ornaments, so the architect needs perspective in order to represent the whole building, ornaments and all. [. . .]

history versus antiquarianism • representation • truth • illusion

Cesare Cesariano (1483–1543)

Translation of Vitruvius's Ten Books on Architecture (1521)

Cesariano, the first self-styled 'professore di architectura,' practised as a military engineer (Gatti, 1971). Cesariano is known above all as the first to have illustrated and commented on the translation of Vitruvius into a modern language, carried out by him with the collaboration of Buono Mauro and Benedetto Giovo. A masterpiece of book illustration and graphic design, the book was considered more accessible than Fra Gioncondo's, the first illustrated Latin edition (1511), and it influenced Durantino's (1524) and Caporali's Vitruvius editions (Zoubov, 1960), and was accepted as authoritative until the publication of Barbaro's (1556). Cesariano's interpretation is held to be a reflection of the opinions of the Milanese circle of Leonardo and Bramante, to which he had belonged as a student and apprentice of the latter (Wittkower, 1973). The Preface is the first instance of an explicit use of architecture to legitimise the power of a modern sovereign – in this case the French king, François 1er, who had just conquered Milan and made the Gothic Cathedral of Milan the symbol of his reign. In its interpretation of the original, Cesariano's text displays the utmost arbitrariness however. While constantly paying tribute to Vitruvius's authority, his lengthy commentary, approximately ten times longer than **De Architectura**, simultaneously takes countless liberties with it. Among the most patent cases of mis-application is the triangulation study Cesariano carries out on the ground plan and façade of the Gothic Cathedral of Milan as an example of classical Vitruvian composition. And, perhaps as a joke, like Leonardo, Cesariano departs both in his commentary and in illustrations from the Vitruvian doctrine by picturing the centre of the body in the circle and the square as the penis, and not, as Vitruvius had specified, the navel. Shockingly, another illustration of Vitruvian man has an erection. To its credit, this book – not Serlio's, as is generally claimed – contains the first published representation of the different orders of columns.

Further reading Baroni, 1940; Battisti, 1958–1967; Bruschi, 1978b; Ciapponi, 1960, 1976; De Pagave, 1878; Ferrari, 1967; Frankl, 1945; Frigerio, 1934; Garin, 1961a; Gatti, 1971; Krinsky, 1967, 1969, 1971; Leoni, 1955; Malaguzzi Valeri, 1913–1923; Pelatti, 1932; Schlosser, 1979; Tafuri, 1966, 193–198, 1968, 1978; Vagnetti, 1973; Vagnetti and Marcuzzi, 1978; Wilinsky, 1969; Wittkower, 1973; Zoubov, 1958.

Dedication

. . . Vitruvius wisely put all these things in ten volumes, rightly believing that no other thing [architecture] is more worthy of a great prince by virtue of its great worth. It is only natural that he wished to dedicate it to Augustus Cesar, monarch of the universe. Taking from this example, I am compelled to dedicate to you [François 1er] this work, translated into our Italian mother tongue with commentary and historical background and that some wise men have taken upon themselves to publish. To your blessed and glorious majesty I humbly dedicate it as worthy of such a Prince ... with the hope that it will provide you with great pleasure. After completing the heavy task of governing your kingdom, I trust you will deign look upon these pages and see the admirable genius of the ancient and noble inventions necessary to human life. I will not over reach myself by praising the glories of the sublime French Crown, for you are covered and adorned with countless triumphs more than any other prince of these times ...

Book I, Chapter II What Architecture Consists Of

Cesare Cesariano
1483–1543

Now look at the figure on the page opposite (ground plan of the Cathedral of Milan). Clearly it is laid out according to triangular ichnography. It is distinct from quadrature as one can see from the way the members are distributed and by the intercolumniation. Triangulation was almost like a rule used by the German architects who used it in their design for the sacred building of the Cathedral of Milan. The symmetry is visible along the whole length and modulation of the columns ... Let us use the letters A.B.C.D. on the exterior of the building. Taken together they form two equilateral triangles. And where the interior letters E.F.G.H. are, there are also equilateral triangles. Where the letters a.i.k. are, there is the front of the pentagonal portico. As for I.K.L., they form an equilateral triangle that cuts the precedent line of the middle columns which by alternating correspondence mutually distribute the columns. ... In the centre is the letter O. Also the letters z and R form an equilateral triangle of a length of 64 braccia. Also the same length is the equilateral triangle formed by M.N.O. But the letters P.Q.R. are equilateral triangles located between two centres ...

... Continuing now onto the givens related to the tympanum of the façade of the aforementioned Cathedral of Milan. As for orthography and scenography I apply it to the hexastyle façade. The triangular reasoning is indicated by the letters A.B.C.E.F. that mark the points of the equilateral triangle. The same holds for A.F.G. If the top of the capitals of the columns have a line drawn through them called M to N, they will intersect and form another equilateral triangle with point L. The same for the points A and F. They form a square whose other points are R and S. The latter will, in turn, form the base of an equilateral triangle with the point Q. This forms the top of the big triangle with the letters O.P.Q.

Book III, Chapter I On the Composition of Sacred Buildings and of the Symmetry and Measurements of the Human Body

... And first the human body must be symmetrically drawn on a plane surface. Then we need a line that is perpendicular and that sections the drawing in two, (as in the figure on p. 100.) This line is the one that goes from A on the top to B at the base of the plane. Now we draw the other line that also cuts the plane in two symmetrical parts, that is the right and the left. Whoever wishes to draw a proportional body must follow this model. And in this model one may call A the point over the top of the head of the human figure. One may then extend a line from one extremity of the hand to the other G and o. All the optical distribution is contained between the line of the arms and the line of the chest. But the other collateral lines make up the square indicated by the points H.L.K.G., which is, in turn, divided by H and G and K and L, at the centre of which is the radical centring of the male member that we give the letter O to.

archaic beliefs • body model • classical canon • antiquity • abuses • systemisation of space distribution

Cesare Cesariano
1483–1543

COLVMNARVM EX SEX GENERIBVS CAPITVLORV: BASIV & SPIRAR ALIOR QVOQZ
GENERV CAPITVLOBZ QVOBZ A VITRVVIO SYMMETRIAE PERSCRIPTAE SVT AFFIGVRATIONES.

COLVMNA DORICA PRIMV A VIRILI CORPORE IMITATA.

COLVNA DORICA PRIMO MARONALI MORE ORNA & IMITATA

COLVMNA IONICA QVAE CV OR NATV & SINE STR IIS EFFICI POTEST.

COLVMNA CORINTHIA A VIRGINEA GRACILITATE IMITATA

COLVMNA ATTIGVRGA SIVE QVAE ATTICA DICITVR & PERAEQVATA.

COLVMNA THVSCANICA A COMVNI SYMMETRIA VSV ORNATVQ IMITATA.

HAEC COLVMA POTVTI ALIAE ORARI : SRIARZ RVGIS ET CV SIRIGLIS, EROCHIS & PLOCHIS

li Epiftylii Zophori & corone & fic de fingulis : Li capitelli de quefte fono quafi di tauta uenuftate : quanto li Corinthii : & fono
facti in uarii modi : ma quafi perho con pocha comentatione de fymmetrie diferente ut dictum eft da li Corinthii. La uarietate
de li quali & de altri capitelli imitati da le fymmetrie de le campane & uafi : fi como e fignata la dictione ＆ . & Si como da molti
Romani ædificii ho exemplato alcuni quiui etiam per dimonftrare di quello dice Vitruuio in la præfente lectione li ho affigurati.

Ma il tertio quale Corynthio fi dice ha imitatione de uirginale gracili
tate : per che le uirgine per la tenereza de la ætate con piu fubtili mem
bri figurati receueno li effecti piu uenufti in lo ornato . Ma la prima in
uentione di epfo capitello effere facta cofi fe memora : una uirgine Ci

❦Ma il tertio che Corynthio fi dice &c.
V itruuio quiui defcribe la inuentione del
capitello Corinthyo con breuita del hifto
ria . ❦Matura a le nuptie : ideft epfa uir
gine era Matura ad effere maritata : feu
da ponerla in la religione . per che in qui

25. Cesare Cesariano. *Di Lucio Vitruvio Pollione de Architectura Libri Decem*. 1521. Cesariano's suggestion of six Orders (*genera*, kinds) of architecture, comparing their proportions and details.

EPISTYLIORVM RATIO ZOPHORI AC CORO NAE·TYMPANI
ACROTERIOR·ANGVLARIOR·INCLINATIŌESQ3 EORVM PER
OPTICE INDICATIO·ENTαϭIϭ QVQ3 COLVM NAR·NECNON
STRIAR·AD NORMAM CONFIGVRATIO✍

26. Cesare Cesariano. *Di Lucio Vitruvio Pollione de Architectura Libri Decem*. 1521. Cesariano's illustration of the text of Vitruvius referring to optical illusions due to perspective deformations and the need for architectural corrections.

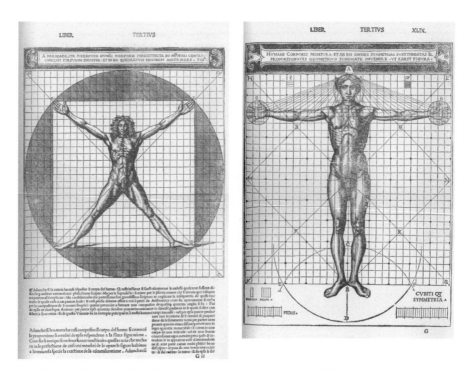

27., 27b. Cesare Cesariano. *Di Lucio Vitruvio Pollione de Architectura Libri Decem*. 1521. The geometrical and proportion structure of the human body as described by Vitruvius inscribed in a circle and a square, interpreted by Cesariano to stress the centrality of the genitals.

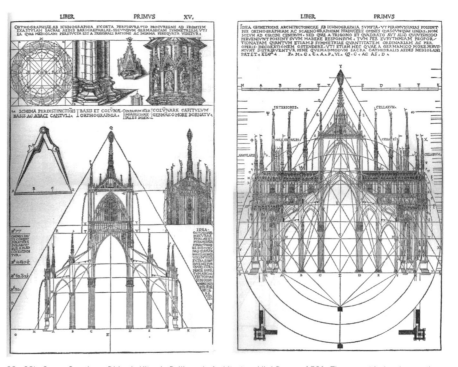

28., 28b. Cesare Cesariano. *Di Lucio Vitruvio Pollione de Architectura Libri Decem*. 1521. The geometrical and proportion structure of the Milano Cathedral based on analogies between similar triangles regulating the proportions of the façade.

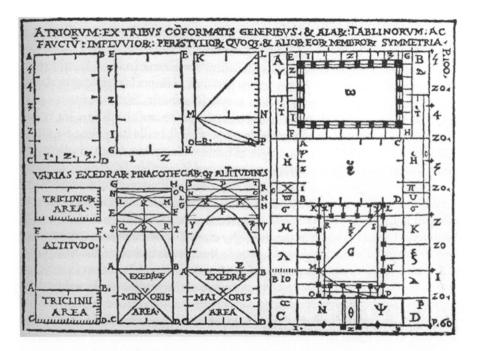

29. Cesare Cesariano. *Di Lucio Vitruvio Pollione de Architectura Libri Decem*. 1521. Proportion structure of an atrium house.

Francesco Giorgi (or Zorzi) (?–?)

Memorandum for S. Francesco della Vigna (1535)

When differences arose concerning the proportions of Sansovino's design for the church of S. Francesco della Vigna in Venice, Giorgi, a learned Franciscan monk attached to the church, was called upon to draw up a report. His recommendations – a practical application of the architectural theory he had expounded in his *De Harmonia Mundi*, combining elements of plotinean neo-platonism with Christian doctrine – were followed (Wittkower, 1962, 102–107).

Further reading Battisti, 1958–1967; Walker, 1958; Yates, 1947.

April 1, 1535. In order to build the fabric of the church with those fitting and very harmonious proportions, something that one can do without altering anything that has been done, I would proceed in the following manner. I would like the width of the nave to be 9 paces, which is the square of three, the first and divine number. The length of the nave, which would be 27, would have a triple proportion that makes a diapason and a diapente. And this mysterious harmony is such that when Plato in the Timaeus wished to describe the wonderful consonance of the parts and fabric of the world, he took this as the first foundation of his description, multiplying proportions and figures according to the fitting rules and consonances until he had included the whole world and each of its members and parts. We, wishing to actually build the church, have thought it necessary and most appropriate to follow that order of which God, the greatest architect, is the master and author. When God wished to instruct Moses concerning the form and proportion of the tabernacle which he had to build, He gave him as a model the fabric of the world and said (as is written in Exodus 25) 'And look that thou make them after their pattern, which was showed to thee on the mount.' By this pattern was meant, according to all the interpreters, the fabric of the world. And rightly, because it was necessary that the particular place should resemble His universe, not in size, of which He has no need, nor in delight, but in proportion, which He wills should be not only in the material places, in which He dwells, but (If we, then, follow the same proportions, we shall content ourselves for the length of the nave of the church with the number 27, which is three times that of the width, and the cube of the primary number, beyond which [number 27] Plato, in the description of the world, would not go, nor would Aristotle in his first book of 'De Caelo') having command of the measurements and forces of nature allow this number to be transgressed in any one body. The truth is that one can increase the measures and numbers, but they should always remain in the same ratios. And whosoever should presume to transgress this rule would create a monster, and break and violate the natural laws. So perfect is it. Similarly, I recommend the orders of the columns and pilasters to be designed according to the rules of the Doric art, of which I approve in this building as being proper to Him to whom the church is dedicated and to the brethren who have to officiate in it. Lastly it remains to speak of the front, which I wish should be in no way a square, but it should correspond to the inside of the building, and from it one should be able to grasp the form of the building and all its proportions. So that inside and outside, all should be proportionate. And this is our final intention, . . . that nobody will be able to dare, nor be any more at liberty, to change anything. S. Francesco a Vigna, Venice, April 1st, the 25th of the same month, A.D. 1535.

I F(rate) Francesco Giorgio, . . . have made the above description so that everybody may understand that what one undertakes in this church, is done in accordance with good principles and proportions and so I commend and pray that it may be done.

archaic beliefs • body model

Francesco Giorgi
(or Zorzi)

Albrecht Dürer

Etliche Unterricht Unterweisung der Messung Befestigung der Statt, Schloss und Flecken, 1527

30. Albrecht Dürer. *Etliche Unterricht zu Befestigung der Statt, Schloss und Flecken*. 1527. Plan of a town from the first original architectural treatise in a modern language.

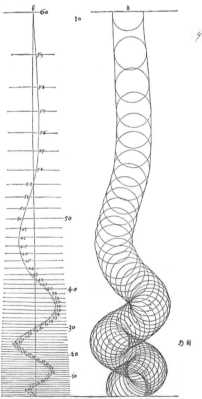

31. Albrecht Dürer. *Unterweisung der Messung (The Painter's Manual)*. 1525. Abstract shape for a spiral column. In contrast to previous treatises based on the circle, the square and regular shapes for design. The book applies mathematical tools to generate 'screw-line' profiles, irregular and 'deformed' shapes. It includes faces inscribed in warped grid frameworks, in contrast to Pacioli's normative human face, explain its variability.

Sebastiano Serlio (1475–1564)

The Books on Architecture (1537–1575)

In contrast to traditional architectural treatises, Serlio's books based on material left by his teacher Peruzzi, rely heavily on illustration to convey information and contain no theoretical commentary whatsoever. This format, that of a set of practical handbooks for architects and amateurs, although initiating a long tradition, was a great novelty at the time (Ackerman, 1972, 24; Blunt, 1973; Dinsmoor, 1942, 65–67) and stands in stark contrast to the more theoretical genre of the Albertian treatise of architecture. Books I and II (1545) are devoted to geometry and perspective. Book III (1540) is an illustrated catalogue of Roman antique buildings – a valuable substitute for untravelled readers. Upon its publication, and dedication to the French king Francis I, Serlio was named 'peintre et architecteur de Roy' (Adhémar, 1954) and settled in France, moving from his native Italy. In book IV (1537), the five orders, which have since become canon, are presented together for the first time (Schlosser, 1979, 407). Books V (1547), IV (written 1547–1550; unpublished until the twentieth century), VII (1575) and VIII (now lost) are respectively on churches, domestic architecture, architectural irregularities and military architecture. Serlio also stands out from the tradition of the other *trattatisti* in the attention he pays to the architecture not only of the rich and famous of the day, but also to the middle classes and even the poor (Rosenfeld, 1978). The subtitle of the book is telling: *'on all the habitations which are the custom today, beginning with the lowliest cottage, or what we call hut, and rising from rank to rank, to the most sumptuous palace for a prince, both the villa and the city house'* (Hart and Hicks, 2001). *Different Dwellings from the Meanest Hovel to the Most Ornate Palace.'* In this he may have influenced Alvise Cornaro (1557–1575) (Rosenfeld, 1978). Reprinted often and widely translated (Flemish, 1539?; French, 1542; German, 1542; Latin, 1569; English, 1611), Serlio's books enjoyed a great vogue and became the main channel through which the Italian Renaissance and mannerist architecture spread to the rest of Europe (Blunt, 1973).

Further reading Ackerman, 1972, 24; Adhémar, 1954; Argan, 1932, 1946; Benevolo, 1968; Blunt, 1973, 1980; Colombier, 1946; Dinsmoor, 1942, 65–67; Forssman, 1961; Hauser, 1965; Marconi, 1969; Ramirez, 1981a; Rosci, 1956, 1966, 1967; Rosenfeld, 1969, 1970; Santaniello, 1970; Schlosser, 1979, 407; Shearman, 1963; Treves, 1941; Tzonis and Lefaivre, 1984a; Wilinsky, 1961; Wolters, 1969.

Book IV: On the Five Styles of Buildings

The author to the readers

Gentle Reader, I have formulated some rules concerning architecture on the assumption that not only exalted intellects could understand this subject, but that every average person might also be able to grasp it, depending, however, on the greater or lesser extent of their interest in this art. These rules, as will be described below, are divided up into seven books. Since the subject suited it, I wished to begin publishing the rules with this, the fourth book, because it is more relevant and more important than the others for the understanding of the different styles of buildings and their ornaments. As for all the pleasant things which you will find in this book, you should give the credit not to me but to my teacher, Baldassare Peruzzi from Siena, who was not only most learned in this art – both in theory and in practice – but was also very kind and generous in teaching those who were interested – particularly me; what little I know, I owe it all to his kindness, and I intend to follow his example with those who do not disdain to learn from me, so that everyone can possess some knowledge of this art which is as delightful to the mind when thinking of what is to be made, as it is to the eyes when it is made. This art, through the fine quality of the famous and excellent intellects which I have mentioned, flourishes as much in this century as did the Latin language in the times of Julius Caesar and Cicero. Therefore be kind and well-disposed towards, if not the result, at least the desire which has been very strong in me to satisfy you with this work, and where you find that my weak ability has not been able to cope with the great weight of my task, go to stronger minds which may carry the burden for me and fill in where I have been wanting.

Sebastiano Serlio
1475–1564

In the first book I will discuss the principles of geometry and the different intersections of lines so as to enable the architect to understand perfectly everything which he will produce.

In the second, I shall show in words and figures sufficient perspective to enable the architect, when he wishes, to reveal his concept in a visible design.

In the third, there will be the *Icnografia* – that is the plan – the *Orthografia* – which is the elevation – and the *Sciografia* – which means the receding side – of a majority of the buildings in Rome, Italy and abroad; all carefully measured, and with their names and where they are to be found written alongside.

In the fourth, which is this one, there is a discussion of the five styles of building and their ornaments (Tuscan, Doric, Ionic, Corinthian and Composite), and with these styles the art of the understanding of the various elements is almost completely embraced.

In the fifth I shall discuss many types of temples designed in different forms – that is, rotunda, square, hexagonal, octagonal, oval, cross-shaped – with their plans, front and side elevations carefully measured.

In the sixth book we shall discuss all the habitations which are the custom today, beginning with the lowliest cottage or what we call a hut, and rising from rank to rank to the most sumptuous palace for a prince, both the villa and the city house.

In the seventh and last book I shall conclude with the many situations which can occur for the architect: in various places and on strangely shaped sites; in restorations or the rebuilding of houses; and how we are to make use of other buildings, and anything of like kind (whatever they may be, and even if they have been used previously).

Now in order to proceed in a more logical manner, I shall start from the strongest and least ornate Order: that is the Tuscan, which is the most Rustic, the strongest and of the least delicacy or gracefulness.

The ancients dedicated buildings to the gods, matching them to their natures, robust or delicate accordingly: for example, Doric work for Jupiter, Mars and Hercules – these Doric forms taken from a man; the Ionic for Diana, Apollo and Bacchus – the work taken from the form of a matron that is, that which combines both robustness with delicacy (Diana, from her feminine nature is delicate, but in her hunting she is robust; similarly, Apollo for his beauty is soft, but at the same time he is robust because he is a man; I would say the same for Bacchus); on the other hand they wanted the Corinthian style, taken from the form of a virgin, to be dedicated to the goddess Vesta, tutelary deity of virgins. However, in these modern times it seems to me that the procedure should be different, but not too far from the ancients. What I mean is that, following our Christian customs, I would (as far as I could) dedicate sacred buildings, according to their types, to God and to His Saints, and I would give secular buildings, both public and private, to men according to their rank and professions. They say therefore that Tuscan work – as it seems to me – is suitable for fortresses; for example, for city gates, fortified hill towns, castles, treasuries and places where munitions and artillery are kept, prisons, sea ports and other similar things for use in war. Although it is indeed true that Rustic work – that is, different bonds of roughly worked stones with several others a little more delicately cut because of the pleasure which the sculptors derived from it – was sometimes mixed by the ancients with Doric, sometimes even with Ionic and Corinthian work, nevertheless, since Tuscan work is really the roughest, least ornamented of all of the others, it seems to me that Rustic suits and is more fitting to Tuscan work than to any other. This is manifestly seen to have been observed by the Tuscans both in their greatest and principal city, which is Florence, and outside the city on their villas. As many very beautiful buildings and sumptuous constructions built of Rustic work can be seen there as exist throughout the rest of Christendom. They were, however, mixed with that amount of rusticity and delicacy which appealed to the architects, and for that reason I would say that such work is more suited to Tuscan than any other type. Therefore, gathering together several ancient examples and some of my own, I shall show in different ways how to build city or fortress gates with such types of work; also for public or private places, façades, loggias, porticos, windows and niches, bridges, aqueducts and various other ornaments – all of which could fall to the worthy architect to design. It is also certainly possible, not departing too much from that which the ancients built, to mix and combine this Rustic work with Doric, and again with Ionic and sometimes with Corinthian, if anyone wished to satisfy a whim. However, perhaps it could be said that this was more licentious than reasoned, because the architect should proceed very modestly and be very cautious, especially in public and solemn works, where it is praiseworthy to preserve decorum.

At the beginning of this book I wished to imitate the ancient writers of comedies, some of whom, when they were to perform a comedy, used to send out a messenger who, in a few words, told the spectators all that the comedy was about. Therefore since, in this volume, I am going to discuss the five styles of buildings, that is, Tuscan, Doric, Ionic, Corinthian and Composite, I thought that, at the beginning, the forms of all the types to be described should be seen here. Although only the principal proportions and measurements for the columns and their ornaments have been marked so as to provide a general rule, nevertheless, in its place each thing shall be recorded in minute detail. This is, however (as I said), only to show a general rule at a single glance. So as to be better understood by everyone, I shall place at the outset of each Order the Vitruvian terms accompanied by those used today, common to the whole of Italy. First, the Tuscan pedestal (I mean the dado), should be a perfect square, the Doric pedestal is to be that much more of a square as it is to take a line from one corner to another of a perfect square and swing it up for the vertical, the Ionic pedestal should be a square and a half, the Corinthian pedestal is to be a square and two-thirds of that square, the Composite pedestal should be two perfect squares – for all these only the dado, without its mouldings above and below, is intended. Do not be surprised that the following chapter is the fifth, which some might have expected to be the first. Because the first book on geometry will occupy one chapter, the second book on perspective

Sebastiano Serlio
1475–1564

will occupy two, the third on antiquities will occupy one, which makes a total of four, therefore the following chapter for this reason will be the fifth.

Book IV, Chapter V: On Tuscan Work and its Ornaments

Sebastiano Serlio
1475–1564

This is to be found in the writings of Vitruvius in the seventh chapter of the fourth book: the height of the Tuscan column with its base and capital should be seven parts, taking the measurement from its thickness at the base. The height of the base should be half the column. Once this has been divided into two parts, one is to be for the plinth [editor's note: a square or rectangular base for column, or door framing] pilaster or the other should be divided up into thirds; two parts are to be given to the torus, the other will be for the collar. The protrusion of the base is to be made in the following way: first, draw a circle the thickness of the column at the bottom and put it in a square; around the square which you have drawn, draw a circle touching the four corners – this will be its protrusion. Although all the other bases have square plinths, nevertheless the Tuscan one must be round in accordance with the text of Vitruvius. The height of the capital should be the same as the base. Divide it into three parts: one is to be for the abacus; the next should be divided into four parts, three are to be for the echinus [editor's note: the convex projecting moulding of eccentric curve supporting the abacus of the Doric capital. Hence the corresponding feature in capitals of other orders, which often had egg-and-dart ornamentation], the last should be for the ring; the remaining third part is to be for the frieze – the astragal with its necking should take up half of this. But with this divided into three, two are to be for the astragal and one should be given to the necking. The projection of the necking should be the same as its height, and even though it is joined to the capital it is, however, a member of the column. The column in the upper part should be diminished by a quarter part, and in this way the capital in the upper part will not be larger than the column at the bottom. The way to diminish the column is this: divide the trunk of the column into three parts, the third part at the bottom should be perpendicular, that is, plumb, and the remaining two-thirds are to be divided into as many equal parts as you wish. Then on the third part of the column draw a semi-circle, and from the lines that fall from the outside edges of the capital come in an eighth part – which will be in total the quarter part. Under the necking, here drop two plumb lines upon the semi-circle, and the part of the circle which remains from that line to the very edge of the column should be divided into as many equal parts as those of the two-thirds of the column. Having done this on both the left- and right-hand sides, draw the horizontal lines from the two sides of the semi-circle and place on each line its number, in sequence going down – in the same way place the numbers in the same sequence on the lines that divide the column. It is certain that the first line from the circle will coincide with the line under the necking. Then bring up the second line of the circle onto the second line of the column, and then bring up the third line of the circle onto the third line of the column, and then bring up the fourth line of the circle onto the fourth line of the column. When you have done this, draw a line from the base of the semi-circle to the fourth line, then draw a line from the fourth line to the third line, and then draw a line from the third line to the second line, then draw a line from the second line to the first line. Having done this on both sides of the column, even though the said lines are in themselves straight, nevertheless they create a curved line – the careful craftsman, with hand work, then smoothes out all the angles on it which occur where the lines join. Although this rule is made for the Tuscan column, which diminishes by a quarter part, it could nevertheless serve for every type of column; the greater the number of parts, both of the column and the semi-circle, the more correct the diminution will be.

A   Plinth, called abacus or 'cimasa'.

B   Echinus, called 'uovolo'.

C   Ring, called 'quadretto' or 'regolo'.

D   Hypotrachelium [editor's note: in some columns, that part of the capital and the annulet of the echinus, or the space between two neck mouldings] called frieze.

E   Astragal [editor's note: a bead, usually half-round, with a fillet on one or both sides. The term is used to describe the classical moulding consisting of a small convex moulding decorated with a string of beads or bead-and-reel shapes], called 'tondino'.

F   'Quadretto' [editor's note: the same as 'neck' in the classical orders, the space between the bottom of the capital and the top of the shaft, which is marked by a sinkage or a ring of mouldings], called necking.

G   Top scape, that is, the thickness of the column at the top.

H   Bottom scape, that is, the thickness of the column at the bottom.

I   'Quadretto', called 'gradetto', some call it a 'listello', others a collar.

K   Torus [editor's note: a bold projecting moulding, convex in shape, generally forming the lowest member of a base over the plinth], called 'historic', others call it by different names.

L   Plinth, called 'socle'.

M   Protrusion of the base, called 'sporto'.

N   Bottom scape of the column, that is, its thickness at the bottom.

O   Top scape of the column, that is, its thickness at the top.

Sebastiano Serlio
1475–1564

The columns drawn above (they may also be pilasters) have to be of the dimensions mentioned previously, governed, however, by whichever Order they may be.

Once the column with its base and capital is completed the architrave, frieze and cornice must be placed above it. The architrave is to be as tall as the capital. The frieze is to be the same height, and the fascia should be a sixth of this. Similarly the cornice and its members should be the same height and divided into four parts: one for the cymatium [editor's note: the crowning moulding of a classical cornice, especially when it has the form of a cyma, though it may also be an ovolo or cavetto], two for the corona, and the remaining part should be given to the cyma below it. The projection of the whole is to be at least as much as its height, and in the bottom of the corona some channels should be cut, larger or smaller depending on the works, according to the judgement of the architect. But since this work is very solid and its members plain, the architect, in my opinion, could certainly take the licence of adding some members which appear suited to such a type – this ought to be when more delicate work is required. . . . In addition I praise coronas that project more than their quadrate, provided that the stones can be supported by the buildings. Projections of this sort lend commodity and decorum: commodity, because if there are ambulatories above them, there will be more space, and also they will protect the works from the rain; decorum, because at the optimum distance the work will seem larger and where the stonework is reduced because of the delicacy, the greater projection will make it appear larger.

Although I said above that the Tuscan column with its base and capital should be seven parts, following the text of Vitruvius, and this proportion and shape is certainly good and accepted, nevertheless, because the first columns were six parts (taking this measurement from a human foot, which is a sixth of the body) and also because Doric' columns should be seven parts (the ancients added an extra part to give them more height), it seems to me that on such authority and because this column is of a more robust style, it should be shorter than the Doric. Therefore, in my opinion, with its capital and base, it is to be six parts. All this should be as a general rule, observing, however, all the rest of the measurements which we mentioned on the above column and its ornaments. Since neither Vitruvius nor any other architect as far as I have seen has ever given a rule for stylobates (called pedestals) – because in antiquity, as far as can

Sebastiano Serlio
1475–1564

be seen, these elements were built by architects according to the situations or the architects' needs (whether for raising columns or for raising steps up to porticoes or for any other elements which go with porticoes) – I would judge that, as long as we are not constrained by necessity, each pedestal should be matched to the style of the column, using provable guidelines. It is quite clear that the pedestal should at least be quadrate, I mean the dado without the base and head. Since the Tuscan column, then, is the most solid of all the Orders, its pedestal should be a perfect square; its front is to be the same width as the plinth of the base of the column, and its height should be divided into four parts. One part is to be added for the plinth at the base and the same should be added for the head; these members are to be without any carving whatsoever. As the column is divided into six parts, so the pedestal will, in itself, be in six parts proportioned to the column.

In this present volume I have promised to describe only the different styles of buildings and their ornaments. Therefore I shall not mention here how to arrange the gates of cities and fortresses, with their flanks, cannon emplacements and their other defensive constructions, and leave that task to the military architect, responding to the dictates of the sites and the situations which arise. But I will certainly discuss the way in which, once a city or fortress gate has been arranged, I think it should be ornamented, showing this in some figures. Every city gate has to have a door which is called a relief door (others call it a *porticella*). However, in order to preserve the symmetry, meaning proportional correspondence, it is necessary to make another which is false. The measurements of the gate are to be established in this way: whatever the width of the aperture, add half of this to the height. The height should be divided into six parts; one part is to be the pilastrade on the right- and left-hand sides. The front of the pilasters should be a third the width of the gate, and their height with the capitals and bases is to be five parts. The height of the bases, and thus the capitals, should be a third of the pilaster, nevertheless still observing the rule given for the initial column. The architrave, frieze and cornice should be as tall as the width of the front of the pilaster, according to the rule given on the initial Order. The relief door should be between the pilasters and its width is to be the same as the front of the pilaster, and the height should be double the width. Its pilastrades are to be a third part of that door. The elevation above the gate should be at the discretion of the architect, but we shall show the proportion of the pediment (called frontispiece) in two ways on the Doric Order.

Since the architect must have many ideas to satisfy himself and others, he could again ornament a city or fortress gate in another way, observing the following rule: however wide the aperture of that gate, its height should produce a 'sesquialtera', that is, two parts in width and three in height. Its pilastrade should be an eighth the width of the door, and the column is to be a quarter of it. But since a third part of the column is inset, fixed with other stones into the wall and placed there more for ornament than to bear weight, it should be made seven parts high – even eight would be permitted in a situation where the architect wanted to give the gate more gracefulness. The opening of the side doors should be half that of the principal door and their pilastrades are to be like those on the large one. Their height should be such that the fascia which supports the arch is their *supercilium* or what we call architrave. If a single piece of stone required for such an element cannot be found, the voussoirs should be built as shown in the figure. Thus the proportion of those doors will be 'superbipartiens tertias' – that is, three parts in width and five in height. There should be xv voussoirs in the arch. For the bases, capitals, architrave, frieze and cornice, the rule given on the initial column should be observed. The elevated part in the middle should be at the discretion of the architect, as I said for the others. The more such works are roughly hewn, the more they shall preserve the decorum of a fortress.

Sebastiano Serlio
1475–1564

A city or castle gate could be built in another way, plainer and even stronger, by following the figure seen below. The proportion should be such that the width of the opening of that gate is to be the same as the height up to the fascia which supports the vault. The height from the fascia upwards should be equal to the semi-circle – but, as ever, at the discretion of the architect that height may be more or less depending on the need, especially if he is constrained by circumstance. On both the left- and right-hand sides two smaller doors should be built thus, as I said for the others. Their width is to be half that of the central door, and the same amount of masonry should be left between the large door and the two small ones. Their height is to be double their width. Thus the fascia which bears the arch will also be a support for the voussoirs of those doors; the fascia could even be made to be the *supercilium* itself, that is, architrave, for that door. This door, as I said, could be built larger or smaller as the architect wishes, not, however, deviating much from the forms given.

Diversity of invention sometimes leads the architect to conceive things which he would perhaps never have imagined. For this reason, the figure shown below will give great commodity and utility to buildings, according to the situations which may arise for the architect – in a fortress wall, for example, provided that the wall was of a good thickness, building this work on the inner part. First it would do service as a loggia to provide cover and give more space for an ambulatory above, something which would be suitable for defence. For greater security during bombardment, all the openings could be infilled with earth. On occasions the architect might have to build near a hill. In this situation, in order to prevent the rain-water streams which continuously run down the said hill washing away the soil from the lowest parts, the building must be constructed up against the hill on a structure like this one. This would not only be a protection against such a threat, but also a fine ornament to its building. (131r) Raffaello from Urbino made use of a similar invention on Monte Mario a short way out of Rome, for the villa of Clement VII – it had been begun in his Cardinalate. Girolamo Genga used the same invention to the advantage of his patron on a beautiful building on the imperial hill a short distance outside Pesaro, as a support for a cistern also built against a hill, but with some very delicate brickwork.

[111]

The ancients used different types of bonding for this Rustic work, as can be seen below. The architect can adapt this invention to various things, depending on the situations that arise. Its measurements should be such that the opening is a perfect square, the masonry between one opening and the next being a quarter part smaller. The *supercilium*, called architrave, should be a quarter part of the opening and made up of an odd number of voussoirs which – converge towards the centre. In the same way, above that draw a semi-circle divided into ix equal parts, all the lines drawn towards the centre of the circle to form its voussoirs, and set the three blocks between them with the fascia above. In this way the work will be very strong and will last forever. However, to make the voussoirs of the architrave more secure it will be necessary to infill the semi-circle with brick-work (that is, terracotta) and for greater ornament it could be built in lattice-work as the ancients used to do – similar bonding can be seen in Rome on SS. Cosma e Damiano, still very strong despite its great antiquity.

Sebastiano Serlio
1475–1564

The intelligent architect could make use of this gate in various places, as was mentioned at the beginning, but not for fortresses because the passage – I mean to say vestibule – would not be suitable for manoeuvring artillery or large defensive weapons. Nevertheless, the exterior could be used for any gate whatsoever. The proportion is to be as follows: its opening should be twice as high as it is wide; the voussoirs of the semi-circle should be ix in number, all their lines drawn to the centre of the circle; the horizontal fascia which supports the arch is to be a seventh the width of the gate; the distance from the fascia to the pavement should be divided up into seven-and-a-half parts and there should be six courses of stones, three being one-and-a-half parts each and the other three one part each – this is how the seven-and-a-half parts are to be distributed; the height of the central voussoir should be half the width of the gate; the fascia which runs above the voussoirs is to be the same height as the foot of the voussoirs, but the central voussoir should be a quarter wider than the others.

The following gate could be used for all the buildings mentioned at the beginning, since it is Rustic work. It would be especially suitable for a country villa as a gate for the courtyard. This can be observed in many places along the roads in Italy in front of the houses of noblemen, since gates like this make such places very imposing. Its proportion should be as follows: the height of the opening to the underside of the arch is to be twice the width; the pilastrade should be a fifth the width of the opening – the same for the pilastrade of the arch; the pilaster should be double the pilastrade in width and its thickness a sixth of its front; the height of the base is to be a quarter of the front of the pilaster; the height of the capital should be a third of the pilaster; the smooth fascia, which is in place of the architrave, is to be the same height as the capital – similarly for the frieze and the cornice. However, for the individual members, that is, the bases, capitals and cornices, the rule given on the initial Order should be observed. The impost that supports the arch is to be the same height as the capital and divided up following the very same initial rules. However, concerning the other members, that is, the voussoirs and the other stones, they can be easily deduced with a pair of compasses, as can be seen. If, for greater ornament, you want to build a pediment – something that is indeed a very fine ornament – two methods for this can be seen shown on the Doric order.

Book VI: On All the Habitations Which Are the Custom Today Beginning with the Lowliest Cottage, or What We Call Hut, and Rising from Rank to Rank, to the Most Sumptuous Place for a Prince, both the Villa and the City House

On the House of the Poor Peasant, through four degrees of limited means

Although I said I wanted to begin with the meanest hovel of a poor peasant, I shall however omit the humble hut of the poor beggar and discuss the poor man living off his own labours with his small household, who has little land and who needs at least one room to sleep in and in which to have a fire. This should not be less than X feet on each side and it is marked C. If on the other hand this poor man has some farm animals it will be necessary, particularly if he has oxen, to build a small stable attached to the house that ought not to be less that VII feet in width. There should be a small window in the wall towards the fire so that the oxen, seeing the fire during the night, will not be afraid during the day, as Vitruvius and other good men advise. It would also be good if there was a small window in this stable towards the east so that the first rays of the rising sun will enter and produce the same effect that was mentioned regarding the fire. [...] If this peasant is a little wealthier in goods he could build a portico on the front of the house, at least VII feet wide. [...] Further, if this peasant had a larger household and was a little wealthier on the scale of limited means, in addition to the portico he could have an oven and a cantina. These places should be at either end of the portico and of the same width. [...] Thus this house will serve for four degrees of limited means.

Sebastiano Serlio
1475–1564

anticlassicism • deformation • freedom • naturalism • classical canon • antiquity • abuses • representation • truth • illusion • urbanisation of architecture • planning • social reform and democratization

32. Sebastiano Serlio. *I Libri dell'architettura*. 1537–1575.
Scenes for three kinds of theatre: satire, 32b. tragedy and 32c.
comedy.

Toſcano
parte
VI.

Doríca
parte
·VIII·

i onica
parte
VIII·

corintha
parti
IX

cōpoſita
parti
·X·

Proportione
quadrata

Proportio
ne della a
ſchiancio .

Propor-
tione d̄lla
metá più.

Propor-
tione di
duo terzi
più

Propor-
tione ad-
dopp¹ata

DEL-

33. Sebastiano Serlio. *I Libri dell'architettura*. 1537–1575. Table comparing five kinds (*genera*), manners, or orders of architecture that Serlio establishes as canonical (in contrast to Vitruvius's three) in this treatise. His proposal will become a norm for the following three centuries.

Saranno per modo di essempio diuersi casamenti di diuerse larghezze, la faccia de' quali sarà minore che la parte di dietro verso li giardini: li quali casamenti saranno, ò per qualche incendio, ò da guerre talmente rouinati che solamente sarà restato alla faccia dauanti alcuni vestigij de' confini, nè si vedrà fondamento alcuno, che li quattro confini a,b,c,d, essendo questi talicasamenti di più persone, nè si cognosca altre partitioni che come ho detto nella parte dauanti, talmente che ciascuno conosce la sua parte delle vestigie della faccia, ma li confini di dietro non si reggono se non li due angoli a,b. Potrà in questo accidente l'Architetto presupporre per l'antecedente, che la linea a,b, sia la linea maggiore, & che la parte dauanti c,d, sia la linea minore. Et con la regola, ch'io ho dimostrato nella passata carta, darà a ciascuno la sua rata parte, si come si dimostra nella figura qui sotto.

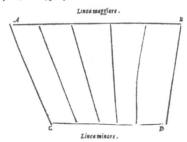

Vorrà tal volta l'Architetto accrescere vna cornice, cioè d'vna piccola farne vna maggiore proportionatamente, con tutti i suoi membri: con la regola passata si potrà accrescere quanto li piacerà, & quanto la cornice hauerà da essere maggiore dell'altra, sia tanto più allungata la linea B,C, come si dimostra qui sotto.

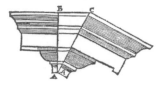

34. Sebastiano Serlio. *I Libri dell'architettura.* 1537–1575. Serlio, like Dürer, was interested in irregular shapes and solving problems of deformation of regular shapes due to optical or 34b. compositional factors, establishing the idea of an oblique architecture to solve such problems.

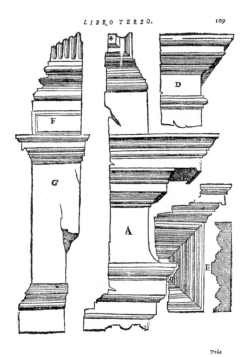

LIBRO TERZO.   109

Pola

35. Sebastiano Serlio. *I Libri dell'architettura.* 1537–1575. Table of architectural, 'exploded', details of an antique building.

36. Sebastiano Serlio. *I Libri dell'architettura*. 1537–1575. Fragment of the façade of the building of the Colosseum of Rome showing its system of construction and details of elements.

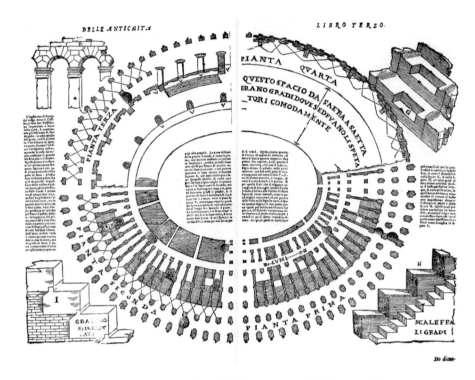

37. Sebastiano Serlio. *I Libri dell'architettura*. 1537–1575. Plan and section of the Colosseum of Rome.

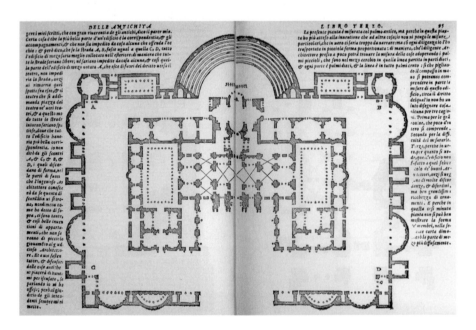

38. Sebastiano Serlio. *I Libri dell'architettura*. 1537–1575. Plan of the Thermae of Diocletian.

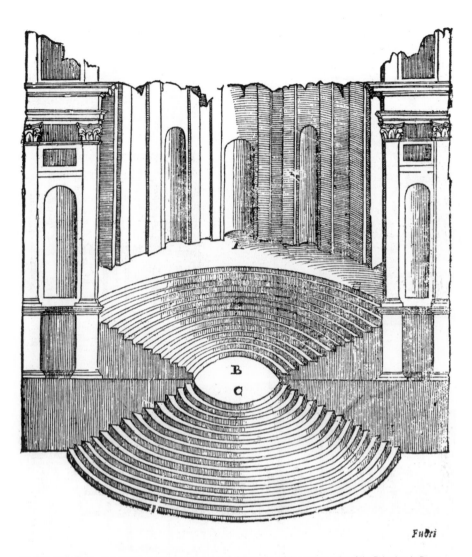

Fuori

39. Sebastiano Serlio. *I Libri dell'architettura*. 1537–1575. Perspective of the upper exedra of the Belvedere in Rome.

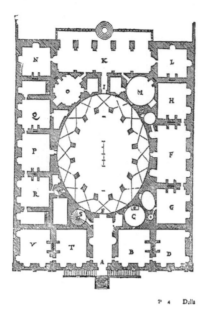

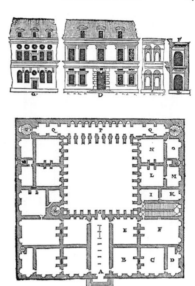

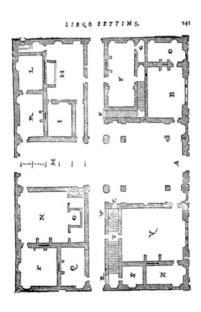

40., 40b., 40c. Sebastiano Serlio. *I Libri dell'architettura*. 1537–1575. Plans of regular, right-angle based residential buildings.

41. Sebastiano Serlio. *I Libri dell'architettura*. 1537–1575. Illustration of how an irregular, deformed medieval façade can be transformed into an ordered orthogonal, antiquated one.

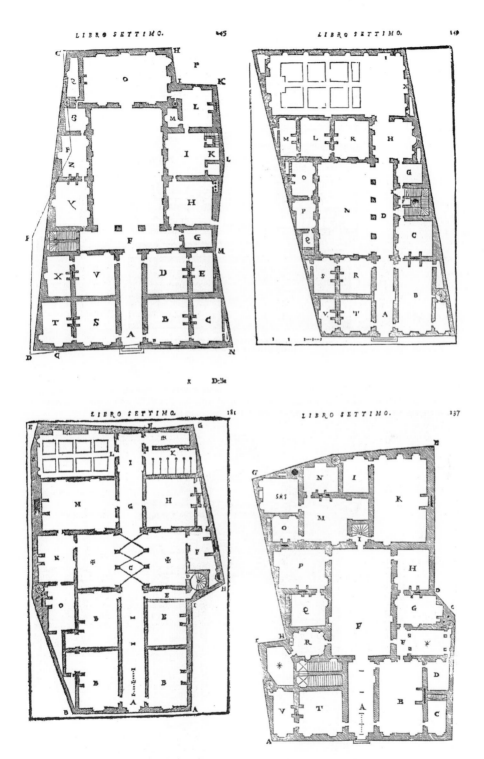

42., 42b., 42c., 42d. Sebastiano Serlio. *I Libri dell'architettura*. 1537–1575. Plans of residential buildings adapted to irregular, non-rectangular (oblique) sites.

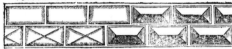

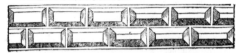

43. Sebastiano Serlio. *I Libri dell'architettura*. 1537–1575. Six manners or ways of rusticating masonry walls, ranging from the most natural and rough to the most geometrical and regular 'representing partly the work of nature and partly the work of artifice'. Serlio here introduces the rustic as a sixth manner, preceding the Tuscan and the Doric.

44. Sebastiano Serlio. *I Libri dell'architettura*. 1537–1575. Illustration of a gate from *The Sixth Book* containing thirty examples exploring possible combinations of the various manners of architecture – here the Doric with the Corinthian – with the rustic representing a dramatic conflict rather than a harmonious concord between the brutal and the polished, the brutal–natural and the civilised–artificial.

Pietro di Cataneo

I Quattro primi libri di architettura, 1554

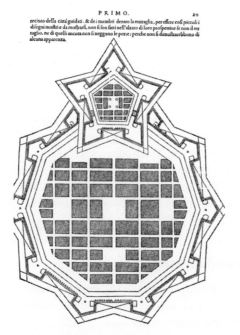

45. Pietro di Cataneo Senese. *I Quattro primi libri di architettura.* 1554. Prototype plan of a town consisting of a dual system of a pentagonal surveying unit and a decagonal surveyed one, the surveying unit superimposed on the top rather than in the centre. Both town units are fortified with the newly invented defence system of triangular bastions and both are embedded with an orthogonal grid of building blocks and rectangular squares. Notice the unresolved conflict between polygonal and orthogonal geometries.

Francesco de Marchi

Dell 'Architettura militare, 1599

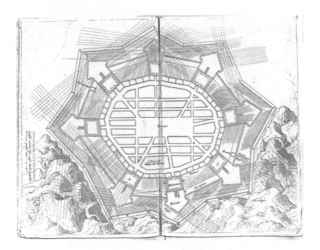

46. Francesco de Marchi. *Dell'Architettura militare.* 1599. Plan of a town prototype defended by an octagonal and triangular fortification containing an orthogonal and radial street network of building blocks and rectangular squares. Notice the unresolved conflict between polygonal and orthogonal geometries. Fire lines are superimposed on the plan to show the total ballistic control offered by the scheme.

[123]

Giorgio Vasari (1511–1574)

Lives of the Painters, Sculptors and Architects (1550)

Giorgio Vasari
1511–1574

This book of Vasari's, a painter of some repute, is the first book of history of art. It also includes architecture and garden design. It is widely held to be one of the most important sources on the thinking behind the artistic and architectural production in the mid-sixteenth century, a period in full so-called mannerist departure from the more Albertian, rationalist early Renaissance. His text on the Palazzo T decorated with frescoes by Giulio Romano, excerpted here, is the first to celebrate an architecture of illusion in the service of *terribilità*. His text on the famous Bòboli gardens in Florence by the architect Tribolo propounds a similar search for emotional engagement in design. The description emphasises the water works – water had never before been used as a sculptural element to such a degree – and the grotesque, which reaches a pitch unprecedented in garden design. This is one of the first instances where architecture is seen as a rhetorical device, capable of arousing strong emotions and prefigures the aesthetics of the picturesque and romanticism.

Giulio Romano, Painter (1492–1546)

Passing the great loggia, decorated with stucco, arms and other curious ornaments, we come to some rooms full of such various fancies that the mind is bewildering for Guilio being very imaginative and ingenious, to show his ability, intended to make a room similar to the Psyche room, the walls of which should correspond with the painting and create an illusion. As the place was marshy he laid the foundations deep and double, building a round room with thick walls so that the four external angled walls should be strong enough to bear a double barrel-vault. He then made the windows, door and chimneypiece of rustic stone, so twisted that they looked as if they leaned to one side and would fall. In this strangely built place he began to paint the most curious idea imaginable: Jove fulminating the giants. On the vaulting is the throne of Jove foreshortened, and a round Ionic temple on perforated columns, with a canopy over the seat in the middle. His eagle is there, the whole being on the clouds.

Lower down angry Jove is fulminating the giants, with Juno assisting; lower still, while the strange-faced winds blow on the earth, the goddess Ops turns at the noise with her lions, as do the other gods and goddesses, especially Venus, who is next to Mars and Modus, who with wide-open arms seems to be expecting the heavens to fall and yet remains immovable. The Graces stand in fear with the Hours near them, and each goddess is fleeing in her chariot. The Moon, with Saturn and Janus, moves towards an opening in the clouds to get away from the noise and fury, and so does Neptune, who, with his dolphins, seems to be trying to rest on his trident, while Pallas and the nine Muses wonder what this portends. Pan embraces a nymph who is trembling with fear, and he wishes to take her away from the tumult and lightnings which fill the heavens. Apollo stands on the chariot of the sun and some of the Hours attempt to stop the horses. Bacchus and Silenus, with satyrs and nymphs, exhibit the utmost fear, and Vulcan, with his huge hammer on his shoulder, looks towards Hercules, who is speaking of the matter to Mercury.

Near them stands the trembling Pomona, while Vertumnus and all the other gods exhibit the emotion of fear, which is presented with indescribable force both in those standing and in those fleeing. On the lower part, that is to say on the walls below the arching of the vault, are the giants, some under mountains and huge rocks, which they are carrying on their strong shoulders to mount to heaven. But Jove fulminates and all heaven is incensed against them, so that it not only strikes terror into the rash daring of the giants, hurling mountains at them, but all the world seems overturned and the end of all things at hand. We see Briareus in a dark cavern almost covered by the huge masses of rock, the other giants lying crushed and some killed under the fragments.

Through the cleft of a dark cave many giants may be seen fleeing, struck by the thunders of Jove and about to be crushed like the others. Elsewhere Giulio did other giants with temples, columns and parts of mountains falling, making a great slaughter among them. Between these falling walls is the fireplace, and when a fire is lighted the giants seem to be burning. Pluto in his chariot is drawn by shrivelled horses, and flees to the centre accompanied by the Furies, and thus Giulio decorated the chimneypiece most beautifully with this idea of fire. To make the work more terrible, he represented huge giants struck in various ways by the lightning and thunderbolts, falling to earth, some killed, some wounded, and some crushed beneath mountains and ruins. No more terrible work of the brush exists, and anyone entering the room and seeing the windows, doors and other things so twisted that they appear about to fall, and the tumbling mountains and ruins, will fear that all is about to come about his ears, especially as he sees the gods fleeing hither and thither. A marvellous feature is that the painting has neither beginning nor end, and is not interrupted in any way, so that objects near the buildings seem very large, and those in the distant landscape are gradually lost, and the room, which is not more than fifteen braccia long, looks like an open country, and the floor being of small round stones set with a knife and the walls at the junction being painted like them, there seem to be no corner stones, and the place looks extremely large.

Giorgio Vasari
1511–1574

Niccolo, called *Il Tribolo*, Sculptor and Architect (1500–1550)

[...] On the north side the meadow is as large as the area of the palace, stables and private garden together. From it one mounts to the principal garden, surrounded by an ordinary wall, and as one gradually ascends the garden rises clear into full sunshine, as if there was no palace in front. From the top there is a view not only of the palace, but of the surrounding plain as far as the city. In the middle of the garden are high and thick cypresses, laurels and myrtles growing wild, and forming a labyrinth surrounded by a hedge two-and-a-half brachia high, so regular that it looks as if it had been produced by the brush. In the middle of the labyrinth Tribolo made a beautiful marble fountain, as the duke desired. At the principal entrance by the lakes Tribolo wished to extend the avenue for more than a mile, to the Arno, and that the water from the fountains should accompany it to the river in channels at the sides, to be filled with various fish. He wished to make a loggia in front of the palace and, after passing an open court, to have another palace like the old one in every respect on the side of the stables, which would have formed a very large palace and a fine façade.

On passing the court at the entrance to the great garden of the labyrinth, and mounting the steps to it, one entered a clearing thirty brachia square, made to receive a large fountain of white marble, to rise fourteen brachia above the ornamentation, and that the water should issue from the mouth of a statue at the summit, six brachia high.

At the end of the meadow there were to be two loggias opposite each other, thirty brachia by fifteen, with a marble bas-relief of twelve brachia in the middle of each, and outside a cistern of eight brachia to receive the water from a vase held by two figures. In the middle of the labyrinth Tribolo intended to make the water pass through spouts, but the marble basin, afterwards put there had to be far smaller than the one of the principal fountain, and at the top there was to be a bronze figure spouting water. In the middle, at the end of the gardens there was to be a door with marble cherubs spouting water in every direction, and double niches at the corners containing statues, like those on the side walls at the junction of the avenues traversing the garden, which are covered with verdure.

The door gives access by some steps to another garden as broad as the first, but not so long, at the base of the mountain. It was to contain two other loggias at the sides, and a cave in the wall opposite the side against the hill, with three cisterns to catch water, and two fountains in the wall on either side, and two others opposite with the door between, these containing as many fountains as the lower garden, the upper one receiving the water. It was to be filled with orange trees since it is protected by the walls and the mountain from the north and other contrary winds. Two flights of steps, one on each side, led up to a wood of cypresses, mulberry trees, yews, laurels and other evergreen trees, finely spaced out. In the middle there was to be a fine lake, according to Tribolo's design. As it narrowed to a corner, it was necessary to make a loggia with a pointed end, from which, on mounting steps, there was a view of the palace, the fountains, the gardens, and all the country round as far as the ducal Villa of Poggio a Caiano, Florence, Prato, Siena, and the surrounding country for many miles. On Piero completing the aqueduct as far as Castillo, taking in all the watery of la Castellina, he died of a severe fever after a few days. Tribolo therefore took up the task, and recognised that the water, although plentiful, would not suffice for what he proposed to do, and it would not rise as high as was necessary.

The duke then permitted him to bring water from Petraia, more than one hundred and fifty breccia above Castello, where it is both plentiful and good. He made an aqueduct like the other, and high enough to reach the lakes and principal fountain by another channel. He then began the grotto for the three niches and the fountains on either side, one of which was to have a large stone statue of Monte Asinaio, to spout water from its mouth into a cistern, from which the water was to pass to the fountain which is now behind the steps of the labyrinth garden, and to enter the vase on the shoulders of the River Mugnone, standing in a large niche of grey stone, beautifully decorated and covered with spungite; a representation of the fact that the Mugnone rises in Monte Asinaio. Tribolo then made his Mugnone, a figure in grey stone four brachia high, in a fine attitude, holding a vase on one shoulder and emoting it into a cistern, while the other shoulder rests on the ground, the left leg is crossed over the right.

Behind is a nude female figure representing Fiesole, rising amid the spungite in the middle of the niche, holding the moon, the ancient device of the city. Below the niche is a large basin supported by two large goats, one of the duke's devices, with festoons and masks hanging about them. The water issues from the lips of the goats to the bottom of the basin, passes round the walls of the labyrinth garden, where there are fountains between the niches, and oranges and pomegranates between these. In the second garden Tribolo had arranged for a Alonte delta Falterona similar to his Monte

Asinaio, from which the statue representing the Arno was to receive its water. But as neither figure was ever completed, I will speak of the fountain and of the Arno which Tribolo did. The river holds a vase to its side, and leans on a lion with a lily in its claws, the vase receiving its water from a hole in the wall, behind which la Falterona was to be. As the long basin is exactly like that of Mugnone, I say nothing except that it is a pity that such a beautiful work is not in marble. Continuing his conduit, Tribolo brought the water from the lot under the orange garden, and the next one to the labyrinth, which it encircled, and in the middle he made the water-spout. He then united the waters of Arno and Mugnone under the level of the labyrinth in bronze channels, finely devised, filling the pavement with slender jets, so that by turning a tap all those who come to see the fountain are sprinkled, and escape is not easy, because Tribolo made a stone seat about the fountain, supported by lions intermixed with marine monsters in bas-relief, a difficult task as it is on a slope and he had to make a level surface and seats too. He next began the fountain of the labyrinth, making marine monsters encircling the base, in marble, so carved with their tails intertwined that it is a unique work of its kind. He then did the marble basin, first carried out at Castello, with a large marble bas-relief, from the villa of Antella, brought by M. Ottaiano do' Medici from Giuliano Salviati. Before making the basin Tribolo did some cherubs dancing, to decorate this, holding festoons of marine objects beautifully carved.

Giorgio Vasari
1511–1574

He also gracefully executed the cherubs and masks for spouting water, and proposed to erect a bronze statue three brachia high on the top, to represent Florence, to which the waters of Arno and Mugnone flow. For this figure he had made a (model, which was to wring water out of its hair. After bringing the water to the first quadrangle of thirty braccia beneath the labyrinth, he began the great fountain. This was octagonal, and devised to receive all the waters mentioned into the first basin, from the labyrinth and from the main conduit as well. Each of the eight sides forms a step of $1/5$ a braccia high, and at each angle is a projection with a corresponding one on the steps, which rise to the height of $2/5$ at the angles, so that the middle point of the steps is indented, giving them a quaint appearance, but very convenient to mount. The rim of the fountain is shaped like a vase, and the body of it is round. The pedestal is octagonal and continues in this shape almost up to the button of the tazza, forming eight pedestals on which are seated eight cherubs of life-size, in various attitudes, with entwined arms and legs, forming a rich ornament. The tazza, which was round and eight braccia across, discharged water evenly all round into the octagonal basin, like a fine rain. Thus the cherubs are not touched, and seem to be playing and avoiding the bath in a charmingly childish manner, an idea unequalled for its simple beauty.

Opposite the four sides of the crossing of the garden four bronze cherubs are lying at play in various attitudes, all made from Tribolo's design though done by others. Above the tazza another pedestal begins, at the base of which four cherubs are on projections, squeezing the necks of some geese who are spouting water brought from the principal conduit leading from the labyrinth, which rises exactly to this height. Above the cherubs is the remainder of the shaft, which is made of small tubes from which the water flows in a curious way, and assuming a square shape, it rests upon some well-made masks. Above them is a smaller basin, at the edges of which are four goats' heads tied up by the horns spouting water into the great basin, and combining with the cherubs to make the falling rain already mentioned. Another shaft followed higher up, with other ornaments and cherubs in half-relief, forming a round top, which serves as a base for a figure of Hercules crushing Antaeus, designed by Tribolo and executed by others. From the mouth of Antaeus water issues in a great quantity, instead of his spirits being supplied from the great conduit of Petraia, rising sixteen braccia from the level where the steps are and falling into the larger basin. Through this aqueduct pass the waters from the lake and grotto, as well as those of Petraia, and, joined to those of Castellina, go to the fountains of Falterona and Monte Asinaio, and thence to those of the Arno and Mugnone. Reunited at the fountain of the labyrinth, they go to the great fountain where the cherubs with the geese are. They were to flow thence according to Tribolo's design by two conduits to the basins of the loggias, and thence each to its private garden.

anticlassicism • deformation • freedom • naturalism • emotions • passions • sentiments • legitimation • representation of power • representation • truth • illusion • rhetoric • signification • narrative

Giovan Battista Bellucci (1506–1554)

New Inventions for Making Fortresses of Various Forms (completed c. 1554; published 1598)

The author studied architecture in Rome. This work, like those of Castriotto and de Marchi, was probably composed in major part in Rome between 1534 and 1545, when Pope Paul III had summoned the greatest fortification experts in Italy in order to consult them on fortification design (de la Croix, 1960, 180). Bellucci was among the first representatives of the split between military and civil architects and one of the most belligerent proponents of his generation for the creation of a modern architectural practice based on the use of technical knowledge and experience instead of on the imitation of antique prototypes and theoretical speculation (ibid. 175–176).

Further reading Promis, 1863–1874; Straub, 1964.

Chapter I

p.50. But because men endowed both with the capacity for the speculative and the operative are rare, I feel that the right thing, in order to insure the perfection of a fortification, is to see that the person in charge of speculating be a soldier who by experience of war knows how to speculate well about it when the case arises. As for the operative one, he should be a stonemason because he understands the correct principles of architecture.

p.51. All the fortifications made in Italy by architects without the consultation of soldiers in Italy as in Florence with Antonio Sangallo [...] have shortcomings, and important shortcomings, and a leader should ask for the consultation of soldiers when building a fortified structure and should hand over to them all the work related to it and not to scholars because neither proportions nor books know how to fight.

p.52. You should not give the job to architects, masons, master carpenters, nor scholars because their like will never carry out the task well if they do not have the experience of the world which in our time wages war differently from in the past. What is needed is not to be found in books or pat architecture for we need to be less forceful than inventive.

p.53. Architects and scholars, as I have said before, should have nothing to do with fortifications because they have never been involved with armies and know nothing about waging war and pulling a piece of artillery nor how to install an encampment [. . .] but, instead, it would be good if architects limited themselves to making palaces, churches, tombs, cornices, architraves, bases, columns, crests, terms, masks and trophies. Fortification requires good shoulders, good parapets, good sorts and good men . . .

efficiency • economisation • fit • utility • mechanisation of architecture • social control • defence

Daniele Barbaro (1516–1570)

Translation of Vitruvius's Ten Books (1556)

Barbaro was a Venetian patrician and patron of Andrea Palladio. His translation of Vitruvius differs from Cesariano's thanks to its scientific reasoning. Like other commentators in the tradition initiated by Alberti, he notes the inconsistencies of Vitruvius's text. The one new departure of his book is his enthusiastic panegyric of industrial architecture in the form of the Arsenal of Venice. In this he takes the opportunity of Vitruvius's chapter on ports to praise the port, the Arsenal and the hydraulic engineering works of Venice. Alberti had praised the Cloaca Maxima of Antiquity. Barbaro praises these modern utilitarian works. His admiration for the machines in the Arsenal prefigures Galileo's more famous passage (1638).

In our times we do not have the perfect things the ancients had. This is because there is not one among the new buildings that attempts to imitate those marvellous buildings and because rarely are those architects who make theatres, amphitheatres, circuses, palestras, gates, basilicas and temples today willing through art and practice, and with spirit and judgement, to embrace the kind of ambitious undertakings worthy of the ancient buildings that, according to the quality of their temples, are reputed great; and the first great feat of contemporary times that occurs to me is the fortification of the city that with thick and high walls on top of extremely wide and deep foundations. They stand for a magnificent and excellently beautiful idea. But in contemplating great things, I cannot help but think of the port of the Venetians and the building of the boats and ships that are used today. I cannot say that its grandeur is the stuff of the selection of marbles or the magnificence and superbness of the materials that the ancients used to use in their own buildings . . . Nor I will say, however, that in their port that houses all things for the production of these things related to shipping they have superseded everything that went before. In our day we can see where the wooden boats, and big ships, and small vessels, and barges and galleons are built to perfection in terms of all the capabilities, safety and comfort one could possibly desire. Neither do I wish to say that this is the kind of marvel that appeals immediately to every man of judgement. This is because it is born of something even more admired and worthy of being desired and studied namely a long and unviolated freedom that has given birth to this greatness. Such wonders are not so numerous nor is there a power so big that in such a short time made this possible as the Venetians have done. This abundance and this experience has grown little by little naturally (so to speak) and with the genius of the city ... Because one sees the marvellous order of things in one sweep of the eye including all the equipment of a ship, and all the instruments, all the apparatuses with marvellous order not only from one's place with so much facility and felicity I would say that one can hardly believe how the whole thing moves. The cuts, the capstan, the wheels, the winches are so ingeniously made and positioned and ordered that there is no weight so great that it is not capable of being moved with great speed. Similar huge things do not have the same effect upon the viewer because they are not as well ordered and fast. But now, in the opinion of the great Nicolo Zeno, the whole is reduced in one ordered system that is so beautiful and functional that one cannot help marvelling at the quantity and size of the objects, at their order (as we have already said), and born from a loving study, industrious judgement of that gentleman I was fortunate enough to visit the Arsenal with observing how the heaviest things are moved with such little effort. Still other instances of greatness of the city are offered. Divine providence and the nature of things which terrify all great hearts instill the love of country that brings every comfort. The sea and the earth, that are equal are in constant war over which one will finally occupy the place of this lagune.

legitimation • representation of power • mechanisation of architecture

Pirro Ligorio (1510–1583)

Book of Antiquity (late 1550s)

In Dante's *Inferno* and Alberti's *Hypnerotomachia Poliphili* (1499) the grotesque had been described. Here it is polemically defended. This unpublished text by the archaeologist, and architect of the Villa d'Este, Pirro Ligorio, stands in contrast to the writings of Vasari and Barbaro (1556), and, ultimately, Vitruvius, that condemned the grotesque, the most extreme of the departures from the canonical repertory. Pirro's reasoning could not be further from the search for absolute values. He argues in favour of it on the grounds that his predecessors had condemned, namely that there is a relation between it and dream visions and that it is symbolic of an existential condition that arises out of the unconscious (Mueller Profumo, 1985, 144–145).

Further reading Coffin, 1966; Gaston, 1988; Lazzaro, 1990; Lotz, 1996; Smith, 1976.

The grotesque elements embody representations of vain desires for vague and unreasonable things that run quickly from mouth to mouth and that produce incertitude and that appear in vain dreams in which natural and true things are replaced by merely apparent things. This is akin to child's play, ... that arises from a desire to see again things that are over and that are remembered with anxious effect, either because one fears the evocation of the images or because of desires one has in dealing with vision according to the opinion of Artemediorus and Seneca ... Although they appear to be fantastic material to the general public, all are vital symbols and things not lacking in mystery ... There we deal with fantastic forms and as they were outlined in dreams they combine with moral and fantastic things related to the gods ... They have not been used for a fantastic finality nor to demonstrate vicious assumptions nor to adorn and invade a variety of halls. They were made in order to provoke stupor or, to put it differently, produce admiration among poor mortals, to indicate even though this is only by approximation, the gestation and wholeness of the ideas just as much as the imaginings of the intellect ... and to show the accidents, to yield to the insatiable appetite of created things ... Those things adumbrated by the poets and philosophers of transmigration such as the subtle Empedocles, a famous physicist, such as Pythagoras with his pythagorian works ... many poets of transmutation recount many pythagorian things – transmigrations of men into trees, beasts, rivers and animals variously filled with spirits [...]

anticlassicism • deformation • freedom • naturalism • archaic beliefs • body model

Philibert de l'Orme (1510–1570)

New Inventions for Building Economically (1561)

Philibert de
l'Orme
1510–1570

Son of a master mason, Philibert received a humanist education in his native Lyon, at that time a thriving economic and cultural centre. Having risen to the post of 'Surintendant des bastimens royaux' under Henri II, Philibert fell from grace after the king's death. During the next five years, before regaining royal favour under Catherine de Medici, he turned to writing. From 1568 on, his two publications were issued jointly as one treatise – the first by a Frenchman. The plan of the book is novel: its *eleven* books chronologically follow the process of building (Blunt, 1958a, ch. IV). It covers the relation of architect to patron and to manual labourers and goes on to principles of stereotomy (the first book to do so), vaulting, chimney construction and roofing. Four books are devoted to the orders. Philibert's thinking is steeped in hermeticism. It also embraces ingenuity, novelty and economy, rejecting the strict adherence to established Italian prototypes. Here, his influence was strong until the second half of the seventeenth century in France. His work was re-edited in 1568, 1576, 1626 and 1648 (Tzonis *et al.*, 1982).

Further reading Bilodeau, 1997; Blomfield, 1973; Brion-Guerry, 1955; Hautecoeur, 1948–1963; Lefranc, 1916; Tzonis, 1982; Wiebenson, 1982, 1993.

New Inventions to Build Well at Small Expense

Chapter II
Concerning the fashion and manner in which beams may be made of a number of pieces

After having understood through the discourse contained in the first book the manner in which all sorts of roofs may be made for the great residences that Kings and Princes desire today (such as great halls and chambers more than thirty feet wide), the necessity of making use of wood for beams led me to imagine a new invention to make them of two hundred or three hundred pieces, and even more if so desired, as his Majesty the late King Henry saw for himself in my residence near Tournelles in Paris. For which I had had done two beams, one of two hundred twenty-five pieces and the other of two hundred and sixty-three, not counting the pins, which were used only to maintain the pieces in place until the beams had been installed. They were tested with two jacks in the presence of his Majesty, as referred to above, and other Princes and Lords, the aforesaid beams being pressed in such a manner that the entire roof was lifted, breaking the walls of the building where they were. And whatever pressure or force that could be imposed upon them with the jacks, despite the fact that I have since attempted to break them, they could not be lowered by so much as half a finger's breadth. It is my sincere belief that if in their place there had been installed four bigger beams of the type we are accustomed to using, they would have broken if they had had to endure such a great force, or at the very least, would have sagged so much that they would have appeared more fit to make arches than to be used as supporting beams in a building. I had ordered them made in such a manner that you may see in [...] drawings [...]; they measure fourteen feet within the construction and may be used for a residence of twenty-five feet in width because it is my desire to fit corbels on which the beams can sit over a span of one half-foot and as much, but no more, within the wall. This is done in order that, if any piece should become rotten, through the passage of time, or for other reason, it should be a simple matter to remove it and to put in a new one without breaking the walls or demolishing any part, as is customary when replacing a beam in the old manner. For it is necessary to ruin walls and floors at the point where such a beam bears upon them and to create much disorder thereby. Before going on, I am of the opinion that the beams and the method described here by us should be used for common residences no more than eighteen or twenty feet wide because it is easy to find wood to make them. But for building from twenty-four feet, and up to thirty, forty and fifty, or as much as you wish, this method will be very useful, of greater advantage and allow greater savings, providing a means to make a thing possible that heretofore has been impossible. It should not be forgotten that halls and chambers which are great in width must have heights in proportion and the dimensions that are required thereby. Thus it will not be displeasing if the beams are disposed in a basket handle form or shall have some curve and part of a circumference, which I find more pleasing than beams that are completely straight, for they will be seen particularly well when used in building. The wider and higher the said halls are, the greater their majesty and beauty. This invention is therefore for the necessity of the place, for which wood cannot be found to make the beams that are customary. [...]

Philibert de
l'Orme
1510–1570

The conclusion to the present work with certain instructions for the undertaking and execution of buildings

In so far as it appears to me to be insufficient to have shown heretofore the manner in which all sorts of buildings should be constructed and how to conduct that construction from the foundations up to their highest points, if I do not show in like manner how the Architects, Commissioners, Controllers and other persons in charge of such buildings must know how to conduct the business of their Estate and be in accord all together, lest many errors occur, accompanied by wastage of money, and by intolerable mockery and repentance therefore. For this reason, desirous as I am to inform at length all those concerned of that which they must do, and even the Lord himself, in order that he make no mistake, and to ensure that his will is done perfectly and duly, I have decided for the end and conclusion of the present work to show and to illustrate the unity and intelligence that must exist between the Lord, the Architect, the masters of the works, and other persons, likewise the obedience that must be given by the Architect to the Lord, and all workers, Controllers and Officers to said Architect, in order that all things ordered by him and arranged for the rightful construction of the works should be done correctly. I have therefore decided to write the present additional discourse the better to show how the Lord must know how to choose and to employ the men in each Estate to which they belong, for otherwise it would be both ridiculous and dangerous for one man to do the work of the Estate of another, without having learned it and also to make known that when the Architect has arranged all those things that must be done each day, both by the Master Masons and the other workers (paid either by the day or on completion) that it is necessary, principally for large edifices, to assign a Controller for the upkeep in writing of lists, registers and contracts. Said Controller must have some knowledge and intelligence of the mason's art and other works that are to be performed, if that is possible, for otherwise he will be able to control and supervise neither the workers nor the works, nor the satisfactory or unsatisfactory character of the materials and the nature of these, nor the carpentry and other works and less capably the manner in which they are used. And, what is more, he will be unable to know if the workers concerned are competent, nor will he be able to declare the works to be satisfactory on completion either by measurement or by evaluation. Moreover, he will be unable to judge value, nor cause works to be altered when defects are found in them. With the result that the Estate of the Controller is here of great importance and very necessary for good order and the saving of money for the Lord, to whom he must report and be unfailingly loyal and obey the commands of the Architect. Otherwise, he will not be able to do the work of a Controller in a manner that is profitable to his master and Lord, and even less acquire honour in doing so. For if he takes no advice from the Architect and does as it appears to him to be necessary, an infinity of errors will ensue, as I have seen happen often, with unbearable expense for the purse of the master and Lord, all this having been done without the knowledge of the Architect, who in some cases dares say nothing, nor show that he is aware of it, for fear of displeasing certain persons, and it may be that he would not be thanked for speaking out. For this reason, I advise the Architect to be very attentive to his own responsibilities and to leave aside those of others. In some great enterprises there are a small number of Commissioners placed above the Architect, to whom the same obedience is owed as to the Lords, in so far as they have all powers to dispose of funds, which explains that they must be told what is being done and what is to be done, in order to ensure that they take the trouble to obtain money for the works desired. It is also necessary for a Commissioner, like the Architect, to be in all things attentive in order to ensure that the masters and workers are not exploited or robbed by the Controllers, or indeed by the servants of the latter, as I have myself seen done. For if by chance an agreement is reached on work, it is necessary to give the Controller his commission before the said contract can be finalised, or if not, afterwards, or the poor labourers will be worked and insulted in diverse ways. When the time has come to make the measurements of the land they ensure that they are very well paid to certify same and to place upon them their seals. There is an infinity of other examples of avarice, on which I prefer to remain silent rather than set them down in writing. I do not say that all act in this manner, for I have known and now know several who are honest men. It is also necessary for the Lord to have certain persons to ensure that the labourers do their work, as Superintendents and others do, and who likewise cause the materials to arrive and to be employed.

[...] the Architect, having ordered that which is necessary for the execution of the works for which he is responsible, should withdraw and remain alone in his office, study, chamber, library or garden, according to his convenience, as you can see represented here [...] below, said figure showing a wise man in a garden before the Temple of prayer, with three eyes. One eye to admire and adore the holy divinity of God, and to contemplate His works that are so admirable, and also to observe past

Philibert de
l'Orme
1510–1570

times. The second to observe and measure the present time and give orders to conduct in due manner and direct those things that are present. The third to look forward to the future and things to come in order to prepare and be forearmed against the attacks, wrongs, calamities and great miseries of this melancholy world, in which we are subject to so many calumnies, trials and travails, that it is impossible to enumerate them. I also show him with four ears, thus illustrating that he must listen much more than he must speak.

[...]

[...] to return to our Wise Man, symbolising the Architect, I show him with an abundance of four hands to illustrate that he has many things to do and to manage at the same time if he wishes to master the sciences that are required for him. Furthermore, he holds a memorial and instruction in his hands to teach and inform those who have need thereof with great diligence and assiduity, this represented by the wings on his feet, which also demonstrate that he does not wish others to be weak and lazy in his business and undertakings. He also shows that to all those who may visit him or come to his garden, he shall not hide his admirable treasures of virtue, his cornucopias filled with pleasing fruit, his basins full of great riches and secrets, his streams and fountains of science, nor his beauteous trees, vines and plants that flower and bear fruit in all seasons. You may see also in the aforesaid figure several admirable beginnings of edifices, palaces and temples, of which the aforementioned wise and learned Architect shall show and teach the structure with good and perfect method, as is shown in the aforesaid figure, in which you may remark also a young apprentice, representing youth, who must seek out the learned and wise to obtain instruction, both in words, in memorials, writings, and in drawings and models, as is shown to you in the form of the memorial placed in the hand of the obedient youth, impatient to learn and know the art of Architecture.

efficiency • economisation • fit • utility • rigorism • essentialism • professional practice • education

Philibert de l'Orme 1510–1570

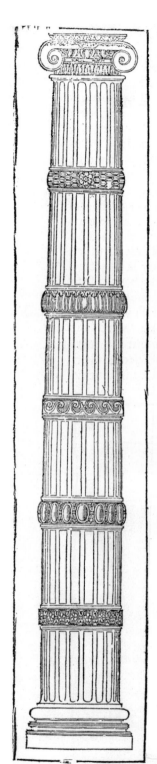

LIVRE VII. DE L'ARCHITECTVRE

47. Philibert de l'Orme. *Le Premier tôme de l'architecture*. 1567–1648. The French Ionic Order and Corinthian column
with manifest remnants of its natural origin.

Quand vous affemblez vos courbes pour faire les hemicycles,
comme i'ay dict cy-deffus, il vous faut cheuiller vne piece contre
l'autre. Mais il côuient que ce foit par fort petites cheuilles, & que
les trous foient côme le bout du petit doigt. Et ne les y conuient
mettre par grande force, afin qu'elles n'empefchent que le joint &
commiffures des courbes ne puiffent joüer l'vn fur l'autre de leur
longueur & largeur du bout des pieces. Ie n'en voudrois point
mettre, n'eftoit que cela aide fort à les bien affembler & mettre en *Grande facilité*
œuure. Apres que le tout eft pofé, ie ferois content que lefdictes *& diligente*
cheuilles fuffent dehors: toutesfois cela ne nuit ny ayde, fi ce n'eft *fert à bien en-*
quand il faut changer quelque piece qui eft pourrie ou gaftée : car *feigner.*
cela entretient l'œuure iufqu'à ce qu'on y aye mis vne autre neuf-
ue. I'ay monftré par cy-deuant qu'aux lieux marquez P, aux en-
droicts efquels y a de petits poincts, faut mettre lefdictes cheuilles.
Ce que vous pourrez encores mieux cognoiftre par la figure cy-
apres mife en la mefme marque P, aux pieces des courbes qui font
figurées plus grandes, afin que l'on en puiffe auoir meilleure co- *Aquoy feruês*
gnoiffance. Il fera fort bon de mettre le moins de telles cheuilles *les cheuilles ne*
qu'on pourra, afin que lefdictes pieces des courbes ne foient tant *ceffe nouuelle*
corrompües, & qu'elles puiffent joüer plus facilement fur leurs *façon.*
joincts & commiffures. Ce qui eft plus ayfé à cognoiftre par la figure fuiuante, que par trop grand difcours, duquel ie me fuis rete-
nu pour n'en eftre befoin.

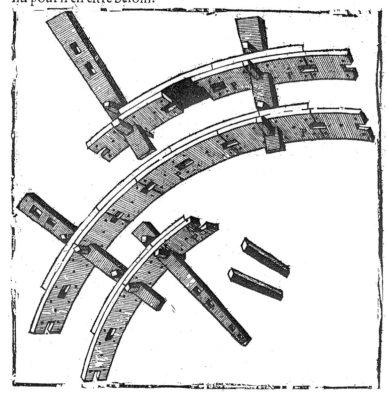

48. Philibert de l'Orme. *Nouvelles Inventions pour bien bâtir à petits frais.* 1561. Construction detail of modular arch ring for a wooden vault.

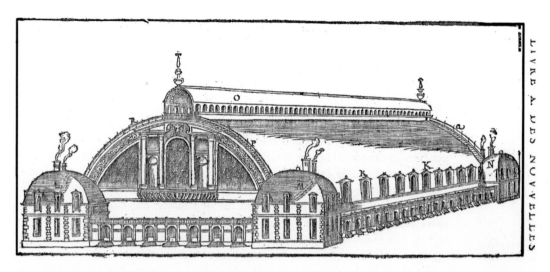

49. Philibert de l'Orme. *Nouvelles Inventions pour bien bâtir à petits frais*. 1561. Proposal for a Basilica to be covered by a wooden vault with a 150-foot opening.

Bernard Palissy (c.1510–1589)

True Recipe by Which the People of France Will be Able to Multiply their Fortunes. Also the Design and Ordonnance of a Fortified City That is the Most Unassailable Ever Heard Of (1563)

Bernard Palissy
c.1510–1589

Palissy was one of the most renowned artists and scientists of the French Renaissance, and is usually credited with having invented the highly prized technique of ceramic glazing, probably in imitation of Chinese pottery. His inventiveness in many areas of the natural sciences earned him an invitation from Francis I, the king of France, to become a lecturer at the Collège de France, the newly founded teaching institution that was to become the centre of cultural revival. A Huguenot, Palissy was sent to the Bastille in 1588, although officially in the service of the royal family, and died there. His artistic views have been called naturalistic and anticlassical (Panofsky, 1968, ch. 5, n.2). Indeed, both in his scheme for a house, formed of living trees, and for a spiral fortress, intended for the protection of his co-religionists of La Rochelle against the Catholics and modelled on a snail, the traditional classical forms are overturned in favour of daringly innovative natural ones.

Further reading Hazlehurst, 1966; Panofsky, 1968b, 219, n.2.

And now to the elms, to be used for the walls and roof of said private study, and shall be placed and dressed in such a manner that the trunks of said elms shall serve as pillars and the branches as architrave, frieze and cornice, as well as the tympanum and frontispiece, observing the correct disposition of the masonry work.

QUESTION: In truth, I think it to be folly for you to wish to observe the rules of architecture in buildings made of trees; you are well aware that trees grow daily and cannot retain for long the dimensions that you might wish to give them and we know that the Architects of ancient times did nothing without certain dimensions and great reflection, witness Vitruvius and Sebastianus, authors of certain books on architecture.

RESPONSE: You were right to be afraid and to challenge me: you have adduced good reasons to prove my folly and to despise the intention for my garden, in light of the fact that it is a thing worthy of such great esteem. If you have read all the books on architecture that you say, you will find that the designers of excellent edifices in ancient times took their designs and examples for their pillars from trees and the human form – take some measurements of their columns and you will find that they are broader at the bottom than at the top, which is one of their methods in making their columns, and also that columns made of trees will always be rarer and more excellent than those in stone. If you wish to accord so much honour to those in stone, which you desire to give preference over those made of the trunks of trees, I say to you that this is against all the provisions of Divine and human law, for the works of the Sovereign and first builder must be held in great honour, more than those of human builders. Likewise, you know that a portrait that has been copied from another can never be held in such great esteem as the original from which it has been copied. This is why stone columns cannot be glorified above those in wood, nor can it be said that they are more perfect, and this is all the more so since those in wood engendered, or at least taught us how to make, those in stone. And also since the Sovereign Geometrician, the first builder, put his hand to them, they must be held in higher esteem than those in stone, however rare they may be, unless they are in jasper or other precious stone. [...]

[...] all such Towns are of poor design, especially as the component members are not attached to the main body. It is very easy to attack the body if the members lend no assistance. Seeing that, I despaired completely of finding examples to follow in Towns built in the present day, and I cast my mind elsewhere to contemplate the images of the designs and other pictures made by Master Jacques de Cerseau, and several other artists, and I looked at the plans and drawings of Vitruvius and Sebastianus and other Architects, in order to determine whether I might not find in those images something that could help me in designing the aforesaid Fortified Town, but it was never possible to find any able to help me in this task. And seeing this, I walked like a man with his mind elsewhere, head lowered, neither acknowledging nor seeing the presence of any other person, by reason of my preoccupation, the aforementioned Town, and I went, in this way, to visit all the most excellent gardens that I could find (doing so in order to see whether there might not be some maze design imagined by Daedalus or some ordered garden that might serve my purpose) and I could find nothing to satisfy me. So I began to wander through the woods, mountains and valleys, in search of some industrious beast which might have made some industrious residence. [...]

Bernard Palissy
c. 1510–1589

Have you ever seen anything made by the hand of man that it fits so precisely as the two shells and attachments of the aforesaid cockles and scallops? In truth, it is impossible for men to make their like. Do you think that all the small concavities and ridges in such shells are made solely as ornaments, as things of beauty? No, no, there is something more here – they increase the strength of the aforesaid fortress, as buttresses placed against a wall consolidate that wall, there can be no doubt of this, and I shall always give credit to Architects of good judgement. Do you think that fish which erect their fortresses in the form of a spiral or an Archimedean screw do so without reason? No, it is not solely to please the eye, there is certainly something more than this. You must know that there are several fish which have such pointed noses that they could eat the greater number of the fish described above if the latter's residences were rectilinear, but when they are attacked by the enemy at the gate, by withdrawing within, they turn as they withdraw, following the spiral, and by this means they ensure that their enemy cannot harm them. And this being considered, it can be seen that it is not to please the eye that they are thus made, but for greater strength. [...]

[...] and I began to think that I could find no better counsel for the design of my Fortified Town and began to observe in order to find the fish that are the most industrious in Architecture and to take counsel from their industriousness. [...] And thus, having spent much time in considering this, I saw that in the shell of the purple whelk there is a number of fairly large points disposed around that shell and I was sure, not without reason, that said horns had been formed as so many walkways and defences for the fortification and retreat of the whelk. And having seen this, I found no better solution for the construction of my Fortified Town than to take as my example the fortress of the aforesaid purple whelk and therefore took up my compasses, ruler and other necessary tools to make my drawing thereof. Firstly, I drew the plan of a great rectangular square around which I drew a great number of houses, to which I added windows, doors and workshops all facing towards the outside of the plan and streets of the Town. At one of the corners of the aforesaid square, I drew a great doorway on which I marked the plan of the house or residence of the principal Governor of said Town in order to ensure that no person should enter said square without leave from the Governor. At the entrance of the square, I drew the plan of certain slope-roofed, low open galleries to shelter artillery pieces, drawing this in such a manner that the walls in front of the gallery should serve for defence and battery, with several openings for cannon fire disposed around it, all facing towards the centre of said square, in order that if enemies should enter the square through a tunnel that it would be but a moment's work to destroy them. This having been done, I drew the beginning of a street starting from the aforesaid gateway, surrounding the houses I had drawn around said square, setting out to build my Town in spiral form and line, following the form and industriousness of the purple whelk. But when I had thought a little on my business, I perceived that the task of a cannon is to fire in straight lines and that if my Town was totally constructed along a spiral line the cannon would be unable to fire down streets and this is the reason for which I resolved to follow the example of the whelk only in so far as it could serve my purpose, and began to draw the first street around and near the square according to a rectangular plan, and having done this, I drew the houses along said street with entrances and exits all facing the centre of the square, thus

Bernard Palissy
c.1510–1589

making a street forming four faces surrounding the first rank surrounding the centre, turning like the shell of the whelk but doing so in straight lines. I immediately drew another street around the first, also turning, and when these drawings were done, complete with the necessary houses along them, I began to follow the same line to draw the third street, but because the square and the two streets around it had greatly expanded the whole, I found it advisable to give eight faces to the second street, doing so for several reasons. When the third street was drawn, with the houses along it, I found my intention to be good and valid, and I drew the plan of another street like the third, that is to say, with eight faces, continuing to turn around the square. This done, I found that the Town was spacious enough and began to draw the houses along said street, up to the outside walls of the Town, which walls I then drew as joined to the houses of the street running along them. When I had completed my drawing in this manner, it appeared to me that my Town was far superior to all others because the outside walls of other Towns are without purpose in times of peace but those I have made are useful at all times as accommodation for those who carry on a number of trades, while guarding said Town. Again, having completed my drawing, I found that the walls of all the houses served as so many fortifying spurs and whatever side cannon were fired against the Town, they would encounter walls everywhere and in this Town there will be just one street, one entrance, and that street turns constantly around the centre in straight lines from corner to corner, leading into the centre, in the middle of the Town and at each corner or angle of the faces of the aforementioned streets there will be a double gateway and a vaulted roof and above each of these a high cannon emplacement or platform in such manner that from the two corners of each face it will be possible to fire from corner to corner while remaining protected by the aforesaid vaulted gateways, with the result that those tending the cannon cannot be attacked in any manner.

anticlassicism • deformation • freedom • naturalism • design methodology • representation • truth • illusion • social control • defence

Alvise Cornaro (1475–1566)

Treatise on Architecture (1567–1575 written)

This Venetian nobleman and scholar belonging to the Aristotelian circle of Padua was one of the leading figures of the so-called 'agrarian revolution' that occurred in the Veneto province in the early and mid-sixteenth century as a result of the collapse of Venetian trade and the ensuing turn towards agricultural exploitation by the Venetian patrician families. As one of the first great landowners in the region, he was concerned about the economic efficiency of this new rural enterprise. He wrote on the canalisation methods for reclaiming the marshland of the coastal deltas and about the design of eco-nomical and practical agrarian residences (Fiocco, 1952, 1958, 1963, 1965). His treatise on architecture reveals an impatience with the courtly version of Vitruvianism and a polemical functionalist approach which must have had a certain influence on the young Palladio (Ackerman, 1972, 22ff.). It also reflects the climate of social consciousness in Venice at the time and is the first treatise to express concern for not only the rich but also for the ordinary citizens of the city, middle class and poor alike (Rosenfeld, 1978, 43–46). The text excerpted here is from the first version of the treatise (c. 1557–1566).

Further reading Bentmann and Müller, 1970; Cavallari-Murat, 1969; Cessi, 1936; Faggin, 1967; Heydenreich, 1969b; Lovarini, 1899; Puppi, 1967, 9–10, 1970, 1973; Rosci, 1966, 26ff., 34ff., 59ff., 1967; Schlosser, 1979, 254; Sereni, 1979.

The beautiful and commodious buildings and edifices which form the main parts of the city, are those that are the most ornamented, honoured and made beautiful and famous. But above all, all the beautiful and comfortable dwellings, houses and abodes of citizens are important, because there is an infinite number of them and they make the city. Without them there would be no city. Architects have written very little of them, and therefore I will write about them in order to teach citizens not just archi-tects. I will not write about theatres, amphitheatres, terms, nor about how to make a city because this never happens, and because these other types of buildings cannot be useful. The divine Vitruvius and the great Leon Battista Alberti have not written about this enough.

urbanisation of architecture • planning

Philibert de l'Orme (1510–1570)

The First Volume of Architecture (1567–1648) (see Philibert de l'Orme, 1561)

Preface

The like is true of the seven arts and disciplines which make Architecture perfect, and the Architect admirable. But, alas! few architects receive so many graces and favours from God to be able to know and to understand them, since it pleases Him to open the senses and the intelligence of each of us for cognisance of His works and of the propor-tionate dimensions, of Architecture, nay of all things, for which He ordained at the first creation certain dimensions, weights and numbers, as we shall deduce at a later time in

Philibert de
l'Orme
1510–1570

fuller measure (God willing) in our Volume and Work on the Divine proportions, where we advise all persons to imitate the dimensions and proportions which we call divine for right and proper reasons, and consequently more worthy of being followed, than those written down, invented and made by man, in edifices both ancient and modern, as these are still to be seen in diverse places. For God is the only, the great and admirable Architect, who has disposed and created by His word alone the entire celestial and elementary and terrestrial machine of the world, with such great order, such great dimensions, and such admirable proportions, that the human mind, without His assistance and inspiration, cannot comprehend them, and most signally the architecture and construction of the human body, not only in the composition and the assembly of its spiritual, humid and solid parts (as these are studied by doctors of medicine) but in the great harmony and more than admirable proportions and symmetry which exist between all its members and parts both interior and exterior. This is studied or is to be studied and known by learned and expert Architects in order to accommodate it to the buildings that they undertake to build with that excellence that is divine, that is, other than that excellence deriving from common and customary proportions. Thus shall we (God willing) set out in detail and demonstrate in familiar fashion in the aforesaid Volume and work, where we speak of the holy and divine measurements and proportions given by God to the Holy Fathers of the Old Testament: such as to the Patriarch Noah for the building of the Ark to protect against cataclysm and deluge; to Moses, for the Tabernacle of the Altar, tables, curtain walls, temple courts, and other things; to Solomon, for the Temple built by him in Jerusalem, and two houses also built by him, one for himself and the other for his wife, daughter of the Pharaoh. A similar example is to be seen in the Book of Hezekiah, that is a man who appeared to him, resembling a creature in bronze and holding in one hand a cord and in the other a reed or a cane, bearing the dimensions and proportions that God alone showed to him for the restoration and the rebuilding of the Temple of Jerusalem. [. . .] Truly, such proportions are so divine and admirable, that I cannot read, read again, contemplate and I must say, adore, sufficiently to satisfy my soul, by reason of the great majesty and divinity of Him who handed down and ordained them.

Certainly, I cannot marvel enough, as so many divine dimensions and proportions have not been determined, observed and practised by the ancients, or by any among the moderns. As for myself, I freely and frankly avow that the Palaces, Castles, Churches and houses that I have by my order had built until the present day, and that are, by the grace of God, prized and praised by men, seem to me to be nothing (albeit that the proportions have been respected as laid down by the art of true Architecture of men) if I compare and measure them against the yardstick of the divine proportions coming from on high (as we have said above) and with those in the human body. With the result that if the aforesaid edifices were to be built again, I would give them an excellence and a dignity far above those that men find in them today.

Book I, Chapter IX

[. . .]

The Architect, seeing himself to be constrained by his Lord and the disposition of his building not being such as to orient it as it should be, must then demonstrate his skill and intelligence in making use of everything and making the old building fit with

Philibert de l'Orme 1510–1570

the new and find new ideas on what should be done, either to build in square, round, oval or triangular form, or in any other manner that may be fitting: ensuring that each element has its own aspect and view and that each and every thing is in its proper place. But above all else it is most proper to seek those things that are necessary for the well-being of the occupants and when one cannot do better it is desirable to change the views from the windows and the doors where these are undesirable. [. . .]

Those things that are obligatory and to which one cannot always give proper order, dimensions and proportions, or which prevent the buildings being oriented as they should, require knowledge and skill that is learnt through long experience and practice in building of a number of edifices and not through the dimensions and proportions that one might impose upon them. To be clear on this matter, the Architect must be familiar with all the rules and precepts of his art, not so much through books as through long and great practice, as we have said, since then he shall immediately find the remedies and aids necessary to him.

Philibert de
l'Orme
1510–1570

Book III Prologue in the Form of an Announcement

In so far as this third book is almost entirely devoted to the setting out and description of certain characteristics and lines that we call Geometric, these being very necessary to Architects, Master Masons, Stone Dressers and Cutters and other persons, to know and to be helped thereby in the areas we shall propose and in the manner we shall describe and which shall be known by the discussion and reading of the aforesaid lines, which cannot be correctly found nor practised other than with the aid and use of the draughtsman's compasses. For this reason, I conceived the intention of thinking out and describing straightforwardly the figure and image that you shall find hereinafter, which shall bring to your attention the excellence of the aforesaid compasses, as well as several excellent things that shall serve as examples and for the instruction and counsel of all those practising or wishing to practise the profession of Architect and also for other persons, with singular pleasure and profit. In the first place therefore I show an Architect, dressed in the manner of a learned and wise man (as he must be) and as if coming out of a cave or other dark place, that is to say a place of meditation, solitude and study, in order to arrive at true knowledge and perfection in his Art. With one hand he pulls up the skirts of his robe, wishing to show that the Architect must be diligent in all activities, and with the other hand he holds and uses a pair of compasses around which a serpent is entwined, in order to signify that he must measure and compare all things and all works and constructions with prudence and mature reflection in order to able to see with certainty the path he must tread between men, a path which has, here and there, traps and thorns, that is to say, barbs, envy, hatred, disappointments, insults, barriers and impediments which harm all good souls and most signally those who wish to practise well the art of Architecture, as I have said at length elsewhere. This is why the greatest possible prudence, well judged and measured, is necessary and useful to them: prudence, I say to you, such as the Serpent represents and which is ordered and recommended by Jesus Christ in His Gospel, saying: *Estote prudentes sicut serpentes et simplices sicut colombe.* This means: Be wise as the serpent and simple as the dove, wishing thereby to show that prudence, joined with simplicity and modesty, leads men to all good and praiseworthy enterprises. For as Gavarre says in his book *Mots Dorés* ['golden words']: so great is the gift of prudence that by it one may

[143]

amend the past, give order to the present and provide for the future and things to come, from which we may infer that he who has not that most marvellous virtue of prudence cannot remedy his loss, nor preserve that which he possesses, nor seek that which he hopes. For this reason, I represent the aforesaid Architect continuing to hold the compasses in his hand, teaching thereby that he must direct all his works (as we have said) by means of measurement; and I have also added to the aforesaid compasses a serpent, as a reminder that it is necessary to be well advised, prudent and cautious, following the example of said serpent. For, as Saint Ambrose writes, sensing the approach of the Enchanter, he puts one ear to the ground and stops the other with the tail of his coat. Thus also the Architect shall win the Palm I propose to him and draw to his attention, as the goal at which he must aim and the path that he must take, wishing to symbolise with the aforesaid Palm a constant and firm determination to withstand labour and pain in all his responsibilities and business, in order to achieve glory, honour and victory, as signified by the said Palm, which is of such a nature, that however you may burden it once or many times, it does not weaken or bend, but rises, resists and strengthens against the burden and load placed upon it, breaking cleanly rather than bending or weakening. However, before the aforesaid Palm can be won, or if you wish, before glory and honour can be achieved, there is more than one obstacle along his way.

In order therefore to be sure of winning the Palm, it is necessary to be accompanied in all things and places by prudence, bearer and (as Saint Bernard writes) carrier of all the other virtues, being so sublime and heroic that it cannot be had by any degenerate and evil person. For this reason I desire that our Architect be a pure soul, one who does not deceive, exploit or harm others. He is not however to be criticised for imitating the serpent, that is to say, for being cautious and well-advised, in order to protect himself from the seduction, malice and deception of evil men. That which he may acquire by means of prudence, said prudence not being that human and vulgar attribute that should rather be termed ruse and trickery (in the manner that the name of vice is commonly given to virtue) but that prudence which occupies the main place among the four Virtues, called Cardinal by the Philosophers, and is none other than premeditation, discretion and foresight in going about one's business, in order that it should be done well and result in a satisfactory outcome. This is the prudence that I desire for our Architect, which, if he may by the grace of God acquire it, shall not make him less wise than well-advised in those things that he must do, in knowing what to say and knowing when to say nothing at the requisite times and knowing how to explain his desires with good grace and to make understood by Kings, Princes, great Lords, and all other persons, his enterprises and conceptions; to know how to discourse upon the works they wish to execute, and to talk of these in the appropriate manner, time and place. For it may happen that saying nothing may be seen as ignorance and simplemindedness; just as saying too much may be seen as folly and temerity. *Omnia tempus habent* (says the Wise Man) *tempus tacendi and tempus loquendi*. Giving to us in this adage leave to speak at one time, and to say nothing at another. For the constant unwillingness to speak indicates great lack of intelligence and the desire to talk too much, even greater folly. This signifies that one must observe the circumstances of place, subject, time and persons. Those circumstances must not be ignored, as I warn you when I place at the highest point in our figure the image of Mercury, source of Eloquence, to show that the Architect not only must know how to talk and discuss his works, but

must also be prompt and diligent to know and understand the proper sciences and disciplines. [. . .] However, I do not wish him to be too mercurial, that is to say, change-
able and talkative, supporting first one side, then the other, through I know not what
inconstancy and frivolity; rather, I wish him to follow and emulate good men, in order
to be good himself, and the learned and wise, in order to receive teaching from them,
accompanied by honour and good reputation, and in doing so he shall acquire fame
and immortal praise. We have added to the aforesaid Mercury his trophies, that is to
say caduceus and horns, not wishing to signify any other thing but that the Architect
shall acquire fame and reputation in all things and in all places, if he but observe that
which is written above. [. . .]

Book III, Chapter XVI

[. . .] certain Architects and Masters who, not understanding the practice of the drawing
of lines and Geometry, say that they see in this a constraint, and find in it some strange
structure that need be of no concern and saying that this is work for Masons. We must
admit, conceding this point to them, that Masons know more of this than such Architects, which goes against reason, for the Architect must be learned in order to
command and order all kinds of work from Master Masons. However, today in many
places, the cart is put (as we say) before the horse, that is to say in more than one place
Masons govern and teach Masters, this being said without wishing to vex the Learned,
whom I praise and honour, but not those who deceive their Lords, wishing to interfere
in an Estate which they do not understand and know nothing except what they have
heard and learned from Master Masons.

Philibert de
l'Orme
1510–1570

Book IV Prologue

The Architect who has knowledge of the aforesaid drawing of lines, certainly has no
excuse for not being able to find an infinity of new and pleasing ideas and not doing
many things which surpass the opinion, ingenuity and knowledge of more than one of
those who style themselves Architects, not forgetting satisfactory explanations accompanied by proper demonstration, provided that they wish to hear and receive them in
return. And the aforesaid demonstrations shall be taken from Geometry, the most
subtle, the most ingenious and the most inventive of all the disciplines and the four
sisters of Mathematics, as Cassiodorus [editor's note: Roman statesman and author,
c.485–585] calls them, because Geometry finds its beginning in things that are self-
evident, and most signally in Arithmetic, which is so necessary for all Estates that with
much reason well-advised men ensure that it is taught to the young. I have great praise
for this and am very much of the opinion that we would be even better advised to
teach, along with the theory and the practice of said Arithmetic, the principles of
Geometry and that all sorts of Estate, from the highest to the lowest, should understand the two aforementioned disciplines. For there is no science, no mechanical art, no
trade that you may name that cannot find aid and profit and use in Arithmetic and
Geometry, which are such excellent disciplines that they make men subtle and ingenious in inventing many singular and profitable things for the public good.

Chapter I. Concerning the vault and trompe *that I designed and had done at the*
Château of Anet to support a private study, in order to accommodate it to the chamber
in which his Majesty the late King Henry was wont to reside

This is a very convenient place to discharge the promise I made in our books on the
New Invention, on how to build well at little cost, to describe and show the design of
the *trompe*, or suspended corbelled conical vault, at Anet in the Château of the late
Duchess of Valentinois. Said *trompe* was made to solve a difficulty posed by the addition
of a private study to the chamber where the late King Henry was wont to reside when
staying at the aforesaid château. The difficulty was that there was no room or space to
create said study in the main body of the new building whose construction had already
begun, nor in the older building that had already been constructed, so much so that
there was nothing there to allow the creation of the aforesaid study. For after the hall
there was the antechamber, followed by the bedchamber of the King and at the side
was the extension containing the robing room. Considering therefore the difficulty and
lack of space in this place and, in addition to this, knowing that it is necessary and more
than reasonable to join private studies to chambers occupied by Kings, great Princes
and Lords (in order that they might withdraw alone and in private either to write or to
deal with matters in secret, or otherwise) I was in great perplexity, for I could not find
the place for the aforesaid study without spoiling the other accommodation and chambers, which had been done along the lines of the older foundations and other walls
whose construction had been commenced before my arrival. So what was the
outcome? I drew my design at a corner close to the bedchamber of the King, looking
from the outside from the garden and it seemed to me to be good to make there a vault
suspended in the air in order to find more easily the space to make the aforesaid private
study. And this was done, it being a *trompe*, shaped conically, this form being stronger
for the support of masonry and loads to be placed upon it, to close around with dressed
stone the aforesaid study and to crown it with a kiln vault also in dressed stone without
the use of any wood at all. [. . .]

Chapter II. The plan of the trompe *and private study of the King projecting from the*
building, being suspended in the air and the manner in which like vaults and
trompes *should be done*

[. . .]

I wish to say and inform the Reader that it seems to me that the term 'trompe', as
used by us herein, has come, or has been taken and usurped, from the likeness between
the form of that vault and the trumpet, the 'trompette' – or 'trompe' or trump, as it is
called in many places. Both are wide at the front and narrow gradually within in the
form of a vault. But that is enough on this point, before going on to the description and
construction of the structure concerned, of which it is question herein for the construction of buildings. Know therefore that it may be constructed with a right, obtuse or
acute angle and with any form you may desire at the front, that is to say straight,
squared with facets, such as the half of a hexagon or an octagon, or indeed quite round.
In this way it is possible to make a *trompe* that is straight, hollow, rampant or in any
other manner that may be imagined, according to necessity and the difficulties of the
building in which it is desired to incorporate it. All sorts of vault can be made in *trompe*
form and all suspended in air, without support from below, except for the two sides

forming the angle, and all using the same method for their design, with much shorten-ing and saving of time, study and labour, for those desirous of knowing the practise thereof.

[...] in order to make better understood the structure of the aforesaid *trompes* and since they are designed by means of certain lines and drawings of that which I shall call Geometry (which can be shown with the help of compasses, in order to find the manner in which they may be made with moulds and panels for cutting and assembling all sorts of stone or wood, as may be used in the construction of buildings) it appears to me that it would be very appropriate at this point if I began by showing those I had done at the aforementioned Château of Anet.

[...]

I am quite certain that no Craftsman in this Kingdom had ever heard tell of a *trompe* like that which I had done in Lyons, it being (as we have said) lowered, angled and skewed, with practically the three-quarters of its arc projecting out from the build- Philibert de
l'Orme
1510–1570 ing, nor like that which I had done at the aforementioned Château of Anet, which is greatly prized by those versed in the art – although if they wished to take the trouble to study and understand the method written down by me here, I am quite certain that they could make and think out more marvellous examples. If I encounter the proper persons therefore, I shall have done others of another sort, which shall be more admired. I found the design and conceived the artifices therefore in that aforemen-tioned year one thousand five hundred and thirty-six, by the means and with the aid of Geometry and much mental labour of which I have not complained since, but rather praised God greatly for the fact that with a single design and a single form of *trompe*, it is possible to make all such vaults.

archaic beliefs • body model • design methodology • representation • truth • illusion • systemisation of space distribution

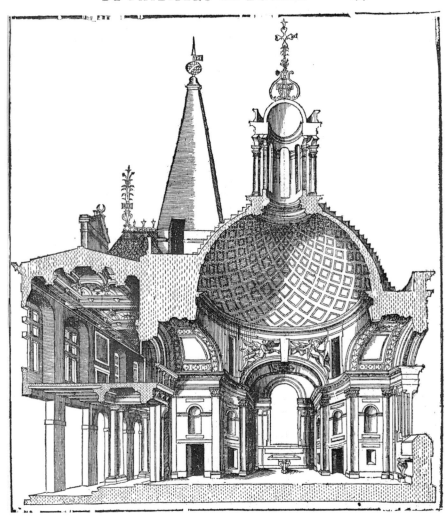

50. Philibert de l'Orme. *Le Premier tôme de l'architecture.* 1567–1648. Perspective section of a church.

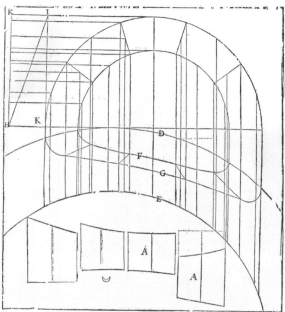

51. Philbert de l'Orme. *Le Premier tome de l'architecture*. 1567–1648. Stereotomy drawings for cutting stones to construct a vault and 51b. fantail *trompe* stair structure.

Afin que vous ayez encores plus de paſſe-temps , & d'occupa-tion, ſi vous la voulez prendre, i'ay tiré d'abondant en vne autre fi-gure cy-apres, la façon comme l'on trouue le cyntre de la ſufdiéte porte en talus biaiſe : ainſi que vous le voyez á la marque L, auec ſa circonference r'alongée , en la ligne M O. Enſemble les pa-neaux de teſte par le deſſus, au lieu ſigné C. Et ceux des commiſ-ſures ou des joinéts marquez B. Qui aura le loiſir de s'y occuper

LIVRE IV. DE L'ARCHITECTVRE

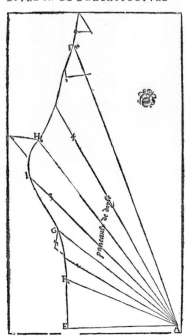

52. Philibert de l'Orme. *Le Premier tôme de l'architecture*. 1567–1648. The Château of Anet and its *trompe*.

Andrea Palladio (1508–1580)

The Four Books of Architecture (1570)

Palladio, originally a stonemason, was taken into the household of the humanist scholar and amateur architect Gian Giorgio Trissino. The latter had known the designs of Bramante and Raphael in Rome and brought his protégé into contact with Cornaro and Serlio (Ackerman, 1972; Puppi, 1973a, 11–12). From then on, Palladio was active in the design of mestic, civic and ecclesiastical buildings in Vicenza, Venice and elsewhere in the Veneto, which made him the most imitated architect in history (Ackerman, ibid., 1972). The success of palladianism, which provided an architectural imagery of power for Venetian patrician businessmen whose great trading and shipping assets were being massively transferred to farm land (Bentmann and Müller, 1970; Puppi, ibid.; Ackerman, ibid.) and to the proto-protestant city leaders of Vicenza, owes much to the format of his books (Ackerman, ibid.), probably influenced by Serlio in their emphasis on illustration. Palladio made Book II and III into catalogues of his own works.

Further reading Ackerman, 1972; Argan, 1930, 1932; Barbieri, 1964; Bentmann and Müller, 1970; Burns, 1975; Cavallari-Murat, 1969; Faggin, 1967; Fiocco, 1952; Forssman, 1962, 1965, 1966; Heydenreich, 1969b; Honour, 1960; Howard, 1980; Lotz, 1962, 1967; Pallucchini, 1959; Pane, 1961; Puppi, 1970, Puppi, 1973a, 11–12, 1973b, 1977; Schlosser, 1979, 414ff.; Sereni, 1979; Spielmann, 1968; Tafuri, 1968; Verga, 1970; Wiebenson, 1980, 1982; Wittkower, 1962, 1974; Zorzi, 1958, 1965, 1967, 1968.

The Four Books on Architecture

The Author's Preface to the reader

Guided by a natural inclination, I gave myself up in my most early years to the study of architecture: and as it was always my opinion, that the ancient Romans, as in many other things, so in building well, vastly excelled all those who have been since their time, I proposed to myself Vitruvius for my master and guide, who is the only ancient writer of this art, and set myself to search into the reliques of all the ancient edifices, that, in spite of time and the cruelty of the Barbarians, yet remain; and finding them much more worthy of observation, than at first I had imagined, I began very minutely with the utmost diligence to measure everyone of their parts; of which I grew at last so solicitous an examiner (not finding any thing which was not done with reason and beautiful proportion) that I have very frequently not only travelled in different parts of Italy, but also out of it, that I might entirely, from them, comprehend what the whole had been, and reduce it into design. Whereupon perceiving how much this common use of building was different from the observations I had made upon the laid edifices, and from what I had read in Vitruvius, Leon Battista Alberti, and in other excellent writers who have been since Vitruvius, and from those also which by me have lately been practised with the utmost satisfaction and applause of those who have made use of my works; it seemed to me a thing worthy of a man, who ought not to be born for himself only, but also for the utility of others, to publish the designs of those edifices (in collecting which, I have employed so much time, and exposed myself to so many dangers) and concisely to jot down whatever in them appeared to be more worthy of consideration; and moreover, those rules which I have observed, and now observe, in building; that they who shall read these my books, may be able to make use of whatever will be good therein, and supply those things in which (as many perhaps there may be) I shall have failed; that one may learn, by little and little, to lay aside the strange abuses, the barbarous inventions, the superfluous expense, and (what is of greater consequence) avoid the various and continual ruins that have been seen in many buildings. [...] I shall therefore first treat of private houses, and afterwards of public edifices. [...] And in all these books I shall avoid the superfluity of words, and simply give those directions that seem to me most necessary, and shall make use of those terms which at this time are most commonly in use among artificers.

Book I, chapter I. Of the several particulars that ought to be considered and prepared before we begin to build

Andrea Palladio
1508–1580

Great care ought to be taken, before a building is begun, of the several parts of the plan and elevation of the whole edifice intended to be raised: for three things, according to Vitruvius, ought to be considered in every building, without which no edifice will deserve to be commended; and these are utility or convenience, duration and beauty. [...] An edifice may be esteemed commodious, when every part or member stands in its due place and fit situation, neither above or below its dignity and use; or when the loggias, halls, chambers, cellars and granaries are conveniently disposed, and in their proper places. The strength, or duration, depends upon the walls being carried directly upright, thicker, below than above, and their foundations strong and solid: observing to place the upper columns directly perpendicular over those that are underneath, and the openings of the doors and windows exactly over one another; so that the solid be upon the solid, and the void over the void. Beauty will result from the form and correspondence of the whole, with respect to the several parts, of the parts with regard to each other; and of these again to the whole. [...]

    [...]

Book I, chapter XII. Of the five orders made use of by the ancients

[...] The measures and proportions of each of these orders I shall separately set down; not so much according to Vitruvius, as to the observations I have made on several ancient edifices. But I shall first mention such particulars as relate to all of them in general. [...]

Book I, chapter XX. Of abuses

Having laid down the ornaments of architecture, that is, the five orders, and shown how they ought to be made; and having placed the profiles of everyone of their parts as I found the ancients did observe them; it seems, to me not improper to inform the reader in this place of many abuses introduced by the Barbarians, which are still followed, that the studious in this art may avoid them in their own works, and be able to know them in those of others. I say therefore, that architecture, as well as all other arts, being an imitator of nature, can suffer nothing that either alienates or deviates from that which is agreeable to nature; from whence we see that the ancient architects, who made their edifices of wood, when they began to make them of stone, instituted that the columns should be left thicker at the top than at the bottom, taking example from the trees, all which are thinner at the top than in the trunk, or near the root. And because it is very probable that those things are depressed upon which some great weight is put, bases were placed under the columns, which, with their *bastoni* and *cavetti*, seem to be crushed with the burden layed upon them. So likewise in the cornice they introduced the triglyphs, modiglions and dentils, which represent the ends of those beams that are put for a support to the floors and roofs. The same also may be observed in all the other parts, if they are considered. Being thus, that manner of building cannot but be blamed which departs from that which the nature of things teaches, and from that simplicity which appears in the things produced by her; framing as it were another nature, and deviating from the true, good and beautiful method of building.

[...]

I know therefore nothing that can be done more contrary to natural reason, than to divide that part which is supposed to shelter the inhabitants and those that go into the house from rain, snow and hail. And although variety and things new may please everyone, they ought not to be done contrary to the precepts of art and contrary to that which reason dictates; whence one sees, that although the ancients did vary, yet they never departed from the universal and necessary rules of art, as shall be seen in my books of antiquities. Also, concerning the projection of the cornices and the other ornaments, making them come out too much is no small abuse. When they exceed that which is reasonably proper for them, especially if they are in a close place, they will make it narrow and disagreeable, and frighten those that stand under them because they always threaten to fall. Nor ought the making cornices which are not in proportion to the columns less to be avoided. If upon little columns great cornices are placed, or little cornices upon great columns, who doubts but that such a building must have a very unpleasing aspect? Besides which, the practice of dividing columns, making certain annulets and garlands round them in order that they may appear to be held firmly united together, ought as much as possible to be avoided. The more solid and strong the columns are in reality not just in appearance, the better they execute the purpose for which they were erected, which is to make the work thereon both strong and secure. I could mention many other such abuses, as some members in the cornices that are made without any proportion to the others, which, by what I have shown above, and by that which has been already said, may very easily be known.

Andrea Palladio
1508–1580

Book II, chapter II. Of the compartment or disposition of rooms, and of other places

In order for homes to be commodious for the use of the family, without which they would be greatly blameworthy and far from being commendable, great care ought to be taken in the principal parts, such as the loggia, halls, courts and magnificent rooms. The ample stairs ought to be light and easy of ascent. In addition, the most minute and least beautiful parts must be accommodated to the service of the greatest and more worthy. This is because as in the human body there are some noble and beautiful parts and some rather ignoble and disagreeable, we see that those stand in very great need of care because without them they could not subsist. So in buildings there ought to be some parts considerable and honoured, and some less elegant, without which the other could not remain free, and so consequently would lose part of their dignity and beauty. But as our Blessed Creator has ordered our members in such a manner, that the most beautiful are in places most exposed to view, and the less comely more hidden, so in building we ought to put the principal and considerable parts in places that are most seen, and the less beautiful in places as much hidden from the eye as possible. This is so that in them may be lodged all the foulness of the house, and all those things that may give any obstruction, and in any measure render the more beautiful parts disagreeable.

I approve therefore that in the lowest part of the fabric, which I make somewhat underground, may be disposed the cellars, the magazines for wood, pantries, kitchens, servants-halls, wash-houses, ovens and such like things necessary for daily use. From which disposition follow two conveniences. The one is that the upper part remains free; and the other, and no less important, is that the said upper apartments are more wholesome to live in, the floor being at a distance from the dampness of the ground. Besides, as it rises, it is more agreeable to be looked at and to look out of. It is also to be observed that in the remaining part of the building there may be great, middle-sized and small rooms, and all near one another, that they may reciprocally be made use of. The small rooms may be divided to make closets where studies or libraries may be placed, riding accoutrements and lumber, which may be every day wanted, and which would not be so proper to be in rooms, where one either sleeps, eats, or where strangers are received.

What contributes also to conveniency is that the rooms for summer be ample, spacious and turned to the north; and those for the winter to the south and west, and rather small than otherwise. We seek the shades and winds in summer, and in winter the sun. Besides, small rooms are much more easily warmed than large. But those which we would make use of in spring and autumn must be turned to the east and ought to look over greens and gardens. In this particular part, studies and libraries ought also to be as the morning is the most proper time of all other to make use of them. But the large rooms with the middling, and those with the small, ought to be so distributed that, as I have elsewhere said, one part of the building may correspond with the other, and that the body of the edifice may have in itself a certain convenience in its members, that may render the whole beautiful and graceful. [...]

Book II, chapter III. Of the designs of town-houses

[...] And here the reader may take notice, that in placing the said designs, I have had respect neither to the rank or dignity of the gentlemen to be mentioned, but that I have inserted them where I thought most convenient, not but they are all very honourable. [...]

Book II, chapter XII. Of the choice of the situation for the building of a villa

[...] And, finally, in the choice of the situation for the building of a villa, all those considerations ought to be had which are necessary in a city house; since the city is, as it were, but a great house, and, on the contrary, a country house a little city. [...]

classical canon • antiquity • abuses • precedent • authority • invention • systemisation of space distribution

Andrea Palladio
1508–1580

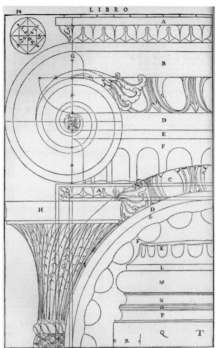

53. Andrea Palladio. *I Quattro libri dell'architettura*. 1570. Temple of Fortuna Virilis side view, part of the frieze, and plan of the angular capital. 53b. Ionic capital.

54. Andrea Palladio. *I Quattro libri dell'architettura*. 1570. Example of a system of four 'winding stairs made at the Chateau of Chambord for Francois I er with four entrances, the one over the other. They can serve four apartments without the inhabitants of one going down the staircase of the other . . . all see one another without giving one another the least of inconvenience'.

55. Andrea Palladio. *I Quattro libri dell'architettura*. 1570. The house for the Counts Valmarana.

[155]

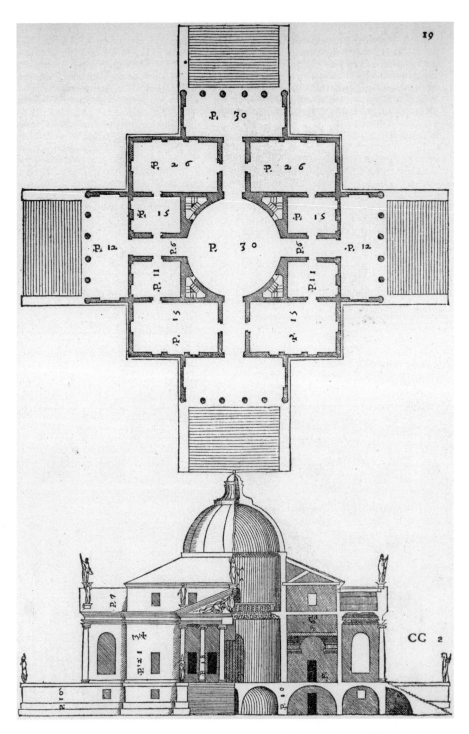

56. Andrea Palladio. *I Quattro libri dell'architettura*. 1570. Villa Almerico, La Rotonda, plan, partial façade and section showing the four 'loggias' at each side made because the site 'enjoys the loveliest views on all sides' 'that give the effect of an enormous theatre'.

Jean Martin

Architecture ou Art de bien bâtir de Vitruve Pollion, 1574

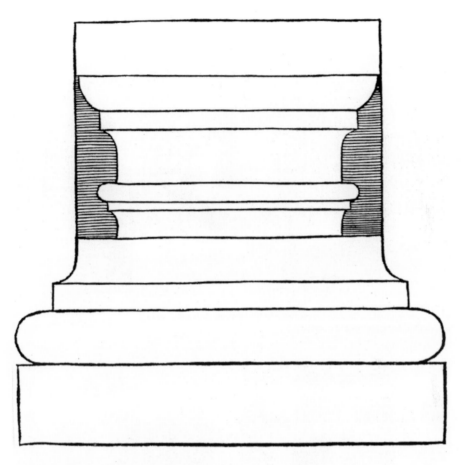

57. Jean Martin, *Architecture ou Art de bien bâtir de Vitruve Pollion*. 1574. The Tuscan Order.

Jacques Androuet Du Cerceau

Les Plus excellents bastiments de France, 1576–1579

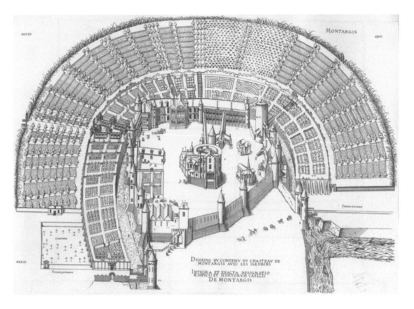

58. Jacques Androuet Du Cerceau. *Les Plus excellents bastiments de France.* 1576–1579. The Château of Montargis with its surrounding gardens and cultivations.

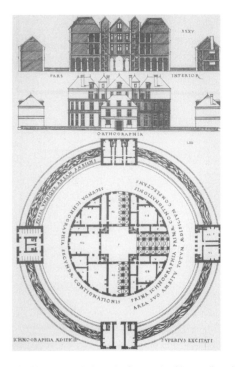
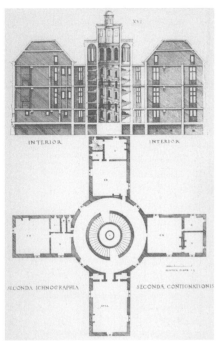

59., 59b. Jacques Androuet Du Cerceau. *Les Plus excellents bastiments de France.* 1576–1579. Two châteaux. Plans, sections and façade.

Giacomo Barozzio da Vignola

Prospettiva, 1583
Cinque Ordini, 1563

60. Giacomo Barozzio da Vignola. *Prospettiva*. 1583.
Man drawing the figure of a woman on a grid paper
without looking at the model, just listening to an
observer who gives a verbal description of the model
seen through a mechanical coordinating device.

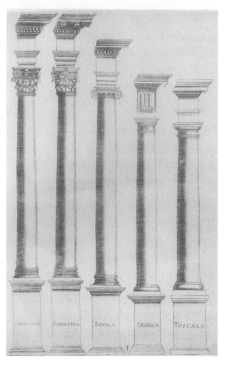

61. Giacomo Barozzio da Vignola. *Cinque Ordini*. 1563.
The five Orders in a simplified description that will
become canonical during the coming four centuries.

[159]

Antonio Rusconi

Dell'Architettura, 1590

*praponendoui loto, et facendo i tetti pendenti, diedero la caduta all'acque,
& fi aficurarono maggiormente, del modo che uediamo efpreffo quì fotto.*

F A mentione Vitruuio, che in Francia, in Ifpagna, in Portogallo, & in
Guafcogna fi facenano de gl'edificij cofi rozi, coperti di tauole fegate di
Rouere, ouero con paglie, & ftrame; come appare nelle due feguenti figure;
& potrafi aggiungere, che fino al di d'hoggi per la Germania fi ueggono
gran parte delle cafe coperte di tauolette di Pino, & che per la Polonia, &
per la Mofcouia poche cafe fi trouano, che non fiano contefte di legnami,
anco nelle Città più nominate, & più celebri.

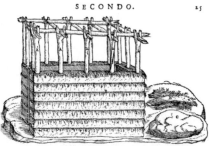

P ER difenderfi poi dalle pioggie, dalle grandini, & dal Sole le copriro-
no di cannuccie, di frondi, e di loto, come ci moftra il diffegno feguente.

E T perche li coperti non reggeuano à foftener le pioggie, et le altre cödi-
tioni infopportabili del Verno, cominciarono ad innalzare i colmi, et fo-

62., 62b. Antonio Rusconi. *Dell'Architettura.* 1590. Illustrations of regional architecture for the text of Vitruvius. Rusconi died in 1587 before the publication of this book. His ambitious plan for an illustrated edition of Vitruvius was cancelled because of the publication of Barbaro's 1556 edition.

Domenico Fontana

Della Transportione dell'obelisco Vaticano et delle fabriche di nostro signore Papa Sisto, 1590

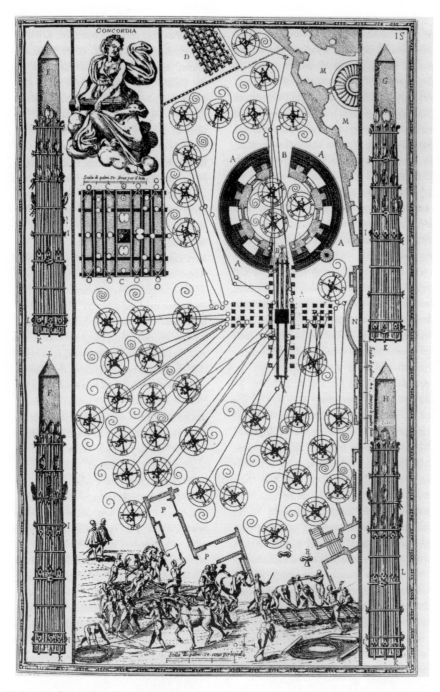

63. Domenico Fontana. *Della Trasportatione dell'obelisco Vaticano et delle fabriche di nostro signore Papa Sisto .V. fatte dal Cavalier Domenico Fontana, architetto di Sua Santità.* 1590. Plan of the operation showing the tower and the watch-like arrangement of the capstans in the piazza and within the sacristy.

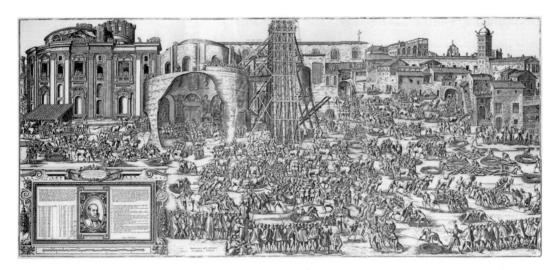

64. Domenico Fontana. *Della Trasportatione dell'obelisco Vaticano et delle fabriche di nostro signore Papa Sisto .V. fatte dal Cavalier Domenico Fontana, architetto di Sua Santità.* 1590. Engraving documenting Fontana's tower, the preparations of the work groups in the piazza before moving of the obelisk, the adjoining sacristy. The unfinished St Peter's is in the background.

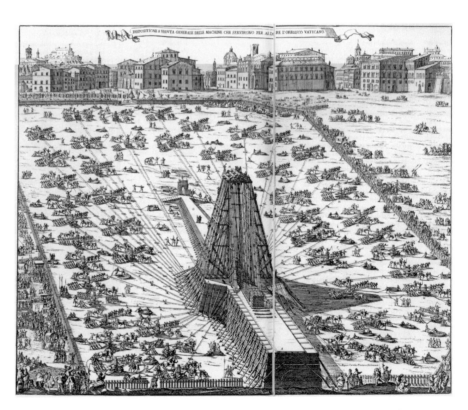

64b. View from the air of the piazza of St Peter's after the obelisk has been moved showing Fontana's machine.

Giovanni Paolo Lomazzo (1538–1600)

The Idea of the Temple of Painting, Sculpture and Architecture (1590)

Lomazzo began his career as a painter but when, in 1571, he was struck with blindness, he turned to writing and became one of the greatest representatives of late mannerist theory in art and architecture with the publication of his three works (1584, 1590, 1591). Two mannerist academies existed at the end of the sixteenth century. One is Accademia della Valle in Bregno, in Milan, presided by him; the other is Zuccaro's in Rome. In the wake of the counter-reformation, both institutions turned their back on the relation of architecture to the real world and limited their discussions to metaphysical and theological matters. Lomazzo claimed that the artistic genius was of the same substance as the divine genius or 'Idea' which commands all nature (Klein, 1970, 1974; Lee, 1967, 1–16; Schlosser, 1979). The following passage contains whole sections from Ficino's commentary on Plato's *Symposium* to this effect. Lomazzo's faith in the universal legitimacy of the rules of the ancients could not be further from Alberti's or that of the French theoreticians of architecture from Perrault onwards, who were all troubled by the arbitrary nature of architectural precepts, along with that of the excessive mannerist architectural forms they went hand-in-hand with. Both the precepts and the forms will come under attack by Perrault.

Further reading Ackerman, 1964, 1967; Blunt, 1940, ch. IX; Gordon, 1948; Hauser, 1951; Klein, 1959; Mahon, 1947; Paris, 1954; Spina-Barelli, 1958; Wittkower, 1962, 119–120.

Giovanni Paolo
Lomazzo
1538–1600

But since architecture above all the other sciences is the one the painter must have most complete knowledge of, and since it presents the greatest diversity that comes to the fore as soon as it is put into practice, as the painters, sculptors, goldsmiths and all the others who use it in their work know all too well, it is necessary to know its true rule in order to exercise it. This rule, in short, can be extracted better than anywhere else from the study of the form of good antique buildings that are, among so many others, the Coliseum and the Pantheon of Rome; and also many modern buildings too, a pure and true architecture, without all that confusing foliage and frames that suffocate all the beauty of the art. This beauty appears when the architect proceeds according to the rules of the precepts of the art that vary and are distinguished according to the different orders of architecture, the Tuscan, the Doric, the Ionic, the Corinthian, the Composite.

It is from proportion that beauty, utility, adaptation and ornamentation of natural bodies first, as among the rational animals, women and children and among non-rational animals, horses and other quadrupedes, birds, dragons and monsters such as the cenocephali, the man eaters, rhinoceri and centaurs, and also demi-gods such as satyres, fawns, silenes, pans and such, and among non-animated objects such as trees, mountains, hills, plains, rivers, seas, sources and everything that is to be found among natural creation. In the second place, proportion generates this beauty even in artificial bodies and objects, such as, among the buildings, even military, and it is by it that we erect correctly all the constructions, however great and economical they may be. It is from her, in addition, that the proportion of clothing, instruments of defence or of entertainment and so many other things comes and that can rejoice our eyes and give them pleasure.

This proportion is the one that is to be found naturally in bodies that are in orthogonal projection (whose parts are not foreshortened or reduced) with very studied contours, drawn according to reasoning and not happenstance, showing the relationships between the proportional parts of the members, so that the object becomes beautiful and adapted to its functions.

IV. We can draw from this the lesson that the artist must give more importance to reason than to the pleasure of one person; because the work must be universal and perfect; and who ever proceeds differently works in a vacuum. This is something that never occurs among those that know that their idea needs no further artifice for its beauty to come through on the work, and that it suffices to put care and solicitude for the body and to chase away the perturbations of cupidity and fear to make us see in their works rational beauty, that is natural to their spirit. . . . All this Ordonnance of the world that we see, we receive through the eyes, not as it is in the matter of bodies, but the way it is in the rays that penetrate the eyes. And as this ordonnance of the world is sustained in light, already incorporeal and separated from its necessary material, we might say that all the beauty of the universe offers itself to us through light. But seeing that beauty is in the eye of the beholder and not in the objects themselves, it will be all the more similar, in docile matter, to the archetype of man infused with a divine ray of light in the angel and in the soul. If matter harmonises also with divine power and with the Idea of the angel, it harmonises also with reason and with the stamp of the Idea in the soul. And the soul approves this fittingness in the harmony in which beauty consists, and which we see, according to the various qualities of matter, come closer or further apart more or less from the form that the soul possesses from the start.

aesthetisation of architecture • archaic beliefs • body model

El Greco (Domenico Theotocopoulos) (1541–1614)

Marginalia to Daniele Barbaro's translation of Vitruvius (c. 1591)

El Greco was a painter who incorporated architecture in his paintings. Indeed he is credited with the architectural frames to his own paintings in Toledo (Marias and Bustamante, 1981). The following text is made up of some of the marginalia he inscribed in his copy of Daniele Barbaro's translation of Vitruvius (1556). These notes were part of the preparation of an anti-Vitruvian treatise on architecture now lost. El Greco considers that architecture should be an exercise of *venustas* more than of *firmitas* and *utilitas* and defends novelty, variety and complexity. He is averse to the very idea of rules in architecture, believes above all in the freedom of invention and proceeds to refute Vitruvius's attachment to archaeological remains, canonical proportions, perspective and mathematics. The radicalness of these ideas, acceptable in art, was far too extreme to have any immediate resonance in architectural circles (Marias and Bustamante, 1981). Here follows an unguarded, private, freely expressed diatribe, giving full vent to a heartfelt contempt unfettered by considerations of polite intercourse, against Vitruvius's rule of proportions, comparing him to an idiot. He also sees Vitruvius's manner of distorting proportions in order to compensate for distance from the eye as responsible for creating monstrous forms. The hand-written passages, transcribed by Marias and Bustamante (1981), contain some unreadable parts. These are indicated by the presence of '. . .'.

Further reading Marias and Bustamante, 1981.

El Greco
1541–1614

Book III, Chapter 1

Nine or ten faces ... of the measurements is as if you learned in a foreign language ... from memory how to make an embassy without knowing what is being said ... it looks like in order to talk about measurements they have to pretend to be something they are not ... except that they seem as though they were donkeys covered in the skins of lions; from such things the wise architect must flee with the certainty that all these measurements will only be deleterious.

As far as I can see this subtle point is nothing but the Baba de spanna (editors: 'an absurdity').

And with this supposed knowledge, that only by seeing things you know beyond any doubt that all you need are measurements ... then the plan are the feet and if in order to make temples one needs to keep in mind the figure of the human body, why make them all the same, based on the same body, both in front and from the back? And why not vary them the same way the human figure is varied? ... but these are measurements that are sophomoric and the product of useless imaginings. Now, in order to claim some knowledge of painting, Vitruvius speaks of the consideration of the perfect human body and about how good sculptors and painters in order to make it give it a height of ten faces, and I say that according to them they have read and they say that this proportion is based on the knowledge of the measurement and that it happens that without it it is not possible to have proportion or consideration because those who are not cognisant of this do not count.

[...] The figure of a well-proportioned and beautiful man is not the same on horseback as on foot. It would therefore be good to change the proportions because on a horse he is higher than our line of vision ... For example the distance to the chin or the beard we could make bigger and greater ... because otherwise the lower lip is not visible ... and the upper one is more thin thanks to the distance that separates it from the eye; and what happens to the nose ... the lip becomes bigger and the ear and the nose more aquiline because from below it does not appear ... and the forehead higher and straighter. And the remedy for the ... of the head that ... would vacillate and for this one should provide perfect proportions for things and leave superfluities. But when is this done well? Not often, as it is shown. It would variety never be permitted ... would be either perfect nor worthy of the name. Anyway, I would not be happy to see a beautiful, well-proportioned woman, no matter from which point of view, however extravagant, not only lose her beauty in order to, I would say, increase in size according to the law of vision, but no longer appear beautiful, and, in fact become monstrous.

representation • truth • illusion

El Greco
1541–1614

Jacques Perret

Des Fortifications et artifices, architecture et perspective, 1601

65., 66. Jaques Perret. *Des Fortifications et artifices, architecture et perspective.* 1601. Aerial views of two town prototypes designed by Perret, architect and engineer of King Henry the IV of France.

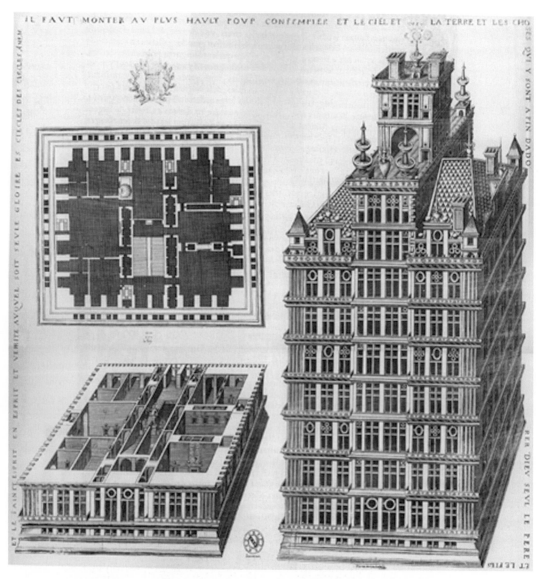

67. Jaques Perret. *Des Fortifications et artifices, architecture et perspective.* 1601. Aerial view, plan and section of an extraordinary eleven-floor building.

Federigo Zuccaro (1543–1609)

The Idea of Painters, Sculptors and Architects (1608)

Federigo studied painting under his elder brother Taddeo (1529–1566), the chief exponent of the mannerist tradition in Rome during the mid-sixteenth century. In 1553, he established the Academy of Saint Luke in his own Palazzo in that city, becoming 'Principe' there in 1590 (Pevsner, 1940). His writings, like those of Lomazzo, bear the neo-Scholastic, neoplatonic stamp of the counter-reformation (Schlosser, 1979, 388). According to Federigo, the work of art, '*disegno externo*', or external design proceeds directly from the mind of the artist, which, as it participates directly in the mind of God, contains an a priori 'Idea' of perfect beauty, '*disegno interno*', or internal design. Personal judgement and subjective contemplation are held up as the supreme arbiters in design decisions.

Further reading Blunt, 1940; Croce, 1964; Gordon, 1948; Hauser, 1951, 128; Heikamp, 1959, 1960; Mahon, 1947; Rosci, 1956; Wittkower, 1943, 1973.

Federigo Zuccaro
(1543–1609)

Chapter III. Definition of Internal Design

Accepting that there is such a thing as what is called internal design in general, I propose a definition for it. This is because it is logical that once one has explained the meaning of a word, one then passes onto the essence of the thing. And, basically, I say that design is not material, it is not body-like, but it is rather without any substance whatsoever. It is, in fact, form, idea, order, rule, state and object of the intellect, the stuff which intentions are made, and which is also to be found in all external things, whether divine or human. Following the doctrine of the philosophers, I declare that internal design in general is an Idea that forms representations expressly and distinctly in the intellect of the intended thing that is, also, an integral part of the intellect. And in order to better understand this definition, one must observe that there are two kinds of operations, one external, that involves drawing, forming, painting, sculpting, making. And the other internal, that involves intention and will. And as it is necessary that all the external operations have a term to describe them, in order to be understood and perfect, that is the thing operated on, as in drawing and painting end up in a made and coloured thing. Sculpture yields the Colossus; architecture yields the Palazzo, the Temple or the theatre. In this way it is necessary for the internal operation to have a product in order to be complete and perfect ... Design is a known thing and object, in which the intellect knows what things are represented in it.

Chapter XII. On Sensitive Human Design

In order to better deal with the formation of internal human design in general, I want to demonstrate how necessary it is in order for it to be formed in our intellect, and that the internal sense, that is fantasy, be cogitated at the same moment. The one will see clearly that there are other designs outside the external and internal intellect, and that to divine sufficiently and completely the design it is necessary after having divided it into internal and external, to divide again, between sensible and intellectual and these in turn are divided into speculative and practical. Thus it is sensible to subdivide even more between sensed, fantasised and cogitated. These are divisions that may seem new, and somewhat closer to caprice than to truth. Nevertheless, in the present discourse we will demonstrate their truth, necessity and propriety and as the same philosopher of the book on the soul [Aristotle] teaches this beautiful doctrine.

aesthetisation of architecture • archaic beliefs • body model

Vincenzo Scamozzi (1552–1616)

Of The Idea of Universal Architecture (1615)

This is the last treatise to provide, as the title implies, a grandiloquent, bombastic, pompous defence of the notion that architectural compositional rules were absolute and that a universal vision of architecture was possible, combining both civil and military concerns (de la Croix, 1960). It was the bulkiest of its kind written in Italy (Wittkower, 1962, 123), with its over one thousand pages. It is divided into two parts. The first is speculative and attempts to present architecture both as an art whose purpose is to please and persuade, like rhetoric, and as an empirical science. Like Lomazzo and Zuccaro, he pins his theoretical discussion on a faith in the existence of the platonic Idea, a kind of unvariable inner sense of perfection (Panofsky, 1960, 1968). The second is a practical handbook in the tradition of Serlio, on the orders but with claims to more exhaustive treatment (Herrmann, 1958). The book was debated often by the Académie Royale d'Architecture and in general widely read and translated in the seventeenth century.

Further reading Barbieri, 1952; Barocchi, 1960–1962; De la Croix, 1960; Donin, 1948; Germann, 1980, 156–157; Gordon, 1975; Jannaco, 1961; Pallucchini, 1936, 1961; Puppi, 1967; Wittkower, 1962, 123, 1973; Zoubov, 1960.

Volume I, Chapter I, p.3

What Architecture is: On the Power of the Title of Architect, and How He is Able to Speculate on All the Beautiful Forms Thanks to His Idea

Because all the sciences and all the Fine Arts are praised, commended and held in high esteem and honour either by their capacity for speculation or for the certainty of their demonstrations, and because they are held as excellent either thanks to the nobility of the subject that we deal with here, that is how they can be used to govern the attention of mankind and to administer republics and reigns, or thanks to the practicality of their results, consequently, if we pursue this consideration, without any doubt we will discover that Architecture is not only a science, but that in fact it is the greatest of all sciences, and among all the sciences truly the worthiest and deserving of every praise. This is because, as we will demonstrate, it is sublime in its speculations, beyond doubt in its demonstrations, and the noblest in subject with which it deals. It is also the most excellent in the method it uses to demonstrate, the most necessary to political and civil life thanks to the commodity that it brings to the human race because it is the only one that embellishes the world . . .

Vitruvius justly said, after all, that *Architecture was a science endowed with several disciplines and erudition that are carried out in the other arts*. And because, as we have already said, the sciences occupy the first position of nobility and certainty, so it is that Architecture without a doubt resides among the principle sciences. It is capable of embracing the multiplicity of the disciplines which are subaltern to it and of the kinds of erudition that adorn it. First among them is mathematics, and all the doctrines that it supports. [. . .]

On the basis of the authority of Vitruvius, Plato, Aristotle, Pappus and many others that I do not mention, one sees that Architecture, undoubtedly, is a speculative science, excellent in doctrine and erudition and extremely noble and singular in the way it investigates the causes and reason of things that are related to it. And, as has been demonstrated countless times, Architecture is manifestly a science, as Plato said, because it has its own way of demonstrating that is certain and beyond doubt and because it can be taught and demonstrated like mathematics and other similar sciences, as Aristotle would say. And it demonstrates how to build good, useful and beautifully ornamented buildings and to know and understand the principle of things and that it always leads to practical results. This is also why it is always easy to understand the feelings, the reasoning and also the greater intelligence of its masters. [. . .]

Vincenzo
Scamozzi
1552–1616

Architecture can be thought of in two ways: one, pertaining to its excellence and purity of science, and one pertaining to the aims of the work. In this case, as Savio would say, it is the equal of all the sciences and all the liberal arts, not only in theory but also in practice. Because, as a philosopher considers bodies in their nature simply by way of their causes and in abstract and without any material related to them, so the practical physicist considers their organisation with their parts and members. That is why it is non-scientific. Therefore, by speculating with his Idea, with his intellect in other words, the architect discovers the causes of all forms, and parts of buildings and their material, and efficient causes and their aims (that are first to be found in intentionality). This is what makes Architecture a pure form of science.

Volume II, Book 6, Chapter V, p.16

[. . .] And if we proceed examining well in general all the things that they (the Moderns) have believed and declared we find that everything is based on the opinions of Vitruvius, or else they hardly deviate from them. So much so that one could say that the greatest part have not experienced the proportions of the antique buildings. They have neither seen them, nor observed them, not even the best examples which are living sources and embody all the forms of the most perfect ornaments.

But returning to the columns, the Tuscan cannot be reduced to six modules as the Moderns claim it can, nor to seven as Vitruvius and, similarly, Pliny write. He mentions that the Tuscan has seven modules, and the Doric six, and the Ionic and Corinthian both nine modules, although the Temple of Diana at Ephesus contained eight modules, and above only seven. And both used the Roman order that was in use for temples then. In such a way that one and the other can be made very small when they are compared to all the orders and placed on the level above the others below as desired. And all the more when they are without bases and without capitals, because all the shaft of all these columns gets bigger as it does with the other orders as they pass from hand to hand. So it is that the Moderns shape these columns that are thicker than the orders that are slimmer and more delicate such as the Corinthian and other similar ones.

archaic beliefs • body model • classical canon • antiquity • abuses

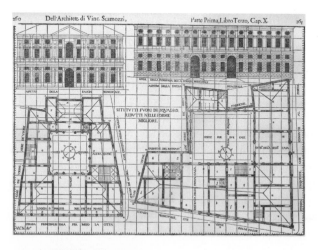

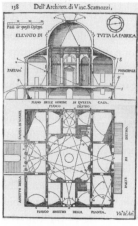

68. Vincenzo Scamozzi. *Dell'Idea dell'architettura universale*. 1615. Façades and plans of buildings inscribed in a grid framework. 69b. Section and plan demonstrating the penetration of sunlight in the building.

Daniel Speckle

Architectura, 1589

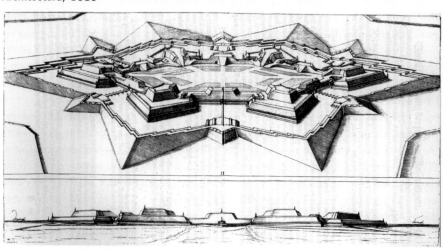

69. Daniel Speckle. *Architectura*. 1589. Two views of a town illustrating the new kind of optimal fortification whose angular bastions and low wall profile is designed with the help of geometry by Speckle, architect and engineer from Strasbourg.

Teofilo Gallaccini (1564–1641)

Treatise on the Errors of the Architects (written 1621; published 1767)

This architectural critic was not an architect but an amateur – a physician by education. Although written in the early seventeenth century, his work appeared in print only once attacks on the baroque came into fashion. Its character is that of a moralistic polemic against the unhealthy, dishonest excesses of mannerist princely architecture. It called for a return to the rationality and virtue embodied in nature. Far ahead of its time, it stood in sharp contrast to the more dominant dogmatic, mystifying spirit of Lomazzo, Zuccaro and Scamozzi and heralds in the functionalist approach of Laugier, and the followers of Lòdoli of the eighteenth century – when, in fact, it was published for the first time.

Further reading Battisti, 1959; Kaufmann, 1952; Schlosser, 1979.

Teofilo Gallaccini
1564–1641

(P.3) Part One. Preface

Medicine is a science truly salutary, praiseworthy and, in its origins, divine, and more ancient that any other, a marvellous natural magic, imitator of nature and her minister, joined by a common good not only for mankind but also for lowly animals, plants and minerals; one of the things it does is to study poisons: not because poison is its aim, that is taken for granted, but in order to conserve health and consequently longevity of life. Nor is it for use since it is so opposed to life, and the enemy of nature and all living things. It is because from its knowledge it is possible to block its effects and to prolong life. So with Architecture, principal minister to the glory of Princes, Republics, imitator of the works of nature, guarantor of human comforts, of public and private ornaments, of the defence of all states, in peace as well as in war, and in their conservation. This expertise, or art is envied by Princes and glorious noble people because it is like imitating the supreme Architect of the marvellous and immense structure of the Universe (from whence it arises that there is not one man who if he not be deprived of invention or of the use of his intellect and does not derive pleasure from construction). The Kings, Emperors, Monarchs of the world and Popes, owe their power in great part to the way in which it represents their heroic virtue, and their magnificence. Architecture is like a goodness, a political ornament, extremely noble in appearance, however diverse the buildings of the City or State. In Architecture, I say, knowledge of all the errors, that occur all the time, is one of the things (although for its natural condition it would be damaging) to warn against if one wishes to please. In so doing, our aim is not to teach architects to commit errors. Because, just as in all contemplative science one finds the truth of things and not lies. And in every moral science it is necessary to find the good, the just, the honest and the appropriate. Thus the aim of every art is nor to make errors in acting, nor to ever depart from the straight reason of their discipline. Because among the human arts there is not one that teaches how to sin – of which the only master is misuse. The aim here is to introduce knowledge of the errors of a misused Architecture, so that a member of the profession is able to avoid them, and to become excellent.

(P.23) Chapter II. Of the Errors That Are to be Found in Foundations

The errors in buildings that are to be found in the establishment of foundations are very damaging. This is because they are responsible for the ruin of the entire building and cannot be corrected without the greatest difficulty and without incurring the greatest danger. But it is not possible to have perfect knowledge of these unless one knows beforehand what the different kinds of foundations are. Let us say, then, that foundations are either in dry, solid and firm ground, or in a marshy area, or in water. One might also say there are natural foundations and others that are artificial . . .

Part II, Chapter VII. Of the Errors that Occur in the Non-observance of Decorum

Among all the errors that are committed by Architects, one goes against the perfection and the beauty of buildings. And thanks to it their appearance shows no sign of grace or nobility. Neither do they produce a sense of marvel in those who behold them. And this arises from the non-observance of decorum, which I think is easy to understand once the following has been said. Let us say, then, that decorum is nothing but a kind of beauty and a grace in things that is born from a certain correct distribution, according to which every part goes with every other. But to apply this definition one must say that the decorum of buildings is none other than a beauty residing in the fitness of the parts among themselves that occurs depending on a correct and proportional disposition is given to each part that is suited to it. To convey this idea of the errors in this way, let us say that buildings imitate the human body, and thus are composed of members, because we find in it the head, the shoulders, the hips, the belly and the legs. And to each member are assigned its particular ornaments and the ones that belong to the shoulders, hips and the rest cannot be applied to the head, and vice versa. It is of the utmost importance, therefore, to make sure the proper ornaments go in the right places. . . .

Teofilo Gallaccini
1564–1641

Chapter IX. Of the Errors of Superfluity and of Defect

Nature, who is the Mistress of the Arts, is never defective nor superfluous in her works. Neither should any of the imitative arts be overly prolix nor overly niggardly. In the right kind of Architecture, that is the kind that imitates Nature, must not go against necessity, nor let itself do anything that is not necessary. But nevertheless buildings often err in this way, in being superfluous, that is not necessary. And the errors of niggardliness are of different types: they are either defects in the right thickness of the walls, or of the proportioned space of places, according to length and height; or in the absence of certain parts that reinforce and secure the foundations; or the defects of lighting.

classical canon • antiquity • abuses

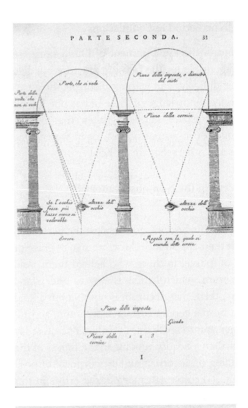

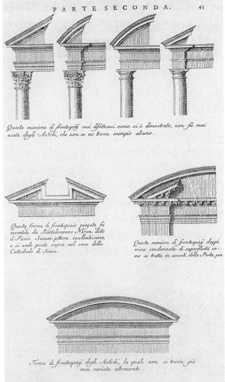

70., 70b. Teofilo Gallaccini. *Sopra gli errorri degli architetti.* 1767 (written 1621). Illustrations of errors of architecture that Gallacini, a medical doctor, claimed resembled 'poisons'.

Ben Jonson (1572–1637)

Neptune's Triumph (1624)

This masque – a masque is a Renaissance court entertainment, lavishly produced and involving highly allegorical action accompanied with song and dance – contains a thinly veiled attack on the architect Inigo Jones, the first English architect to be inspired by Italian-inspired Renaissance architectural forms. This personal invective by the famous poet and playwright, presenting Jones as a charlatan upstart, is the expression of a widespread resistance among the artists of the time to the idea that an architect was anything more than a lowly manual worker, or cook as he is portrayed here (Gordon, 1975). This is one episode in the long struggle by architects to assert themselves as on a par with other liberal artists during the Renaissance.

Further reading Orgel and Strong, 1973.

Poet
You are not His Majesty's confectioner? Are you?

Cook
No, but one that has a good title to the room, his
Master-cook. What are you, Sir?

Poet
The most unprofitable of his servants. I, sir, the poet. A
Kind of a Christmas Engine; one that is used at least once
A year for a trifling instrument of wit or so.

Cook
Were you ever a Cook?

Poet
A Cook? No surely.

Cook
Then you can be no good poet: for a good poet differs
Nothing from a master-cook. Either art is the
Wisdom of mind.

Poet
As how, Sir?

Cook
Expected, I am, by my place, to know how to please the
Palate of the guests; so, you, are to know the palate
Of the times: study the several tastes, what every Nation,
The Spaniard, the Dutch, the French, the Walloon, the
Neapolitan, the Briton, the Sicilian, can expect from you.

Poet
That were a heavy and hard task, to satisfy expectation,
Who is so severe an exactness of duties; ever a tyrannous

Mistress: and most times a pressing enemy.

Cook

She is a powerful great Lady, Sir, at all times, and must
Be satisfied: So must her sister, Madam Curiosity, who
Has as dainty a palate as she, and these will expect.

Poet

But, what if they expect more than they understand?

Cook

That's all one, Mr Poet, you are bound to satisfy them.
For, there is a palate of the Understanding, as well as of the
Senses. The Taste is taken with good relishes, the sight
With fair objects, the Hearing with delicate sounds, the
Smelling with pure scents, the Feeling with soft and plump
Bodies, but the Understanding with all these: for all
Which you must begin at the Kitchen. There, the Art of
Poetry was learned, and found out, or nowhere: and the
Same day, with the Art of Cookery.

Poet

I should have given it rather to the cellar, if my suffrage had been asked.

Cook

O, you are for the Oracle of the Bottle, I see Hogshead
Trismegistus: He is your Pegasus. Thence flows the
spring of your muses, from that hoof.
Seduced Poet, I do say to thee, –
A Boiler, range, and dresser were the fountains
Of all the knowledge, in the universe,
And that's the kitchen. Where a master-cook –
Thou dost not know the man! nor can thou know him!
Till thou hast served some years in that deep school,
That's both Nurse, and Mother of the Arts,
And hear him read, interpret, and demonstrate.
A master-cook! Why, he is the man of men,
For a professor! He designs, he draws,
He paints, he carves, he builds, he fortifies,
Makes citadels of curious fowl and fish,
Some he dry-ditches, some motes round with broths;
Mounts marrow-bones; cuts fifty-angled custards;
Rears bulwark pies; and, for his outer works,
He raises ramparts of immortal crust;
And teaches all the tactics at one dinner:
What ranks what files to put his dishes in;
The whole Art Military! Then he knows
The influence of the stars, upon his meats;
And all their seasons, tempers, qualities,

Ben Jonson
1572–1637

[176]

And so, to fit his relishes, and sauces!
He has Nature in a pot! above all the chemists,
Or bare-breeched brethren of the Rosie-Crosse!
He is an architect, an engineer,
A soldier, a physician, a philosopher,
A general mathematician!

design methodology • professional practice • education

Ben Jonson
1572–1637

Pierre Le Muet

Manière de bien bâtir pour toutes sortes de personnes, 1623

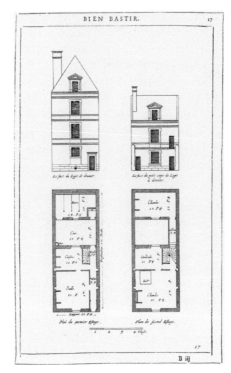

71. Pierre Le Muet. *Manière de bien bâtir pour toutes sortes de personnes*. 1623. Plan and elevation of one of the simplest and lower cost building prototypes for a town house. The book deals with thirteen different sites and the prototypes are developed in a systematic almost combinatorial manner. It contains Le Muet's inventions but also reflects contemporary Parisian practice. Aimed as a practical guide, it proved to be extremely popular, reprinted in fifty-three editions.

Joseph Furttenbach

Architectura Universalis, 1635

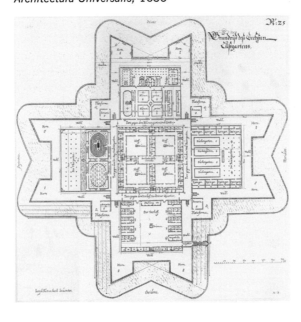

72. Joseph Furttenbach. *Architectura Universalis*. 1635. Plan of a town prototype with palace building and gardens.

Sir Henry Wotton (1568–1639)

Elements of Architecture (1624)

The author was one of the most cultured men of his day and served many years in Italy as English Ambassador to Venice. Upon his return he published his book, the first English treatise to be based on High Renaissance architectural theory (O.C.A., 1220). Wittkower (1974, 99) believes that his extremely critical analytical method stems from his early friendship with Francis Bacon. Wotton was influenced by Vitruvius and Alberti, but, as one of the first independent architectural critics in history, the one dominating idea he adopts in his treatise is the moral duty to "censure" architects (ibid.). The book addresses itself not so much to professionals as to the increasingly interested architectural public of the court of James I and Charles I (ibid.). It was reprinted and incorporated into other publications no less than sixteen times before 1750 (ibid.).

Further reading Harris, 1990.

Now as almost all those which have delivered the elements of logic do usually conclude with a chapter touching method; so I am here seized with a kind of critical spirit and desirous need to shut up these building elements with some methodical direction how to censure fabrics already raised. For indeed without some way to contract our judgement, which among other so many particulars would be lost by diffusion; I should think it almost harder to be a good censurer than a good architect. Because the working part may be helped with deliberation but with the judging must flow from an extemporal habit. Therefore (not to leave this last Piece without some light) I could with him that cometh to examine any noble Work, first of all to examine himself, whether perchance the sight of any things before (which remain like impressed forms) have not made him apt to think nothing good, but that which is best; for his humour was too sore. Next, before he come to settle any imaginable opinion, let him by all means seek to inform himself precisely of the age of the work upon which he must pass his doom. And if he shall find the apparent decays to exceed the proportion of time then let him conclude without further inquisition, as an absolute decree, that either the materials were too slight, or the seat is nought. Now, after these premises, if the houses be found to bear his years well (which the method of censuring is contrary to the method of composing) from the ornaments (which first allure the eye) to the more essential members, till at last he be able to form this conclusion that the work is commodious, firm and delightful; which (as I said in the beginning) are the three capital conditions required in good buildings, by all authors both ancient and modern. And this is, as I may term it the most scientific way of censuring.

design methodology

Michelangelo Buonarroti, the Younger (1568–1646)

Untitled Draft of a Letter to Pope Urban VIII about the Palazzo Barberini in Rome (c.1625)

The author, grandnephew of Michelangelo, is known mainly as a poet in the 'rustic' tradition of Tasso (Jannaco, 1961, 312–319; Rossi, 1968). The following text appears to have been written in response to a request by Maffei Barberini, Pope Urban VIII, for consultation regarding his projected palace on the Quirinal Hill in Rome (Blunt, 1958b; Hibbard, 1971, 222–226; Wittkower, 1973, 112–115). This proposal is noteworthy for transferring to architecture the notion of 'sprezzatura', usually translated as 'wilful neglect', made famous by Castiglione's *Courtier* in relation to art, literature and manners (Waddy, 1975).

Further reading Shearman, 1963.

Francis Bacon
1561–1626

I say first that one should decide whether the present building should receive additional acccessories that improve it and make it more commodious or whether you would like to give more nobility to a building ... and this with a certain disharmonious disunion. I say that there are two ways of doing things well: either with magnificence and pomp, or else truly with a *sprezzatura* that, carried out successfully, makes it more pleasing to the eye. In the first case, one will search to give the particular building everything in terms of fitness to the site. In the second, it will be necessary ... to use hard work and grace, because lacking in the first requirement [fitness] it makes a virtue out of necessity. [...] *Sprezzatura* in buildings can be of two types. The first is when you do not wish to make an incremental change to a building, such as enlarging a room, improving the lighting conditions, broadening the stairs or that kind of thing. That kind of *sprezzatura* is not the one that I am considering here because it is far from being relevant to the immediate concern of the present design. The other *sprezzatura* with just as much concern for commodity is to be seen just as much of an intrinsic form which does not profess to create a sublime thing but rather something with 'maniera' or rustic or grotto-like or something of the same nature, representing something which is new and consequently, by the same turn, more attractive. Whichever concept of *sprezzatura* one chooses, I think it is necessary one way or the other to decide which approach to adopt.

anticlassicism • deformation • freedom • naturalism

Francis Bacon (1561–1626)

'On Building' (1625), The Essays (1597–1625)

Bacon, the renowned English philosopher, upturned one of the basic tenets of Renaissance classicism – the search for aesthetic pleasure based on harmonious proportions and ornamentation – in favour of an extreme functionalist approach when he advocated that utility be the sole guiding principle in domestic architecture, even at the cost of 'uniformity'. It marks one of the first precedents in what was to become the 'rigorist' revolt against the excesses of the baroque by Gallacini, Laugier and the followers of Lòdoli.

Further reading de Zurko, 1957.

Houses are built to live in, and not to look on; therefore let use be preferred before uniformity, except where both may be had. Leave the goodly fabrics of houses, for beauty only, to the enchanted palaces of the poets; who built them with small cost. He that builds a fair house upon an ill seat, committeth himself to prison. [. . .]

I say you cannot have a perfect palace except you have two several sides; a side for the banquet, as is spoken of in the book of Hester, and a side for the household; the one for feasts and triumphs and the other for dwelling. I understand both these sides to be not only returns, but parts of the front; and to be uniform without, though severally partitioned within; and to be on both sides of a great and stately tower in the midst of the front, that, as it were, joineth them together on either hand. I would have on the side of the banquet, in front, one only goodly room above the stairs, of some forty foot high; and under it a room for a dressing or preparing place at times of triumphs. On the other side, which is the household side, I wish it divided at the first, into a hall and a chapel (with partition between) both of good state and bigness; and those not to go all the length, but to have at the further end a winter and a summer parlour, both fair. And under these rooms, a fair and large cellar sunk under ground; and likewise some privy kitchens, with butteries and pantries, and the like. [. . .]

Francis Bacon
1561–1626

Beyond this front is there to be a fair court, but three sides of it, of a far lower building than the front. And in all the four corners of that court fair staircases, cast into turrets, on the outside, and not within the row of buildings themselves. But those towers are not to be of the height of the front, but rather proportionable to the lower building. Let the court not be paved, for that striketh up a great heat in summer, and much cold in winter. But only some side alleys, with a cross, and the quarters to graze, being kept shorn, but not too near shorn. The row of return on the banquet side, let it be all stately galleries: in which galleries let there be three, or five fine cupolas in the length of it, placed at equal distance; and fine coloured windows of several works. On the household side, chambers of presence and ordinary entertainment, and some bed chambers; and let all three sides be a double house, without through lights on the sides, that you may have rooms from the sun, both for forenoon and afternoon. Cast it also, that you may have rooms for both the summer and winter; shady for summer, and warm for winter. You shall have sometimes fair houses full of glass, that one cannot tell where to become to be out of the sun or cold. For inbowed windows, I hold them of good use; (in cities, indeed, upright do better, in respect of the uniformity towards the street) for they be pretty retiring places for conference; and besides, they keep both the wind and sun off; for what which would strike almost through the room doth scarse pass the window. But let them be but few, four in the court, on the sides only.

Beyond this court, let there be an inward court, of the same square and height; which is to be environed with the garden on all sides; and in the inside, cloistered on all sides, upon decent and beautiful arches, as high as the first storey. On the under storey, towards the garden, let it be turned into a grotto, or place of shade, or estivation. And only have opening and windows towards the garden; and be level upon the floor, no whit sunken under ground, to avoid all dampishness. And let there be a fountain, or some fair work of statuary in the midst of this court; and to be paved as the other court was. These buildings to be for privy lodgings on both sides; and the end for privy galleries. Whereof you must foresee that one of them be for an infirmary, if the prince or any special person should be sick, with chambers, bed-chamber, antecamera, and recamera, joining to it. This upon the second storey. Upon the ground storey, a fair gallery, open, upon pillars; and upon pillars, to take the prospect and freshness of the garden. At both corners of the further side, by way of return, let there be two delicate cabinets, daintily paved, richly hanged, glazed with crystal glass, and a rich cupola in the midst; and all other elegancy that may be thought upon. In the upper gallery too, I wish that there may be, if the palace will yield it, some fountains running in diverse places from the wall, with some fine avoidances. And thus much for the model of the palace.

efficiency • economisation • fit • utility • systemisation of space distribution

René Descartes (1596–1650)

Discourse on Method (1637)

René Descartes
1596–1650

This brief passage on cities is no less radical than the rest of the *Discourse* in its espousal of rationality. It puts forth the novel view that new cities built *ex-nihilo* are by definition better than ones built up piecemeal over centuries because they eliminate disorder. Never before had the rejection of historical precedent and the search for innovation based on scientifically defined method been so absolute.

Part II

I was then in Germany, to which country I had been attracted by the wars which had not yet come to an end. And as I was returning from the coronation of the Emperor to join the army, the setting in of winter detained me in a place where, having no society to divert me, nor cares or passions to trouble me, I stayed shut up the whole day alone in a stove-heated room, and where I had absolute leisure to pursue my own thoughts. One of the first considerations that occurred to me was that there is very often less perfection in works composed of several portions, and carried out by the hands of various masters, than those on which one individual alone has worked. Thus we see that buildings planned and carried out by one architect alone are usually more beautiful and better proportioned than those which many architects have tried to put in order and improve, making use of old walls which were built with other ends in view. In the same way also, those ancients cities which, originally were mere villages, have become in the process of time great towns, are usually badly constructed in comparison with those which are regularly laid out on a plain by a surveyor who is free to follow his own ideas. Even though, considering their buildings each one apart, there is often as much or more display of skill in the one case than in the other, the former have large buildings and small buildings indiscriminately placed together, thus rendering the streets crooked and irregular, so that it might be said that it was chance rather than the will of men guided by reason that led to such an arrangement. And if we consider that this happens despite the fact that from all time there have been certain officials who have had the special duty of looking after the buildings of private individuals in order that they may be public ornaments, we shall understand how difficult it is to bring about much that is satisfactory in operating only upon the works of others . . .

It is true that we do not find that all the houses in a town are razed to the ground for the sole reason that the town is to be rebuilt in another fashion with streets made more beautiful; but at the same time we see that many people cause their own houses to be knocked down in order to rebuild them, and that sometimes they are forced so to do where there is danger of the house falling on themselves, and when the foundations are not secure. From such examples I argued to myself that there was no plausibility in the claim of any private individual to reform a state by altering everything, and by overturning it throughout, in order to set it right again.

design methodology • urbanisation of architecture • planning

Galileo Galilei (1564–1642)

Dialogues Concerning Two New Sciences (1638)

Galileo Galilei
1564–1642

This work is the first exposition of the modern scientific theory of proportion. Employing empirical observation and geometric verification, Galileo disproves the neo-platonic principle that 'harmonious' proportions that derive from the perfect 'Forms' of the divine 'Idea' are universally applicable; he shows that, on the contrary, proportions necessarily vary according to the size and material of natural bodies. There can be no doubt that this theory and this type of reasoning revolutionised architectural thinking and practice (Tzonis and Lefaivre, 1984b).

Further reading Dijksterhuis, 1964; Geymonat, 1965; Tzonis and Lefaivre, 1984b.

Salviati: The constant activity which you Venetians display in your famous arsenal suggests to the studious mind a large field for investigation, especially that part of the work which involves mechanics; for in this department all types of instruments and machines are constantly being constructed by many artisans, among whom there must be some who, partly by inherited experience and partly by their own observations, have become highly expert and clever in explanation.

Sagredo: You are quite right. Indeed, I myself, being curious by nature, frequently visit this place for the mere pleasure of observing the work of those who, on account of their superiority over other artisans, we call 'first rank men'. Conference with them has often helped me in the investigation of certain effects including not only those which are striking, but also those which are recondite and almost incredible. At times also I have been put to confusion and driven to despair of ever explaining something for which I could not account, but which my senses told me to be true. And notwithstanding the fact that what the old man told us a little while ago is proverbial and commonly accepted, yet it seemed to me altogether false, like many another saying which is current among the ignorant; for I think they introduce these expressions in order to give the appearance of knowing something about matters which they do not understand.

Salviati: You refer, perhaps, to that last remark of his when we asked the reason why they employed stocks, scaffolding and bracing of larger dimensions for launching a big vessel than they do for a small one; and he answered that they did this in order to avoid the danger of the ship parting under its own heavy weight [*vasta mole*], a danger to which small boats are not subject?

Sagredo: Yes, that is what I mean; and I refer especially to his last assertion which I have always regarded as a false, though current, opinion; namely, that in speaking of these and other similar machines one cannot argue from the small to the large, because many devices which succeed on a small scale do not work on a large scale. Now, since mechanics has its foundation in geometry, where mere size cuts no figure, I do not see that the properties of circles, triangles, cylinders, cones and other solid figures will change with their size. If, therefore, a large machine be constructed in such a way that its parts bear to one another the same ratio as in a smaller one, and if the smaller is sufficiently strong for the purpose for which it was designed, I do not see why the larger also should not be able to withstand any severe and destructive tests to which it may be subjected.

Salviati: The common opinion is here absolutely wrong. Indeed, it is so far wrong that precisely the opposite is true, namely, that many machines can be constructed even more perfectly on a large scale than on a small; thus, for instance, a clock which indicates and strikes the hour can be made more accurate on a large scale than on a small. There are some intelligent people who maintain this same opinion, but on more reasonable grounds, when they cut loose from geometry and argue that the better performance of the large machine is owing to the imperfections and variations of the material. Here I trust you will not charge me with arrogance if I say that imperfections in the material, even those which are great enough to invalidate the clearest mathematical proof, are not sufficient to explain the deviations observed between machines in the concrete and in the abstract. Yet I shall say it and will affirm that, even if the imperfections did not exist and matter were absolutely perfect, unalterable and free from all accidental variations, still the mere fact that it is matter makes the larger machine, built of the same material and in the same proportion as the smaller, correspond with exactness to the smaller in every respect except that it will not be so strong or so resistant against violent treatment; the larger the machine, the greater its weakness. Since I assume matter to be unchangeable and always the same, it is clear that we are no less able to treat this constant and invariable property in a rigid manner than if it belonged to simple and pure mathematics. Therefore, Sagredo, you would do well to change the opinion which you, and perhaps also many other students of mechanics, have entertained concerning the ability of machines and structures to resist external disturbances, thinking that when they are built of the same material and maintain the same ratio between parts, they are able equally, or rather proportionally, to resist or yield to such external disturbances and blows. For we can demonstrate by geometry that the large machine is not proportionally stronger than the small. Finally, we may say that, for every machine and structure, whether artificial or natural, there is set a necessary limit beyond which neither art nor nature can pass; it is here understood, of course, that the material is the same and the proportion preserved. [. . .]

Salviati: [. . .] And this which I have said about the ability to support itself must be understood to apply also to other tests; so that if a piece of scantling [*corrente*] will carry the weight of ten similar to itself, a beam [*trave*] having the same proportions will not be able to support ten similar beams.

Please observe, gentlemen, how facts which at first seem improbable, will, even on scant explanation, drop the cloak which has hidden them and stand forth in naked and simple beauty. Who does not know that a horse falling from a height of three or four cubits will break his bones, while a dog falling from the same height or a cat from a height of eight or ten cubits will suffer no injury? Equally

Galileo Galilei
1564–1642

harmless would be the fall of a grasshopper from a tower or the fall of an ant from the distance of the moon. Do not children fall with impunity from heights which would cost their elders a broken leg or perhaps a fractured skull? And just as smaller animals are proportionately stronger and more robust than the larger, so also smaller plants are able to stand up better than larger. I am certain you both know that an oak two hundred cubits [*braccia*] high would not be able to sustain its own branches if they were distributed as in a tree of ordinary size; and that nature cannot produce a horse as large as twenty ordinary horses or a giant ten times taller than an ordinary man unless by miracle or by greatly altering the proportions of his limbs and especially of his bones, which would have to be considerably enlarged over the ordinary. Likewise the current belief that, in the case of artificial machines the very large and the small are equally feasible and lasting is a manifest error. Thus, for example, a small obelisk or column or other solid figure can certainly be laid down or set up without danger of breaking, while the very large ones will go to pieces under the slightest provocation, and purely on account of their own weight. And here I must relate a circumstance, which is worthy of your attention, as indeed are all events, which happen contrary to expectation, especially when a precautionary measure turns out to be a cause of disaster. A large marble column was laid out so that its two ends rested each upon a piece of beam; a little later it occurred to a mechanic that, in order to be doubly sure of it not breaking in the middle by its own weight, it would be wise to lay a third support midway; this seemed to all an excellent idea; but the sequel showed that it was quite the opposite, for not many months passed before the column was found cracked and broken exactly above the new middle support. [...]

Galileo Galilei
1564–1642

Second Day

Sagredo: [...] From what has already been demonstrated, you can plainly see the impossibility of increasing the size of structures to vast dimensions either in art or in nature; likewise the impossibility of building ships, palaces, or temples of enormous size in such a way that their oars, yards, beams, iron-bolts, and, in short, all their other parts will hold together; nor can nature produce trees of extraordinary size because the branches would break down under their own weight; so also it would be impossible to build up the bony structures of men, horses, or other animals so as to hold together and perform their normal functions if these animals were to be increased enormously in height; for this increase in height can be accomplished only by employing a material which is harder and stronger than usual, or by enlarging the size of the bones, thus changing their shape until the form and appearance of the animals suggest a monstrosity. This is perhaps what our wise Poet had in mind, when he says, in describing a huge giant:

> Impossible it is to reckon his height,
> So beyond measure is his size.

To illustrate briefly, I have sketched a bone whose natural length has been increased three times and whose thickness has been multiplied until, for a correspondingly large animal, it would perform the same function, which the small bone

[185]

performs for its small animal. From figure 73 you can see how out of proportion the enlarged bone appears. Clearly then if one wishes to maintain in a great giant the same proportion of limb as that found in an ordinary man he must either find a harder and stronger material for making the bones, or he must admit a diminution of strength in comparison with men of medium stature; for if his height be increased inordinately he will fall and be crushed under his own weight. Whereas, if the size of a body be diminished, the strength of that body is not diminished in the same proportion; indeed the smaller the body the greater its relative strength. Thus a small dog could probably carry on his back two or three dogs of his own size; but I believe that a horse could not carry even one of his own size.

mechanisation of architecture • scientification

Galileo Galilei
1564–1642

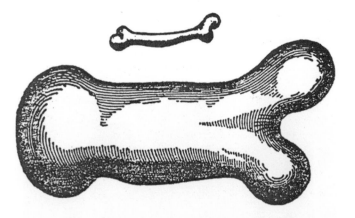

73. Galileo Galilei. *Discorsi intorno a due nuove scienze*. 1638. Illustration showing that, in nature, the proportions of two homologous skeleton elements cannot be invariant when the size changes, contradicting traditional theories.

74. Galileo Galilei. *Discorsi intorno a due nuove scienze*. 1638. Illustration showing a loaded cantilevered element.

André Félibien

Description de la grotte de Versailles, 1676

75. André Félibien. *Description de la grotte de Versailles*. 1676 Engraving of the grotto of Versailles designed by Charles Perrault and built in 1664. The sculpture represents Apollo, the Sun – and symbolically Louis XIV – returning to his mother, Thetis surrounded by her nymphs and, on the two sides, his horses with the Tritons.

Georg Andreas Böckler

Architectura Curiosa Nova, 1664

 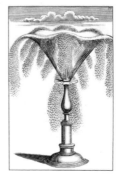

76., 76b., 77., 77b. Georg Andreas Böckler. *Architectura Curiosa Nova*. 1664. Different types of fountains. The book by an architect and engineer treated waterworks as an art form. It contained an inventive typology of shapes of jets generated by mechanical devices.

Roland Fréart de Chambray (1602–?)

Parallel of Antique and Modern Architecture (1650)

In 1640, Roland Fréart de Chambray was sent to Rome with his brother, Paul Fréart de Chantelou, by Richelieu to bring back to Paris the best artists of the time with the aim of making France the new artistic centre of the time. De Chambray, an architect, was a champion of the simplicity of ancient architecture and criticised the liberties of mannerism. His work is a visual comparison of the order's ten most important French and Italian architects from Alberti to Delorme. In it, he seeks to establish the first principles of the ancients as an absolute model. Anticipating the work of such eighteenth-century theoreticians as Germain Boffrand, Marc-Antoine Laugier and Julien David Le Roy, he reduced the number of orders to the original Vitruvian three. The book was extremely well received both in France (Tzonis *et al.*, 1982) and England where it was translated by John Evelyn in 1664.

Further reading Bilodeau, 1997; Blomfield, 1973; Hautecoeur, 1948–1963; Middleton, 1963; Tzonis *et al.*, 1982; Wiebenson, 1993.

p.2. Some architects think that imitation is the work of apprentices and that in order to be masters it is necessary to produce some novelty . . . They believe that in imagining a kind of particular cornice, or something else, that they can create a new order, and that this, and this only, constitutes invention . . . The Doric, Ionic and Corinthian . . . contain all that is not only beautiful but necessary in architecture, there being only three manners of building, without it being necessary to rely on the Tuscan not on the Composite that I purposefully removed to the end of this treatise and detached from these as they are superfluous and almost useless.

p.3. It is the very least of my thoughts to broach novelties. On the contrary, I would, if it were possible, ascend even to the very source of the Orders themselves, and derive from thence the Images, and pure Ideas of these incomparable Masters, who were indeed their first Inventors, and be instructed from their own mouths; since doubtless the further men have wandered from their principles, transplanting them as it were into a strange soil, the more they are become degenerate, and scarce recognisable to their very authors.

p.5. Honest Vitruvius in his time well foresaw the ill consequence which those of the profession would introduce out of their love of novelty, which already began it seems to incline them to libertinism, and the disdain of the Rules of that Art, which ought to remain most sacred and inviolable; so that we must look on this as on a grey-headed evil which grows worse and worse daily, and has become now almost incurable: notwithstanding, would our modern architects but yet fix any limits to the freedom they have taken. . . . But our architects never entering into this consideration, have fallen into an error which admits of no excuse, by forcing the weaker to support the stronger. Scamozzi is the first that has spoken of this in his *Treatise of the Five Orders*, where he assigns to the Corinthian the most eminent place. However, to avoid all contest, I find it safest, never to mix them together at any time, seeing it was never practis'd by the Ancients; [. . .] I went and drew from antiquity itself before examining the modern authors. They are the best books, and their beauty has been universally recognised for the past two thousand years, and it is on the basis of these that one should ground one's studies.

p.6. It is quite simple to precisely determine what the word Order means for architects. Of all the moderns, only Scamozzi has thought of giving a definition. He believes it is a kind of excellence that vastly increases the gracefulness and beauty of sacred or profane buildings ... Father Vitruvius called this 'ordonnance' and this word is today in use among painters when they wish to express the elegant composition of the painting ... Nevertheless, it is not exactly the intention of the architects, and Vitruvius, doing much to explain this to us, added that it is a fitness or regular lay-out of the individual members of a work and a comparison of all the proportions to symmetry.

p.7. It is necessary to approach things in detail and to consider them materially in each of their parts so that it touches the imagination more fully and yields its idea to us through its form. This idea is what we must search out for architecture does not consist in words and so its demonstration must be sensorial and visual. [...] If we wish to define order exactly and to provide an understanding which is clear, one must proceed as in an anatomical study, and say that the column with its base and its capital crowned by an architrave, frieze and cornice form a kind of building that we call an order, then that this is the case with all the other orders, and that the differences between the orders consists in the proportions of their parts and the form of their capitals.

p.22. It is from this consideration that I pulled from among the ranks of the other masters the exceptional Palladio and Scamozzi, who having set themselves the task of imitating antique architecture by the study of its admirable monuments that remain still in the old city of Rome, followed a much more noble manner with much more elegant proportions than those of the school of Vitruvius.

p.24. It would not be fair in this overview to attribute as much rigour to Serlio as to his companion because having set out to follow Vitruvius, who is a famous author and venerated by architects, he completed his task honourably. On the other hand, Vignola took another path, in truth more noble, and the same as the one I too am following here, failed to avoid certain pitfalls. The Doric profile he gives is taken from the first order of the temple of Marcellus, the worthy example of the species that is to be found amidst the antiquities of Rome, of which I too have made a choice to serve as models. With this difference, however, that I observed precisely all the measures of the original which are much altered in the work of this author.

classical canon • antiquity • abuses • precedent • authority • invention

Count Emanuele Tesauro (1591–1675)

The Aristotelian Telescope (1654)

Tesauro was for twenty-four years a Jesuit. In this, his main work, he transferred concepts from Aristotelian rhetoric to all areas of art, including architecture. Hence the allusion to Aristotle in the title of the book. We have here one of the first systematic attempts to look at architecture as a language and to formalise its own particular type of metaphors and symbols. Tesauro was writing for a courtly society, which tended to indulge in 'precieux', 'gongorist', abstruse art forms based on the cult of the pun or epigram ('agutezza') that had to be deciphered in order to be understood. Accordingly, the kind of architectural language which Tesauro was concerned with was one which departed from the common style and spoke only to a select group of 'cognoscenti' (Battisti, 1960). Hence the second allusion in the title, appropriately metaphorical, esoteric and epigrammatic, to the telescope ('*canocchiale*'), the device par excellence for discerning phenomena imperceptible under ordinary conditions. The work enjoyed great popularity, going through over a dozen editions before the end of the century.

Further reading Croce, 1964; Tagliabue, 1955; Tatarkiewicz, 1970–1974, III, 388–395; Weinberg, 1961.

pp.86–87. There is no painting, no sculpture that merits the glorious title of ingenious if it is not epigrammatic or pun-like. And I say the same holds for architecture. Its scholars are called engineers because of the cleverness of the ingenuity of their works. This appears in the many bizarreries of the delightfully playful ornamentation on the façades of sumptuous buildings: florid capitals, arabesque-bearing friezes, triglyphs, metopes, masques, cariatids, terms and medallions. They form metaphors out of stone and mute symbols that add to the delight of the work and the mystery of the thrill. There is no shortage of such expressions of wit and cleverness in military architecture where they manufacture defensive and offensive weapons: emblems swarming with human bodies amidst their shields; rams's heads protruding from walls with their bronze horns; ostriches, scorpions, swans, cranes, all ingenious but fierce and homicidal metaphors. But all this is nothing compared to some of the metaphorical subtleties of some noble architects that would make Nature herself envious. This is the case with the Portico Olympico that pictures the seven liberal arts. It is conceived with so much genius that you would have wished to write a poem about it. It is itself a poem in stone with seven verses. Each one describes one of the seven muses housed in her own school, giving assurances to her disciples of great progress to come where even mutes would have been able to talk. Another great feat of ingenuity is one in which marble is made to speak and, no less, to be heard. This is what an architect from Syracuse did in order to please Dionysius. He made a statue of him that, like the suspicious tyrant he was, always listened to what was said about him by those beholding it. Indeed, he sculpted its ear in such a way, with the right channels and hollows, as to be able to capture what was said and placed it near a location that courtiers frequented. [...] Unhappy courtiers, whom even the stones spied on, testifying to the proverb that 'the walls of the kings have ears'.

Then there is also the ingenuity of an Egyptian architect who, in making on the earth that which nature herself makes most frightful in the secret recesses of the clouds. With a thundering metaphor he made men fall to the ground, then laughed at their terror. In the labyrinth of Egypt, one of the seven miracles of the world, that at each step created another human miracle, there was something even more famous. Once you approached a gate of the temple dedicated to the god of thunder such a loud thunderous clap was released that one thought it was the end of the world.

rhetoric • signification • narrative

Count Emanuele
Tesauro
1591–1675

Jean de La Fontaine (1621–1695)

Account of a Trip to the Limousin (1663)

De La Fontaine was among the first to flout the principle of regularity in architecture, so central to Renaissance classicism, in the name of 'variety'. His own writings, the celebrated **Fables** in particular, display the same stylistic predilection in literary style (Lapp, 1971, 30).

Monsieur Chateauneuf and I lunched very well and proceeded to visit the Prince's quarters. It had been added onto several times, partly under François Ier, partly even earlier by his predecessors. Towards the front was the main building that his father had begun. The three halls in it present, thank God, no symmetry whatsoever and have no bearing or relation to one another. The architect avoided this as much as he could. What François Ier ordered done, judging from the outside, I found most appealing of all. There are many small galleries, small windows, small balconies, small ornaments, without regularity and without order. This makes for something great that is quite delightful.

anticlassicism • deformation • freedom • naturalism

Giovanni Pietro
Bellori
1615–1696

Giovanni Pietro Bellori (1615–1696)

Idea of the Painter, Sculptor, and Architect Chosen from the Superior Natural Beauty of Nature (written 1664; published 1672)

Originally delivered as a lecture before the Academy of S. Luke in Rome (1664), this brief text served as an introduction to Bellori's major theoretical work on the arts (1672), **Vite de pittori, scultori et architetti Moderni** where he attacked the 'Moderns' Michelangelo, Bernini and Borromini, giving prominence instead to Raphael. The book is dedicated to Colbert, who had already founded the Académie Royale d'Architecture (1661). Bellori combined here for the first time the conflicting principles of ideal representation, espoused by the more radical late mannerist theoreticians Lomazzo and Zuccaro, and the Aristotelian notion of imitation (Panofsky, 1960, 1968, 57–63). 'Idea' is redefined in more conservative terms than Lomazzo and Zuccaro as an image of selected and embellished nature. Bellori thus redirected theory of the arts into a new synthesis and was the first to formulate what the French theorists of the seventeenth and eighteenth centuries were to call '*la belle nature*' (Lee, 1967, 14–16).

Further reading Battisti, 1976; Donahue, 1946; Pevsner, 1940; Previtali, 1976; Venturi, 1936.

The idea and deity of beauty current among the ancient scholars was formed in their mind through the constant observation of the most beautiful parts of natural things, whose ugly and vile side gave birth to the other idea that is also a result of experience. This is following what Plato said about the idea of perfect cognition of anything having to begin in nature. Quintillian upholds the view that as all things perfected through art and human ingenuity are born of nature herself, from which is derived the true Idea. Thus, those who without knowing the truth depend on practical reasoning draw semblances instead of figures. These are dissimilar to beauty, they rob ingenuity and copy the ideas of others, thus making their work not the children of nature but her bastards [. . .]

Bramante, Rafael, Baldassare, Giulio Roman, and ultimately Michelangelo, by forcing themselves to restore ruins to their first idea and appearance, chose forms that were more elegant than the antique buildings. But today instead of having such extremely wise men, we have come to have many who ingratiate themselves by copying antiquity almost without any of the sense of ingenuity and without any of the invention that is to be found in the originals. Each of them, however, claims to be in possession of a new idea of architecture of a new type, presenting it in the public squares and on the façades. These are men who are surely void of any of the sciences that belong to architecture, whose name they falsely subscribe to. They do nothing but deform buildings and entire cities with frenetic angles, *sprezzature* [editor's note: irregularities caused by wilful neglect] and distortions of lines, badly outlined bases, capitals and columns, with swarms of stucco details, trifles and disproportionate shapes. And although Vitruvius condemned similar novelties and proposed good examples to follow. But good architects follow the most excellent forms of the orders; painters and sculptors chose the most elegant natural beauties, and their works arise and remain above nature, that is the ultimate aim of these arts, as we have established.

Jean-Baptiste
Colbert
1619–1683

aesthetisation of architecture • anticlassicism • deformation • freedom • naturalism • archaic beliefs • body model • classical canon • antiquity • abuses

Jean-Baptiste Colbert (1619–1683)

Observations on the Plans and Elevations of the Façade of the Louvre (1664–1665) and *Letter to Louis XIV* (28 September 1665)

Colbert entered the service of Louis XIV and exercised his authority in all domains related to government policy and public administration. As *Surintendant des Batiments*, one of his functions was to be in charge of overseeing the designs for the projected new façade of the Louvre, the most prestigious architectural project of the times internationally. His *Observations* are a report, which he prepared about the proposals submitted by Bernini who had been invited to Paris by the king to design the building. Colbert's devastating criticism is written from a staunchly functional standpoint and, not surprisingly in light of the recent rebellion of *La Fronde* [editor's note: an uprising of the old aristocracy against the crown during the early years of Louis XIV's reign], with a mind to military safety. In the end, he won out over Bernini who was forced to abandon the project and the city. Colbert tackled the problem of city planning in Paris (1672) in the same non-compromising spirit of pragmatism. In his letter to Louis XIV, he is daringly critical of the monarch's plan to abandon the Louvre, centrally located in Paris, for the more remote Versailles, which would be more difficult to administer from.

Further reading Egbert, 1980; Herrmann, 1973; Pevsner, 1940; Schiavo, 1956; Tzonis *et al.*, 1975.

Observations on the Plans and Elevations of the Façade of the Louvre

It must be ensured in the plan of the building that there be, as close to the gate as shall be possible without harming the beauty and magnificence of the gateway, a guardroom for those guarding the gate during the day and for the bodyguards at night, accompanied by a room for the officers.

It would be very necessary for Cavalier Bernini to see once or twice the entrance to the Louvre from ten o'clock in the morning until midday in order, considering the great number of carriages and the crowds of people, that he might judge whether the place at his disposal before the Louvre is sufficient to contain all that is required.

Although his excellence Cavalier Bernini has at his disposal a very extensive set of apartments for all seasons of the year, it is nevertheless necessary that he consider at all times both our climate and the manner in which our kings live. As it is certain that we have only four or five summer months and that during this time our kings are never in Paris, it is necessary to consider the winter apartment as that in which our kings will reside on almost all occasions and that in consequence it must be made more pleasing to the eye, better arranged and more comfortable than all the others. To which Cavalier Bernini will reply, if it so pleases him, that all the agreeable apartments that he shall add to the Louvre, either at the front or at the back of the building, are oriented at the front to the rising and midday sun and the north, and at the back, to the setting sun and the north, and that the accommodation exposed to the midday sun, which is almost the only accommodation where kings shall reside, remains in the same state as before, it not being possible that they be accommodated at the front due to the noise made by carriages and guards, with the result that it can already be said that all the expense that His Majesty shall make may produce no greater comfort for his ordinary accommodation than that which he occupies at the present time, considering that it would remain unchanged.

Jean-Baptiste
Colbert
1619–1683

For the same reasons, that is the long winter and the fact that our kings are ordinarily resident during that season, it is necessary that Cavalier Bernini should consider the means of walling in with ease and good illumination all the great arcades of the building containing the rooms and apartments because if no means is found of doing this with ease it will be impossible to spend winter there without great discomfort, nor even to preserve the vaulting of the arcades if these are exposed to rain and snow.

It is necessary to ensure that all pipes for water and the discharge of ordure and waste should flow extremely easily and that the aqueducts are large, wide and spacious, providing connections everywhere throughout the place.

It is necessary to ensure that the discharge of excrements is easy, that the privies are located in convenient places, such that evil smells may never incommode the apartments or the inside spaces of the Louvre, and that easily used discharges should be present on all floors. It is necessary to consider this point as one of the most important, on which is dependent the health of the royal personages.

Examine the location at which all the water may be taken for the Louvre, considering the points of arrival, distribution and discharge, in such manner that any rupture of the piping cannot at any time compromise the solidity of the foundations. Choose the highest possible location for the creation of a water reservoir with sufficiently capacious volume for all necessary instruments in case of fire. Ensure that it is possible to draw water with pumps from the aforesaid reservoir into three or four other reservoirs on the topmost floor, near the attics, to remedy the same accident.

It would be very necessary for Cavalier Bernini to see for himself the disposition of the premises for food and drink for the King and Queen in order to see the arrangement and number of rooms that are necessary in order that he may be able to place them at the locations that are most convenient for the service of their Majesties.

Letter to Louis XIV

His Majesty is returning to Versailles. I beg him to allow me to say on this topic just two words on thoughts which frequently occur to me and for which, if it pleases your Majesty, my zeal may be deemed to be the explanation.

This residence has much more to do with the pleasure and entertainment of His Majesty than his glory and since His Majesty makes known to all persons the degree to which he prefers the latter to the former, and since this is assuredly his innermost thinking, such that it is with every confidence that one may speak freely thereof to his Majesty without risk of displeasing him, I would feel it to be a betrayal of the loyalty that I owe him if I did not say that it is mete indeed that after so great and so intense an application to the affairs of his State, earning the admiration of all, that His Majesty should devote some energy to his pleasure and entertainment, whilst nevertheless remaining particularly attentive to the need to avoid such causing prejudice to his glory.

Jean-Baptiste
Colbert
1619–1683

However, if His Majesty wishes to discover where in Versailles over 500,000 ecus have been spent over the last two years, he will assuredly have difficulty in doing so. His Majesty might wish to reflect upon the fact that it is evident from the accounts kept by the treasurers of these buildings that during the period in which such large sums have been spent on this residence, the Louvre has been neglected, and the Louvre is assuredly the most superb palace that exists in the world, and the most worthy of the grandeur of His Majesty [. . .] And God preserve us from the many occasions requiring the engagement of some great war, which, by removing the means of finishing this superb edifice, will give His Majesty for many years the displeasure of no longer having the time or the opportunity to do so.

His Majesty knows that apart from glorious action in war, nothing is more revelatory of the grandeur and spirit of princes than buildings, and that all posterity measures their reputation by the yardstick of the superb buildings they have erected during their lifetime. What a pity it would be if the greatest and most virtuous king that ever there was, possessing that genuine virtue that makes the greatest princes, should be measured by the yardstick of Versailles! Nevertheless, there is good reason to fear this misfortune.

For my part, I admit to His Majesty that, notwithstanding his reluctance to increase expenditure, if I had been able to foresee that this expense was to have been so great, I would have been minded to employ it in works paid in small cash sums, in order for it to pass unseen.

His Majesty will also observe, if it pleases him to do so, that he is in the hands of two men who frequent His Majesty almost entirely at Versailles, that is to say, in pleasure and entertainment, and who are unaware of the extent of His Majesty's love of glory, from whatever source it may come, and that the scope of their intelligence, according to their conditions, various private interests, the thought they devote to paying court to His Majesty, combined with the patronage at their disposal, will drag His Majesty from design to design intended to make these works immortal, if His Majesty does not remain on his guard against them.

To reconcile all these considerations, that is to say to give to His Majesty the glory that is rightfully his, and likewise his entertainment, His Majesty could promptly close all the accounts for Versailles, determine a sum to be applied there each year, and it may perhaps be a good idea to separate this sum entirely from the other building funds, and then to devote his energy to finishing the Louvre once and for all. And if peace continues for many years, to erect public monuments to carry His Majesty's glory and grandeur further than those the Romans erected in ancient times.

efficiency • economisation • fit • utility • luxury • hedonism • consumption • scientification

Sir Christopher Wren (1632–1723)

Surveyor's Report on the Condition of St Paul's Cathedral (1666)

Sir Christopher
Wren
1632–1723

Wren, a scientist and an architect, is perhaps best remembered as the designer of St Paul's Cathedral in London after the Great Fire of 1666. The essence of his approach, as an architect and as a scientist, is empirical observation. His reports (1666, 1669) consist of a minute observation of structural defects in two Gothic churches and a proposal for ways to correct them on the basis of proven building principles. His **Tracts** (1670s), four in all, were probably draughts for a comprehensive but never completed treatise on architecture (Sekler, 1956, 52–57). To the question of whether beauty in architecture was absolute or relative, Wren offered a novel compromise solution, eschewing the extreme positions of Perrault and Blondel.

Further reading Bennet, 1972; Harris, 1990; Jardine, 2002; Summerson, 1953.

I shall presume therefore to enumerate as well the defects of comeliness as firmness, that the one may be reconcil'd with the other in the restitution. And yet I should not propose any thing of mere beauty to be added, but where there is a necessity of rebuilding, and where it will be near the same thing to perform it well as ill.

First, it is evident by the ruin of the roof, that the work was both ill design'd, and ill built from the beginning: ill design'd, because the architect gave not butment enough to counterpoise, and resist the weight of the roof from spreading the walls; for, the eye alone will discover to any man, that those pillars as vast as they are, even eleven foot diameter, are bent outwards at least six inches from their first position; which being done on both sides, it necessarily follows, that the whole roof must first open in large and wide cracks along by the walls and windows, and lastly drop down between the yielding pillars.

This bending of the pillars was facilitated by their ill building; for, they are only cased without, and that with small stones, not one greater than a man's burden; but within is nothing but a core of small rubbish – stone, and much mortar, which easily crushes and yields to the weight: and this outward coat of free-stone is so much torn with age, and the neglect of the roof, that there are few stones to be found that are not moulder'd, and flaw'd away with the Salt-peter that is in them; an incurable disease, which perpetually throws off whatever coat of plaister is laid on it, and therefore not to be palliated.

From hence I infer, that as the outside of the church was new flagg'd with stone of larger size than before, so ought the inside also: and in doing this, it will be as easy to perform it, after a good Roman manner, as to follow the Gothick rudeness of the old design; and that, without placing the face of the new work in any part many inches further out or in, than the surfaces of the old work; or adding to the expence that would arise were it perform'd the worse way.

This also may be safely affirm'd, not only by an architect, taking his measures from the precepts and examples of the ancients, but by a geometrician (this part being liable to demonstration) that the roof is, and ever was, too heavy for its butment; and therefore any part of the old roof new pieced will still but occasion further ruin, and the second ruin will much sooner follow than the first, since 'tis easier to force a thing already declining . . .

The middle part is most defective both in beauty and firmness, without and within; for, the tower leans manifestly by the settling of one of the ancient pillars that supported it. Four new arches were, therefore, of later years, incorporated within the old ones, which hath staighten'd and hinder'd both the room, and the clear through view of the nave, in that part, where it had been more graceful to have been rather wider than the rest . . .

I cannot propose a better remedy, than by cutting off the inner corners of the cross, to reduce this middle part into a spacious dome or rotundo, with a cupola, or hemispherical roof, and upon the cupola (for the outward ornament) a lantern with a spiring top, to rise proportionably, tho' not to that unnecessary height of the former spire of timber and lead burnt by lightning.

By this means the deformities of the unequal intercolumnations will be taken away; [. . .]

scientification

Sir Christopher Wren (1632–1723)

Surveyor's Report on the Condition of the Cathedral Church of Salisbury (1669)

(See Wren, 1666)

Almost all the cathedrals of the gothick form are weak and defective in the poise of the vault of the Ailes; as for the vault of the Navis, both sides are equally supported, and propped up from the spreading by the bows or flying buttresses, which rise from the outward walls of the Ailes; but for the vaults of the Ailes, they are indeed supported on the outside by the buttresses, but inwardly they have no other stay but the pillars themselves, which (as they are usually proportioned) if they stood alone without the weight above, could not resist the spreading of the Ailes one minute. True indeed, the great load above the walls and vaults of the Navis, should seem to confirm the pillars in their perpendicular station, that there should be no need of the butment inward; but experience hath shown the contrary, and there is scarce any gothick cathedral, that I have seen, at home or abroad, wherein I have not observed the pillars to yield and bend inwards from the weight of the vault of the Aile; but this defect is most conspicuous upon the angular pillars of the cross, for there, not only the vault wants butment, but also the angular arches that rest upon that pillar, and therefore both conspire to thrust it inward towards the centre of the cross: and this is very apparent in the fabrick we treat of: for this reason, this form of churches has been rejected by modern architects abroad, who use the better and Roman art of architecture.

scientification

Jean Dominique Cassini (1625–1712)

The Manuscript of the Anecdotes of the Life of J.D. Cassini (written *c.*1669; published 1810)

Cassini, an astronomer working in Italy, was called on by Colbert and put in charge of the organisation of the Paris Observatory under construction. He then directed the scientific works that were carried out there. On the subject of architectural construction he is critical of Perrault's designs for a more scientific approach to construction (Tzonis and Lefaivre, 1984b).

Further reading Petzet, 1967; Wolf, 1902.

Vincent Sablon
1619–1693

[...] The edifice of the Observatory. [...] Its plan was the work of an architect rather than that of an astronomer. [...] The Count of Angivilliers [...] pointed out to me that the Royal Observatory was not a building simply devoted to astronomy, but that it must be considered as a public edifice, as one of the monuments most deserving of praise from the century of Louis XIV, and, as such, worthy of a religious respect allowing neither its destruction nor its alteration. Do what you will, he added, provided that you preserve its façade and its proportions. It was therefore no longer a question of what would be best done for astronomy, closing me in with restrictions laid down for me [...]

Finally, in order to ensure that I am correctly understood, I shall try to add an example to the precept by suggesting designs for the Observatory that will meet all the required conditions. This will perhaps lack a perfect concordance with the rules of the art or of building, and I shall take no account either of the beauty of the proportions, the embellishments or the decorations that only artists can add, it being their responsibility to remedy that lack.

It is thus a canvas, a sort of programme that I shall be proposing to the architects, one that I invite them to complete for themselves. [...]

[...] It is in this domain that the genius of the architect shall have free rein to go through its paces. Until the present time, we have, as it were, held that genius on a leash by means of the obligations, the dimensions and the forms that we have imposed upon it, but here we ask no more than rooms and the windows, without interfering with the proportions, the disposition of the parts or the decoration, nor the external or internal forms.

[...]

mechanisation of architecture • scientification

Vincent Sablon (1619–1693)

History of the August and Venerable Church of Chartres (1671)

The author, a priest attached to the Cathedral of Chartes, wrote an enthusiastic description in verse to his Gothic cathedral as part of a guidebook to the building. In opposition to the classicists of the age, he praised the Gothic stonemasons for their technical skills (Frankl, 1960, 339–340) and the Gothic forms for their beauty.

[...] This church is marvellous in its architecture, marvellous in its art, no less than in its structure, marvellous inside, marvellous outside, and marvellous in its whole extent. It is immense and vast, and ancient in structure, the Gothic order adorns it with mosaic, and by their ornament and their antiquity they make it venerable for posterity. From the bowels of a mountain its mass composed, by artful invention crosswise disposed. Its superb length in arches deployed, on a hundred stout pillars its burden carried, and a hundred flying buttresses on various elevations, by various works the building furnished, by a gifted mason artfully built, with not a sign of marble or porphyry, or those ornaments which the vulgar admire, but the skilled architect designed to show that nothing resists his exceptional art. [. . .]

rigorism • essentialism

André Félibien (1619–1695)

Description of the Grotto of Versailles (1672)

André Félibien
1619–1695

Like André Félibiens's **Entretiens sur les vies et sur les ouvrages des plus excellents peintres anciens et modernes** (1666) reprinted four times before 1688 (Tzonis et al., 1982), this text, by the first secretary of the Académie Royale d'Architecture, expounds a liberal theory of beauty in architecture and misgivings about the authority of the classical canon. The present text, more extreme than the former, praises the imitation of natural roughness and irregularity in design (Miller, 1983).
Further reading Bilodeau, 1997; Fontaine, 1909; Wiebenson 1982, 1993.

There are two kinds of grotto: one which is the work of nature, and the other which is made by art; and since art can only aspire to great beauty when it is imitating nature well, so nature never produces anything so beautiful as when it seems that art has had a hand in its production. Those whose curiosity has led them to explore the caves of Tibiran in the Pyrenees will have seen three which seem to form a complete apartment, with a remarkably convincing imitation of the rich ornamentation used in the wall panelling and ceilings of the most sumptuous rooms. The vaults of these subterranean chambers are lined with rock crystals, and their walls with kinds of pilasters formed by the solidification of water which has fallen in droplets at different intervals from the ceiling of the caves, making the fluting which can now be seen. Between these pilasters are what look like niches occupied by figures, also of solidified water deposits, in the place of statues; and would look still more like statues, had chance and nature been capable of executing what they seem to have designed: but as they work blindly, what they do has neither proportion nor symmetry. This is why nature, to make up for these faults, often uses in her productions the wealth of materials and variety of colour of which she is mistress.

Art in itself is a poor workman; but seeing clearly what it does, and being guided by the light of reason, it works in orderly fashion. It imitates all that nature produces, and when it wishes to make an accomplished work, it joins forces with nature, working in concert with her: nature provides the material, to which art gives form.

Versailles could be said to be a place where art labours alone, one that nature has abandoned to allow the king to conjure up there, by a kind of creation if I may use such an expression, many magnificent works and an infinity of extraordinary sights; but nowhere in this royal house has art so happily succeeded as in the Grotto of Thetis.

[199]

This grotto is a rectangular building standing close to the palace, by the water tower façade. It is a heavy mass of rusticated stone pierced by three large arches with iron doors worked even more ingeniously than richly. Above the middle door there is a golden sun, whose rays spread outwards to form the iron bars of all three doors of the grotto; and as these doors face west, when the evening sun strikes them their gold takes on a new lustre, their faint rays become veritable shafts of light.

Three large bas-reliefs decorate the façade of the building. The middle one depicts the sun descending into the sea. The other two are filled with tritons and sirens, who rejoice at the sun's arrival. Other reliefs in the form of medallions show water nymphs frolicking on the backs of dolphins; all this decoration alludes in some way to the being who gives form to the whole building.

For to better appraise this building's beauty and spirit, it is important to realise that it is designed to represent the palace of Thetis, where the Sun retires after having completed his daily course and spread his rays all over the earth.

André Félibien
1619–1695

To convey an idea of the dwelling-place of Thetis, whom the poets depicted as a sea deity, the building raised had to look as if it were not the work of men but of nature, set in a watery realm, embellished as befitted its situation, and enriched by the most precious objects of the sea.

Not everyone who has tried to make grottoes in palaces and pleasure-grounds has succeeded. They thought that to make a cool retreat from the heat of summer they should build their grottoes underground, and adorn them with statues and all the finest riches that art can devise. Others have built them at the bottom of garden walks, and covered them with pebbles and charming paintings. The latter, strictly speaking, make what the Italians call *loggie*, or lodges offering comfort, repose and shelter from the heat. Paintings are well suited to them, and make them more enjoyable, as in the *loggie* of the Palazzo Ghisi in Rome, painted by Raphael. But it is evident that the rocaille and seashells have no connection with the paintings; they mock and disfigure nature instead of making a good imitation of it. The grottoes built underground would be more tolerable if ungarnished by over-accomplished works of art which are not suited to them; and we must note again that they are not greatly used anyway, for as they are sometimes too cold and the air in them too damp and unhealthy, no sooner has one entered than one wishes to leave again to breathe a milder air.

The Grotto of Versailles is made for its occupants to remain inside for as long as they wish, without exposure to an excess of cold. And yet, since it is lit only by the three doors which open into it, it cannot be called a loggia or a summer-house, for it has every appearance of a grotto hewn from rock and decorated by the hands of the deities who live in it. It is built in such a way that inside, corresponding to each of the three doors, are three recesses, separated by two thick piers. And though they are built to carry the vault, one sees that they are also there for decoration, and the middle recess is Apollo's resting place, while those on either side are for his horses.

The grotto has no other light than that which enters through its openings; and since air comes through these openings and cools as it circulates to and fro, it makes the interior mild and pleasant, and one never tires of being there; for besides the beauty of the grotto itself, it also offers an even more splendid view framed in each of the three openings, like a triptych in which nature herself represents, with an admirable handling of perspective, the gardens and nearby hills.

But to make the grotto seem natural and at the same time extraordinary, art has everywhere sought to cover its traces as far as possible; and the better to imitate nature, it has borrowed everything it deemed suitable to compose the different works with which the grotto is adorned.

If those who have applied their endeavour to the execution of so beautiful a work deserve some honour for having brought it to so high a degree of perfection, how then to limit the honour due to he who was the primary impetus of all these noble inventions, by whose light we move not only in our pursuit of perfection in art but also in our attempts to make this art have some special connection with the great Prince for whom it is undertaken? For just as the poets imagined that after completing his daily course the Sun retired to the palace of Thetis to rest after the exertions of the day, others saw that this ingenious fiction could make a pleasant theme for a grotto in Versailles, where the King might go from time to time to take a rest from his great and illustrious fatigues, without this place of repose preventing him from promptly returning to his tasks as eagerly as the Sun who rises from his watery retreat to light the world again. This is the idea on which the place I have just described is based, and which men must see with their own eyes to admire still more its accomplishment. [. . .]

André Félibien
1619–1695

anticlassicism • deformation • freedom • naturalism • legitimation • representation of power

Jean Le Paultre (1618–1682)

Recueil Général du Chasteau de Versailles, 1677

78. Jean Le Paultre's engravings of night time celebrations at the court of Louis XIV at Versailles.

Sir Christopher Wren (1632–1723)

Tracts on Architecture (1670s)

(See Wren, 1666)

Tract I

Architecture has its political use; publick buildings being the ornament of a country; it establishes a nation, draws people and commerce; makes the people love their native country, which passion is the original of all great actions in a common-wealth. The emulation of the cities of Greece was the true cause of their greatness. The obstinate valour of the Jews, occasioned by the love of their temple, was a cement that held together that people, for many ages, through infinite changes. The care of public decency and convenience was a great cause of the establishment of the Low countries, and of many cities in the world. Modern Rome subsists still, by the ruins and imitation of the old; as does Jerusalem, by the temple of the Sepulchre, and other remains of Helena's zeal.

Architecture aims at eternity; and therefore the only thing incapable of modes and fashions in its principles, the Orders. The Orders are not only Roman and Greek, but Phoenician, Hebrew and Assyrian; therefore being founded upon the experience of all ages, promoted by the vast treasures of all the great monarchs, and skill of the greatest artists and geometricians, every one emulating each other; and experiments in this kind being greatly expenseful, and errors incorrigible, is the reason that the principles of architecture are now rather the study of antiquity than fancy.

Beauty, firmness and convenience are the principles; the two first depend upon geometrical reasons of opticks and staticks; the third only makes the variety.

There are natural causes of beauty. Beauty is a harmony of objects, begetting pleasure by the eye. There are two causes of beauty, natural and customary. Natural is from geometry, consisting in uniformity (that is equality) and proportion. Customary beauty is begotten by the use of our senses to those objects that are usually pleasing to us for other causes, as familiarity or particular inclination breeds a love to things not in themselves lovely. Here lies the great occasion of errors; here is tried the Architect's judgement: but always the true test is natural or geometrical beauty.

Geometrical figures are naturally more beautiful than other irregular figures; in this all consent as to a law of nature. Of geometrical figures, the square and the circle are most beautiful; next to straight lines, equal and geometrical flexures; an object elevated in the middle is more beautiful than depressed.

Position is necessary for perfecting beauty. There are only two beautiful positions of straight lines, perpendicular and horizontal: this is from nature, and consequently necessity, no other than upright being firm. Oblique positions are discord to the eye, unless answered in Paris, as in the sides of an equilateral triangle: therefore gothick buttresses are all ill-favoured, and were avoided by the ancients, and no roofs almost but spherick, in all positions, the ribs answer. Cones and multiangular prisms want neither beauty or firmness, but are not ancient.

Views contrary to beauty are deformity, or a defect of uniformity, and plainness, which is the excess of uniformity; variety makes the mean variety of uniformities makes complete beauty: uniformities are best tempered, as Rhymes in Poetry, alternately, or sometimes with more variety, as in stanzas. In things to be seen at once, much variety makes confusion, another vice of beauty. In things that are not seen at once, and have no respect one to another, great variety is commendable, provided this variety transgresses not the rules of opticks and geometry.

An architect ought to be jealous of novelties, in which fancy blinds the judgement; and to think his judges, as well as those that are to live five centuries after him, as those of his own time. That which is commendable now for imitated, and when it is unknown which was the original; but the glory of that which is good of itself is eternal.

. . .

A walk of trees is more beautiful than the most artificial portico; but these not being easily preserved in market-places, they made the more durable shades of porticoes; in which we see they imitated nature, most trees in their prime, that are not sapplings, or dotards, observe near the proportion of Doric pillars in the length of their bole, before they part into branches. This I think the more natural comparison, than that to the body of a man, in which there is little resemblance of cylindrical body.

Tract II

. . . when the imitation of groves was forgot, the diameters were advanced to seven; then to eight; then to nine; as in the Ionick Order; then, at last, to ten, as in the Corinthian and Italick Orders: and herein the architects had reason, for the great expense is in raising and carving of the columns; and slenderer columns would leave them more opportunity to show their skill in carving and enriching their works in the capitals and mouldings. Thus the Corinthian Order became the most delicate of all others, and though the column was slenderer, yet bore a greater weight of entablature than the more ancient Orders.

. . .

It seems very unaccountable, that the generality of our late architects dwell so much upon this ornamental, and so slightly pass over the geometrical, which is the most essential part of architecture. For instance, can an arch stand without butment sufficient? If the butment be more than enough, 'tis an idle expense of materials; if too little, it will fall; and so for any vaulting: and yet no author hath given a true and universal rule for this; nor hath considered all the various forms of arches . . .

classical canon • antiquity and abuses • nature nurture and fashion

Claude Perrault (1613–1688)

The Ten Books of Vitruvius, Corrected and Translated with Notes and Figures (1673)

Perrault was educated as a physician. In spite of his lack of architectural training, Colbert Louis XIV's minister, gave him some of the most architecturally significant projects of the time in France: to make a new translation of Vitruvius (1673), to write a study of proportions and the Orders, the main design problem since the Renaissance (1673), to build the Paris Observatory and, finally, to design the façade for the main royal residence, the Louvre (Herrmann, 1973). This is not wholly surprising. Claude's brother, Charles (1688) was the closest collaborator of Colbert's (Herrmann, ibid.). More importantly, Claude was a member of the academy of sciences, the newly formed, highly regarded, small scientific elite supported by the Crown whose main task was to transfer the innovative logico-empirical methods to all the important fields of inquiry. He himself carried out work in chemistry, anatomy and physics in addition to architecture. Up until

Scamozzi (1615), architectural theoreticians had taken for granted that the rules of beauty were 'positive' or absolute, a position defended and expanded on by Blondel (1675). Perrault argued, on the contrary, that they were 'arbitrary', that they were admired only because of custom and the association made automatically in the mind of the viewer between the building and the authority of its powerful, courtly owner. This definition of beauty relied on anthropological and archaeological data (Desgodetz, 1682) and on a systematic reading of all Renaissance and antique treatises. The iconoclastic thesis dealt a jarring blow to the classical canon and Perrault was reviled throughout the next hundred years as being responsible for the undoing of good taste (Briseux, 1752), but it qualified him in the eyes of Colbert to undertake the design of the Louvre façade which, it was hoped, would initiate a tradition distinct from that of the Italians and more in keeping with the modern absolutist state. In general, the views of Perrault on beauty, because of their sociological insight and cultural relativism, are well in advance of their time (Tzonis, 1972, Ch. 7).

Further reading Bilodeau, 1997; Blomfield, 1973; Blunt, 1973; Brönner, 1972; Cassirer, 1909; Ciapponi, 1976; Egbert, 1980; Fontaine, 1909; Gillot, 1914; Hautecoeur, 1948–1963; Hernandez, 1972; Herrmann, 1973; Jones, 1936; Margiotta, 1953; Petzet, 1967; Pevsner, 1940; Rykwert, 1982; Tatarkiewicz, 1970–1974, III; Tzonis, 1972; Vagnetti and Marcuzzi, 1978; Wolf, 1902.

Claude Perrault
1613–1688

Book I, Chapter II

13. Founded on authority

All of Architecture is founded on two principles, of which one is positive and the other arbitrary. Its positive foundation is custom and the useful and necessary ends for which an edifice is built, such that it is Solid, Salubrious and Comfortable. The foundation that I term arbitrary is Beauty, which is dependent on Authority and Habit.

14. Habit

Vitruvius seems to be saying that Habit is the main authority in Architecture, when he argues that the custom among the Ancients of ornamenting all the rooms in their residences in the same manner, was an inviolable law, despite the fact that this goes against reason, reason dictating that chambers and private studies should be more ornate than staircases and vestibules.

Book III, Chapter II

Aesthetic taste in our century, or at least that in our own nation, is different from that of the Ancients and that may derive to some extent from the Gothic, since we like airiness, light and free space. That has led us to invent a sixth manner for the disposition of Columns, which is to pair them, associating them two by two and also join into one space the two spaces between columns.

[...]

Mr Blondel, in his learned 'Lessons on Architecture', of which he has made a Course of Study, devotes three whole chapters [...] to showing that the universal custom of today of pairing Columns is a licence that should certainly not be tolerated and since no person, as far as I know, had sought before the reasons which might have led to this new practice, he discusses at length essentially the refutation of those I have given above. This matter seems to me to be important enough to deserve examination, and I believe that it will not be found to be irrelevant that I add to this memorandum my own reply to the refutation thus given.

The principal objection on which most emphasis is placed is founded on a prejudice and a false premise that it is not permitted to diverge from the customary practices of the Ancients, that all things which do not imitate their manner must be deemed bizarre and capricious, and that if this Law is not kept inviolate, the door is opened to licence such as to sow disorder in all the Arts. But since this justification proves too much, it must prove nothing, for there are many more disadvantages in closing the door to pleasing new ideas, than in opening it to ideas that are so ridiculous that they annihilate themselves. If this Law were to exist, Architecture would never have reached the point to which the inventions of the Ancients have brought it, all those inventions having been new ideas in their own time; and we should not seek new means of acquiring knowledge that we lack, and that we acquire every day in Agriculture, in Navigation, in Medicine, and in all the other Arts, the perfection of which the Ancients endeavoured to achieve, in which they never claimed to have succeeded; at least, there is no one among them who ever cast Anathema on those who sought to add to the rules that we imagine to have been prescribed for us by those great Personages who, all the evidence suggests, would have been surprised to see the manner in which posterity honours them [. . .]

Claude Perrault
1613–1688

Book VI, Chapter II

3. I do not believe that we must doubt

This maxim from Vitruvius meets with the approval of the majority of the Architects and Sculptors who hold that the judicious practice of this change in proportions is one of the finest things in their art, for they claim that it allows them to remedy the bad effects that disadvantageous aspects may cause in Constructions when they corrupt or at least prevent the true proportions from being seen, due to the foreshortening of objects that are seen from an oblique angle. This remedy will for example involve ensuring less apparent diminution for very large columns than for small ones.

    [. . .]

But not all Architects and Sculptors believe that we must always have regard to these reasons and there are some who consider that such precautions should be employed only rarely. Their argument is that our vision is not as subject to error as Vitruvius claims, not simply because in fact vision, like the other senses of the outside world, is never in error, but because our judgement of what we see, which is the only thing to which one may attribute the errors committed, is ordinarily very sure and almost infallible when long habit and frequently repeated experience perfected by a certain age has led on so many occasions to the correction of initial errors, with the result that such mistakes recur only rarely. For in fact almost nobody fears that the floor of a long gallery may touch his head when he reaches the end because he perceives that end to be at the same level as his forehead and nobody worries at how he will pass through a door which he sees from afar as being covered entirely by a finger tip. For our judgement is so correct that if the walls of a gallery, which although parallel nevertheless appear to come together at the far end, are slightly widened, we perceive this to have been done, or if a paved way had been given a slope towards the far end, where it would normally appear to rise, despite it being on a level, nobody would fail to notice it.

We see also quite well if a face is round, or if it is long, despite seeing it at a high window; and a tall, thin body will certainly not appear short and thickset at like location, and no extraordinarily tall person will ever be taken for a dwarf. But what is more important still is that the certainty of this judgement is a thing that all possess without ever giving it a thought, despite the fact that it can be acquired only by a number of reflections of common sense, the purpose of which is to think upon the effects of the external senses, for it is by means of such reflection and the judgement of common sense that we do not take a spark for a Star, or a white sheet of paper for a great white wall, nor an oval for a circle, nor a tall window for a square one when the distance and situation of such objects leads to their appearing to be other than they in fact are. The reason for this is that common sense immediately adds to the image in the eye those circumstances of which it is aware, such as the distance and situation of the object seen, and the size of the things to which it is compared, preventing that image from being taken for that of another thing. For the images of a spark and a sheet of paper, when such objects are close to us, are indeed very like those of a Star or a white wall when the latter objects are distant from us. Likewise, an oval and an oblong rectangle seen at an oblique angle and from a distance create the same effect in our eye as a circle and a perfect square when seen directly. This happens in the same manner in vision and in hearing as in all the other actions in which practice and custom create in us habits and such ease that we perform a hundred things that are necessary to accomplish them without ever giving them a thought ... without reflecting upon our actions.

[...]

The assumption that all aspects of vision depend solely on the eye ... is not true, because vision always uses the judgement of common sense to correct it. And it hardly ever happens that our vision lacks this judgement, otherwise perspective and painting would always deceive us [...] there are few cases in which the aforesaid rule for changes in proportions is relevant. For if we suppose that it is desired to place a statue at a great height, it is quite possible to make it colossal, but this is done in order for it to appear colossal and not in order to prevent distance making it appear too small, because when it is necessary for a thing to be small, it is also necessary for that thing to appear small.

[...]

The intention I had in communicating to the public the thoughts that are my own on the alteration of the proportions of objects has not met with the success that I had hoped, because my intention was not to *attract attention to myself*, as the common expression has it, but merely to oblige the learned to instruct me on a question that I believed to be beset with some difficulty. I see however that it appears that no reasonable response is to be given to me, lest prejudice be done to the authority of the Ancients, who are claimed to be above all argument. I was led into error by the fact that I would never have thought that this obstinate admiration for the Ancients could have gone so far, for I believed that veneration was felt for the works of those great men and for the precepts which they handed down to us, because these were always founded on reason, when they were of a nature to be governed by reason, such as is the case herein. However, I see that this is not the case, and that there can be no question of examining whether all that the Ancients said is logical or not, but to admire it,

Claude Perrault
1613–1688

to follow it blindly and if one is wise, to prefer to copy Serlio, Palladio, Vignola and Samozzi, rather than to attract insults by believing that one can encourage the learned to cultivate and perfect an Art that demands much intelligence, judgement and logic. Nor did I believe that the Architects of our time were incapable of logical reasoning, as the Author gives us to understand when he says that the arguments I use to support my opinion *'are things too metaphysical for them'* but it is his characteristic exaggeration that leads him to feel excessive veneration for the Architects of the ancient world and to treat with excessive contempt those of the present, given their works of beauty in which more intelligence and reason is to be seen than is necessary to forestall the belief that they are lacking in any of the qualities necessary for those who devote their efforts to perfect the Arts and to persuade us that it is not impossible to add something to the inventions of the Ancients.

Claude Perrault
1613–1688

design methodology • nature • nurture • fashion • precedent • authority • invention •
representation • truth • illusion

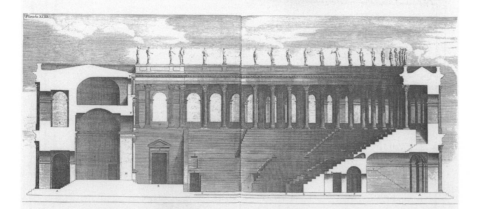

79. Claude Perrault. *Les Dix livres d'architecture de Vitruve, corrigés et traduits*. 1673. Illustration of reconstructed Roman theatre.

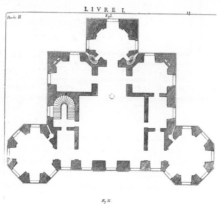

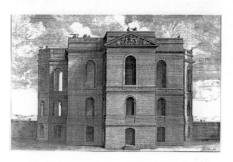

80b. Claude Perrault. *Les Dix livres d'architecture de Vitruve, corrigés et traduits*. 1673. The observatory of Paris designed by Claude Perrault. Notice the observation rooms conceived by analogy to fortification towers.

80. Claude Perrault. *Les Dix livres d'architecture de Vitruve, corrigés et traduits*. 1673.

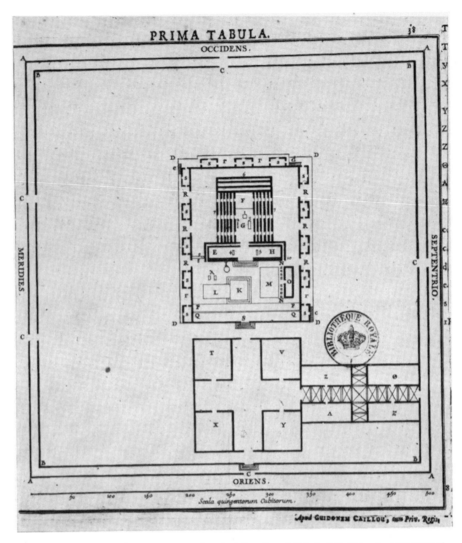

81. Claude Perrault. *Temple of Herod*. 1678. Plan. From Louis Compiègne de Veil, *De Cultu Divino*. Perrault's design of the Temple was prepared for the Latin edition of Maimonides' *Mishneh Torah* by de Veil. Perrault ignored the long tradition of fictitious reconstructions and tried to stay close to the Maimonides text, establishing a new scientific method of reconstruction based on authentic texts as close as possible to the time of the artefact. Perrault, however, probably ignored the existence of drawings of the Temple by Maimonides himself.

François Blondel (1617–1686)

Lessons of Architecture (1675)

Blondel was a military engineer who lectured on mathematics at the Collège de France and became a member of the Academy of Sciences before being named as first director of the Academy of Architecture when it opened in Paris in 1671. His *Cours* contains the official doctrine and pedagogical programme of the academy and remained for a full century the leading textbook in France among architects. Blondel upheld the Renaissance belief that beauty in buildings was 'absolute' because it was grounded in the natural order of things. He bolstered his arguments with many references to scientific data, although not always in a way which supported his conclusions reliably. He engaged in a polemical debate over the matter with Claude Perrault (1683) who claimed that, on the contrary, beauty had no timeless, universal norms – that it was, in fact, 'arbitrary'.

Further reading Bilodeau, 1997; Blomfield, 1973, II; Blunt, 1973; Cassirer, 1909; Egbert, 1980; Hautecoeur, 1948–1963; Hernandez, 1972; Herrmann, 1973; Mauclaire and Vigoureux, 1938; Pevsner, 1940; Tatarkiewicz, 1970–1974; Wiebeson, 1982, 1993.

Preface

Since the establishment of the Monarchy, there have been erected no Buildings so august, in such great numbers and in so many places in the Kingdom, as we have seen during the reign of Louis the Great. Not only has this wise Prince taken care to ensure that effort is devoted to the search for those things which may contribute to restoring to Architecture its former glory, but he has also set out to make perfect knowledge of it easy to acquire for all.

It is to this end that His Majesty founded in Paris late in the year one thousand six hundred and eleven the Academy of Architecture, composed of a goodly number of his subjects selected as the most capable in this Art both from those who practise this profession and outside it, in order to work upon the establishment of beauteous Architecture and to dispense public lessons.

His Majesty desired firstly that these Architects should apply themselves seriously to study, assembling on one day in each week to confer and to exchange their knowledge between themselves, since His Majesty judged very rightly that this was the sole means of stripping Architecture of its unwonted ornaments, to remove the abuses that the ignorance and presumption of Labourers had introduced into it and to enrich it with the natural beauty and grace that were the source of its greatness at the time of the Ancients. His Majesty also wished that a register should be maintained to record the decisions taken in each of the Conferences, in which the principal difficulties encountered in Buildings are to be discussed and resolved.

It is also in this Academy that His Majesty desires that the most accurate and correct rules of Architecture should be taught publicly on two days in each week, in order to form within it a seminary, as it were, of young Architects. And to give them greater encouragement and passion for this Art, His Majesty [. . .] will choose a goodly number to be sent at His Majesty's expense to Rome in order that nothing should be lacking in their perfect instruction, and to make them capable of service in the management of the construction of Buildings.

Nevertheless, since it is true that knowledge of the precepts of Architecture does not suffice alone to make an Architect, since that quality presupposes enlightenment in many other spheres, His Majesty wished that during the second hour of the lessons of the Academy there should be public teaching of the other Sciences that are absolutely necessary to Architects, such as Geometry, Arithmetic, Mechanics, [. . .] Hydraulics, Gnomonics, Military Architecture, Perspective, the Stone Working and diverse other parts of Mathematics. [. . .] It is for this reason that I have composed this course of study in Architecture, which has already been dispensed publicly there. [. . .]

It deals solely with practical matters, for having said little on the origin and parts of Architecture, of which the most considerable is that which serves the beauty of Edifices, I now come to the explanation of the Orders in general, of which I speak quite succinctly, reserving the more detailed argument on this topic for the second part, which is more speculative. After this, I apply myself entirely to the proper understanding of the most correct practices which may be used for the employment of the five Orders of Architecture, beginning with those of Vitruvius, [. . .] the practices of the principal Interpreters or Imitators such as Philander, Daniel Barbaro, Cataneo, Serlio, Leone Battista Alberti and others [. . .] I have chosen from among the Moderns the three Architects who have handed down to us precepts that approach most closely the beauty of those Edifices and which have earned the widest possible admiration, these being Vignola, Palladio and Scamozzi.

François Blondel
1617–1686

Book I

Chapter X. Concerning paired columns

Regarding the Columns and Pilasters that Scamozzi placed so near to each other, and which are commonly called 'coupled' or 'paired' Columns or Pilasters, it should be noted [. . .] that it would be no easy matter to find many of these in the Buildings of ancient times. I know well that some can be seen in Rome in a house built by Bramante, [. . .] but his intentions are unknown to us and I know not what may have led Architects of the last century (whom we must nevertheless honour as Restorers of the glory of Architecture) to introduce this manner into most of their Works. [. . .]

I have nothing to say on the love attributed to our Nation for light and free space, since it is admitted at the same time that this still contains elements of the Gothic and in that sense is very different from the taste of the Ancients, nor on the arguments that we must be allowed to add to the inventions of the Ancients, just as Hermogenes was entitled to add to the practices of those who preceded him. I reply that there is nothing truer. It is no doubt the task of new Hermogenes to dare to produce their new ideas in all centuries, and they are entitled to correct the faults of others and their inventions must pass down to posterity as infallible rules.

Nevertheless, it is quite true also that it is this same reasoning that has opened the door in all eras to the disorder to be found in Architecture and in the other Arts. We have almost no Labourers who do not have a very good opinion of themselves and who do not believe themselves to be as capable as Hermogenes. The Gothic Architects filled their edifices with so many inappropriate features only because they believed that they were entitled to add to the inventions of the Greeks and the Romans. And those ridiculous cartouches, those grotesque eccentricities and extravagant ornaments that German Architects continue to affect, along with the great contempt they have for legitimate dimensions in certain parts of Architecture, come simply from the fact that they are convinced that they are just as entitled to seek novelty and to add to the practices of the Ancients, as the Ancients had to seek their own and to add to those that had been produced by Architects before them. Which would lead me to state categorically that it is necessary to obey certain rules and to put a halt to caprice if it is wished to restore the beauty of Architecture, if this argument had not been put forward at greater length in another place.

[...]

Book II, Concerning the Proportions of Columns Placed One Above Another

Chapter I. Concerning the sequences of the Orders of Architecture

The first and principal rule that must be observed when placing Columns on different levels one above the other is that either the larger should invariably be placed below the slimmer columns, or that they should be of the same Order or of different Orders.

François Blondel
1617–1686

And since all Architects are in agreement that the Tuscan Order is the biggest and most massive of all, after which comes the Doric, followed by the Ionic, and lastly the Corinthian or Composite Order, according to the epithets that some have applied to them, that is to say 'Massive' to the Tuscan Order, 'Strength' to the Doric Order, 'Gravitas' to the Ionic Order, 'Genteel' to the Composite and 'Delicacy' to the Corinthian Order.

[...]

Book V

Chapter XIV. An examination of the arguments against the necessity of proportions in Architecture, which are, it is said, approved only through custom

We shall soon have a Volume from Mr Perrault on the same topic of proportions in Architecture, which can only be excellent given its source, although in the Notes he has written on Vitruvius, he seems to have views very far from those of this Author.

Although such a manner of thinking is singular and extraordinary, and I am very much minded to believe it to be not entirely true, I choose nevertheless not to undertake to refute it, because my reflections upon the force of custom have sufficiently convinced me that that person among the Moderns who has named it the *Queen of the actions of men* would, perhaps, have been correct in extending her empire beyond the bounds of Morality and to make her Queen of most of the thoughts, reasoning and knowledge of men, just as much as of their actions.

I would have ample matter for discussion if I wished to discourse upon the enormous differences that may be encountered in mores, opinions and tastes in food, song and a thousand other types, according to the differences between Nations, Epochs, Sexes, Ages and Conditions, etc. and if I wished to say that they stem for the most part from custom, and that it is custom that changes temperament, which overturns natural inclinations, and which makes acceptable the most violent poison in food, or if I wished to go no further than the argument of the Philosopher when he asserts that we normally take as true those things that seem to us to be most clear and most self-evident, without considering that such clarity and self-evidence often come from the ease with which we have in understanding and imagining them, through the habits we have contracted, having so often considered them in the same manner. For although it may be true that our thoughts are spiritual in part, we cannot say that they have no need, in order to be produced, of the ministry of certain bodily organs, which are all the more capable of the changes needed to create habits for the fact that their delicate nature, their softness, their subtlety and the vivacity of their movements, are infinitely greater than the other parts of the body. It is these organs which, in the view of the aforesaid Philosopher, having by the repetition of several like actions been rendered supple and pliant in a certain direction, acquire this facility of movement through which they represent to us objects much more promptly and easily in one manner than in another and thus make those objects seem clearer and more self-evident in that way. [...]

François Blondel (1617–1686)

Concerning this argument, could we not say that this principle is the source of those opinions that are so opposed on the same subjects in Men who speak and think in good faith, and who, following the inclination they first find themselves with regard to that object, either because that inclination has been communicated to them by others in whom they trust, or because of a disregard for common views due to their desire to adopt singular ones, or due to any other concern they may have, have not ceased thereafter to see the aforesaid object from that same standpoint [...] And it is this which makes those accustomed to lying convinced in the end that the lie they have proffered has become true, so often have they said it.

Finally, it is this which leads me to refrain from saying that the disregard shown by Mr Perrault for the proportions of the parts in Architecture is due to his being accustomed thereto, because he could reply to me that the esteem in which we hold these imaginary proportions comes from no other source than the fact that we are accustomed to considering them thus, perhaps under the sway of our teachers, in whose footsteps we have followed blindly like sheep following the sheep who go before them, or perhaps wishing to distinguish ourselves by making others believe that we find beauty in the nature of things which has no other existence than that conferred upon them by our imagination.

Although in fact it is of little importance to Architects that the beauty they give their Constructions should be founded on principles that are natural or customary, since whatever the truth, it is necessary for their work to be agreeable and pleasing to the eye of those who contemplate them. It is however quite appropriate that I should adduce some arguments in the defence [...] of all those who have spoken of Architecture and who have believed that the explanation for the fact that an Edifice built according to the rules is infinitely pleasing to our eye is simply that beauty has become mistress of our mind and senses, because of some cause born within us and inculcated in our minds by nature, rather than by opinion [...]

Book V

Chapter XV, refutation of these arguments

[...] I do not see how one can be entitled to argue that the beauty produced in an Edifice by the legitimate proportions of Architecture is not *convincing*, since there is no person to whom they are not pleasing, who does not approve them immediately on seeing them, and who is not entirely *convinced* that it is from this beauty that all the pleasure and satisfaction they feel derives. Moreover, I do not see how it can be possible to say that this beauty, or rather the proportions that produce it, are not *necessary*, since everybody knows that they are of a necessity so absolute that all the beauty contained in a building vanishes at the very moment that we change some essential thing in its symmetry. With the result that we can say that one thing is necessary to another, if the latter perishes immediately the first is lacking. There is nothing in my view so necessary in Architecture as legitimate proportions, since all beauty, all grace and in the end all that may please us disappears and vanishes like smoke immediately such proportions cease to be present.

But since we are not obliged to believe that the beauty of an Edifice is founded in nature, rather than in opinion and in that to which we are accustomed, although it may be admitted that it is in some way *convincing* and that there is *some necessity* in the proportions of Architecture, it is appropriate at this point to go into greater detail on the topic on which it appears that we have not hitherto applied ourselves other than very superficially.

François Blondel
1617–1686

There is nothing so natural to all animals as the effort to preserve that which is dearest to them, which is life. Thus all things that may contribute to that end are necessarily natural. It is also for the same reason that those things that allow us to live in greater comfort and pleasure are also natural where we are concerned. Hence the fact that we can begin by asserting that the Art of building in general is natural to us. [...]

It is appropriate above all else to agree on one fact, and that is whether the productions of the Arts cause to be born in us some pleasure that is natural to us, or if all things that are pleasing to us in the Works created by Art exist only in our imagination, whether certain dishes cooked in a certain manner by a good Cook appear to us to be savoury and agreeable to the taste only through habit, whether the violence of the various passions that Poetry and Rhetoric sometimes excite in our souls are produced only by the company of others and custom, whether the mixing of harmonies in Music arranged in accordance with certain proportions does not give us a pleasure that is natural to us, and a thousand other examples of this same kind.

For if we say that all these pleasures have no other existence than that we are accustomed to deeming them to be pleasurable, I am quite content to allow in this manner that the satisfaction that our eyes receive from the proportions of Architecture comes solely from custom and habit, but if on the contrary it is desired that the Arts through their productions should be capable of engendering in our senses, or rather in our souls, pleasure which is in our natures [...]

I may therefore be allowed the conclusion that the satisfaction received from the Works of Painting and Sculpture is real in some manner in our minds, because they conform to the beauty that we find in the Objects that those Arts depict [...] the beauty that ravishes us in Architecture has also some real and natural foundation in us which makes that beauty pleasing, because it conforms to, or is made in imitation of the beauty to be seen in the Works of Nature.

It is thus that I say that the beauty of a Column that is nicely straight, round and tapered according to the rules gives us a pleasure that is natural, because it is modelled on the tree [...] a door situated in the middle of a building and the windows to the right and to the left at equal distances from the same middle point, of the same height, of equal width to those with which they are paired, at the same level, etc. gives us natural pleasure because this arrangement imitates closely that which composes the beauty of a human face or body [. . .]

[. . .] the main parts of the entablature and pediments are also in a certain sense natural, since, according to Vitruvius, they are also made in imitation of the ordinary buildings of the first Greeks, who, following at that time the simplicity of the natural world, gave to their Edifices only that which was purely necessary, or at most, a minimum of comfort. [. . .]

I am well aware that Architects later mixed with those parts of Architecture that we may call natural many elements and mouldings that certainly do not come from the same source and which, on the contrary, seem to contradict the normal practices of nature. [. . .] About which we might say with some appearance of truth that all the pleasure they give to the eyes comes only from custom and the authoritativeness of those who first applied them, since far from finding their principle in nature, they appear to be far removed therefrom by virtue of their disposition or appearance, unless there is some more hidden reason, but no less natural, and which is the cause of our pleasure in contemplating them.

[. . .] On the contrary, *we must seek elsewhere the cause and attribute it, if we wish, as did Vitruvius and most of the other Architects, to such an imaginary proportion, deliberately granting it despotic dominance over the movements of our souls, giving obeisance to its orders and renouncing all other pleasure than those that we imagine we derive from it.*

It is in this manner that those who have some esteem for proportions are made to seem ridiculous, and because there are certain other persons who claim that there are no absolute rules related to symmetry and proportion and say that symmetry is the relationship between equality and resemblance, the relationship that the parts which for example are on the right hand have to those on the left hand, or those that are above to those below, etc. And proportion is on the contrary the relationship between the overall size of a building and each of its parts, or between those parts themselves, as for example when the length is equal to or double the width, when a storey is no higher than three-quarters of the height of the storey supporting it, and so on. At which point they allow that the parts that are symmetrical may well contain some part of the beauty of the Edifice, but they have no regard for anything that is said about proportion, *because*, they say, *we cannot see it, and therefore it cannot be cause of an effect that can be perceived, such as the effect of pleasure given by beauty.*

Book V

Chapter XVI, inductive arguments proving that Proportions are the cause of beauty in Architecture and that this beauty is no less founded in Nature than that of harmony in Music

If we could argue on this topic as we can in Mathematics, it would not be difficult to convince each other by force of demonstration, but since we cannot agree so easily on the principles of Physics, we should not be surprised if we often find ourselves to have opposing views and if we defend them with such firmness, without recourse to the reasoned arguments we normally adduce, because they have different effects on different minds according to the different manners in which they are considered, or the different concerns of the observer. I say therefore that if I have no convincing demonstration in favour of proportions, I do not see either that any person has sufficiently strong arguments to persuade me against them and to prevent me from explaining herein my thoughts on them and the reasons which led me to share the opinion of Vitruvius and the other Architects who have believed that the proportions of the parts of an Edifice are the principal and essential cause of its beauty.

And if we reason by induction, I say firstly that after having long considered that two unequal weights are sometimes balanced on the arms of a pair of scales when they are placed at certain distances and that of those same weights the heaviest wins in certain situations over the lightest, but in others the lightest may win over the heaviest. Efforts have been made to seek the reason for such different effects and after some experiments, it was seen finally that the weights were balanced when the lengths of the arms of the scales were in the same reciprocal ratio as the sizes of the aforesaid weights. And as it was seen that the effects were indubitably the same on every occasion that these values were in the same ratio as before, it was categorically pronounced that the resemblance between these proportions was the cause of the resemblance of the effects, and this was made into a *stable, reliable and indubitable principle* of one of the most pleasing parts of Mathematics.

François Blondel
1617–1686

[...]

Now, as it is observed by inspection of several buildings ancient and modern that there are some among them that we have pleasure in seeing and that there are others on the contrary which it displeases us to see, it is not difficult to conclude that there are in Architecture constructions that are elegant and agreeable to the eye and others that are disagreeable. So, if through a long series of observations, we were to discover and to know that a thing was always present in all the dimensions of the agreeable buildings and was never present in the others, might we not presume, with reason, that it was that thing that was the cause of the beauty that engenders the pleasure of Architecture?

It was therefore with this in mind that I sought with great attention and effort the particular dimensions of buildings that are generally assumed to be the most pleasing among those that are known, and since in the examination that I made of them I found that there were certain proportions between the sizes of the main body of the Edifice and its parts and between those selfsame parts, and since I have seen that these proportions, which are common to all agreeable Edifices and are to be seen generally in all their parts, are nevertheless found only rarely (not to say never at all) in disagreeable buildings, and furthermore that they are in most cases subject to the same numerical ratios that create the sweetness of the harmonies of Music, I do not see why there should be surprise if I go so far as to pronounce that it is those proportions which are the cause of beauty and elegance in Architecture and that we must make of them a *stable and reliable principle* for that part of Mathematics in order that through study and contemplation we may draw from them in the future an infinity of consequences and rules to serve in the construction of buildings. And this principle, although it is not founded on any convincing logical demonstration, is not any less sure than those of the other Sciences of which we have just spoken above, it being founded, like them, on induction and on a series of experiments.

[...]

As for the argument that the pleasure we feel in seeing some Edifices comes to us only from custom and habit, and that their beauty, which we imagine to be real and natural, is accompanied by other forms of beauty that are authentic and natural, such as the beauty of a material and the delicacy with which it is worked, I say firstly on the subject of custom and habit that our happiness would be far greater than it is if the habit of seeing things were enough for us to find them agreeable. For the number of ugly and deformed objects is infinitely greater that the number of beauteous objects. And as we have almost no objects before our eyes that are not imperfect, we should be in a continual state of satisfaction and tasting without cease the pleasure given us by custom and habit, to which we can habituate ourselves without interruption by perpetually seeing ugly things. I am well aware that there are many things that become bearable through habit, such as in love, taste, fashion in clothing, dances, gestures and a thousand other things, with which otherwise we would have no business, but I also know that good wine, for example, needs no custom for it to be liked, that we feel joy that we cannot well express on first sight of a beautiful body or a beautiful face, and that for the same reason and through experience there are buildings whose beauty surprises us, ravishes us and fills our souls with pleasure and admiration at the very first time we see them, far from custom or habit being necessary to allow us to savour their delights.

François Blondel
1617–1686

And as for the argument that the proportions of the parts in Architecture please us only because they are accompanied by other forms of beauty that are real and natural (such as for example the material and the working of it) I must first admit that the beauty of a material and the delicacy of the execution of work are infinitely useful in enhancing the excellence of that which the proportions bring into being in an Edifice [...] the beauty of a material and the delicacy with which it is worked serve only to make us more aware of the inadequacy of the Architect when they are applied to a subject that is poorly designed and arranged [...] there are buildings made with ordinary materials without ornament or delicate mouldings and which in their simplicity and the bareness of the parts that compose them never cease to surprise and to give extreme pleasure to those who contemplate them [...] Might we not then say, for the same reason, that all the beauty of a Construction comes entirely from the rightness and precision of the dimensions and proportions applied by the Architect in the building of his Edifice?

[...]

It is thus that we look with pleasure on the great masses of some Gothic buildings whose beauty, produced by the symmetry and proportions of the whole in relation to the parts and between those selfsame parts never ceases to be apparent and to make itself noticed in its essence, as if in spite of the ugly ornamentation surrounding it. And what is more convincing still is that if their dimensions are examined attentively, it will be found that they have approximately the same proportions as those that are given to Edifices constructed according to the rules of good Architecture, at the sight of which we feel such satisfaction.

[...]

Book V

Chapter XIX, conclusion of this treatise on the reason for which certain things please us more than others in Architecture

[...] there is no person who does not see without some irritation a crowd of Soldiers scattered in complete disorder in a landscape. We suffer confusion with distaste *because our soul finds nothing stable or reliable on which to anchor itself in disorder and being affected* at the same time by a thousand objects that distract the soul and divide it without granting it the leisure or the place to form an idea of unity which may satisfy it, the soul is disquieted, is confused. However, if that same number of Soldiers were to be ranged under arms and in battle order by a skilful Captain, if each individual Soldier were adroit in the Exercise and handling of his arms, if the various battalions knew well how to execute their manoeuvres, and if all the Corps were accustomed to performing the Military manoeuvres correctly, there is no person who would not be delighted to observe them. Because *order, disposition, arrangement, number* and *proportion* in the sizes of Battalions, Squadrons, the distances and intervals, precision, regularity, variety and speed of movement of so many different subjects create in our eyes, or rather in our imaginations, *one exemplary unit within an infinite series* in which each object finds its distinct place without trespassing on the others and which, through a concept of universality, produces that *Harmonious Concert* that we call *Beauty*, the source of the pleasure we feel.

[...]

And since we cannot say that the beauty of the harmonies in Music or that of an Army ranged in battle order do not possess real, persuasive beauty rooted in nature, although they have no other existence than that of order and proportions, I do not know by what right it is asserted that the beauty of a building, produced, as we have seen, from the order, form, arrangement and proportions of its parts, possesses nothing real, persuasive or rooted in nature.

I could add to these arguments the comparison I have previously drawn between the pleasure we receive from Architecture and that which we receive from various other Arts such as Poetry, Rhetoric, Drama, Painting, Sculpture and so on, to show that it is everywhere founded on the same principle, and that nature, *which is always the same in every place*, uses means that are quite similar when it wishes to produce the same effects in our soul. [...]

Juan Caramuel
de Lobkowitz
1606–1682

*classical canon • antiquity • abuses • nature • nurture • fashion • precedent • authority • invention • systemisation of space distribution • professional practice • education

Juan Caramuel de Lobkowitz (1606–1682)

Civil Architecture, Orthogonal and Oblique (1678)

This massive, two volume architectural treatise by Caramuel, a Cistercian monk who attained the rank of bishop, mainly known today as a forerunner of structural linguistics, contains a highly original section on what the author calls 'oblique' architecture. Based on an application of the most up-to-date findings in the field of optics, this section is a highly sophisticated attempt to create an immutable canon of autonomous, that is to say purely formal, rules with which to govern architecture (Tzonis and Lefaivre, 1984a).

Further reading Bonet-Correa, 1984; Connors, 1982; de Bernardi Ferrero, 1965; Oechslin, 1969; Ramirez, 1981a; Rosenau, 1979; Rykwert, 1982.

Introduction

A new Art is born; (eighth among the Liberal Arts, tenth among the Muses) of which no one else in the world has written. This is oblique Architecture. I call it thus because it is ordered differently from straight architecture, from the temple of Jerusalem, as well as from arithmetic, geometry, logarithms, painting, statuary, perspective and other different sciences discussed so far in the present book.

Treatise V

Part II of Orthogonal architecture in particular

After having dealt with architecture in general, we take up the pen to write about architecture in particular. In anticipation of the explanation of what the difference is, let us pass onto what the division of architecture is.

Architecture, then, is the art of building (and for this reason Alberti, celebrated for being a great mathematician, apart from being very eloquent, wished that the word general be called, relying on the Greeks on the Latin, Science of Building) and is divided into two parts, of which one is called Orthogonal and the other Oblique.

Juan Caramuel
de Lobkowitz
1606–1682

Othogonal architecture has to do with architecture whose floors are parallel to the horizon, that are made literally straight, and have as perpendiculars the lines which are determined by the plumb. On the basis of such plans are orthogonal walls and salons and rooms governed by Ideas derived from [editor's note: *Alberti's concept of*] quadratura, the instrument that serves to delineate right angles.

Concerning the Oblique, where the ground is inclined (as in the case of staircases, in which every day thousands of errors are committed) such as in passages and gates that are irregular; in round or elliptical temples; in the crowning elements above windows; and the angles which the frontispieces of temples end with.

Treatise VI

What Oblique architecture is

Concerning Orthogonal architecture, not only in past centuries but also in our own, different authors have written with certainty and curiosity about it, perfecting, adorning it, and where it appeared necessary, correcting the ideas of palaces and temples such as in, for example, Vitruvius's *Ten Books*. We have dealt amply with this in the precedent treatise. I now enter into Oblique architecture. In this I have no one to follow or imitate. I have seen many things well worked out in practice and in which the laws of Oblique architecture have been well executed. But I have also observed many mistakes in existing buildings. As there is no other book that deals with Oblique architecture and it is usually masons who wish to do away with architects when the occasion arises and they have to accommodate oblique places that are not amenable to straight delineations. They do so by filling the resulting empty spaces with irregular shaped elements [. . .]

Engraving number VI illustrates the obliqueness of a staircase that slopes downward from A to B. The architects were obliged to place balusters in it, and not knowing how to make them according to the necessary deviation, therefore made them straight, providing them with a triangular base FGH and a similar triangular top, CDE. As a result, the whole has had no proportion whatsoever. I have observed similar stairs in different cities, including Rome, in which the Campidoglio is to be found. With the intemperateness of the weather befalling the bases (CDM and LIK) they have been almost destroyed. And as concerns the kind of the stone necessary for the epistyle, it has, as a result, broken because it cannot bear the weight [. . .]

The staircase of the Vatican, beautiful as it is, contains many errors [...] The columns have no bases and rest directly on the stairs and this is where the first error lies. In addition the capitals also lack tops, and this causes offence to the eye. Other places in Rome contain similar errors, which are equally worthy of censure ...

Article I

Architecture in general is defined as the science of building. It is divided into Orthogonal and Oblique. Accordingly, there is a science of Orthogonal building and a science of Oblique building. [...] I say that to build orthogonally is to build well respecting the laws and rules of the art. To build orthogonally is to erect orthogonal walls and combined with them statues and columns according to the laws of Orthogonal and Parallel lines and straight angles. I deny that to build Obliquely is to build badly, that is to build differently from that which is prescribed by the laws and precepts of the art. On the contrary, to build obliquely is to build walls and other elements that form oblique angles with one another and these can have a good correspondence with one another. From which we can conclude that it is possible for an architect to build Orthogonal architecture obliquely and oblique architecture orthogonally and either to work badly and to commit many mistakes in Orthogonal architecture and to work well without errors in executing Oblique architecture.

Juan Caramuel
de Lobkowitz
1606–1682

Article II

[...] The first architect who made Oblique lines in the heavens and on earth was God. Because coming from heaven the two tropics and Arctic and Antarctic circles parallel to the equinox he made the sun move in a way that describes an ellipse which is a circle that is in an oblique relation to the Zodiac. [...] He erected mountains on earth that grow obliquely, like the rivers and the valleys.

Article III

Note

The ground plan (Ichnographia or Sciagraphia, if you prefer the Greek terms) is governed by laws and distinctions and is either quadrangular (that is square or in the form of a parallelogram) or not. If yes, the ground plan is Orthogonal, and on it are erected walls and columns according to architecture in general. If no, the building is circular or the straight lines of the building fall in such a way as to form slopes or inclinations.

The circular plan is that which is described by an arc from which all the lines that join it to the centre are equal. Look carefully at engraving XXIII. There is in it a circle, which is called an equal circle, and its centre is A. For this reason its circumference forms a plan that is perfectly circular. However, if the circumference follows the line BCDE, then the plan is said to be oval, or elliptical, and not perfectly spherical.

A deformation appears that thus affects the walls that form a plan without right angles appear. If you look at engraving II, and then engraving III, you will see the difference. [...] This demands great art and ingenuity in delineating the columns and arcs in this correspondence. And ultimately in Figure IV there are two walls that are in a relation of non-orthogonality and are inclined contrary to it and this Obliqueness would be beautiful if this deformation was taken into account in a symmetrical way.

Oblique lines, which are much more normal and well known, are nevertheless mostly badly executed. This is the case with most staircases. [. . .] This means the plan of a staircase cannot be carried out well according to whim, but must be inclined in such a way as to form the angle BAM in relation to the horizontal line.

The making of staircases combining circularity with inclination is represented in engraving XXV. And there is an example of this double obliqueness. It is in the Temple of Saint Peter in Rome and it is the Chapel of the Sepulchre of the Apostles. Its material is a precious and beautiful marble.

Article IV

How Oblique delineations are born of Orthogonal ones

Let me say (in this, the first lesson of Oblique architecture) that we should turn to engraving XXXIX of the section called 'Arquitectura Recta'. And that after having seen it and considered it well you will work with me in setting up a demonstration.

Juan Caramuel
de Lobkowitz
1606–1682

You have *db* and *dc*, that are equal among themselves as are the lines *DB* and *DC*. On these points, *c*, *d* and *b*, draw three equal lines that are parallel to the line *DB*. To define the tops of the lines trace the line *acd* and with it the squared rectangle *ABCDA*. You will thus have transformed it into the rhomboid *abcda*. And here I warn you that the square is indicated with big capital letters and the rhomboid with small letters that we call cursive. I add that straight lines that are in one figure are the same as in the other figure. Having carried this out, let us proceed.

The line *DFE* divides the figure in the parts that you want (12 metres seem to be enough). Cross this line with lines that are parallel and which pass through points along the line *DE*. These lines, however secret they are, are indicated by points, and they must exit from the square and arrive to the line *ab*. From there on they get inclined and run parallel to the line *bc*. Then trace the vertical *ed*, because it is the one that dominates the entire delineation. Then take up a compass and make sure the line *mf* is equal to the line *MF*.

That *sg* is equal to *SG*; that *zh* is equal to *ZH*; that *ai* is equal to *AI* and *th k* to *TH K*. And finally *fl* to *FL*. And so on and so forth until the end of the process. And at last with a wise and experienced hand you pass a line through all the points and you will derive an oblique circle *efghikl*. In the same manner that you have derived the first circle, you will be able to derive a second, by assuring that *sn* is equal to *SN*, etc. And passing through these points with your pen, you will describe the circle *mnopqr* etc. With the same diligence, you will then delineate the external circle because *zt* and *ZT* are equal. And passing through those points that I have indicated, with your pen you will describe the circle *stuxy*, etc.

Please do me the favour of pursuing the reading of this doctrine and of considering well these two figures, and to note how in them the secret lines that have the same letters are equal. And you will be made to see how the one transforms the other, and how the Orthogonal is converted into Oblique.

anticlassicism • deformation • freedom • naturalism • representation • truth • illusion • systemisation of space distribution

82. Juan Caramuel de Lobkowitz. *Architectura Civil recta y obliqua*. 1678. The five kinds of architecture corresponding to five kinds of social order.

83. Juan Caramuel de Lobkowitz. *Architectura Civil recta y obliqua*. 1678. The Doric capital and base as examples of orthogonal architecture.

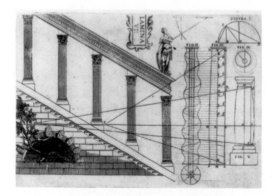

84. Juan Caramuel de Lobkowitz. *Architectura Civil recta y obliqua*. 1678. Orthogonal kind of columns in conflict with the inclined frame of a staircase. 84b. Oblique kind of columns resolving the conflict.

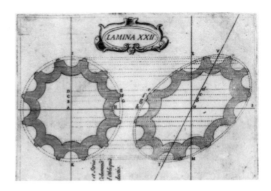

85. Juan Caramuel de Lobkowitz. *Architectura Civil recta y obliqua*. 1678. Orthogonal and oblique kind of Corinthian capital and shaft plan obtained by translating the orthogonal.

86. Juan Caramuel de Lobkowitz. *Architectura Civil recta y obliqua*. 1678. Example of oblique architecture applied in the difficult case of double deformation of orthogonal architecture, a staircase with curvilinear plan.

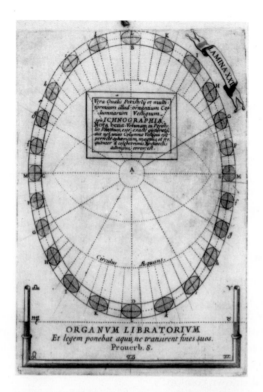

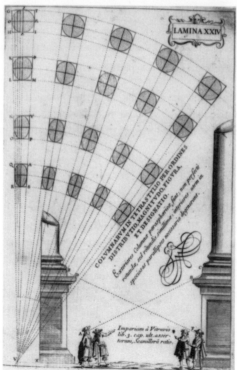

87. Juan Caramuel de Lobkowitz. *Architectura Civil recta y obliqua*. 1678. 89b. Juan Caramuel de Lobkowitz. *Architectura Civil recta y obliqua*.

Guarino Guarini (1624–1683)

Civil Architecture (written after 1678; published 1737)

Guarini was a philosopher who while a Thetine monk in Rome discovered Borromini's architecture and developed into the leading Italian baroque architect of the later seventeenth century (Wittkower, 1973). His line of argument bears some similarity with Perrault's (1683). Both agree that proportion is not a matter of blind obedience to the antique prototypes and rules. But Guarini concludes that the laws of proportion should be completely subjected to laws of perspective with the aim of creating exciting visual effects. The book, one of many by the author (Wittkower, ibid.), was published after his death by his student Vittone.

Further reading Kaufmann, 1955; Mueller, 1968; Oechslin, 1969; Ramirez, 1981b; Wiebenson, 1982; Wittkower, 1962.

First Observation

Architecture concerns, before all else, comfort

This we sincerely declare because the art of building was born of necessity, and need was the first to fashion a shelter; whence even the most barbaric peoples of America had some sort of houses in which to shelter themselves from the inclemencies of the weather; thus men's first purpose in building was to minister to their needs, and to find in their buildings their own comfort.

Second Observation

Architecture should not contrive its buildings in such a way that they run counter to the customs of the country and its people

It follows from the above observation that what runs counter to a country or its people shall not be comfortable. Thus it would be inconvenient for poor peasants to build spacious rooms, or to raise ceilings too high in the colder countries, and so on.

Chapter Three

On the general rules of architecture

Architecture, though based on mathematics, is no less an art that appeals to the senses, which does not seek to displease the senses with reason: thus, even though many of its rules follow the dictates of reason, when its demonstrations prove offensive to the eyes, it shall change them, ignore them and even contradict them; thus it shall not be uninstructive to learn what the architect must observe, to see the purpose of architecture and its way of proceeding.

Sixth Observation

Architecture can amend old rules, and invent new ones

The beauty of buildings consists in the suitable proportions of their parts, to obtain which proportions the Ancients in the person of Vitruvius prescribed certain well-defined rules, which some architects have followed so closely, that *nec latum unguem* would they depart from them; but I view the matter differently, and from what occurs in all other professions consider that some ancient rules can be amended, and other new ones added; and primarily experience itself demonstrates this, for the antiquities of Rome are not precisely in accordance with the rules of Vitruvius, as neither are the proportions of the Baroque, nor those of other Moderns, who observe to every last measure [editor's note: 'Simmetria'] the ancient documents; but as we can see, many new proportions, and many new forms of execution, have been found in our times which were not used by the Ancients.

Guarino Guarini
1624–1683

Seventh Observation

To preserve the appearance of rightful proportions, architecture should depart from the true proportions and rules

This we shall prove: since Architecture aims to please the senses, if the senses are deceived, as often happens, judging a straight object to be crooked, an upright one to be leaning, and a large one to be small, it shall be necessary in such case to gratify them, in such a way that what *is* not but *seems* to be lacking be made to seem right by the addition of more than the due.

Eighth Observation

Architecture should obey the nature of the locality, and accommodate itself to it artfully

To accommodate himself to the locality should be one of the architect's principal intentions. For example: if the locality is misshapen, irregular and cannot comprise a square without great loss of area, while it would better accommodate an oval, the architect should place therein an oval, rather than a square; if the area is surrounded by houses, and can only receive light from above, the architect should choose a type and disposition of building whereby it shall receive light from above, and so on.

Ninth Observation

Agreeable proportions in architecture can be various, without giving disturbance the one to the other

This is proven: for since there is no science, no matter how evident, that is not based on opinions that are not only many but contrary, even in extremely serious matters of faith, customs and interests; then how much more can architecture vary, that takes no delight, if it does not please the senses; nor is governed by any other reason, than the pleasing of a learned judgement, a judicious eye? This can be seen in the diverse proportions that the resourceful and celebrated modern architects use, and in the Antiquities of Rome, which are at variance with the sentiments of Vitruvius. It can also be seen in Gothic architecture, which must have given pleasure in its time, although nowadays it is barely esteemed but rather derided, although those truly ingenious men had erected buildings requiring skills so great, that whoever with a level eye considers them shall see that, although not correct in their proportions, they are marvellous nevertheless, and worthy of much praise.

Tenth Observation

Architecture should not take as much licence as perspective

Guarino Guarini
1624–1683

Perspective succeeds in its purpose and achieves its end when it deceives the eye and makes the surface of the body appear; hence even in an immoderate architecture it can succeed in its end with every praise. Architecture, however, cannot achieve its end of pleasing the eye other than with true proportions, with its ultimate purpose being not to deceive the eye. Perspective moreover need not concern itself with the solidity and strength of the work, but merely with delighting the eye. Architecture however must consider the solidity of the work, hence it cannot be as free to invent as perspective is.

Treatise III: On the Drawing of Elevations

The architect must consider two types of elevation: one that assumes a plane from which his drawing is to rise; the other that assumes no plane but is drawn vertically to be later cast onto a plane to see how much of the plane is covered by it. Therefore there are two types of drawings, one we shall call elevated, and the other depressed; the latter we shall discuss in the following Treaty; for the moment we shall talk only of the former. Vitruvius defines the drawing of elevations as follows: *erecta frontis imago, modiceque picta rationibus, operis futuri figura*, that is the elevation of the front, adroitly shadowed, and showing the forms and the ratios of the future building; in short, an elevation of the façades of the future building, and of each of its proportions.

Item one: On the first principles of elevation drawings

Every art is based on clear, simple and evident principles: thus the drawing of elevations, like the other sciences, has certain first delineations, via which it diversely composes and forms its ideas, which in the following Observations we shall enumerate; and there are in general diverse sorts of projections and other saliences which advance out of the vertical plane of the building and curve in diverse ways to lend grace to the work.

Item two: On the way to effect various curved lines necessary in elevation drawings

For the swelling of columns, for the volutes and spiral forms, it is necessary to know how to trace diverse curved lines, which do not of themselves form any body, as they do not return to the point from which they started: these are principally the parabola, the hyperbola, the spiral line, the conchoid, the undulating line, the line of perspective, which we shall discuss only in so far as they relate to architecture [. . .]

Item twenty-three: On oblique architecture

Serlio, in Book I Chapter 6, gives some teaching of this architecture; and Caramuel dedicates a whole treatise to it, with many diagrams; it is an architecture which is employed not only to diminish or enlarge cornices in keeping with proportions and any given drawings, but is also of use in the architecture of staircases and the forms they may take, and since we intend to discuss staircases it is fitting to advance these considerations.

anticlassicism • deformation • freedom • naturalism • orientalism • representation • truth • illusion

Guarino Guarini
1624–1683

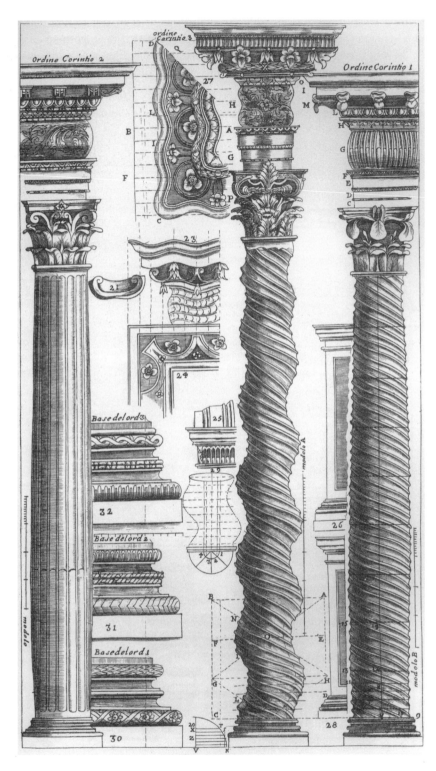

88. Guarino Guarini. *Architectura Civil*. 1678. 'Supreme' canonical, on the left, and twisted and 'undulating', or Salomonic Corinthian order.

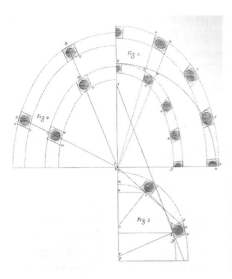

89., 89b. Guarino Guarini. *Architectura Civil*. 1678.
Guarini's treatment of the conflict between canonical
regular rectangular order and irregular containing frame
was to save at all costs the regularity of the elements of
the order. The drawing on the left suggests the shape of
the column to remain indifferent to the elliptical plan of the
colonnade while on the right he suggests a triangle to be
inserted to fill in the anomalous gap generated between the
inclined frame of the stairs and the orthogonal baluster.

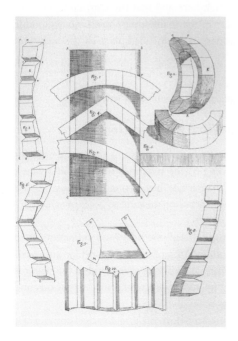

90. Guarino Guarini. *Architectura Civil*. 1678. Structural
detail showing the new sophisticated techniques of
descriptive geometry to represent instructions for stone
cutting.

[231]

Sébastien le Prêtre, seigneur de Vauban (1633–1707)

Letter to Louvois (1681)

Vauban was the most influential military engineer of the seventeenth century and by far the most successful in guaranteeing military victories for Louis XIV. From this letter he appears to have been as much concerned with the expressive capabilities of military architecture than with purely technical qualities. The other work excerpted here, his **Maxims** (1680s), reveal the extremely rationalised systems thinking typical of military operations but applied here to the complex practical tasks involved in managing the building of domestic architecture.

Further reading Jähns, 1889; Parent, 1971.

Sébastien le Prêtre, seigneur de Vauban 1633–1707

Observation by Louvois. The design of the doors that you have sent for the citadel is too large and too magnificent: once again, a way must be found to diminish them considerably. His Majesty is having too many fortified places built to continue to make for them beautiful doors that add nothing to the effectiveness of the place. I beg you to work on diminishing them in order to ensure that they no longer cost more than 12,000 ecus for the pair.

Reply from Vauban. It is not possible to make them less wide or less high given the need for security of closure and the necessity for ease of passage. I fail to see how it is possible to subtract anything from the solidity of their masonry or their different levels. This means that all the changes that you may desire to be made inevitably come down to a few triglyphs, metopes and dentils and the arms and monograms of the King, which form the entirety of the ornamentation of these doors.

[. . .]

You will save by this approximately 400 or 500 ecus, enabling you to claim that they are of very simple design, and even very ugly. I am not however of this opinion, given that the whole of Germany passes through here and that the Germans, who are extremely curious and perceptive connoisseurs in the main, are people who will judge the magnificence of the King and the effectiveness of the fortified place by the beauty of its doors.

[. . .]

efficiency • economisation • fit • utility • legitimation • representation of power

Some Maxims That Are Good to Observe by All Those Who Build (1680s)

1 Whoever wishes to have something built must first undertake to make the cage for the bird, in other words to adjust one's building to the revenues of one's land, one's condition, one's needs and especially to the means one has at one's disposal. To use them otherwise would mean falling either into excess or meanness, both of which are equally loathsome and ridiculous.

2 These conditions duly taken into account with all the necessary reflection, then the issue is to choose the location of one's building in a place with good air and especially that this spot be on one's own land and not on someone else's; where the water is clean, excellent and close, the bottom good, its access practical, close to woods and abundant, easy and reasonably priced building materials.

3 Then examine well the quality of the bottom before making any decision, for if it

were necessary to find a foundation that was very low it would be imprudent for an individual to commit himself and it must never be by constraint or a great necessity that one undertakes to surmount these great difficulties that cost a lot and do not always produce things which are of good quality.

4 After having drawn up a report of all the pieces that can be necessary to house one comfortably and given oneself all the time needed for this study, one must look it over several times over a considerable period of time, and make all the possible reflections and always take away and add in such a way that nothing remains to be desired.

5 Make several plans of the distribution of the building simultaneously, while avoiding all confusion and too great a dependence of the rooms among themselves and also avoiding to mislocate the staircase, the chimneys, etc., and especially do nothing that is contrary to the rules that follow here.

6 Examine many times and at different times these plans and elevations, show them to intelligent acquaintances, listen to their opinions and correct them always to the point at which your mind is content and has no more objections, after which you have a good version made of these drawings and stick to them without any changes.

Sébastien le Prêtre, seigneur de Vauban 1633–1707

7 Having done this, calculate in a detailed way that which the finished building, once you have the key in your hand, is capable of holding, and to this effect look into all the parts in minute detail and do not fool oneself about the price of materials the way people who are not experienced in building always do. After which, add a quarter to the price of the estimate, maybe even a third, in consideration of the hidden costs that almost always arrive from trickery, the changes and augmentations that always occur, bad weather, bad orders, bad materials used in a bad way, cheating of the workers or the negligence of those in charge, bad luck, etc.

8 Estimate also the accompaniments of the house that one is having built, such as gardens, enclosures, orchards, farmyards, avenues, and even the furniture that are always a considerable part of the expense. All these things must be examined thoroughly not once but many times. After which, if one finds oneself in such a situation as to be able to cover this expense, proceed to the collection of the materials a year in advance if it is a considerable building and always start with the most necessary and with that which needs the most expedient attention.

9 Accommodate oneself to the site of the said building, whose greatest length and principal apartments must face the rising sun. For, if this is achieved, one of its ends will face the north and the other the south and, in this way, the main rooms will not be exposed either to the great cold or heat. This is not so general a rule that there are no exceptions, according to the case and place where one is obliged to build.

10 Once all these precautions have been taken and examined, the best will be (if the master is able) to expedite the work as much as possible provided that this does not drive up the price. The reason for this is that this way one is freed from the encumbrance of workers and from the problems associated with them and that through diligence one is able to considerably hasten the pleasure resulting from one's work.

11 The parts that require great care in the construction process are the excavation of the foundations and the transportation of earth, the rerouting of water channels, if there is any, the reinforcement if any is necessary, cut stones, plaster, lime, sand and water, the tiling, the cement, sculpture and painting, carpentry and joining, the floors and coverings, ironwork, locks and nails, plumbing and big furnishings.

12 If all these things are well observed, the person who is having a building erected

will need nothing more than these maxims that will prevent him from falling into the most common traps and that can only be extremely useful because of the good advice they contain.

design methodology • efficiency • economisation • fit • utility • systemisation of space distribution

Sébastien le
Prêtre, seigneur
de Vauban
1633–1707

Anonymous

L'Architecture militaire (?)

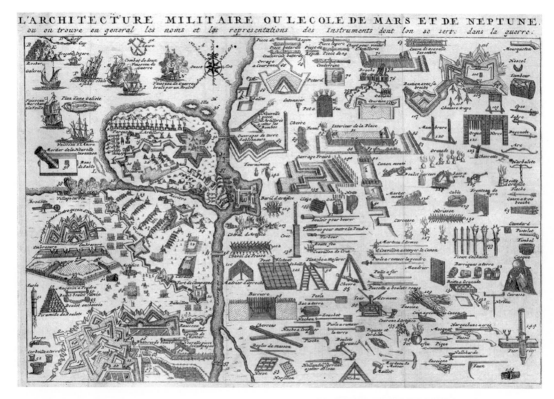

91. Anonymous. *L'Architecture militaire*, end of the seventeenth-century engraving enumerating the elements of military and naval means of attack and defence, mechanical and architectural.

Antoine Desgodetz (1653–1728)

The Antique Buildings of Rome (1682)

Desgodetz, a graduate of the Académie Royale d'Architecture, was sent to Rome, as part of Colbert's policy to systematise architectural knowledge, in order to make scientifically exact measurements of the major Roman monuments. His findings were used by Perrault (1683) (Herrmann, 1958, 1973). Desgodetz's work became the standard authority all over Europe until the nineteenth century (Herrmann, ibid.).

Further reading Bilodeau, 1997; Blomfield, 1973; Hautecoeur, 1948–1963; Lemonnier, 1911–1929; Schudt, 1959; Tzonis et al., 1982; Wiebenson, 1993.

Preface

I have no doubt that my undertaking herein will appear a very rash one: to set out to discuss a topic on which the most learned Architects have already worked and which they appear to have entirely exhausted. And I undertake to do so only with the greatest of reluctance, having some difficulty in convincing myself that I can add something to the excellent Volumes that Palladio, Serlio and Labacco have handed down to us concerning the Edifices of the Ancients and what Monsieur de Chambray has noted in his Parallel Study of Ancient and Modern Architecture. For the veneration that my Masters have inspired in me for the writings of those great Personages has ever led me to read them with respect, and therefore I have never had the thought that anything could be found in them that was not supported by persuasive reasons and I presumed that if any of their arguments was not in accord with that of which the common population is capable, those Authors had others in mind that are unknown to us and on which all our capacities would give us no other right than to guess at them, if we can, in order to derive advantage therefrom.

Given this praiseworthy assumption, I sought that which might have led those celebrated Authors to neglect the detail and accuracy that is lacking in the descriptions and drawings that they have handed down to the public. For, in the end, we cannot say that the dimensions are accurate, nor that the aesthetics and other particulars of the originals are reported in their exact truth, since most of these things are different in the books of each of these Architects. It is a certain fact that even before my observations, which show that they did not present things as they are, they had already contradicted each other. It first came to my mind that these great Authors had not judged correctly how useful such accuracy would be. The excellence and beauty that causes the Edifices of the Ancients to be admired is not dependent on the minute details of their proportions and other circumstances of this nature without which we may say that their works are certainly resplendent, appearing in all their grandeur and all their majesty. But since that these Authors wrote down all the proportions of the parts down to the smallest and least important, I thought that we must believe that if they were not in agreement on those dimensions there might be at least one among their number who recorded the true ones. And the precision with which the great Masters noted down all the dimensions seems to lead us to understand that there are mysteries in the proportions of Architecture that is given solely to the Learned to comprehend and like the course of the Stars and the Organs that serve the most noble functions of Animals, there are movements and conformations of which we know neither the causes nor the purposes, although we may be sure that there is nothing in Beings so perfect that it does not serve some purpose. It may also be that Learned men in Architecture, who are privy to the secrets of this great Mistress of the arts, are alone in knowing the ultimate truth of these proportions and if there are some whose reasons escape their comprehension, it is necessary to judge those that are not yet discovered by those they have discovered, in the certainty at least that these great examples handed down to us by the Ancients could never be imitated too exactly.

My first intention was, once I had undertaken to measure precisely the ancient monuments of Rome, to determine which of these Authors of great reputation should be followed, as having recorded the true dimensions. But when in the field I devoted all the care needed to remove this doubt, I was very surprised to make another discovery that I was not seeking, and that was that those who have hitherto measured the ancient Edifices did not do so accurately and none of the drawings we possess of them is free of very substantial error.

Although it is no great thing to have had the patience to measure all these dimensions and the talent of these excellent men who collected the drawings of ancient Edifices and who gave us such learned explanations saw no great interest in the errors to be seen there, which must be attributed simply to the Labourers they employed to do this work, who could not know many things other than by conjecture and by estimation, since they were almost inaccessible due to their height above the ground, or hidden in the ground covering them, nevertheless, I would never have dared to show myself in public in a capacity so unattractive as that of corrector of Volumes that are generally approved, if I had not been obliged to obey the Powers that be and to defer to authorities that were obliged to overcome both my inclination to refrain from producing my work and the reticence that it is reasonable that my age should inspire in me in the face of an enterprise of this great extent.

It is therefore appropriate, before judging my conduct in publishing this Volume, to know in what spirit I undertook it, the method I adopted to bring it to the state in which it now is, and what led me to publish it, for in truth I undertook it at the start solely for my own instruction.

I saw that in order to unearth that which was hidden and to approach as I desired that which was high up, it would be necessary for me to incur expense and to make efforts that were far beyond my resources. Nevertheless, in the end my zeal and perseverance overcame all these difficulties. For I found the means during the sixteen months I spent in Rome to make my own drawings of all these ancient Edifices, whose plans, elevations and side views I drew, along with all the dimensions that I measured exactly, following the contours of the ornaments in terms of their aesthetics and in the different styles apparent in them. I verified all this several times to confirm for myself a certainty for which I could take responsibility, having had excavated those things that were buried and had raised ladders and other machines to approach those that were very high up, in order to see close-up and measure with Compasses the heights and projections of all the parts, both generally and individually, down to the very smallest.

[. . .]

In comparing and contrasting the measurements made by myself with those recorded by the Authors I have named above, I divide the Authors into two categories, for Palladio, Labacco and Monsieur de Cambray have established precise measurements with which they give the dimensions of all the parts of the Buildings they

Antoine
Desgodetz
1653–1728

[237]

describe. Serlio gives none, and that is why I have related all the proportions of the parts of the Edifices he has drawn to the diameters he gives for the columns, assuming that this diameter has been measured correctly. I compare the dimensions he gives and the measurements provided by the other Authors with the measurements I myself made. [. . .] I drew all the side views in large format to the same scale in order to be able to compare and contrast them at a glance without the need to calculate the various parts.

It will perhaps be found that the great precision of the dimensions I provide has a certain superfluous or affected character about it, when for example I note that over a length of nine or ten fathoms [*toise*], one among the Authors I am studying is in error by six or seven lines. However, I did not believe that in order to avoid criticism for adopting a vain precision I should refrain from setting forth matters as I found them to be, since precision is the only matter at hand herein. For if in one or two places a remark has escaped me on the particulars I have observed, I do not give them as my own, but as having heard them said in the conferences of the Academy. And although those reflections are founded on opinions particular to some members of the Company and not shared by the others, they made a sufficient impression upon me that I could but report them on those occasions where the examples of the practices of the Ancients seemed in some way to confirm them, in such manner nevertheless that the Reader remains entirely free to judge them, and to do so with ease, since he has before his eyes the evidence on which he must judge.

precedent • authority • invention • representation • truth • illusion

Antoine
Desgodetz
1653–1728

92. Antoine Desgodetz. *Les Edifices antiques de Rome.* 1682. Section and orthogonally projected interior documenting with great exactitude the Pantheon in Rome.

Claude Perrault (1613–1688)

The Ordonnance of the Five Species of Columns (1683)

(See Perrault 1673)

Claude Perrault
1613–1688

The Ancients rightly believed that the proportional rules that give buildings their beauty were based on the proportions of the human body and that just as nature has suited a massive build to bodies made for physical labour while giving a slighter one to those requiring adroitness and agility, so in the art of building, different rules are determined by the different intentions to make a building more massive or more delicate. Now these different proportions together with their appropriate ornaments are what give rise to the different architectural orders, whose characters, denned by variations in ornament, are what distinguish them most visibly but whose most essential differences consist in the relative size of their constituent parts.

These differences between the orders that are based, with little exactitude or precision, on their proportions and characters are the only well-established matters in architecture. Everything else pertaining to the precise measurement of their members or the exact outline of their profiles still has no rule on which all architects agree; each architect has attempted to bring these elements to their perfection chiefly through the things that proportion determines. As a result, in the opinion of those who are knowledgeable, a number of architects have approached an equal degree of perfection in different ways. This shows that the beauty of a building, like that of the human body, lies less in the exactitude of unvarying proportion and the relative size of constituent parts than in the grace of its form, wherein nothing other than a pleasing variation can sometimes give rise to a perfect and matchless beauty without strict adherence to any proportional rule. [. . .]

In architecture, there are not only general rules of proportion, such as those that, as we have said, distinguish one order from another, but also derailed rules from which one cannot deviate without robbing an edifice of much of its grace and elegance. Yet these proportions have enough latitude to leave architects free to increase or decrease the dimensions of different elements according to the requirements occasioned by varying circumstances. It is this prerogative that caused the Ancients to create works with proportions as unusual as those of the Doric and Ionic cornices of the Theatre of Marcellus or the cornice of the Façade of Nero, which are all half again as large as they should be according to the rules of Vitruvius. It is also for this very reason that all those who have written about architecture contradict one another, with the result that in the ruins of ancient buildings and among the great number of architects who have dealt with the proportions of the orders, one can find agreement neither between any two buildings nor between any two authors, since none has followed the same rules.

This shows just how ill-founded is the opinion of people who believe that the proportions supposed to be preserved in architecture are as certain and invariable as the proportions that give musical harmony its beauty and appeal, proportions that do not depend on us but that nature has established with absolutely immutable precision and that cannot be changed without immediately offending even the least sensitive ear. For if this were so, those works of architecture that do not have the true and natural proportions that people claim they can have would necessarily be condemned by common consensus, at least by those whom extensive knowledge has made most capable of such discernment. And just as we never find musicians holding different opinions on the correctness of a chord, since this correctness has a certain and obvious beauty of which the senses are readily and even necessarily convinced, so would we also find architects agreeing on the rules capable of perfecting the proportions of architecture, especially when, after repeated efforts, they had apparently explored all the many possible avenues to attaining such perfection. [. . .] For nearly two thousand years architects have tried out solutions varying in dimension from two and one-half to seventeen minutes, some making this projection as much as seven times as large as others without being disconcerted by the preponderance of proportions at variance with the one they would like to have accepted as true and natural. And disconcerted they should have been had any one of these proportions indeed been true and natural, since a true and natural proportion would have had the same effect as do things that offend or give pleasure without our knowing why.

But we cannot claim that the proportions of architecture please our sight for unknown reasons or make the impression they do of themselves in the same way that musical harmonies affect the ear without our knowing the reasons for their consonance. Harmony, consisting in the awareness gained through our ears of that which is the result of the proportional relationship of two strings, is quite different from the knowledge gained through our eyes of that which results from the proportional relationship of the parts that make up a column. For if, through our ears, our minds can be touched by something that is the result of the proportional relationship of two Strings without our minds being aware of this relationship, it is because the ear is incapable of giving the mind such intellectual knowledge. But the eye, which can convey knowledge of the proportion it makes us appreciate, makes the mind experience its effect through the knowledge it conveys of this proportion and only through this knowledge. From this it follows that what pleases the eye cannot be due to a proportion of which the eye is unaware, as is usually the case.

Claude Perrault
1613–1688

A true comparison between music and architecture demands that one consider more than harmonies, which are all by nature unchangeable. One must also consider the manner in which they are applied, which differs with different musicians and countries, just as the application of architectural proportions differs with different authors and buildings. For just as it is impossible to claim that any single way of using harmonies is necessarily and infallibly better than another or to demonstrate that the music of France is better than that of Italy, so it is also impossible to prove that one capital, because it has more or less of a projection, is necessarily and naturally more beautiful than another. And the case is not the same as that of a simple chord, where one can demonstrate that a string played with another that is a little longer or a little shorter than half its length is unbearably discordant, because such is the natural and necessary effect of proportion on sounds.

There are still other inherent and natural effects produced by proportions, such as the movement of bodies in mechanics, but neither should these be compared to the effects produced by proportions for the pleasurable satisfaction of sight. For if one arm of a balance is a certain length relative to the other so that one weight will necessarily and naturally prevail over the other, it does not follow that a certain proportional relationship between the parts of a building must give rise to a beauty that so affects the mind that it transports it, so to speak, and compels it to accept that proportion as inevitably as the relative length of the arms of a balance makes that balance tilt in the direction of the longer arm. Yet that is what most architects claim when they would have us believe that what creates beauty in the Pantheon, for example, is the proportion of that temple's wall thickness to its interior void, its width to its height, and a hundred other things that are imperceptible unless they are measured and that, even when they are perceptible, fail to assure us that any deviation from these proportions would have displeased us.

I would not linger unduly over this question – even though it is a problem whose solution is of the utmost importance for the work I have undertaken and even though I am convinced that anyone who takes the trouble to examine the issue will find no great difficulty in judging that I need not argue my point of view any more than I already have – were it not for the fact that most architects hold the opposite opinion. This shows that we must not consider the problem unworthy of examination, for even though reason appears to be on one side, the authority of architects on the other balances the issue and leaves it undecided; in truth, though, the question is architectural only in so far as certain details and examples taken from architecture serve to show that there are many things that do not fail to please us despite common sense and reason. However, all architects agree on the truth of these examples.

Claude Perrault
1613–1688

Now, even though we often like proportions that follow the rules of architecture without knowing why, it is nevertheless true that there must be some reason for this liking. The only difficulty is to know if this reason is always something positive, as in the case of musical harmonies, or if, more usually, it is simply founded on custom and whether that which makes the proportions of a building pleasing is not the same as that which makes the proportions of a fashionable costume pleasing. For the latter have nothing positively beautiful or inherently likeable, since when there is a change in custom or in any other of the non-positive reasons that make us like them, we like them no longer, even though the proportions themselves remain the same.

In order to judge rightly in this case, one must suppose two kinds of beauty in architecture and know which beauties are based on convincing reasons and which depend only on prejudice. I call beauties based on convincing reasons those whose presence in works is bound to please everyone, so easily apprehended are their value and quality. They include the richness of the materials, the size and magnificence of the building, the precision and cleanness of the execution, and symmetry, which in French signifies the kind of proportion that produces an unmistakable and striking beauty. For there are two kinds of proportion. One, difficult to discern, consists in the proportional relationship between parts, such as that between the size of various elements, either with respect to one another or to the whole, of which an element may be, for instance, a seventh, fifteenth, or twentieth part. The other kind of proportion, called symmetry, is very apparent and consists in the relationship the parts have collectively as a result of the balanced correspondence of their size, number, disposition and order. We never fail to perceive flaws in this proportion, such as on the interior of the Pantheon where the coffering of the vault, in failing to line up with the windows below, causes a disproportion and lack of symmetry that anyone may readily discern, and which, had it been corrected, would have produced a more visible beauty than that of the proportion between the thickness of the walls and the temple's interior void, or in other proportions that occur in this building, such as that of the portico, whose width is three-fifths the exterior diameter of the whole temple.

Against the beauties I call positive and convincing, I set those I call arbitrary, because they are determined by our wish to give a definite proportion, shape, or form to things that might well have a different form without being misshapen and that appear agreeable not by reasons within everyone's grasp but merely by custom and the association the mind makes between two things of a different nature. By this association the esteem that inclines the mind to things whose worth it knows also inclines it to things whose worth it does not know and little by little induces it to value both equally. This principle is the natural basis for belief, which is nothing but the result of a predisposition not to doubt the truth of something we do not know if it is accompanied by our knowledge and good opinion of the person who assures us of it. It is also prejudice that makes us like the fashions and the patterns of speech that custom has established at court, for the regard we have for the worthiness and patronage of people in the court makes us like their clothing and their way of speaking, although these things in themselves have nothing positively likeable, since after a time they offend us without their having undergone any inherent change.

Claude Perrault
1613–1688

It is the same in architecture, where there are things such as the usual proportions between capitals and their columns that custom alone makes so agreeable that we could not bear their being otherwise, even though in themselves they have no beauty that must infallibly please us or necessarily elicit our approval. There are even some things that ought to appear misshapen and offensive in light of reason and good sense but that custom has rendered tolerable. [. . .] For all these things, which should cause displeasure because they contravene reason and good sense, were tolerated at first because they were linked to positive beauties and ultimately became agreeable through custom, whose power has been such that those said to have taste in architectural matters cannot bear them when they are otherwise.

In order to realise how many rules there are in architecture for things that please, albeit contrary to reason, we must consider that the reasons that ought to carry the greatest weight in regulating architectural beauty should be based either on the imitation of nature, such as the correspondence between the parts and the whole of a column, which reflects the correspondence between the parts and the whole of a human body; or on the resemblance of an edifice to the first buildings that nature taught men to make; or on the resemblance that the echinus, cymatium, astragal and other elements have to the things whose shape they have adopted; or, finally, on the imitation of practices in other crafts, such as carpentry, which provide the model for friezes, architraves and cornices and their constituent parts, as well as for modillions and mutules. Nevertheless, the grace and beauty of these things do not depend on such imitations and resemblances, for if they did, the more exact the imitation, the greater would be their beauty. Nor is it true that the proportions and the shape that all these things must have in order to please and that cannot be changed without offending good taste faithfully reproduce the proportions and the shape of the things they represent and imitate. For it is obvious that the capital, which is the head of the body represented by the entire column, has nothing like the proportion a human head should have with respect to its body. [. . .] By the same token, columns do not meet with greater general approval the more they resemble the tree trunks that served as posts in the first hues that men built. [. . .] Nor would cornices please us more were their constituents to represent more exactly the shape and disposition of the elements of wood construction that are their origin. [. . .]

Hence, neither imitation of nature, nor reason, nor good sense in any way constitutes the basis for the beauty people claim to see in proportion and in the orderly disposition of the parts of a column; indeed, it is impossible to find any source other than custom for the pleasure they impart. Since those who first invented these proportions had no rule other than their fancy [*fantaisie*] to guide them, as their fancy changed they introduced new proportions, which in turn were found pleasing. Thus the proportion of the Corinthian capital that was considered beautiful by the Greeks, who gave it a height of one column diameter, was not approved by the Romans, who added another one-sixth column diameter. [...] This only shows, however, that the taste of the architects who approved, or still approve, of the proportion that the Greeks gave their Corinthian capitals must be based on some principle other than that of a positive and convincing beauty, pleasing of itself, inherent in the thing as such – that is, dependent on its having this proportion and no other – and that it is difficult to find any reason for such taste other than prejudice or custom. Indeed, as we have said, the basis for this prejudice is the fact that when countless convincing, positive and reasonable beauties occur in a work that has this proportion, these positive beauties succeed in making a work so beautiful that although the proportion itself may add nothing to its beauty, the reasonably founded love born to the entire work is transferred to each constituent part individually.

Claude Perrault
1613–1688

The first works of architecture manifested richness of materials; grandeur, opulence and precision of workmanship; symmetry (which is a balanced and fitting correspondence of parts that maintain the same arrangement and position); good sense in matters where it is called for; and other obvious reasons for beauty. As a result, these works seemed so beautiful and were so admired and revered that people decided they should serve as the criteria for all others. And in as much as they believed it impossible to add to or to change anything in all these positive beauties without diminishing the beauty of the whole, they found it unimaginable that the proportions of these works could be altered without ill effect; whereas, they could, in fact, have been otherwise without injury to the other beauties. In the same way, when a person passionately loves a face whose only perfect beauty lies in its complexion, he also believes its proportion could not be improved upon, for just as the great beauty of one part makes him love the whole, so the love of the whole entails love of all its parts.

It is therefore true that in architecture there is positive beauty and beauty that is only arbitrary, even though it appears to be positive due to prejudice, against which one guards oneself with great difficulty. It is also true that even though good taste is founded on a knowledge of both kinds of beauty, a knowledge of arbitrary beauty is usually more apt to form what we call taste and is that which distinguishes true architects from the rest. Thus, common sense is all that is needed to apprehend most kinds of positive beauty. [...]

Yet it can be readily appreciated that all these things could have different proportions without affronting or wounding even the most refined and delicate sensibility, which is certainly not the same thing as when a troubled disposition harms a patient without his knowing the precise extent of the disorders that are making him ill. For to be offended or pleased by architectural proportions requires the discipline of long familiarity with rules that are established by usage alone, and of which good sense can intimate no knowledge, just as in civil law there are rules dependent on the will of legislators and on the consent of nations that a natural understanding of fairness will never reveal.

Thus, as we have said, if when considering works with differing proportions, true architects approve only those that are the mean between the two extremes of the examples cited earlier, they do so not because such extremes offend good taste for some natural and positive reason that is contrary to good sense. Rather, they approve the mean only because the excessive proportions of our examples are not in keeping with the usage [*manière*] that we have become accustomed to find pleasing in the fine works of the Ancients, where such extremes are not usually present and where the ancient usage is not so much pleasing in itself as pleasing because it is linked to other positive, natural and reasonable beauties that make it pleasing by association, so to speak.

However, usage of the mean, equally distanced from the extremes observable in the examples put forward, still varies considerably and is not precisely defined in ancient works, which, for the most part, meet with uniform approval. Now even though there is no compelling reason for such usage to be perfectly regulated in order Claude Perrault
1613–1688 for it to please and, consequently, even though in architecture there are, strictly speaking, no proportions that are true in themselves, it still remains to be investigated whether it is possible to establish probable mean proportions that are founded on positive reasons but that do not stray too far from those that are accepted and in current use. [. . .]

And this would not be very difficult to do; for unlike matters pertaining to the durability and convenience of buildings, where it is still possible to introduce innovations of considerable utility, these proportions are things for which no study or research need be undertaken nor any discovery be made. Nor are they at all of the same nature as the proportions required in military architecture and in the construction of machines, where proportion is of the utmost importance.

[. . .] Proportions are not based on positive and necessary reasons, as they are in such things as fortifications and machines, where, for example, the line of defence cannot be longer than the range of the artillery nor one arm of a balance shorter than the other without making these things absolutely wrong and completely ineffectual.

[. . .]

[*Perrault proposes here his method of dealing with proportions*]. Now it is easy to see that the third method is at least simpler and more convenient than the others. [. . .] It is equally obvious that nothing is easier than this method for finding, retaining and imprinting on the memory the proportion a face should have. [. . .] This should at least be considered a likely proportion, since it is founded on the regular division of a whole into three equal parts. This is the method followed by the Ancients and the one Vitruvius has used to justify the proportions he has established in his writings, where he always employs easily remembered, methodical divisions. The method has been abandoned by the Moderns only because they could not make it correspond to the irregular dimensions of the elements in the beautiful works of antiquity, which are very different from what Vitruvius has left us, so that it would have been necessary to alter the dimensions of these ancient works in some way in order to reduce them to the regular proportions the method requires. And most architects are convinced that these works would have lost all their beauty had even a single minute been added to or subtracted from any one of the elements in which the worthy craftsmen of antiquity once deposited these dimensions.

The extent to which architects make a religion of venerating the works they call ancient is inconceivable. They admire everything about them but especially the mystery of proportions. These they are content to contemplate with profound respect, not daring to question why the dimensions of a moulding are neither slightly greater nor slightly smaller, which is something one can presume was unknown even to those who established these dimensions. This would not be so surprising if one could rest assured that the proportions we see in these works had never been altered and differed in no way from those that the first inventors of architecture established. Nor would such veneration astonish us if we were of the same mind as Villalpando, who claims that God, through a special revelation, taught all these proportions to the architects of Solomon's Temple and that the Greeks, who are considered their inventors, learned them from these architects.

Claude Perrault
1613–1688

Yet, preposterous as it may be, the exaggerated respect for antiquity, which architects hold in common with those who profess the humanities and believe that nothing done today can match the works of the Ancients, originates in the genuine respect for sacred things. Everyone knows that the cruel war waged on scholarship by the barbarism of past ages spared theology alone of all the branches of learning it obliterated and that as a result what little remained of culture took refuge, in a sense, in the monasteries. In these places, where intelligence was obliged to seek the noble substance of knowledge concerning nature and antiquity, the art of reasoning and of training the mind was practised. Yet this art, which by nature is proper to all branches of learning, had for so long been practised only by theologians, whose every belief is bound and captive to ancient wisdom, that the habit of utilising the freedom needed for scrupulous investigation was lost. Several centuries passed before people in the humanities were able to reason in anything other than a theological way. This is why, formerly, the only aim of learned inquiry was the investigation of ancient doctrine; whereby, greater pride was taken in discovering the true connotation of the text of Aristotle than in discovering the truth of that with which the text deals.

The docility characteristic of men of letters so sustained and reinforced the spirit of submission ingrained in their way of studying and treating the arts and sciences that they had great difficulty divesting themselves of it. They could not bring themselves to distinguish between the respect due to sacred things and the respect warranted by things that are not: things that, when the truth is to be ascertained, we are permitted to examine, criticise and censure with moderation and whose mysteries we do not consider as being of the same kind as the mysteries of religion, which we are not surprised to find unfathomable.

Because architecture, like painting and sculpture, was often dealt with by men of letters, it was also ruled by this spirit of submission more than the other arts. These people professed to argue from authority in architectural matters, labouring under the assumption that the authors of the admirable works of antiquity did nothing without reasons to justify it, even though these reasons remain unknown to us.

There are those, however, who will not accept as necessarily unfathomable the reasons that make us admire these fine works. After examining everything relevant to this subject and being instructed in it by those who are most expert, they will, if they also consult good sense, be persuaded that there is no great obstacle to believing that the things for which they can find no reason are, in fact, devoid of any reason material to the beauty of the thing. They will be convinced that these things are founded on nothing but chance and the whims of craftsmen who never sought any reason to guide them in determining matters whose precision is of no importance.

I am well aware that whatever I may say, people will have trouble accepting this proposition, and it will be taken as an unorthodox opinion apt to provoke a great many adversaries. Although there are a few honest people who, perhaps because they have not given the matter enough thought, genuinely believe that the glory of their beloved antiquity rests on its being considered infallible, inimitable and incomparable, there will be many others who know very well what they are doing when they cloak in a blind respect for ancient works their own desire to make the matters of their profession into mysteries that they alone can interpret.

Although I may have thoroughly substantiated this unorthodox opinion, my intention is not to profit by it in any way other than to gain leave to change a few proportions that differ from ancient ones only in minor and unremarkable ways. Therefore, I do not believe that people will take issue with me, especially after having declared that I hold for ancient architecture all the veneration and admiration it deserves. If my discussion of it differs from others, my aim is simply to avert the objections that overly scrupulous admirers of the past may raise concerning the drawbacks that they see in my not following to the letter the examples of the great masters and in the risk I run in not gaining credence for my new proposals.

Claude Perrault
1613–1688

Those who want neither to quibble nor to use the authority of antiquity in bad faith will not extend its power to matters that have no need of it [. . .], since the exactitude of these proportions is not what makes the beauty of ancient buildings. The significance of their being altered is outweighed by the importance of having proportions that are truly balanced in all parts of every order in such a way as to establish a straightforward and convenient method.

Should the outcome of my project not be successful, the disgrace should not be a cause of great concern to me, for I would be in illustrious company. Despite considerable abilities, neither Hermogenes, nor Callimachus, nor Philo, nor Chersiphron, nor Metagenes, nor Vitruvius, nor Palladio, nor Scamozzi was able to obtain sufficient approval to have his precepts constitute the rules of architectural proportion. If the objection is raised that the system I propose, even if approved, was not very difficult to discover, that I have hardly changed proportions at all, and that most of them can be found in one or another of the works of the Ancients or Moderns, I will admit that I have indeed not invented new proportions; but this is precisely what I take pride in. I say this because my work has no other aim than to show, without disturbing the conception architects have of the proportions of each element, that they can all be reduced to easily commensurable dimensions, which I call probable. For it seems very likely that the first inventors of the proportions for each order did not determine them as we see them in ancient buildings, where they only approximate such readily commensurable dimensions. [. . .] The carelessness of those who built the ancient buildings we see is the only real reason for the failure of these proportions to follow exactly the true ones, which one may reasonably believe were established by the first originators of architecture.

I cannot see how one might object to this opinion, because I neither know, nor believe that one can know, the reasons that made architects use difficult and fractional proportions unnecessarily and contrive to change the original ones, which were simple whole numbers. [. . .] And finally, for what mysterious reason do no two columns of the portico of the Pantheon have the same thickness? Nor do I believe it possible to guess why Scamozzi, in his treatise on architecture, establishes proportions that are so confused that they are not only difficult to remember but even to understand.

I therefore have cause to believe that if the alterations in proportion introduced by architects after Vitruvius were made for reasons unknown to us, those I propose will be founded on reasons that are clear and explicit, such as the ease of subdividing and remembering them. I also contend that whatever innovations I introduce are intended not so much to correct what is ancient as to return it to its original perfection. I do this not on my own authority, following only my own insight, but always in reference to some example taken from ancient works or from reputable writers. My use of argument and inference is sparing and even when used cannot be objected to, since I submit all my arguments in total deference to all knowledgeable people who care to take the trouble to examine them.

And finally, if the works that survive from antiquity are like books from which we must learn the proportions of architecture, then these works are not the originals created by the first true authors but simply copies at variance with one another, with some of them accurate and correct in one thing, others in another. Therefore, in order to restore the true sense of the text in architecture, if one may so speak, it is necessary to search through these different copies, which, as approved works, must each contain something correct and accurate, and obviously base one's choice on the regularity of divisions, which are not fractional for no reason but simple and convenient as they are in Vitruvius.

As for the sceptics who may question that the works of antiquity are defective copies whose proportions differ from those of the originals, I believe that I have sufficiently established the legitimacy and acceptability of this contention through the arguments elaborated at some length in this Preface. Here, I have attempted to prove that the beauty of ancient works, admirable though it may be, is not enough to justify the conclusion that the proportions to which they conform are true proportions. This I have demonstrated by showing that the beauty of these buildings does not consist in the exactitude of such true proportions, since plainly something may be omitted from them without the beauty of the work being diminished by it. In addition, I have demonstrated that the work would not have more appeal were it to conform to these true proportions while lacking other things wherein true beauty consists, such as the agreeable tracing of profiles and contours and the skilful disposition of all the elements that determine the character of the different orders. For, as we have said, the correct disposition of these elements is secondary to proportion as one of the two parts that together encompass everything pertaining to the beauty of architecture.

I have given a general explanation of the reasons that justify the liberty that I have taken in proposing some changes in the proportions of the orders and am reserving for the treatise that follows the details of each alteration. It now remains for me to state my reasons for making changes in the characters that distinguish the orders, which is to make even greater license than to tamper with proportions, since such changes are more easily recognised, the eye being able to detect them without the aid of ruler or compass.

Those who find it unjustifiable to change anything in the rules that they believe were established by the Ancients may take the liberty of deriding my arguments and censuring the boldness of my project. It is not to them I speak, for there is no arguing with those who deny principles. And I maintain one of the first principles in architecture, as in all the other arts, should be that since no single principle has ever been completely perfected, even if perfection itself is unattainable, one may at least approach it more closely by reaching for it. I also maintain that those who believe in the possibility

Claude Perrault
1613–1688

[248]

of reaching for perfection are more likely to aspire to it than those who believe the opposite.

[...]

Among those who have written about the architectural orders, there is no one who has not added to or corrected something in what it is claimed the Ancients established as inviolable rules and laws. These writers, who, apart from Vitruvius, are all modern, made such alterations after the example of the Ancients themselves, who, instead of books, left works of architecture into which each put something of his own invention. Now these innovations have always been considered the fruit of studious research undertaken by able and inventive minds in order to perfect those things in which the Ancients had left some flaw. Although some of the changes were not approved, others affecting matters of even considerable significance were accepted. In fact, enough of them were applied to show that a change of opinion in affairs of this kind is in no way a reckless undertaking and that a change for the better is not as difficult as the ardent admirers of antiquity would have us believe.

Claude Perrault
1613–1688

classical canon • antiquity • abuses • nature • nurture • fashion • precedent • authority • invention • systemisation of space distribution

Tofcan.　Dorique.　Ionique.　Corinthien.　Compofite.

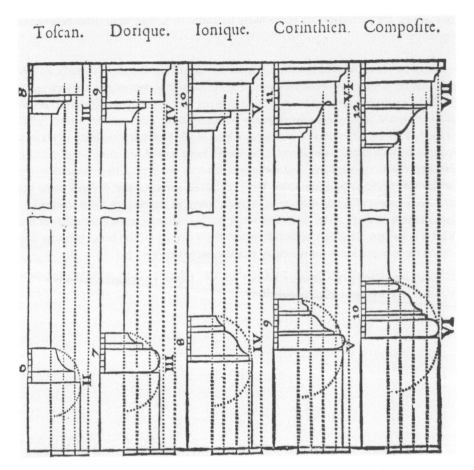

93. Claude Perrault. *Ordonnance des cinq especes de colonnes*. 1683. Perrault's version of the five Orders of architecture. Proportions for pedestals.

Sir William Temple (1628–1699)

The Gardens of Epicurus (written 1685; published 1692)

It has been said that Whiggism – the liberal, bourgeois movement in England that started in the late seventeenth century – is the first source of the 'landscape' garden and of the pre-romantic aesthetics of the 'picturesque' (Pevsner, 1944). Temple was a Whig as well as a diplomat, statesman and essayist. His description of the *shawaradgi* of Chinese gardens was an important argument for the overthrow of the artificial pomp and rigid regularity of the baroque garden (Clark, 1943) and of the constraining absolutist policies, which it was seen to symbolise.

Further reading Harris, 1990; Hilles, 1965; Hunt, 1976; Hussey, 1927; Lang, 1972; Malins, 1966; Ogden, 1949; Sirén, 1950.

What I have said of the best forms of gardens is meant only of such as are in some sort regular; for there may be other forms wholly irregular that may, for aught I know, have more beauty than any of the others. But they must owe it to some extraordinary dispositions of nature in the seat, or some great race of fancy or judgement in the contrivance which may reduce many disagreeing parts into some figure which shall yet upon the whole be very agreeable. Something of this I have seen in some places but heard more of it from others who have lived much among the Chinese, a people whose way of thinking seems to lie as wide of ours in Europe as their country does. Among us, the beauty of building and planting is placed chiefly in some certain proportions, symmetries, or uniformities; our walks and our trees ranged so as to answer one another, and at exact distances. The Chinese scorn this way of planting and say a boy who can count to a hundred may plant walks of trees in straight lines and over against one another, and to what length and extent he pleases. But their greatest reach of imagination is employed in contriving figures, where the beauty shall be great and strike the eye, but without any order or disposition of parts that shall be commonly or easily observed. And though we have hardly any notion of this sort of beauty, yet they have a particular word to express it; and, where they find it hit their eye at first sight, they say the Sharawadgi is fine or is admirable or any such expression of esteem. And whoever observes the work upon the best Indian gowns or the painting upon their best screens or porcelain will find their beauty is all of this kind [that is] without order. But I should hardly advise any of these attempts in the figure of gardens among us; they are adventures of too hard achievement for any common hands; and though there may be more honour if they succeed well, yet there is more dishonour if they fail, and it is twenty to one they will; whereas, in regular figures, it is hard to make any great and remarkable faults.

anticlassicism • deformation • freedom • naturalism • orientalism

Robert de Cotte (1656–1735)

Journey to Italy (1689)

A student of Jules-Hardouin Mansart, de Cotte worked on Versailles with him and married into his family, eventually rising to the Mansart's old rank of Architect of the King and director of the Académie de l'architecture (Lemonnier, 1911–1929, vol. 4). His description, while on a trip to Rome in the 1680s, of a revered piece of Italian architecture such as the Rotunda as lacking in proportion is similar in spirit to Desgodetz's almost contemporary description of Roman antiquities (1682) and reveals how concerted the rejection of Italian precedent was among the French architectural establishment.

We commenced by visiting every thing and the church of St Peter, which we saw but slightly.

I find it extraordinarily tall, which, however, is not surprising because of the beautiful proportions and the height is noticeable only in the individual parts, which are colossal. All is of the latest magnificence, the architecture, sculpture and painting being so well-ordered that every thing fits together in beautiful proportions. This church was designed by Michelangelo, except for the portal and the porch, which are not as good as the rest.

The main square in front of the portal is large, decorated by a circular colonnade with four rows of columns in the Doric order designed by Bernini, but this number of columns, instead of creating a happy effect, creates confusion and resembles a forest. In the centre, the columns in the rear have a thicker diameter than those in the front, but that is not apparent. The gallery that comes to the colonnade and porch, which leads on one side to the porch and on the other side to the grand staircase, slopes following the level of the ground; that is fairly against the rules but does no harm, the top of the colonnade's entablature joining the impost of the portal. The interior of the galleries is vaulted with double arches on pilasters, and between those pilasters are windows in culs-de-four; that is in a dry, bad taste.

Near there is the Rotunda, once called the Pantheon, an edifice that Agrippa had built and dedicated to the gods. The entire structure dates back to Antiquity. Pope Urban VIII had bronze ornaments built on the inside and outside vaults, the pediment and the roof. This work was of the latest magnificence, every thing was encrusted with marble and decorated with architecture of the Corinthian order . . . [but] there are no proportions.

The pilasters project not, so it appears that the cornice of the attic is ancient and that it was removed from an earlier building and reused. There are openings around the attic, half of them false, the rest real. That makes a sort of window surrounded by a decorative frame and a small term. These openings appear ancient but the pedestal has blocked up part of them, which means that they have no proportions, part of the openings being a kind of loggia or tribune in the thickness of the walls. The vault is filled with recessed square compartments: there are 50, one on top of the other, and 28 all around the edge, which means that they are extremely large. They were filled with bronze ornaments that made them appear small but now there is no proportion. This church is lit only from above by an opening 27 inches in diameter, which means that it rains inside. Upon close examination, I found that this church had no proportion [. . .]

What caused me to observe this was that the edifice was built without a peristyle, having only a square forecourt carrying a pediment that is still visible and that is more elevated than the porch. It is sure that if the whole structure had been built together, the workers would have taken their measurements to connect the architecture.

classical canon • antiquity • abuses

Charles Augustin D'Aviler (1653–1701)

Lessons of Architecture (1691)

This work whose author was a member of the Académie Royale d'Architecture is part of the movement in France initiated by Colbert to systematise the rules of architecture and thus to establish architecture as an autonomous field of inquiry. The first edition included a dictionary of over 5,000 terms and after a general definition of the column, D'Aviler enumerated no less than 104 types (Nyberg, 1967). It was reprinted six times before 1756 (Tzonis *et al.*, 1982).

Charles Augustin
D'Aviler
1653–1701

Further reading Bilodeau, 1997; Blomfield, 1973; Herrmann, 1973; Wiebenson, 1982, 1993.

Notice

Since the obscurity of its terms is one of the biggest obstacles on the way to the knowledge of an art, and after having reflected how difficult it would be to understand, without clarification, most of those in this book, which contains over five thousand belonging to the art of building and those who depend on it; I have judged it quite necessary to give an explanation of them in the form of a Dictionary containing accurate and concise definitions. Discourse was no vehicle for this task, as the explanation of the terms would have interrupted its train, and caused confusion and obscurity; not even plates and diagrams could fully supply this shortcoming, no matter how precise and correct they are. Thus the only approach open to me was this Dictionary, where I have attempted to explain the words not in everyday usage and which belong to the art of building.

But since, no matter how precise a definition is, it can never be fully elucidated except by means of a diagram or an example, I have been careful to commit to the plates contained in this book, and to refer to common examples, all the terms which might be clarified in this way. To this end I have drawn widely on the architecture of Antiquity, and the most illustrious buildings of Paris, its environs and even of foreign countries; and the reflections that they have given me occasion to make may serve as rules for the formation of good taste, and for an acquaintance with the beauties and the defects of the most acclaimed buildings, ancient and modern.

The variety of the matter treated will be seen as sufficient if one considers that no architect who has written has made mention of more than ten or twelve columns, while more than a hundred are contained in this Table, none of them imaginary, and classed according to their material, construction, form, disposition and use: the same is observed for all the other things explained therein.

Architecture has so vast a scope that one cannot expect to be able to study everything in a single country. Different nations build according to their particular tastes and needs; the diversity of temperatures serves as a gauge for the distribution and form of their buildings; the choice of materials and the manner of employing them vary too in keeping with the different climates. Therefore there is no better way to complete one's studies than to travel.

When the imagination is furnished with these fair notions, an expedient can be devised for testing their strength, and seeing whether any progress has been made; and when one is assured of this progress, one may dedicate oneself entirely to practice, without which study becomes, in a sense, useless. Learning, criticism, the knowledge acquired during travel, skill in producing excellent drawings, are of little use unless they are put into practice, for it is practice which makes the true architect. Practice teaches him to detect, merely by examining drawings, what can and cannot be executed in the actual building; practice gives him absolute authority over all his workmen, and reveals to him the secrets of their different professions; and it is acknowledged that an architect needs not only to be conversant in sculpture, structural carpentry, joinery and metal-work, but also to have a notion of the price of all these things so that he can match them to the expenditure available for the project. Workmen are entirely deferent of the views of the architect who guides them, once they see that he combines theory with practice; for ultimately it is through practice that buildings are built and the project is brought to fruition.

Charles Augustin
D'Aviler
1653–1701

professional practice • education

Charles-Augustin d'Aviler

Cours d'architecture, 1691

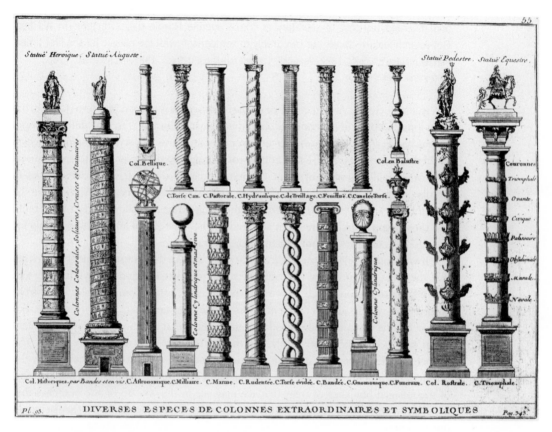

94. Charles-Augustin d'Aviler. *Cours d'architecture*. 1691. Table of different kinds of 'extraordinary and symbolic columns' beyond the 'ordinary' columns. A demonstration of possible diversity and variety.

Jean-François Félibien des Avaux (1658–1733)

Dissertation Touching upon Ancient Architecture and Gothic Architecture (1699)

The author, a historian and connoisseur, was the son of the elder André Félibien (1666) and inherited his post of secretary of the Académie Royale d'Architecture. In his text, Gothic architecture comes out favourably in comparison with the classic for the first time.

Further reading Bilodeau, 1997; Fontaine, 1909; Frankl, 1960; Pace, 1981; Tzonis et al., 1982; Wiebenson, 1982, 1993.

It is true that Gothic Architecture, or at least that which is termed 'modern' Gothic, has been long practised in Italy and we should not be surprised by this. The different populations had become accustomed over several centuries to this style of building, which created apparently light, delicate edifices of a design so daring as to astonish. Among the considerable number of great Churches built in this style in various places in Europe, there are older examples that lack neither solidity nor beauty. Some are to be seen that have been preserved down to our day as intact as if they had just been built, and those same churches are often admired by the most skilful architects, not only for their goodly construction, but also for their general design.

If we consider, even closely, those that were built in the purest Gothic style, we see that the most extraordinary characteristics they seem to offer to the eye initially and which seem to be completely opposed to nature, are founded on examples taken from nature itself, where all the different styles of building find their ultimate source. For here in brief is what may have produced the edifices that are most massive and rough-hewn and those which, conversely, are the lightest and most delicate in aspect. The former have kept something of the rusticity of the caves and caverns inhabited by the northern peoples in the distant past and the latter take their example from the lightness of the foliaged branches of trees that we may see in the woods, or the branches that people in warm climates make themselves in order to provide shade for themselves in open country.

This is the reason why in the latter edifices mentioned above we see an infinity of very slim columns. They are like so many branches and trunks of trees. In some cases several rise together into the air from the top of the same pillar that serves as a trunk for them. Sometimes these small columns are grouped in bundles from the very bottom of the edifice. They hide very high massive pillars that support the vaulted roof. They support transverse arches resembling other very slim and supple branches and consequently are very suitable to bend according to the manner in which they are seen. The use of stilted arches and ogives helped reduce the thrust of the main arches, thus leading to a marked diminution of their loading and thickness. Lastly, the Architects who built these edifices in the best manner of the style discussed here justified the principles of their Art using arguments that it was impossible to counter in a time when ignorance of letters, the difficulty of recovering a single Book on true Architecture, being that of Vitruvius, and moreover the almost complete destruction of all the buildings of Antiquity, prevented any argument against modern edifices.

Gothic Architecture could no longer be destroyed except by corrupting itself. It was necessary for those who practised to erase their Works completely, down to the idea of the basic principles of their Art and that is in fact what happened, as soon as they had reduced that Art to a confused amalgam of an infinite multitude of ornaments and an unbridled excessiveness in their design. The last Gothic edifices came, due to these excesses, to resemble, as it were, those delicate Works that we call today 'filigree', in which almost none of the simplicity, disposition and solidity of the older Churches mentioned above was now to be seen.

[...] Thus it is not sufficient for an edifice to be built solidly, for that solidity must be apparent to the eye, in a manner appropriate to the very nature of the edifice concerned. Nor is it sufficient for a building to be ornamented with highly exquisite Works: such ornamentation must be placed there as if by necessity and such that the character, usage and dignity of the building seems to require it.

It is on these principles of solidity and authentic and apparent beauty that the Architecture of Antiquity is founded. Whence the fact that ancient columns were worked to resemble tree trunks and not the supple branches to which the columns of Gothic Constructions are compared and which seem to be suitable at best for the support of foliage and flowers in garden bowers, or coverings in light fabric for tents and pavilions in a camp.

François de Salignac de la Mothe Fénelon 1651–1715

Let us conclude simply by saying in general terms how far Greek and Roman Architecture are contributors to the design of Gothic Architecture, whether Ancient or Modern. It will suffice to reflect on a very central defect of both these latter styles of building. In brief, Gothic columns are so ill-proportioned that the gross character of some led initially to distaste, and the excessive weakness of others eventually led to the conclusion that it was necessary to abandon entirely in any edifice whatsoever the progression of two designs so ill-suited. At the same time it was recognised that columns according to the five orders of Greek and Roman Architecture, although very distant from the gross or extremely feeble character of Gothic columns, themselves evidenced a different, highly agreeable progression in five distinct dimensional proportions. And in fact these proportions make it possible to erect all five orders one above the other: that is to say, the Doric on the Tuscan, the Ionic on the Doric, and the Composite with the Corinthian, one over the other and both above the Ionic, such that the disposition of these orders of columns, embellished in five different styles, produces in an edifice variety, beauty and magnificence beyond compare. Therefore, Gothic buildings would be poorly esteemed today except for the grandeur of several of these Constructions, and a sometimes happy choice of overall proportions to be observed in certain Churches, but this is so as if by chance, and rarely with all the precision that would seem to be appropriate for them.

anticlassicism • deformation • freedom • naturalism • classical canon • antiquity • abuses • rigorism • essentialism

François de Salignac de la Mothe Fénelon (1651–1715)
The Adventures of Télémaque (1699)

Fénelon, theologian and Bishop of Cambrai, led the Quietest heresy in France which was critical of the absolutist tendencies of Louis XIV. He held views that greatly prefigure the liberal philosophical currents of the enlightenment. He wrote the moralistic novel Télémaque in order to hold up the hero as a model for the young heir to the French throne who was his pupil. The work contains descriptions of buildings and towns, which the author offers as alternatives to those of his day. In his much quoted *Letters* (1713; 1714) he dwells on the analogy between architecture and rhetoric, favouring the Greek ideals of simplicity, usefulness and nearness to nature to what he terms the vain and refined luxury of the Gothic. He has been cited among the forerunners of Laugier (Hermann, 1962, 25).

Further reading Atkinson, 1960; Hautecoeur, 1948–1963; Hilles, 1965; Lombard, 1954.

Book I

François de
Salignac de la
Mothe Fénelon
1651–1715

They came to the entrance to Calypso's grotto, where Telemachus was surprised to behold a scene of rustic simplicity and objects fit to charm the eye. There was no gold, nor silver, nor marble, nor columns, nor paintings, nor statues to be seen there, it is true: but this grotto was hewn from the living rock, and covered all over with little stones and seashells; its floor was matted with a young vine whose supple tendrils spread evenly over every part of it. The gentle zephyrs kept this place, despite the fiery sun, delightfully cool; fountains, gushing softly in meadows sewn with amaranths and violets, here and there formed pools as pure and as clear as crystal; a thousand budding flowers dotted the meadow which surrounded the grotto. Here they found a grove of those densely-leafed trees which bear golden apples and whose blossom, which returns every season, gives off the sweetest of perfumes; this grove seemed to crown those lovely meadows, and formed a shade which the sun's rays could not pierce. Inside, all that could be heard was birdsong, or the chatter of a brook which, rushing over a boulder, fell in foamy cascades to flow off across the meadow.

The goddess' cave was set in a hillside. The sea was visible from it, sometimes clear and smooth as a looking-glass, sometimes crashing madly against the rocks, heaving upwards into mountainous waves as it broke itself against them with great clamour. On the other side a stream could be seen, verged with lime-blossom and high poplars whose magnificent heads rose cloudwards. The various streams which divided the countryside into islets were playful in their demeanour: some flowed quick and clear, others seemed hardly to move; others described great meanders and came back on themselves as if they wished to return to their source and could not bring themselves to leave these enchanted banks. In the distance could be seen hills and mountains which vanished into the heavens, and whose bizarre outline traced a horizon perfectly formed for the pleasure of the eye. The closer mountains were covered in green vines hanging in festoons: their grapes more vivid than purple bulged from under their leaves, the vines sagging under the weight of their fruit. The fig, the olive, the pomegranate and all the other trees covered the countryside, making a huge garden of it.

Book II

This town [Thebes] extended over an immense area and seemed to us to have more people than the most thriving towns of Greece. Public order perfectly provides there for the tidiness of the streets, for the watercourses, the comfort of the bath-houses, the cultivation of the arts and the safety of the public. The squares are adorned with fountains and obelisks; the temples are of marble, simple yet majestic in their architecture. The palace of the prince is like a city in itself: one sees there nothing but marble columns, pyramids and obelisks, colossal statues, furniture of solid gold and silver.

Book V

[...] in Crete. Everyone works there, and no-one thinks of getting rich; each man believes himself amply paid for his work with a mild and orderly life, where all that is truly necessary in life is there to be enjoyed in peace and abundance. Valuable furniture, showy dress, sumptuous feasts and gilded palaces are not permitted. Garments are in one piece, of fine, brightly-coloured wool without embroidery. Meals are frugal; [...] the houses are clean, comfortable, pleasant, but without ornament. Excellence of architecture is cultivated there: but it is reserved for the temples of the gods: men would not dare to have houses comparable to those of the immortals. The greatest riches of the Cretans are their health, strength, courage, the peace and union of their families, the freedom of all citizens, the abundance of necessary things, the contempt of superfluity, industriousness and a horror of idleness, the emulation of virtue, submission to law and fear of the righteous gods.

Book X

And people soon came rushing there from all parts. Trade in this city was like the ebb and flow of the sea. Treasures poured in like wave upon wave. Everything arrived and everything left freely. Everything that entered was useful; everything that left, left other riches in its place. Severe justice presided over the port where so many nations congregated. Plain dealing, good faith, candour seemed, from the heights of those magnificent towers, to beckon to merchants from the most distant shores; each of these merchants, whether he came from oriental lands where the sun rises every day from the bosom of the waves, whether he arrived via that great sea where the sun, its course spent, quenches its fires; each of these merchants lived as peacefully and safely in Salento as in his homeland.

For the hinterland of the city, Mentor visited all the shops, all the artisan's studios, and all the public squares. He prohibited all merchandise from foreign lands likely to introduce luxury and sloth. He prescribed rules on dress, nourishment, furniture, the size and decoration of houses, for all stations of society. He banished ornament of gold and silver; and he said to Idomeneus: I know only one way of making your people modest in their expenditure, and that is for you to set them the example. You need a certain majesty in your bearing; but your authority will be sufficiently marked by your guards and your retinue of officers [...]

[...] He restricted the use of architectural ornament, such as columns, pediments and porticoes, to temples; he prescribed models for a simple and gracious architecture, for making, in limited space, a bright and comfortable house for a sizeable family, such that it should acquire a healthy aspect, that each dwelling be separated from the other, that its order and cleanliness be easy to maintain, and its upkeep inexpensive.

He argued that every house of a more considerable size should have a small peristyle, with small sleeping chambers for the free occupants of the house. But he most severely prohibited superfluous ornament and magnificence in these dwellings. These various models for houses for families of various sizes helped embellish and impose order on one part of the city, at little expense; while the other part, already completed in accordance with the caprice and splendour of its inhabitants, was, despite its magnificence, less agreeable to look at, and less comfortable. This new city

François de
Salignac de la
Mothe Fénelon
1651–1715

[259]

was built in very little time, since the neighbouring coast of Greece supplied good architects [. . .]

anticlassicism • deformation • freedom • naturalism • rigorism • essentialism • social reform • democratisation

Michel de Frémin (?–?)

A Critical Report on Architecture, Containing the True and False Architecture (1702)

Frémin, a layman, wrote his book on a popular level as a series of forty-eight 'letters' to an imaginary correspondent who was planning to build a house for himself (Nyberg, 1963). The author not only greatly admires the Gothic construction skill but goes even further and derides Modern architecture for its structural deficiencies (Hautecoeur, 1948–1963, III, 461; Hermann, 1962, 37), thus anticipating Laugier (1753) and Souf-flot (1741). He is an early formulator of the functionalist aesthetic. His definition of 'vraye architecture' is one which gives to the viewer the impression of rational design by eliminating ornaments (Tzonis and Lefaivre, 1984b). This book, like that of Cordemoy, written slightly later, which it influenced (Middleton, 1962, 1963) testifies to the growing popularity of architectural criticism among non-architect writers and readers (Nyberg, 1963).

Further reading Bilodeau, 1997; Wiebenson, 1982, 1993.

There are errors that are in breach of the rules, and errors that are in breach of good taste. The former are invariably actual errors and include all things that can be done in Buildings which deviate from and go against reason; the latter are errors only with respect to certain aesthetic tastes, that is to say, to certain persons, they appear to be errors, but not to others.

In order to determine which are actual errors, it is necessary to determine what is true and sound Architecture: that is the key standpoint from which it is possible to see clearly whether the Architect is intelligent or ignorant and which will permit us to judge correctly the rightness or wrongness of an edifice.

Architecture is an Art of building according to the object, according to the subject and according to the place. In giving this definition, I mean that Architecture certainly does not consist only of knowledge of the five Orders. My assertion is that the latter knowledge is the smaller part of Architecture and that an Architect who can speak only of the dimensions of the five Orders is a very diminutive, very limited Architect.

I say therefore that Architecture is an Art of Building according to the object, according to the subject, and according to the place, by which I mean that the first pre-occupation of any Architect in designing his building is to conceive the purpose for which a Building has been commissioned from him – this is what I mean by the word 'object'. He must, having understood thoroughly the specific use to which the Building is to be put, imagine and dispose all things that are naturally appropriate to that use. He must plan in his head the entirety of his Edifice, look closely at whether what he has conceived shows perfect unity, whether in that unity all the parts have their allotted place, and are mutually proportionate. This is what I understand by building according to the 'subject'. And when he has seen that all that he has conceived is appropriate to the object and is naturally related to it, he must compare all that he has imagined with the situation of the land, observe the effect that his edifice will have in the location marked out, analyse the reflections that the light will make on his edifice, as well as the effect of shadows and the winds to which the edifice may be subject, either from neighbouring Buildings or by other things that may project on to it their shadows and turbulent winds. Without such attention, without such analysis, all that is done in Building is false Architecture.

In the building of Notre Dame, the designing Architect considered first the general view and then, entering into the detail of each of the parts that were necessary to conform to the object, he reflected upon them. He considered that this Church, which according to the circumstances of the time in which he was living, was not to be very spacious, because the Paris of that time was very restricted and very small, was nevertheless destined to be so one day, according to hopes for the future, and that he should therefore make it extensive. He considered that since the city was to be a Metropolis, it should have most singular spaces and dispositions, because the criteria applying to a Church of this kind are quite different to those applying to a Parish Church. He considered that if he reduced his ideas to the simple extent of his land, he would not provide the quantity of space that would be appropriate to hold a large number of people. He considered that a Church where there is almost continuous singing must have a construction that closes that singing within and prevents its dispersal. He knew that the whole of the Sacrifice is done only that it may be seen, and therefore far from removing it from sight or surrounding it with columns, it was necessary to contribute to that spectacle and to help it to be seen. So what did this Architect do? With respect to his idea of the future, he made a great Nave, doubling its volume by including galleries. With respect to the harmony of the singing, which becomes fuller and more melodious when it is concentrated, he lowered the vaulted ceilings of the side aisles. With respect to the need for light, while lowering the vaulted ceilings, he enlarged the high windows, thereby multiplying the sources of light. With respect to the spectacle of the Sacrifice, he reduced the size of the pillars to a middling thickness, and made them round so as not to impede the view with corners, as is the case when pillars are square.

[...]

I will speak to you now of the *Sainte Chapelle*. This is, once again, a model of true Architecture, that is to say a Construction in which the intelligent management of the Architect provides lessons on the manner in which private Chapels should be built. [...] All the provisions which in fact should be made to ensure that the Prince may see, at one glance, all that is happening throughout the place. [...] He has disposed separate Chapels in a manner such that several Masses may be celebrated at the same time in order to satisfy the piety of different persons. He has included another almost at the same level as the apartments of his Master, either to ensure that the latter should not be tired by climbing stairs or bored by descending them, or to allow the admission of a purer and clearer air, knowing as he does that in the calm reflection that deep piety inspires, the spirits are almost at a halt and the body then becomes more susceptible to foul odours than is the case when busy and in movement. He has included a very private Oratory, with ingenious window openings where the Prince, far removed from ill-smelling breath and columns of air that copious lunches have infected and in which the tartar of Champagne wine evaporating from overloaded stomachs has spread incommodious acids, can, sheltered from this contagion, pray in salubrious circumstances. He has included no upper gallery, not that this construction is devoid of the

Michel de Frémin
??–??

[261]

commodities of the faith, but apparently he was as good a Doctor as he was an Architect, as Vitruvius argues Architects must be, for he knew that from the bottom of a Church where all manner of men are entitled to assemble, the air mixed with the smell of malodorous feet, along with soiled garments, being agitated by the friction between the particles with which these odours fill their mass, could rise to infect an upper gallery and attack his Master, either in his sense of smell, or by instilling nausea. He judged therefore that it was more expedient to refrain from including such a gallery. He took his reflections further, he sought a unity for his Nave, that is to say he did not wish to burden it with a multiplicity of Side Altars, Columns or Pillars, nor with side aisles, nor with Constructions that might hide from the gaze of the Prince, or those assigned to protect him, all those things that it is important to see.

[...]

Michel de Frémin
??–??

That is what I term good and sound Architecture. On the basis of my depiction of it for you, it will be easy for you to judge Constructions of the same kind. But in order to judge bad Architecture, take as your example Saint Eustache, as I have said.

[...]

What ignorance as to the effects of solid bodies when they are carried by other bodies! What ignorance as to the natural uses of a Church and of the ultimate ends to which it must be directed!

[...]

If you lack knowledge of the rules of the Art, you have only to make use of those given you by Physics. They will lead you on a righter path and in reminding you of this I can promise you that if you take good heed of them you will arrive at a quite complete design. You would not have believed that with the simple principles of Physics it would be possible to build a house and to make it absolutely regular, for following this axiom you will think that an old Tutor of Philosophy must necessarily be an excellent Architect. It is nevertheless true, taken in the sense that I intend. We can see in Paris a door of a College of which I am told the Director's valet was once the Architect, a door which is truly meritorious. For this reason, I argue that if we do not know Nature well, it will never be possible to design a pleasing residence. I am not talking here about the actual building of it, since that involves other rules, but about the arrangement of its parts and its general disposition.

This is so because how could it be designed well without knowledge of the nature of the air nor the quality of the land on which it is intended to build it? How could we place correctly a Staircase, Kitchens or Stables, if we knew nothing about the variations and changes in the winds? How could we locate windows correctly, if we did not know how the light that is to pass through them will illuminate the interior of the house, and if certain shadows might not make it too obscure, ensuring that the illumination is inadequate.

[...]

The sense of fitness in a Building must be one of the principal concerns of the Architect. This is an Art which regulates the entirety of the Construction, the aim being to place in each of its parts each thing in the manner in which it should be so placed by both nature and necessity.

This Art [*the art of fitness*] teaches us the necessary locations, the necessary proportions and the necessary dispositions. It teaches us how to choose materials, how to put them together and how to work them. It teaches us to reconcile the work undertaken and end for which it is undertaken [. . .] in order to practise it according to all its rules, it is necessary to have [. . .] a universality of knowledge of all that must contribute to the Building with respect to its object, its subject and its location, as well as particular knowledge of all that must be in the Building with respect to the person of the Master who has commissioned it, to his family and to his condition in society [. . .]

Comparison of Buildings is the most practical method of proceeding and consequently the most effective for expressing one's thought. Three or four examples of houses will teach you more than any pair of written volumes of theory. I will admit to you immediately that in Paris I see few private Buildings that could be put forward as models of true Architecture and in which the rules of fitness have been scrupulously and exactly followed [. . .]

It is this sense of fitness that makes true Architecture, and fitness is governed by prudence and wisdom. The reasoning is simply as follows – I have a house to build, what should I do? It is a house – that is my object. As a house it is intended to house me, so therefore is it lodging that I seek? My social condition is such and such, my occupation is such and such, my family is such and such and its domestic situation such and such – what is fitting for my person, my family, my condition, my domestic situation? I have such an area on which I wish to build: this is its nature, its orientation – what is the quality of the air which predominates there? How can I ensure that this air remains pure and salubrious? What disposition should I give my rooms to prevent the entry of turbulent winds which would make them unhealthy? Shall I [. . .] situate my garden along a great length and include no more than a small courtyard with two or three arches of no interest? Reasoning in this way, what should be the preoccupations of the draughtsmen? What can one say of baths placed where cellars should be, the inclusion of galleries where there should be apartments? The filling of the main space of the place, where a staircase should be? Dividing the external faces of the building into arcades, removing thereby the windows which would make my days in the building happy ones? What can one say of the example of Simathie, who included a superb doorway to a house deprived of a courtyard? What about Thiridor, who made a staircase capable of accommodating six persons abreast to enter an apartment deprived of a spacious main storey? This is obviously an excess of imprudence. When my accommodation is designed as it should be with respect to my person, my condition, my family, and even the idea that those around me have of me – for this is also one of the great rules of fitness – I shall have defined that which is specific to me, and then my draughtsman shall work within the proportions laid down for my house, and he should do his work according to the rules and good taste [. . .] This simple and natural grace that he shall instil in my house shall be neither a breach of good manners, nor a breach of logic – quite the contrary, in providing simplicity as the only ornamentation, my Architect shall be praised, and my Building shall be judged pleasing – but if he makes me a great entrance door and raises as a consequence the floors of my second storey in order to succeed in this, I shall be obliged to suffer a staircase of horrible length and a slope sharp enough to put a crick in my neck and frightening to descend [. . .] The profusion of sculptural ornamentation that I may include in the friezes along the staircase and all the luxurious handrails with which I may embellish it, the corbels and masks with which I overload it, far from inspiring a favourable opinion of my method in undertaking the task, shall inspire the thought that I have done nothing intelligent, wise or sensible. [. . .] It is important that your house should be your house, that is to say, it is

Michel de Frémin
??–??

important that it should be executed in such a manner that you find it filled with all the comfort and convenience that you desire and that as experience shows that which is found attractive by the ancestors is not always to the taste of the children, your house should be arranged to please them in order that they should be content with it in their turn, rather than wishing to change it. That will in fact be so if you take care to follow the rules of fitness to the letter. The rules of fitness, correctly followed, will be to the taste of all reasonable persons. If the same considerations applied in Architecture as in Medicine, I would say to you that you should deliver yourself into the hands of your Architect, but the difference that exists in the authority exercised by these two Arts does not permit such submission.

All that remains for me is to say a brief word about what I mean by the sense of fitness for the social condition of the person commissioning a building. Such fitness is the science of refraining from including anything in a Building which is above the dignity and social condition of the Master. If this is done it is inappropriate, involving forgetfulness of his social estate or failure to adhere to the rules of modesty and prudence.

I could give you another type of example of this lack of fitness in the houses of some men, who, made vain by fortune too quickly gained to be legitimate, convince themselves that making ostentatious display of their wealth by applying it even in those places in their houses where it is indecent to make such display, will seek to confuse Champagne with Young Wine, and in the brilliance they grant themselves, either to triumph over others of whom they were once the servants, or to excite a burgeoning concupiscence in themselves, to which a sudden and naturally inspired abundance lends wings, they brave public opinion and the pain it has in witnessing their triumph and its despair at their arrogance.

[...]

Ornamentation is only necessary in a Building when it has a natural place therein.

[...]

I make a distinction in Buildings between grace and beauty. Beauty is an assembly of a number of things that are rich, magnificent and superb. Grace is the distribution and arrangement of those things.

[...] the multiplicity and sumptuousness of the Columns [...] confer no grace; the Nave is great, the concept noble and intelligent, the Architect had imagination, but he let himself go too far in the direction of beauty he wished to place there. If he had been a categorical Architect, by which I mean one of those men who consider every aspect of what they reflect upon and omit nothing in their projects, his design, which doubtless had grandeur, would have been graceful and pleasant [...] It is not enough in Architecture (*true architecture*) to build in order to build, one must build in relation to the reason for building in the first place.

[...] in constructions where there is a desire to go to extremes, creating sublime elevations, the result is often failure. A symbol must signify that which must be signified and hieroglyphs indicate what one wishes to signify: when one gives free rein to an excess of ornamentation, one spoils the construction [...]

design methodology • efficiency • economisation • fit • utility • scientification • systemisation of space distribution

Michel de Frémin
??–??

Abbé Jean-Louis de Cordemoy (1631–1713)

Extract from a Letter by the Author . . . to the Remarks of M. Frézier, Ingénieur Ordinaire du Roy, proffered in the *Journal de Trévoux* in the Month of September 1709 (1710)

Because of the 'graeco-gothic' ideal expounded in his book, **Nouveau Traité de Toute l'Architecture** (1706), combining elemental Grecian directness with the structural ingenuity of Gothic buildings, Cordemoy has been seen as a predecessor of the early functionalist theoreticians, Soufflot (1741) and Laugier (1753, 1765) (Hermann, 1962; Middleton, 1962, 1963). The book was written for entrepreneurs, workmen and laymen in a systematic fashion (Nyberg, 1967). Taking his cue from Frémin (1701), Cordemoy criticises modern structures for their overly heavy construction and traces this grave fault to St Peter's in Rome (Herrmann, ibid.). Cordemoy (1710) was engaged in a lively polemic with Frézier (1709) who decried the former's lack of knowledge of engineering and his excessive reliance on the authority of the ancients (Nyberg, ibid.). Here follows an answer to Frézier's attack on him in one of the leading intellectual journals of the time, the **Memoires de Trévoux**. It was published in that same journal.

Abbé Jean-Louis de Cordemoy 1631–1713

The public is awaiting my response to the remarks of M. Frézier.

He says firstly that to *weed out abuse in the works of those who have acquired themselves a reputation in architecture, one must at least be something of a builder, which is to say, have some idea of building, be acquainted with the materials used, etc.* I might repudiate this maxim. For every day one sees persons with some taste for painting who can clearly discern the beauty of the draughtsmanship in a painting, its use of colour, its handling of light and shade and so on, and the defects which may be found therein, without knowing the manner of drawing, the mixture of colours, or even having the first idea of how to paint. The same holds for the other arts. But I would rather forgive my Reverend Father his maxim. How does he know that I have not *some idea of building, etc.*? Is it because he feels I decide too freely on the defects of *certain works, which have hitherto earned the admiration of all Europe*? This proves nothing: for I can assure him that I have more than *some* idea of all that he points to. I am, without wishing to brag, a competent draughtsman. I even paint in a manner not unpleasant to those with a measure of taste. I might also say that I know how to handle a hammer and chisel; and that I have devised the odd piece of architecture that has been found passable enough.

If one examines what I say about churches, one will see not a sign that I have *that of St Peter of Rome stripped of the great beauty which architects and connoisseurs have concurred in praising since its completion.* One shall see only that it would be much more beautiful, if it had free-standing columns. M. Frézier would rather not see this. For myself I might further say that this is a foible I have in common with the Ancients, whose allegiance I shall always plead: that *I side with them* is at least indication that I have some taste, for I am told that *it is dangerous to think otherwise to these great men*; that *prejudice is in their favour*; and that *far from surpassing them, we should be happy if we could emulate them.* With this last precept I particularly concur. And if one dare reproach those great men Bramante and Michelangelo for anything, it is that they did not do everything in their capability to imitate in St Peter's of Rome, the foremost church of the Christian world, what the early faithful took great pains to use in theirs, that is, colonnades.

M. Frézier then asks me needlessly to *produce for him a drawing to my taste*. Sidonius has just given it to him. And if he is not content with that, Eustathius priest of Constantinople shall give him another. This ingenious architect oversaw, on the orders of Constantine, the building of the celebrated Church of the Holy Sepulchre. Eusebius tells us it was of prodigious size and height.

For the *treatise on stone-cutting* that he also requests of me, all can be found in the excellent Louvre portico. Would not this great range of columns suffice in a vast building such as St Peter's of Rome, and with more justification than in Val de Grace à Paris, to add at the same time to its dégagement and its magnificence?

I shall only ask him if he believes that the ordonnance and treatment of this modern architecture are within the bounds of correctness. For myself I am convinced that they are not. One cannot deny that the Order of architecture, which is no more than bas-relief in our arcuated churches, should be disposed not only in such a way to lead one to believe that if it were detached from the walls it could support the rest of the building unassisted, but also in a manner which does not offend the eye.

I am well aware that most architects believe a building to be all the more beautiful the more ornament it has; and this is what leads them to multiply pilasters in an inappropriate manner, for in doing so they also multiply half-bases, half-capitals and breaks in the entablature. But all these things are very poor in effect. One should avoid inasmuch as is possible, therefore, not only these false beauties resulting from interpenetrating pilasters, but also the habit of placing two pilasters together to form a re-entrant angle, even if this is found in some much-acclaimed works. For they necessarily presuppose a mutual penetration contrary to that precise correctness which is so pleasing in architecture.

If however it occurred that necessity were such that a re-entrant angle was absolutely impossible to avoid, the proportions should then be changed to give each pilaster a little more than half its diameter.

rigorism • essentialism

Anthony, Earl of Shaftesbury (1671–1713)

Characteristics of Men, Manners, Opinions, Times (1711)

Shaftesbury was a convinced Whig like Temple (1685) but preferred to advance his liberal ideals in his writings on moral philosophy rather than through active political life (Pevsner, 1944). His work is written in the form of a dialogue between a philosopher who sees in nature the model for all fields of human behaviour and a sceptic who is won over in the end (ibid.). Shaftesbury was the first to use wilderness as a symbol of nature in her primitive, true, good, beautiful state in order to criticise the rigid rule imposed upon her, and implicitly upon society, by absolutist princely patrons, and precedes Burke and Kant in formulating the sensitivity of the sublime (Lefaivre and Tzonis, 1996). He contributed much to the development of the pre-Romantic aesthetics of the eighteenth century, and his anti-baroque views had an influence on Burlington's neo-palladian circle (Wittkower, 1974, 103–104).

Further reading Hilles and Bloom, 1965; Hussey, 1967b.

(98–102) ... I sing of Nature's order in created beings, and celebrate the beauties which resolve in thee, the source and principle of all beauty and perfection.

'Thy being is boundless, unsearchable, impenetrable. In thy immensity all thought is lost, fancy gives over its flight, and wearied imagination spends itself in vain, finding no coast nor limit of this ocean, nor, in the widest tract through which it soars, one point yet nearer the circumference than the first centre whence it parted... wood of numerous spreading branches (which seem so many different trees) 'tis still, I suppose, one and the self-same tree. Now should you, as a mere caviller, and not as a fair sceptic, tell me that if a figure of wax, or any other matter, were cast in the exact shape and colours of this tree, and tempered, if possible, to the same kind of substance, it might therefore possibly be a real tree of the same kind or species, I would have done with you, and reason no longer. But if you questioned me fairly, and desired I should satisfy you what I thought it was which made this oneness or sameness in the tree or any other plant, or by what it differed from the waxen figure, or from any such figure accidentally made, either in the clouds, or on the sand by the sea shore, I should tell you that neither the wax, nor sand, nor cloud thus pieced together by our hand or fancy had any real relation within themselves, or had any nature by which they corresponded any more in that near situation of parts than if scattered ever so far asunder. But this I should affirm, 'that wherever there was such a sympathising of parts as we saw here in our real tree, wherever there was such a plain concurrence in one common end, and to the support, nourishment, and propagation of so fair a form, we could not be mistaken in saying there was a peculiar nature belonging to this form, and common to it with others of the same kind'. By virtue of this, our tree is a real tree, lives, flourishes, and is still one and the same even when by vegetation and change of substance not one particle in it remains the same.

Anthony, Earl of
Shaftesbury
1671–1713

At this rate indeed, said I, you have found a way to make very adorable places of these sylvan habitations. For besides the living genius of each place, the woods too, which by your account are animated, have their Hamadryads, no doubt, and the springs and rivulets their nymphs in store belonging to them, and these too, by what I can apprehend, of immaterial and immortal substances.

We injure them then, replied Theocles, to say 'they belong to these trees', and not rather 'these trees to them'. But as for their immortality, let them look to it themselves. I only know that both theirs and all other natures must for their duration depend alone on that Nature on which the world depends; and that every genius else must be subordinate to that one Good Genius.

... May one not inquire 'what substances they are of? whether material or immaterial?'

(110–111) 'O mighty Genius! sole animating and inspiring power! author and subject of these thoughts! thy influence is universal, and in all things thou art inmost. From thee depend their secret springs of action. Thou movest them with an irresistible unwearied force, by sacred and inviolable laws, framed for the good of each particular being!' as best may suit with the perfection, life, and vigour of the whole. The vital principle is widely shared and infinitely varied, dispersed throughout, nowhere extinct. All lives, and by succession still revives. The temporary beings quit their borrowed forms and yield their elementary substance to new-comers. Called in their several turns to life, they view the light, and viewing pass, that others too may be spectators of the goodly scene, and greater numbers still enjoy the privilege of Nature. Munificent and great, she imparts herself to most and makes the subjects of her bounty infinite. Nought stays her hastening hand. No time nor substance is lost or unimproved. New forms arise, and when the old dissolve, the matter whence they were composed is not left useless, but wrought with equal management and art, even in corruption, Nature's seeming waste and vile abhorrence. The abject state appears merely as the way or passage to some better. But could we nearly view it, and with indifference, remote from the antipathy of sense, we then perhaps should highest raise our admiration, convinced that even the way itself was equal to the end. Nor can we judge less favourably of that consummate art exhibited through all the works of Nature, since our weak eyes, helped by mechanic art, discover in these works a hidden scene of wonders, worlds within worlds of infinite minuteness, though as to art still equal to the greatest, and pregnant with more wonders than the most discerning sense, joined with the greatest rot or the acutest reason, can penetrate or unfold.

'But 'tis in vain for us to search the bulky mass of matter, seeking to know its nature; how great the whole itself, or even how small its parts. 'If, knowing only some of the rules of motion, we seek to trace it further, 'tis in vain we follow it into the bodies it has reached. Our tardy apprehensions fail us, and can reach nothing beyond the body itself, through which it is diffused. Wonderful being (if we may call it so), which bodies never receive except from others which lose it, nor ever lose, unless by imparting it to others. Even without change of place it has its force, and bodies big with motion labour to move, yet stir not, whilst they express an energy beyond our comprehension.

Anthony, Earl of
Shaftesbury
1671–1713

(120–133) The wildness pleases. We seem to live alone with Nature. We view her in her inmost recesses, and contemplate her with more delight in these original wilds than in the artificial labyrinths and feigned wildernesses of the palace. The objects of the place, the scaly serpents, the savage beasts, and poisonous insects, how terrible, or how contrary to human nature, are beauteous in themselves, and fit to raise our thoughts in admiration of that divine wisdom, so far superior to our short views. Unable to declare the use or service of all things in this universe, we are yet assured of the perfection of all, and of the justice of that economy to which all things are subservient, and in respect of which things seemingly deformed are amiable, disorder becomes regular, corruption wholesome, and poisons (such as these we have seen) prove healing and beneficial.

'But behold! through a vast tract of sky before us, the mighty Atlas rears his lofty head covered with snow above the clouds. Beneath the mountain's foot the rocky country rises into hills, a proper basis of the ponderous mass above, where huge embodied rocks lie piled on one another, and seem to prop the high arch of heaven.... See! with what trembling steps poor mankind treads the narrow brink of the deep precipices, from whence with giddy horror they look down, mistrusting even the ground which bears them, whilst they hear the hollow sound of torrents underneath, and see the ruin of the impending rock, with falling trees which hang with their roots upwards and seem to draw more ruin after them. Here thoughtless men, seized with the newness of such objects, become thoughtful, and willingly contemplate the incessant changes of this earth's surface. They see, as in one instant, the revolutions of past ages, the fleeting forms of things, and the decay even of this our globe, whose youth and first formation they consider, whilst the apparent spoil and irreparable breaches of the wasted mountain show them the world itself only as a noble ruin, and make them think of its approaching period.... But here, mid-way up the mountain, a spacious border of thick wood harbours our wearied travellers, who now are come among the

ever green and lofty pines, the firs and noble cedars, whose towering heads seem endless in the sky, the rest of the trees appearing only as shrubs beside them. And here a different horror seizes our sheltered travellers when they see the day diminished by the deep shades of the vast wood, which, closing thick above, spreads darkness and eternal night below. The faint and gloomy light looks horrid as the shade itself; and the profound stillness of these places imposes silence upon men, struck with the hoarse echoings of every sound within the spacious caverns of the wood. Here space astonishes; silence itself seems pregnant, whilst an unknown force works on the mind, and dubious objects move the wakeful sense. Mysterious voices are either heard or fancied, and various forms of deity seem to present themselves and appear more manifest in these sacred sylvan scenes, such as of old gave rise to temples, and favoured the religion of the ancient world. Even we ourselves, who in plain characters may read divinity from so many bright parts of earth, choose rather these obscurer places to spell out that mysterious being, which to our weak eyes appears at best under a veil of cloud. . . .'
Here he paused a while and began to cast about his eyes, which before seemed fixed. He looked more calmly, with an open countenance and free air, by which, and other tokens, I could easily find we were come to an end of our descriptions, and that whether I would or not, Theocles was now resolved to take his leave of the sublime, the morning being spent and the forenoon by this time well advanced.

Anthony, Earl of
Shaftesbury
1671–1713

Section II

Methinks, said he, Philocles (changing to a familiar voice), we had better leave these unsociable places whither our fancy has transported us, and return to ourselves here again in our more conversable woods and temperate climates. Here no fierce heats nor colds annoy us, no precipices nor cataracts amaze us. Nor need we here be afraid of our own voices whilst we hear the notes of such a cheerful choir, and find the echoes rather agreeable and inviting us to talk.

I confess, said I, those foreign nymphs (if there were any belonging to those miraculous woods) were much too awful beauties to please me. I found our familiar home-nymphs a great deal more to my humour. Yet for all this, I cannot help being concerned for your breaking off just when we were got half the world over, and wanted only to take America in our way home. Indeed, as for Europe, I could excuse your making any great tour there, because of the little variety it would afford us. Besides that, it would be hard to see it in any view without meeting still that politic face of affairs which would too much disturb us in our philosophical flights . . . How sorry am I to lose the noble Amazon! How sorry . . .

'Tis true, said I, Theocles . . . Your genius, the genius of the place, and the Great Genius have at last prevailed. I shall no longer resist the passion growing in me for things of a natural kind, where neither art nor the conceit or caprice of man have spoiled their genuine order by breaking in upon that primitive state. Even the rude rocks, the mossy caverns, the irregular unwrought grottoes and broken falls of waters, with all the horrid graces of the wilderness itself, as representing Nature more, will be the more engaging, and appear with a magnificence beyond the formal mockery of princely gardens. . . . But tell me, I entreat you, how comes it that, excepting a few philosophers of your sort, the only people who are enamoured in this way, and seek the woods, the rivers, or seashores, are your poor vulgar lovers?

Say not this, replied he, of lovers only. For is it not the same with poets, and all those other students in nature and the arts which copy after her? In short, is not this the real case of all who love lovers either of the Muses or the Graces?

However, said I, all those who are deep in this romantic way are looked upon, you know, as a people either plainly out of their wits, or overrun with melancholy and enthusiasm. We always endeavour to recall them from these solitary places. And I must own that often when I have found my fancy run this way, I have checked myself, not knowing what it was possessed me, when I was passionately struck with objects of this kind.

Anthony, Earl of
Shaftesbury
1671–1713

No wonder, replied he, if we are at a loss when we pursue the shadow for the substance. For if we may trust to what our reasoning has taught us, whatever in Nature is beautiful or charming is only the faint shadow of that first beauty. So that every real love depending on the mind, and being only the contemplation of beauty either as it really is in itself or as it appears imperfectly in the objects which strike the sense, how can the rational mind rest here, or be satisfied with the absurd enjoyment which reaches the sense alone?

From this time forward then, said I, I shall no more have reason to fear those beauties which strike a sort of melancholy, like the places we have named, or like these solemn groves. No more shall I avoid the moving accents of soft music, or fly from the enchanting features of the fairest human face. If you are already, replied he, such a proficient in this new love that you are sure never to admire the representative beauty except for the sake of the original, nor aim at other enjoyment than of the rational kind, you may then be confident. I am so, and presume accordingly to answer for myself. However, I should not be ill satisfied if you explained yourself a little better as to this mistake of mine you seem to fear. Would it be any help to tell you, 'That the absurdity lay in seeking the enjoyment elsewhere than in the subject loved'? The matter, I must confess, is still mysterious. Imagine then, good Philocles, if being taken with the beauty of the ocean, which you see yonder at a distance, it should come into your head to seek how to command it, and, like some mighty admiral, ride master of the sea, would not the fancy be a little absurd?

Absurd enough, in conscience. The next thing I should do, 'tis likely, upon this frenzy, would be to hire some bark and go in nuptial ceremony, Venetian-like, to wed the gulf, which I might call perhaps as properly my own. Let who will call it theirs, replied Theocles, you will own the enjoyment of this kind to be very different from that which should naturally follow from the contemplation of the ocean's beauty. The bridegroom-Doge, who in his stately Bucentaur floats on the bosom of his Thetis, has less possession than the poor shepherd, who from a hanging rock or point of some high promontory, stretched at his ease, forgets his feeding flocks, while he admires her beauty. But to come nearer home, and make the question still more familiar. Suppose (my Philocles) that, viewing such a tract of country as this delicious vale we see beneath us, you should, for the enjoyment of the prospect, require the property or possession of the land.

The covetous fancy, replied I, would be as absurd altogether as that other ambitious one. O Philocles! said he, may I bring this yet a little nearer, and will you follow me once more? Suppose that, being charmed as you seem to be with the beauty of those trees under whose shade we rest, you should long for nothing so much as to taste some delicious fruit of theirs; and having obtained of Nature some certain relish by which these acorns or berries of the wood became as palatable as the figs or peaches of the garden, you should afterwards, as oft as you revisited these groves, seek hence the enjoyment of them by satiating yourself in these new delights. The fancy of this kind, replied I, would be sordidly luxurious, and as absurd, in my opinion, as either of the former.

Can you not then, on this occasion, said he, call to mind some other forms of a fair kind among us, where the admiration of beauty is apt to lead to as irregular a consequence? I feared, said I, indeed, where this would end, and was apprehensive you would force me at last to think of certain powerful forms in human kind which draw after them a set of eager desires, wishes and hopes; no way suitable, I must confess, to your rational and refined contemplation of beauty. The proportions of this living architecture, as wonderful as they are, inspire nothing of a studious or contemplative kind. The more they are viewed, the further they are from satisfying by mere view. Let that which satisfies be ever so disproportionable an effect, or ever so foreign to its cause, censure it as you please, you must allow, however, that it is natural. So that you, Theocles, for aught I see, are become the accuser of Nature by condemning a natural enjoyment.

Anthony, Earl of Shaftesbury 1671–1713

Far be it from us both, said he, to condemn a joy which is from Nature. But when we spoke of the enjoyment of these woods and prospects, we understood by it a far different kind from that of the inferior creatures, who, rifling in these places, find here their choicest food. Yet we too live by tasteful food, and feel those other joys of sense in common with them. But . . .

We who were rational, and had minds, methought, should place it rather in those minds which were indeed abused, and cheated of their real good, when drawn to seek absurdly the enjoyment of it in the objects of sense, and not in those objects they might properly call their own, in which kind, as I remember, we comprehended all which was truly fair, generous, or good. So that beauty, said I, and good with you, Theocles, I perceive, are still one and the same. . . . Thus . . . we returned again to the subject of our yesterday's morning conversation . . . my love of this mysterious beauty . . . and consider that all sound love and admiration is enthusiasm: is there a fair and plausible enthusiasm, a reasonable ecstasy and transport allowed to other subjects, such as Architecture, painting, music; and shall it be exploded here? Are there senses by which all those other graces and perfections are perceived, and none by which this higher perfection and grace is comprehended? Is it so preposterous to bring that enthusiasm hither, and transfer it from those secondary and scanty objects to this original and comprehensive one? Observe how the case stands in all those other subjects of art or science. What difficulty to be in any degree knowing! How long ere a true taste is gained! How many things shocking, how many offensive at first, which afterwards are known and acknowledged the highest beauties! For 'tis not instantly we acquire the sense by which these beauties are discoverable. Labour and pains are required, and time to cultivate a natural genius ever so apt or forward. But who is there that once thinks of cultivating this soil, or of improving any sense or faculty which Nature may have given of this kind? And is it a wonder we should be dull then, as we are, confounded and at a loss in these affairs, blind as to this higher scene, these nobler representations? Which way should we come to understand better? Which way be knowing in these beauties? Is study, science, or learning necessary to understand all beauties else? And for the sovereign beauty, is there no skill or science required? In painting there are shades and masterly strokes which the vulgar understand not, but find fault with; in architecture there is the rustic; in music the chromatic kind, and skilful mixture dissonancies: and is there nothing which answers to this in the whole?

I must confess, said I, I have hitherto been one of those vulgar who could never relish the shades, the rustic, or the dissonancies you talk of. I have never dreamt of such masterpieces in Nature. 'Twas my way to censure freely on the first view. But I perceive I am now obliged to go far in the pursuit of beauty, which lies very absconded and deep; and if so, I am well assured that my enjoyments hitherto have been very shallow. I have dwelt, it seems, all this while upon the surface, and enjoyed only a kind of slight superficial beauties, having never gone in search of beauty itself, but of what I fancied such. Like the rest of the unthinking world, I took for granted that what I liked was beautiful, and what I rejoiced in was my good. I never scrupled loving what I fancied, and aiming only at the enjoyment of what I loved; I never troubled myself with examining what the subjects were, nor ever hesitated about their choice.

Anthony, Earl of Shaftesbury 1671–1713

... in medals, coins, embossed work, statues, and well-fabricated pieces, of whatever sort, you can discover beauty and admire the kind. True, said I, but not for the metal's sake. 'Tis not then the metal or matter which is beautiful with you? No. But the art? Certainly. The art then is the beauty? Right. And the art is that which beautifies? The same. So that the beautifying, not the beautified, is the really beautiful? It seems so. For that which is beautified, is beautiful only by the accession of something beautifying, and by the recess or withdrawing of the same, it ceases to be beautiful? Be it. In respect of bodies therefore, beauty comes and goes? So we see. Nor is the body itself any cause either of its coming or staying? None. So that there is no principle of beauty in body? None at all. For body can no 'way be the cause of beauty to itself? No way. Nor govern nor regulate itself? Nor yet this. Nor mean nor intend itself? Nor this neither. Must not that, therefore, which means and intends for it, regulates and orders it, be the principle of beauty to it? Of necessity. And what must that be? Mind, I suppose, for what can it be else? ... the beautiful, the fair, the comely, were never in the matter, but in the art and design; never in body itself, but in the form or forming power,' ... What is it but the design which strikes? What is it you admire but mind, or the effect of mind? 'Tis mind alone which forms. All which is void of mind is horrid, and matter formless is deformity itself.

Of all forms then, ... those ... are the most amiable, and in the first order of beauty, which have a power of making other forms themselves. From whence methinks they may be styled the forming forms [...] The dead forms [...], which bear a fashion, and are formed, whether by man or Nature, but have no forming power, no action, or intelligence [...] Next, [...] the second kind, the forms which form, that is, which have intelligence, action, and operation [...] Here therefore is double beauty. For here is both the form (the effect of mind) and mind.

[...]

Thus architecture, music, and all which is of human invention, resolves itself into this last order. Right, said I; and thus all the enthusiasms of other kinds resolve themselves into ours. The fashionable kinds borrow from us, and are nothing without us. We have undoubtedly the honour of being originals.

anticlassicism • deformation • freedom • naturalism • regionalism • nationalism • sublime

Joseph Addison (1672–1719)

The Spectator (1712)

Addison, like Temple (1685) and Shaftesbury (1711), was a Whig and a key figure in the propagation of the picturesque taste in England (Pevsner, 1944). He too was outspoken in his criticism of the rigidity and pomp of the baroque formal garden, preferring to this product of 'art' the unaffected beauty of nature.

Further reading Clark, 1943; Hipple, 1957; Hunt, 1976; Hussey, 1967a, 1967b; Jacques, 1976; Malins, 1966; Martin, 1976; Pevsner, 1944; Tuveson, 1960; Wiebenson, 1978; Wittkower, 1974, 103–104.

No. 412: *Monday June 23 1712*

Joseph Addison
1672–1719

. . . Divisum sic breve fiet opus. Mart.

I shall first consider those pleasures of the imagination, which arise from the actual view and survey or outward objects: and these, I think, all proceed from the sight of what is great, uncommon, or beautiful. There may, indeed, be something so terrible or offensive, that the horror or loathsomeness of an object may overbear the pleasure which results from its greatness, novelty, or beauty, but still there will be such a mixture of delight in the very disgust it gives us, as any of these three qualifications are most conspicuous and prevailing.

By greatness, I do not only mean the bulk of any single object, but the largeness of a whole view considered as one entire piece. Such are the prospects of an open champaign country, a vast uncultivated desert, of huge heaps of mountains, high rocks and precipices, or a wide expanse of waters, where we are not struck with the novelty or beauty of the sight, but with that rude kind of magnificence which appears in many of these stupendous works of nature. Our imagination loves to be filled with an object, or to grasp at anything that is too big for its capacity. We are flung into a pleasing astonishment at such unbounded views, and feel a delightful stillness and amazement in the soul at the apprehension of them. The mind of man naturally hates everything that looks like a restraint upon it, and is apt to fancy itself under a sort or confinement, when the sight is pent up in a narrow compass, and shortened on every side by the neighbourhood of walls or mountains. On the contrary, a spacious horizon is an image of liberty, where the eye has room to range abroad, to expatiate at large on the immensity or its views, and to lose itself amidst the variety of objects that offer themselves to its observation. Such wide and undetermined prospects are as pleasing to the fancy, as the speculations of eternity or infinitude are to the understanding. But if there be a beauty or uncommonness joined with this grandeur, as in a troubled ocean, a heaven adorned with stars and meteors, or a spacious landscape cut out into rivers, woods, rocks and meadows, the pleasure still grows upon us, as it arises from more than a single principle.

Everything that is new or uncommon raises a pleasure in the imagination, because it fills the soul with an agreeable surprise, gratifies its curiosity, and gives it an idea of which it was not before possessed. We are, indeed, so often conversant with one set of objects, and tired out with so many repeated shows of the same things, that whatever is new or uncommon contributes a little to vary human life, and to divert our minds, for a while, with the strangeness of its appearance: it serves us for a kind of refreshment, and takes off from that satiety we are apt to complain of in our usual and ordinary entertainments. It is this that bestows charms on a monster, and makes even the imperfections of nature please us. It is this that recommends variety, where the mind is every instant called off to something new, and the attention not suffered to dwell too long, and waste itself on any particular object. [. . .] For this reason there is nothing that more enlivens a prospect than rivers, jetteaus, or falls of water, where the scene is perpetually shifting, and entertaining the sight every moment with something that is new. We [. . .] find our thoughts a little agitated and relieved at the sight of such objects as are ever in motion, and sliding away from beneath the eye of the beholder.

No. 414: *Wednesday June 25 1712*

Joseph Addison
1672–1719

There is something more bold and masterly in the rough careless strokes of Nature, than in the nice touches and embellishments of art. We have before observed, that there is generally in Nature something more grand and august, than what we meet with the curiosities of art. When, therefore, we see this imitated in any measure, it gives us a nobler and more exalted kind of pleasure than what we receive from the nicer and more accurate productions of art. On this account our English gardens are not so entertaining to the fancy as are those in France and Italy, where we see a large extent of ground covered over with an agreeable mixture of garden and forest, which represent everywhere an artificial rudeness, much more charming than that neatness and elegancy which we meet with in those of our own country.

I would rather look upon a tree in all its luxuriancy and diffusion of boughs and branches, than when it is thus cut and trimmed into a mathematical figure; and cannot but fancy that an orchard in flower looks infinitely more delightful, than all the little labyrinths of the most finished parterre.

No. 415: *Thursday June 26 1712*

Greatness, in the works of architecture, may be considered as relating to the bulk and body of the structure, or the manner in which it is built. As for the first, we find the Ancients, especially among the eastern nations of the world, infinitely superior to the Moderns.

The Wall of China is one of these eastern pieces of magnificence, which makes a figure even in the map of the world, although an account of it would have been thought fabulous, were not the wall itself still extant.

In the second place we are to consider greatness of manner in architecture, which has such force upon the imagination, that a small building, where it appears, shall give the mind nobler ideas than one of twenty times the bulk, where the manner is ordinary or little.

Let anyone reflect on the disposition of mind he finds in himself, at his first entrance into the Pantheon at Rome, and how his imagination is filled with something great and amazing; and, at the same time, consider how little, in proportion, he is affected with the inside of a Gothic cathedral, though it be five times larger than the other; which can arise from nothing else, but the greatness of the manner in the one, and the meanness in the other.

Among all the figures in architecture, there are none that have a greater air than the concave and the convex; and we find in all the ancient and modern architecture, as well as in the remote parts of China, as in countries nearer home, that round pillars and vaulted roofs make a great part of those buildings which are designed for pomp and magnificence. The reason I take to be, because in these figures we generally see more of the body, than in those of other kinds. There are indeed figures of bodies where the eye may take in two thirds of the surface; but as in such bodies the sight must split upon several angles, it does not take in one uniform idea, but several ideas of the same kind. Look upon the outside of a dome, your eye half surrounds it; look up into the inside, and at one glance you have all the prospect of it; the entire concavity falls into your eye at once, the sight being as the centre that collects and gathers into it the lines of the whole circumference: in a square pillar, the sight often takes in but a fourth part of the surface, and, in a square concave, must move up and down to the different sides, before it is master of all the inward surface. For this reason, the fancy is infinitely more struck with the view of the open air, and skies, that passes through an arch, than what comes through a square, or any other figure.

Joseph Addison
1672–1719

anticlassicism • deformation • freedom • naturalism • emotions • passions • sentiments • orientalism • view • movement

Stephan Switzer

Ichnographia, 1718

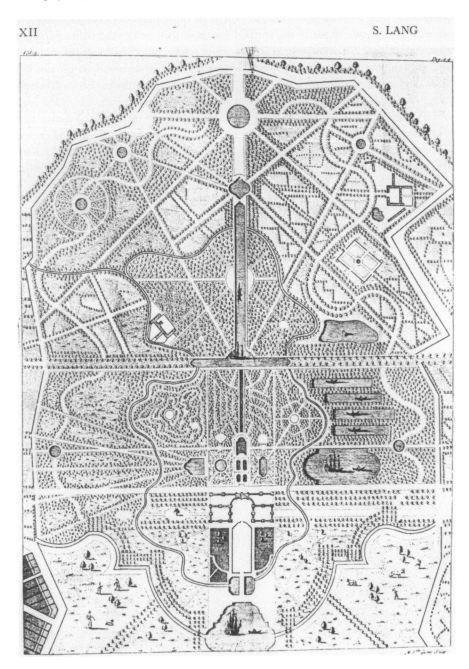

95. Stephan Switzer. *Ichnographia*. 1718. 'A Forest or Rural Gardens' showing two spatial schemes superimposed, a traditional regular using bilateral symmetry and multiple radiating patterns and a new kind employing irregular serpentine lines.

J.A. Corvinus

Marly-le-Roi, Mid-seventeenth century

96. J.A. Corvinus. *Marly-le-Roi*. Mid-seventeenth century

Andrea Pozzo

Perspective Pictorum et Architectorum, 1693–1700

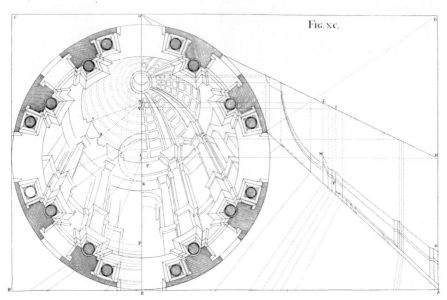

97. Andrea Pozzo. *Perspectiva Pictorum et Architectorum*. 1693–1700

98. Andrea Pozzo. *Perspectiva Pictorum et architectorum Andrea Putei e societate Jesu.* 1693–1700

Le père Bernard de Montfaucon

L'Antiquité expliquée, 1716

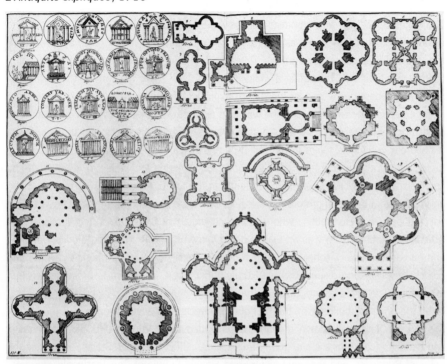

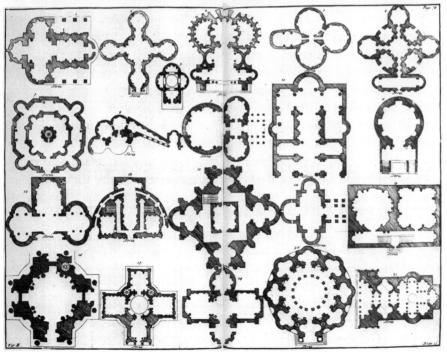

99., 100. Le père Bernard de Montfaucon. *L'Antiquité expliquée*. 1716. A very rare for its time illustration of existing building plans, a first step towards a descriptive taxonomy of architecture.

Johann Bernhard Fischer von Erlach (1656–1723)

Outline of a Historical Architecture (1721)

Johann Bernhard
Fischer von
Erlach
1656–1723

The Viennese sculptor and architect Fischer von Erlach initiated the Austrian baroque and created its most spectacular masterpieces – the *Hofbibliothek*, *Karlskirche*, *Schoenbrunn*, the Imperial Stables, among others – reflecting the grandiose ambitions of the Habsburg Empire just as it was becoming a major European power, at the turn of the eighteenth century. Besides having one of the most prolific architectural practices of the time, and being exceptionally well travelled, he was also extremely learned, as this book, **Outline of a Historical Architecture**, shows. Contemporary scholars have confirmed the veracity of his sources, which he refers to himself (Kunoth, 1957; Sedlmayr, 1956). He picked up his architectural erudition from the court of Queen Christina of Sweden in Rome where he spent sixteen years before returning to Vienna at the age of thirty-nine. The book is based on the precedents of two proto-archaeologists who were in Rome at the time: the art theorist and painter Piero Bellori, who was the custodian of Christina's art collections, and Athanasius Kircher, who was an Egyptologist, and wrote on Roman and biblical antiquity and on eastern Asia. Fischer also used Roman medals, travel descriptions by Dutch and French travellers and discussions with Christopher Wren. The work is broken down into four books. The first presents, besides the Temple of Solomon, which was widely believed to be the origin of building by the baroque architects, the Seven Wonders of the World. The second, less well-known monuments, included Celtic monuments like Stonehenge and his own design for a stone quarry in Salzburg, called the 'Rock Stage', as well as the baths of Budapest, and the great cistern and Haghia Sophia of Constantinople, the great bridge of Isfahan, the entrance to the residence of the King of Siam, the Great Wall of China and the Pagoda of Nanking. As for the Fourth Book, it contains Fischer's own works that he regards as no less than the natural continuation of these marvels. Indeed, his works do share a common feature with the architectural wonders presented in the book: a cultivation of baroque excess, both in its cult of gigantism and ornamentation. Although this is one of the most unabashed public relation operations by an architect – he classified his own buildings according to the social rank of the patron – it does not detract from the fact that the book is also the first comparative history of architecture, intended to be truly international in its scope. His introduction to the collection reveals a preoccupation similar to Kircher's (1697) and d'Aviler's (1691) for increasing the formal vocabulary of architecture beyond the more traditional scope of classical Greek and Roman models to include Middle Eastern and Asian precedents. Still, there was no equivalent in any other field at the time for this highly original and daring concept of a truly universal, global 'international style', even if the purpose of the enterprise is to project himself as its chief representative. A telling detail of this 'internationalism' is the rejection of the euro-centric Vitruvian doctrine. Indeed, whereas Vitruvius had attributed the Corinthian Order to the city of Corinth, Fischer sees its origins in the Temple of Solomon. Consisting of ninety plates, mostly engravings by J.A. Delsenbach, it was based more on images than text, like Vignola's. It was extremely popular, going through three German and two English editions between 1721 and 1737.

Further reading Aurenhammer, 1973; Kunoth, 1956; Oechslin, 1972.

Preface

It is neither to amuse the reader with superfluous talk nor to follow the fashion of those who wish to present themselves falsely as authors that I attach this Preface to the present book. The vain fancy of having it admired is even further from my intentions. Its sole purpose is to apologise for any mistakes that I believe are inevitable in such a work. I have had to rely on the accounts of others and to the operations of an engraver who often required more time than I could give. Those whom the author has the privilege of being acquainted with know that I undertook the work out of a kind of amusement at a time when the victorious armies of his Imperial Majesty [Emperor Charles VI] left little place for concerns related to civil architecture. As far as the others are concerned, if they are among those who are disinterested judges whom the reputation of others does not upset, they will see that I have attempted to supply art lovers with samples of architectures of all kinds and architects with sources for new inventions rather than to instruct the learned . . .

Johann Bernhard
Fischer von
Erlach
1656–1723

As the main goal was to present the most famous buildings that time has destroyed, I have had to rely on the most authentic witnesses, such as contemporary histories and ancient medallions that have preserved the images of what are now mere ruins. These ruins are of little use in giving an idea of the original buildings in the same way that the skeleton of a dead body is in giving the impression of the grandeur and shape of the living person. As for the modern drawings we have of some ancient buildings, that some undertake on the basis of vague and arbitrary imaginings, I hold them in low esteem. The judicious reader will observe easily, if he gives himself the trouble to, that what I present as the seven wonders of the world have little to do with much of what others have presented. In certain cases, however, I have benefited from the elucidations and research of others. In such cases, I have given praise where praise is due. Among others, let us mention the famous Villalpando's description of the Temple of Solomon; Palladio, Serlio, Bramante, Ligorio and several others whose drawings have served to repair the injuries of time on the most considerable monuments of antiquity and the memory of their illustrious makers.

Moreover, I have taken no liberty whatsoever in the ornaments. Invention has not been part of this enterprise, only reference to authority and reasonable conjecture.

I flatter myself in thinking that with all these attentions in mind, this essay on architecture will please not only the eyes of curious persons of good taste, but also their minds, and that it will serve to cultivate the sciences and the arts in general. History itself will find here the means of nurturing the memory of readers and of expressing things more clearly and distinctly than verbal descriptions could. Graphic designers will see in it that the tastes of nations differ no less in architecture than in dress or in the preparing of food, and that by comparing them one will be able to make a judicious choice among them. And they will recognise that use can authorise certain *bizarreries* in the art of building . . .

First Book. On Some Jewish, Egyptian, Syrian, Persian and Greek Antique Buildings

The Temple of Solomon

The author proposes in this work to give the public a general idea of the diversity of the buildings of antiquity. The drawing, which is a wordless description, often requires a verbal explanation. One without the other is not expressive enough. The verbal descriptions of this book will not extend beyond what is necessary to inform those who are not versed in architecture. As for those who know architecture, they will know that any detail one gives in a book in no way suffice to give an idea of the real thing. The Temple of Solomon is no exception. The subject is vast and one might well recall that Roman architecture owes its perfect handling of the Corinthian order to that excellent structure. The Phoenicians had transferred its knowledge to the Greeks, and they to the Romans.

The Palace of the Emperor Diocletian

Johann Bernhard
Fischer von
Erlach
1656–1723

If Misters Son and Wheler in their curious research on Greece had been better at drawing, one might have a more exact knowledge of the most well preserved Roman antiquities of all, that the furore of barbarians has not succeeded in destroying. The etymology of the word Spalato, that the moderns believe to be formed of Palatium, is believable enough, since the seal of that city still bears a palace and that, indeed, Spalato was born of the ashes of the ancient Salon of the palace that the Emperor Diocletian had had built for his retirement ... Eusebius teaches us that a fire caused by a lightning was the first tragedy to strike this palace. What remains of its old walls and what is now part of the great walls of the city is a great square whose side, that gives onto the sea, comes into view first as one approaches it from the sea.

The surprising structure of rocks in England called Stonehenge, Chorea Gigantum, or the Dance of the Giants

It is near Salisbury in a plain where stones of a prodigious height are stacked up one next to the other, some bearing others horizontally in such a manner as to form gates. The structure is less remarkable by the size of the stones than by their arrangement. One sees right away that these are monuments whose origins are so old that there is not trace of their foundation left. But those who think they are other than burial stones would do well to reflect on the fact that the ancient Gothic graves were surrounded by upturned stones, as we can see from the engravings of *Svecia Illustrata*, and in the Danish monuments in Worms.

Plan of the Imperial Baths of Budapest in Hungary, renowned for its waters as well as for the excellence of Arabic architecture

[...]

Mosque that the Sultan Orcanus built in Bursa in Asia Minor

[...]

View of the Great and Magnificent Mosque of the Great Sultan Achmed in Constantinople in the year 1610

[...]

The Soleimanye Mosque, built in Constantinople par Sultan Suleiman with peristyle and garden that contains the mausoleums of Suleiman II and his wife

[...]

The Great Cistern of Constantinople in the Meidan near the Hippodrome. The 224 columns of freestone which supports it underground are all almost covered with water at a height that permits small boats to pass. We had this elevation brought from the Orient with its plan and with some other Turkish buildings to communicate them to the curious because of their uniqueness

[...]

The great and magnificent Temple of Haghia Sophia, near the caravanserai

[...]

View of a part of the great city of Mecca with the holy place which is so famous and where according to the Mohammedans the house of Abraham and the fountain of Ishmael still stand and where, finally, Mohammed wrote his Koran. It is visited every year by Turkish caravans

[...]

Johann Bernhard
Fischer von
Erlach
1656–1723

View of the Palace of the Kings of the Persians in Isfahan seen from the Meidan. The biggest and most regular square in the world. It is 700 feet long and 250 large and is surrounded with houses that have a structure as big as a canal bored with water and trees. In the centre there is a mast surmounted with an apple that serves as a target for galloping horsemen that aim at it with arrows

[...]

View of the great bridge of Ali-Verdi-Chan of Isfahan on the Sendrud River. It is named after the person who had it constructed, Ali-Verdi-Chan. It is 300 geometric feet long and 20 wide. On either side there is a covered loggia covered with a platform which is just as easy to use and open to the breeze there as the lower one is shaded. There is a third, vaulted gallery under the bridge from one end to the other that is very pleasant when the water level is very low

[...]

View of the residence of the King of Siam, with the magnificent entrance of the French Ambassador that is constructed on the River Menam with 150 balloons, or boats belonging to the Siamese state

[...]

Plan and elevation in perspective of the imperial court of Peking, representing the fore-courts oriented towards the four corners of the world, and second fore-courts, first entrance to the court, the first court, the second court, the third court and the four gardens each comprising eight magnificent pleasure houses. In the distance, the Great Wall that separates China from Tartary

[...]

The Famous Pagoda near Nanking, with its courts, walks, baths and the magnificent 9-storey-high porcelain tower. The extent of its domain is 42 miles round

[...]

Tsing Dao, or the road of the pillars in the Chinese province of Chen Xi, where the tops of mountains have been joined by a 30 stadia long bridge in order to cut all the detoura on the way to the capital. This bridge is supported by beams but mostly, where the valleys are too deep, by pillars of stone of such a height as to inspire horror, and of such a width that can accommodate 4 horses across. On either side there are iron railings

history versus antiquarianism • orientalism

Johann Bernhard
Fischer von
Erlach
1656–1723

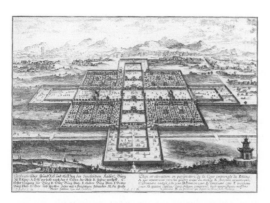

101. Johann Bernhard Fischer von Erlach. *Entwurf einer historischen Architecktur*. 1721. Plan and elevation of the Imperial Court of Peking.

102. Johann Bernhard Fischer von Erlach. *Entwurf einer historischen Architecktur*. 1721. The tomb of Mohammed in Medina.

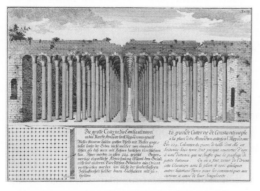

103. Johann Bernhard Fischer von Erlach. *Entwurf einer historischen Architecktur*. 1721. The Great cistern of Constantinople called Atmeidan, containing 224 columns of hewn stone. They are almost completely submerged in water.

104. Johann Bernhard Fischer von Erlach. *Entwurf einer historischen Architecktur*. 1721. The royal palace of Babylon, with gardens hung on twenty walls.

Daniel Defoe (1660–1731)

A Tour Through the Whole Island of Great Britain (1724–1727)

With the keen observation of a specialised reporter, Defoe details the realities of country and city life. He sees both realities as part of a purely commercial world with hardly any sentimental tint. The famous novelist thus sheds a uniquely revealing light on the underlying economic realities that prompt the establishment of country estates outside London and accompany the rise of the picturesque movement (Williams, 1975, 80–81).

Further reading Manwaring, 1965; Williams, 1975, 80–81.

The reason of my taking notice of this badness of the roads, through all the midland counties, is this; that as these are counties which derive a very great trade with the city of London, and with one another, perhaps the greatest of any counties in England; and that, by consequence, the carriage is exceeding great, and also that all the land carriage of the northern counties necessarily goes through these counties, so the roads had been ploughed so deep, and materials have been in some places so difficult to be had for repair of the roads, that all the surveyors' rates have been able to do nothing; nay, the very whole country has not been able to repair them; that is to say, it was a burden too great for the poor farmers; for in England it is the tenant, not the landlord, that pays the surveyors of the highways.

This necessarily brought the country to bring these things before the Parliament; and the consequence has been, that turnpikes or toll-bars have been set up on the several great roads of England, beginning at London, and proceeding through almost all those dirty deep roads, in the midland counties especially; at which turn-pikes all carriages, droves of cattle, and travellers on horseback, are obliged to pay an easy toll; that is to say, a horse a penny, a coach three pence, a cart four pence, at some six pence to eight pence, a wagon six pence, in some a shilling, and the like; cattle pay by the score, or by the head, in some places more, in some less; but in no place is it thought a burden that ever I met with, the benefit of a good road abundantly making amends for that little charge the travellers are put to at the turn-pikes.

Several of these turn-pikes and tolls had been set up of late years, and great progress had been made in mending the most difficult ways, and that with such success as well deserves a place in this account.

[...]

Labour is dear, wages high, no man works for bread and water now; our labourers do not work in the road, and drink in the brook; so that rich as we are, it would exhaust the whole nation to build the edifices, the causeways, the aqueducts, lines, castles, fortifications, and other public works, which the Romans build with very little expense.

But to return to this new method of repairing the highways at the expense of the turn-pikes; that is to say, by the product of funds raised at those turn-pikes [...]

This improving of the roads is an infinite improvement to the towns near London, in the convenience of coming to them, which makes the citizens flock out in greater numbers than ever to take lodgings and country-houses, which many, whose business called them often to London, could not do, because of the labour of riding forward and backward, when the roads were but a little dirty, and this is seen in the difference in the rents of houses in those villages upon such repaired roads, from the rents of the like dwellings and lodgings in other towns of equal distance, where they want those helps, and particularly the increase of the number of buildings in those towns, as above.

[...]

The benefit of these turn-pikes appears now to be so great, and the people in all places begin to be so sensible of it, that it is incredible what effect it has already had upon trade in the countries where it is more completely finished; [...] the benefit in abating the rate of carriage is wholly and simply the tradesmen's, not the carrier's.

Yet the advantage is evident to the carriers also another way; for [...] they can bring more weight with the same number of horses, nor are their horses so hard worked and fatigued with their labour as they were before; in which ones particular 'tis acknowledged by the carriers, they perform their work with more ease, and the masters are at less expense.

The advantage to all other kinds of travelling I omit here, such as the safety and ease of gentlemen travelling up to London on all occasions, whether to the term, or to the Parliament, to Court, or on any other necessary occasion, which is not a small part of the benefit of these new methods.

Daniel Defoe
1660–1731

[...]

From Richmond to London, the river sides are full of villages, and those villages so full of beautiful buildings, charming gardens and rich habitations of gentlemen of quality, that nothing in the world can imitate it; no, not the country for twenty miles round Paris, though that indeed is a kind of prodigy.

[...]

It is since the Revolution that our English gentlemen began so universally to adorn their gardens with those plants, we call ever greens, which leads me to a particular observation that may not be improper in this place; King William and Queen Mary introduced each of them two customs, which by the people's imitating them became the two idols of the town, and indeed of the whole kingdom; the queen brought in (1.) the love of fine East-India callicoes [...], which afterward descended into the humours of the common people so much, as to make them grievous to our trade, and ruining to our manufacturers and the poor; so that the Parliament were obliged at last to prohibit the use of them: (2.) The queen brought in the custom or humour, as I may call it, of furnishing houses with china-ware, which increased to a strange degree afterwards, piling their china upon the tops of cabinets, scrutores and every chimney-piece, to the tops of the ceilings, and even setting up shelves for their china-ware, where they wanted such places, till it became a grievance in the expense of it, and even injurious to their families and estates. [...]

The king on his part introduced (1.) the love of gardening; and (2.) of painting. In the first his majesty was particularly delighted with the decoration of ever greens, as the greatest addition to the beauty of a garden, preserving the figure in the place even in the roughest part of an inclement and tempestuous winter.

With the particular judgement of the king, all the gentlemen in England began to fall in; and in a few years fine gardens, and fine houses began to grow up in every corner; the king began with the gardens at Hampton-Court [editor's note: one of the largest royal residences of England built in 1515 by Cardinal Wolsey], Kensington [editor's note: partly designed by Christopher Wren, Kensington Gardens were originally the grounds of Kensington Palace in London, adjoining Hyde Park], and the gentlemen followed every where, with such a gust that the alteration is indeed wonderful throughout the whole kingdom.

[287]

Daniel Defoe
1660–1731

But I find none has spoken of what I call the distant glory of all these buildings. There is a beauty of these things at a distance, taking them *en passant*, and in perspective, which few people value, and fewer understand; and yet here they are more truly great than in all their private beauties whatsoever. Here they reflect beauty and magnificence upon the whole country, and give a kind of a character to the island, of Great Britain in general. The banks of the Seine are not thus adorned from Paris to Roan, or from Paris to the Loign above the city: the Danube can show nothing like it above and below Vienna, or the Po above and below Turin; the whole country here shines with a lustre not to be described. Take them in a remote view, the fine seats among the trees as jewels shine in a rich coronet; in a near sight they are mere pictures and paintings; at a distance they are all nature, near hand all art; but both in the extremest beauty. In a word, nothing can be more beautiful; here is a plain and pleasant country, a rich fertile soil, cultivated and enclosed to the utmost perfection of husbandry, then bespangled with villages; those villages filled with these houses, and the houses surrounded with gardens, walks, vistas, avenues, representing all the beauties of building, and all the pleasures of planting. It is impossible to view these countries from any rising ground and not be ravished with the delightful prospect. For example, suppose you take your view from the little rising hills about Clapham [editor's note: Clapham is a residential district in London, south of the Thames], there you see the pleasant villages of Peckham [editor's note: Peckham is a residential district four miles south east of London], Camberwell [editor's note: this is a municipality in the same area as the former districts], with some of the finest dwellings about London; with all the villages mentioned above, and the country adjoining filled with the palaces of the British nobility and gentry already spoken of; looking north, behold, to crown all, a fair prospect of the whole city of London itself; the most glorious sight without exception, that the whole world at present can show, or perhaps ever could show since the sacking of Rome in the European, and the burning the Temple of Jerusalem in the Asian part of the world.

Add to all this, that these fine houses and innumerable more, which cannot be spoken of here, are not, at least very few of them, the mansion houses of families, the ancient residences of ancestors, the capital messuages of the estates; nor have the rich possessors any lands to a considerable value about them; but these are all houses of retreat. Like the bastides [editors' note: a bastide is a medieval settlement built for defence purposes and generally laid out with a geometric plan] of Marseilles, gentlemen's mere summer-houses, or citizen's country-houses; whither they retire from the hurries of business, and from getting money, to draw their breath in a clear air, and to divert themselves and families in the hot weather; and they that are shut up, and as it were stripped of their inhabitants in the winter, who return to smoke and dirt, sin and seacoal (as it was coarsely expressed), in the busy city; so that in short all this variety, this beauty, this glorious show of wealth and plenty, is really a view of the luxuriant age which we live in, and of the over-flowing riches of the citizens, who in their abundance make these gay excursions, and live thus delicious all the summer, retiring within themselves in the winter, the better to lay up for the next summer's expense.

[. . .]

Supposing now, the whole body of this vast building to be considered as one city, London, and not concerning myself or the reader with the distinction of its several jurisdictions; we shall then observe it only as divided into three, namely. the city, the Court, and the out-parts.

The city is the centre of its commerce and wealth. The Court of its gallantry and splendour. The out-parts of its numbers and mechanics; and in all these, no city in the world can equal it. Between the Court and city, there is a constant communication of business to that degree, that nothing in the world can come up to it. As the city is the centre of business, there is the Custom-house, an article, which, as it brings in an immense revenue to the public, so it cannot be removed from its place, all the vast import and export of goods being, of necessity, made there.

Here, also, is the Excise Office, the Navy Office, the Bank, and almost all the offices where those vast funds are fixed, in which so great a part of the nation are concerned, and on the security of which so many millions are advanced.

Here are the South Sea Company [editor's note: a company incorporated in 1711 for the purpose of exclusive trade with the South Seas, and of taking up the unfounded National Debt], the East India Company [editor's note: a company formed for carrying on an East Indian trade, especially. The English company was incorporated in 1600], the Bank, the African Company, &c. whose stocks support that prodigious paper commerce, called stock jobbing; a trade, which once bewitched the nation to its ruin, and which, though reduced very much, and recovered from that terrible infatuation which once overspread the whole body of the people, yet is still a negotiation, which is so vast in its extent, that almost all the men of substance in England are more or less concerned in it, and the property of which is so very often alienated, that even the tax upon the transfers of stock, though but five shillings for each transfer, brings many thousand pounds a year to the government; and some have said, that there is not less than a hundred millions of stock transferred forward or backward from one hand to another every year, and this is one thing which makes such a constant daily intercourse between the Court part of the town, and the city; and this is given as one of the principal causes of the prodigious conflux of the nobility and gentry from all parts of England to London, more than ever was known in former years, viz. that many thousands of families are so deeply concerned in those stocks, and find it so absolutely necessary to be at hand to take advantage of buying and selling, as the sudden rise or fall of the price directs, and the loss they often sustain by their ignorance of things when absent, and the knavery of brokers and others, whom, in their absence, they are bound to trust, that they find themselves obliged to come up and live constantly here, or at least, most part of the year.

Daniel Defoe
1660–1731

But let the citizens and inhabitants of London know, and it may be worth the reflection of some of the landlords, and builders especially, that if peace continues, and the public affairs continue in honest and upright management, there is a time coming, at least the nation hopes for it, when the public debts are being reduced and paid off, the funds or taxes on which they are established may cease, and so fifty or sixty millions of the stocks, which are now the solid bottom of the South-Sea Company, East-India Company, Bank, &c. will cease, and be no more; by which the reason of this conflux of people being removed, they will of course, and by the nature of the thing, return again to their country seats, to avoid the expensive living at London, as they did come up hither to share the extravagant gain of their former business here.

What will be the condition of this overgrown city in such a case, I must leave to time; but . . . in time, 'tis to be hoped, all our taxes may cease, and the ordinary revenue may, as it always used to do, again supply the ordinary expense of the government.

Then, I say, will be a time to expect the vast concourse of people to London, will separate again and disperse as naturally, as they have now crowded hither. What will be the fate then of all the fine buildings in the out parts, in such a case let any one judge.

efficiency • economisation • fit • utility • urbanisation of architecture • planning

Jean Courtonne (1671–1739)

Treatise on Perspective with Some Remarks on Architecture (1725)

The author was an architect and professor at the Académie Royale d'Architecture. His treatise is especially good at presenting perspective for use by architects. In addition it documents Courtonne's most important built projects, his novel idea that interior design was as important as exterior design (Blomfield, 1973; Hautecoeur, 1948–1963; Lemonnier, 1911–1929; Wiebenson, 1982, 1993).

Jean Courtonne
1671–1739

Digression on Several Difficulties Regarding Architecture in Relation to Optics or Perspective

Before giving perspective elevations of several considerable buildings, of which I was the architect, I believe it is appropriate to say some thing here about the conformity and close union that has always existed between perspective and architecture; this connection is so natural that it is almost impossible to attain perfection in the latter without having a very thorough knowledge of the former. Indeed, so many different parts are found in the greatest edifices, some more recessed than others, that one must admit in good faith that their effect cannot be judged from a simple geometrical elevation.

If, for example, the structure in question is the dome of a church, whose plan is always in the interior, and consequently very far from the elevation of the facing walls, I say that it is very difficult to judge from a geometrical elevation the height that must be given to all of the parts, as well as to others that are more or less further in; because not being on the same plane as the facing walls, there is no sure rule for determining the proportions they must be granted, because of both their distance from the outer walls and the profusion of the eaves, and other bodies that can block the view of several parts that absolutely must not be hidden. 'Tis therefore necessary to leave things up to chance, and assume, without knowing it, that from a certain distance one will be able to see all those parts in their true proportions, and in the manner in which one wants them to appear.

No matter how much one may flatter oneself for having the most consummate experience, 'twill always be true to say that an Architect is not very sure of his success, because he works only by conjecture and has no certain rules on which he can ground himself. I know full well that the greatest resource will be in such structures, which inspire action, and which provide him with several ideas; but since one does not always repeat the same thing (which must even be avoided), the difference of subjects, their plans and their exterior appearance, gives rise to new difficulties, out of which one is not sure of finding a way with honour when one is lacking a sure guide of how to conduct oneself.

It must not be said here that by means of a diagonal line drawn through the cross-section or the profile of the middle of the Edifice, one can become familiar with the parts that can be seen from any point chosen at will: for by this artifice, which is very crude, one can only know a single point, that which is encountered at the place of the cross-section, and one is still unaware of the effect that other parts will have on the right or the left and which shape must be given to all the parts of this dome and to the accompanying structures so that they will have all the gracefulness befitting them.

What I have just said about domes can be applied as well to all sorts of edifices in which some parts that are higher than others can be found, and which are more deeply-set than the facing walls; the result is the same difficulty which one believes can be remedied with infrequently used models, if they are not made considerably large enough, and which cause great expense, because they are always made unnecessarily, and in addition to that, because the model is always smaller than the structure to be built, the eye is not in the right place, and easily discovers what it would see only imperfectly when the edifice is completed.

One can be convinced of the truth of what we have just said if one carefully examines the perspective elevation of the large pyramid whose drawing I give afterwards: for the geometrical elevation upon which it was based is much higher than, and does not have the same proportions as, the perspective drawing below, even though this same perspective drawing was based on the geometrical measurements according to the rule. But the principal difference between them arises not only from the plan of the pyramid, which is deeper than the walls of the octagon, but more from the large talus of the same pyramid, which, as it rises, consequently recedes further from view. And it is to find the true proportion that I have had recourse to perspective, which can never deceive me, and has caused me to know what I must take into account to give the whole mass the gracefulness that is necessary to it.

Jean Courtonne
1671–1739

I have made this argument only to conclude that, because Perspective can give sure rules for knowing true proportions, it is necessary to look in those parts of which we have just spoken. All possible care must be taken when studying such an advantageous science.

It is necessary, for that effect, to put the geometrical plan of the parts that can be seen from a certain viewpoint chosen at will in perspective, for the distance as well as the height of the viewpoint, and on each shortened point of the plan, to raise as many perpendicular lines, reduced and transferred to the Perspective scale, in the way we have explained in the first two parts of this treatise; for if that is executed with all the necessary precaution, the set-back parts, as well as those in the front, will appear the same on the perspective elevation, and in the same way that the structure was completed. And then they can be increased or decreased depending on the effect that they have on the drawing, and one will be sure to see things after the perfect execution of the edifice in the same state that they were shown on the said drawing, provided that one stands at the same distance and the same height as the eye, as that which was assumed by placing the Drawing in Perspective.

On Distribution

What we can say here about Architecture being only a digression, and only in relation to Perspective, is that one must not expect the body of a structure to be able to contain all the notions which might lead to the perfection of this Art; I will only lightly touch upon what will appear to be some connection with the subject of this treatise.

Leaving aside, therefore, that which regards strength and salubrity, which I view as foreign to my subject, I will speak only in passing of the distribution and decoration of buildings.

By distribution I mean the use that an architect must make of a place in which one wants to build an edifice of any kind; it is this part that must be regarded as the main and the most essential one, all the others being, so to speak, subordinate to it. Indeed, when you put columns on top of columns, when your profiles are more regular and more delicate than those of Palladio and the most famous Architects of our times, and when you have used the most skilful Sculptors on the decoration of your Edifice, what success would you achieve, if your land is unevenly distributed? If all the necessary conveniences are lacking? If the main rooms do not have the grandeur, the nobility and the openness befitting them? If the windows are poorly arranged? If the Doors and Fireplaces are badly located? In a word, if you have failed in some essential point that detracts from the quality of a Master, or from that of the Building?

Jean Courtonne
1671–1739

It is true that this part is much larger than it was a hundred or so years ago, and that our Frenchmen have taken distribution to a point that puts them well above other Nations, and ahead of all that our Forefathers were able to do in this domain: in France, as well as in Italy, we have Palaces and Houses built in previous centuries, on the exterior of which reigns a rather beautiful Architecture, while nothing about the interior distribution corresponds to it: there are no conveniences; it seems that our Architects have affected to banish daylight, and to make dusk reign all year long; it is often difficult to find the proper place for a bed; fireplaces take up too much space in the bedrooms, which would seem large, if in addition to that defect the doors were not so small, giving a poor idea of the places in to which they lead. But if by virtue of the happy discoveries that have been made in the past century the French have invented a new Art of distribution, and have surpassed their Neighbours, and have left them only the glory of imitating us, we must make every imaginable effort to strengthen that reputation; and despite the difficulties that might arise in this type of fencing match, the Architect must win the prize, because that is where his genius will appear, and all the other parts depend on it and necessarily have a relationship to it . . . by combining the exterior with the composition of the interior, one causes a secret pleasure to be born in the soul of the Spectators, who know not the reason for the satisfaction they feel nor to what it must be attributed, though they see in what they admire naught but Windows, Pilasters, Masks, Consoles, and other similar ornaments that they have noticed in other places a hundred times, without experiencing the same emotion.

I can not prevent myself from saying here that it is very difficult, not to say impossible, to achieve this perfect relationship between the interior and exterior parts of a building, when an Architect is not the perfect master of his project, and when his ideas are interfered with, most often for trivialities.

But the natural arrangement of the rooms of an edifice, in which the nobility, the grandeur and the proportions that befit them must be conserved, is what makes a distribution perfect: their difference lies not in the figure, as several people might imagine, among which one sees what constitutes the beauty of the plan, by giving each room a different shape, some of them circular, some oval, some square, and still others composed of all these figures, which gives a plan the appearance of a cut flower-bed, especially when the rooms on the right are symmetrical with those on the left, which is necessary for creating a more pleasing distribution.

It is not difficult to show the error of this commonly-held opinion; for symmetry, which is one of the main sources of the beauty of Architecture, must only be in the parts that present themselves to the eye at the same time: but with regard to the totality of the rooms, we know that the main beauty consists of the variety that they are given, in terms of the size, the different ornaments and the use that will be made of them, because nothing would be more boring than seeing a continual repetition of the same thing, in a series of so many rooms that compose the large Apartments.

But one must not imagine that this diversity should include various shapes, and that it is necessary to make round, oval and square rooms; that would only needlessly increase expenses for the extraordinary thickness of the walls, and at the same time decrease the size of those rooms, without augmenting their beauty. I say not that these figures can not be used in some cases, such as in Vestibules or large Salons, when they are in the middle of a façade, and project from the courtyard or garden side: but that must happen only rarely, and these extraordinary figures must be used only in irregular plans, or to correct the lay of the land. When these figures are appropriately placed, they reveal the genius and capacity of the architect.

Robert Castell
d. 1729

Naught remains for me to say about distribution in general, save that in no part of the plan must there be a part so small that it has not a particular use, and of which one can not make sense: that is where it will be seen whether the land is carefully organised, and whether, through a lack of cleverness, there are no empty spaces.

representation • truth • illusion • systemisation of space distribution

Robert Castell (d. 1729)

The Villas of the Ancients (1728)

Castell, a classical scholar rather than an architect, presents the Younger Pliny's villas, described in the latter's famous **Letters**, as an ideal mixture of irregularity and rule. Written after irregularity had been established as fashionable by Addison (1712) and Pope (1731), this book influenced the transition away from the stiff, regimented forms of the formal garden towards the new aesthetics of natural simplicity and informality embodied in the landscape garden (Clark, 1943, 165). Castell was a member of the neo-palladian circle of Lord Burlington, a patron of the arts and letters, who drew around him the chief cultural figures of the movement propagating the English villa and landscape park.

Further reading Harris, 1967, 1990; Hussey, 1967b, 40; Pevsner, 1944.

[. . .] It may not be improper to enquire into the first rise of gardens, and of what they at first consisted, by which a judgement may be the better passed on this before us. The invention of this art seems to have been owing to the first builders of villas, who were naturally led to search for the most beautiful places in which to build them; but as it was hardly possible to meet with any, that within the compass designed for the pleasure of the villa, should contain every thing that was completely agreeable, it was necessary to supply by care and industry whatever was wanting in the natural face of the country: but at first they aimed at nothing further than the disposition of their plantations, for by the small knowledge we can arrive at, in the gardens of the first ages, they seem to have been no more than select, well-watered spots of ground, irregularly producing all sorts of plants and trees, grateful either to the sight, smell, or taste, and refreshed by shade and water. Their whole art consisting in little more than in making those parts next to their villas that, as it were accidentally, produce the choicest trees, the growth of various soils, the face of the ground suffering little or no alteration; the intent of gardens being within a fixed compass of ground, to enjoy all that fancy could invent most agreeable to the senses. But this rough manner, not appearing sufficiently beautiful to those of a more regular and exact taste, set them upon inventing a manner of laying out the ground and plantations of gardens by the rule and line, and to trim them up by an art that was visible in every part of design. By the accounts we have of the present manner of designing in China, it seems as if from the two former manners a third had been formed, whose beauty consisted in a close imitation of nature; where, though the parts are disposed with the greatest art, the irregularity is still preserved; so that their manner may not improperly be said to be an artful confusion, where there is no appearance of that skill which is made use of, their rocks, cascades, and trees, bearing their natural forms. In the disposition of Pliny's garden, the designer of it shows that he was not unacquainted with these several manners, and the whole seems to have been a mixture of them all three. In the Pratulum nature appears in her plainest and most simple dress; such as the first builders were contented with about their villas, when the face of the ground it self happened to be naturally beautiful. By the care used in regulating the turning and winding walks, and cutting the trees and hedges into various forms, it shows the manner of the more regular gardens; and in the Imitatio Ruris, he seems to hint at the third manner; where, under the form of a beautiful country, hills, rocks, cascades, rivulets, woods, buildings, etc. were possibly thrown into such an agreeable disorder, as to have pleased the eye from several views, like so many beautiful landscapes; and at the same time have afforded at least all the pleasures that could be enjoyed in the most regular gardens. The main body of this garden was disposed after the second of these three manners; through its winding paths one, accidentally as it were, fell upon those pieces of a rougher taste, that seem to have been made with a design to surprise those that arrived at them, through such a scene of regularities, which (in the opinion of some) might appear more beautiful by being near those plain imitations of nature, as lights in painting are heightened by shades.

aesthetisation of architecture • anticlassicism • deformation • freedom • naturalism • orientalism • view • movement

Robert Castell
d. 1729

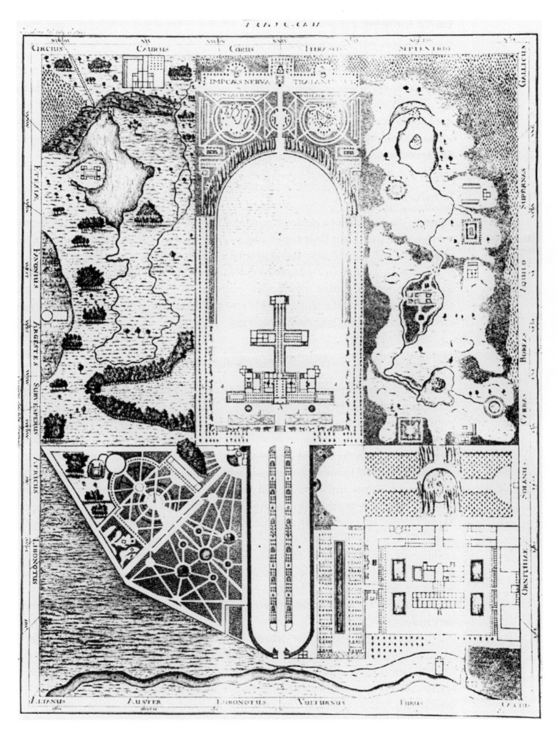

105. Robert Castell. 'Plan of Tusculanum'. *The Villas of the Ancients Illustrated*. 1728. Imaginary reconstruction combining the design of Roman-like regular buildings, French garden regular patterns with *irregularity* and *artful confusion* of disorder and natural *rougher taste*.

Batty Langley (1696–1751)

New Principles of Gardening (1728)

This book, dedicated to the king, exemplifies the kind of practical handbook that, according to Wittkower, was opposed to the elegant publications destined for the gentry and their architects (1974, 109). These books appeared often in pocket-size form and were cheap (ibid.) and they flooded the market. It was one of the great popularisers of natural beauty and picturesque taste.

Further reading Harris, 1977, 1990; Hussey, 1967b.

Introduction

Batty Langley
1696–1751

For since the pleasure of a garden depends on the variety of its parts, it is therefore that we should well consider their disposition, so as to have a continued mix of harmonious objects that will present new and delightful scenes to our view at every step we take, which regular gardens are incapable of doing. Nor is there anything more shocking than a stiff regular garden; where after we have seen one quarter thereof, the very same is repeated in all the remaining parts, so that we are tired, instead of being further entertained with something new as expected.

Part IV. Sect. II. Of the Disposition of Gardens in General

On this very point depends the whole beauty or ruin of a garden, and therefore every gentleman should be very cautious therein [. . .]

Now these unpleasant forbidding sort of gardens owe their deformity to the insipid taste or interest of some of our theoretical engineers, who, in their aspiring garrets cultivate all the several species of plants as well as frame designs for situations they never saw. Or to some nursery-man who, for his own interest advises the Gentleman to such Forms and Trees as will make the greatest draught out of his nursery, without regard to anything more. And sometimes to a coxcomb who takes upon himself to be an excellent Draughtsman as well as an incomparable gardener. Of which there has been and are still too many in England, which is witnessed by every unfortunate garden wherein they come. Now as the Beauty of Gardens in general depends upon an elegant disposition of all their parts which cannot be determined without a perfect knowledge of its several ascendings, descendings, views, etc. How is it possible that any person can make a good design for any garden whose situation they never saw?

To draw a beautiful regular draught is not to the purpose for although it makes a handsome figure on the paper, it has a quite different effect when executed on the ground. Nor is there anything more ridiculous, and forbidding than a garden which is regular; which, instead of entertaining the eye with fresh objects, after you have seen a quarter part, you only see the very same part repeated again, without any variety. And what still greatly adds to this wretched method is that to execute these stiff regular Designs, they destroy many a noble oak and in its place plant, perhaps, a clumsey-bred Yew, Holley, etc. which, with me, is a Crime of so high a Nature, as not to be pardoned.

There is nothing adds so much to the Pleasure of a Garden, of those great beauties of nature, hills and valleys, which, by our regular coxcombs have never been destroyed and at a very great expense also in levelling.

For, to their great misfortune, they always deviate from nature instead of imitating it.

social control • defence • nature • nurture • fashion • social reform • democratization

Batty Langley
1696–1751

106. Batty Langley. *New Principles of Gardening*. 1728. Garden design combining elements of French formal garden with new elements of irregularity.

107. Batty Langley. *New Principles of Gardening*. 1728. Garden design combining two incomplete regular formal garden patterns with a twisting whirlwind labyrinth pattern.

Juste-Aurèle Meissonnier

Oeuvres (1723–1735)

108. Juste-Aurèle Meissonnier. *Oeuvres*. 1723–1735. Interior design with complex silverwork in the forefront containing figures of cherubs, imaginary animals, shell, plant and water twisted, twirling motifs.

109. Juste-Aurèle Meissonnier. *Oeuvres*. 1723–1735. Frontispiece representing a blown-up cartouche design framed by irregular shell-like rocaille and twisted classical motifs accompanied by foliage while a regular classical building appears hidden in the background.

Alexander Pope (1688–1744)

Moral Essays: Epistle to Lord Burlington (1731)

Known chiefly as one of the major poets and satirists of the English Augustan period, Pope is one of the founders of the 'landscape movement' and among those most responsible for the discredit of the regular, stiff formal garden. Much more original in his views than the landscape architects of the time (Hussey, 1967b, 41), he promoted anti-baroque aesthetics of natural simplicity and irregularity (Pevsner, 1944) both in his writings and in his own garden at Twickenham. His influence was widespread, particularly among the circle of writers and architects patronised by Lord Burlington, associated with the rise of the English villa and landscape park. The present text, a letter in verse form, is dedicated to his patron.

Further reading Clark, 1943; Gilmore, 1972; Hilles, 1965; Hipple, 1957; Hunt, 1976; Hussey, 1967a, 1967b; Jacques, 1976; Lang, 1972a; Malins, 1966; Martin, 1976; Pevsner, 1944.

Alexander Pope
1688–1744

T' is strange, the Miser should his Cares employ, To gain those Riches he can ne'er enjoy:
Is it less strange, the Prodigal should wast His wealth, to purchase what he ne'er can taste?
Not for himself he sees, or hears, or eats; ~ Artists must choose his Pictures, Music, Meats:
[. . .]
You show us, Rome was glorious, not profuse,
And pompous buildings once were things of Use.
Yet shall (my Lord) your just, your noble rules
Fill half the land with Imitating Fools;
Who random drawings from your sheets shall take,
And of one beauty many blunders make;
Load some vain Church with old Theatric state,
Turn Arcs of triumph to a Garden-gate;
Reverse your Ornaments, and hang them all
On some patch'd dog-hole ek'd with ends of wall,
Then clap four slices of Pilaster on't,
That, lac'd with bits of rustic, makes a Front;
Or call the winds thro' long Arcades to roar,
Proud to catch cold at a Venetian door;
Conscious they act a true Palladian part,
And, if they starve, they starve by rules of art.
Oft have you hinted to your brother Peer,
A certain truth, which many buy too dear:
Something there is more needful than Expence,
And something previous ev'n to Taste – 'tis Sense:
Good Sense, which only is the gift of Heav'n,
And tho' no science, fairly worth the seven:
A Light, which in yourself you must perceive;
Jones and Le Notre have it not to give.
To build, to plant, whatever you intend,
To rear the Column, or the Arch to bend,

To swell the Terras, or to sink the Grot;
In all, let Nature never be forgot.
But treat the Goddess like a modest fair,
Nor over-dress, nor leave her wholly bare;
Let not each beauty ev'ry where bespy'd,
Where half the skill is decently to hide.
He gains all points, who pleasingly confounds,
Surprises, varies, and conceals the Bounds.
Consult the Genius of the Place in all;
That tells the Waters to rise, or fall,
Or helps th' ambitious Hill the heav'ns to scale,
Or scoops in circling theatres the Vale,
Calls in the Country, catches opening glades,
Joins willing woods, and varies shades from shades,
Now breaks, or now directs, th' intending Lines;
Paints as you plant, and, as you work, designs.
Still follow Sense, of ev'ry Art the Soul,
Parts answ'ring parts shall slide into a whole,
Spontaneous beauties all around advance,
Start ev'n from Difficulty, strike from Chance;
Nature shall join you, Time shall make it grow
A Work to wonder at – perhaps a STOWE.
Without it, proud Versailles! thy glory falls;
And Nero's Terraces desert their walls:
[. . .]
At Timon's [editor's note: the name of a noted misanthrope of Athens] Villa let us
pass a day,
Where all cry out, 'What sums are thrown away!'
So proud, so grand, of that stupendous air,
Soft and Agreeable come never there.
Greatness, with Timon, dwells in such a draught
As brings all Brobdingnag before your thought.
To compass this, his building is a Town,
His pond an Ocean, his parterre a Down:
Who but must laugh, the Master when he sees,
A puny insect, shiv'ring at a breeze!
Lo, what huge heaps of littleness around!
The whole, a labour'd Quarry above ground.
Two Cupids squirt before: a Lake behind
Improves the keenness of the Northern wind.
His Gardens next your admiration call,
On ev'ry side you look, behold the Wall!
No pleasing Intricacies intervene,
No artful wildness to perplex the scene;
Grove nods at grove, each Alley has a brother,
And half the platform just reflects the other.
The suff'ring eye inverted Nature sees,

Alexander Pope
1688–1744

[301]

Trees cut to Statues, Statues thick as trees,
With here a Fountain, never to be play'd,
And there a Summer-house, that knows no shade;
Here Amphitrite sails thro' myrtle bowers;
There Gladiators fight, or die, in flow'rs;
Un-water'd see the drooping sea-horse mourn,
And swallows roost in Nilus' dusty Urn.
[. . .]
'Tis Use alone that sanctifies Expence,
And Splendour borrows all her rays from Sense.
His Father's Acres who enjoys in peace,
Or makes his Neighbours glad, if he increase;
Whose chearful Tenants bless their yearly toil,
Yet to their Lord owe more than to the soil;
Whose ample Lawns are not asham'd to feed
The milky heifer and deserving steed;
Whose rising Forests, not for pride or show,
But future Buildings, future Navies grow:
Let his plantations stretch from down to down,
First shade a Country, and then raise a Town.
You too proceed! make falling Arts your care,
Erect new wonders, and the old repair,
Jones and Palladio to themselves restore,
And be whate'er Vitruvius was before:
Till Kings call forth th' Idea's of your mind,
Proud to accomplish what such hands design'd,
Bid Harbours open, public Ways extend,
Bid Temples, worthier of the God, ascend;
Bid the broad Arch the dang'rous Flood contain,
The Mole projected break the roaring Main;
Back to his bounds their subject Sea command,
And roll obedient Rivers thro' the Land;
These Honours, Peace to happy Britain brings,
These are Imperial Works, and worthy Kings.

Alexander Pope
1688–1744

anticlassicism • deformation • freedom • naturalism • regionalism • nationalism

John Searle

Plan of Pope's Garden at Twickenham (1745)

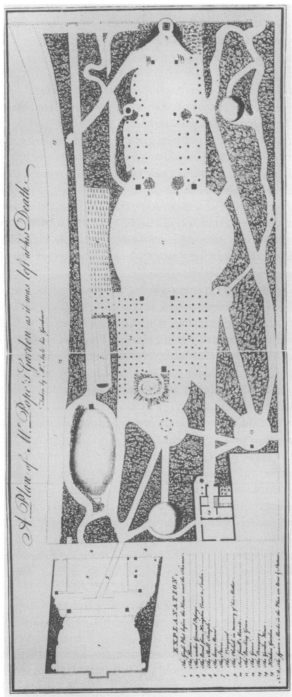

1. Plan of Pope's Garden by J. Serle, 1745, British Museum

110. John Searle. Plan of Pope's Garden at Twickenham 'as it was left at his Death', combining formal with irregular patterns. 1745.

Robert Morris (1701–1754)

Lectures on Architecture (1736)

Morris was an architect associated with the Palladian Burlington circle. A classicist who saw in Palladio the chief reviver of the great ancient tradition, he developed a system of rules for harmonic proportions. What makes it original is the attempt to link norms of proportion with sensualistic theories of pleasure.

Further reading Harris, 1990; Kaufmann, 1955; Placzek, 1970; Summerson, 1963b.

As Nature requires a Sameness, when Art is made use of to add Lustre to her Beauty; so Art never more agreeably pleases us, than when she has a Resemblance of Nature [...] when both are blended or mingled together. [...]

    ... I think our modern way of planning gardens is far preferable to what was used 20 years ago, where, in large parterres, you might see men, birds, and dogs, cut in trees; or, perhaps, something like the shape of a man on horseback – (pardon this digression). In architecture men have fell into methods equally absurd. In some places, may be seen little boys supporting a burden of a monument that had been the labour of 10 or 12 persons to place there; or a Corinthian column set in a fish-pond, and a Tuscan at the entrance of a summer-house. I say, such inconsistencies in nature always hurt the imagination, and we view such objects with more pain and surprise than any pleasure they can possibly give us.

    A champaign open country requires a noble and plain building, which is always best supplied by Doric order, or something analogous to its simplicity. If it had a long extended view, it would be best to range the offices in a line with the building; for at different views it fills the eye with a majestic pleasure. A situation near the sea requires the same, or rather a rusticity and lowness. The vapours of the sea, by its saline qualities, expand themselves some distance, and always are decaying principle; and with the boisterous winds which blow from it, must, consequently, require a power forcible enough to withstand its corrosive quality.

    The cheerful vale requires more decoration and dress; and if the view is long, or some adjacent river runs near it; the Ionic Order is the most proper; where nature seems too wanton in dress, and is gay in verdure, she requires art to assist and embellish her, and the liveliness of the Ionic Order can deck and garnish the glebe. If the spot be an ascent, and some distant hills or wood environ the back part (in which I suppose the front or south aspect), then a few ornaments may be scattered in proper parts, to give it an enlivening variety, but care must be had not to use superfluity. If it be on an eminence, and surrounded with woods, the principal avenues should be spacious: porticos give a grateful pleasure to us in the view, and more so, if the front is not contracted by the avenue, nor continue too near it, to take off the proper shades and keeping of design.

    The Ionic Order is of the three Greek Orders the most applicable to situations of various kinds; and if I say her measures and proportions more pleasingly attract the eye, it is not without reason: the parts are analogous to nature, in which she has been so nicely poised between the rusticity of the Doric and the luxurance of the Corinthian, that I am more apt to believe the Ionic Order was invented as a mean between the Doric and the Corinthian, than that the Ionic was in so beautiful proportion before the Corinthian Order was invented.

The silent streams, the gay, the wanton scene, requires the Corinthian Order; where nature is gilded with lively landscapes, where the verdure is blended with flowers, which she decks herself with, and where the partly-coloured painting of some opening lawn garnishes her in all her pride; then the architect must have recourse to fancy, must mingle his flowers with nature . . .

In delineating the plan or elevation of a building, the outline is to be first formed, as in the plan and profile before us, which are composed of 3 cubes, as represented by the circumscribing circles. It is from thence the internal parts, as well as the ornamenting and disposing the proper voids, and decoration of the front, are to be regulated; and those internal parts are proportioned by first determining the height of the principal storey, as may be seen at the end of the plan; each storey being figured 10 feet in the clear, this, as a standard to the whole, gives the length and breadth of each room by some of those pro-portions: so that by dividing the height of the room which you intend to allot by some of the proportions, into a certain number of equal parts, the same parts are the standard by which you assign some allotted parts for the length and breadth of the said room . . .

Robert Morris
1761–1754

Before I proceed to more particular observations, it may not be improper to explain how the proportions affect imagination. The external parts of a building, at a proper distance, are circumscribed by the retina of the eye: the internal parts terminate the rays of sight, which strike on the retina, and circumscribe them within the focus or point of sight, by a reverberation of rays. So that all external objects are more distinctly and more intelligibly . . . viewed and considered, by having a proper distance assigned for the point of sight. Whereas, the internal parts being so near the eye, it must roll or travel from place to place, and the ideas of the objects only can affect the senses. This general observation will be of use to show that the idea of an external cube, being strongly seated in the imagination, by only viewing two sides of an internal one, the same idea will render such proportion equally agreeable. It is to be further understood that all cube rooms, exceeding 28 or 30 feet, requiring the parts to be proportion'd to it self, must render them difficult to be comprehended at one view; therefore an 18 feet cube for rooms is preferable to one of 40 feet. And all internal parts do not so immedi-ately strike the idea as an external one, where a proper distance can be had to take in all its parts at one view; but if a cube be viewed in profile, nor having any depth to be con-ceived at the same instant, an internal cube may equally affect the eye, since at the entrance into a room, the one side and height may be comprehended the same as a building thus viewed in profile, which is only considered as a square or unison . . .

It is in a great measure custom that familiarises us to proportion. A double square for doors or windows, or any other proportion with which we are more immediately acquainted, have so strong a propensity in the mind, that any parallelogram, a little dif-ferent from it more or less, may easily be discerned. For the truth of this assertion, I appeal to yourselves, whether the eye is not capable of so nice a distinction. I mention this only to show that the first principles of the art being firmly seated in the mind, it will be difficult to impose a proportion on you, that is different from such which have been familiar to you in the theory, or practice of the art.

[. . .]

I say, the country architect has as many different things to meet with, and sur-mount, that are not needful to be known by the architect who is wholly employed in buildings in the city; and few architects, perhaps, have a nice and distinguishing judge-ment for both . . .

As the design before us is small, the little garden I would plant should be proportioned, and care should be taken so to lay out and dispose of the several parts, that the neighbouring hills, the rivulets, the woods and little buildings interspersed in various avenues, &c. to give the more agreeable and entertaining views, should render the spot a kind of agreeable disorder, or artful confusion; so that by shifting from scene to scene, and by serpentine or winding paths, one should, as it were, accidentally fall upon some remarkably beautiful prospect, or other pleasing object . . .

aesthetisation of architecture • anticlassicism • deformation • freedom • naturalism • representation • truth • illusion

Robert Morris
1761–1754

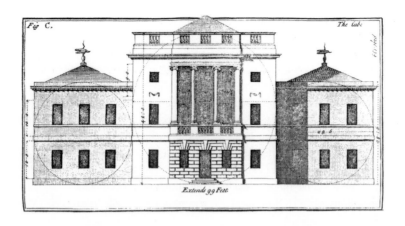

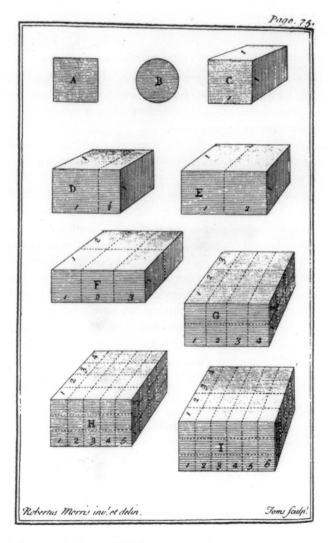

111. Robert Morris. *Lectures on Architecture*. 1736. House composed of three elementary cubes. 111b. Combination of cubical elements.

Amédée-François Frézier (1682–1773)

The Theory and Practice of Stone Cutting and Wood Working (1737–1739)

Frézier looks back to Gothic practice and contrasts the inexpensive lightness of its vaulting with the excessive consumption of material in contemporary baroque buildings (Hermann, 1962). As an army-trained 'ingénieur du Roi', he criticises technically unsound designs in the name of structural economy. His book on stone cutting or stereotomy, the key construction problem, is introduced by a manifesto for a truly functionalist approach to architectural design based on sound scientific principles (1737–1739). In his writings (1738), Frézier is one of the first to present the natural simplicity of the primitive hut as ideal from the structural point of view.

Further reading Bilodeau, 1997; Herrmann, 1962; Middleton, 1962, 1963; Nyberg, 1967; Wiebenson, 1982, 1993.

Preliminary Discourses

First discourse. On the usefulness of theory in the arts relating to architecture

I propose in the present Volume to provide a Theory of the Cutting of Solid Objects as shall be necessary for the demonstration of the use that may be made thereof in Architecture for the construction of vaults and the *working of stone and wood*, which no person has hitherto done and because I adopt an approach to this different from those who have discussed this subject, who have restricted themselves so much to Practice that they seem to have little regard for Theory, or to be ignorant of it. I shall attempt to demonstrate its usefulness.

Vitruvius, who can be cited as a perceptive connoisseur of the Arts, because he is acknowledged to be a celebrated Architect and he was in addition the Engineer of Augustus, made a distinction between two things viz. *Construction* and *Reasoning*. The one, he said, is the affair of Persons who have learnt this Art; the other is the task of the Learned. Not all people think as correctly as him, since men in their great majority have so little knowledge of the Arts that they believe it possible to become skilful in them by experience. They regard Theory as a futile occupation, its object being merely chimerical, yielding no benefit at all for the Arts. We have seen, they say, Great Men in Civil Architecture and even in Military Architecture, who have distinguished themselves with their Works being neither Geometers nor Algebrists, and therefore it is possible to become skilful in the Arts without knowledge of such Sciences.

Before use was made of Geometry and Mechanics in Architecture, men made vaulted roofs of the same materials as today, but they could not be sure of the balance of the forces induced by *Thrust*, nor of the resistance offered by the *abutments or buttresses* which that thrust will try to topple over, with the result that since they did not know how to keep to a middle way between too much and too little in terms of the thickness of those abutments, they tended to go to superfluous expense on materials, or saw their walls fall down due to insufficient strength. Experience still provides us with fairly frequent examples of this, to the shame of those who dabble in construction without knowledge of Geometry or Mechanics and to the great prejudice of those who have commissioned the building. Arches of different kinds have also been constructed – circular, low, high and rampant – but it was not known what the best type of curve was in particular circumstances. Unexpected difficulties were encountered in the execution

of work and the only solution known was that of the Gordian knot, that is by demolishing and recutting those parts of the vault that did not sit squarely until the eye was the
least offended by its ugliness, the outcome being a considerable waste of time and
materials. Because proceeding by trial and error in this way achieves success only by
chance, such constructions lasted only a limited time, cost a great deal to build and satisfied only rarely the Connoisseur's eye and intellect.

Why then should Practitioners so despise Theory and see it as nothing in comparison with that experience whose merits they never cease to trumpet? I can see two
reasons for this: the first is to distract attention from the shame they feel at not being
able to justify their Constructions in any other manner than as imitations of those that
are considered to be good and the appropriateness they have seen in past practice,
feeling that they are not enlightened enough to analyse the causes thereof. This reason
derives from the vanity of the human heart; men, in order to be better than their
equals, claim to despise that which they lack and seek to display ostentatiously that
little they have, hence the mutual contempt that exists in the world and the fact that
science, whose beauty and utility are little known by the multitude, is not elevated to
the rank that it merits above practice used alone. The lack of attention and often of
knowledge on the part of persons in high positions encourages false judgements on the
merit of everyday things, given that it can be seen that the effort devoted to acquiring
knowledge useful for the needs of life or for the enrichment of the mind is usually quite
useless for the obtaining of fortune. This would be enough to discourage any emulation, stop all progress in the Arts and bring back past centuries of barbarous ignorance,
if Nature had not provided a remedy for man's blind injustice. Nature has attached to
such effort the rewards provided by inner satisfaction which alone is capable of sustaining us in the face of the disdain of foolish indifference and presumptuous ignorance.
Indeed, without the attractions of the sciences and a certain love of Virtue, what could
lead any reasonable man to devote long, lacklustre evenings solely to the Public good,
there being in the Public a multitude of persons more disposed to criticise than to
recognise merit, preferring to note the slightest defect rather than that which deserves
their attention and their praise?

The second reason for the views of those who prefer Practice used alone to Theory
may be genuinely deduced from the foundation of their ignorance, because they
attribute to it the effects of Theory, which is unknown to them.

[...]

Most people deprived of knowledge of Theory [...] lacking basic principles, they
succeed only with great effort and long practice in gleaning a few fragments of knowledge of things that pose no problem for those who have knowledge of Theory. Hence
the fact that they praise to the skies the least among them and believe themselves to be
great men because they have explored some of the easier paths of Practice, although
these self-proclaimed Discoverers cannot be sure of the accuracy or the success of their
trial and error, in which they see neither the difference between cases nor the proofs,
with the result that they often believe that they have succeeded when all they have in
fact done is come close to the truth without having taken the surest and shortest path
to arrive there.

[...]

Of the knowledge necessary to us, that of Stone Working, although among the
most neglected, is not the least important. I have seen in my own experience that it is

Amédée-François
Frézier
1682–1773

just as indispensable for an Engineer as for an Architect because he may be sent, as I was, to far Colonies and even to Provinces where there is a lack of skilled Labourers capable of executing certain portions of Fortifications, and where skill is needed in building *walls of stone*. The proof of this which I had just experienced in my second return to America, led me to the idea of writing a Treatise on this, encouraged therein by the extreme scarcity of Books on that subject, and secondly by the imperfect manner in which that subject had been treated hitherto.

Second discourse. Presentation and analysis of the subject discussed here

The idea that has become attached to *Stone Working* is not what comes first to mind since it does not relate exactly to the Work done by the Craftsman who cuts the stone, but to the Science of the Mathematician who manages that work with the intention of building a vaulted roof, or a construction with a defined shape based on the assembly of a number of small units.

[. . .]

design methodology • efficiency • economisation • fit • utility • scientification

Amédée-François Frézier (1682–1773)

A Theoretical and Critical Dissertation on the Orders of Architecture (1738)

In a previous book, **Théorie et Pratique de la Coupe des Pierres et des Bois** (1737–1739), Frézier looks back to Gothic practice and contrasts the inexpensive lightness of its vaulting with the excessive consumption of material in contemporary baroque buildings (Herrmann, 1972). As an army-trained 'ingénieur du roi', he criticised (1709) Cordemoy for the opposite evil: proposing technically unsound design principles in the name of structural efficiency. These criticisms will be echoed later in Patte's treatments of Soufflot's designs for the Eglise Sainte Geneviève (1801). For more information, see Frézier 1737–1739.

Further reading Bilodeau, 1997; Middleton, 1962, 1963; Wiebenson, 1982, 1993.

[. . .]

Our notion of beauty and ugliness is usually the consequence of the fact that we are accustomed to seeing certain things, or to hear them praised and approved because they are conformed in one manner rather than another, but fashion is not always the surest rule for judging the *beautiful* and the *ugly*, since there are frequent vicissitudes in fashion that transform one into the other. This rule can be found only in minds free of prejudice which, after having seen and combined several works from different times and different nations, are in a position to distinguish those forms of beauty that are purely natural, which make themselves felt despite the overlay of habits created by fashion, from those preferred by reason. It is necessary therefore, to examine the Orders of architecture, to find this sort of mind. They are however rare, even among those persons in the profession who would appear to be the natural judges thereof, and it can be asserted, without exaggeration, that we must not always rely on their decision. [. . .]

Most architects drink in like their mother's milk, from their very childhood, the principles that their teachers give them, or they adopt them for reasons of reputation. They regard their precepts as laws they are not permitted to break, however vain and

Amédée-François
Frézier
1682–1773

infantile they may be. Later, their studies are guided by self-interest, their task, in betterment of their fortune, is to study the aesthetic taste of the century, of the nation in which they live, and particularly of those who spend money on the buildings whose construction or supervision they have the ambition of undertaking, with the aim of obtaining preference over the competitors who put themselves forward. However, since the wealthy persons with whom they deal are not always the most enlightened, they are offered only projects based on fashionable models, in which they are unable to distinguish the good from the bad, or, if they are desirous of novelty, they seek to produce that novelty at any price. Hence the bizarre variations that gradually arise in fashion and which are termed in society good or bad *taste*, according to whether they are close to, or far from that which is novel.

It is an easy matter to prove that most of these self-proclaimed decorative designs are devoid of genuine beauty, given that our fashions are neither constant nor universal. The Orientals, the Occidentals, the inhabitants of the North and those of the South have their customs in building and decorative designs to suit their taste: are our peoples the only ones to have the best taste and common sense to themselves? Those persons who have never travelled are sometimes little enough enlightened to arrive at just such a rash assumption, but to relieve them of this illusion, they need only be told that we adopt new ideas from foreigners every day. [...]

Amédée-François
Frézier
1682–1773

Can we say that one or other of these nations has always had constant rules for beauty in the decorative aspect of their architecture? No, we certainly cannot, since they themselves have varied over quite short periods of time. [...] Were our ancestors right? Are we? This is a question to which it is no easier to reply than another we could raise on the different styles in our clothing. We are agreed on the necessity of wearing clothes and of protection from the harm the air may do to us, but not on the grace of its style. This latter depends on how accustomed we are to see objects formed in certain ways, so much so that that which does not conform to the fashion is intolerable and ridiculous – now, the laws of fashion are not restricted to the style of our clothes, they extend to all things and buildings are no less subject to them. [...]

All these changes, you will say, are allowed by comfort, but this argument is not unchallengeable. [...]

I ask also if it is comfortable to admit cold air into a bed chamber through a door opening that would be of sufficient size for the entrance to a barn, rather than making that opening proportionate to our size and our needs. [...]

Since fashion reigns over the essential parts of edifices, it is not surprising that it varies in terms of the arrangement of the decoration thereof, leaving aside sculpted ornamentation, in which we have gone from an excessively bulky relief to a confused profusion of slight arabesques and imagined Chinese dragons, bat's wings and other grotesque devices. We have also progressed, in the construction of vaulted roofs, from Gothic lightness at small expense to a superfluous consumption of materials, as is to be seen in modern churches. However, since the time, some two hundred years ago, when we rediscovered a taste for the architecture of the ancient world, abandoning completely the Gothic style, how many architects have not written volumes in an effort to fix the ancient Orders at certain determined dimensions, each according to his taste, which he finds the best possible! But nothing proves more effectively the futility of the rules they set out to impose upon us than the discord between them and the insane variations with which they have littered architecture. [...]

[311]

Amidst this variety of aesthetic tastes and opinions, is it not permitted to establish a few principles on which reasonable men may agree? And might there not exist a natural architecture independent of the caprice of designers? [...] No person can fail to have observed that the imitation of a natural thing gives us pleasure, and that it is only by imitation that painting, sculpture, music and the theatre please us and give us joy, and when it is perfect, the object copied from pleasing nature gives us greater pleasure than the original. [...] If there is then some universal rule for the Orders, it can be founded only upon the imitation of natural architecture. [...]

The question may be asked, what is this natural architecture? Must we go back to the construction of the houses built by the first men? No monument thereto now exists, not even in the histories [...]

The Origin of the Orders of Architecture

Amédée-François
Frézier
1682–1773

Let us examine the initial establishment of a colony in a country of uninhabited forests, such as our islands in America once were. It will be seen that one begins by setting tree trunks in place, on which pieces of wood are laid horizontally in order to support a roof and other pieces inclined in relation to the horizon and to each other in order to provide the slope required to allow water to drain off, over a structure of tree bark, leaves or branches, reeds or any other thing under which it is possible to shelter from the sun and the rain. [...] The Germans, our ancestors, built in exactly this manner [...]

If we must keep to a faithful imitation of natural architecture, is it not ridiculous to divide up into three ranks of Orders, as if in three storeys, the front elevation of a building that is well known to possess only one? [...] this is no more than a decorated panel with nothing behind it, signifying nothing. In a word – it means that these are simply stones piled up without rhyme or reason. If you brought a savage imbued with common sense, for there are more among us in Europe than is commonly thought, and if you place him before the famous portal of Saint Gervais, he will think to see three habitations placed one above the other. He will reach that conclusion not only because of the division, but also through an idea of what is necessary for the solidity of an edifice, which must not be constructed of several lengths of tree trunk placed end to end where just one is required. Lastly, if, after having explained to him that cornices represent the projecting edges of roofs, we took him into our modern churches, what would he say when he saw many inside and projecting even further outward? He would be unable to prevent himself from laughing at the extravagant superfluity of such projecting elements in a place covered over with a vaulted ceiling itself covered over with a roof. However little esteem we may have for Gothic architecture, he would no doubt prefer it, in so far as it does not parade such inappropriate imitation, for there is no need to have studied the matter to conclude that we must take account of the purpose of objects and verisimilitude in the disposition of decorative elements. He would also see that such projections from the wall are harmful in that they cover part of the stained glass windows from sight and interrupt the free passage of the light that must come through them. They even seem to diminish the space in the place and create a disagreeable impression [...] but this is nevertheless what we see in all new churches, which Italy parades as marvels of the art. How disgraceful! cry the enthusiasts for cornices. How disgraceful to see an Order of architecture deprived of that ornament, which is the principal among them!

classical canon • antiquity • abuses • precedent • authority • invention • rigorism • essentialism • scientification

Jacques-Germain Soufflot (1713–1780)

A Report on Gothic Architecture (written 1741)

The unconventional union of Gothic and classical principles is what Soufflot advocates in his paper delivered before the Academy of Lyon. He had, in fact, taken ideas from Frémin and Cordemoy (Middleton, 1962, 1963) and profited from the calls by Frézier for greater engineering knowledge among architects; and, like his friend, the engraver, Cochin (1754, 1780–1790), he was protected by Marigny, *Surintendant des Bâtiments* and brother of Madame de Pompadour. Soufflot's famous building is the Eglise Sainte Geneviève, which became the Pantheon after the French Revolution. In it, the first neo-classical building in France (Summerson, 1963, 36–37), he puts his new principles to use, in opposition to the currently popular baroque style.

Jacques-Germain
Soufflot
1713–1780

Further reading Blomfield, 1973; Collins, 1954; Erikson, 1974; Hautecoeur, 1948–1963; Herrmann, 1962; Kask, 1971; Kaufmann, 1949; Lemonnier, 1911–1929; Middleton, 1959; Prost, 1860; Tadgell, 1978.

[. . .] If we enter a Gothic church, our eyes, deceived by its proportions, procure for our souls a pleasure that at first surprises and astonishes, leading us to say, as we admire it: 'Look at the prodigious length and height of the nave!' We might easily think that we will never reach the end of it. We walk down it and are surprised to reach it much sooner than be believed we would . . . If, on the contrary, we enter one of our own churches . . . our soul is enchanted by the balance between the whole and the parts, the idea that has been given of it to us takes our judgement unaware for a moment and in the end we say: 'I thought this church was much larger.' We believe ourselves to be near the far end, we direct our footsteps there, and soon we seem to be ever more distant the more we progress, and it is then that we are surprised at such a vast space, and we believe that we have never seen a church so long . . .

In the former, closer examination destroys, we might say, the pleasure. In the latter, it gives rise to pleasure.

The first reason I shall give for this is that we judge all things by comparison. It is certainly the case that a man of no more than middling height but of slim build will appear taller than another who is in fact taller but is of more corpulent build, until we see them side by side. If the church of Milan seems to be even higher than all other Gothic churches, it is because its height has been taken to three times its width.

The second [reason] is that the pillars in these edifices are closer together than in our churches, and there are more of them, and we therefore assume that only a very large space could contain them all.

The third is that there are no cornices to hide anything from view, and whose parts interrupt the gaze as is the case in our churches. [. . .] the only conclusion I wish to draw from this is that despising as we do utterly the bizarre and chimerical ornamentation of the Goths, we could, without going to the extremes they do in their propor-

[313]

tions, draw profit from them and find between their churches and ours a middle way which would remedy that defective initial glance and make us think and say of that which had this happy characteristic: *Omne tulit punctum* . . .

If there are barriers that prevent us advancing along the path to perfection, are we not able to overcome them? Should such freedom not be granted, if not to all architects, at least to those who combine profound theory with long experience, who would use that freedom only with great prudence, not in the manner of most today, with real capriciousness and a pernicious desire for novelty at the expense of good sense, but rather with a praiseworthy desire to give to their constructions a perfection capable of making their daring design admirable for ever?

rigorism • essentialism

Jacques-Germain
Soufflot
1713–1780

Charles-Etienne Briseux

L'art de bâtir les maisons de campagne (1743–1761)

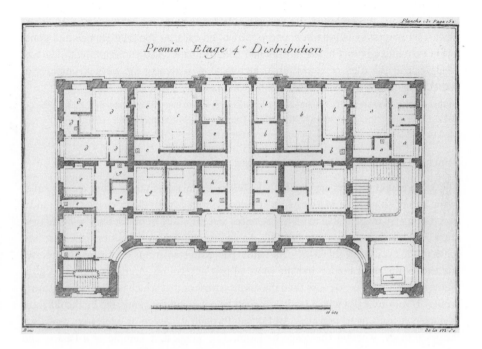

112. Charles-Etienne Briseux. *L'art de bâtir les maisons de campagne*. 1743–1761. Plan of the first floor of a country house with the innovative element of the corridor to provide privacy from the service personnel.

Gabriel-Germain Boffrand (1667–1754)

Book of Architecture (1745)

Boffrand was a pupil of Hardouin Mansart and one of the most sought after architects of his day. He was a member of the Academy of Architecture and represented its outlook. Against all the *'folles nouveautés'* of the rococo, he calls, as the poet Horace had done, to the immutable norms of the Greeks and early Romans. Also consistent with Horace, he developed the idea of character in architecture, searching for ways to impress or pathetically move the spectator according to the rules of *'convenance'*.

Further reading Blomfield, 1973; Hautecoeur, 1948–1963; Herrmann, 1962; Kaufmann, 1933; Lee, 1967; Lemonnier, 1927; Middleton, 1962, 1963; Tzonis, 1975; Wiebenson, 1982, 1993.

Gabriel-Germain
Boffrand
1667–1754

Principles drawn from Horace's *Ars Poetica*

The Sciences and the Arts are so closely linked that principles in the former are principles in the latter. All parts of Mathematics are closely united, with Geometry as the foundation. Geometry is applicable to all the Sciences and the study of one subject will add new knowledge to that of another. Painting, Sculpture and Poetry are sisters: the first two speak to the eyes, the third to the ears. Music paints diverse events of Nature, it expresses and excites the most tender and the most violent of passions. Architecture, although it seems that its object is no more than the employment of that which is material in Nature, is open to various styles which lead to its parts being, as it were, animated by the different characters it leads us to perceive. An Edifice, through its design, is expressive as if on a theatrical Stage, whether the scene be Pastoral or Tragical, a Temple or a Palace, and whether it is a public Edifice destined for a certain manner of use, or a private House. These different edifices, through the arrangement of their parts, their structure and the manner in which they are decorated, must announce their purpose to the observer, and if they do not, true expression is falsified, and they are not as they should be.

The same is true of Poetry: there are different forms and a style agreeable to one will not be found so by another. Horace provided some excellent principles in his *Ars Poetica*, and although he never reflected upon Architecture, it seemed to me that they were so closely related that I could make that link and a very proper application of them to those that have been given to us for Architecture by the Ancients and by the Moderns, and that they could enrich them still further, conferring upon them a more sublime character.

If we wish to build an Edifice that is grave in character, we make it solid and weighty. If we wish to appear light, we make it dry and spare. [. . .]

If we wish to build a sublime Edifice, we ornament it to excess, creating pompous decoration that degenerates into confusion. If we wish to build a simple Edifice, we make a building that is merely uninteresting and devoid of dignity. [. . .]

The ornamentation that must be used only on the exterior of a house must not be used inside it. Each room must be arranged in the manner suitable to the master of the household, and given the size and decoration suitable for his use. [. . .]

The contours of the architectural mouldings and the other parts that compose a building are in Architecture like the words of discourse. All Edifices are formed by just three sorts of line – the straight line, the concave line and the convex line. These three lines also form the shapes of all architectural mouldings that make up the contours of a building. New ones must be created only with great care and they should be used only in those places where they may be put.

The Orders of Architecture employed in the constructions of the Greeks and the Romans are, to the different styles of building, that which the different genres of Poetry are to the various subjects which it may address.

The Greeks allowed three Orders, the massive Order they named 'Doric', the lighter one, which is the 'Corinthian' Order and that midway between these two extremes, which they named 'Ionic'. It is very difficult to design an Edifice well when its only ornament is its simplicity.

A man who does not know these different characters and who does not make them felt in his constructions is not an Architect.

[...]

Each thing must be done in accordance with the nature of the Edifice.

[...]

... often, the Architect plays his part in this, ruining the owner through ignorance, while the owner ruins him through economy.

[...]

Charles de
Secondat, baron
de Montesquieu
1689–1755

In Architecture, as in other things, good sense is acquired by the frequentation of good people and men of good taste, by reading the Philosophers, through long experience of correct working and by knowledge of the style of life in the country where one is building.

[...]

It is to be hoped that those who commission buildings should be more aware of that which is of concern in good Architecture. In France, the only object is comfort and there is no regard for exterior decoration. The façades of most of the great houses are no more distinguished those of the houses of tradesmen. Conversely, in Italy much attention is paid to the public face and exterior decoration, while comfort is neglected. Might we not hope that with so many examples of comfortable houses in France that a taste for public decoration may be introduced?

Perfect success is achieved when the useful has been combined with the agreeable.

aesthetisation of architecture • rhetoric • signification • narrative

Charles de Secondat, baron de Montesquieu (1689–1755)

An Essay on Taste (1748)

This is a section of the Enlightenment philosopher's article on taste prepared for Diderot and d'Alembert's great '**Encyclopédie**'. In it, he inveighs against lavish decoration, trigger-ing Piranesi's statement that 'the rigorists reason like Montesquieu' (1765). Hardly so extreme in his views, Montesquieu clearly emphasised the necessity for surprise and con-trast in keeping with rococo taste. His views were evidently congenial to English theoreti-cians of the sublime, notably Gerard and Burke. The article also included some comments on natural gardens which were immediately translated in England.

Further reading Coleman, 1971; Knight, 1968.

The constitution of human nature in its present state opens to the mind three different sources of pleasure; one in its internal faculties and essence, another is its union with the body; and a third in those impressions and prejudices that are the result of certain institutions, customs and habits.

These different pleasures of the mind constitute the proper objects of *taste*, those objects which we term beautiful, good, agreeable, natural, delicate, tender, graceful, elegant, noble, grand, sublime and majestic, as also the qualities to which we give the name of *Je ne sais quoi*. When, for instance, the pleasure we enjoy in the contemplation of any object is accompanied with a notion of its utility to us, we call that object: *good*; but when an object appears merely agreeable, without being advantageous we then term it *beautiful*.

Concerning the Pleasures of the Mind

Charles de Secondat, baron de Montesquieu 1689–1755

The mind, besides those pleasures which it receives by the organs of sense, enjoys others which are peculiar to its spiritual nature, and are absolutely independent of external sensation, such are the pleasures that arise from curiosity, from the ideas of its own existence, grandeur and perfection, from the faculty of taking a general and comprehensive view of things, of contemplating a great variety of objects, and of comparing, combining and separating its own ideas. These pleasures, which are attached to the nature of every intelligent being, depend not upon the external senses, but reside in the very essence of the soul; and it is needless to inquire whether the soul enjoys them, in consequence of its union with the body, or not; all that is necessary for us to know is that it enjoys them always, and that they are the true and proper objects of *taste*. We shall not, therefore, take any notice here of the distinction that may be made between the pleasures that the soul derives from its own essence, and those that result from its union with the body, but shall comprehend both their kinds of enjoyment under the common name of *natural pleasures*. These pleasures we must, however, distinguish from others that have certain connections with them, and which we may call *acquired pleasures*. In the same manner, and also for the same reasons, we distinguish between the *taste*, which is *natural*, and that which is *acquired*.

It is of great use in researches of this kind to know the source of those pleasures of which *taste* is the rule or measure: since the knowledge of our pleasures, whether *natural* or *acquired*, will contribute much towards the rectifying of the two kinds of *taste* that correspond to them. We cannot truly appreciate our pleasures, nor indeed enjoy them with a proper relish, if we do not carefully examine the nature of those pleasures, and their first springs in the human constitution.

[...]

The constitution of our nature is an arbitrary thing; we might have been otherwise constituted than we are at present; and, in that case, our perceptions and feelings would have been quite different from what they now are. [...]

If the sense of sight had been more feeble and confused than it actually is, it would have been necessary to have introduced into the plans of the architect fewer ornaments, and more uniformity; but the contrary rule must have taken place had our sight been more distinct, piercing and comprehensive.

[...]

And as the perfection of the arts consists in their presenting to us their perspective objects in such a manner as will render them as agreeable and striking as is possible; so a different constitution of our nature from the present would, necessarily, require a change in the present state of the arts adapted to the change which that new constitution would occasion in the means of enjoyment, in the manner of being agreeably affected.

[...]

Concerning Curiosity

The human mind is naturally formed for thinking or perceiving, and *curiosity* is necessary to such a being: for as all things are connected in nature, and every idea and object are in the great chain of being immediately preceded by their causes, and as immediately followed by their effects, so we cannot desire the knowledge of one object without being desirous also of arriving at the knowledge of those that are intimately related to it. Thus when we see the part only of an excellent piece of painting, we are eagerly desirous of the sight of what remains concealed from our view, and the eagerness of this desire is proportioned to the pleasure we received from what we had already seen.

It is, therefore, the pleasure, which we have received from one object that carries forward our desires towards another; hence the mind is always bent upon the pursuit of something new, and never enjoys a permanent repose.

Thus may we always be sure of administering pleasure to the mind, by presenting to its contemplation a multitude of objects, or even, a greater number than it expected to see.

By these observations we may be enabled to explain the reason, why we receive pleasure both from the view of a regular garden, and also from a rural prospect, in which there is neither order nor proportion. The pleasure we receive from these different objects arises originally from the same cause, even from the natural desire we have of seeing a multitude of objects. This desire renders us eager to extend our views, and to wander from place to place; the mind, under its impulse, abhors all limits, and would willingly enlarge the sphere of its contemplation, and even of its actual presence, and thus one of its great pleasures, is to take in a large and distant prospect. But this pleasure is not easily attained: in towns and cities our view is obstructed by various ranges of buildings; in the country it is limited and interrupted by many obstacles. What then is to be done? Why, we must have recourse to art, which comes to our assistance, and discloses nature which was concealed from our sight; in this case we are more pleased with art than with nature, that is to say, with nature veiled and unseen. But when nature presents itself to us in extensive prospects, in variegated landscapes, where the eye can roam uncontrolled through meadows and woods, through rising grounds and flowery plains, the mind is quite otherwise elated and transported with these rural scenes than with the gardens of *Le Notre*; because such is the fecundity of nature, that it is always new and original, whereas art copies and resembles itself in all its productions. This also is the reason why in painting we are more pleased with a rural landscape, than with a correct plan of the finest garden upon the earth; because the painter represents nature in those scenes, where she appears with the greatest beauty, with the most striking variety, where the eye can ramble at liberty, and behold her in all her charms with pleasure and delight.

Charles de
Secondat, baron
de Montesquieu
1689–1755

Concerning the Pleasure that Arises from Variety

If order be thus necessary in all sorts of productions, *variety* is no less so; without *variety* the mind falls into a lifeless inactivity and languor; for similar objects appear to it as if they were wholly the same; so that if a part of a piece of painting was disclosed to our view, which carried a striking resemblance of another part of the same piece that we had already seen, this second part would be really a new object without appearing such, and would be contemplated without the least sensation of pleasure. The beauties we discern in the productions of art, as well as in the works of nature, consisting entirely in the pleasure they administer, it is necessary so to modify their beauties as to render them the means of diversifying our pleasures as far as is possible. We must employ our industry in offering to the eye of the mind objects which it has not as yet seen, and in exciting within it feelings different from those which it may have already experienced.

Charles de Secondat, baron de Montesquieu 1689–1755

[...]

Uniformity carried on to a certain length renders every thing insupportable. [...] If the accounts given of the famous *Vista* or alley that extends from *Moscow* to *Petersburg* be true, the traveller, pent up between these two seemingly endless rows of trees, must feel the most disagreeable attitude and satiety in the continuance of such a dull uniformity. Nay, even prospects which have the charm of *variety*, cease to please, if they be repeated without much alteration, and are for a long time present to the mind. Thus the traveller, who has been long wandering through the *Alps*, will descend satiated with the most extensive views, the most romantic and delightful landscapes.

The human mind loves *variety*, and the reason is, as we have already observed, that it is naturally framed for contemplation and knowledge. Then the love of variety is subordinate and adapted to the attainment of knowledge; or, in other words, an object must be sufficiently *simple* to be perceived with ease, and sufficiently *diversified* to be contemplated with pleasure.

There are certain objects which have the appearance of variety, without the reality; and others that seem to be uniform, but are, in effect, extremely diversified.

The Gothic architecture appears extremely rich in point of variety, but its ornaments fatigue the eye by their confusion and minuteness. Hence we cannot easily distinguish one from the other, nor fix our attention upon any one object, on account of the multitude that rush at once upon the sight; and thus it happens that this kind of architecture displeases in the very circumstances that were designed to render it agreeable.

A Gothic structure is to the eye what a riddle is to the understanding; in the contemplation of its various parts and ornaments the mind perceives the same perplexity and confusion in its ideas that arise from reading an obscure poem.

The *Grecian* architecture, on the contrary, appears uniform; but as the nature, and the number also of its divisions are precisely such as occupy the mind without fatiguing it, it has consequently that degree variety, that is pleasing and delightful. Greatness in the *whole* of any production requires of necessity the same quality in the *parts*. Gigantic bodies must have bulky members; large trees must have large branches, etc. Such is the nature of things. The *Grecian* architecture, where divisions are few, but grand and noble, seems formed after the model of the great and the sublime. The mind perceives a certain majesty which reigns through all its productions.

Thus the painter distributes the figures that are to compose his work into various groups; and in this he follows nature and truth, for a crowd is almost always divided into separate companies. In the same manner in every complex piece of painting we see the lights and shades distributed into large masses, which strike the eye at a distance, before the whole composition is distinctly perceived.

Concerning the Pleasure which is the Effect of Surprise

The same disposition that renders variety agreeable to the mind, is also the occasion of those pleasures which it receives from surprise. This feeling of surprise pleases both from the nature of its object, and the quickness and rapidity with which it acts upon the mind, which perceives either an object it did not expect, or an object presented in a different manner from that which it imagined beforehand.

Surprise is excited by such objects as are either marvellous, new or unexpected; and in those cases where we are struck with the marvellous, the principal feeling is accompanied with an accessory sensation which arises from this, that the object which we contemplate as marvellous is also new and unexpected.

Charles de Secondat, baron de Montesquieu 1689–1755

Hence games of hazard attract the whole attention of the mind, and affect in a lively and agreeable manner by presenting to it a continual train of unexpected events; and hence also arises the pleasure we take in those games in which we are associated with partners, for they are also a combination of unforeseen events produced by the joint influence of dexterity and hazard.

[...]

Surprise may be excited either by the object itself that is presented to our view, or by the manner in which we perceive it, and the circumstances under which we consider it; for an object may appear, in our perception, greater or less than it is in reality; it may appear different from what it actually is; and even in those cases where we see it as it is, we may see it under circumstances which excite an accessory feeling of *surprise*. Thus in the view of any work the mind may be struck with the circumstantial or accessory idea of the difficulty of its production, of the person that contrived and finished it, of the time or manner in which it was executed, or of any other circumstances that are intimately connected with it.

Concerning those Beauties that Result from a Certain Embarrassment and Perplexity of Mind

The mind is frequently struck with surprise from its not being able to reconcile the past with the present, what it sees with what it has seen. There is in *Italy* a vast lake called *Il lago maggiore*, whose borders are entirely wild and barren: but, upon sailing about fifteen miles in this little ocean, we find two islands called the *Borromees*, about a quarter of a mile in circumference; and in these distinguished spots nature seems to have lavished all those rural beauties that the most exuberant fancy can paint. The mind is astonished at this singular contrail, and recalls upon this occasion the pleasure it has received from the prodigies of romance, where the reader is transported from craggy rocks and barren deserts into smiling landscapes and enchanted ground.

[...]

anticlassicism • deformation • freedom • naturalism • representation • truth • illusion

Jacques-François Blondel (1705–1774)

French Architecture (1752–1757)

Blondel was the voice of official architecture during the revival of royal patronage under Louis XV during the 1740s. Besides being one of the most prolific architectural writers in history, he maintained one of the most active architectural practices of his day. In addition, he opened his own private school before being invited to join the royal academy. His **Architecture** (1752–1757) was a call to order after the sway of rococo degeneracy that had followed the death of Louis XIV, a plea for the return to the grandiose ideals and national tradition of that great sovereign's epoch. **Nécessité** (1754) elaborates on the need of the new monarchy to impose itself through its architecture. Completed after his death by his student Patte, his six volume *Cours* (1771–1777) stands as the fullest elaboration of the academic approach to architecture, an eclectic compromise embracing ornamentation, functionality and construction. It remained the authority in original or plagiarised forms through the nineteenth century up to the mid-twentieth century at the French Ecole des Beaux-Arts and its imitators throughout Europe and in America. Blondel's emphasis on ornamentation and architecture for art's sake expressed in that work and in **Distribution** (1737–1738) set him apart from the functionalist, neo-classical circles of Laugier and Soufflot although their own positions owed much to his strictures against the excesses of the rococo. The work of Boullée, Ledoux and Lequeu and the writings and buildings of the Camus de Mézières (1780) would have been difficult to conceive without the impact of his ideas on monumentality and character in architecture.

Further reading Bilodeau, 1997; Blomfield, 1973; Collins, 1954; Erikson, 1974; Hautecoeur, 1948–1963; Herrmann, 1962; Kask, 1971; Kaufmann, 1949; Lemonnier, 1911–1929; Middleton, 1959; Prost, 1860; Tadgell, 1978; Wiebenson, 1982, 1993.

French Architecture

Book I, chapter III. An introduction to Architecture containing the general principles of that Art

No person can be unaware that the buildings of the Greeks and most of those of the Romans were satisfactory more due to the magnificence of their exterior than their interior comforts. The lessons drawn from the history of Architecture and the descriptions handed down to us by all the Authors of those times provide adequate proof that those peoples, when giving to public buildings all the perfection of Architecture, preferred solidity and salubrity above all other things in private buildings and there was far from being in the interiors of their residences the same comforts that French Architects are able to bestow on theirs. It would even appear that for some fifty years now the latter have invented a new art in this regard; all our neighbours would agree with this assertion and those who exercise the profession of Architect acknowledge that before this time our buildings in France, like those in Italy, offered in truth an exterior decoration of quite pleasing design, but an interior that offered little comfort and an apparent effort to banish light. It was even difficult to find the space for a bed and the principal furnishings; the fireplaces occupied the greater part of each room and the smallness of the doors yielded little idea of the places to which they afforded entrance. But now that perfection is considered to consist in the disposition and natural arrangement of the rooms throughout the building and now that nobility, grandeur and goodly proportions are sought, as compatible with a sense of fitness, residences, although less spacious, are better provided with doors and windows and symmetry is to be seen in them with greater regularity. It is to this disposition of parts that we refer and not that which has been imagined by some Architects who see beauty as involving the design of each room with a different shape, making some walls circular, others rectangular, making the plan of some polygonal and making others in a combination of all these, which gives the interior plan of such a building the appearance of a geometric grass lawn. They also misapply symmetry to the right and left of the apartments, this being a symmetry that is as unimportant for the interior of a building as it is important for the exterior, it being necessary that the exterior shapes should be in perfect proportion. Although we surpass the Ancients in such disposition of the parts, we are obliged to acknowledge that they were far superior to us where the exterior decoration of their edifices is concerned. To be persuaded of this, one needs merely to glance at the fragments that have come down to us from antiquity and we are forced to allow that our most beautiful Architecture from the last century is recognised as such only because it comes close to those excellent originals.

Jacques-François Blondel 1705–1774

However, despite all the precepts that the ancients have left for us with respect to the exterior and the discoveries of French Architects concerning the disposition of the parts of the interior, there can be no doubt that we see very few buildings in which it is not evident that the interior has been sacrificed to the exterior, or that the latter has been neglected in order to arrive at a more advantageous arrangement of the apartments inside. The result is that in the former we see a truly admirable exterior ordonnance, while most of the rooms inside are without comfort and without symmetry. Conversely, inside the latter, we see an elegant disposition, but the exterior is without satisfying proportion and affords no sense of fitness, which leads me to believe that the limited study of these matters by most Architects is the cause of the lack of intimate satisfaction observable in some of our buildings.

If it is true however that disposition and decoration are the two most important aspects of a building and that each has been brought to a very high degree of perfection already, the only task now, in order to excel in the art of construction, is to study widely recognised examples of beauty and the general laws applicable to different types of building and to reflect upon the types of licence of which we are occasionally obliged to make use in Architecture, following the examples provided of the most widely approved monuments, and upon the abuses that have crept into our buildings through inadvertence or some other cause.

General precepts concerning the interior disposition of parts

Interior disposition must be the primary concern of the Architect. Even decorative work is absolutely dependent on a precise plan of the building. It is this disposition that determines lengths, widths and heights in an edifice. When one neglects the intimate relationship which must exist between the interior and the exterior of a building, it is impossible to make it pleasing to intelligent persons, because they are struck by a certain private joy when an edifice satisfies the organ of vision through the harmony of its parts disposed within the entirety of its whole.

A sense of fitness, which we have declared to be the first principle of Architecture, is all the more essential in the interior of a building than in its exterior arrangement. If such a sense of fitness is to govern the plan of a building, each room must be situated according to the manner of its use and in accordance with the nature of the edifice and it should have a form and proportions related to its intended use. This signifies that the residence of a private person must not possess an interior disposition of its parts resembling the Palace of a Sovereign, nor must the residence of a Prince resemble a hunting lodge. Thus within the overall diversity of buildings, we may construct single, semi-double, double or even triple buildings, according to requirements.

In general, a distinction is made between three sorts of apartment in a building – those for society, those for display and those for comfort.

Apartments for society are intended for social gatherings of family and friends. For that purpose they must be situated in a storey made pleasing in such a manner that it may be joined to the other apartments in order to make of the main enfilade [editor's note: the alignment of a series of doors axially through a sequence of rooms] a whole vista that will, in the event of festivities, herald the magnificence of the owner to all. Such apartments must be arranged in such a manner that no rooms intended for domestic servants are to be found along their alignment.

Jacques-François Blondel
1705–1774

State apartments are intended for the display of magnificence or to serve as the personal residence of the master of the household. There he will deal with weighty matters and welcome persons of importance. There he will lock up his personal jewellery, paintings and valuable furniture. Such apartments must be laid out in order to communicate with the apartments intended for social gatherings, with the various rooms comprising them opening up at a single glance to the eye and in a single enfilade the interior magnificence of the main body of the residence, which shall be manifest in the luxurious materials employed or the ornamentation chosen and shall attract from without those persons who enjoy visiting the houses of Great Men. The Townhouse ... may be regarded in this respect as one of the most considerable to be found in Paris.

Conversely, an apartment intended for comfort is an apartment which in a building of importance is rarely open to strangers, since it is intended for the withdrawal of the master or the mistress of the household. It is there that they sleep in winter or where they retire if indisposed, and it is there that they deal with private matters and welcome their friends and their family. This sort of place allows persons from outside the freedom to visit the state apartments without the necessity of standing on ceremony sometimes found embarrassing between persons of the same social rank. When the space available on the land does not allow these apartments to be placed near the state apartments, they are situated in an intermediate storey.

The rooms which generally form the apartments of which we speak above are usually described as state, social or private rooms. In the first of these categories, we are referring to those that seem to be of absolute and real necessity, because it appears to be indispensable that any edifice built for the protection of men should be provided with those rooms that are necessary and related to the estate of the master commissioning it. It is from this necessity that the diversity of buildings arises, although built for the same purpose, and from which come the different storeys that one is obliged to construct one above the other if the owner must build in an area where space is limited, either due to the nature of his occupations, or the Important Personages with whom he has dealings. It is ordinarily in this part of the building that an Architect invariably has new opportunities to show his talents, by proving himself capable of combining those things that are necessary with the harmony of the whole and ensuring that those things are directly matched with the parts related to construction and decoration: the first of these requires that the voids should be proportional to the solid portions, and the second requires that the doors providing entry to the building should be proportional to the totality of the edifice and that the windows should be of a size proportionate both to the diameter of the rooms and to the disposition of the exterior faces of the building.

Those rooms whose purpose is social are also governed by their own rules because of the relationship they have with the general orientation of the building, with its situation and the disposition of its parts, and because attention must be paid to the necessary relationship between these rooms and the overall size of the building, in order that those same rooms, the state rooms, and those intended for private withdrawing, should be sufficiently provided with antechambers and free areas where domestic servants may remain present and perform their duties, without interrupting the business of the masters of the household. If no provision is made for this, the occupants would not enjoy a comfortable manner of living, and the natural desire to cherish that which is specifically ours and to avoid that which harms us would not be satisfied.

Jacques-François
Blondel
1705–1774

Concerning the disposition of the state apartments, those intended for display, it is difficult to give any systematic description, since this type of disposition, which is totally determined by a concern for magnificence, is governed by the different customs of nations, which means that that which we in France invariably consider to be appropriate in principle, is seen differently by our neighbours, due not only to the diversity of the customs of nations and the variety of their climates, but also to prejudice.

[...]

Principles concerning the exterior decoration of buildings

I.

That which bears loads must have a degree of solidity commensurate with that which is placed above it. What is delicate and ornate must not be placed below that which is rustic and simple. Great edifices and vast places must be composed of parts of great size. The grandiose and the sparse cannot go hand in hand. All parts of the same decorative work must be proportionate, linked and in the same style. It is not appropriate to include in the same storey of a building or inside the same room elements of Architecture or ornaments that are rustic and simple with other parts of a more delicate character, although these two types of element may be correctly placed separately. The rustic and the simple must have little ornamentation; the delicate and elegant must be more ornate.

II.

However much variety is given to the contours of a building, one must always employ the usual Architectural moulding and refrain from introducing any in the Gothic style on the pretext of novelty. The beauty of Architectural moulding consists in the distribution of its elements, in proportions appropriate to their different characters and in the art of mixing alternately the round and the square, the small and the large, being attentive to bringing them out more or less according to whether they are closer or further from the eye of the spectator, or situated in places with much, or little space.

When the Orders of Architecture are employed in a building, attention must be paid to avoiding any deviation from the general proportions established by the masters of the art. [...] This observation leads to the conclusion that if the height of a building is not sufficient to dispose in it columns to their full effect, it is more prudent to abandon them completely and to seek the benefit of decoration of another type. [...]

IV.

The faces of pilasters and columns must never be interrupted by any element of Architecture that is horizontal and unrelated to their main shaft, it not being appropriate for bases, cornices and imposts, often inserted in the space between columns, to exceed in size half the diameter of the columns, or to project beyond the front faces of the pilasters, given that these elements of Architecture will divide the full height of the column's shaft, and thus constitute a licence that is invariably improper.

V.

Jacques-François
Blondel
1705–1774

Good taste dictates that columns should never overlap each other, and nor should pilasters, nor their bays and capitals, which must remain totally detached and separate from each other. [...]

VI.

In the ancient world, paired columns are hardly to be found [...] and we may conclude therefore that the moderns are alone in using this method and even, according to the view of those who claim to have taken their principles from the ancient world, that method is merely tolerated, due more to habit than because it is truly fitting.

[...]

X.

Architects have always differed on whether it is tolerable that an Order should be interrupted by a floor and consequently occupy more than one storey. If one considers the origin of Architecture and the order of construction, it appears fitting that each storey should have its own separate Order. Vitruvius, when speaking of private buildings and courtyards in the ancient world, does not admit of two Orders, but one Order alone which supports the entablature, above which is the roof of the building, and he places a floor between the two in order to separate the ground floor from the storey immediately above. It is true that he includes isolated columns, but the pilasters that are behind and joined directly to the plain, flat surface of the wall are a cause of dispute [...]

XI.

When a Church has a dome supported by a separate structure and which is elevated above the vaulted ceiling in the middle of the Church, it is reasonable to place a second Order of Architecture on the interior walls and on the outside of such a dome, and even to add a third to the lantern, ordinarily the termination of such edifices, because the body of the Church, that of the dome and that of the lantern are visibly separate one from the other. [...]

XIII.

Raking cornices on pediments must continue without interruption from their beginning to their summit: it is totally contrary to the rules of good taste not only to interrupt them with projections or ledges, but also to cut or roll them or remove parts of their length, since because such cornices originally represented the edge of a roof with two gutters, a pediment of this kind cannot be open at the top to avoid giving a false impression of the solidity of the roof's edge, crest, etc. [...]

XIV.

Cornices with architraves are as satisfactory in an Attic Order as they are to be condemned in the regular Orders because its pilaster has less units of height than columns, and it is therefore fitting that its entablature should appear to be commensurate with its smaller proportions [...]

XV.

Doors and windows must never exceed in height the bottom of the architraves of the entablature, nor must they cut into, on any pretext whatsoever, the cornices or bases delineating the various inner storeys and it is in this that an Architect is obliged to allow the disposition of his exterior decoration to be governed by the considerations of appropriateness that have determined the building's interior disposition.

> [...]

Jacques-François
Blondel
1705–1774

XVII.

Concerning the ornamental Sculpture used as an accompaniment to Architecture, it must be observed that it is not its quantity that increases the beauty of the decoration of the building, but the discernment with which it is disposed at the places where it is fitting. It is necessary to avoid confusion in this regard and to ensure that the elements of such ornamentation are harmonised and proportionate in form, robustness, elegance and other qualities and analogous to the character of the Architecture or the architectural elements in which they are incorporated. [...]

XIX.

Concerning the decorative work on the outside and the inside of buildings, the Architecture must prevail. All elements of ornamentation should be governed by it, and all confusion between the ornaments should be eliminated. All the parts of the building that are, by contrast, unornamented should be used to set apart the decorated parts and to frame them.

XX.

Fashion in Architecture (according to Mr Boffrand, celebrated Architect of our times) is the tyrant of aesthetic taste. It is certain that in all eras it has been a great obstacle to the perfection of that art, because novelty pleases the common people and the true principles are known only to a small number of Architects, whereas most men see genius in eccentricities born of a disordered imagination. It is fashion that during the course of a century brings about infinite variation in the form and style of the ornamentation which occupies a place within Architecture, whereas it should be no more than an accessory. Lastly, it is fashion to which we owe the habit of the last some 30 years of employing a confused mixture of curved and straight lines both in the plans and in the elevations of buildings, without distinction as to the places where these can be used appropriately and without considering that these different lines should be employed exactly as are sounds in Music, which on different strings may express joy, sadness, love, hate, grace, terror, etc. and which are employed only when it is necessary to cause those varied emotions to be felt.

Such disorder in Architecture doubtless comes simply from lack of knowledge of the properties of these different lines and an improper application of the principles, which takes us away equally from perfection and good taste. Fashion is succeeded by habit, which in many cases is no more tolerable, given that habit in Architecture has invariably permitted in the various nations inappropriate practices contrary to the principles of good taste. Such defects are those to be seen in the fretwork ornamentation of constructions in the Gothic style, ogival tierce-point vaults, Church spires of bizarre and eccentric form, although elegant and robust, Indian-style ornamentation and roofing, pediments that are regular but interrupted, whose shapes are more or less worthy of criticism, according to the degree of deviation from the principles of proper Architecture.

After having spoken of the most essential principles relating to good taste, we shall conclude with the recommendation that it is necessary to avoid that which is contrary to nature and a sense of that which is fitting and consequently that, in normal edifices, entablatures, vaulted ceilings or other burdens must not be borne by human figures. [...]

Concerning the licence that one is sometimes obliged to use in Architecture and which must be avoided as far as is possible

It has always been dangerous in the art of building to introduce licence, due to the abuse that may be made of it by those of low intelligence. I have long felt that it would be more fitting to remain silent on the elements of licence that are used in building. However, since our best Architects have not always subjected their decorative work to the principles they have laid down, and since we regard their works as genuine examples of beauty, an infinite number of forms of licence have sprung from this, far more than is warranted by the necessity that they have sometimes been obliged to take into account in certain circumstances and therefore to circumvent the rules, in which they have been followed by almost all nations. It is such licence that we shall discuss here in order that those who exercise this art should not take instances of it as examples to be followed, without having first thoroughly understood the true reasons for its use in the decoration of buildings.

[...]

aesthetisation of architecture • classical canon • antiquity • abuses • design methodology

Jacques-François Blondel 1705–1774

Giovanni Poleni

Memorie istoriche della gran cupola del Tempio Vaticano, 1748

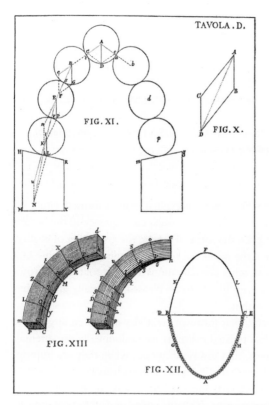

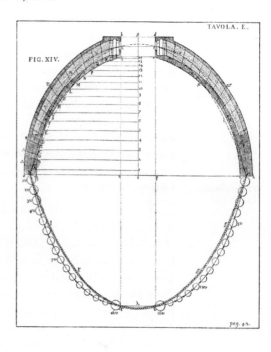

113., 113b. Giovanni Poleni. *Memorie istoriche della gran cupola del Tempio Vaticano, e de'danni di essa, e de'ristoramenti loro*. 1748.
Illustrations of the analogy between the chain catenary vault and the thin vault loaded by its own weight. It was first described by Hooke in 1676.
Here it was used by Poleni to examine the firmness of the dome of St Peter's in Rome.

William Hogarth (1697–1764)

The Analysis of Beauty (1753)

The famous English satirist and painter presents a theory of beauty here where 'fitness' is the main principle. By obeying this rule, the architect steers a mid-way course, avoiding 'both the strict academic canon of regular and monotonous forms and the other extreme of lawlessness and disorder.' The book popularises the functionalist idea of beauty which had been put forth as early as 1567 by Danti (Woodfield, 1971). It was widely read and rapidly translated. Winckelmann and the German neo-classicists were interested in its views (Antal, 1962).

Further reading Antal, 1962; Burke, 1943; Dobai, 1968; Hipple, 1957; Kaufmann, 1944; Mirabent, 1937; Tzonis, 1972; Wittkower, 1962; Woodfield, 1971.

Chapter I. Of Fitness

Fitness of the parts to the design for which every individual thing is formed, either by art or nature, is first to be considered, as it is of the greatest consequence to the beauty of the whole. This is so evident, that even the sense of seeing, the great inlet of beauty, is itself so strongly biased by it, that if the mind, on account of this kind of value in a form, esteem it beautiful, though on all other considerations it be not so; the eye grows insensible of its want of beauty, and even begins to be pleased, especially after it has been a considerable time acquainted with it.

It is well known on the other hand, that forms of great elegance often disgust the eye by being improperly applied. Thus twisted columns are undoubtedly ornamental; but as they convey an idea of weakness, they always displease, when they are improperly made use of as supports to any thing that is bulky, or appears heavy.

The bulks and proportions of objects are governed by fitness and propriety. It is this that has established the size and proportion of chairs, tables, and all forts of utensils and furniture. It is this that has fixed the dimensions of pillars, arches, &c. for the support of great weight, and so regulated all the orders in architecture, as well as the sizes of windows and doors, &c. Thus though a building were ever so large, the steps of the stairs, the seats in the windows must be continued of their usual heights, or they would lose their beauty with their fitness: and in ship-building the dimensions of every part are confined and regulated by fitness for sailing. When a vessel sails well, the sailors always call her a beauty; the two ideas have such a connection!

Chapter II. Of Variety

How great a share variety has in producing beauty may be seen in the ornamental part of nature. The shapes and colours of plants, flowers, leaves, the paintings in butterflies' wings, shells, &c. seem of little other intended use, than that of entertaining the eye with the pleasure of variety.

All the senses delight in it, and equally are averse to sameness. The ear is as much offended with one even continued note, as the eye is with being fixed to a point, or to the view of a dead wall.

Yet when the eye is glutted with a succession of variety, it finds relief in a certain degree of sameness; and even plain space becomes agreeable, and properly introduced, and contrasted with variety, adds to it more variety. I mean here, and everywhere indeed, a composed variety; for variety uncomposed, and without design, is confusion and deformity. Observe, that a gradual lessening is a kind of varying that gives beauty. The pyramid diminishing from its basis to its point, and the scroll or voluta, gradually lessening to its centre, are beautiful forms. So also objects that only seem to do so, though in fact they do not, have equal beauty: thus perspective views, and particularly those of buildings, are always pleasing to the eye.

Chapter IV. Of Simplicity, or Distinctness

Simplicity, without variety, is wholly insipid, and at best does only not displease; but when variety is joined to it, then it pleases, because it enhances the pleasure of variety, by giving the eye the power of enjoying it with ease.

There is no object composed of straight lines, that has so much variety, with so few parts, as the pyramid: and it is its constantly varying from its base gradually upwards in every situation of the eye (without giving the idea of sameness, as the eye moves round it), that has made it esteemed in all ages, in preference to the cone, which in all views appears nearly the same, being varied only by light and shade.

William Hogarth
1697–1764

[...]

The oval also, on account of its variety with simplicity, is as much to be preferred to the circle, as the triangle to the square, or the pyramid to the cube; and this figure lessened at one end, like the egg, thereby being more varied, is singled out by the author of all variety, to bound the features of a beautiful face. [...]

Chapter V. Of Intricacy

The active mind is ever bent to be employed. Pursuing is the business of our lives; and even abstracted from any other view, gives pleasure. Every arising difficulty, that for a while attends and interrupts the pursuit, gives a sort of spring to the mind, enhances the pleasure, and makes what would else be toil and labour, become sport and recreation. [...]

This love of pursuit, merely as pursuit, is implanted in our natures, and designed, no doubt, for necessary and useful purposes. It is a pleasing labour of the mind to solve the most difficult problems; and with what delight does it follow the well-connected thread of a play, or novel?

The eye hath this sort of enjoyment in winding walks, and serpentine rivers, and all sorts of objects, whose forms, as we shall see hereafter, are composed principally of what I call, the *waving* and *serpentine* lines.

Intricacy in form, therefore, I shall define to be that peculiarity in the lines which compose it, that *leads the eye a wanton kind of chase*, and from the pleasure that gives the mind, entitles it to the name of beautiful: and it may be justly said that the cause of the idea of grace more immediately resides in this principle.

Chapter VI. Of Quantity

Forms of magnitude, although ill-shaped, will however, on account of their vastness, draw our attention and raise our admiration. Huge shapeless rocks have a pleasing kind of horror in them, and the wide ocean awes us with its vast contents; but when forms of beauty are presented to the eye in large quantities, the pleasure increases on the mind, and horror is softened into reverence.

How solemn and pleasing are groves of high grown trees, great churches and palaces? Has not even a single spreading oak, grown to maturity, acquired the character of the venerable oak?

Windsor Castle is a noble instance of the effect of quantity. The hugeness of its few distinct parts strikes the eye with uncommon grandeur at a distance, as well as nigh. It is quantity, with simplicity, which makes it one of the finest objects in the kingdom, though void of any regular order of architecture.

Chapter VII. Of Lines

[...]

First, objects composed of straight lines, only, as the cube, or of circular lines, as the sphere, or of both together, as cylinders and cones, &c.

Second, those composed of straight lines, circular lines, and of lines partly straight, and partly circular, as the capitals of columns, and vases, &c.

William Hogarth
1697–1764

Third, those composed of all the former together with an addition of the waving line, which is a line more productive of beauty than any of the former, as in flowers, and other forms of the ornamental kind: for which reason we shall call it the line of beauty.

Fourth, those composed of all the former together with the serpentine line, as the human form. [...] Note, forms of most grace have least of the straight line in them.

It is to be observed, that straight lines vary only in length, and therefore are least ornamental.

That curved lines as they can be varied in their degrees of curvature as well as in their lengths, begin on that account to be ornamental.

That straight and curved lines joined, being a compound line, vary more than curves alone, and so become somewhat more ornamental. That the waving line, or line of beauty, varying still more, being composed of two curves contrasted, becomes still more ornamental and pleasing, insomuch that the hand takes a lively movement in making it with pen or pencil.

And that the serpentine line, by its waving and winding at the same time different ways, leads the eye in a pleasing manner along the continuity of its variety, if I may be allowed the expression; and which by its twisting so many different ways, may be said to enclose (though but a single line) varied contents; and therefore all its variety cannot be expressed on paper by one continued line, without the assistance of the imagination, or the help of a figure. See the figure, where that sort of proportioned, winding line, which will hereafter be called the precise serpentine line, or *line of grace*, is represented by a fine wire, properly twisted round the elegant and varied figure of a cone.

Chapter VIII. Of What Sort of Parts, and How Pleasing Forms are Composed

This way of composing pleasing forms is to be accomplished by making a choice of a variety of lines, as to their shapes and dimensions; and then again by varying their situations with each other, by all the different ways that can be conceived.

[...]

When you would compose an object of a great variety of parts, let several of those parts be distinguished by themselves, by their remarkable difference from the next adjoining, so as to make each of them, as it were, one well-shaped quantity or part.

[. . .] Hitherto, with regard to composition, little else but forms made up of straight and curved lines have been spoken of, and though their lines have but little variety in themselves, yet by reason of the great diversifications that they are capable of in being joined with one another; great variety of beauty of the more useful sort is produced by them, as in necessary utensils and building: but in my opinion, buildings as I before hinted, might be much more varied than they are, for after *fitness* has been strictly and mechanically complied with, any additional ornamental members, or parts, may, by the foregoing rules, be varied with equal elegance; nor can I help thinking, but that churches, palaces, hospitals, prisons, common houses and summer houses, might be built more in distinct characters than they are, by contriving orders suitable to each; whereas were a modern architect to build a palace in Lapland, or the West Indies, Paladio must be his guide, nor would he dare to stir a step without his book.

Have not many Gothic buildings a great deal of consistent beauty in them? Perhaps acquired by a series of improvements made from time to time by the natural persuasion of the eye, which often very near answers the end of working by principles; and sometimes begets them. There is at present such a thirst after variety, that even paltry imitations of Chinese buildings have a kind of vogue, chiefly on account of their novelty: but not only there, but any other new-invented characters of building might be regulated by proper principles. The mere ornaments of buildings, to be sure, at least might be allowed a greater latitude than they are at present; as capitals, friezes, &c. in order to increase the beauty of variety.

Nature, in shells and flowers, &c. affords an infinite choice of elegant hints for this purpose. [. . .] Some Gothic spires are finely and artfully varied, particularly the famous steeple of Strasbourg.

anticlassicism • deformation • freedom • naturalism • rigorism • essentialism

Marc-Antoine Laugier (1713–1769)

Essay on Architecture (1753)

Laugier entered the Jesuit order at fourteen and succeeded through his talents as an orator in becoming by 1749 the King's preacher. He left the order in 1756 and made a career as an 'homme de lettres', becoming editor of the 'Gazette de France', one of the most prominent journals of the time. Besides writing commercially successful books on art criticism, music and history, he published two works on architecture and town planning (1753, 1765). They contain his eloquent plea, in the tradition of Frémin (1701) and Cordemoy (1706), for the abandonment of heavy construction and over-ornamentation of baroque architecture (Hermann, 1962; Middleton, 1962, 1963; Nyberg, 1963). In the first book Laugier, calls for a functionalist aesthetic in architecture and town planning based on the simplicity and essentialism found in nature. The second is more daring in its espousal of innovation in the form of a radical stripping away of ornamentation. It could be seen as an early forerunner of the Miesian doctrine of 'less is more'. Both writings had a great impact and helped to move public opinion in favour of the neo-classicism of Soufflot. The *Essai* was translated into English and German. Goethe singled it out (1771) for attack because of its extreme minimalism and lack of expressiveness.

Further reading Bilodeau, 1997; Wiebenson, 1982, 1993.

Chapter I. General Principles of Architecture

It is the same in architecture as in all other arts: its principles are founded on simple nature, and nature's process clearly indicates its rules. Let us look at man in his primitive state without any aid or guidance other than his natural instincts. He is in need of a place to rest. On the banks of a quietly flowing brook he notices a stretch of grass; its fresh greenness is pleasing to his eyes, its tender down invites him; he is drawn there and, stretched out at leisure on this sparkling carpet, he thinks of nothing else but enjoying the gift of nature; he lacks nothing, he does not wish for anything. But soon the scorching heat of the sun forces him to look for shelter. A nearby forest draws him to its cooling shade; he runs to find a refuge in its depth, and there he is content. But suddenly mists are rising, swirling round and growing denser, until thick clouds cover the skies; soon, torrential rain pours down on this delightful forest. The savage, in his leafy shelter, does not know how to protect himself from the uncomfortable damp that penetrates everywhere; he creeps into a nearby cave and, finding it dry, he praises himself for his discovery. But soon the darkness and foul air surrounding him make his stay unbearable again. He leaves and is resolved to make good by his ingenuity the careless neglect of nature. He wants to make himself a dwelling that protects but does not bury him. Some fallen branches in the forest are the right material for his purpose; he chooses four of the strongest, raises them upright and arranges them in a square; across their top he lays four other branches; on these he hoists from two sides yet another row of branches which, inclining towards each other, meet at their highest point. He then covers this kind of roof with leaves so closely packed that neither sun nor rain can penetrate. Thus, man is housed. Admittedly, the cold and heat will make him feel uncomfortable in this house which is open on all sides but soon he will fill in the space between two posts and feel secure.

Such is the course of simple nature; by imitating the natural process, art was born. All the splendours of architecture ever conceived have been modelled on the little rustic hut I have just described. It is by approaching the simplicity of this first model that fundamental mistakes are avoided and true perfection is achieved. [...] The parts that are essential are the cause of beauty, the parts introduced by necessity cause every licence, the parts added by caprice cause every fault. This calls for an explanation; I shall try to be as clear as possible.

[...] We still have in France a beautiful ancient monument, which in Nimes is called the *Maison Carrée* [editor's note: a Corinthian temple of the first or second century in Nimes, in the South of France] and accords with the true principles of architecture: a rectangle where thirty columns support an entablature and a roof – closed at both ends by a pediment – that is all; the combination is of a simplicity and a nobility which strikes everybody.

[...]

Article I: the column

(1) The column must be strictly perpendicular, because, being intended to support the whole load, perfect verticality gives it its greatest strength. (2) The column must be freestanding so that its origin and purpose are expressed in a natural way. (3) The column must be round because nature makes nothing square. (4) The column must be tapered from bottom to top in imitation of nature where this diminution is found in all

Marc-Antoine
Laugier
1713–1769

plants. (5) The column must rest directly on the floor as the posts of the rustic hut rest directly on the ground. All these rules find their justification in our model; all deviations from this model without real necessity must, therefore, be considered as so many faults.

[...]

Chapter V

Article II: on the layout of streets

The streets of a great town cannot make communication easy and convenient unless they are sufficiently numerous to prevent lengthy detours, sufficiently wide to forestall any obstructions and perfectly straight to shorten the way. Most streets of Paris are, on the contrary, in default of all this. There are large and much visited quarters which are connected with other quarters by one or two streets only; this regularly causes great congestion or at least makes considerable detours unavoidable. [...] The streets are mostly so narrow that one cannot pass through them without danger and so winding and so full of senseless bends and corners that the way between one place and another becomes twice as long.

One must look at a town as a forest. The streets of the one are the roads of the other; both must be cut through in the same way. The essential beauty of a park consists in the great number of roads, their width and their alignment. This, however, is not sufficient: it needs a Le Notre to design the plan for it, someone who applies taste and intelligence so that there is at one and the same time order and fantasy, symmetry and variety, with roads here in the pattern of a star, there in that of a *patte d'oie*, with a featherlike arrangement in one place, fanlike in another, with parallel roads further away and everywhere *carrefours* of different design and shape. The more variety, abundance, contrast and even disorder in this composition, the greater will be the piquant and delightful beauty of the park. One should not believe that *esprit* has a place only in higher things. Everything which is susceptible of beauty, everything which demands inventiveness and planning is suitable to set off the imagination, the fire, the verve of a genius. The picturesque can be found in the pattern of a parterre as much as in the composition of a painting.

Let us carry out this idea and use the design of our parks as a plan for our towns. It is only a question of measuring the area and making the same style roads into streets and *carrefours* into squares. There are towns with perfectly aligned streets, but since the plan was made by uninspired people, a boring accuracy and cold uniformity prevail which makes one miss the disorder of towns of ours that have no kind of alignment at all; everything is related to a single shape, to a large parallelogram transversed lengthwise and crosswise by lines at right angles. Everywhere we have only boring repetition of the same objects, and all quarters look so much alike that one is mistaken and gets lost. A park which was only an assemblage of isolated and uniform squares and where all roads differed only numerically would be very tedious and dull. Above all, let us avoid excessive regularity and excessive symmetry. Dwelling too long on the same sentiment will blunt it. Whoever does not vary our pleasures, will not succeed in pleasing us.

It is therefore no small matter to draw a plan for a town in such a way that the splendour of the whole is divided into an infinite number of beautiful, entirely different

Marc-Antoine
Laugier
1713–1769

details so that one hardly ever meets the same objects again, and, wandering from one end to the other, comes in every quarter across something new, unique, startling, so that there is order and yet a sort of confusion, and everything is in alignment without being monotonous, and a multitude of regular parts brings about a certain impression of irregularity and disorder which suits great cities so well. To do this one must master the art of combination and have a soul full of fire and imagination which apprehends vividly the fairest and happiest combinations.

There is no other town which provides such fine scope for the inspiration of an ingenious artist as Paris. It is an immense forest varied by the contrast between plain and hill and, in the very middle, crossed by a great river which, dividing into several branches, forms islands of different sizes. Supposing the artist were allowed to slice and carve as he liked, how much he could profit from so favourable a diversity. What happy thoughts, ingenious turns, variety of expression, wealth of idea, bizarre connections, lively contrasts, what fire and boldness, what a sensational composition! It will doubtless be said that inventing the plan will be a pure loss because of the difficulty and even impossibility of executing it. Why should the thing be impossible? So many provincial towns, with meagre resources, have had the courage to contemplate rebuilding the town on a new plan, hoping to achieve it with the help of time and patience. Why despair of giving Paris such a fitting embellishment? In the capital of a great kingdom like France the resources are infinite. We only need to begin; time will complete it all. The greatest projects demand only resolution and courage provided they meet no physical obstacle, Paris is already one of the greatest cities in the world. Nothing would be more worthy of a nation as bold, ingenious and powerful as the French than to start on a new plan which in time will make Paris the most beautiful city in the universe.

Article III: on the decoration of buildings

When the plan of a town is well mapped out, the main and most difficult part is done. It remains, however, to regulate the exterior decoration of the buildings. If one wants a well-built town, the façades of houses must not be left to the whim of private persons. Every part that faces the street must be determined and governed by public authority according to the design which will be laid down for the whole street. It is necessary to settle not only the sites where it will be permitted to build but also the style in which to build.

[...]

As to façades of houses, they need regularity and much variety. Long streets where all houses seem to be one single building, because one has observed a rigorous symmetrical scheme, are a thoroughly boring sight. Too much uniformity is the worst of all faults. It is therefore necessary that in the same street the façades are free of this ugly uniformity. To build a street well, uniformity is only needed for façades which correspond and run parallel. The same design should extend over a whole section which is not crossed by another street and must never be repeated in any similar section. The art of varying the design depends on the various forms given to the buildings, on the amount of ornaments applied and on the different way in which they are combined. With these three means each of which is almost inexhaustible one is able, even in the largest towns, never to repeat the same façade twice.

It would, even with variation in design, be a great fault if all the embellishing decoration were the same. The beauty of a painting consists in gradation of light which passes insensibly from the darker to lighter parts and in a sweet harmony of colours which is not at all incompatible with some bold contrasts or, rather, becomes more marked when among the complementary colours there are some which upset the tranquillity through the effect of dissonance. Do we wish to decorate our streets in an exquisite style? Then we must not use ornaments in profusion; let us apply much that is simple, a little that is casual together with elegance and magnificence. As a rule one should change from the casual to the simple, from the simple to the elegant, from the elegant to the magnificent, should occasionally proceed abruptly from one extreme to the other using contrasts the boldness of which attracts the eye and produces strong effects, abandon from time to time symmetry and give in to caprice and eccentricity, blend the soft with the hard, the delicate with the rough, the noble with the rustic, and never depart from the true and natural. It seems to me that in this way one can display on the different houses of a town that pleasant variety and delicate harmony that make the charm of the decoration.

Marc-Antoine
Laugier
1713–1769

[...]

Paris is large enough so that one can use all types of decoration on its buildings. Its bridges, embankments, palaces, churches, great *hôtels*, hospitals, monasteries and public buildings provide the occasion for frequent interruption of the form of ordinary houses by quite singular forms. By knocking down the dreadful hovels which overload, narrow and disfigure most of our bridges and putting in their place beautiful large colonnades stretching from one side to the other, by facing all banks of the river and changing them into wide embankments, by lining all these embankments with façades enriched, some more, some less, by a decoration of fine gradation according to a well understood overall design, a scene will present itself from one end of the Seine to the other which will not be matched by anything in the world. Then if people, walking on both sides of the river through ingeniously laid out and perfectly aligned streets, pass in succession municipal buildings, *hôtels*, palaces, church façades and squares; if they see façades of private houses on which, with regularity preserved, the casual, the simple, the elegant and the magnificent are artistically blended and judiciously selected and set off to great advantage by contrasting one against the other; if, lastly, now and then buildings come into view of bizarre design and shape decorated in the style of the *grand pittoresque*, then I doubt that their eyes could ever tear themselves away from such a fascinating spectacle. Paris would, in its external appearance, no longer be merely an immense city, it would be a unique masterpiece, a marvel and delight. I wish that this scheme of embellishment, of which I have outlined the principles and have fixed approximate rules, would find connoisseurs who appreciate it, amateurs who favour it, devoted citizens who kindly consent to it and intrepid magistrates who seriously consider it and make efficient preparations to having it executed. I know that everything which aims at something useful has preference over that which simply intends to please. However, one can pursue the useful without neglecting the agreeable and must remember that a project which tends to give strangers a grand idea of our nation and attracts them in great numbers is a project that is not without usefulness.

anticlassicism • deformation • freedom • naturalism • rigorism • essentialism • urbanisation of architecture • planning

Ch. Eisen. inv.

114. Marc Antoine Laugier. *Essai sur l'architecture*. 1753. Frontispiece showing the primitive 'natural' hut as the new norm with architecture turning its back on classical historicist details.

William Hogarth

The Analysis of Beauty, 1753

115. William Hogarth. *The Analysis of Beauty*. 1753. Demonstration of the omnipresence of the spiral line in all beautiful objects, natural or artificial.

Charles Nicolas Cochin

'Supplication to the Goldsmiths', *Mercure de France* (December 1754)

Although professionally an engraver, Cochin was one of the chief figures, because of his lively, polemical and abundant writings, in moving public opinion in the direction of neo-classicism in all the arts from the 1750s to the French Revolution. He opposed the Greek models he had come into contact with during his trips to Herculanum to the excesses of the rococo and the mid-century baroque. He was a protégé of Madame de Pompadour and her brother, the Marquis of Marigny, in charge of the royal buildings. He was a close friend of Soufflot and defended him vociferously against his detractor, Pierre Patte.

Further reading Eriksen, 1974; Herrmann, 1962.

Charles Nicolas
Cochin
1715–1790

Be it most humbly represented to these gentlemen that however great the efforts made by the French nation for many years now to accustom its reason to bend to the wantonness of their fancy, it has not been completely able to succeed. Wherefore these gentlemen are supplicated to be so obliging as to observe henceforward certain simple rules dictated by good sense, from which we cannot hear the principles of our understanding. It would be a very noble act on the part of these gentlemen if they would condescend to our weakness and pardon us the real impossibility in which we find ourselves of turning off all the lights of our reasoning faculty out of politeness to them.

[...] We may at least hope to obtain from them that when things can be made right-angled they will be kind enough not to twist them, that when arches can be semi-circular they will be so kind as not to undulate their outlines with those serpentine contours that they appear to have adopted from the writing masters and that are so fashionable that they are used even in the plans of buildings. They are called 'forms' by those who use them, but they forget to add the word 'bad' that is inseparable from them. We consent nevertheless to their serving us this twisted ware to all provincials and foreigners who are poor enough connoisseurs to prefer our modern taste to that of the last century. The more these inventions are scattered among foreigners the more we may hope to maintain the superiority of France. We beg them to consider that we furnish them with fine straight wood and that they burden us with expense by working it into all these sinuous forms, that in bending our doors in order to subject them to the circularities that it pleases the good taste of our modern architects to give to all our rooms, they make us spend much more than if they were to make them straight, and that we find no advantage in them since we pass just as well through a straight door as though through a rounded door. As for the curves of the walls of our apartments we find no other convenience in them except that we do not know where to place them anymore or how to set up our chairs or other furniture against them. The carvers are prevailed upon to accept the assurances we give them, we who have no interest in deceiving them, that regular straight, right-angled, round and oval forms are as rich a decoration as all their inventions and that since to execute them precisely is more difficult than to execute all those grasses, bats' wings and other paltry ornaments which are in current circulation, they will honour their talents more. And that finally the eyes of a great many honest folk, of whom we are one, will be under an inexpressible obligation to them if they are no longer angered by irrational disproportion and by so great an abundance of twisted and extravagant ornaments.

And if we ask for too many things at once, let them at least grant us this one grace, that from now on the principal moulding that they now usually torment, will become and remain straight in conformity with the principles of good architecture. We will then consent to their making their ornaments twist around and over it as much as corresponds with their good graces, and we will consider ourselves the less unfortunate because a man of good taste, if such an apartment comes into his possession, will be able to knock away all such stuff with a chisel, and rediscover the plain moulding, which will provide him with a sensible decoration that will cause his reason no suffering.

It is obvious that a good number of the complaints that we have addressed to the carvers may with good reason also be addressed to architects. The truth is we do not dare to. These gentlemen are less easily governed. There is hardly one of them that even begins to doubt his talents and that does not boast of them with utter confidence. We cannot really on our credit with them convert them even with the best reasons in the world. If we were bold enough we should have invited them respectfully to examine from time to time the old Louvre, the Tuileries and other royal buildings of the last century which are universally recognised for their goodness, and not to give us the chance to so often think they have never laid eyes on them although they are so close. We should have begged them to spare us those dreadful angled forms they have all agreed on for the salient parts of all façades and we should have assured them in the sincerity of our conscience that all the obtuse and acute angles are disagreeable in architecture, and that only the right-angle is capable of producing a positive effect. This means they would lose their octagonal salons. But why should a right-angled salon not be as beautiful? It would no longer be necessary to squeeze cornices in interiors in order to avoid the difficulty of distributing the ornaments proper to them successfully. They would not have been reduced to substituting grasses or other miserable fantasies for the modillons, denticules and other ornaments invented by persons more learned than they and accepted by all nations on the basis of sound reflection. We should have begged them to respect the natural beauty of the stones they draw from the quarry straight and with right angles, and to be so kind as not to spoil them in order to make them conform to shapes that mean eliminating half their volume and give public proofs of deranged minds. We should have begged them to deliver us from the boredom of seeing arched windows on every house from the ground floor to the garrets in such a fashion that it seems as if a pact had been sworn to make no others. Even the window-frames want to jump on the bandwagon and twist themselves in the prettiest manner possible with no other advantage except to give a great deal of trouble to the carpenter and difficulty to the glazier when he has to cut panes into these baroque forms.

We should also have been able to take them on about that general mould which they seem to use to cast all carriage gates by making the moulding of the cornice always turn up into an arched form without being followed by those of the architrave so that the cornice looks false. And if they add their beloved console, however useless it may be, they never know where to place it. Beyond the middle of the pilaster it is ridiculous. And in the middle it does not receive the full weight of the arch. Even while granting that the mansard roof is a wonderful and marvellous invention, worthy of being passed down to generations to come, if only it could be made of marble we would perhaps have been able to beg them to be more sparing with it. In its place they could have offered an attic storey, for example, which being perpendicular and of stone

Charles Nicolas
Cochin
1715–1790

would appear more regular and more in keeping with the rest of the building. For, in the end, one tires of always seeing a blue house on the top of a white one.

How many favours should we not have had to ask of them without in vain hoping they might be willing to grant us even one? So far as they are concerned, all we can do is sigh in silence and wait for the time when their invention runs out and they themselves become exhausted. It seems that this time is near, for they only repeat themselves and there is ground for hope that the desire for novelty will bring back the ancient style of architecture.

aesthetisation of architecture • anticlassicism • deformation • freedom • naturalism • classical canon • antiquity • abuses

Charles Nicolas
Cochin
1715–1790

Charles Nicolas Cochin (1715–1790)

'On a Very Bad Joke' (1755)

(See Cochin 1754)

Let us consider the advancement of the art. What great expansion have we not given to it? We have multiplied the number of excellent architects to the point where they are almost countless. A line of talent that bristles with difficulties under the system of ancient architecture becomes, under ours, the easiest thing in the world. Experience shows that even a master-mason with the most basic gifts for drawing and taste, after he has worked for a while under our orders, is allowed to declare himself an architect and be as good as we are, barring very little. Let us add that to the glory of France and to her advantage, foreigners are beginning to adopt our taste and there is every appearance that they will come here in droves just to learn from us. The English, so jealous of our superiority in all the arts, have become so wild about it that they have abandoned their Inigo Jones and taken up the habit of copying exactly the works of Palladio. What may perhaps diminish this advantage is the foolhardiness that has allowed some of our decorations for doors and chimney-pieces to be engraved. For at first they were the butt of jokes in other nations of Europe, because they did not feel all their beauty, but since then they have been able to resist imitating them. Unfortunately these prints disclose our secret which in any case is not difficult to learn, and a great number of geniuses able to catch these light graces may pop up in any country. If this should happen, as citizens of the world, we will console and applaud ourselves on having turned all men into architects at very little expense. These great advantages have cost us some pains.

There remain a few grumblers who spread it abroad everywhere that good taste is lost and that there are very few architects who understand that sort of decoration that essentially characterises the architect. We destroy all these arguments by affirming out loud that what differentiates the architect is the art of distribution. In vain do they urge that distribution is not so difficult as we wish to make out and that it is quite obvious that any private person with a little intelligence can arrange his house in a manner convenient to himself according to the requirements of his rank, and that the difficulty which a private person cannot remove, nor we either, and which is exact, symmetrical and in what is called good taste, both outside and inside. But here precisely is the point which will always make us victorious. As our style of architecture has no rules to bind it, as it is convenient and, so to speak, docile we have acquired a large number of partisans who will always support us because they are gratified by the facility with which we satisfy their fancies. We would like to see the gentlemen of the Antique school try and decorate the outside of a building under all the conditions which we have imposed on them. Since at first the loudest protests were directed against our exterior decorations, because they were exposed to the sight of everyone, and since empty space costs nothing to decorate and leaves no point on which criticism can fasten we brought in the fashion for a multiplicity of windows which succeeded perfectly. For it is infinitely agreeable to have three windows in a room which formerly would have hardly had two. It is true that this makes for more cold in winter and more heat in summer, but what does that matter to us? It is not less certain that everyone wants a house to be pierced all over by windows and that our gentlemen of the Antique who only know how to decorate the solid parts of buildings find no work.

aesthetisation of architecture • anticlassicism • deformation • freedom • naturalism • classical canon • antiquity • abuses

Morelly (?–?)

The Code of Nature (1755)

Almost nothing is known about the author, who assumed the pen-name of Morelly. He is recognised as one of the most influential of French enlightenment thinkers. His **Code** applies directives to architecture and city planning, which are in accordance with a social programme, already entirely communistic in its conception, where all citizens share equally in work and in the distribution of goods.
Further reading Wagner, 1978.

The Organisation of Society

III. All citizens without exception from the age of twenty-one until the age of twenty-five shall be obliged to work in agriculture unless exempted by reason of some infirmity.

IV. In each city, the body of young people assigned to agricultural work shall comprise labourers, gardeners, shepherds, woodcutters, groundbreakers and brush-clearers, hauliers by land or water, carpenters, bricklayers, blacksmiths and other professions associated with architecture. Those young persons who have carried on one of the six professions termed 'primary' here shall for the designated time be able to leave to work in that which had been earlier learned, or may remain in agriculture for so long as their physical strength permits.

Building Statutes

II. Around a great square of regular shape shall be erected the public stores for all provisions and public assembly rooms within an overall structure of uniform and agreeable disposition.

III. Outside this structure shall be ranged in symmetrical order the living quarters of the city, all equal, of identical design and divided symmetrically by streets.

IV. Each tribe shall occupy a designated town area and each family a spacious and comfortable lodging. All the buildings shall be of uniform design.

V. Each defined area of the town shall be disposed in such a manner that it may be expanded whenever necessary without disturbance to its symmetry. Such expansion shall not exceed certain limits.

VI. At some distance, around the living areas of the city, shall be built galleries of workshops for all the mechanical occupations, and intended for all bodies of workers, the number of which shall not be more than ten, for it has been stated in *Statute V on distribution*, that there shall be for each town no more than a sufficient number of workers for each mechanical occupation.

VII. Outside this area of workshops shall be erected a further rank of edifices destined for the accommodation of those persons employed in agriculture and the occupations dependent thereon, in order also to serve as workshops for those occupations, as barns, cellars, stables for livestock and tool stores, these being in all cases commensurate with the service required by each town.

VIII. Outside all the above areas, at a some distance, shall be erected at the most salubrious location a spacious and comfortable building for the accommodation and treatment of all citizens who are sick.

IX. On another side of the town shall be erected a comfortable place of retirement for all citizens who are infirm or rendered decrepit by age.

X. In another location shall be erected in the least pleasant and the most deserted place a building surrounded by high walls divided into many small accommodations closed by iron grilles where shall be shut in all those deserving of removal from society for a time. *See the Criminal Law Statutes.*

XI. Nearby shall be the place of burial, surrounded by walls within which shall be separately constructed in very robust brickwork sorts of caves that shall be fairly spacious and strongly defended by grilles, in order to be placed there in perpetuity and to serve as graves for those citizens meriting capital punishment, that is to say those deserving to be removed permanently from society. *See the Criminal Law Statutes.*

XII. In general, all the buildings in each town shall be constructed, maintained and rebuilt by the bodies of workers assigned to architecture.

social reform • democratisation • urbanisation of architecture • planning

Count Francesco
Algarotti
1712–1764

Count Francesco Algarotti (1712–1764)

Essay (1756)

The writings of Algarotti, a nobleman and amateur of the arts and letters, are an exposition of the ideas of his former schoolteacher and Italy's main rigorist theoretician, Carlo Lòdoli, the chief Italian critic of baroque 'abuses' in the name of 'idea', who never published himself. Lòdoli upheld the principles of light construction out of wood when possible over more expensive and wasteful stone construction in particular, in the same spirit that Laugier (1753) defended the primitive hut against the excesses of the French baroque architecture of the day. Although Algarotti did not hold to the extreme functionalist views of the master, taking every opportunity to rebuke the principles of honesty, simplicity and rationality in building, he documented them more clearly in works like his **Saggio** (1756) and in his **Lettere sopra l'architettura (1742–1763)**, both excepted in the present book, than did the more faithful disciples, Milizia (1781, 1781, 1787, 1797) and Memmo (1786).

Further reading De Zurko, 1957; Gengaro, 1937; Grassi, 1966; Kaufmann, 1944, 1955, 1958; Meeks, 1966; Tzonis, 1972.

p.60. No one has brought to the attention of the public a greater number of abuses than an honourable man of our times [editor's note: i.e. Carlo Lòdoli]. And these abuses have been perpetrated not by barbarians but by practitioners of our own country that is reputed to be correct and masterful in all kinds of disciplines. Nothing holds him back, not the authority of the times nor the nobility of the example. He has subjected everything to the rigorous examination of reason. And he has no other aim but truth, which he teaches, showing its many facets and appearances, just as Socrates once did in philosophy, pointing to sophistries and denouncing them as vain fallacies. In the same way this honourable man intends to purge architecture [. . .]

p.64. The philosopher [Lòdoli] is firm in his fundamental belief that good architecture must, in his words, shape, ornament and reveal and that this applies equally, whether to matters of function or of representation. Then he goes further, pointing out the terrible consequences that occur when this is not materialised. And this brings him to condemn this or that part of a building. Taken all together, of course, among ancient and modern buildings, it is the ancient ones that get the biggest credit for being beautiful and touted as if they were works of art. Yet many of these buildings that are of stone look like they are wood. Then the columns. They look like they are supporting beams of the roof when in fact the roof is supported by the chimney. This kind of abuse just goes on and on. The more stone buildings are reputed to be beautiful, the more their every part and member clearly and obviously represents a wooden structure. This is an abuse that is greater than anything he could ever have imagined. And because it has been for so long anchored in the minds of men, it is necessary to use every force of reason to combat them. To be far from the function and representation is one and the same thing for a building. They are to be seen in the most obvious contradictions. Why on earth not let stone represent stone, wood, and so on for all materials, instead of something else? Everything that is taught and practised in architecture is opposed to this. Architecture should have a quality that is characteristic, pleasing or rigid in its component parts, consistent with its force of resistance, to the essence of a word or the nature of the material it is made of. [. . .]

p.72. Now, when men are trying to reduce architecture to art, is it not natural for them to realise that of all the materials that there are to build with they should choose one and one only and to the forms it naturally allows? That guaranteeing the stability and that determining the rules of ornamentation a building renders a building delightful to the eye, and also produces function and fitness? And with all the materials, is it not natural to think that they should prefer one which can best serve the greatest amount of demands of stability, change and ornamentation above all others? This way they could arrive at an architecture where only the necessary exists, which by definition is perfection in all the arts. Variety through the multiplication of changes made possible through the choice of the material, and unity deriving from the character of a single material.

Count Francesco
Algarotti
1712–1764

rigorism • essentialism

Sir William Chambers

Designs for Chinese Buildings (1726–1796)

(See Chambers 1759)

'Of the Art of Laying out Gardens Among the Chinese'

Sir William
Chambers
1726–1796

The gardens which I saw in China were very small; nevertheless from them, and what could be gathered from Lepqua, a celebrated Chinese painter, with whom I had several conversations on the subject of gardening, I think I have acquired sufficient knowledge of their notions on their heads.

Nature is their pattern, and their aim is to imitate her in all her beautiful irregularities. Their first consideration is the form of the ground, whether it be flat, sloping, hilly, or mountainous, extensive, or of small compass, of a dry or marshy nature, abounding with rivers and springs, or liable to a scarcity of water; to all which circumstances they attend with great care, choosing such dispositions as humour the ground, can be executed with the least expense, hide its defects, and set its advantages in the most conspicuous light.

As the Chinese are not fond of walking, we seldom meet with avenues or spacious walks, as in our European plantations: the whole ground is laid out in a variety of scenes, and you are led, by winding passages cut in the groves, to the different points of view, each of which is marked by a seat, a building, or some other object.

The perfection of their gardens consists in the number, beauty and diversity of these scenes. The Chinese gardeners, like the European painters, collect from nature the most pleasing objects, which they endeavour to combine in such a manner, as not only to appear to the best advantage separately, but likewise to unite in forming an elegant and striking whole.

Their artists distinguish three different species of scenes, to which they give the appellations of pleasing, horrid and enchanted. Their enchanted scenes answer, in a great measure, to what we call romantic, and in these they make use of several artifices to excite surprise. Sometimes they make a rapid stream, or torrent, pass under ground, the turbulent noise of which strikes the ear of the newcomer, who is at a loss to know from whence it proceeds: at other times they dispose the rocks, buildings and other objects that form the composition, in such a manner as that the wind passing through the different interstices and cavities, made in them for that purpose, causes strange and uncommon sounds. They introduce into these scenes all kinds of extraordinary trees, plants and flowers, form artificial and complicated echoes, and let loose different sorts of monstrous birds and animals.

In their scenes of horror, they introduce impending rocks, dark caverns and impetuous cataracts rushing down the mountains from all sides; the trees are ill-formed and seemingly torn to pieces by the violence of tempests; some are thrown down, and intercept the course of the torrents, appearing as if they had been brought down by the fury of the waters; others look as if shattered and blasted by the force of lightning; the buildings are some in ruins, others half consumed by fire, and some miserable huts dispersed in the mountains serve at once to indicate the existence and wretchedness of the inhabitants. These scenes are generally succeeded by pleasing ones. The Chinese artists, knowing how powerfully contrast operates on the mind, constantly practise sudden transitions, and a striking opposition of forms, colours and shades. Thus they conduct you from limited prospects to extensive views; from objects of horror to scenes of delight; ... from complicated forms to simple ones; distributing, by a judicious arrangement, the different masses of light and shade, in such a manner as to render the composition at once distinct in its parts, and striking in the whole.

Where the ground is extensive, and a multiplicity of scenes are to be introduced, they generally adapt each to one single point of view: but where it is omitted, and affords no room for variety, they endeavour to remedy this defect by disposing the objects so that being viewed from different points, they produce different representations; and sometimes, by an artful disposition, such have no resemblance to each other.

In their large gardens they contrive different scenes for morning, noon and evening; erecting, at the proper points of view, buildings adapted to the recreations of each particular time of the day: and in their small ones (where as has been observed, one arrangement produces many representations) they dispose in the same manner, at the several points of view, buildings, which, from their use, point out the time of day for enjoying the scene in its perfection.

Sir William
Chambers
1726–1796

Their rivers are seldom straight, but serpentine, and broken into many irregular points; sometimes they are narrow, noisy and rapid, at other times deep, broad and slow. Both in their rivers and lakes are seen reeds, with other aquatic plants and flowers; particularly the Lyen Hoa, of which they are very fond. They frequently erect mills, and other hydraulic machines, the motions of which enliven the scene: they have also a great number of vessels of different forms and sizes. In their lakes they intersperse islands; some of them barren, and surrounded with rocks and shoals; others enriched with every thing that art and nature can furnish most perfect. They likewise form artificial rocks; and in compositions of this kind the Chinese surpass all other nations. The stone they are made of comes from the southern coasts of China. It is of a bluish cast, and worn into irregular forms by the action of the waves. They cover them, in different places, with trees, shrubs, briars and moss; placing on their tops little temples, or other buildings, to which you ascend by rugged and irregular steps cut in the rock.

When there is a sufficient supply of water, and proper ground, the Chinese never fail to form cascades in their gardens. They avoid all regularity in these works, observing nature according to her operations in that mountainous country. The waters burst out from among the caverns, and windings of the rocks. In some places a large and impetuous cataract appears; in others are seen many lesser falls. Sometimes the view of the cascade is intercepted by trees, whose leaves and branches only leave room to discover the waters, in some places, as they fall down the sides of the mountain. They frequently throw rough wooden bridges from one rock to another, over the steepest part of the cataract; and often intercept its passage by trees and heaps of stones, that seem to have been brought down by the violence of the torrent.

In their plantations they vary the forms and colours of their trees; mixing such as have large and spreading branches, with those of pyramidal figures, and dark greens with brighter, interspersing among them those that produce flowers; of which they have some that flourish a great part of the year. They likewise introduce trunks of decayed trees, sometimes erect, and at other times lying on the ground, being very careful about their forms, and the colour of the bark and moss on them.

Various are the artifices they employ to surprise. Sometimes they lead you through dark caverns and gloomy passages, at the issue of which you are, all of a sudden, struck with the view of a delicious landscape, enriched with every thing that luxuriant nature affords most beautiful. At other times you are conducted through avenues and walks, that gradually diminish and grow rugged, till the passage is at length entirely intercepted, and rendered impracticable, by bushes, briars and stones: when unexpectedly a rich and extensive prospect opens to view, so much the more pleasing as it was less looked for.

Another of their artifices is to hide some part of a composition by trees, or other intermediate objects. This naturally excites the curiosity of the spectator to take a nearer view; when he is surprised by some representation totally opposite to the thing he looked for. The termination of their lakes they always hide, leaving room for the imagination to work; and the same rule they observe in other compositions, wherever it can be put in practice.

Though the Chinese are not well versed in optics, yet experience has taught them that objects appear less in size, and grow dim in colour, in proportion as they are more removed from the eye of the spectator. These discoveries have given rise to an artifice, which they sometimes put in practice. It is the forming of prospects in perspective, by introducing buildings, vessels and other objects, lessened according as they are more distant from the point of view; and that the deception may be still more striking, they give a greyish tinge to the distant parts of the composition, and plant in the remoter parts of these scenes trees of a fainter colour, and smaller growth, than those that appear in the front or fore-ground; by these means rendering what in reality is trifling and limited, great and considerable in appearance.

The Chinese generally avoid straight lines; yet they do not absolutely reject them. They sometimes make avenues, when they have any interesting object to expose to view. Roads they always make straight; unless the unevenness of the ground, or other impediments, afford at least a pretext for doing otherwise. Where the ground is entirely level, they look upon it as an absurdity to make a serpentine road: for they say that it must either be made by art, or worn by the constant passage of travellers; in either of which cases it is not natural to suppose men would choose a crooked line when they might go by a straight one.

What we call clumps, the Chinese gardeners are not unacquainted with; but they use them somewhat more sparingly than we do. They never fill a whole piece of ground with clumps: they consider a plantation as painters do a picture, and group their trees in the same manner as these do their figures, having their principal and subservient masses.

This is the substance of what I learnt during my stay in China, partly from my own observation, but chiefly from the lessons of Lepqua: and from what has been said it may be inferred, that the art of laying out grounds, after the Chinese manner, is exceedingly difficult, and not to be attained by persons of narrow intellects. For though the precepts are simple and obvious, yet the putting them in execution requires genius, judgement and experience; a strong imagination, and a thorough knowledge of the human mind. This method being fixed to no certain rule, but liable to as many variations as there are different arrangements in the works of the creation.

anticlassicism • deformation • freedom • naturalism • orientalism

Sir William
Chambers
1726–1796

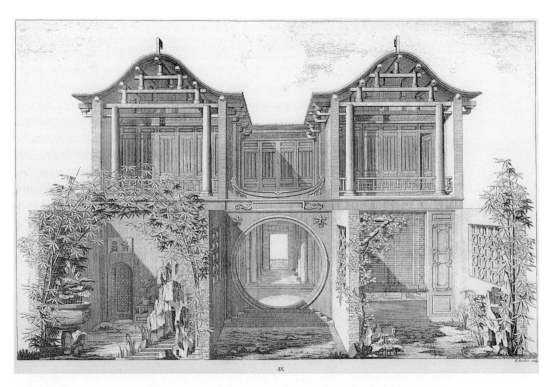

116. Sir William Chambers. *Designs for Chinese Buildings*. 1757. Reconstruction of a section of a Chinese house.

117. Sir William Chambers. *Gardens and Buildings at Kew*. 1763. View of Kew Gardens with a reconstructed Chinese pagoda, a Moorish mosque and Pavilion.

Edmund Burke (1729–1797)

Philosophical Enquiry into the Origin of our Ideas on the Sublime and the Beautiful **(1757)**

It is largely due to this popular treatise that the second half of the eighteenth century was provided with a growing taste which has been dubbed 'pre-romantic'. With his sensationalist and emotional approach and his exaltation of sublimity, of strong contrasts and natural effects, Burke subjected the classical conceptions of architectural beauty, based on laws of proportion or fitness, to a detailed analysis, then refuted them. This work reveals most clearly the break with the past and ushers in the age of subjective sensibility (Wittkower, 1962). Chambers was familiar with Burke's theories (Harris, 1967; Wiebenson, 1968) and evidently they influenced Boullée (Rosenau, 1953; Wiebenson, ibid.).

Further reading Harris, 1967; Hilles, 1965; Monk, 1935; Nicolson, 1963; Rosenau, 1953; Tuveson, 1951; Wiebenson, 1968; Wittkower, 1962; Wood, 1972.

Part I. Sect. VII. Of the Sublime

Whatever is fitted in any sort to excite the ideas of pain, and danger, that is to say whatever is in any sort terrible, or is conversant about terrible objects, or operates in a manner analogous to terror, is a source of the sublime; that is, it is productive of the strongest emotion which the mind is capable of feeling. I say the strongest emotion, because I am satisfied the ideas of pain are much more powerful than those which enter on the part of pleasure. Without all doubt, the torments which we may be made to suffer, are much greater in their effect on the body and mind, than any pleasures which the most learned voluptuary could suggest or than the liveliest imagination, and the most sound and exquisitely sensible body could enjoy. Nay I am in great doubt whether any man could be found who would earn a life of the most perfect satisfaction, at the price of ending it in the torments, which justice inflicted in a few hours on the late unfortunate regicide in France. But as pain is stronger in its operation than pleasure, so death is in general a much more affecting idea than pain; because there are very few pains, however exquisite, which are not preferred to death; nay, what generally makes pain itself, if I may say so, more painful, is that it is considered as an emissary of this king of terrors. When danger or pain press too nearly, they are incapable of giving any delight, and are simply terrible; but at certain distances, and with certain modifications, they may be, and they are delightful, as we every day experience. The cause of this I shall endeavour to investigate hereafter.

Part II. Sect. I. Of the Passion Caused by the Sublime

The passion caused by the great and sublime in *nature* when those causes operate most powerfully, is astonishment; and astonishment is that state of the soul, in which all its motions are suspended with some degree of horror. In this case the mind is so entirely filled with its object, that it cannot entertain any other, nor by consequence reason on that object which employs it. Hence arises the great power of the sublime, that far from being produced by them, it anticipates our reasonings, and hurries us on by an irresistible force. Astonishment, as I have said, is the effect of the sublime in its highest degree; the inferior effects are admiration, reverence and respect.

Sect. II. Terror

No passion so effectually robs the mind of all its powers of acting and reasoning as fear. For fear being an apprehension of pain or death, it operates in a manner that resembles actual pain. Whatever therefore is terrible, with regard to fright, is sublime too, whether this cause of terror be endured with greatness of dimensions or not; for it is impossible to look on anything as trifling, or contemptible, that may be dangerous. There are many animals who though far from being large, are yet capable of raising ideas of the sublime, because they are considered as objects of terror. As serpents and poisonous animals of almost all kinds. And to things of great dimensions, if we annex an adventitious idea of terror, they become without comparison greater. A level plain of a vast extent of land is certainly no mean idea; the prospect of such a plain may be as extensive as a prospect of the ocean; but can it ever fill the mind with any thing so great as the ocean itself? This is owing to several causes, but it is owing to none more than this, that the ocean is an object of no small terror. Indeed terror is in all cases whatsoever, either more openly or latently the ruling principle of the sublime.

Edmund Burke
1729–1797

[...]

Sect. III. Obscurity

To make any thing very terrible, obscurity seems in general to be necessary. When we know the full extent of any danger, when we can accustom our eyes to it, a great deal of the apprehension vanishes. Every one will be sensible of this, who considers how greatly night adds to our dread, in all cases of danger, and how much the notions of ghosts and goblins, of which none can form clear ideas, affect minds, which give credit to the popular tales concerning such sorts of beings. Those despotic governments, which are founded on the passions of men and principally upon the passion of fear, keep their chief as much as may be from the public eye. The policy has been the same in many cases of religion. Almost all the heathen temples were dark. Even in the barbarous temples of the Americans at this day, they keep their idol in a dark part of the hut, which is consecrated to his worship. For this purpose too the druids performed all their ceremonies in the bosom of the darkest woods, and in the shade of the oldest and most spreading oaks. No person seems better to have understood the secret of heightening, or of setting terrible things, [...] than Milton. ... [In] his description of Death.

> The other shape,
> If shape it might be called that shape had none
> Distinguishable, in member joint, or limb;
> Or substance might be called that shadow seemed,
> For each seemed either; black be flood as night,
> Fierce as ten furies, terrible as hell
> And shook a deadly dart. What seemed his head
> The likeness of a kingly crown had on.

In this description all is dark, uncertain, confused, terrible and sublime to the last degree.

Sect. IV. Of the Difference between Clearness and Obscurity with Regard to the Passions

It is one thing to make an ideal clear, and another to make it *affecting* to the imagination. If I make a drawing of a palace, or a temple, or a landscape, I present a very clear idea of those objects; but then [...] my picture can at most affect only as the palace, temple, or landscape would have affected in the reality. On the other hand, the most lively and spirited verbal description I can give raises a very obscure and imperfect *idea* of such objects; but then it is in my power to raise a stronger *emotion* by the description than I could do by the best painting. This experience constantly evinces. The proper manner of conveying the *affections* of the mind from one to another is by words; there is a great insufficiency in all other methods of communication; and so far is a clearness of imagery from being absolutely necessary to an influence upon the passions, that they may be considerably operated upon without presenting any image at all, by certain sounds adapted to that purpose; of which we have a sufficient proof in the acknowledged and powerful effects of instrumental music. In reality a great clearness helps but little towards affecting the passions, as it is in some sort an enemy to all enthusiasms whatsoever.

> [...]

Edmund Burke
1729–1797

Sect. V. Power

Besides these things which *directly* suggest the idea of danger, and those which produce a similar effect from a mechanical cause, I know of nothing sublime which is not some modification of power. And this branch rises as naturally as the other two branches, from terror, the common stock of every thing that is sublime. The idea of power at first view seems of the class of these indifferent ones, which may equally belong to pain or to pleasure. But in reality, the affection arising from the idea of vast power is extremely remote from that neutral character. For first, we must remember that the idea of pain, in its highest degree, is much stronger than the highest degree of pleasure; and that it preserves the same superiority through all the subordinate gradations. From hence it is that where the chances for equal degrees of suffering or enjoyment are in any sort equal, the idea of the suffering must always be prevalent. And indeed the ideas of pain, and above all of death, are so very affecting, that whilst we remain in the presence of whatever is supposed to have the power of inflicting either, it is impossible to be perfectly free from terror. Again, we know by experience, that for the enjoyment of pleasure, no great efforts of power are at all necessary; nay we know that such efforts would go a great way towards destroying our satisfaction: for pleasure must be stolen, and not forced upon us; pleasure follows the will; and therefore we are generally affected with it by many things of a force greatly inferior to our own. But pain is always inflicted by a power in some way superior, because we never submit to pain willingly. So that strength, violence, pain and terror are ideas that rush in upon the mind together. [...] Thus we have traced power through its several gradations unto the highest of all, where our imagination is finally lost; and we find terror quite throughout the progress, its inseparable companion, and growing along with it, as far as we can possibly trace them [...] as power is undoubtedly a capital source of the sublime, this will point out evidently from whence its energy is derived, and to what class of ideas we ought to unite it.

Sect. VI. Privation

All *general* privations are great, because they are all terrible; *Vacuity, Darkness, Solitude* and *Silence*. With what a fire of imagination, yet with what severity of judgement, has Virgil amassed all these circumstances where he knows that all the images of a tremendous dignity ought to be united, at the mouth of hell! Where before he unlocks the secrets of the great deep, he seems to be seized with a religious horror, and to retire astonished at the boldness of his own design.

[...]

Sect. VII. Vastness

Greatness of dimension is a powerful cause of the sublime. This is too evident, and the observation too common to need any illustration; it is not so common to consider in what ways greatness of dimension, vastness of extent or quantity, has the most striking effect. For certainly, there are ways, and modes, wherein the same quantity of extension shall produce greater effects than it is found to do in others. Extension is either in length, height, or depth. Of these the length strikes least; a hundred yards of even ground will never work such an effect as a tower a hundred yards high or a rock or mountain of that altitude. I am apt to imagine likewise that height is less grand than depth; and that we are more struck at looking down from a precipice, than at looking up at an object of equal height, but of that I am not very positive. A perpendicular has more force in forming the sublime than an inclined plane; and the effects of a rugged and broken surface seem stronger than where it is smooth and polished. It would carry us out of our way to enter in this place into the cause of these appearances; but certain it is they afford a large and fruitful field of speculation. However, it may not be amiss to add to these remarks upon magnitude; that, as the great extreme of dimension is sublime, so the last extreme of littleness is in some measure sublime likewise.

[...]

Edmund Burke
1729–1797

Sect. VIII. Infinity

Another source of the sublime is *infinity*; if it does not rather belong to the last. Infinity has a tendency to fill the mind with that sort of delightful horror, which is the most genuine effect, and truest test of the sublime. There are scarce any things which can become the objects of our senses that are really, and in their own nature infinite. But the eye not being able to perceive the bounds of many things, they seem to be infinite, and they produce the same effects as if they were really so. We are deceived in the like manner, if the parts of some large object are so continued to any indefinite number that the imagination meets no check which may hinder its extending them at pleasure.

Whenever we repeat any idea frequently, the mind by a sort of mechanism repeats it long after the first cause has ceased to operate. After whirling about, when we sit down, the objects about us still seem to whirl. After a long succession of noises, as the fall of waters, or the beating of forge hammers, the hammers beat and the water roars in the imagination long after the first sounds have ceased to affect it; and they die away at last by gradations which are scarcely perceptible. If you hold up a straight pole, with your eye to one end, it will seem extended to a length almost incredible. Place a number of uniform and equidistant marks on this pole, they will cause the same deception, and seem multiplied without end. The senses strongly affected in some one manner, cannot quickly change their tenor, or adapt themselves to other things; but they continue in their old channel until the strength of the first mover decays. [. . .]

Sect. IX. Succession and Uniformity

Succession and *uniformity* of parts are what constitute the artificial infinite. 1. *Succession*; which is requisite that the parts may be continued so long, and in such a direction, as by their frequent impulses on the sense to impress the imagination with an idea of their progress beyond their actual limits. 2. *Uniformity*; because if the figures of tile parts should be changed, the imagination at every change finds a check; you are presented at every alteration with the termination of one idea, and the beginning of another; by which means it becomes impossible to continue that uninterrupted progression, which alone can stamp on bounded objects the character of infinity. It is in this kind of artificial infinity, I believe, we ought to look for the cause why a rotund has such a noble effect. For in a rotund, whether it be a building or a plantation, you can nowhere fix a boundary; turn which way you will, the same object still seems to continue, and the imagination has no rest. But the parts must be uniform as well as circularly disposed, to give this figure its full force; because any difference, whether it be in the disposition, or in the figure, or even in the colour of the parts, is highly prejudicial to the idea of infinity, which every change must check and interrupt, at every alteration commencing a new series. On the same principles of succession and uniformity the grand appearance of the ancient heathen temples, which were generally oblong forms, with a range of uniform pillars on every side, will be easily accounted for. From the same cause also may be derived the grand effect of the isles in many of our own old cathedrals. The form of a cross used in some churches seems to me not so eligible, as the parallelogram of the ancients; at least I imagine it is not so proper for the outside. For, supposing the arms of the cross are every way equal, if you stand in a direction parallel to any of the side walls, or colonnades, instead of a deception that makes the building more extended than it is, you are cut off from a considerable part (two thirds) of its *actual* length; and to prevent all possibility of progression, the arms of the cross taking a new direction, make a right angle with the beam, and thereby wholly turn the imagination from the repetition of the former idea. Or suppose the spectator placed where he may take a direct view of such a building; what will be the consequence? The necessary consequence will be that a good part of the basis of each angle, formed by the intersection of the arms of the cross, must be inevitably lost; the whole must of course assume a broken unconnected figure; the lights must be unequal, here strong, and there weak; without that noble gradation, which the perspective always effects on parts disposed uninterruptedly in a right line. Some or all of these objections will lie against every figure of a cross in whatever view you take it. I exemplified them in the Greek cross in which the faults appear the most strongly; but they appear in some degree in all sorts of crosses. Indeed there is nothing more prejudicial to the grandeur of buildings than to abound in angles; a fault obvious in many; and owing to an inordinate thirst for variety, which, whenever it prevails, is sure to leave very little true taste.

Edmund Burke
1729–1797

Sect. X. Magnitude in Building

To the sublime in building, greatness of dimension seems requisite; for on a few parts, and those small, the imagination cannot rise to any idea of infinity. No greatness in the manner can effectually compensate for the want of proper dimensions. There is no danger of drawing men into extravagant designs by this rule; it carries its own caution along with it. Because too great a length in buildings destroys the purpose of greatness which it was intended to promote; the perspective will lessen it in height as it gains in length; and will bring it at last to a point; turning the whole figure into a sort of triangle, the poorest in its effect: of almost any figure, that can be presented to the eye. I have ever observed that colonnades and avenues of trees of a moderate length were without comparison far grander than when they were suffered to run to immense distances. A true artist should put a generous deceit on the spectators, and effect the noblest design by easy methods. Designs that are vast only by their dimensions are always the sign of a common and low imagination. No work of art can be great, but as it deceives; to be otherwise is the prerogative of nature only. A good eye will fix the medium, betwixt an excessive length, or height (for the same objection lies against both), and a short or broken quantity; and perhaps it might be ascertained to a tolerable degree of exactness, if it was my purpose to descend far into the particulars of any art.

Edmund Burke
1729–1797

Sect. XI. Infinity in Pleasing Objects

Infinity, though of another kind, causes much of our pleasure in agreeable, as well as of our delight in sublime images. The spring is the pleasantest of the seasons; and the young of most animals, though far from being completely fashioned, afford a more agreeable sensation than the full grown; because the imagination is entertained with the promise of something more, and does not acquiesce in the present object of the sense. In unfinished sketches of drawing, I have often seen something which pleased me beyond the best finishing; and this I believe proceeds from the cause I have just now assigned.

Sect. XII. Difficulty

Another source of greatness is *difficulty*. When any work seems to have required immense force and labour to effect it, the idea is grand. Stonehenge, neither for disposition nor ornament, has any thing admirable; but those huge rude masses of stone, set on end, and piled each on other, turn the mind on the immense force necessary for such a work. Nay the rudeness of the work increases this cause of grandeur as it excludes the idea of art and contrivance; for dexterity produces another sort of effect which is different enough from this.

Sect. XIII. Magnificence

Magnificence is likewise a source of the sublime. A great profusion of things which are splendid or valuable in themselves is *magnificent*. The starry heaven though it occurs so very frequently to our view, never fails to excite an idea of grandeur. This cannot be owing to any thing in the stars themselves, separately considered. The number is certainly the cause. The apparent disorder augments the grandeur, for the appearance of care is highly contrary to our ideas of magnificence. Besides, the stars lie in such apparent confusion as makes it impossible on ordinary occasions to reckon them. This gives them the advantage of a sort of infinity. In works of art, this kind of grandeur, which consists in multitude, is to be very cautiously admitted; because a profusion of excellent things is not to be attained, or with too much difficulty; and, because in many cases this splendid confusion would destroy all we admire, which should be attended to in most of the works of art with the greatest care; besides it is to be considered that unless you can produce an appearance of infinity by your disorder, you will have disorder only without magnificence.

[...]

Sect. XIV. Light

Edmund Burke
1729–1797

Having considered extension, so far as it is capable of raising ideas of greatness, *colour* comes next under consideration. All colours depend on *light*. Light therefore ought previously to be examined, and with it, its opposite, darkness. With regard to light; to make it a cause capable of producing the sublime, it must be attended with some circumstances, besides its bare faculty of showing other objects. Mere light is too common a thing to make a strong impression on the mind, and without a strong impression nothing can be sublime. But such a light as that of the sun, immediately exerted on the eye, as it overpowers the sense, is a very great idea. Light of an inferior strength to this, if it moves with great celerity, has the same power; for lightning is certainly productive of grandeur, which it owes chiefly to the extreme velocity of its motion. A quick transition from light to darkness, or from darkness to light, has yet a greater effect. But darkness is more productive of sublime ideas than light.

[...]

Here is an idea not only poetical in a high degree, but strictly and philosophically just. Extreme light, by overcoming the organs of sight, obliterates all objects, so as in its effect exactly to resemble darkness. After looking for some time at the sun, two black spots, the impression which it leaves, seem to dance before our eyes. Thus are two ideas as opposite as can be imagined reconciled in the extremes of both; and both in spite of their opposite nature brought to concur in producing the sublime. And this is not the only instance wherein the opposite extremes operate equally in favour of the sublime, which in all things abhors mediocrity.

Sect. XV. Light in Building

As the management of light is a matter of importance in architecture, it is worth enquiring how far this remark is applicable to building. I think then, that all edifices calculated to produce an idea of the sublime ought rather to be dark and gloomy, and this for two reasons; the first is that darkness itself on other occasions is known by experience to have a greater effect on the passions than light. The second is that to make an object very striking, we should make it as different as possible from the objects with which we have been immediately conversant; when therefore you enter a building, you cannot pass into a greater light than you had in the open air; to go into one some few degrees less luminous, can make only a trifling change; but to make the transition thoroughly striking, you ought to pass from the greatest light, to as much darkness as is consistent with the uses of architecture. At night the contrary rule will hold, but for the very same reason; and the more highly a room is then illuminated, the grander will the passion be.

Part III. Sect. XXVII. The Sublime and Beautiful Compared

On closing this general view of beauty, it naturally occurs that we should compare it with the sublime; and in this comparison there appears a remarkable contrast. For sublime objects are vast in their dimensions, beautiful ones comparatively small; beauty should be smooth and polished; the great, rugged and negligent; beauty should shun the right line, yet deviate from it insensibly; the great in many cases loves the right line, and when it deviates, it often makes a strong deviation; beauty should not be obscure; the great ought to be dark and gloomy; beauty should be light and delicate; the great ought to be solid, and even massive. They are indeed ideas of a very different nature, one being founded on pain, the other on pleasure; and however they may vary afterwards from the direct nature of their causes, yet these causes keep up an eternal distinction between them, a distinction never to be forgotten by any whose business it is to affect the passions. In the infinite variety of natural combinations we must expect to find the qualities of things the most remote imaginable from each other united in the same object. We must expect also to find combinations of the same kind in the works of art. But when we consider the power of an object upon our passions, we must know that when any thing is intended to affect the mind by the force of some predominant property, the affection produced is likely to be the more uniform and perfect, if all the other properties or qualities of the object be of the same nature, and tending to the same design as the principal.

[...]

Edmund Burke
1729–1797

Part IV. Sect. XIII. The Effects of Succession in Visual Objects Explained

If we can comprehend clearly how things operate upon one of our senses, there can be very little difficulty in conceiving in what manner they affect the rest. To say a great deal therefore upon the corresponding affections of every sense would tend rather to fatigue us by a useless repetition, than to throw any new light upon the subject, by that ample and diffuse manner of treating it; but as in this discourse we chiefly attach ourselves to the sublime, as it affects the eye, we shall consider particularly why a successive disposition of uniform parts in the same right line should be sublime, and upon what principle this disposition is enabled to make a comparatively small quantity of matter produce a grander effect, than a much larger quantity disposed in another manner. [...] Let us set before our eyes a colonnade of uniform pillars planted in a right line; let us take our stand, in such a manner, that the eye may shoot along this colonnade, for it has its best effect in this view. In our present situation it is plain that the rays from the first round pillar will cause in the eye a vibration of that species; an image of the pillar itself. The pillar immediately succeeding increases it; that which follows renews and enforces the impression; each in its order as it succeeds, repeats impulse after impulse, and stroke after stroke, until the eye long exercised in one particular way cannot lose that object immediately; and being violently roused by this continued agitation, it presents the mind with a grand or sublime conception. But instead of viewing a rank of uniform pillars, let us suppose that they succeed each other, a round and a square one alternately. In this case the vibration caused by the first round pillar perishes as soon as it is formed; and one of quite another sort (the square) directly occupies its place; which however it resigns as quickly to the round one; and thus the eye proceeds, alternately, taking up one image and laying down another, as long as the building continues. From whence it is obvious that at the last pillar, the impression is as far from continuing as it was at the very first; because in fact, the sensory can receive no distinct impression but from the last; and it can never of itself resume a dissimilar impression: besides, every variation of the object is a rest and relaxation to the organs of sight; and these reliefs prevent that powerful emotion so necessary to produce the sublime. To produce therefore a perfect grandeur in such things as we have been mentioning, there should be a perfect simplicity, an absolute uniformity in disposition, shape and colouring. Upon this principle of succession and uniformity it may be asked, why a long bare wall should not be a more sublime object than a colonnade; since the succession is no way interrupted; since the eye meets no check; since nothing more uniform can be conceived? A long bare wall is certainly not so grand an object as a colonnade of the same length and height. It is not altogether difficult to account for this difference. When we look at a naked wall, from the evenness of the object, the eye runs along its whole space, and arrives quickly at its termination; the eye meets nothing which may interrupt its progress; but then it meets nothing which may detain it a proper time to produce a very great and lasting effect. The view of a bare wall, if it be of a great height and length, is undoubtedly grand: but this is only *one* idea, and not a *repetition* of *similar* ideas; it is therefore great, not so much upon the principle of *infinity*, as upon that of *vastness*. But we are not so powerfully affected with any one impulse, unless it be one of a prodigious force indeed, as we are with a succession of similar impulses; because the nerves of the sensory do not (if I may use the expression) acquire a habit of repeating the same feeling in such a manner as to continue it longer than its cause is in action; besides, all the effects which I have attributed to expectation and surprise in Section II can have no place in a bare wall.

anticlassicism • deformation • freedom • naturalism • emotions • passions • sentiments

Julien David Le Roy 1724–1803

Julien David Le Roy (1724–1803)

The Ruins of the most Beautiful Monuments of Greece (1758, revised 1770)

The architecture of Ancient Greece had only been available through preserved literary descriptions, legends and monuments that were Roman rather than Greek before Le Roy's book. His is the first published documentation. It was undertaken under the direct influence of the Englishmen James Stuart and Nicholas Revett. Because the French had better relations with the Ottomans than the English, Le Roy's access to the monuments was much facilitated. In contrast to the Englishmen, who spent three years doing their research in Athens, Le Roy left after three months. To their more meticulous and slow approach, he opposed an approach to documentation that was journalistic. And whereas the Englishmen were concerned with widening the limits of archaeological knowledge, Le Roy was interested in translating Greek architecture into stylistic terms that were meaningful for practising architects. In particular, Le Roy's emphasis on the colonnade initiated a long tradition of incorporating the element as a basic part of urban design. As a result of all of these factors, although Le Roy did not return to Europe until almost half-a-year after Stuart and Revett, he managed to get his book published ahead of theirs. *Les Ruines* not only appeared four years earlier than *The Antiquities of Athens, Measured and Delineated*, it also had a greater impact on architecture and did more to directly stir a new and vital interest in Greek architecture (Wiebenson, 1969).

p.I The principles in general are a small number of essential and fertile ideas that represent in an abridged manner the substance of the sciences and arts from which they have been drawn and in which serve as a guide for us. They are more or less certain in relation to the object of the particular science or art they belong to, they even have different degrees of certainty within the same science or art. This latter truth does not seem to me to have been sensed strongly enough by the authors who have written on architecture; some of them struck with the evidence of certain principles have looked upon them as incontestable truths, others contemplating those with a less solid foundation have taken them to be arbitrary. The object of the present writing is to sort out as much as possible the nature of the different principles of this art, to make known the ones that are constant and to which all artists that set out to erect buildings must bend themselves to on the one hand and, on the other, the ones that we are permitted to stray from sometimes. A just appreciation of these principles would help us avoid two very dangerous problems in architecture, namely that which consists in admitting no rules, and to take capriciousness as one's guide in the composition of monuments, and that which consists in accepting too great a number of rules and to thus impede the imagination of architects and turn this sublime art into a kind of craft where no one does anything but imitate without choice that which has already been done by ancient architects.

Julien David Le Roy 1724–1803

p.IV The writings of the ancients, their medals, their statues, their engraved stones, their inscriptions, these treasures that the barbarians deprived us of are not the only monuments that are able to provide us with knowledge of the power, the genius and the taste of the most famous nations of antiquity and on the communication that went on between them. The buildings of a small number of famous cities have cast new light for us onto this interesting part of history.

p.III (1770 edition) If one examines the writings of Vitruvius, if one considers the temples that still stand in Greece and in different parts of Asia, one will recognise that in each species, without passing into another class, was able to present very different masses. This is because the proportion of the façades of these buildings could differ according to the number of columns that ornamented them, according to the type of columns, according to the proportion the architect gave them, and lastly according to the disposition of the steps that served as a kind of basement for the building.

Vitruvius determines on the basis of truth the number of columns that each species of temple must bear on its façade, but one still finds in Greece a great number of examples that prove that the architects of this nation did not subject themselves to it in a servile way. The Temple of Minerva in Athens for example is peripheral and it has eight columns although Vitruvius only gives six to this species of temple. [. . .] Not only did the Greeks refuse to give the same number of columns to each species of temple, often they even decorated them with different orders. As they gave but a height of six diameters to their Doric columns and sometimes more than ten to the Corinthian ones, this prodigious difference in proportions perforce produced very striking varieties in the massing of the buildings and in the character of the façades of the temples according to the order that had been used there.

p.VII The spectacle that the history of art offers us, well capable of pricking the curiosity of those who love to follow progress is to see how the original primitive ideas of some creative geniuses have influenced the various works that men did subsequently. Their essays in architecture offer striking examples of this. The stone erected by the Phoenicians on the tomb of a famous man, imitated in other monuments of the same type, and made bigger, more colossal, was the starting point of the obelisk. The same stone represented, on the contrary, by masses of stones piled up, large at their base, pointed towards the top, gave birth to the idea of the pyramids. The origins appear to us to be all the more likely as we know that pyramids were tombs and obelisks were often devoted to immortalising the memory of heroes or the benefactors of humanity. We discover also in the form of the huts of different peoples, that antiquity has left us some traces of, the model of the oldest temples that are known to us.

classical canon • antiquity • abuses • history versus antiquarianism • precedent • authority • invention

Julien David Le
Roy
1724–1803

118. Julien David Le Roy. *Ruines des plus beaux monuments de la Grèce*. 1758. The temple of the winds in eighteenth-century Athens.

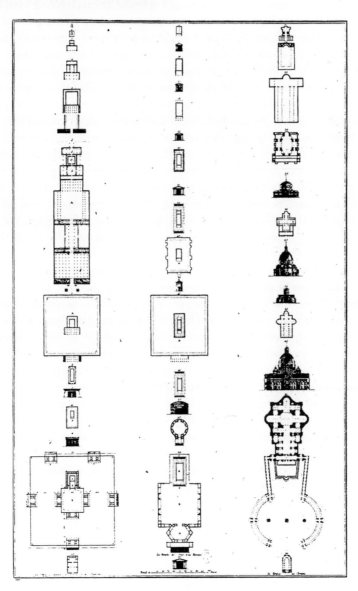

119. Julien David Le Roy. *Ruines des plus beaux monuments de la Grèce*. 1758. Proposal for a taxonomy of buildings showing historical precedents of temples of the Egyptians, Hebrews, Phoenicians on the left, Greeks and Romans in the centre and the Christians on the right demonstrating a progress in complexity.

Count Francesco Algarotti (1712–1764)

Letter to a Gentleman in Venice (1759)

(See introduction for Algarotti 1756)

Bologna, 14 April 1759

Count Francesco
Algarotti
1712–1764

Too austere for your liking, then, seem those men who should like no ornament in architecture that does not have its reason, and who maintain that every thing must be necessary. You on the contrary are of the same opinion as Cicero; that the pediment of the temple of Capitoline Jupiter would have been a splendid accomplishment even if placed above the clouds, where there is no threat of rain. As far as I am concerned I confess that in place of a pediment above the clouds I would have preferred a fine terrace. But this is not the reason why I should embrace wholly and unconditionally the system of those purists. To want everything in view to also have a true function, as they express it, is to want too much. Whatever could be the function of the foliage of the Corinthian capital, the volutes of the Ionic, the fluting on columns, the animals and such like things usually carved? Are these then to be banished from a well-formed edifice because they support nothing, buttress nothing, because they are not of absolute necessity? In painting, robes serve to cover gracefully and at the same time to reveal the figure, that is, the nude underneath. Thus ornaments in architecture serve to embellish the building, and to accent its essential parts at the same time as its outline. And just as a certain flourish, or the occasional quirk or excess is permitted in the painting of robes, so we should allow the same of ornaments on buildings. We ought never to condemn the saw, *licencia sumpta pudenter.*

We should, however, condemn out of hand those ornaments which show the thing quite differently from what by nature it ought to be. Palladio for example disapproves, and rightly so, of the abusive practice of breaking the pediments of doors, windows and loggia in the middle, there being nothing, he says, more contrary to reason than splitting that part whose purpose is to protect the occupants of and those entering the house from rain, snow and hail. Which we can take as a jibe at Michelangelo, who took such liberties, and sometimes bent the rules. I am now thinking of the cornice, and in particular the Doric cornice placed ornamentally over alleys even by architects of repute. Is there nothing more absurd than placing triglyphs, that is, feigned roof beams, with their ends exposed where, if they were really there, they could catch fire and cause the building to collapse? You will surely remember the floor of the church of Santa Giustina in Padua. Its inlay of different kinds of stones makes them look like cubes, with pieces of crossed wood: and so realistically is it contrived that in walking over it one is almost on one's guard against stumbling, and one walks with raised legs. So much art, and more money, spent on creating an illusion of something, that if it really existed, would have to be cleared away.

Then we see on the façades of churches something I have never liked, despite the fact that it was commonly practised by the greatest of architects. This is using two or more Orders placed one above the other. Should not the cornice of the lower Order be an external expression of the flooring which divides the lower storey from the upper? This is undoubtedly not its purpose and intention in the view of universal wisdom. And how incongruous, that the two Orders on the façade of the church show this on the exterior, suggest that it is divided into two storeys, and once we are inside we find it to be of one storey only, or as they say, right below the roof?

Where several architectural Orders can fittingly be placed one above the other is on the façades of palazzi; for here they indeed show the different storeys into which the building is divided internally. Except that it would be desirable that the salience of the cornices of the lower Orders should be somewhat restrained, something of which architects are not usually aware – in this way the purpose of the principal cornice, of the uppermost order, would be better appreciated, and which with an emphatic projection should afford shelter from rain, protecting the building underneath.

No finer aspect can a façade present, in my opinion, than when the lower order is crowned with a simple fascia, and the cornice is reserved for the uppermost order.

classical canon • antiquity • abuses • rigorism • essentialism

Alexander Gérard (1728–1795)

An Essay on Taste (1759)

Alexander Gérard
1728–1795

The first edition (1759) and the second (1764) appended to this essay by the Scottish philosopher, Alexander Gerard, a translation of three French texts on the subject of taste, by Voltaire, Montesquieu and d'Alembert. He was, like them, a figure of the Enlightenment. One of the greatest influences on him was Hume, whose theory of associationism he uses in order to ground his own theory of taste on established principles of psychology (Grene, 1943; Hipple, 1957). Gerard was instrumental in making taste into an accepted criterion for beauty in architecture, thus dislodging the traditional reliance on traditional canon and precedence.

Further reading Knight, 1968.

Sect. II Of the Sense or Taste of Grandeur and Sublimity

Grandeur or sublimity gives us a still higher and nobler pleasure, by means of a sense appropriated to the perception of it; while meanness renders any object, to which it adheres, disagreeable and distasteful. Objects are sublime which possess quantity or amplitude, and simplicity in conjunction. Considerable magnitude or largeness of extension, in objects capable of it, is necessary to produce sublimity.

Grandeur in works of architecture may, in some instances, arise from their largeness: for we generally estimate the magnitude of things by comparison with those of the same species: and though no edifice is equal in quantity to many works of nature by no means accounted great; yet lofty palaces and pyramids, far exceeding the bulk of other buildings, have a comparative magnitude, which has the same influence upon the mind, as if they had been absolutely large. But still the principal source of grandeur in architecture is association, by which the columns suggest ideas of strength and durability, and the whole structure introduces the sublime ideas of the riches and magnificence of the owner.

Objects impress us more or less according to the degree of attention which we bestow upon them. Custom enables us to apply our minds more vigorously to objects than we could at first. It is not only difficult to form a complete conception of new objects, but when they excite neither surprise nor curiosity, it is sometimes even difficult to attempt conceiving them, and to bring ourselves steadily to contemplate them. Custom wears off this indisposition; begets an aptitude and previous bias to the emotions, which beauty and deformity inspire; and thus renders us prone to their peculiar sentiments. Works of taste fall in with the predominant temper, and on that account easily engage the attention, affect deeply, and excite the liveliest perceptions.

Sensibility of taste arises chiefly from the structure of our internal senses, and is but indirectly and remotely connected with the soundness or improvement of judgement. The want of it is one ingredient in many sorts of false taste; but does not constitute so much one species of wrong taste, as a total deficiency or great weakness of taste. Sensibility may sometimes become excessive; and render us extravagant both in liking and disliking, in commending and blaming. But, in truth, this extravagance proceeds much less commonly from excess of sensibility than from a defect in the other requisites of fine taste; from an incapacity to distinguish and ascertain, with precision, different degrees of excellence or faultiness. Instead of forming an adequate idea of the nature of the beauty or deformity, we go beyond all bounds of moderation; and when we want to express our sentiments, can do it only in general terms, tumid and exaggerated.

Alexander Gérard
1728–1795

anticlassicism • deformation • freedom • naturalism • emotions • passions • sentiments

Giovanni Battista Piranesi

Carceri d'invenzione, 1760

120. Giovanni Battista Piranesi. *Carceri d'invenzione*. 1760. Visionary design of strong emotions – an awe-inspiring interior in ruins.

Sir William Chambers (1723–1796)

A Treatise on Civil Architecture (1759)

Chambers' treatise has been described as the Englishman's Palladio and Vignola, for it was the leading authority in England into the nineteenth century (Harris, 1968). Its aim was to provide a course of instruction on the five orders and their embellishments, a narrower focus but in much the same spirit as the *Cours* by François Blondel almost 100 years earlier. The emphasis was on decoration, as the title suggests, and in this area the influence of the then-current philosophical discussions on grandeur and the sublime by such writers as Gerard (1759) and Burke (1757; see Harris, 1967) is apparent, as was his opposition to Laugier and the Italian *rigoristi*. The third edition (1791), with an expanded title, *Treatise on the Decorative Part of Civil Architecture*, bears significant alterations and additions. Among these is the polemical opposition to the then-current neo-classical surge of interest in the antiquities of Athens occasioned by the publication of the Steuart and Revett's book on that topic. It was an echo of Piranesi's earlier polemical writings. Chambers' other works were more original, for example his *Designs of Chinese Buildings* (1757), *A Dissertation on Oriental Gardening* (1772) and *Letter to a Gentleman Who had Objected to Certain Parts of his Treatise on Oriental Gardening* (1772) also cast a revealing light on his love of ornament. He was among the first to import Chinese architecture to Europe, as a result of his service in Canton, China, as an employee of the Swedish East India Company (Harris, 1968).

Further reading Harris, 1990; Kaufmann, 1955.

Of Pilasters

I am not ignorant, that several authors are of a different opinion: a certain French Jesuit in particular; who some thirty years ago, first published an essay on architecture, which from its plausibility, force and elegance of diction, went through several editions; and operated very powerfully on the superficial part of European connoisseurs. He inveighs vehemently against pilasters, as against almost every other architectonic form but such as were imitated by the first builders in stone, from the primitive wooden huts: as if, in the whole catalogue of arts, architecture should be the only one confined to its primitive simplicity, and secluded from any deviation or improvement whatever.

To pilasters, the essayist objects, because they are, in his opinion, nothing better than bad representations of columns. Their angles (says he) indicate the formal stiffness of art, and are a striking deviation from the simplicity of nature; their projections, sharp and inconvenient, offend and confine the eye; and their surfaces without roundness, give to the whole order a flat air: they are not susceptible of diminution, one of the most pleasing properties of columns; they are never necessary, and to sum up the whole, he hates them: his aversion was first innate, but has since been confirmed by the study of architecture.

Concerning the reverend father's inborn aversion, much need not be said; and several others of his objections, as they consist more of words than meaning, seem not to require any refutation; but, to assert that pilasters are not susceptible of diminution shows very little acquaintance either with books of architecture, or with buildings.

And we go back to the origins of things and consider pilasters, either as representing the ends of partition walls, or trunks of trees, reduced to the diameter of the round trunks which they accompany, but left square for greater strength; the reason for diminishing them will, in either case, be strong and evident.

It is likewise an error to assert that pilasters are never necessary; but that columns will at all times answer the same end: for, at the angles of all buildings, they are evidently necessary, both for solidity and beauty; because the angular support, having a greater weight to bear than any of the rest, ought to be so much the stronger; so that its diameter must either be increased, or its plan altered from a circle to a square; but chiefly as it obviates a very striking defect; occasioned by employing columns at the angles of a building; which is, that the angle of the entablature is left hanging in the air without any support: a sight very disagreeable in some oblique views, and in itself very unsolid.

It is indeed customary in porches, and other detached compositions, to employ columns at the angles; it is judicious so to do: for of two defects, the least is to be preferred. And although Father Laugier, the writer whose objections I have now cited, could see no reason for rejecting detached pilasters, when engaged ones were suffered; yet there is a very substantial reason, which is that a detached pilaster in some oblique views appears thicker than it does in front, nearly in the ratio of seven to five; and consequently if, when seen in front, it appears well proportioned in itself, and with regards to the columns it accompanied; it never can appear so, when viewed upon the angle. [...]

Engaged pilasters are employed in churches, galleries, halls, and other interior decorations, to save room: for as they seldom project beyond the solid of the walls, more than one quarter of their diameter, they do not occupy near so much space, even as engaged columns. They are likewise employed in exterior decorations; sometimes alone, instead of columns, on account of their being less expensive. [...]

Another disagreeable effect of undiminished pilasters is likewise obviated by rejecting them: indeed, I am at a loss to account for it; and, as it is diametrically opposite to a received law in optics, I imagined it might be the result of some defect in my own sight; till by enquiry, I found others were affected in the same manner. It is this; the top of the shaft always appears broader than the bottom; as any one may observe, by casting a glance on the pilasters of St Paul's. [...]

T.-N. Loyer (?–?)

Follow-up on my First Dissertation on How to Decorate Apartments (1762)

This is the first example of the reversal of over-ornamentation in interior design. It is a rejection of inessential decoration. The interior uses only essential architectural elements such as the Doric column in the name of the truly beautiful, of masculinity, simplicity and the relation to needs and functionality. It strives towards richness, agreeableness and a lack of confusion (Eriksen, 1974).

A taste for what is good is always in harmony with reason and it is on this first principle that all correct rules have been based. In all that is intended to present itself agreeably to our sight, unity of effect is required. In order to attain to this, it is essential to know the means of doing so. Only the course which leads to good architecture is able to bring us to this goal.

[367]

For we perceive in effect that on all occasions when a man wishes to decorate an apartment with some taste, whatever use it serves, he is always obliged to turn to principles which architecture alone supplies. She gives us the forms which may be required for all needs, she apprises us of all the properties. She has collected everything that is likely to grant grace to whatever is desired to represent. She has, in fact, enriched herself for our benefit and we will lack no resources if we consult her truly.

This cautious path is the one that the ancient architects followed most scrupulously, and without in any way belittling the genius that was theirs, they always advanced on it with steady steps towards the truth, keeping themselves to the rules adopted by the most enlightened of mankind.

We will judge the truth of this if we are willing to examine with attention the works executed during the great centuries of Greece and Rome, and we will make the same judgement when we see the works of the past two centuries. Encouraged by the example of all those skilful artists of today I have sought the ancient path and when I have found myself with some houses to decorate I have taken from the principles of architecture everything that could be of use to my aims.

T.-N. Loyer
?–?

I am of the opinion that a right-angled design is always the best form that we can use in all sorts of decoration, especially in rooms of a regular form intended for peristypes, vestibules, assembly rooms, etc. I agree that it would be ridiculous and an offence against the correct rules to terminate the angles of these rooms by a circular design or by other forms that always seem artificial and misplaced. But the nobler decoration conform more to the rules of the art. I believe that smooth turns for angles ought to be tolerated, that they are necessary even to correct the ugly defect produced by the obliquity of an irregular room like that which is the subject of discussion.

The pilasters which decorate this room are thirteen-and-a-half inches wide, project an inch-and-three-quarters, and are ten feet six inches high including the base and the capital. The height in relation to the width of the pilasters is a sixth more than the correct proportion, but this disproportion, far from creating an unpleasant effect gives more lightness and elegance to this Order which by itself would be a little heavy especially in interior decorations, where the ceiling seems to absorb the features beneath.

The chimney-breast is of right-angled design relieved at the sides by a flat projecting member half-an-inch thick on a continuous ground two inches wide. The front face is decorated with a pilaster nine inches wide recessed in the wall and forming a double frame which rises from the socle above the mantelpiece to a point just below the architrave of the entablature where it crosses over and terminates along the attic. The mirror which is proportioned to the chimney-breast is also of rectangular form and in height is one-and-three-quarters times its width; it is framed by a moulding four inches wide whose principal members are carved with antique ornaments. This mirror is surmounted by a projecting member which forms the attic. It rests with pendant drops on the crossing of the pilaster and rises in right-angled form above the architrave and frieze to a point below the cornice whose first mouldings serve to crown its upper edge. They perform the same service for each of the triglyphs placed at either end perpendicular to the pilasters. In the panel of this attic is a garland in the same taste and similar to those of the overdoors of which I just spoke.

The entablature that runs transversally to the pilasters is made up of architrave, frieze and cornice. Its proportions are relative to the diameter of the pilasters. But to give greater richness to the architrave I have divided the large service into two parts, one above and one below, in concordance with the rules of this order.

The triglyphs which decorate the frieze are distributed at equal intervals and although I have compressed their width by almost one tenth, I am still left with metopes a sixth wider than those of the regular proportion; but the garland with swags hung from two nails with which each metope is decorated corrects this disproportion and at the same time provides a decoration that is agreeable, abundant and without confusion.

Here, gentlemen, you have what I have thought it proper to introduce into the scheme of decoration of which I have tried to speak. I have limited myself to employing only the riches of architecture. I have followed the rules and forms which are truly regular, only permitting myself licence in cases of necessity and in such cases licence and the rules are not mutually destructive. I have banished all arbitrary forms that often display only the anarchy of genius and little knowledge. In the end, I have carefully avoided all affected contours that are fit to tire the eyes of the person of taste and discerning connoisseur.

Johann Joachim
Winckelmann
1717–1768

classical canon • antiquity • abuses

Johann Joachim Winckelmann (1717–1768)

Remarks on the Architecture of the Ancients (1762)

Winckelmann was one of the leading figures of the neo-classical movement whose influence extended to all the arts, including architecture. His life story has become almost legendary. The son of a poor cobbler, he early developed a fervent love for classical antiquity and ancient art and devoted his life to these two causes. His first book, entitled **On the Imitation of the Painting and Sculpture of the Greeks** (1755) established his renown. He was the first historian to draw a sharp distinction between Greek art and its Roman copies, and to base upon this distinction a preference for the 'noble simplicity and calm grandeur' of the original over the degenerate, secondary, Roman versions. The book was widely translated and contributed much to the rise of Greek revival architecture (Wiebenson, 1969) throughout Europe and America. The present book is an application of his new, rigorist aesthetic principles to architecture.

Further reading Greenhalgh, 1978; Honour, 1968; Kaufmann, 1955; Praz, 1972; Rosemblum, 1967.

Chapter II: Concerning Ornamentation in Architecture

After the basic essentials of architecture comes its embellishment, that is the theme of the present chapter. First, I will discuss it in general, then in particular.

A building without decoration is like a healthy person who is reduced to poverty, something no one looks upon as a good thing. Sameness or monotony can be read as a defect in architecture just as much as in writing or in other works of art. Decoration is synonymous with variety. Both in writing and building it provides a change for the intellect and for the eye, and when decoration is combined with simplicity in architecture, the result is beauty. This is because whatever is good and beautiful is that way because it is the way it should be. This means the ornamentation should be suited to the general as well as particular purpose. As far as the first is concerned, it should look like an addition. And as regards the second, it should not change the nature of the place nor its function. It should be thought of as clothing that serves to cover up nakedness. The larger the groundwork of the building, the less decoration it needs – a precious stone should only be set in a gold wire in order to enhance its full sparkle.

Ornamentation was as rare in antique buildings just as in the antique statues. In the former one sees neither ogee-mouldings [editor's note: an ogee moulding is one having the shape of double curve formed by the union of a convex and concave line, resembling an S-shape] nor roundels. The same is true of antique altars. Under the Consulate of Dolabella, shortly before the reign of Augustus, an arch was built in the Claudian aqueduct. And over it there was a projecting travertine cornice that ran diagonally, but in the straight line, something it would have been not so easy to carry out in subsequent times.

Later on, however, architectural variety became a goal achieved through curved elevations or concave and arched lines. The straight members and parts were fragmented and thus diversified. But this variety that adapted itself to each architectural order in a different way was actually not viewed as decoration, which indeed was sought after so little by the ancients that the word that stood for it was applied only to ornamentation in clothes. It was only in later times that the Roman word for decoration was also applied to works of the intellect. For since true good taste went into decline and appearance was put before substance, decoration was no longer looked on as mere addition but entire squares that had been kept empty were suddenly full of it. The result of this was meaningless architecture: for if each part is small, the whole will be small as well, as Aristotle says. Architecture suffered the same fate as the old languages, that became richer after they lost their beauty; this can be proved by the Greek as well as the Roman language, and as architects could neither equal nor surpass their predecessors in beauty, they tried to look richer. . . .

Michelangelo, whose fertile imagination could not be blocked by economy or imitation of the ancients began to spread out in terms of ornamentation and Borromini, who exaggerated these ornaments, created a deterioration in architecture which spread throughout Italy and other countries and will survive, because our times are going even further away from the severity of the ancients, and people are very like the kings of Peru, who had gold plants and flowers in their gardens, and whose greatness was shown by their decadent taste.

classical canon • antiquity • abuses

Johann Joachim
Winckelmann
1717–1768

Robert Adam

Ruins of the Palace . . . at Spalatro, 1764

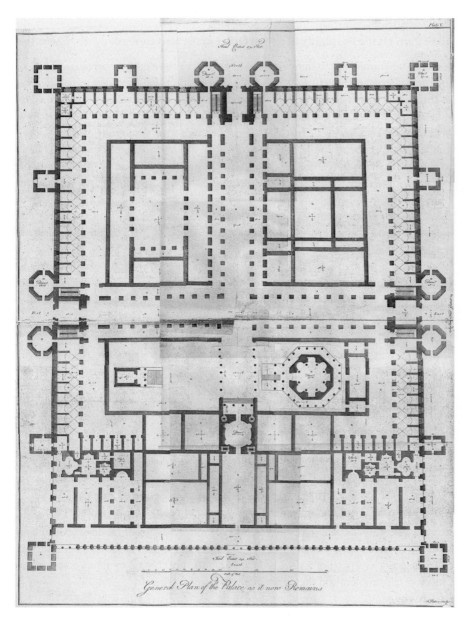

121. Robert Adam. *Ruins of the Palace . . . at Spalatro*. 1764. Plan of the palace.

Marc-Antoine Laugier (1713–1769)

Observations on Architecture (1765)

(p.251)

Sixth Part. Of the Possibility of a New Order of Architecture

It would be humiliating to think that the Greeks have the exclusive privilege of inventing the orders of architecture. Why would other nations be forbidden to get involved in the quarry that the Greeks first exploited, to penetrate beyond the borders where they stopped? This quarry is immense, it is indefinite. Let us be brave enough to believe that there is still a great number of beauties that genius is capable of apprehending and producing in the light of day. All the arts, before genius brought its flame to theirs, are like a universe shrouded in darkness. One only feels a small number of objects within it, by groping at it. Imagination enclosed them in a narrow circumference and sees only amorphic chaos in their arrangement and links. Light illuminates this unknown universe and immediately sight loses itself in its immensity, marvels are created and multiply at every step. It was a small circle of regular things, distinct and striking.

Genius is the light that gives reality and shine to the beautiful effects of nature. Genius seems to create anything because it has the capability to discover everything. Nature seems to have set itself the rule to conceal its riches from us. She only gives us slight indications, in order to excite us to work, only remedy to the anguish of living, to make us taste the pleasures of discovery, the prize that soothes our pain and constantly encourage us to new efforts.

Nature is constantly mixing gold and mud. She keeps her treasures in deep abysses which she only permits access to with great difficulty. Genius comes, removes vulgar coverings, dismisses defective accidents, and lifts the gold out of the mud. And that which seems common and trivial, in passing through its container gains an uncalculable value and price.

Let us not say that arts have boundaries. Destined to activate the riches of nature, their sphere is necessarily indefinite. If they stop at boundaries, it is because genius has ceased to preside over their progress. This is the reason architecture has remained at the point that the Greeks left it at. We are worthy enough to go beyond the ancient limits. Let us dare believe that there are beauties beyond these. Let us take the torch of genius in hand, let us penetrate where only the Greeks have gone, and let us bring back unknown marvels from there.

The point is to create a new order of architecture. Let us establish first the conditions of the problem and then indicate the ways of solving it.

(p.265)

Sixth Part, Chapter II. Ways of Solving the Problem

There are only two ways to innovate in architecture. The first is to invent new mouldings whose form is unknown heretofore. The second is to combine in a new way old mouldings.

We call mouldings all the irregularities of the surface. These irregularities can only be in either straight or curved lines, in relief or recessed. The straight mouldings which are in relief or recessed can only have three differences among each other. They form either a straight angle or an acute angle or an obtuse angle.

The ones with a straight angle are called quartered. The ones with an acute angle are called acutangles, those with an obtuse angle are called obtusangles.

rigorism • essentialism • urbanisation of architecture • planning

Denis Diderot (1713–1784)

'My Say on Architecture', 'A brief Corollary on What Went Before' in *Essais sur la Peinture* (written 1766?; published 1793)

This, translated as 'My Say on Architecture' and 'A Brief Corollary on What Went Before', originally belonged to a work partly published in 1766, entitled **Essays on Painting**. Republished in its entirety under the Directoire, it had some success and good reviews. But the real impact was felt among the German romantics. In 1796, Goethe introduced Schiller to the piece. It was admired for its rejection of the 'classical lie' which defined beauty as the outcome of the alliance of art and nature. Goethe saw Diderot's description as consistent with the true laws of nature (Goethe, 1772; Mortier, 1955; Rouge, 1949). **Further reading** Knight, 1968.

Denis Diderot
1713–1784

My Say on Architecture

My purpose here, my friend, is not to examine the character of the different orders of architecture. And even less to weigh the advantages of Greek and Roman architecture against the prerogatives of the Gothic, to show you how the latter expands the space within a building through the height of its vaults and the lightness of its columns, destroys the imposing mass of the building from the outside through the multitude and the bad taste of its ornaments; nor to argue in favour of the analogy between the obscurity of the stained glass and the incomprehensible nature of the adored being and the dark thoughts of the beholder. It is rather to convince you that without architecture, there is no painting and no sculpture, and that it is in art, that has no substitute under the sun, that the two imitative arts owe their origin and progress.

I will end here my chapter on architecture. All its art is contained in these three words: solidity or security, fitness and symmetry. From whence one may conclude that this system of measures of the rigorous Vitruvian orders seem to have been invented to lead to monotony and to suffocate genius.

I will not end this paragraph without giving you a small problem to resolve.

It is said of Saint Peter's in Rome that its proportions are so perfectly applied that the building loses its size and scale when seen for the first time; so much so that it can be said that *Magnus esse, sentiri parvus* [It may well be big, but it feels small].

Upon which, one could reason thus. What good is it to have such admirable proportions? To make a great thing appear small and common? It would seem that it would have been better to shun them in this case, and that it would have been of more use to produce the opposite effect, and to have given grandeur to an ordinary and common thing.

One answer is that, in truth, the building would have appeared bigger at first sight if one had sacrificed the proportions artfully. But, then, the question is which was to be preferred? To produce a great and sudden admiration or one that began small, grew little by little, to at last become great and lasting through thoughtful and detailed examination.

One might allow that, everything being equal, a thin and slender man will look taller than a well-proportioned one; but one may also ask which one of these two men we will admire most; and whether the first would agree to let himself be reduced to the more rigorous proportions of antiquity, at the risk of losing something of his apparent height.

One may ask, furthermore, whether the narrow building made bigger through art winds up being perceived as small as it is in reality, as opposed to the big building that the art of proportions have given an ordinary and common appearance to, winds up being perceived as big thanks to the effect of the decrease of the unfavourable proportions by the necessary ensuing comparison of the beholder himself to parts of the building.

Denis Diderot
1713–1784

One reply is that it is not surprising that a man would sacrifice his apparent height by accepting rigorous proportions because he is not ignorant of the fact that it is this very rigour in the proportion of his limbs that he will obtain the real satisfaction of meeting, as perfectly as possible, the real functions of life; that proportion is what power, dignity, grace, in a word beauty which utility is always the basis of. But it is not the same case with a building because it has one single object, one single aim.

We deny that the comparison of the beholder with parts of the building creates the expected effect and repairs the unfavourable illusion of the first impression. To near a given statue that suddenly becomes colossal, is very surprising, however, that is for certain. One perceives the building as much bigger than we thought. But as soon as our back is turned, the general power of all the other parts of the building dominate once again and restore the building, big in itself, to an ordinary and common appearance. In such a way that, on one hand, each detail appears great, while all the rest appear small and common. While in the opposite system of irregularity, every detail appears small while all the rest remains extraordinary, imposing and large.

The talent of increasing the size of objects through the magic of art, and that of concealing enormity through the understanding of proportions, are assuredly two great talents: but which is the greatest of the two? Which is the one the architect should prefer? How should Saint Peter's in Rome have been fashioned? Was it better to reduce it to an ordinary and common effect through the strict obedience to proportions rather than to give it an imposing appearance, through a less severe and regular order?

One should not choose too hastily, for Saint Peter's, thanks to its celebrated proportions, after all, either never obtains, or obtains only in the long run, that which we would have granted it constantly and suddenly in another system. What is an accord that impedes the general effect? What is a fault that gives value to the whole?

There is the quarrel between Gothic and architecture and Greek or Roman architecture, proposed in its full force. [...]

Another question: if we impoverish architecture in subjecting it to measures, modules, it should need to recognise only the rule of variety of fitnesses. Wouldn't we do the same for painting, sculpture and all the other arts, children of drawing, in subjugating the figures to given heights of heads, and these heads to given lengths of noses? Would we not, in so doing, have turned science, conditions, characters, passions, and other organisations, a silly matter of rule and compass? ...

A Brief Corollary on What Went Before

But what do all these principles mean, if taste is nothing but whim, and if there is no eternal, immutable rule of beauty?

If taste is a matter of whim, if there is no rule of beauty, where do the delicious emotions come from that arise so suddenly, so involuntarily, so tumultuously in the depth of our souls, that dilates or tightens them, that force tears of joy, of pain, of admiration from our eyes at the sight of a great physical phenomenon or on hearing the tale of a great moral trait? Be silent, Sophist! You will never persuade my heart that it is wrong for it to quiver, my entrails that they are wrong to throb.

The true, the good and the beautiful are closely bound together. Add to the two first a rare, stunning circumstance and the true will be beautiful, and the good will be beautiful. If the solution to the problem of the three bodies is nothing but the movement of three given points on a scrap of paper, it is nothing, just a pure speculation. But if one of these three bodies is the star that lights up our day, the other, the planet that lights up our night; and the third, the globe we dwell on: suddenly, the truth becomes great and beautiful. [...]

Michelangelo gave to the dome of Saint Peter's in Rome the most beautiful form possible. The geometer, de la Hire, struck with this form, traced its profile, and found that it is the curve of the greatest resistance. Who is it that inspired this curve to Michelangelo, among the infinite number of curves he could have chosen? The daily experience of his life, that's what. It is this curve that suggests to the master carpenter, just as much as to the sublime Euler, the angle of the mainstay of a wall that is threatened with ruin. The same as that which gives the wing of a windmill the inclination which is the most favourable to the movement of rotation. The same, again, that is often involved, in its subtle calculation, elements that the geometry of the Academie would not know how to grasp.

Experience and study. These are the preliminaries for one who makes and for one who juges. But then I demand sensitivity. But the same way we see men who practise justice, goodness, virtue from nothing but a well understood interest, the spirit and a taste for order, without feeling their delights and pleasures, there can also be taste without sensitivity, and sensitivity without taste. Sensitivity, when it is extreme, is undiscerning. Everything moves it indiscriminately. One will tell you, 'That is beautiful'. The other will be moved, transported, inebriated. [...] He will mumble. He will be unable to find the words that express the state of his soul.

The happiest, beyond any doubt is the latter. The best judge? Another matter. Cold, severe, calm observers of nature often know better the delicate chords that must be plucked. They create enthusiasms without being enthusiasts themselves. [...]

Whence the uncertainty of any work of genius. It is alone. It is appreciated only by being related to nature immediately. And who knows how to get there? Only another man of genius.

aesthetisation of architecture • representation • truth • illusion

Denis Diderot
1713–1784

Giovanni Battista Piranesi (1720–1778)

Diverse Manners of Ornamenting Chimneys (1769)

Giovanni Battista
Piranesi
1720–1778

In **Parere sull' Archittetura**, Piranesi, one of the most renowned artist–engravers in history, composed as a dialogue between Didascalo, a master who defends tradition, and a novice, Protopiro, who argues for the novelties of the rigorist position of Laugier (1753, 1765) and Winckelmann (1755) (Wilton-Ely, 1978, ch. 4). In the end, Didascalo, Piranesi's mouthpiece, gets the better of his opponent. Piranesi, whose views have been characterised as 'negative Utopian' (Tafuri, 1976), embraced the ideals of the heavily ornamented late-empire Roman architecture in opposition to the rigorists like Laugier and Wincklemann who preached a new neo-classical rationalism in architectural form and a theory of functional simplicity. No less critical of baroque architecture than the rigorists, rather than join the attempts to correct and reform, he chose to take its excesses and push them to their utmost, near freakish, extremes (Yourcenar, 1961). The following text is a succinct statement of his position.

Further reading Fleming, 1962; Kaufmann, 1958; Wilton-Ely, 1972, 1978; Wittkower, 1938, 1975.

The study of Architecture, having been carried by our ancestors to the highest pitch of perfection, seems now in decline, and returning again to barbarism. What irregularities in columns, in architraves, in pediments, in cupolas; and above all what extravagance in ornaments! One would think that ornaments are used in works of architecture, not to embellish them, but to render them ugly. I know indeed that in this caprice those for whom the buildings are made has often more part than the architect who makes the design.

Let the architect be as extravagant as he pleases, so he destroy not architecture, but give to every member its proper character. Let the artist be free to drape statue or figure in paintings as he likes best, let him adjust the folds and garments with the greatest variety he is able; but let it be always so that it may appear a human body and not a block covered with drapery. Let all the variety of graces be given too with it. This the ancients had in view: we ought to follow their manner, and observe the kinds of ornaments used by them, the manner in which they disposed them to make them harmonise with the whole.

It will perhaps appear to some people, the poorness of whose ideas renders them above measure lovers of simplicity, that these my designs are overloaded with ornaments, and the saying of Montesqieu will once more be objected to me, *that a building loaded with ornaments is an enigma to the eyes, as a confused poem is to the mind*; and I again answer that I am as much an enemy to enigmas and confusion as Montesquieu or anyone else is, and that I am as much as any one else against a multiplicity of ornaments that can only offend the eye and confound it. Not to be so would be a mistake of the same kind as that committed by someone who blamed the confusion and assault in a bad concert to the multiplicity of voices and instruments rather than on the ignorance of the composer or the bad quality of the musicians. In the same manner precisely, what offends and confounds the eye, in a work of architecture, is the want of the *high* and *low*, which constitutes as well in art as nature a certain variety of degrees, and pre-eminence of merit, so that some parts appear principal, and others serve only to accompany the first. Let the architects artfully make use of this precaution, and I am certain that a multiplicity of ornaments will not present to the eye a confusion of objects, but a graceful and pleasing disposition of things.

That is, the multiplicity of ornaments ought not so much to be measured by their quantity and number, as by the quality of the works they are employed in.

Even the grotesque has its beauty, and gives pleasure; and that, the Chinese manner be as far distant from the Grecian, and perhaps more so than the Egyptian and Tuscan, we are delighted to have our rooms and apartments fitted up after the Chinese manner. Mankind is too fond of variety to be always pleased with the same decorations: we are alternately pleased with the gay and the serious, and even with the pathetic, nay the horror of a battle has its beauty, and *out of fear springs pleasure*.

The law, which some people would impose upon us of doing nothing but what is Grecian, is indeed very unjust. Must the genius of our artists be so basely enslaved to the Grecian manners, as not to dare to take what is beautiful elsewhere, if it be not of Grecian manners, not of Grecian origin? But let us at last shake off this shameful yoke, and if the Egyptians, and Tuscans present to us, in their monuments, beauty, grace and elegance, let us borrow from their stock, not fertilely copying from others, for this would reduce architecture and the noble arts to a pitiful mechanism, and would deserve blame instead of praise from the public, who seek for novelty, and who would not form the most advantageous idea of an artist, as was perhaps the opinion some years ago, for a good design, if it was only a copy of some ancient work. No, an artist, who would do himself honour, and acquire a name, must not content himself with copying faithfully the ancients, but studying their works he ought to show himself of an inventive, and, I had almost said, of a creating genius; and by prudently combining the Grecian, the Tuscan, and the Egyptian together, he ought to open himself a road to the finding out of new ornaments and new manners.

aesthetisation of architecture • emotions • passions • sentiments • orientalism

Pierre Patte (1723–1804)

A Report on the Most Important Objects in Architecture (1769)

Patte, a student of Boffrand, Le Camus de Mézières and J.F. Blondel at the Académie Royale d'Architecture who built a career as an architectural writer and critic, was one of the most influential theoreticians in his field in the eighteenth century. In his **Monuments** (1765) he described and illustrated with his own engravings each one of the numerous squares dedicated to Louis XV. The book has been seen as the authority on the functionalist aesthetic principles which were at work during the greatest period of French city planning (Blomfield, 1973, II). For Patte, **Les objects les plus importants** ('the most important objects in architecture') the title of his book of 1769, are not the Orders, proportion or ornamentation. They are related rather to purely functional aspects since they are capable of leading to rationally correct solutions. His praise for Gothic structural efficiency echoes that of Frezier. In this tradition, he attacks the pseudo-functional notions of 'convenance' and 'distribution' which he sees merely as pretexts for many architects to disregard truly functional aspects of construction. From the early conception of Soufflot's design for the Dome of the Eglise Sainte-Geneviève in the 1770s, Patte was antagonistic, seeing it as an example of pseudo-functionalism which dismissed true principles of construction. Within a few months, one of the most celebrated eighteenth-century architectural quarrels flared up and split the world of architecture for years (Middleton, 1962, 1963). Patte's most adamant opponent – Soufflot's staunchest defender – was Cochin. In 1801, Patte was still preoccupied with the issue, as revealed in his **Analyse Raisonnée** (Mathieu, 1940; Mondain-Monval, 1918).

Article the Second. On Harmful Urban Disposition. Concerning the Most Advantageous Manner in which the Parts of a Town Should be Disposed

Despite the multitude of Towns that have been built until the present day in all parts of the world, none has yet existed that can be truly cited as a model. Chance has no less presided over their general disposition than over their initial location. To be convinced of this, one need only glance at them to see that all are simply masses of houses arranged without order, without reference to any overall well-argued plan and that the entire merit of the most praised of Capitals consists solely in a few areas that are moderately well built, in a few streets that are passably well laid out, or in a few public monuments that may be commended either due to their overall size or the good taste shown in their architectural design. Everywhere it will be seen that all things have been sacrificed to grandeur, to magnificence, but no effort has ever been made to procure true well-being for men, to preserve their lives, their health, their property, or to ensure that the air is salubrious in their respective lodgings.

Pierre Patte
1723–1804

If we look closely at a large Town, what strikes the eye immediately is the ordure that flows openly in the gutters before it enters the sewers and the foul odours that it gives off as it passes. Further, the blood of slaughterhouses flows down the middle of the street and offers some horrible and revolting spectacle at every step.

[...]

In short, Towns may be seen everywhere to be places of dirt, disease and discomfort.

Regarding the disposition of streets, one should not imitate Babylon, all of whose houses were separated by ploughed earth and spacious gardens adjoining them, which gave to that City an immense size. Neither should one take as an example the Cities of China, whose streets, although moderately wide, have in most cases only a ground floor. There is no doubt that such arrangements make Towns extremely extensive and give them more the appearance than the reality of Grandeur. And neither do all our great Capitals in Europe, Paris, Lyons, Venice, Naples, whose streets are very narrow, and whose houses rise as high as five or six storeys, which makes these Cities generally unhealthy, deserve to serve as models.

It is not necessary to indicate the place that should preferably be assigned to public monuments in the disposition of a Town or City. Their allotted purpose should cause us to feel which place would be most fitting for them, and what size. There are some that should be placed on the river bank, and others on the outskirts, others in the centre, and yet others scattered among the various areas of a Town or City. The essential point is to envisage, when situating them, their use, the convenience or needs of the inhabitants and above all to proceed in a manner suited to ensuring the greatest possible space for those that will be the most frequented.

In the case of markets for example, it is necessary to avoid the inconveniences that are to be observed in most of those in our Towns and Cities in Europe. [...] On the contrary, in Turkey, Persia and the Orient, the bazaar is an ornament of the Town and is built in stone with gateways at the entrances. Bazaars announce their purpose with great and long galleries illuminated by domes where goods and commodities of all kinds are sheltered from the rain and heat.

Apart from the fact that such abuses corrupt the air of a Town, how unseemly it is to observe that in all areas of Capitals as well ordered as Paris, London, Madrid and others the inhabitants relieve themselves publicly in the streets in full view of the world and show themselves thus in full daylight, this at almost every step one takes, under the gaze of the weaker sex in postures so ill suited to the demands of decency, being a breach equally of good manners and modesty. In Constantinople, any person relieving himself in the street is beaten. In Great Cairo, Damascus and in all those places we regard as barbarous, no such practice is tolerated.

[...]

First, although porticos provide permanent shelter from rain, sun and accidents caused by carriages to those on foot, it is far from being the case that they are embellishments in a Town. They usually vary in shape from building to building, as well as in height. Since the middle of the street is used now only by carriages and beasts of burden, it is completely neglected, hence the fact that the streets become a species of sewer for which no person is willing to take responsibility. Moreover, porticos darken the ground floors of houses and shops, and make the streets dangerous at night.

Second, the pavements for those on foot are no less responsible for the neglect of the middle of the street than are the porches of the buildings. The unpleasantness of the streets of the English Capital are well-known in this regard. [...]

Third, the disposition of the streets of Paris, Madrid, Naples and other cities, although more advantageous with respect to the houses and cleanliness, are the daily cause of accidents because their streets are generally too narrow and the way for carriages is not distinct from that for persons on foot, with the result that the latter are frequently trampled by horses, or risk being knocked down. Another unpleasant fact is that it is hardly possible to walk in the street without being covered in mud by carriages or drenched by water draining from the roofs when it rains.

The Chinese are the only people which seems to have taken some precautions in this regard in the disposition of their main streets, which in some cases may be up to one hundred and twenty feet wide. They divide this space into three parts: the middle part is reserved for persons on foot and palanquins, and the two other parts, running along the fronts of the houses, are intended for the passage of beasts of burden and carriages.

Pierre Patte
1723–1804

§ III. How the cleanliness of a Town or City may be ensured by uniting the sewers with the water conduits

[...] with the help of our system there would be no further need, where repairs to the pipes are concerned, to remove the paving of the streets and thus to hinder passage in the public thoroughfares. Within such an underground aqueduct one would remedy with ease all the accidents that may arise, which could not be either frequent or grave, given that the conduits would be placed in robust and spacious manner and would not therefore suffer from the weight of carriages or their own weight, as is the case when they are made in lead or placed in the earth without precaution.

But another utility of the highest importance offered by such underground vaults placed under the public thoroughfare is that they make it possible to do without all the carts that continually occupy it. [...] In all the above explanations, the reader will have noticed how many advantages such arrangements would provide for any Town. Its cleanliness, salubrity, the distribution of its water supply and the removal of its ordure would be done with ease and without difficulty. The more thought is given to this, the more I am convinced that the reader will be persuaded that it is only by the unification of the sewers with the conduits for water that it may be hoped to equip any Town fittingly and successfully.

§ IV. On the manner in which septic tanks may be rectified and the air purified in houses

By means of our method of underground aqueducts, it is also easy to modify the septic tanks that cause in the houses of a Town such daily infection and spread foul odours throughout the neighbourhood when it is necessary to empty them. One need only locate the privies on the ground floor in all cases and to make their discharge tank shallow and in the form of a funnel. Then, by placing at the bottom a pipe solidly fixed and inclined towards the aqueduct, the excrement would be led there as it is deposited. With the intention of accelerating their flow, it would be necessary to proceed so as to direct through the small tank that we are dealing with here all the waters of the house, that of the roofs, those which come from the kitchens, those of the inner courtyards and others. Through this process, these places would be constantly washed through and the ordure carried away regularly and there could therefore be no odour in the house due to their remaining there.

Article the Third. Instructions to a Young Architect

Be this as it may, I exhort you not to be discouraged and to work ever harder to perfect yourself, both in theory and in practice. For skill in drawing does not suffice alone for excellence in Architecture. On the contrary, nothing is more commonplace than an excellent Draughtsman making a very mediocre Architect, witness Oppenore, Meissonnier [editor's note: Juste Aurèle Meissonnier was a French designer born in Turin. First a goldsmith, he was appointed designer to the king under Louis XV, a position he held until his death], Germain and Pinault. Architectural drawing, if unenlightened by experience, is no more than an agreeable illusion of which the actual execution of the building usually destroys the charm: it is no more than a pretty picture of Architecture and that is all. You must believe that there is an immense difference between the effect produced by an edifice on paper and that which it produces on the site. The dome of the *Invalides* drawn geometrically as it stands will appear heavy, cumbersome, without aesthetic proportions, but what elegance it has in the execution! Is there anything so graceful and so happily achieved? That the distinctive quality of a great Architect – to be able to judge in advance that which one's thoughts will become once in place, to assess the effect of the frontispieces, foreshortened sections and perspective of a projected design so that all the diverse parts of its whole should be so interlinked that from their assembly springs that form of mute harmony where nothing is contradictory, nothing confused, where nothing interrupts the unity of the design, but on the contrary where all tends to aggrandise objects, to highlight them, producing a form of magical enchantment for the eye. It is the meeting of practice and theory that will instruct you on all such relationships.

[...]

Examine the constructions of the Goths, whose edifices should be studied ceaselessly by all Builders, instead of simply contenting themselves with admiring them. You will see with what intelligence they dispose their materials.

It is customary to use stone for construction in the manner in which nature has disposed it during its formation, that is to say stone which is found in layers must be placed in the same manner in buildings, but conversely stone formed in the mass and whose parts therefore do not testify to any particular position, such as marble, sandstone and rock, may be laid in any manner. It is experience which has taught us that stone laid down in layers has greater consistency and solidity when used in buildings in accordance with its position in the quarry. One could hardly find a better comparison than that between the great resistance of the different stony masses in their employment than that with the pages of a book: if one places a weight on a book perpendicular to its edge, it may be remarked that the weight will tend to separate the pages, but if on the contrary one places that same weight horizontally on the book, on its flat face, it can be seen that it joins the pages one to another with even greater firmness.

This does not mean that stone has not often been employed other than in accordance with its natural layering. The Gothic builders habitually formed their small columns in this manner.

There are many experiments that would be desirable to discover what loads may be supported by the different types of stone, for example, what weight a pillar two feet in diameter and of a given height [...] may bear without breaking or crumbling [...] But what is this relative weight and to what level may it increase? This is what remains to be demonstrated. Failing such knowledge, we constantly trust to chance and multiply structural elements without necessity, tending to include more rather than less: it would appear that the Goths knew more than we in this respect ...

Pierre Patte
1723–1804

efficiency • economisation • fit • utility • urbanisation of architecture • planning

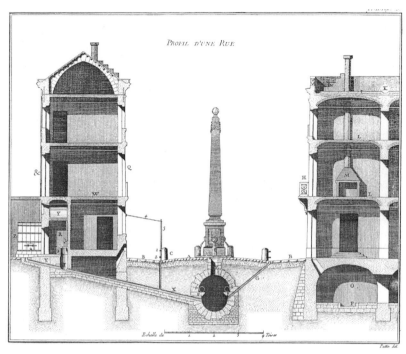

122. Pierre Patte. *Mémoire sur les objets les plus importants de l'architecture*. 1769. Section of buildings and street showing foundations and the piping of drainage, sewage and heating as an integrated system.

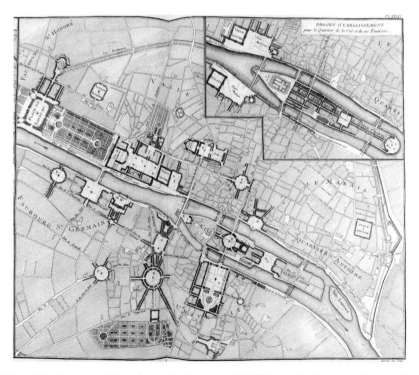

123. Pierre Patte. *Monuments érigés en France à la gloire de Louis XV*. 1765. Plan of Paris showing different locations proposed for placing the statue of Louis XV as well as modifications of the public spaces and the urban tissue.

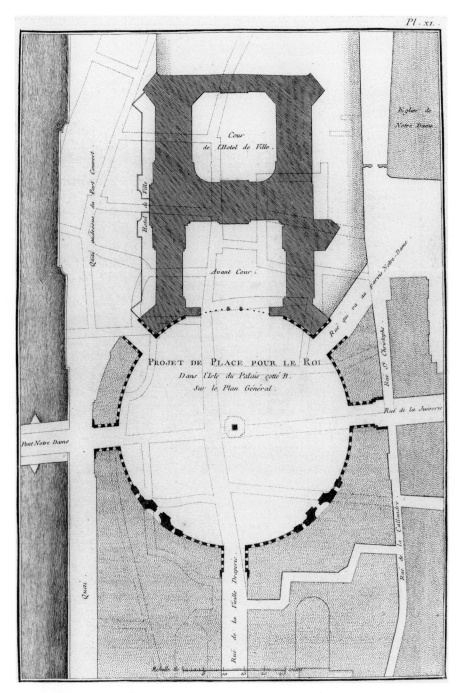

124., 124b. Pierre Patte. *Monuments érigés en France à la gloire de Louis XV*. 1765. Proposals for inserting regularly shaped public spaces in the old irregular tissue of historical Paris. Notice the indifference with which the interiors of the buildings affected are treated.

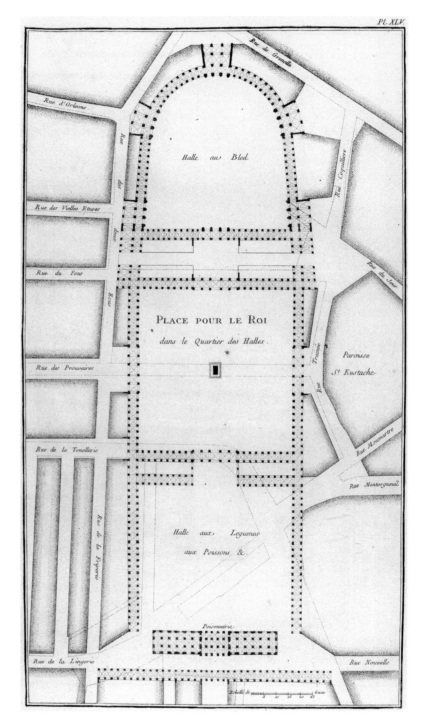

Pierre Patte. *Monuments érigés en France à la gloire de Louis XV*. 1765.

Charles Nicolas Cochin (1715–1790)

Letter from an Architectural Engraver to Monsieur Patte (1770)

(See Cochin 1754)

Like you, I have read that Mr Parent has written about the thrust of vaults, archivolts, keystones, counter-keystones, and their action on their piedroits, and that they determine their force, depending on their weight and thrust; I am also aware that in his treatise on mechanics, Mr de la Hire has also demonstrated the arrangement that the archivolts of a vault can be given to make it durable, and that he has established the exact rules for finding the strength that the piedroits or supporting walls must have to resist the thrust under any and all circumstances. After that, my dear Colleague, according to you it is no longer permissible to attempt new research, nor to employ new means; operating on other principles would be to risk or, to put it a better way, to work towards the collapse of a building ... to these new discoveries, to this profound study, to acquired experience, and to the careful calculations of Mr Soufflot we are going to owe the construction of a dome that will prove to posterity the progress that we have made in our time in the art of building, by casting aside the slavish principles to which, before him, all vaults and domes seemed to be subjected, and I confess in good faith that until then I had believed in the observations and theories of Parent and de la Hire ... and if the reason of construction requires variety, then why should one want to make a dome, and the means to build it, a dogma, a determined axiom, and deprive it of the arbitrariness that is the wellspring of genius, masterpieces and discoveries? ... It seems to me, however, considering the treatise that you have printed, based on his principles (first plate, first figure in your Dissertation on the dome of Saint Genevieve), that this dome or this so-called rule does not produce a fine effect on the proportions of a church, neither inside nor outside. That may be because the *roof of the church* on which you are planning to build it requires it to have a better, stronger and more elegant form. In truth, my dear Colleague, how can one presume to forbid rules, when the means of rejecting them are so weak (*how can less than nothing be extracted from nothing*)? For rules can be false or lost only if, for the project as a whole, the good effect of any edifice, the optical point from which it must be seen, comes into conflict with how they are used. After that, how must one operate? You do not know, and neither do I; for Fontana has mentioned nothing about it; and if he had, you would have as well.

Let us return to architecture. Where has Mr Patte learned what he announces to us as an undeniable principle: that everything must be elevated, from the lowest foundations to the rooftop, with the footing set back or banked? If that were true, then none of the Gothic churches would still be standing today. Experience disproves it; just let him observe our admirable parish. On the contrary, in general, although the Gothic churches do not do justice to the taste of their architects, they do infinite justice to their intelligence in the art of building lightly and sturdily at the same time: it can even be said that, in this respect at least, they were superior to the Italians.

How do we know whether Mr Soufflot, who is especially familiar with all the edifices of this type, and who has ceaselessly conducted research on them, would not have found the means to combine the noble decoration of the Greeks with the lightness of Gothic architecture? Mr Patte, verily, has not envisaged things from that angle; but why would we not grant that degree of confidence to the experience of Mr Soufflot, which is proven, rather than to Mr Patte, which is more than dubious? If we consider that the vault which can have the most thrust does not bear on the wall, why would we not assume that Mr Soufflot would have combined his thrusts with the resistance, that the thing would be in perfect balance, and that therefore the pillars would only have to carry a load that would act perpendicularly, and in that case, exert a force that is more than sufficient? That is what I am convinced of, and what I believe I owe to the esteem of Mr Soufflot among the experienced architects.

The little scoundrel has discovered that the algebraic equation is false in relation to the construction and the form of the dome of Saint Genevieve church. A young German, one of his talented friends, has done it as well as he has, but Mr Patte had badly explained to him what he was asking. Do not be surprised, Mr Patte is a manufacturer of neither algebra nor architecture; he is merely a merchant. You are familiar with the hazards to which we expose ourselves when we fail to develop ...

rigorism • essentialism • scientification

Louis-Sébastien Mercier (1740–1814)

The year 2440 (1770)

This Utopian work of fiction depicts an inhabitant of the *Ancien Régime* Paris, who after a slumber of almost 700 years, is given a guided tour of the new Paris. In its conceptions of city planning, the book seems to anticipate twentieth-century developments. Like almost all Mercier's many novels, it reveals a radically critical attitude towards the conservative cultural and social values of the *Ancien Régime*.

Chapter VII: The New Paris

See how all these houses are equipped with what is most necessary and most useful to life. What cleanliness! What freshness of the air is the result! Look at these comfortable, elegant buildings. No longer constructed are those dreadful chimneys whose fall threatens every passer-by. No longer do roofs have that Gothic slope which, at the slightest wind, causes tiles to slide down into the most populous streets.

We climbed to the top of a house up a well-lit stairway. What a pleasure it was for I who love an open view and clean air, to discover a terrace ornamented with pots of flowers and covered over with a perfumed bower. The top of each house had a similar terrace – so much so that the roofs, all of equal height, together formed a sort of vast garden and the Town, seen from high on a tower, was crowned with flowers, fruit and verdure.

I have no need to add that the Hôtel-Dieu general hospital was no longer enclosed in the centre of the city. If some stranger or some citizen, I was told, fell ill away from his native country or family, we do not imprison him, as you did in your time, in a disgusting bed, lying between a corpse and a dying man, there to breathe the poisoned exhalations of death, thus transforming what was no more than an inconvenience into a cruel illness.

We have divided the Hôtel-Dieu into twenty smaller houses scattered throughout the city. By this means, the bad air that this pit of horror once exhaled is dispersed and has ceased to be a danger to the capital. [...]

We no longer see that horrible mixture, that revolting confusion, heralding more a place of vengeance rather than one of charity. Each patient has his own bed and may expire without accusing human nature [...] When one's suffering comes only from nature, one suffers in silence.

Chapter XLIV and Last: Versailles

I arrive, my gaze seeks out that superb palace where once were determined the destinies of more than one Nation. How surprised I was! I saw only ruins, broken walls, mutilated statues, a few porticos half toppled over allowed a confused glimpse of splendour: I was walking through the ruins when I came across an old man sitting on the capital of a column. 'Oh!' I said to him. 'What became of this vast palace?' He replied, 'It collapsed.' 'How so?' 'It collapsed in on itself. A man, in his sinful and impatient pride, wished to force nature to his will, piling construction upon construction; greedy in his capricious will, he tired his subjects. Here all the money of the Kingdom was swallowed up. Here flowed a river of tears to form those fountain basins of which no trace now remains. This is all that remains of a colossus built by a million hands at the price of so much painful effort. This palace was wrong from its very foundations. It was made in the image of the grandeur of he who built it. The kings who succeeded him were obliged to flee lest they be crushed. May these ruins cry out to all sovereigns that all those who abuse a transient power reveal no more than their weakness to the generation that follows them...' With these words, his tears flowed in torrents and he looked up to the sky with great melancholy. 'Why do you weep?' I asked. 'Everybody is happy and these ruins certainly do not herald public destitution.' At this he raised his voice, crying, 'Ah! Alas, know thou that I am that Louis XIV who built this triple palace. Divine Justice has rekindled the light of my days on earth in order that I may contemplate more closely my unhappy works... How fragile are the monuments of sinful pride!... I weep now and will weep forever... Ah! Why did I not know...' I was about to question him when one of the serpents still numerous in that place darted from a broken stub of column around which it had been entwined, bit me on the neck, and I awoke.

[...]

The End

[...] Who built the circuses, theatres and baths? [...] Crowned monsters whose tyrannical pride crushed one half of the people to delight the eye of the other half. The enormous pyramids of which Egypt boasts are monuments to despotism. Republicans build aqueducts, canals, roads, public squares, markets, but every palace built by a monarch is the germ of impending calamity.

efficiency • economisation • fit • utility • social reform • democratisation • urbanisation of architecture • planning

Louis-Sébastien
Mercier
1740–1814

Jacques-François Blondel (1705–1774)

Lessons on Architecture (Vol. I) (1771)

(See Blondel 1752)

Introduction

[. . .]

The skilful Architect draws the onlooker into the mysteries of Art. To do so he must avoid all sterile superfluity in his designs; he must learn to manage his resources so that the particular character to be given to each edifice is not confused. He must be able, using happy transitions from the grave to the elegant, from the simple to the complex, to vary his works by employing in some cases masses that are strong or light, shortened or pyramidal forms, rectilinear or sinuous, in others, giving more or less movement to his design, either by using continuous masses, or preferring projecting sections and intermediate masses. Without departing from the spirit of fitness (*convenance*), he must often prefer proud and masculine beauty to a sweet, naïve character, and sometimes, on the contrary, he will employ the light and delicate gracefulness of Art.

In order to succeed in choosing with good taste that which we must imitate and that which we must reject in the works of our predecessors, we have already said, and we repeat it here, students of Architecture must see drawing as the basis of all their work, not in order to become Painters, Sculptors or Decorative Artists themselves, each of the latter Arts requiring that one devote oneself wholly to it, but because in order to be good Architects they must be at least moderately capable of drawing the overall design, the ornamental work, the surrounding landscape, and must know the rules of perspective and the art of modelling if they are to be at the very least capable of assessing correctly the talents of the Artists they must one day associate in work. They should nonetheless be quite convinced that it is also dangerous for them to be in complete ignorance of the Sciences, although they must avoid giving themselves up to that study with an energy and enthusiasm that almost always carries the student beyond the goal he must set himself. For, in the first case, with cold designs deprived of the ornamentation that should embellish them, they will be obliged to hand over their design to other hands, who will often not do them justice, with the result that these beauties, which should be no more than accessories in Architecture, become obstacles to the primordial beauties which form its essence.

[. . .]

Today, through an irresponsibility that is just as blameworthy, the *gravitas* suited to exterior decorative work is applied inside apartments: our furniture is designed in a manner experience has taught us to avoid, by which I mean those square forms whose corners are so offensive to the eye, and impede the movements of persons assembled in our places of residence and in many cases, the excuse is used that these shapes are in imitation of those of the Greeks, without reflecting that they employed them only in their Temples or in the exterior decoration of their public edifices and that they are never fitting, or only very rarely, in those things that are intended merely for comfort or for everyday use. What could be more absurd for example that to overload the panelling of a lady's boudoir with the same garlands of oak and laurel used in Rome to decorate the Triumphal Arches intended to hand down to posterity news of the victories of Heroes? A perhaps even more culpable carelessness are those Chinese rock piles and ornaments used so copiously for twenty years now in all our buildings and even inside our Places of Worship. Students should beware – imitation requires discernment [...]

It was in vain that the principles of the art were laid down by the great masters, the title of creator seems to some of those who emulate them to be preferable to that of imitator, with the result that under the pretext of making new styles of column they have invented the idea of overloading the main shaft with various bumps, themselves overloaded with inappropriate decorative ornamentation. They have shortened columns to convert the order into the Attic form, they have twisted the shafts, invented new bases, placed symbols on their capitals, thinking to symbolise the Orders. They have abused pedestals and have even failed to shrink from shortening their entablatures: most of these liberties came in with Borromini, doubtless an Architect of genius, but also as incorrect as he was lax. [...]

Jacques-François
Blondel
1705–1774

Chapter II. The Precepts of the Art, Taken From the Proportions of the Orders of Greek and Roman Architecture

[...]

[...] that mute poetry, that smooth, firm and vigorous colouring, in a word, that tender, touching strong or terrible melody that can be borrowed from Poetry, Painting or Music and can be added to the diverse compositions made in Architecture. In addition, our manner of reasoning, seeking and feeling may perhaps not be that of most of our Contemporaries, nor that of our Successors [...]

Concerning originality in Architecture

We say: 'This design is a new one, the style of its ordonnance is original, quite unusual, very uncommon', when we see in the decoration that the creative genius of the Architect has been able to go beyond the boundaries of the Art, without however travelling too far from the precepts handed down, the intention being to apply widely in his buildings interesting forms of Architecture and certain allegories in its ornamentation, but both must start out from the intention with which the edifice was constructed. Such a design is one in which the movement to be seen in the disposition of the visible masses of the building is in harmony with the pyramidal parts of its façades, that which has nothing trivial in it, manifesting through the character of its Architecture a grave but noble disposition of its parts – pleasant but simple, grand but never gigantic. Such types of form are also justly admired when they are used in a manner commensurate with the type of the edifice [...]

Concerning pyramidal Architecture

We commonly say: 'This Architecture is pyramidal in style', when we wish to express the fact that the Architect has built for this reason a top floor above that which marks the top of the building proper, or when, without recourse to this method, he has planned, in making the building's frontispiece project quite far, that it should dominate sufficiently through an optical effect, although he has kept the storeys of his façades at the same height.

[...]

Concerning the sense of what is fitting in Architecture

We say that the design of a building is fitting when we have observed that the exterior disposition of its parts and the main parts of its decoration bear an absolute relation to the intention which originally gave rise to its construction, when a sense of that which is fitting has presided over it, and that a feeling for what is appropriate has been observed exactly, and the Designer has incorporated into his design the style and the character which he needed to choose in order to express [...] We should beware, to ignore the role of colour in Architecture is to remain content with that which is merely habitual, to fail to see the poetry of this Art: an edifice must announce itself for what it is at the first glance.

Concerning genuineness of style in Architecture

Jacques-François
Blondel
1705–1774

We say metaphorically that 'This Architecture is genuine' when we wish to express the fact that it preserves in all its parts the style that is intrinsic to it, without mixture of any kind. This is Architecture that is decisive, it situates each element in its allotted place, it has recourse only to ornamentation that is necessary for embellishment; it avoids inappropriate variety based on contrast where symmetry and regularity are to be preferred. Finally, genuine Architecture is an Architecture that pleases the eye through the impression formed of the type of the edifice observed.

[...]

Concerning correctness in Architecture

Genuine Architecture pleases the eye of all. Correct architecture pleases only the enlightened intellect. [...]

Architecture that is correct, as we understand it here, springs more from the Architect's reasoning and meditation than from strict application of precepts [...]

Concerning unity in Architecture

Artists in modern Italy have degenerated still further by losing sight of the originals: they have preferred unity to beauteous simplicity, the interpenetration of Architectural elements, their mutilation, and contrasting forms.

Unity consists in the art of reconciling in one design solidity, comfort and satisfactory disposition of the parts, without any of these three aspects harming the others. It involves avoidance of mixtures of styles, or different types of expression in the decoration, avoidance of any Architectural or Sculptural element that has not been taken from the same source, the display in the same storey of several different Orders in terms of diameter and character, ensuring that the entablatures, if scalloped at their beginning, should not continue with dentils within the continuity of the decoration. It entails the avoidance of any interruption where it is not absolutely necessary, in the continuous level of the architraves and cornices of the pediments, nor in the various visible storeys of the building, unless it has been determined that this liberty is made indispensable in the exterior decoration of the disposition of the building due to some interior constraint relating to solidity or comfort. It involves avoidance of excessively ornate frontispieces and excessive simplicity in those parts of the façade that are set back. It involves avoiding the impression of too much movement in the planes of the building when the simplicity of the façades seems to prohibit, in the overall disposition, excessive use of changes of plane in the frontispieces and parts of the façade set further back. It involves avoiding excessive unevenness in the height of the top of the façade in the main body of the building, eschewing the belief that in order to break monotony it is necessary to change the form or the proportions of the openings in the same storey of a building. It involves bewaring the inclusion of too much unevenness in the piers between the bays of the façade, although such variation seems to be authorised by the repetition of the bodies subdividing it. It involves taking care in the wings of a building, although these may be lower than its main body, to make use of the same style of Architecture in the storey continued in the wing. [. . .]

Concerning variety in Architecture

We describe Architecture as being 'varied' when in the façade of a residential building we see, without the rules of unity being breached, a praiseworthy difference in the forms of the openings and in the unevenness of the junctions between walls compared with the piers and cornerstones of the doors and windows. It is necessary that the repetition of the frontispieces and pavilions should permit such variety. Provided that it is always founded on the same style of ordonnance, it is preferable to the monotonous repetition that is often entailed by the alternating voids and solids in the disposition of a public edifice, of which economy, solidity and simplicity must determine the character, but in a great private Townhouse, in the house of a wealthy person, such exactness tends more towards sterility than to the beauty of symmetry. [. . .] Moreover, one must be aware that such variety is undeniably more appropriate inside than outside a building because the decoration of the different rooms in apartments must necessarily be differentiated and the disposition of façades must necessarily be unified. It is even necessary that state, social and private apartments should be differentiated [. . .] being treated on the basis of a style and manner to match the different orders of Citizen, a variety that a sense of what is fitting inevitably imposes, that good taste permits and which is in many ways preferable to habit in the Art which leads to the placing of the same ornamentation, the same symbols and the same allegories in edifices of different types. [. . .]

By 'style' in Architecture we mean the correct style which one must choose to suit the purpose of the building. Style in the disposition of façades and the decoration of apartments is the intrinsic poetry of Architecture, which alone will help make truly interesting all the designs of an Architect.

Concerning the nature of Symbolic Architecture and Sculpture

It is said when speaking of a building that its Architecture is symbolic when the style that characterises its decoration appears to be taken from the reasons that led to its being constructed [. . .] beautiful Architecture is sufficient unto itself. The Architect must begin with the plain flat walls of his design and be content with them before seeking to add ornamentation, and the latter must often spring from the Architecture itself, otherwise such ornaments will be regarded as inappropriate accessories.

Jacques-François
Blondel
1705–1774

Concerning the differences that must be understood between light, elegant and delicate Architectures

Delicate Architecture, considered from the point of view of construction, is an Architecture which, like all the most pleasing Gothic buildings, offers little solid matter in its structure but involves industrious activity for the construction of vaults, panaches, *trompes* and groining of all kinds for the construction of our places of worship, our public edifices and the residences of great personages [. . .] a delicate Architecture is also one, since it is to be seen close up inside, and at a short distance outside, must have a relief that is not pronounced, must be in good taste and appropriate as a base for bevelled, cursive, mild and subtle ornamentation.

Concerning naïveté in Architecture

Jacques-François
Blondel
1705–1774

By 'naïveté' in Architecture we refer to an Architecture which in its disposition allows to be seen an expression that is sincere, natural, and so on, and with no pretensions other than the style intrinsic to it. [. . .]

Concerning what should be understood by mystery in Architecture

This term could be applied to Architecture in which one sees that the Architect, far from displaying grandly and openly all the elements of his Art, has truly penetrated its mysteries in order to apply only those rules that are most strongly approved, or conversely to mask in the construction of his edifice part of the secret of the manner in which the stone has been worked.

Concerning what may be called grand Architecture

By 'grand' Architecture we normally mean an Architecture that makes apparent all the height we can give to it, compatible with that of the edifice, and irrespective of the type of the latter, by, for example, using only a single order in the frontispiece of a place of worship [. . .]

Concerning what is understood by bold Architecture

Architecture is also called 'bold' when, in relation to the structure concerned, far from hiding the mystery of the Art, it trumpets all the resources available for its construction due to knowledge of the art of working stone and industrious reflection upon its structure. A bold construction is also one which, in relation to the economy of the material, appears elegant in its points of support, softly curved in its vaulting and light in the proportions dictated by the overall disposition of its parts. [. . .]

Concerning what is to be understood by awe-inspiring Architecture

We may understand by 'awe-inspiring' Architecture, an Architecture whose expression is deep, seems to announce through the external disposition of its parts, the security of the interior of the edifice, because it offers, at first impression, a real and apparent solidity, not only in the firmness of its elements, but also in the choice of materials used [. . .]

Concerning abuses in Architecture

In Architecture, licence may sometimes be regarded as a resource. The abuses of which we wish to speak here can never be seen as other than mediocrity in this Art. [. . .]

Concerning fashion in Architecture

Fashion in Architecture is usually considered by the great Masters as the source of all that Art's vicissitudes. It is fashion that is in turns oppressive, frivolous or delicate, bends to the opinion of the Artist and to the often ill-assured taste of the building's owner. It is fashion that shows no constancy whatsoever in its rules, nothing certain in its forms, nor anything truly interesting in its details. Architecture that is governed by fashion is inevitably deprived of the correctness necessary to it and leaves in the mind of he who contemplates it no more than a vague conception of the beauties of the Art.

Concerning what is meant by flat Architecture

Jacques-François
Blondel
1705–1774

We say: 'This Architecture is flat, has too little relief' in order to express its lack of projecting surfaces and the lack caused by this in the decoration of a building that must be seen from a certain distance. [. . .] One should beware of this, since too little relief is prejudicial to the character of an architectural design, taking away from it the sense of plenitude which is the source of all the merit of the exterior decoration, giving to it that sense of certainty, and that articulation of its elements which provides it with its full aesthetic effect. Inside a building, this is another matter, since there one must avoid an excessive harshness: a tender, light architectural design and soft-curved Sculpture are preferred. A lesser degree of space, moderate light, more precious materials in most cases, all these must guide the genius and pen of the Artist.

[. . .]

Chapter V. Concerning Taste in Art, or the Manner of Avoiding All That May be Contrary to it

All know that aesthetic taste is something real: the difficulty is to define it. And what is it in fact? In what does it consist? On what does it depend? Can it be governed by fundamental principles, or not? To conclude, is it an attribute of the mind, or an affect of the soul? Whatever the truth, let us say that we use the term '*taste*' to express in a general way the ultimate degree of perfection, that taste, as we understand it, is the natural Judge of the Fine Arts, that have been reduced to constant and positive principles only to please it, and that, in a word, taste in those same Arts is not artificial, but natural, that it is innate in us but can be perfected and it then becomes a lamp to guide Artists in all their works.

It may be changed, modified or augmented by natural taste, with the result that it may be said that acquired taste, in order to be perfected, has need of natural taste.

This taste may also be divided into active taste and passive taste – the former is the lot of the Artist, and the latter that of the Connoisseur.

Taste in Architecture may be acquired only through the comparison of masterpieces of the Great Masters. Theory alone is not enough to cause genius to flower. It is true that it prepares the way, but enthusiasm, by enabling the Artist to overcome obstacles, will raise it to the summits of perfection. [. . .]

Aesthetic taste is needed in order to emulate successfully, otherwise even the most beautiful models will degenerate in the hands of a Copyist.

Discretion is therefore needed when emulating the creations of those Nations so celebrated in the past.

[. . .]

Taste in Architecture is to be seen particularly in the manner of shaping a building, this being the most essential of the requirements for an Architect, who is never free of the obligation to demonstrate his skills in this area. In order to acquire this degree of perfection, the science of Mathematics, profound theoretical knowledge of the precepts, study of the best Authors: all such knowledge is insufficient without taste and experience. The art of defining the contours of a building does not depend on genius. Genius may understand the fundamental rules of the Art and follow them up to a certain point, but only taste is entitled to choose – in a word, it is aesthetic taste that must be the arbiter of the genius of the Architect. Neither must the aim be to innovate; and taste must be commensurate with the matter at hand. A meditative spirit is needed, free of constraints, a controlled imagination without servitudes. The Artist must know how to take account of the qualities of his materials to give to the shapes he designs a form of expression that will be commensurate with each material. He must plan for the distance from which his mouldings will be seen, he must consider the volume of air that must surround them and he must work upon the style of Architecture that will place them in the visual scene in a manner that confers upon them that character of firmness or lightness, ornateness or simplicity so appropriate for ensuring that the parts are dependent upon the whole, and finally, he must dare to allow himself on some occasions a particular style that only aesthetic taste can allow in this part of Architecture.

[. . .]

Jacques-François
Blondel
(1705–1774)

aesthetisation of architecture • classical canon • antiquity • abuses • rhetoric • signification • narrative

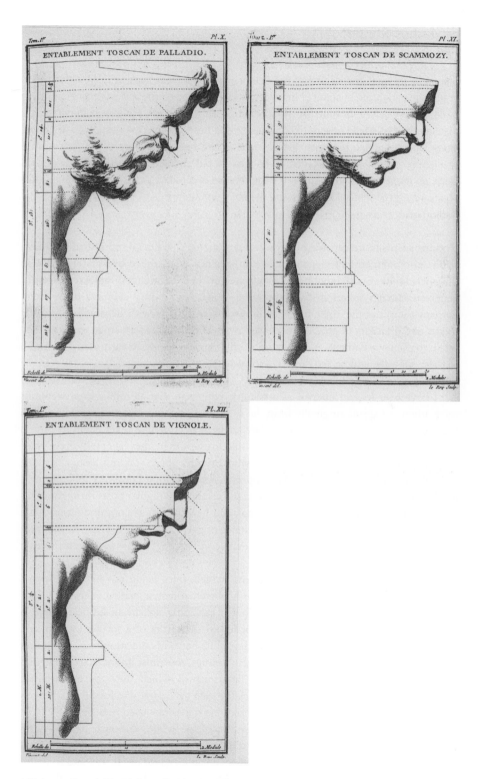

125. Jacques François Blondel. *Cours d'Architecture*. 1771. Anthropomorphic profiles of the *genera* of architecture bridging abstract formal theory with imitative theory of 'character'.

Sir James Steuart (1712–1780)

Critical Observations on the Buildings and Improvements of London (1771)

Steuart, a political philosopher of the Scottish Enlightenment, was, with Montesquieu in France, the advocate of some of the most optimistic conjectures and arguments in favour of capitalism before its triumph (Hirschmann, 1977, passim). He saw commerce as a mechanism that would ensure public interest and freedom from the despotism of princes along with economic progress. He believed in the need of a 'mercantile people' in a 'modern economy' to be managed by benevolent but strong statesmen. Accordingly, his views on improving London stress the importance of a public works programme capable of advancing commercial interests and the common welfare.

Further reading Hirschmann, 1977.

Nothing seems more capable of affording satisfaction to a liberal mind than the many public improvements of elegance and convenience which have been lately made in this metropolis. Every inhabitant participates of their advantages, and every man of generous feelings shares in the reputation which his country acquires from them. Perhaps then it is the right of every individual to discuss with decent freedom the merits and demerits of public works, and even of private undertakings as far as they relate to public ornament. A discussion of this sort may serve to turn men's attention to these subjects, and be the means of introducing a greater correctness of taste to the future.

I have ever looked upon it as a peculiar happiness that all public improvements must among us spring originally from the spirit of the people, and not from the will of the prince. In the one case, whenever they are fairly begun, they never fail to be carried on with unremitting zeal and activity: while in the other, they generally have their beginning and end with the monarch who protects them. Of this last, a striking example is seen in France. Louis XIV, a prince, fond of glory, pompous and enterprising, [. . .] cut canals, extended public roads, and established regular posts throughout his kingdom. He regulated police of his capital, and he added to its commodiousness and its decoration, by lighting and a better manner of paving its streets. There he stopped; and there the nation stopped with him. France at this day, is just as far advanced in those articles as she was a century ago. [. . .]

But this very national spirit in England, which, once being put in action, exerts itself with so much vigour and effect, finds however, at first, a terrible enemy in vulgar prejudice, which must be overcome before it can fairly act. In an arbitrary state, a prince, a minister, may have his eyes opened to the errors of a former system, and immediately adopt a new one, without restraint: but with the multitude it requires time; they seldom reason, and it is to their feelings you must apply. Habit sanctifies every thing with them; and even that deformity to which they are accustomed, becomes beauty in their eyes. *As fine as London upon the Bridge*, was formerly a proverbial saying in the city: and many a serious sensible tradesman used to believe that heap of enormities to be one of the seven wonders of the world, and next to Solomon's temple the finest thing that ever art produced. When first the reformation in the streets was begun, from the same cause every nuisance had its advocate. It was said to be for the ease of the horses that the midway should be paved with huge rocks, and the footpath with sharp pebbles for the benefit of the feet. The posts were defended to the last;

and the pulling down of the signs, which choked up and disgraced the streets, regretted as a barbarous invasion on the monuments of national taste. [. . .]

But almost every other square in London seems formed on a quite different plan; they are gardens, they are parks, they are sheep-walks, in short they are every thing [. . .] but what they should be. [. . .] A garden in a street is not less absurd than a street in a garden; and he that wishes to have a row of trees before his door in town, betrays almost as false a taste as he that would build a row of houses for an avenue to his seat in the country [. . .]

[. . .]

A passion for building in town seems to arise among the nobility at present; how many handsome structures then, may not be erected along those sides, where at present there are only stables and timber-yards? [. . .]

On a supposition then that men of rank and fortune should hereafter be induced to rear up their mansions in Oxford Road; it may not be presumptuous to hint at some errors which have been too commonly adopted in fabrics of that sort. To such, a gateway with a spacious court within is both stately and commodius; but the front to the street should still present something that intimates a relation to the society in which you live; a dead wall of twenty or thirty feet high, run up in the face of your neighbours, can only inspire horror and dislike. I am sorry upon this subject to instance Burlington House. How many are there, who have lived half a century in London, without knowing that so princely a fabric exists? It has generally been taken for a jail. None, I am confident, ever passed under its gloomy wall, late at night, without thinking of ghosts, robbery and murder. The formidable entrance, that betrays no marks of *humanity*, but what are daubed over the doors, recalls to the imagination. [. . .]

Sir James Steuart
1712–1780

It is strange that great men should not see the impropriety of this taste in a government like ours. It may produce respect in Algiers or Tunis; but here it can only excite disgust. Disgust once conceived, the transition from the house to the owner is easy and natural; and I will venture to pronounce (however whimsical it may appear), that he who thus immures himself in a free country, will hardly ever attain consideration or power. At Paris, the *Hotels* of the great are indeed all constructed with *Porte Cochères* [editor's note: this is a doorway large enough to let a vehicle pass from street to parking area] and courts; at the bottom of which the grand apartments lie; but then the *Façades* to the streets are gay and ornamented; and their bandeliered Swiss and powdered lackeys at the gates, give the whole an air of life and intercourse with their fellow citizens, which must be agreeable everywhere. [. . .]

But there is another style, which has been a good deal affected by our great men of late, and is perhaps the most judicious for those who have no ground property in town. I mean what is called a street house. Many a nobleman, whose proud seat in the country is adorned with all the riches of architecture, porticos and columns, 'cornice and frise with bossy sculpture grave', is here content with a simple dwelling, convenient within, and unornamented without. This is pardonable where only a house is rented for a winter residence, without any idea of property annexed: but where a family mansion is intended to be built, something ought to be produced suitable in dignity, to the name it bears. [. . .]

For it cannot be denied that where men congregate in large bodies, it gives more scope to the passions than in smaller societies. The manifold relations in which mankind then stand to one another, and the various combinations of interest among them, beget new situations, from which new vices must naturally arise: but from the same source do not the opposite virtues flow? [. . .] It is different as to crimes which are cognisable by the laws. They unquestionably will be more frequent in great towns; but it is the business, and it is in the power of the laws, to control them. [. . .]

It is the duty of the magistrate to watch over, and restrain, the disorders of the people; and this is only to be effected by wholesome regulations, carried into execution by an active and vigilant police. Every other way is a solecism in politics. To reform a city by desolation is like putting a man to death to teach him better manners. [. . .]

urbanisation of architecture • planning

Sir William Chambers (1723–1796)

Dissertation on Oriental Gardening (1772)

(See Chambers 1759)

Their [the Chinese] scenes of terror are composed of gloomy woods, deep valleys inaccessible to the sun, impending barren rocks, dark caverns, and impetuous cataracts rushing down the mountains from all parts. The trees are ill formed, forced out of their natural directions, and seemingly torn to pieces by the violence of tempests: some are thrown down, and intercept the course of the torrents; others look as if blasted and shattered by the power of lightning . . .

. . . The buildings are in ruins; or half consumed by fire, or swept away by the fury of the waters: nothing remaining entire but a few miserable huts dispersed in the mountains, which serve at once to indicate the existence and the wretchedness of the inhabitants. Bats, owls, vultures, and every bird of prey flutter in the groves; wolves, tigers and jackals howl in the forests; half famished animals wander upon the plains; gibbets, crosses, wheels and the whole apparatus of torture, are seen from the roads; and in the most dismal recesses of the woods, where the ways are rugged and overgrown with weeds, and where every object bears the marks of depopulation, are temples dedicated to the king of vengeance, deep caverns in the rocks, and descents to subterraneous habitations, overgrown with brushwood and brambles; near which are placed pillars of stone, with pathetic descriptions of tragical events, and many horrid acts of cruelty, perpetrated there by outlaws and robbers of former times: and to add to both the horror and sublimity of these scenes, they sometimes conceal in cavities, on the summits of the highest mountains, foundries, lime-kilns and glass-works; which send forth large volumes of flame, and continued columns of thick smoke, that give to these mountains the appearance of volcanoes.

orientalism

Sir William Chambers (1723–1796)

Letter to a Gentleman Who Had Objected to Certain Parts of his Treatise on Oriental Gardening (1772)

Chambers was Architect of the Works in England and a member of the French Academy of Architecture in Paris. In this text, the influence of the then-current philosophical discussion by such writers as Burke (1757) on grandeur and the sublime is apparent

(Harris, 1967, 1970). Like Jacques-François Blondel's **Cours** (1771–1777), this text was among the first written by an architect about the 'terrible' in architecture and garden architecture, and was greatly responsible for spreading the popularity of the notion. Chambers also composed other works, among them **A Treatise On the Decorative Part of Civil Architecture**, which became the leading authority in England into the nineteenth century.

Further reading Harris, 1967, 1970a, 1990; Kaufmann, 1955; Summerson, 1963b.

With respect to the Terrible, it appears to me useful nay even necessary in a *large Work*, as well for the purposes of variety and contrast, as to employ many rude and ungrateful Tracts of land, constantly intervening in extensive compositions which it is sometimes impossible to adorn, and which can never be adorned without considerable expense, a mixture of this mode would be singularly useful in most of Our English Gardens, which from a perpetual smiling sameness in all their parts, are extremely dull and unentertaining. If any disgusting ideas are excited in the application of the *Terrible* in decorating grounds the fault must be in the Composer, and not in the objects, which are of a nature to produce the Sublime in the highest degree.

Johann Wolfgang
von Goethe
1749–1832

  I cannot give up Water works, they are at present indeed exploited in England. But are the English never wrong and prejudiced? All other European nations (even those most famed for taste) still make use of and admire them. Water works are certainly productive of much pleasure and animation in the Scenery of Gardens, where they are well contrived as those of Marli and in some of the Villas near Rome. They as well as *Electrical Effects* might (I am persuaded) be brought in to enliven our Gardens, this however I speak in a Whisper, but the Connoisseurs should hear me, who seem to have laid down as an invariable axiom that the English style of Gardening is alone right, and that whatever differs from it is absolutely absurd and wrong.

  [. . .]

anticlassicism • deformation • freedom • naturalism

Johann Wolfgang von Goethe (1749–1832)

On German Architecture (1772)

Goethe presents the mistaken view that Gothic architecture is Germanic in origin (in fact its origins in Europe are French, and are generally traced back to Suger Saint-Denis) in this early text, his first publication. However, influenced by von Herder's nationalist theory of cultures, it presents the first example of a polemical espousal of a regionalist architecture based on nationality in opposition to the neo-classical approach of abbé Laugier, against whom he inveighs personally, which he sees as imperialistic and counter to the spirit of the German *Volk* (Tzonis and Lefaivre, 1989, 1996). It is also noteworthy for the romantic image it holds up for the architect. In his autobiography, Goethe later expressed the opposite point of view: a positive attitude with regard to classicism (1811).

Further reading Frankl, 1960; Germann, 1972; Pevsner, 1945; Robson-Scott, 1965; Rouge, 1949.

What accomplishments have you achieved that justify your arrogance! The Genius of the Ancients, rising from its tomb, seems to have you bound in chains, Latin foreigner! You roam among sacred ruins to discover their proportions, you put together villas out of their glorious remains, you look upon yourself as guardian of the mysteries of Art because you can calculate the measurements of gigantic buildings down to the inch and to its fractions! Had you but felt, instead of measured – had the spirit of the masses you gape at been brought to bear upon you, then you would not have imitated only because it has already been done and it is beautiful. You would have created your own designs out of necessity and truth, and as a result living sculptured beauty might have welled from them.

As things stand, you have based a claim for truth and beauty on your own wants. The splendour of the effect of columns struck you; and you, too, wanted to use them, and walled them in; you too, wanted colonnades, and encircled the forecourt of St Peter's with marble walks which lead from nowhere to nowhere so that Mother Nature, who despises the improper and unnecessary, drove your rabble to prostitute this splendour into public cloacae, so that men turn away their eyes and hold their noses before the Wonder of the World.

Johann Wolfgang von Goethe 1749–1832

These are the ways of the world. The artist's whim serves the rich man's wilfulness. The topographer gapes and our *dilettanti*, called philosophers, lathe out of protoplastic fables about the rules and history of the fine arts up to the present, and true men are murdered by the evil Genius in the forecourt of the mysteries. It is rules, more than examples, that harm the man of genius. Before his day, a few people may have worked out a few parts. But school and rule fetter all power of perceiving and acting. What does it profit us, O neo-French philosophising connoisseurs, that the first man who sensed his needs, rammed in four tree-trunks, joined up four poles on top, and topped all with branches and moss? From that, you decide what is proper to meet our needs today, as if your new Babylon were to be ruled by you with innocent patriarchal fatherliness.

But it is wrong that your hut is the world's first-born. Two poles crossed at the top at one end, two at the other, and one pole across like a ridge is, as you can see every day in the huts of field and vineyard. This is an invention much more primeval, from which you cannot derive your rule of style. Not one of your conclusions can soar into the region of truth: all float in your system's atmosphere. You try to teach us what we need, because by your principles that which we really do need cannot be justified. You have the column close to your heart; and in other parts of the world you become a prophet of it. You say columns are the first essential component, they are pure, manifold greatness when they stand there in rows! But take care not to use them with impropriety. Their nature is to stand detached. And woe to the wretches who have riveted their slender shoots to lumpish walls!

And yet, my dear Abbé,[1] it seems to me that in repeated condemnations of the impropriety of walling columns in which made the moderns the stuff of masonry, even into the intercolumnia of ancient temples – that this might have roused some thought in you. If your ear were not deaf to truth, those stones might have sermonised to you. The column in no way is a component of our dwellings. On the contrary, it speaks against the essence of all our building. Our houses do not arise out of four columns in four corners; but from four walls and four sides, which are there instead of all columns, and exclude all columns, and where men stick them on, they are a burdening superfluity. The very same holds true of our palaces and our churches, a few excepted, which I need not heed.

---

1. Editor's comment: Goethe is referring here to the Abbé Laugier, prime representative in his view of imperialist French neo-classicism, compared to which Goethe prefers the Gothic.

Your buildings thus describe planes, and the more widely they stretch, and the more boldly they rise to heaven, the more unendurably their uniformity press upon the soul. Ah, but another Genius came to our help! That genius which ministered thus to Erwin of Steinbach, saying, 'Make varied the vast wall, which thou must carry heavenwards, so that it rises like a most sublime, wide-arching Tree of God, who, with a thousand boughs, a million twigs, and leafage like the sands of the sea, and tells forth to the neighbourhood the glory of the Lord, his master.'

When for the first time I went towards the Cathedral of Strasbourg, general notions of Taste filled my head. By hearsay I honoured the harmony of the masses, the purity of the forms, was a sworn enemy of the tangled arbitrariness of Gothic ornament. Under the Gothic heading, I piled up, like the article in a dictionary, all the synonymous misunderstandings of the confused, the unregulated, the unnatural, the patched-up, the botched, the over laden, which had ever passed through my head. Foolishly as a people, which calls all the foreign world 'barbarie', I named Gothic all that did not fit into my system, from the neatly-turned gay coloured cherub-dolls and painting our bourgeois nobility adorn their house with, to the solemn remnants of older German Architecture, whose few fantastical frettings made me join in the universal song: 'Quite squashed with ornament'. And so, as I walked towards the Cathedral, I shuddered in prospect of some malformed, curly-bristled ogre.

Johann Wolfgang von Goethe 1749–1832

With what unlooked-for emotions did the sight surprise me, when I stepped before it! A sensation of wholeness, of greatness filled my soul; which, composed of a thousand harmonising details, I could savour and enjoy yet by no means understand or explain. So it is, men say, with the bliss of Heaven. How often have I come back to enjoy this sacredly profane bliss, to enjoy the gigantic spirit of our elder brethren in their works. How often have I come back, to behold it from every side, from far and near, in every differing light, its dignity and glory. Heavy it is on the spirit of Man, when his brother's work is so sublimely reared that he must only bend and worship. How often has the twilight, with its friendly stillness, refreshed my vision wearied with wide-eyed exploration, when it made the numberless parts melt into whole masses; and how, simple and great these masses stood before my soul, and my power rapturously unfolded in enjoyment and understanding. Then appeared to me, in faint divining, the genius of the great master mason. 'Why art thou astonished?' he whispered to me. 'All these masses are there of necessity, and dost thou not see them in all the other churches of my town? Only I have raised their arbitrary proportions into harmony. How above the main porch, which lords over two smaller ones to either side, the wide rose-window opens, answering to the nave; and commonly but a hole for daylight, how, high above, the bell-loft asked for the smaller windows! All was necessary; and I shaped it into beauty. But, ah, when I hover through the dark, sublime openings, which seem to gape there empty and vain! In their brave slender form have I hidden the mysterious forces which were there to raise high into the air those two spires, of which, alas, only one now sadly stands, lacking the five pinnacled crown I destined for it, so that the provinces about it should do homage to it and its kindly brother.' And so he parted from me, and I sank down into a sadness of compassion, until the birds of morning, which haunt its thousand openings, made jubilee towards the sun, and roused me from my slumber. How freshly I sparkled in the morning scented brilliance! How happily I stretched out my arms towards it, opened my eyes to the great harmonious masses, quickened into numberless small parts! As in works of eternal Nature, down to the minutest fibril, all is shape, everything depends on the whole. How the firm-grounded gigantic building lightly rears itself into the air! How filigreed [editor's note: a filigree is jewel work of a delicate kind made with threads and beads, usually of gold and silver], all of it, and yet for eternity! To thy teaching, Genius, I owe it that I reel no longer at thy depths, that into my soul distils a drop of that blissful stillness of the spirit, which can look down upon its own creation, and, like God, can say that it is good.

And now shall I not rage, O holy Erwin, if the German learned in art listens to envious neighbours and misjudges his advantage over them, and misunderstanding the word Gothic, belittles thy work, when he should thank God he can announce loudly: this is German architecture, this is ours, when the Italian can boast none of his, and even less the Frenchman.

And if you wanted not to concede this advantage, then prove to us that the Goth already built like this – you will have difficulty. And, beyond all, if you cannot demonstrate that there went a Homer before Homer, willingly will we leave to you the story of little efforts that succeed or fail, and tread in worship before the work of the master who first created from the scattered elements before the work of the master who first created a living whole from scattered elements. And you, my dear brother in the spirit of seeking after truth and beauty, shut your ears to all word-strutting about fine art. Come, enjoy, open your eyes. Beware. Desecrate not the name of your most noble artist, and hurry, come close, and behold his glorious work. If the impression upon you is loathsome, or non-existent, then farewell. Harness up and begone to Paris.

But I join you, dear youth, standing there moved, unable to blend the contradictions crossing in thy soul, feeling now the restless might of the great unity, now scolding me for being a dreamer who sees beauty where you see only strength and roughness. Let no misunderstanding divide us, be not girdled for rough greatness by the soft doctrine of modern beauty-lisping, lest your sick sentiment in the end bear smooth littleness. They would make you believe the fine arts have sprung from that bent presumed in us for beautifying all things around. Untrue! In that sense by which it might be true, the genteel and the artisan might use the words, but not the philosopher.

Art is plastic long before art refines; and yet is great true art? Yes. Greater and truer than the very fine. For in man there is a plastic nature, which as soon as his existence is secure, becomes active. As soon as man has nothing to worry him or make him fear, the demi-god gropes around for matter to breathe his spirit into, quickening in his own peace; and thus with fantastical strokes, with horrid shapes, high colours, the savage decorates his cocoa-shell, his feathers and his body. Let the plastic art be composed of the most arbitrary forms, still it will cohere, without proportions of form; for One Feeling has worked it into a characteristic whole.

This characteristic art is the only true art. If, out of ardent, united, individual, independent feeling, it quickens, unconcerned, yes, unconscious, of all that is strange, then born whether rough savageness or civilised sensibility, it is whole and living . . .

Come here, and experience the deepest sense of truth and beauty of proportions, quickening out of the strong, rough, German soul out of the straight, gloomy, pope-ridden stage of the *medium aevum*. And our *aevum*? It has renounced its Genius, it has sent its sons round to collect strange growths for their damnation. The light Frenchman, who makes still worse a patchwork – he has at last the kind of cunning needed to

Johann Wolfgang
von Goethe
1749–1832

fit together his plunder into one whole, he builds out of Greek columns and German vaults his Magdalene's wonder-temple.

emotions • passions • sentiments • regionalism • nationalism

Claude-Henri Watelet (1718–1786)

Essay on Gardens (1774)

Watelet, a painter, was, with Morel (1776), the importer into France of picturesque garden design. He was important in developing the view that design could affect the sentiments (Lefaivre and Tzonis, 1977). He influenced Le Camus de Meziàres who dedicated his book (1780) to him. Watelet's views are dependent on authors like Pope, Whately and Rousseau (Wiebenson, 1978, 41).

Further reading Lefaivre and Tzonis, 1977; Pevsner, 1974; Tzonis and Lefaivre, 1975a; Wiebenson, 1978.

An Embellished Farm

The dwelling shall be placed upon the slope of a hill from which the gaze shall be able to travel with greater ease to the buildings and enclosures destined to derive profit from the generous benefits of Nature.

The enjoyments of the countryside must be a tissue of desires excited without artificiality and satisfactions provided without effort.

It is necessary therefore that the house, designed in order to associate what is useful with what is pleasurable, should be oriented in a manner to allow to be seen without impediment the establishments that surround it [...]

[...] A collection of buildings, courtyards and enclosures draws my eye and excites my curiosity. I was then rather incurious as to the garden, which promised only monotonous uniformity.

I walk down the hill therefore, my imagination in pastoral mode. The desire is formed, it must now be maintained and satisfied. But the more aesthetic taste has been perfected in the human society of which I am part, the more artifice must be delicately balanced. This is work in which the useful and the agreeable, cleverly combined, must be of mutual service and never mutually prejudicial. It is on this point that the Art I serve is truly a liberal Art. Therefore, the learned possessor of this principle and faithful to its observance has disposed all things in a fitting manner, even down to the roads by which he leads me there. This is the exposition of his Novel. The slope of the land on which I walk is a gentle one, and the paths moderately sinuous. They do not tend in any geometrical direction, towards the place where I wish to arrive, but they are not tortuous to the extent that they cause excessive delay to my journey. Ah! Is that not what is most fitting for man? There is nothing so similar to the progression of our thoughts as the routes they form in this vast countryside. You rarely see such paths travelling straight. Indecision is doubtless a more comfortable state for us than exactitude, and more natural than precision.

But already, travelling along my sinuous and gently sloping path, I have come across some pleasing views, and then lost them to view, only to come across them once again with all the more pleasure. At all times I am protected from the sun by trees that seem to have grown by chance, or by the shelter provided to me by small hedges that surround crops of all kinds. I reflect upon their diversity. The efforts to maintain them are of interest to me. My steps slow noticeably and I am ready to stay them in order to enjoy my impressions the more. The shade afforded by a stand of trees under which there is a lawn and a small fountain brings me to a halt and invites me to take a few moments of rest.

If I sit, my eyes are drawn to a scene of choice and I prolong without regret a necessary relief.

It is in this way that a modest artifice will add to enjoyment based on need. But while the intention may make itself visible here, it must not be too obvious.

To invite while not obliging, that is the finest among the agreeable Arts.

In places intended for leisurely walking, distances and happy discontinuities must therefore determine when rest is taken.

It will appear as if chance had determined the form and the pleasurable features.

Claude-Henri
Watelet
1718–1786

The pretexts to stay one's progress may in some cases be the dimensions or arrangement of a few trees of extraordinary nature disposed in a felicitous grouping, in others the discovery of a spring promising and providing refreshment in its waters, or a grand vista requiring a few moments for the eyes to explore it, or a picturesque point of view that draws the eye, or an unexpected object that brings the walker to a halt, fixing his attention.

But having reached the bottom of the little hill, I see the buildings of the farm and am all the more interested when I note the great care taken everywhere. The outer walls are built and maintained with satisfying meticulousness: stone is combined with brick. This diversity has produced a kind of base, and a distinct crown and in this modest variety has been found a means of decoration that does not deviate from that which is appropriate. Opposite the main entrance, tall trees, disposed in a semicircle but without exaggerated symmetry, offer shade of which the workers and those visiting the farm may often have need. A few benches have been prepared for their rest and in the shade a fountain, whose waters are supplied by the hillside we have just descended, flows into a stone basin, whose shape and proportions are made pleasing by their rusticity. Whosoever has travelled in Italy will not be ignorant of the attractiveness of such objects, many of which are commonplace, due to the effect provided by the simplicity of their shapes and the felicitous relationship between their principal parts.

[...]

We are already entering the farmyard. It is surrounded by all the requisite buildings and their various uses are indicated over their entrance with the result that a few glances are enough to give me the impression that I am a resident of the place, of whose main features I have gained knowledge at a glance.

What would be the point here of an ostentatious wealth of ornamentation and superfluities? This is displeasing, or annoying, when it is excessive. O happy were the inhabitants of the countryside, if only they knew the value of what they enjoy, or could enjoy! [...]

anticlassicism • deformation • freedom • naturalism • emotions • passions • sentiments • view • movement

Jean-Jacques Rousseau (1712–1778)

Reveries of the Solitary Walker (1776–1778)

Rousseau's eloquent call for a return to the good, beauty and truth of nature had an unparalleled influence on the rise of romanticism and sentimental naturalistic conceptions in all the arts including architecture, and on the abandonment of the pomp and regularity of the baroque aesthetics of the *ancien régime*. This is his last work and, although unfinished, contains his most developed description of the soothing effects of nature upon the shifting states of the human soul.

Further reading Atkinson, 1960; Kaufmann, 1943; Røstvig, 1954, 1958; Tzonis, 1972.

Fifth Walk

Of all the places where I have lived (and I have lived in some charming ones) none has made me so truly happy or left me such tender regrets as the Island of Saint-Pierre in the middle of the Lake of Bienne. This little island, which the people of Neuchâtel call the '*Île de la Motte*', is scarcely known even in Switzerland. To my knowledge it has never yet been mentioned by any traveller. Yet it is very agreeable and wonderfully well situated for the happiness of those who like to live within narrow bounds – and even if I may be the only person ever to have had such a life thrust on him by destiny, I cannot believe that I am the only one to possess so natural a taste, though I have never yet encountered it in anyone else.

   The shores of the Lake of Bienne are wilder and more romantic than those of Lake Geneva, since the rocks and woods come closer to the water, but they are no less pleasing. There may be fewer ploughed fields and vineyards, fewer towns and houses, but there is more natural greenery and there are more meadows and secluded spots shaded by woodlands, more frequent and dramatic changes of scenery. Since these happy shores are free of broad roads suitable for carriages, the region is little visited by travellers, but it is fascinating for those solitary dreamers who love to drink deeply of the beauty of nature and to meditate in a silence which is unbroken but for the cry of eagles, the occasional song of birds and the roar of streams cascading down from the mountains. In the middle of this beautiful, nearly circular expanse of water lie two small islands, one of them inhabited, cultivated and some half a league in circumference, the other one smaller, uninhabited, untilled and bound one day to be eaten away by the constant removal of earth from it to make good the damage inflicted by waves and storms upon its neighbour. Thus it is that the substance of the poor always goes to enrich the wealthy.

   There is only one house on the whole island, but it is a large, pleasant and commodious one, belonging like the island to the Hospital of Bern, and inhabited by a Steward together with his family and servants. He keeps a well-stocked farmyard, with fish-ponds and runs for game-birds. Small as it is, the island is so varied in soil and situation that it contains places suitable for crops of every kind. It includes fields, vineyards, woods, orchards and rich pastures shaded by coppices and surrounded by shrubs of every variety, all of which are kept watered by the shores of the lake; on one shore an elevated terrace planted with two rows of trees runs the length of the island, and in the middle of this terrace there is a pretty summer-house where the people who live around the lake meet and dance on Sundays during the wine harvest.

It was on this island that I took refuge after the stoning at Môtiers. I found the place so delightful and so conducive to the life that suited me, that resolving to end my days there, I was concerned only lest I might not be allowed to carry out this plan, conflicting as it did with the scheme to carry me off to England, the first signs of which I was already beginning to detect. Troubled by forebodings, I could have desired that this place of refuge be made my lifelong prison, that I be shut up here for the rest of my days, deprived of any chance or hope of escaping and forbidden all communication with the mainland, so that not knowing what went on in the world, I should forget its existence and be forgotten by those who lived in it.

[...]

What then was this happiness, and wherein lay this great contentment? The men of this age would never guess the answer from a description of the life I led there. Precious *far niente* was my first and greatest pleasure, and I set out to taste it in all its sweetness, and every toiling I did during my stay there was in fact no more than the delectable and necessary pastime of a man who has dedicated himself to idleness.

Jean-Jacques
Rousseau
1712–1778

The hope that they would ask nothing better than to let me stay in the isolated place in which I had imprisoned myself, which I could not leave unaided and unobserved, and where I could have no communication or correspondence with the outside world except with the help of the people surrounding me, this hope encouraged me to hope likewise that I might end my days more peacefully than I had lived until then, and thinking that I would have all the time in the world to settle in, I began by making no attempt at all to install myself. Arriving there unexpectedly, alone and empty-handed, I sent in turn for my companion, my books and my few belongings, which I had the pleasure of leaving just as they were, unpacking not a single box or trunk and living in the house where I intended to end my days, as if it had been an inn which I was to leave the following day. Everything went along so well as it was that to try to order things better would have been to spoil them. One of my greatest joys was above all to leave my books safely shut up and to have no escritoire. [...] I filled my room with flowers and grasses, for I was then in the first flush of enthusiasm for botany, a taste soon to become a passion [...] My morning exercise and its attendant good humour made it very pleasant to take a rest at dinner-time, but when the meal went on too long and fine weather called me, I could not wait until the others had finished, and leaving them at the table I would make my escape and install myself all alone in a boat, which I would row out into the middle of the lake when it was calm; and there, stretching out full-length in the boat and turning my eyes skyward, I let myself float and drift wherever the water took me, often for several hours on end, plunged in a host of vague yet delightful reveries, which though they had no distinct or permanent subject, were still in my eyes infinitely to be preferred to all that I had found most sweet in the so-called pleasures of life. Often reminded by the declining sun that it was time to return home, I found myself so far from the island that I was forced to row with all my might in order to arrive before nightfall. At other times, rather than strike out into the middle of the lake, I preferred to stay close to the green shores of the island, where the clear water and cool shade often tempted me to bathe. But one of my most frequent expeditions was to go from the larger island to the smaller one, disembarking and spending the afternoon there, either walking in its narrow confines among the sallows, alders, persicarias and shrubs of all kinds, or else establishing myself on the summit of a shady hillock covered with turf, wild thyme and flowers, including even red and white clover which had probably been sown there at some time in the past, a perfect home for rabbits, which could multiply there in peace, without harming anything or having anything to fear.

[...]

When the lake was not calm enough for boating, I would spend the afternoon roaming about the island, stopping to sit now in the most charming and isolated corners where I could dream undisturbed, and now on the terraces and little hills, where I could let my eyes wander over the beautiful and entrancing spectacle of the lake and its shores, crowned on one side by the near-by mountains and on the other extending in rich and fertile plains where the view was limited only by a more distant range of blue mountains.

As evening approached, I came down from the heights of the island, and I liked then to go and sit on the shingle in some secluded spot by the edge of the lake; there the noise of the waves and the movement of the water, taking hold of my senses and driving all other agitation from my soul, would plunge it into a delicious reverie in which night often stole upon me unawares. The ebb and flow of the water, its continuous yet undulating noise, kept lapping against my ears and my eyes, taking the place of all the inward movements which my reverie had calmed within me, and it was enough to make me pleasurably aware of my existence, without troubling myself with thought. From time to time some brief and insubstantial reflection arose concerning the instability of the things of this world, whose image I saw in the surface of the water, but soon these fragile impressions gave way before the unchanging and ceaseless movement which lulled me and without any active effort on my part occupied me so completely that even when time and the habitual signal called me home I could hardly bring myself to go.

[...]

Such, apart from unforeseen and troublesome visits, was the way I spent my time on this island during the weeks I lived there. I should like to know what there was in it that was attractive enough to give me such deep, tender and lasting regrets that even fifteen years later I am incapable of thinking of this beloved place without being overcome by pangs of longing.

[...]

Everything is in constant flux on this earth. Nothing keeps the same unchanging shape, and our affections, being attached to things outside us, necessarily change and pass away as they do. Always out ahead of us or lagging behind, they recall a past which is gone or anticipate a future which may never come into being; there is nothing solid there for the heart to attach itself to. Thus our earthly joys are almost without exception the creatures of a moment; I doubt whether any of us knows the meaning of lasting happiness. Even in our keenest pleasures there is scarcely a single moment of which the heart could truthfully say: 'Would that this moment could last for ever!' And how can we give the name of happiness to a fleeting state which leaves our hearts still empty and anxious, either regretting something that is past or desiring something that is yet to come?

But if there is a state where the soul can find a resting-place secure enough to establish itself and concentrate its entire being there, with no need to remember the past or reach into the future, where time is nothing to it, where the present runs on indefinitely but this duration goes unnoticed, with no sign of the passing of time, and no other feeling of deprivation or enjoyment, pleasure or pain, desire or fear than the

Jean-Jacques Rousseau 1712–1778

[407]

simple feeling of existence, a feeling that fills our soul entirely, as long as this state lasts, we can call ourselves happy, not with a poor, incomplete and relative happiness such as we find in the pleasures of life, but with a sufficient, complete and perfect happiness which leaves no emptiness to be filled in the soul. Such is the state which I often experienced on the Island of Saint-Pierre in my solitary reveries, whether I lay in a boat and drifted where the water carried me, or sat by the shores of the stormy lake, or elsewhere, on the banks of a lovely river or a stream murmuring over the stones.

What is the source of our happiness in such a state? Nothing external to us, nothing apart from ourselves and our own existence; as long as this state lasts we are self-sufficient like God. The feeling of existence unmixed with any other emotion is in itself a precious feeling of peace and contentment which would be enough to make this mode of being loved and cherished by anyone who could guard against all the earthly and sensual influences that are constantly distracting us from it in this life and troubling the joy it could give us. But most men being continually stirred by passion know little of this condition, and having only enjoyed it fleetingly and incompletely they retain no more than a dim and confused notion of it and are unaware of its true charm. Nor would it be desirable in our present state of affairs that the avid desire for these sweet ecstasies should give people a distaste for the active life which their constantly recurring needs impose upon them. But an unfortunate man who has been excluded from human society, and can do nothing more in this world to serve or benefit himself or others, may be allowed to seek in this state a compensation for human joys, a compensation which neither fortune nor mankind can take away from him.

It is true that such compensations cannot be experienced by every soul or in every situation. The heart must be at peace and its calm untroubled by any passion. The person in question must be suitably disposed and the surrounding objects conducive to his happiness. There must be neither a total calm nor too much movement, but a steady and moderate motion, with no jolts or breaks. Without any movement life is mere lethargy. If the movement is irregular or too violent it arouses us from our dreams; recalling us to an awareness of the surrounding objects, it destroys the charm of reverie and tears us from our inner self, bowing us once again beneath the yoke of fortune and mankind and reviving in us the sense of our misfortunes. Complete silence induces melancholy; it is an image of death. In such cases the assistance of a happy imagination is needed, and it comes naturally to those whom Heaven has blessed with it. The movement which does not come from outside us arises within us at such times. Our tranquillity is less complete, it is true, but it is also more agreeable when pleasant and insubstantial ideas barely touch the surface of the soul, so to speak, and do not stir its depths. One needs only enough of such ideas to allow one to be conscious of one's existence while forgetting all one's troubles. This type of reverie can be enjoyed anywhere where one is undisturbed, and I have often thought that in the Bastille, and even in a dungeon with not a single object to rest my eyes on, I could still have dreamed pleasantly.

But it must be admitted that this happened much more easily and agreeably in a fertile and lonely island, naturally circumscribed and cut off from the rest of the world, where I saw nothing but images of delight, where there was nothing to recall painful memories, where the company of the few people who lived there was attractive and pleasing without being interesting enough to absorb all my attention, and where I could devote the whole day without care or hindrance to the pastimes of my choice or to the most blissful indolence. It was without doubt a fine opportunity for a dreamer

Jean-Jacques
Rousseau
1712–1778

who is capable of enjoying the most delightful fantasies even in the most unpleasant settings, and who could here feed on them at leisure, enriching them with all the objects which his senses actually perceived. Emerging from a long and happy reverie, seeing myself surrounded by greenery, flowers and birds, and letting my eyes wander over the picturesque far-off shores which enclosed a vast stretch of clear and crystalline water, I fused my imaginings with these charming sights, and finding myself in the end gradually brought back to myself and my surroundings, I could not draw a line between fiction and reality; so much did everything conspire equally to make me love the contemplative and solitary life I led in that beautiful place. Would that it could come again! Would that I could go and end my days on that beloved island, never leaving it nor seeing again any inhabitants of the mainland who might recall the memory of the calamities of every kind which it has been their pleasure to heap upon me for so many years! They would soon be forgotten for ever; of course they might not similarly forget me, but what could that matter to me, so long as they were kept Jean Marie Morel 1728–1810 from troubling my quiet retreat? Set free from all the earthly passions that are born of the tumult of social life, my soul would often soar out of this atmosphere and would converse before its time with the celestial spirits whose number it hopes soon to swell. I know that mankind will never let me return to this happy sanctuary, where they did not allow me to remain. But at least they cannot prevent me from being transported there every day on the wings of imagination and tasting for several hours the same pleasures as if I were still living there. Were I there, my sweetest occupation would be to dream to my heart's content. Is it not the same thing to dream that I am there? Better still, I can add to my abstract and monotonous reveries charming images that give them life. During my moments of ecstasy the sources of these images often escaped my senses; but now, the deeper the reverie, the more vividly they are present to me. I am often more truly in their midst and they give me still greater pleasure than when I was surrounded by them. My misfortune is that as my imagination loses its fire this happens less easily and does not last so long. Alas, it is when we are beginning to leave this mortal body that it most offends us!

anticlassicism • deformation • freedom • naturalism • emotions • passions • sentiments • view • movement

Jean Marie Morel (1728–1810)

Theory of Gardens (1776)

Morel was the official architect of the Prince de Conti and designed the gardens of La Malmaison. Along with Watelet, he is responsible for popularising picturesque garden design in France (Lefaivre and Tzonis, 1977; Wiebenson, 1978).

Introduction to Geometrical Gardens

Even our most accredited tastes and opinions are often naught but prejudices that blind habit petrifies and slavish imitation perpetuates: reason struggles against them in vain; habit and imitation, which are more powerful, stifle and subjugate it; our mores, our customs, most of the arts imagined for our pleasures, all are subject to their authority. To prove their power and show how far their influence extends, I will mention, in order to adhere to the topic on which I am proposing to write, the type of garden that we have brought to our countryside. The boredom that results from its monotony and uniformity has been generally acknowledged for a long time.

What could have been in the mind of the first man who, indeed, taking in hand the materials that he borrowed from nature with the plan of creating a garden out of it, dared to mutilate them and attempted to arrange them in an order that was contrary to that which nature indicated to him? . . . He did not therefore think that by substituting the dryness of the ruler and methodical compass for easy and freehand drawing with a pencil, the art of gardens would be necessarily limited to a cold and mechanical combination of geometrical figures; that those figures, too few to produce variety in the effects, and almost always chosen at random, would spawn naught but monotonous and, consequently, uninteresting decorations? And that, lastly, the geometrical forms and their symmetrical distribution, leaving the genius of the composer inactive, would offer the imagination no resource, no understanding of the combinations of taste, and therefore no means of stirring the emotions?

A style that is so poor in its effects, so limited in its means, has, however, constantly been preferred to the free and adventurous march of nature, to the exciting variety of its tableaux, to the richness and charms of its scenes.

It is, one cannot doubt, this resemblance that all the gardens of this kind have to each other, the uniformity that reigns in all its parts, that results in the boredom we must constantly endure. That feeling affects us even more promptly in those lavish gardens where charm has been sacrificed to luxury, where a profusion of art ornaments and rich materials abounds, where architecture and sculpture are used as embellishments, where water is harnessed and forced to spring out in thin sprays and struggles to follow a direction opposite to that which nature has intended for it, flowing uphill when it should be flowing down. It is to this lavish monotony, which may at first glance astonish and flatter the owner's pride but which will always be charmless and without any attraction for the heart; it is to this lavish monotony, I say, that necessary accounts for the instinct which forces him to leave his pompous gardens . . .

anticlassicism • deformation • freedom • naturalism • emotions • passions • sentiments

Jacques-François Blondel (1705–1774)

Lessons on Architecture . . . continued by P. Patte (Paris 1777)

(See Blondel 1752)

Taste in the interior decoration of apartments in France has undergone several revolutions in the past century. Under Louis XIV, it was treated with the same severity as the exterior of buildings. Apartment doors, windows, fireplaces and cornices were in an austere and serious style: seldom did any one take the liberty of giving them any thing except geometrical, round, oval, square or rectangular shapes: the profiles and ornaments were always in the most masculine style: in the hands of such men as Perrault, Mansart and Le Brun, these sorts of decorations certainly were graceful, noble and dignified: they gave the most important air to the interior of grand apartments, as any one can judge by the models that still remain standing today, i.e., the Chateaux at the Tuileries, the Louvre, Versailles and elsewhere. But in the hands of their imitators they quickly degenerated; in the end they became unbearably heavy and monotonous: they

Jacques-François
Blondel
1705–1774

[410]

were overburdened with a multitude of ornaments placed without any order and with confusion; which caused people to imperceptibly tire of them.

Around 50 years ago, excesses in the opposite direction were commonplace; geometrical forms were abandoned, interior decorations were twisted and turned every which way, under the pretext of varying them, lightening them and brightening up the apartments. Such men as Lajoux, Pinault, Meissonier and their Copiers, if it may be permitted to say so, turned their backs on Architecture in a way. In our decorations only extraordinary twists and turns, a confusing jumble of attributes placed without reason, and combined with ornaments of a bizarre imagination, in which one finds a ridiculous heap of twisted cartouches, rocailles, dragons, reeds, palms and all sorts of imaginary plants, were allowed for a long time; so much so that Sculpture reigned as an absolute mistress over Architecture. The numerous engravings that have found their way into the hands of the Publick, independently of the great number of apartments with this bad taste in decoration that still survive, provides some idea of the extravagance of these frivolous compositions.

Jean-Baptiste Le Roy
1720–1800

That there has been a return to good taste is something we owe to Mssrs Servandoni, Cartaud, Boffrand and a few other of our best Architects who have not allowed themselves to be carried away by the new style. In comparison with their works, the absurdity of this monstrous combination becomes obvious: we are gradually returning to more sensible, less bizarre forms; and the return of classical taste at last having spread its influence to our decorative arts, especially during the past 15 years, it can be said that the interior decoration of apartments, and the style of their furnishings, have, in a way, become a new art. Less severity, more delicacy and more variety in the forms have been added to the good style of the last century's decoration: their projections and their profiles have been given hardly any relief, in order to make them appear lighter. By adopting geometric forms, at the same time, depending on the circumstances, these Architects have created less serious contours that are more capable of producing a pleasing whole and at the same time less uniformity in the layout of the apartments. Lastly, the ornaments that are admired on the finest ancient structures have been applied to interior decoration, such as acanthus leaves and laurel leaves, festoons, egg-and-dart motifs, dentils, fluting, guilloches, scrolls, medallions, etc., and in such a way that Architecture has once again taken its rightful place ahead of Sculpture.

aesthetisation of architecture • anticlassicism • deformation • freedom • naturalism • archaic beliefs • body model

Jean-Baptiste Le Roy (1720–1800)

Précis for a Work on Hospitals (1777 composed; 1787 published)

During the last years of the *Ancien Régime* the members of the Académie Royale des Sciences, among them Le Roy, were called on to provide solutions to the problems of hospital design for the overcrowded Paris of the day. The present report to the Academy contains one of the first explicit references to a building as a machine (Fortier *et al.*, 1975; Foucault *et al.*, 1976).

Further reading Fortier, 1975; Foucault *et al.*, 1976; Rosenau, 1970; Tzonis, 1977.

Uncertain of whether I had any predecessor in this domain, I sought out that which had been written upon it. Imagine my surprise when I saw that in the multitude of books of all kinds that fill our libraries, there is not one that discusses the construction of hospitals, whereas there are a great number on palaces, theatres and many other edifices, so true is it that mankind always prefers those things that are brilliant and even frivolous, to those that offer no more than the tedious utility.

However, when I became aware of the plans that had been made for the rebuilding of the Hôtel-Dieu in another place, the volume that I desired on hospitals seemed to me to be even more necessary, for I saw with the greatest astonishment that, far from profiting by the observations of physics and modern medicine on this matter, what was proposed to us in 1773 for a hospital of this size were plans that could have been produced two centuries earlier.

Jean-Baptiste Le Roy
1720–1800

This is because, sacrificing, as is quite often the case in our nation, the essential to the subsidiary, the authors of the plans seemed to have forgotten that decorative work is the smallest part of such an edifice and that the fundamental object, the essential aim that should prevail is to build in a manner likely to preserve, at least as far as that is possible, an air that is pure and free from the corruption that invariably reigns in hospitals with many inmates.

But, reflecting further on what might have prevented those architects from directing their efforts towards the object that I have just described, I conceived, through the knowledge that I had of the talents and the capacity of several among them, that it was solely due to a lack of knowledge of the observations which I have just spoken above.

These diverse considerations led me to think it necessary to remedy the lack of any treatise on the building of hospitals, and that this was essential at a time when there was ceaseless discussion of the rebuilding of the Hôtel-Dieu in another place. And finally, I considered that it was of the greatest importance at the present time to make known, by means of a volume intended solely for that very purpose, the observations of physics and medicine capable of enlightening the government and municipal officers, the architects and the public on the proper construction of such edifices.

[. . .]

I go on to set out the rules deriving from these various observations and which must determine our choices of the situation, disposition and plan of a hospital. I then discuss at length the properties of the air to which it is necessary to pay close attention in order to direct its movement and to cause it to circulate in those places where it is desired that it be renewed. I next apply these considerations to the construction of hospital wards, and I end this part with a description of the hospital design I have announced.

[. . .]

I go on to lay down the rules which must guide the construction of hospitals and I examine the standard plan for such buildings. I do not speak of the plan of the Hôtel-Dieu, which is no more than a formless pile of buildings amassed together. I speak of other hospitals built in a more regular fashion. These buildings are ordinarily given a square, or a rectangular shape, or may be laid out in a cross. I analyse the effects of the air in hospitals built in these different ways and I show clearly that they cannot satisfy the purpose one must necessarily have in mind.

In the first types, that is those with a square or rectangular form, the air is as if stagnant in the inner courtyard and around the building, since the same wind could never move this fluid on more than one side and nor could it renew the air in the wards, even if their windows were open.

In hospitals whose plan is in the form of a cross, with a cupola where the arms meet in order to draw in the air and to cause it to circulate through the wards, either such a cupola will be useless or this fluid will be highly corrupted in those parts of the wards that are near to it, since the air is gathered together there from all parts of the building. In the former case, the cupola is good for nothing, this being a good reason to reject it, and in the latter, the cupola is a source of great harm, which is yet another reason to reject it.

All the above brings us inevitably to the plan and disposition of the parts that I propose for hospitals in order to ensure that they promote the protection of the sick by maintaining air that is as pure as possible.

The observations that I have described, showing that the disposition of a hospital in which all wards are connected is absolutely incapable of satisfying the proposed purpose; it is absolutely necessary to separate them, which I have therefore done.

Jean-Baptiste Le Roy
1720–1800

In order to gain an idea therefore of the hospital I propose, the various wards and rooms should be imagined as entirely separated one from the other and ranged like the tents in a camp or like the pavilions in the gardens at Marly. They are to be seen thus in the elevation of my hospital, along its length. By means of this disposition, each ward forms something similar to an island in the air and is surrounded by a considerable volume of that fluid, which the winds may remove and renew easily due to the unimpeded access they enjoy on all sides. Since the air is thus renewed, it will serve to renew that in the wards, without it being possible for the corrupted air in some to be carried into the others.

Having established the order and disposition of the wards of the hospital, I would have resolved only part of my problem, if I had not sought then to give them an internal plan to allow the air to be renewed ceaselessly and in such a gradual manner that the patients are not incommoded in any way, this being a consideration of the utmost importance. However, the internal plan can be determined only in accordance with the properties of the air by virtue of which it is able to move and adopt such and such a movement. It is in this connection that I set them out in detail, as I have already announced, in order to make better known how the plan I give the wards produces, as a consequence of those properties, a continual renewal of the air, without however leading to any very perceptible movement.

I am not deluding myself – the true theory of the circulation of the air, a theory that is equally applicable to its movement in mines and chimneys, it is from that theory that I arrive at the plan for the wards.

[...]

And when I propose such an experiment, I do not propose it with vain purpose, I would in truth wish it to be done in a ward constructed to a small scale to serve as a model for those that are to compose the hospital I have imagined, for I do not claim in any way that this disposition of the ward is so perfect that it cannot be improved or even altered. I propose it only as one which, after much reflection, seems to me to be the best according to the experiments on this fluid of which we have knowledge. Indeed, a hospital ward is truly, if I may express it thus, a machine for the treatment of the sick and it must be considered from that standpoint. Now, no machine can be brought to perfection without a large number of trials and experiments. I say again that it will never be possible to perfect the disposition and construction of hospital wards unless they are considered in this way.

I must add that in the case of contagious diseases, such as smallpox, malign fever, scurvy and other like sicknesses, one must include wards that are distant from those that form the main body of the hospital and they should be situated, to use the expression of sailors, *downwind* of them, in order that their corrupted air may not, or only very rarely be carried towards them.

mechanisation of architecture • scientification • environmental control and determinism

Jean-Baptiste Le
Roy
1720–1800

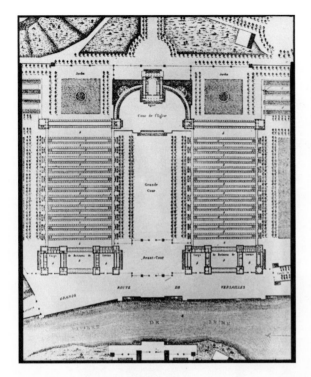

126. Jean-Baptiste Le Roy. *Plan Général d'un projet d'Hôtel-Dieu*. 1773–1777. Plan for a hospital. In contrast to the centralised plan of Petit, which Le Roy criticises as not sufficiently segregating patients to avoid contagion, he proposes a linear scheme. While inspired by the pavilion arrangement of the Marly gardens (in 93 above), it can be easily seen as a predecessor of modern linear plans applied massively in the twentieth century.

Antoine Petit

Mémoire sur la meilleure manière de bâtir un hôpital de malades (1774)

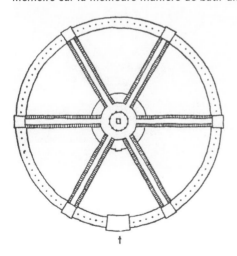

127. Antoine Petit. *Mémoire sur la meilleure manière de bâtir un hôpital de malades*. 1774. Wheel-shaped hospital plan prototype. The wards for keeping patients radiate from the centre in a panoptic manner.

B. Seeley

Plan of Stowe Gardens, 1777

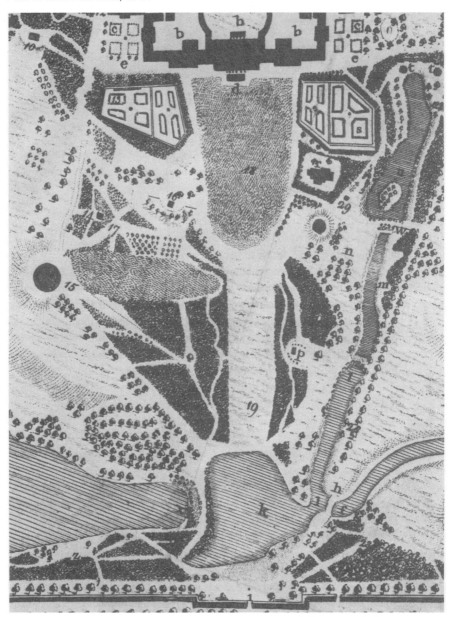

128. B. Seeley. *Plan of Stowe Gardens*. 1777. The gardens designed by William Kent who, in the words of Horace Walpole, saw that 'all Nature was a garden', manifest an approach to design that does not try to impose on the existing site any universal norms but exploits the opportunities offered the given region. It combined regular arrangements with natural freedom and was considered as the original source of the English garden and the most representative artefact of Britishness in the eighteenth century.

Nicolas Le Camus de Mézières (1721–1789)

The Genius of Architecture (1780)

Camus, architect of the functional Halle aux Blés in Paris, claimed to be the first to write on the analogy of proportions of architecture with human sensations. The bulk of the contents of the book was intended to provide a guide to interior design (Wiebenson, 1968). The author went on to explore the effect of all the artificial and natural means available as well as the relation of interior to outside surroundings (ibid.).

Further reading Bilodeau, 1997; Hermann, 1973; Wiebenson, 1982, 1993.

Introduction

No one has yet written on the analogy of the proportions of Architecture with our sensations; we find only scattered fragments, superficial and, as it were, set down by chance. [...]

Hitherto it has been customary to work in accordance with the proportions of the five Orders of Architecture, used in the ancient buildings of Greece and Italy: this is a priceless model, and we cannot do better. But how many Artists have employed these Orders mechanically, without taking the opportunity to combine them into a whole with a character all its own, capable of producing certain sensations; they have not been inspired by the analogy and relation of those proportions with the affections of the soul.

We sometimes see examples of Architecture that surprise and impress, but leave the judgement uncertain: there remains something to be desired. Why is this so? [...] When we look at some great fabric, our sensations are of contradictory kinds. [...]

What are the causes of these various effects? Let us try to distinguish them. Their existence is in no doubt; and this becomes still more apparent if we combine Painting and Sculpture with Architecture.

[...]

The arrangements of forms, their character, and their combination are thus an inexhaustible source of illusion. We must start from this principle whenever we intend to arouse emotion through Architecture, when we set out to address the mind and to stimulate the soul, rather than to build by piling one stone on another, indiscriminately copying arrangements and ornaments that are imposed by convention or borrowed without reflection. Effects and sensations spring from the considered intention that governs the ensemble, the proportions and the agreement of the various parts.

Bedchamber

The bedchamber that completes the state apartments will often serve only for show. It is too large. There is a preference for a room with a lower ceiling, in which one feels better enclosed and in which one can be oneself. But a bedchamber there must be, for propriety's and custom's sake, and it must be in keeping with the rest of the apartment. It will be meant for ostentation, if you will; all the more reason to give it a character that inspires repose and proclaims tranquillity. Avoid, therefore, the noise from the courtyards, and anything that might distract. This is the palace of sleep, and all must be simple and uniform. The light is to be dim and faint, as it is painted at the moment of the waking of Venus, when the Graces inform her of the coming of dawn. Gauze curtains, drawn across the windows at two-thirds of their height, will admit only so much light as is appropriate to the place. The shadows, however, must not be too heavy. The Artist who concerns himself with decoration must adopt as a principle that the brighter and stronger the light, the harder the shadows become. Light and shadows influence the character of a room, and the effects that flow from it. The arrangement and the choice of furnishings contribute to the same ends. The bed will accordingly be placed at the end of the room, in the centre of its width, and generally facing the windows. The chimneypiece will be halfway along the side wall, beyond the bed; otherwise, it would be too close, and symmetry would be lost; a setback or a segment of a circle will indicate the depth to be occupied by the bed. All will then be in due order, and the decoration will be in keeping.

The glass over the mantel will be the same both in dimensions and ornament as the one opposite to it, beneath which will stand one of those commodes that are called *Régence*. The room may be hung with tapestry or damask, all framed with gilt borders. The panels to left and right are to be the same. A tranquil and sedate ensemble must give a sense of the nature of the room, as we have said. Its proportions will be Ionic: this Order represents a proportional mean between the others and is well suited to such an effect. Furnishings contribute to the character more than is thought: their design and arrangement will be determined by the Artist who has devised the ensemble and not by the Upholsterer, whose task is only to execute. The proportions, the forms and the choice of colours will thus be in the province of the Architect. All too often, the Upholsterer decides on the entire furnishing and does so without any regard to the principles enunciated here; self-interest is his only guide, and the consonant effect of the whole is lost. It is therefore the Artist's duty to attend to these details and to direct the work; only he knows what he intends, and only he can employ all the necessary means to a single end, namely, the ensemble that establishes the desired character and inspires the proper sensations.

By preference, the colour green will be chosen for the hangings of a bedchamber; it has something of foliage about it, and sleep seems all the sweeter. Green is to be favoured for its uniformity, and the evenness of its shades contributes to the mild and tranquil impression that is conducive to repose. The panels will be framed with gilt mouldings, but these will have simple profiles; they will show little relief and almost no ornament. A few pictures may be admitted if tastefully arranged; too many would disturb repose.

The bedchamber, as we have said, is the sanctuary of sleep. Beds may take on pleasing shapes, and those called *à la Polonaisre* convey the idea through their elegance, their pyramidal forms, and their domed canopies; their plumed tops have a pleasing effect, but one must have the wit to keep these ornaments in proportion with the rest of the room and to compose them to suit the condition and the age of the persons for whom they are intended.

Alcoves are out of favour at the present time; not only are they inconvenient for service, in case of sickness above all, but they fail to provide for a sufficient circulation of air. It is difficult to find room in them for beds of any elegance or ornateness; and taste, luxury and health have united to dispense with them.

Beds in niches had fewer disadvantages; but still they did not offer all the necessary convenience. The closets that were commonly placed to left and right of them were not easily reconciled with the magnificence of a state bedchamber, and such arrangements are now proscribed and relegated to subsidiary apartments of little importance.

Nicolas Le Camus
de Mézières
1721–1789

In general, therefore, a detached bed is to be preferred, placed, as we have observed, at the back of the room, as if it were in the sanctuary of the temple. For the rest, opulence and even magnificence will set the tone for the whole room. But, once more, beware of that excess of ornament that seems to depart from the character proper to a bedchamber.

The room that follows is similar and no less interesting; this is the boudoir.

Boudoir

The boudoir is regarded as the abode of delight; here she seems to reflect on her designs and to yield to her inclinations. With such thoughts in mind, dictated as they are by the manners of our age, spare no pains to make the room as pleasing as you can. All is to be subordinate to luxury, comfort and taste. The proportions of the Corinthian Order are elegant, and here they are appropriate. Impart a tone of dignity and self-regard; this room is a lady of fashion to be adorned. The air of delicate gallantry from which there is no departing demands that the masses be light and rhythmical, the forms not pronounced. Take care to avoid the harsh shadows cast by undue brightness. A dim, mysterious light will be obtained by the use of gauze artfully disposed over part of the windows.

Nicolas Le Camus de Mézières 1721–1789

This is a room where there must be no lack of openings and reflections; looking glasses will produce the necessary effect. Take care, however, that they do not form the principal part of the furnishings. When used to excess, they create a sad and monotonous effect. Place them so as to leave, between each one and the next, at least twice as much space without a glass as with a glass: these intervals of repose may be adorned with fine, rich hangings. Against each panel a picture will be artfully hung with heavy tassels and silk cords braided with gold. The subjects will derive from the pleasing and amorous themes of mythology. The triumph of Amphitrite, Psyche and Cupid, or Venus and Mars, all suggest compositions apposite to the character of the room. Here, all must be convenient and all must please. In keeping with the dimensions of the room, those details made to be seen close must satisfy by their harmony. The burden of the whole is this: that enjoyment is close at hand. To the boudoir let us add private closets that are made with artistry and apt in their design.

Where the windows are to the East, the light will be softer; the prospect must be a pleasing one, as far as possible. In the absence of natural beauty, have recourse to Art: here, taste and genius must come to the fore. The magic of painting and perspective must be applied to create illusions. If a view of a private garden can be procured, then arbours, trellises and aviaries will have a fine effect. Birdsong and an artful cascade, whose waters charm the eye and the ear alike, will seem to summon Love. Often, too, such sounds cause a sweet slumber to overcome our senses, and airy dreams set our souls adrift. Varied statues divert us with the subjects that they represent. Orange trees and myrtles, planted in choice vessels, enchant the eye and the nostrils. Honeysuckle and jasmine twine like garlands around the Deity who is worshipped at Paphos. A well-contrived variety affords the interesting spectacle of the beauties of nature. Here the soul rejoices; its sensations are akin to ecstasy. This is the retreat of Flora; here, decked in her liveliest hues, she waits in secret for the caress of Zephyrus. Here, the beauty and mildness of spring will always prevail. Maintain, therefore, the freshness of the shrubs and flowers; renew them as the seasons progress; it requires no more than care. The principal garden and the greenhouse will come to your aid.

[419]

The boudoir would be still more delightful if the recess in which the bed is placed were to be lined with looking glasses, their joints concealed by carved tree trunks artfully arranged and leafed and painted to resemble nature. This would repeat to form a quincunx, which would be multiplied by the glasses. Candles, their light softened by gauzes in various degrees of tautness, would improve the effect. One might believe oneself to be in a grove; statues painted and suitably placed would enhance the pleasure and the illusion.

Let us continue to survey the details. The chimneypiece may be adorned with ormolu in a delicate design on veined white marble. All the other marbles must be of the same colour to sustain the cool, ornamental and magnificent air that must prevail in this place.

Opposite the window or the chimneypiece, a niche is required for a daybed, or an ottoman; this niche must be decorated with looking glasses all around, even on its ceiling.

Nicolas Le Camus de Mézières 1721–1789

An alcove or rather recess ten or twelve feet deep, if discreetly lit, will gain in effect by enhancing the air of mystery. Glasses all around; a well-proportioned dome in the centre of the ceiling; and a bed placed directly beneath, detached on every side and decked *a la Polonaise*, would create a pleasing effect.

The colours of the furniture and hangings are not without influence on the desired character of the room. Red is too harsh; yellow would create unpleasing reflections; green would appear too serious. White and blue are the only admissible colours.

The furniture and the frames of the glasses and of the hangings must be gilt and carved; the cornice that crowns the room may be similarly enriched; but the carving must be delicate; as for the gilding, let it not be used in excess. It must be applied only to the ornaments and some of the fillets, and the whole must be no more than heightened and picked out in gold on a fine white ground. Levity is the whole charm of this room, which is frivolous by nature.

It follows from these principles that the mouldings in general must not be too pronounced, nor must they be too weak; never fall into a vice through seeking to avoid a fault.

The ceiling may represent an azure sky with few clouds; it need be enlivened only by a pair of doves taking wing to join Venus' chariot.

The panelled dado will be white and the mouldings gilt and carved, as in the rest of the room.

The parquet will be laid in compartments or in marquetry, and in the winter a fine carpet will cover it.

One cannot devote too much care to a decoration of this kind; the masses may vary, but take care to keep to a circular plan. This form is appropriate to the character of the room; it is sacred to Venus. Consider a beautiful woman. Her outlines are gentle and well rounded; the muscles are not pronounced; the whole is governed by a simple, natural sweetness, whose effect we recognise better than we can express it; this stems from a tender quality that is already apparent in the cradle. We can give no better example. Such are the notions that may serve as guides; add only lightness in the ensemble and grace in every part.

Take care to avoid looking glasses that are curved in plan; they create reflections that are distorted and elongated in relation to the degree of curvature.

We must also observe that all possible attention is to be given to the purity, the colour and the setting of glasses. The least flaw, the least scratch, the slightest fault, and they must be rejected.

It would be absurd if a nymph desirous of contemplating her own charms were to find, instead of a regular form, a crabbed and crooked figure. The fixing of glasses in itself may sometimes occasion such mishaps, which arise in any that are out of alignment, out of square, or out of plumb. They are easily remedied, unless the glasses in a single frame fail to match in thickness or in colour. These faults are of the essence; they must never be tolerated. Change the glasses, or the eye will be fatigued or, as our ladies of fashion themselves would put it, 'teased'. For then the face, or any object reflected in the glass, seems fractured and divided between two complexions, which occasions the most disagreeable disparity: one does not expect to be vexed in such a manner in one's own boudoir.

This delightful retreat must arouse none but the sweetest emotions; it must confer serenity upon the soul and delight upon all the senses. It must aim for the ultimate perfection: let desire be satisfied without impairing enjoyment.

Nicolas Le Camus
de Mézières
1721–1789

Looking Glasses

Since we are on the subject of the quality of glasses, it should be noted that few of them are perfect; their selection is a matter deserving of the closest attention. The purest and clearest are to be placed level with the eye; they must be large enough to show the figure at full length. If a second glass be added above, it must, as I say, be of the same colour and the same thickness as the glass that it surmounts; but in this piece, which must be one-third as large as the one beneath, a few flaws may be tolerated if necessary. Glasses enclosed in a single frame must never differ in these two qualities of colour and thickness. The fault is too obvious and becomes intolerable. There is a great art in their fixing. A glass that is inclined a little more or a little less often conceals its flaws, so that they can be detected only with difficulty, and then only from the side; often, indeed, they are effaced altogether. The flaws in glasses placed against the light between two windows are very hard to detect, and it is here that the worst are placed; the Glaziers take care to set up their faulty glasses here in the hope that they will not be rejected. Without close attention to this point, one will be cheated: the Merchants, apart from their ordinary discount of one inch in height and in breadth, enjoy additional discounts in respect of flaws in the glass; and there are some glasses for which the price is reduced by more than one-third. Most Merchants accept them, and their great art is then to pass them off as unflawed. But take care: in disposing of them or in exchanging them for others, one would lose more than half their cost. An attentive Architect cannot therefore be too careful or too strict in his examination. His duty demands it; and if there are some positions in an apartment where flawed glasses might pass, it is not the Merchant who should have the profit, but the client, since every glass has its intrinsic value and the makers have a tariff of discounts according to the number of flaws.

May I be excused this digression, which is a matter of economy and not of decoration.

Let us proceed to the dressing room. To lovely women, every moment is precious, and they know how to dispose of their time; they count the minutes, and every one bears the hallmark of pleasure.

[421]

Dressing Room

The dressing room is the place where the Graces hold counsel: they are simple and unaffected; their greatest charm springs from nature. This idea and the character of the Graces themselves must preside at the making of their chamber. They are slight and delicate of person, neither too tall nor too small. Their abode must be in keeping. Its proportions will be Ionic, the proportional mean between the Doric and Corinthian Orders.

The dressing room belongs by its nature to the private apartments. In general, twelve feet wide by fifteen or sixteen feet long and nine feet high are the most suitable proportions. This room must be parqueted; the ceiling is to have a cornice; but if the cornice be ornamented, this must be done with restraint, lightness and taste.

The whole chamber will be wainscoted to its full height; the panels will be handsome in shape, well framed and symmetrically placed.

All ostentation is to be avoided: magnificence offends the Graces and puts them to flight; they take pleasure only in noble simplicity.

Eliminate sharp angles in the form of this room; it is highly advisable to have canted corners in which looking glasses will be mounted. Segments of circles make a very fine effect, and the wainscoting, in such cases, can take on this form instead of a flat panel; but then the corner glasses are inset in a recess, which is rectilinear in plan; as, in general, the canted panels are not wide, such recesses are not unpleasing, and they have the advantage of softening the effect of the room as a whole. If the reflections of the reveals in the glass give rise to complaint, have them painted to represent half a mosaic, which together with its reflection will appear whole and produce a fine effect. You will be glad of this when you cast your eyes upward and see how the angles of the ceiling have become less pronounced. The doors and fireplaces must be so placed that they do not interfere with the position of the dressing table, which must be lit from the East. It would be inconvenient to have the dressing table in line with the doors. To be in its natural place, it must have a favourable light. This need for light must not cause it to be placed too close to the chimneypiece; the fire might cause discomfort and is incompatible with the scents and pomades. The entrance must therefore be at the far end of the room, but not opposite the window. A glass is best in the latter position, especially as objects are reflected in the glass above the dressing table; and it is not without interest to observe the arrival of those who come to pay homage. The door must therefore be in one of the side walls.

The chimneypiece will be in veined white marble; its consoles will be rounded in plan, and the mantel will follow their contour. The top of the opening cannot be placed too low; and the view afforded by the glass over the mantel will be all the better if another is placed on the opposite wall. These repetitions are necessary, so that one may see oneself from every side.

This room will be parqueted and wainscoted to its full height and painted white or two very pale shades of grey; the same will apply to the frames and borders of the glasses, with the exception that the moulding nearest to the glass itself will be gilt. This trace of gilding will counter the excessive sameness, which might otherwise bring in a touch of melancholy. The dressing table sets up a kind of constraint, which must be softened. To this end, place in each panel of the wainscoting a print of some agreeable subject, enclosed in a gilt frame with flat, plain mouldings to avoid dust. These prints

Nicolas Le Camus
de Mézières
1721–1789

[422]

will give variety to the room and enliven it. The cornice will be of a simple, light, and low profile, and that of the wainscoting will be similar.

Flowers must be placed in a number of vases around the room; have no fear of overloading the mantel with them. It would be pleasing to set in the corners little stands bearing finely designed vases. These would contain flowers, which would be all the fresher if their stalks were to stand in water. These vases may be of copper, enamelled in lapis lazuli and with gilt trimmings.

The hardware of the doors and windows will produce a finer effect polished and varnished than gilt; the braided bell ropes will form swags, with white and blue as their basic colours.

Such is the aspect of a dressing room, always remembering that cleanliness and grace must be its principal ornaments; let the whole room proclaim the exquisite freshness enjoyed by those who emerge from it.

Nicolas Le Camus
de Mézières
1721–1789

Closet for Clothing

The closet for clothing and accessories will adjoin the dressing room, or at least must not be far from it. This chamber will be furnished with large wardrobes with well-fitting doors, in which there will be shelves and hangers. Its most advantageous aspect is Northerly: the light is even; the fabrics will be less exposed; feathers and furs will keep better; and insects dislike this aspect. There must be no fire; smoke might penetrate the doors of the wardrobes, however well closed. This room will be paved with freestone; parquet is less suitable, because it harbours vermin. This will not be a high room; nine feet will suffice. It will have a ceiling; where there is a cornice, this will serve as a crown for the presses. In the centre of the room will be a large cloth-covered table, where the dresses and other articles that are needed may be spread out. Any chairs that may be placed here must not have cloth seats, because of the insects; use straw or cane. Straw is best, especially in frames of acacia wood.

The linen room will be discussed when we come to the lodgings set aside for the lady's maids.

Closet of Ease

This must not be far from the bedchamber and the dressing room; it is paved with freestone and ceiled, with a cornice if desired. Shelves will be placed in the corners to hold various vessels, potpourris and scented waters. There must also be small cabinets, made to the height of benches or sunk into the walls, to hold the various accessory objects that this place requires.

As for the closestool, it is placed in a niche contrived for the purpose, usually in the centre of one of the lateral walls.

This place may be heated by flues from a stove in the adjacent room. The light should come from the North; a fanlight above a door may serve, but only as a last resort. This closet must have a second door leading to a lobby so that the servants may attend to it without passing through the principal rooms of the apartment. The whole is painted in white or grisaille. Although of little consequence, these rooms demand some thought if they are to be arranged to best advantage. Nothing must be neglected: the least corner must have its use, either for the napkins or for a little fountain with a marble scallop shell or a basin to receive the water that falls when one washes one's hands, and which is ordinarily carried off by a little discharge, which leads to a sink or to the outside. Arrange this room artistically, but always bear in mind that it must be in keeping with the rest of the apartment. When a closet is pretty, one does not suppose the other rooms neglected.

Water Closet

This room closely resembles the foregoing; it serves much the same purpose, except that it is not in such general use. It is called *cabinet à l'Anglaise*, because it came to us from the English. The bowls are marble troughs to receive the matter, and this is soon washed away when one lifts the plug with its valve and turns the faucet, which gives water in abundance and carries away whatever is in the bowl; the plug closes hermetically, so that the odours cannot pass; it is even covered by a little water, so that no vapours may escape. There are also little conduits from which water springs when one desires to wash oneself, a custom that combines cleanliness and health. A cistern is usually placed in the mezzanine above. Delicacy suggests the attachment of a cylinder of hot coals, so that the water shall not be too cold in winter. Water is drawn from this same cistern to supply a little fountain for washing the hands, which is emptied by an overflow pipe. It is easy to give an artful arrangement to this room. The seat must never be placed facing the door, but to the right or left. It most commonly occupies a niche, square in plan, and to either side there are shelves for white napkins. At the height of the seat there is a little press in which to drop the day's soiled linen. The frames that support the little shelves for linen and scented waters normally taper to serve as a base for a vase full of perfumes and scents. This room is paved with freestone or with marble; it has a ceiling and a cornice. It is pointless to lavish ornaments upon it. The wainscoting must be simple and massive, with the look of architecture rather than of woodwork, and with panels that are either in relief or recessed in the walls; for it is generally to be painted to resemble marble, well polished and varnished. The effect is more solid than stucco but lacks its brilliance. The same decoration may be made in plaster; but observe that the arrises are never sharp enough, which is a great disadvantage. To remedy this, you may leave your walls quite smooth and paint them to look like marble. Shadow and perspective will create whatever masses you may desire. The windows in this room will face North, so that the odours may be less in evidence; the fermentation of the matter is less promoted by cold than by heat.

But, once again, this room must not offer an elegance that would be out of keeping with the rest; without a just relation between the parts and the whole, there is no architecture.

Baths

The baths demand several rooms; they require an anteroom, a room for the bathtubs, a vapour bath, a small bedroom and a number of private closets.

Anteroom to the Baths

This anteroom is at the end of a passage; it leads to the bathroom, to the water closet, to a number of cabinets, which serve as lobbies, and to the stair to the mezzanine above, where the cistern is and where the lady's maids have their lodging.

This room is paved with freestone, has a ceiling with a cornice, and is generally

Nicolas Le Camus
de Mézières
1721–1789

wainscoted to its full height. It should be painted in grisaille: its aspect is of no consequence.

There will be a stove, and it is ordinarily from here that all the flues convey heat to the closets, water closet and baths.

Bathroom

Diana descends to her bath. It is here that you must strive to divert her in the form of the room, in its arrangement and in its ensemble. The proportions are to be Corinthian; this room demands elegance and lightness, and there must be some play in its plan. The light should be full, without being multiplied by too many windows; one will suffice, and this will face the bath. The aspect, where possible, will be to the East and will look out along a walk that ends in a grove, where Art will weave its most elegant spells. The sense of idleness that accompanies the bath calls for objects of distraction. Melancholy thoughts intrude; the mind must be diverted. The bath itself, as we have said, will be so placed as to enjoy a pleasing outlook. If gauzes seem to banish an indiscreet daylight, it is for Art and taste to draw them aside.

Nicolas Le Camus
de Mézières
1721–1789

The bath is not to stand on the floor, for it could not then be entered without too much effort. It must be sunk, so that its rim stands, at most, eight or nine inches above the floor. This makes access more convenient and obviates the dangers attendant on stepping into the bath. One might desire to have the bath in the centre of the room rather than in a niche; it would be more easily attended by the servants, and one would have the advantage of a clear view all around. There must be at least three looking glasses, one opposite the window, another over the mantel, and the third opposite the second. These glasses will extend as low as possible, so that one may see oneself from every angle. The mantel must be fifteen inches at most above the fireplace opening, which should be two-and-one-quarter feet wide. Veined white marble is the most appropriate material for the chimneypiece and for the floor.

The entire room should be finished in the same marble: it might also be painted with trelliswork, so that in the bath one would see jasmine and honeysuckle all around; it would be an easy matter to contrive in the walls a few little waterfalls, which would be reflected in the glasses and which, by their murmur, would make the room more agreeable.

The shape of this room may be octagonal, and the ceiling painted to represent the sky, which would form an azure dome above the arbour just described; a few birds, seeming to swoop through the air, might add animation to the scene. For greater animation, bring in a birdcage, standing low and to the full width of the window. The movements of the birds and their singing would help to dispel the ennui of the bath. For absolute tranquillity, a canopy, or rather a bed *à la Polanaise,* might be placed over the bath to support curtains whiter than snow. But Diana sometimes ranges through the forests, and her skin may be marred by the heat of the Sun. In such a case, blue curtains will have a better effect. Foresight is all. What is proper for a blonde has not the same advantages for a brunette.

The entry must have two doors, so arranged that one is closed when the other opens. Diana is in her bath; let no Actaeon surprise her.

In the matter of decoration, it would be possible to go further, and give the whole its proper character. Why not represent it as a grotto, worthy of Amphitrite, sparkling with all the riches of the deep? Why not create a chamber from Neptune's palace? How many interesting objects might be gathered there! Looking glasses, suitably placed, would reflect groups of columns; and these would form the basis of the decorative scheme. The resulting splendour of openings and perspectives would have the finest possible effect, inclining the soul towards a sensation of delight.

The chariot of the Sovereign of the Deep might serve as the bath itself, harnessed to sea horses whose nostrils would spout jets of water and lace the rocks with rivulets of silver to delight the eye; one might be in the midst of the seas. The bath itself would nevertheless be served by faucets dispensing hot and cold water, as is the custom.

Shall we enrich this composition? Let us add birdsong, as we have suggested, to animate it and give it life. Before and behind some of the openings we place birdcages. We plant trees; with winter in mind, let us add some that are artificial; let illusion reign supreme. Let us set the foreground with terracing, with aquatic herbs, and with various seashells scattered on the shore. In default of nature, silver gauze may replace the crystal waters; their sound may be imitated by some further device. Let us set all the magic of optics to work; this is the moment for the Artist to display all his talents, and make known the extent of his Art. He may give his fancy free rein, but, above all, he must divert. His invention may be prompted by pictures and prints or by stage decorations.

Nicolas Le Camus
de Mézières
1721–1789

Let us take every opportunity that arises to improve the ease of service; neglect nothing that may tend to greater convenience.

Baths such as these must far exceed the advantages of bathing in a river, for here the soul enjoys a healthful tranquillity, which is beyond price. A bath is never a matter of indifference; its advantages derive from the manner of taking it. Let us try to make it pleasurable as well as healthful.

We may regret that no public baths have been established in France; such baths would have a twofold advantage in that they would serve as schools of swimming, a useful and, one might even say, an essential accomplishment. In many circumstances, this might be a means of saving life; and it would be one more occasion for the Artist to produce an Architecture that would bring us closer to the taste of the Ancients, both in the distribution of the plan and in the decoration, and would allow our Arts to compete with those of Greece and Rome.

If it were our intention to imitate the bath of Diana, other, and no less agreeable, compositions would suggest themselves. We might counterfeit a kind of boscage formed by various trees, some evergreen and some aromatic, mingled with groups of rose, honeysuckle, myrtle, and orange bushes standing in tubs, which might be partly concealed from view by other plants in low pots.

In compositions of this kind, what an abundance of ideas mythology can yield if only we set our minds to it and if we give free rein to a sound and rational imagination! This is the palace of the Gods; these apartments that we have to decorate are theirs, and it is for us to impose our customs upon them.

We shall not speak of the baths of the ancients in any spirit of comparison with our own: they were magnificent, but they were public; and their character is not to be reconciled with the manners of our time, which combine the utmost sensuous refinement with the utmost delicacy.

We shall say nothing of the manner of the Turks: to supplement the use of water for bathing, they have sweat rooms to provoke perspiration; such a method could do nothing but harm in climates such as ours. We have other ways of making ourselves perspire.

There are also vapour baths; such matters belong to the province of Medicine. We speak of the decoration of baths; this is our sole concern.

Vapour Baths

The entrance to this will adjoin that of the bathroom. Like the bathroom itself, it will have an inner and an outer door and will be enclosed on every side.

[. . .]

Bedroom Adjacent to the Bath

This room will be very simple, small in size, and very sparingly lit. A Westerly exposure is appropriate; it is here that gauze curtains are necessary; their effect is to form a half-light, propitious to sleep.

In this room, neatness is the only requirement; nothing frivolous, and no ornaments. It will suffice to have wainscoting to the full height of the room, painted a very light grey, the chimneypiece in white marble, the bed in the same colour with a little border in which blue predominates; this will convey a fitting air of simplicity and freshness to the whole. An alcove, fashioned as a niche, is appropriate to this room; it seems more conducive to repose. On either side of this will be a closet, unless other special ones exist; these are essential for the sake of good order; repose will be the less disturbed, and the servants will work more conveniently.

This chamber will be parqueted and ceiled, with a cornice adorned with few and simple mouldings, so that everything seems expressly made to avoid catching the attention. A laboured pretension, or too much opulence, or too much contrivance might dispel the gentle vapours of Morpheus [editor's note: Ovid's name for the god of dreams, son of sleep]. Remove all distractions, respect the rights of sleep, and endeavour to preserve it for a few precious moments. Give the room Tuscan proportions, as its serious character demands. Do not hesitate to place a number of looking glasses in it; they will imitate a lovely pool, whose tranquillity seems to summon and detain the presence of sleep. Let monotony prevail; it numbs the senses and binds them captive; one yawns and falls asleep.

Nicolas Le Camus de Mézières 1721–1789

Closet for the Bath

Closets of this kind serve expressly to hold all the accessories that relate to the bathroom; dresses and linen are placed here during the bath, and the servants in attendance withdraw here when they are not required.

Here, in particular, everything must have its place; it would be displeasing to see clothes strewn here and there. Neglect nothing that would tend to establish order and cleanliness. These closets must convey an impression of perfect arrangement. [. . .]

Closet of Ease

There must be a closet of ease; we have said enough on the subject in speaking of the bedchamber, and reference may be made to this.

Such are the dependencies of the apartment of a lady, always remembering that

[427]

above these rooms, which should not in general be too high, there is an entresol, with lodgings for the lady's maids; each will require two rooms with fire-places, and they will share a third, large enough for their usual work, where there must be a stove. Two other rooms may be added, one for a seamstress and the other for the wardrobe maid. Provide a staircase to communicate with the closets and the bedchamber.

aesthetisation of architecture • emotions • passions • sentiments

Francesco Milizia (1725–1798)

Principles of Civil Architecture (1781)

Francesco Milizia
1725–1798

A man of letters who made a career out of architectural criticism, Milizia was one of the most prolific leaders of the 'rigoristi' movement in Italy. Like Algarotti (1756) and Memmo (1786), he owed his success to the fact that he popularised the ideas of another, his old school teacher Carlo Lòdoli, who never published himself. The voluminous treatise of the *Principi* is an attempt to construct an exhaustive and rational system of new rules for architecture, covering questions of composition, the Orders, proportion and location of buildings. A functionalist answer to Blondel's *Cours* (1771–1779), it turns its back on the past and looks to scientific laws for direction. The passage dealing with the need for architectural rules of proportion to be consistent with the principles of optics is indicative of this tendency. In his *Arte* (1781), Milizia demands that in architecture everything be justified by necessity and condemns the merely ornamental. His scandalous guidebook *Roma* (1787) comparing, unfavourably, the baroque sacristy of St Peter's with the city's main sewage system, the Cloaca Maxima, earned him a condemnation from the Pope and a prohibition to ever enter the city again. The article on 'autorità' in his *Dizionario* (1797) railed against the baroque architects who clung to tradition. Milizia believed that the legacy of antiquity was exhausted, that it no longer made sense to look backward and that a truly revolutionary architecture was at hand. In his *Art of Seeing* (1810), in addition to expounding the desirability of a revolutionary architecture, he anticipates the impact on the dissemination of architecture of the advent of the new mass media (the new printing technology).

Further reading De Zurko, 1957; Gengaro, 1937; Grassi, 1966; Herrmann, 1962; Kaufmann, 1952 and 1960; Meeks, 1966; Prozillo, 1971; Tzonis, 1972; Ulivi, 1942.

Chapter I

On the essence of architecture

p.110 I. Architecture is an art of approximate imitation, like painting, sculpture, eloquence, poetry and music. No other difference obtains between them, than that some of these arts have their natural models before them, and they need only open their eyes, contemplate the objects around them, and from these objects form a system of imitation. Architecture has no such model. Where are the dwellings built by the hands of nature, that architects may take as an example for imitation? The palace of a monarch is not modelled on the palace of the universe; just as harmony is not modelled on the music of the celestial bodies, the sound of which has never, until now at least, struck any ear. Architecture does in fact lack a model formed by nature, but has another formed by men, using their natural industry in building their first dwellings. The primitive cabin is natural architecture; the primitive cabin is the origin of the beauty of civil architecture.

p.111 Now, if the exemplar of architecture is that first uncouth creation, the cabin, it is from this rustic model that architecture must take the fairest parts, imitating them, refining them, disposing them in a manner which is natural and convenient to the use of the building, in order that from the variety of elements, combined in a manner fitting to their object, there results a pleasing whole.

IV. But since architecture was born from necessity, everything that is beautiful in it must be present by dint of necessity. It would be deplorable if the artifice of pleasure manifested itself: art blushes to be discovered: hence all that is done for mere ornament is vicious.

V. In architecture, therefore, ornament must result from necessity; nothing should be seen in a building that does not have its proper function, that is not integral to the building itself; hence all that is on view should have a function.

VI. Therefore the origin, and the analysis, of early natural architecture is the great standard which should guide architects in their works, and regulate judgements in the examination of such works. If these principles are lost from view, if they are trampled underfoot as vile and abject, we may say farewell to architecture: it is turned on its head, it is no longer a science, no longer an art: it is arbitrary, prey to tasteless abuse.

Francesco Milizia
1725–1798

The final principles here expressed are all positive and constant, unalterable by changing trends, independent of authority, inflexible to instances, universal in every country whatever its climate, because they derive from the very nature of the thing, and from good sense. That which belongs to good sense, belongs equally and always to all the nations of the world. Together these principles constitute the true and essential beauty of architecture; they are its metaphysics, which is nothing other than the science of first principles. Every art, every science has its first principles, founded on general and constant observations. Therefore every science and every art has its metaphysics, but a metaphysics far removed from the tiresome jargon of the scholastics, which is empty of sense and leads into error, imposture and fanaticism.

Whosoever raises himself to the first principle, sees in a glance the concatenation of parts, and how their relations converge on the first general principle. He sees all errors, truth, consequences: all becomes clear to him and admits of the most rigorous demonstration.

Every inquiry into the beauty of architecture, therefore, depends on a continuous and reasoned inquiry into what is natural and true. It follows that no authority or example is reliable, that is opposed to reason; it is valuable only in so far as it conforms to reason, and serves both to illustrate it better and to make it clearer.

Chapter XII

On the improvement of the orders and the invention of a new order

Are the three Greek orders susceptible of improvement? And who shall venture to apply the *non plus ultra* to the arts and the sciences?

Greater harmony of precision can indeed be found in the proportions of the whole and the parts; better forms of elements can be found, and disposed more gracefully. The Ionic capital has in fact been refined into a better system than it was before; why should we be unable to come up with another quite different, and still more beautiful, system? The same can be said of some other elements of the other orders.

It is in our working of foliage especially that we can do ourselves greater honour.

Art hitherto has rarely employed leafage either of the fairest, or the most correctly accomplished, kind. It is precisely here, that nature is rich in beauties without end, and reveals an astonishing fecundity in the diversity and forms of its productions. The artist, therefore, must seek after and study these beauties of nature. He shall discover therein an infinity of models, which shall suggest to him a thousand ideas on how to pleasantly delineate and vary elements and ornaments. If our artists could only wander the countryside and accompany nature in those its products with the most beautiful forms, which we describe as freakish and bizarre, and rid them of the solecisms by which they often seem to have been blighted when they leave the hands of unadorned nature; if, in short, sound judgement and refined taste were to guide their observations and bring them to an appropriate application, they would every day extend the sphere of the arts, and continually add to the stock of their wealth.

Francesco Milizia
1725–1798

Chapter I

On architectural proportions

The rules of proportion depend absolutely on that part of the optical sciences known as perspective: that is, the way in which we see objects at different distances and in different situations. An architectural object seems pleasant to us when its principal or essential parts are conjugated in such a way that the eye is struck by the most, then least, significant parts successively, according to the various grades of importance which these parts have in the composition, in order that their diverse images impress themselves on the mind before it is struck by other, subordinate elements. These subordinate elements, however, must also be treated in such a manner that they do not become absorbed by the former, but rather are equally capable of exciting distinct ideas which are suitable to the ends for which they are intended. Such an effect may also in some way be produced by the different forms and situations of the parts; for simple forms operate more promptly than complex ones, and the salient reveals itself sooner than the recessed, as the near sooner than the far. But the principal cause and the mainspring of such an effect are the just relations of their dimensions: on our sight these prevail.

p.113 A building shall be well proportioned, therefore, if the eye easily comprehends all of its parts, if the impressions made on this organ are not diffuse, and if they form, so to speak, an accord of impression.

Chapter II

On vision as it relates to architecture

An object renders itself visible by the simple impulse or reflection of rays of light, which travel from the surface of the object to the retina or the back of the eye, where they depict the image of the object, which is seen in the place to which the faculty of sight is directed, so to speak, by the rays.

Sight is a kind of touch, although rather different from ordinary touch. To touch something with our body or with our hands, we need to draw close to that thing; or it must draw sufficiently close to us to allow us to touch it. But we cannot touch it with our eyes, no matter its proximity to us, if it is not in a condition to send light back to us in quantities large enough to make impressions on this organ, or to depict itself from a perceptible angle.

The smallest angle at which men can see objects is approximately one minute.

I Laws of vision concerning the distance of objects

Three things concur in determining the distance from which we can apprehend a far-off object. 1. The size of the angle that the object forms in our eye. 2. The intensity of light from the object itself. 3. The degree of brightness of the neighbouring and intermediate objects that are seen at the same time. Each of these causes influences the effect of vision, and by weighing and comparing them together we shall determine in all cases the distance at which a given object can be apprehended.

1. The first more general, and in most cases the most reliable, means we have of judging the distance of objects, is the visual or optical angle formed by the optical or visual rays which come from the edges of the object to the centre of our eye. It is evident that the closer the eye draws to the object, the larger the visual angle becomes. Thus:

Rule I. The distance of an object is in inverse proportion to the visual angle, that is, the smaller the visual angle, the greater the distance of the object.

Francesco Milizia
1725–1798

Rule II. The brighter the object or the livelier its colours, the closer it appears to us.

Rule III. Poorly lit objects appear larger and more distant by reason of the dullness or darkness of their colour. Black obscuring their outlines makes objects smaller.

p.114 Rule IV. The more distinctly the parts of an object are seen, the nearer that object seems to us; and conversely it shall appear more distant to us, the more confusedly its parts are seen.

Rule V. If the distance between two visible objects forms an imperceptible angle, the objects, even though far apart, shall appear to be contiguous: whence, a continuous body being nothing other than the result of many contiguous bodies, if the distance between many visible objects is only apprehended at sensible angles, all these different bodies shall make but one continuous body.

Rule VI. An object appears larger and more distant, the more intermediate objects there are between the former and the observer; and the brighter and more distant these intermediate objects are, the larger the principal object appears to us, especially if it is less brightly lit than the other objects.

(p.115)

II. Laws of vision with regard to the size of objects

The size, or extension, of visible objects can be known by means of the optical angle combined and compounded with the apparent distance of the object.

An object appears larger (all other things remaining equal), the greater the angle at which it is seen; from which it follows that the same object may appear now larger, now smaller, depending on its greater or lesser distance from the eye. And this is what we call apparent size.

To judge of the real size of an object, we must have regard to distance, for, if a near object can appear at the same angle as a distant object, we must of necessity estimate the distance; and if the distance apprehended is great, though the optical angle is small, we may judge that a distant object is large, and vice versa.

Rule VII. The chord, or subtendent, of a circle appears to have the same angle at all points of its circumference, even if one of its points is considerably closer to the object than the others. And the diameter appears the same size at all points on the circumference of the circle.

[431]

Rule VIII. If the eye is fixed on one point on the circumference of a circle, and a chord within that circle moves in such a way that its extremities always touch the circumference of the circle, that chord shall always appear to have the same angle: whence, the eye being trained on any angle of a regular polygon, all sides shall appear to have the same angle.

It follows therefore that the proper object of sight is not the measurement of distances or sizes: this is the object of touch, of the rule and the compass. As for sight, it has only light and colours as its proper objects.

p.116 Rule IX. When the objects employed go unnoticed by most observers, such as orders, vases, trophies etc., the size conferred on them should accord with the rules of optics, in order that, from the point from which they are viewed, they appear of the just and required size. But where conspicuous objects are employed, such as statues etc., they should be left almost their natural size, in order that they appear as large as they really are.

III. Laws of vision concerning diverse positions of the eye relative to the object

Rule X. If the eye is above a horizontal plane, objects shall appear to rise the more they recede, until finally they shall appear to be on a level with the eye. Therefore a man standing on the seashore fancies that the sea rises the further out he casts his gaze.

Rule XI. When many objects are placed under the plane of the eye, the more distant objects shall appear taller, and vice versa.

Rule XII. If the same objects are all in a plane above the eye, the more distant objects shall appear the lower. Thus the sky seems to stoop down and touch the earth, while the latter seems to rise up and unite with the sky. Therefore in cornices the elements which are to the rear should be inclined forward slightly.

Rule XIII. The upper parts of objects of a certain height appear to be inclined forwards: this is how frontispieces, towers etc. appear.

p.117 [. . .] and in order that statues which stand on the top of buildings should appear upright, they should be placed leaning back a little.

Rule XV. With regard to the breadth of objects, experience itself shows that their extent cannot be seen distinctly and comfortably in a single glance, if the angle is not between eight and nine degrees.

It follows therefore, that accomplished effects in practice cannot always be deduced from accomplished drawings on paper; and conversely, unpleasant drawings on paper are no sure proof of the disagreeable outcome of the building. No less are small models sufficient for communicating the effect of the full-scale execution.

aesthetisation of architecture • representation • truth • illusion • rigorism • essentialism

Ribart de Chamoust (?–?)

The French Order Found in Nature (1783)

Nothing much is known about Ribart de Chamoust. The following text expressed the French Enlightenment at its most idealistic: democratic, enamoured with simplicity and passionate about Rousseauesque natural freedom which the author sees as embodied in a new French order of architecture, whose idea goes back to Philibert de l'Orme's sixteenth-century treatise.

By the word *type*, I mean Man's earliest attempts to subjugate Nature, to make it propitious to his needs, suitable to his uses and favourable to his pleasures. The physical objects that the Artist rightly and sensibly chooses in Nature to kindle the fires of his imagination and keep them burning are what I call *archetypes*.

Section II

On the Greek type and masses in general

I do not leave the types of the Greeks aside; on the contrary, I make them my own, and employ them with the utmost care, because some of them strike our senses in the most pleasing manner, and are the most suitable to our climate. According to Vitruvius, tree trunks were the models for columns; a roof and a ceiling placed on the trunks were the exact forerunners of the entablature. All my inventiveness in this regard consists only of the manner in which I consider this type.

It is necessary to know what constitutes an Order, and for all those who know it, to seek to invent new ones. It is necessary to develop Nature, to follow its march through History and in monuments, in order to avoid resorting to composites, which has been the case up until the present.

Nowhere is it said that trees whose tops have been cut off, which our forefathers originally used to hold up the roofs of their rustic dwellings, must always be planted one by one, at regular intervals, and around a quadrilateral or circular plan. They took them, according to appearances, as they found them in the woods; and it is certain that, aside from regularity, they more commonly found them on triangular or polygonal plans than on others. Why do we remain attached to squares and rectangles, on which nothing, so to speak, but boring parallelepipeds can be built? Changing the plans, and consequently all the columns, is how we will naturally arrive at producing new masses, and at easily diversifying them.

If the Orders followed up until the present day have seemed opposed to changing masses, the one that I propose seems on the contrary to demand it: the result will be an endless diversity in our edifices, less repetitive decorations, a more intelligent distribution, un-hoped-for conveniences, discoveries advantageous to construction, hitherto unsuspected furnishings, in short, a thousand useful and pleasing objects that can only expand the range not only of Architecture, but of all the Arts in general. How will the eye, one will ask me, become accustomed to all the new forms of masses? A modern Philosopher [Smith] answers in my stead: there is not one, no matter how bizarre, whose use will not make it pleasing.

Section III

The French Order glimpsed in the Greek type, and its development

I was walking in the shadow of tall trees on my estate, in a gorge that leads into the Marne. Young trees, placed three by three in a fairly regular pattern, although planted haphazardly, came into sight. The groups of these trees formed and ordered by their unity a kind of natural, hexagonal and extraordinary room. At this sight, my first idea about changing masses came to mind and became stronger, especially since I saw how it fit in with the concept of a French Order that had already occurred to me. Perrault, I said to myself, by coupling columns, going against accepted practice, pleased everyone.

Why, I wondered, on the one hand, by arranging them in sets of three, like those trees were, would I not increase the beauty resulting from their openness or their closeness, so sought after by the Ancients, as much as he had, and, on the other, facilitate those clear spaces to which the Moderns sacrifice so much? I walked through that room with a certain pleasure, and took it as an archetype.

The following spring, some tender shoots sprouting at the tops or the forks of the cut trees formed capitals that must have looked more genuine than those of Callimachus. Several large, naturally coiled roots, or twisted in the even distribution of the ground, marked the bases. A lawn that my Miller made next to his drainage ditch was in the rough shape of a stylobate. I thought that I had naught more but ornaments to desire. This type offered me the proportions of the parts, the union of the columns and the space between them; and there I already glimpsed the newness of masses and distributions.

Ribart de
Chamoust
??–??

Section IV

Comparing the three columns to the three Graces

After having found and chosen in pure Nature the parts that, according to avowed principles, could lead to the primitive composition of a beautiful whole; after having arranged them to form beautiful harmony, and assembled all that determines an Order, the only thing that was left for me to do was to give it brilliance and elegance: for that I had imagined a second type. Drawing, Sculpture and the Visual Arts came to my assistance, and fertilised my studies.

In the three columns of each group, I pictured the three Graces, who are always depicted as being inseparable . . .

So that one might easily make the comparison between the two groups, I have enclosed the drawing of a small national Monument that I had modelled in clay. I thought that to the eye, this would provide a better sense of the relationships between them than mathematical demonstrations. Not that I have neglected them, I am aware of their force; but not every one finds them amusing. I satisfied myself with adapting the scales resulting from my operations to this drawing.

Observations on the ornaments of the national or French monument

The three Virgins who dominate the national or French monument are nothing new. They can be found in the Edda. In them I find the Magnanimity, Affability and Generosity that still typify the French Nation today, and which makes her domination desired all over the world.

It seems that the occupations our Ancients gave them were the forerunners of the earliest impulses which became the driving force behind the movement of our State: knowledge, industry, gaiety and activity.

Section V

On the specific characteristics of the French Order

The French Order is lighter, more elevated and more ornamented than the others. In that respect it owes all to Nature, and principally to the three Graces, who embellish beauty itself.

The top of the trunk, decorated by leaves, forms, like the vase in the Corinthian order, the body of the French capital, which I also call the fork or the head of the column. It is crowned by an abacus which, being triangular, round on the sides and having cut sections, exactly represents our French capital. Also, in stead of roses or sunbursts, I have placed on its sides knots of ribbons, or, rather, cockades fastened to the braid with a button. In stead of the shoots that sprout from the trees of this type, I have placed large lily leaves in order to decorate them more simply and pleasingly. I have arranged them in such a way that they form a large fleur-de-lys on each of the three sides; and from whatever side one turns to examine the group of columns, one always sees the three fleurs-de-lys from the arms of France in the three capitals seen together. I believe that one may encounter naught better to symbolise the Nation. Naught is simpler, I must admit, but simplicity is not the easiest thing to achieve ...

If the capitals of the Temple of Jerusalem were as the third Book of Kings described them, or as Villalpando has depicted them ... they would surely bear no resemblance to those I give to the French Order ... I do not believe, after all, that one imagines I have borrowed nothing from the various attempts of the last century's Architects; comparison alone will prove that the Order I give is all mine.

Ribart de
Chamoust
??–??

Section XI

On distribution

Grouping the columns together in sets of three, and the form of their grouping, gives birth to a distribution quite different from that which is practised nowadays. The plans of a building in the French Order and the rooms that compose it, naturally come back to equilateral triangles with cut corners, to regular diamonds, to hexagons that are regular or lengthened on two parallel sides, to rectangles ending in equilateral triangles or half-hexagons, and to a thousand other figures that would be too boring to list here. What I must point out, however, is that the French order can be used in quadrilateral plans as much as the other Orders, and that it appears to be much more suitable to all sorts of circular plans than they are ...

The French Order will result in vast peristyles, spacious and well-lighted galleries, likely themselves to be peristyles and a second Order, magnificent rooms lit from above by the intervening spaces between the columns, as Egyptian rooms were; it will be easy to find convenient furnishings for the apartments, such as the bedrooms, studies, wardrobes and alcoves with their open plans; staircases will take new shapes, and given the multiplicity of walls and courtyards, it will be easier to light them; the number of landings as well as of entrances and exits will naturally increase.

The rooms, whose form will be less repetitive, will be more likely to have diversity in their ornaments; the greatest task will always be to arrange them symmetrically in relation to the doors, windows, fireplaces and beams.

From the change in the building's plan will follow that of the garden; everything, the flower-beds, the groves, the rows, will become new and continue to vary. For example, the rows, as they are made now, represent the covered walkways of the Ancients; when they are placed in relationship to the French Order, they will take, if you will, five or six different forms because of the arrangement of the trees.

On decorum

The French Order is suitable only to public buildings, and to private edifices that require grandeur and magnificence . . .

It is not only the richness and majesty associated with this Order that must determine its use, but also the extent of its masses, the spacious rooms that can be laid out and the strength it can give any building that must look like a monument and immortalise a Nation . . .

The effects of a vault and a dome carried on large arches will be felt; that of the intimate union which reigns between the two ways of presenting the groups of columns, that of a new Order peculiar to the French Order, and lastly, that of windows that are differently shaped depending on the requirements of convenience and use.

With regard to ornaments, I believe that they will appear without profusion, well-chosen and affixed with a noble simplicity. The trophies that one sees will only herald the gentleness of a peaceful reign, the joy of an unshakeable State, and the happiness of a free People. The Figures above the doors represent the Sciences, the Arts and the Talents that particularly distinguish the French, while those which hold up the large pedestals on the floor offer the more than venerable love that the Nation, by its gaiety and affability, inspires towards it in the four corners of the globe.

anticlassicism • deformation • freedom • naturalism • classical canon • antiquity • abuses • regionalism • nationalism

Antoine-Chrysostôme Quatremère de Quincy 1755–1849

Antoine-Chrysostôme Quatremère de Quincy (1755–1849)

On Egyptian Architecture (1785 composed; 1803 published)

The archaeologist, sculptor and antiquarian Quatremère played an important role in forming the cultural policies of France under Napoleon, along with others like his friend and protector, the painter J.L. David. Quatremère preferred the grandeur and ornamentation of Egyptian architecture to the simplicity of Greek architecture advocated by Laugier and Winckelmann. This orientalist position is expressed in the present text which won the prize of the Académie des Inscriptions et Belles-Lettres in 1785.

Further reading Collins, 1965; De Zurko, 1957; Lavin, 1992; Schneider, 1910.

There can be no doubt that all those things which in the arts relate to abstract principles of the impressions that they make upon our souls, can only be properly comprehended by those who have personally experienced those impressions. No description can be given of sensations, no drawing may stimulate them, and they arise solely from an immediate vision of the monuments. It is to be regretted that those travellers who have been in a position to receive such impressions have had neither the talent nor the inclination to pass them on to us in their descriptions of the monuments of Egypt. They remained content with very superficial drawings.

But such drawings without descriptions are nevertheless more valuable than the most extensive descriptions without drawings, especially for those able to read between their lines. Any person in the habit of this form of interpretation, and who has often had occasion to compare with the monuments themselves the drawings made by travellers, and to define for himself in this area a rule of criticism, must not despair of acquiring from the simple viewing of the drawings a tolerably exact idea of the actual effect and some of the other qualities of the Architecture concerned.

But this art has a multitude of different parts on which one may, simply on the basis provided by drawings, give a pronouncement as judiciously as when one has seen the originals.

Let us suppose that the aim should be above all not to assess the fine subtleties of the manner, the appropriate relationships between elements, the graces of the shapes, and the delicacy of the ornamentation or proportions that escape the most meticulous draughtsman, but only to grasp the specific character, the originating principle, the types and the general system of a form of Architecture, to discover within it its particular genius and the nature of its principal shapes, its masses, its planes and its essential details – for this, it will be agreed that a study of the copies may, up to a point, replace the viewing of the originals.

Antoine-
Chrysostôme
Quatremère de
Quincy
1755–1849

I would add that the theory of Egyptian Architecture, whatever the theory that it is eventually succeeded in building on the basis of the most certain information and the most detailed notions, could never become a conventional object of study for those who exercise the art of building.

There is no pretension here to divine or to lay down the rules for an Architecture that, very probably, had no rules, and it will be considered that the conditions of the programme have been met if, according to the information existing today, we succeed in imparting knowledge with some method and with the order that such a subject entails, on the taste, characteristic shapes, main elements, general disposition, genius, general aspect, decorative style and means of construction of Egyptian Architecture. [. . .]

First Part. An Effort to Determine Some of the Causes that Influenced the State of Architecture in Egypt

It can be seen that an opinion is fairly generally established among authors who have written on Architecture and that nobody, it seems to me, has yet sought to debate an opinion that tends to locate the origin of this art in a primitive nation, and to confer the honour of having discovered it on a people who *invented* it and handed it down to its neighbours, whence it passed from people to people and to all nations.

Since Egypt is in many respects the first people to be known to us historically [. . .] the cradle of Architecture has been situated in Egypt and we have attributed its invention to the Egyptians.

The use of the notion of *invention* is perhaps misleading and based on a misunderstanding in more than one respect. First, if Architecture is considered solely from the point of view of a straightforward need, the form of industry it involves could not be classed as an art, to which the idea of invention would be applicable, or such an invention, of whatever kind it may be, would be made at all times and by all peoples.

If we go on to consider Architecture from the point of view of construction, it is more a science than an art, and a science based on studies and observations whose development must in all respects go hand-in-hand with the growth of human societies themselves.

If, lastly, we consider it from the point of view of pleasure, as a luxury in human societies, it is necessary to say that the instinct for pleasure, like the taste for variety, is everywhere quite natural to mankind, so much so that in all times and in all countries similarities concerning more than just one point could be singled out, indicating that Architecture is an art whose aim is always to please and imitate.

Architecture was not invented by a single, specific people. It is necessarily a universal consequence of the needs of mankind, and of the pleasures that in human societies become one with their needs. The invention of Architecture must be placed in the same category as that of language, that is to say, neither can be attributed to a single man, since both are attributes of man. If language belongs to humanity, do the languages that are the local variations of a general faculty belong to local human societies or to nations? We make a distinction between languages we call mother tongues, that is to say, those whose origin is unknown, and those which are composites or derivatives of previously existing languages. Their links are indicated or demonstrated by analogies between their vocabularies or their structure. In that research, it would be a grave mistake, by confusing the general principles of universal grammar, which belong to language, with the rules of syntax specific to individual languages, if we claimed to establish parentage between two languages solely on the basis that they both have declensions and conjugations. As far as I know, nobody has, in this field, made any such mistake.

Antoine-
Chrysostôme
Quatremère de
Quincy
1755–1849

Conversely, however, we might say that almost nobody has escaped a very similar error where Architecture is concerned. The general maxims of the art of building common to all forms of Architecture have almost always been confused with the particular principles and original givens of individual forms of Architecture, with the result that links and relationships have been imagined between the most distant forms.

[...]

If that were to be so, it is absolutely necessary that there should be observed in the architectural works of peoples who are totally different, the most distant, the most separated one from another, certain similarities from which no consequence may be deduced liable to establish the reality of a communication of aesthetic taste, style or basic principle between them.

Just as it is important to make a careful distinction between that which, in Architecture, comes from the inspirations of nature, human instinct, or the forces of general causality, so it would be desirable to take care in determining the local causes that must have modified in a variety of ways the production of that art, in recognising in each land the originating principle from which it developed, and the particular needs that influenced the initial direction it took [...] will help discern, among the similarities that are observed, which of them must be attributed to the general action of a universal principle, and which are revelatory of a spirit of imitation or borrowing.

It is also necessary to recognise an indigenous principle in Egyptian Architecture. And if, in all its edifices, taken as a whole or considered in all their details, we find a perfect conformity with the taste and style of the underground constructions, we shall conclude that, having had so different an origin from that of the Greeks, it would have been difficult for Egypt to have communicated to them either its aesthetic taste or its principles. The conclusion to be drawn from this is that Greek borrowing from Egypt could only have been the borrowing of details or elements accessory to the constitution of its Architecture.

Perhaps another conclusion to be drawn from this is that both these styles of Architecture must be considered as without generic relationship linking them. [...]

For those who understand the nature of systematic imitation by Architecture of its models, and for those who are aware of what should be understood here by the notions of 'model' and 'imitation', any minute discussion of such matters would be but a tedious pleasantry. These notions are of little importance in themselves, and since it is not relevant here to verify the detail of them, it is beyond the scope of the present type of critique to deal with them.

What is argued here is that the material used in the earliest houses in Egypt, those which influenced the taste and the forms of architectural imitation, was stone and not wood. What is sought to be proved here, is that the intrinsic and specific character of its Architecture adopts none of the forms or combinations specific to carpentry, and that, in conclusion, it modelled itself on a type of structure quite different from that of the Greeks, and that structure is that of the underground works.

We do see however some columns in Egypt that are a quite manifest imitation of trees and plants natural to that country. The same is true here as that which will be repeated later, that in Greek Architecture the column was not an imitation of the tree, but simply beams assembled and already shaped by the carpenter. This analogy that one finds in Egypt, between some columns and certain trees, is a decorative one detracting nothing from the constitutive system as a whole. [. . .]

Antoine-
Chrysostôme
Quatremère de
Quincy
1755–1849

What also appears certain is that Egypt is not by its nature a country rich in wood, and especially wood for carpentry. [. . .] This is no mean argument in support of our claim with respect to the probability of the originating principle of Egyptian Architecture. Because art takes necessarily as its model in this area not that which is rare but that which is general in a country, not what is exceptional, but that which is founded on habit.

All things in the temples of Egypt are redolent of mystery, which was the initial foundation of its religion, and which must be that of all religions, for religion has as its principal object the prevention of the human mind from seeking that which it will never find. It is the antidote for curiosity, that passion of man, whose action is salutary when limited to the discovery of things that are within his grasp, but the most pernicious of curses when pride, which is its basic principle, revolts against his weakness, and despite his inability to discover the truth, breaks down all the ramparts of wisdom that time has raised between man and the void. Mystery, the soul of Egyptian worship, imbues all the monuments left by its arts.

Architecture's much vaunted artistic representation is of a kind far different from that of the other arts.

We have seen that in truth primitive houses, whose construction is suggested by need, have become everywhere a form of model for imitation by the art. But that model is undoubtedly not nature. We certainly cannot see as the productions of nature such gross attempts at the art of building, and we can describe as an art of representation or imitation only that art which imitates nature. This docility in the art, this servitude to the forms of the first buildings, produces only a resemblance that is more or less arbitrary, and is far from being a complete representation of the model. If the representational or imitative virtues of Architecture were limited to that, there can be no doubt that the general opinion of men would not have elevated it to the rank of a representational art.

It must be said that Architecture represents or imitates nature not in any given object, not in a positive model, but by transferring to its works the laws that nature

[439]

follows in its own creations. This art does not copy any particular object, it does not repeat any particular construction, it imitates the worker and follows his action. To conclude, it imitates or represents not in the way a painter represents his model, but like a pupil who seeks to adopt the manner of his master, who does not do what he sees done, but how he sees it being done.

There is no single source for decorative work. It is only through abstraction that it can be reduced to a general principle. It is certain that the taste for ornamentation springs from the nature of the human mind. The successive needs for rest and movement is one of these abstract causes used to explain the major part of the actions and feelings of men. It is a necessity for the soul to change situation as it is for the body to change position. How can the soul change its situation? It does so by moving from one sensation to another. [...]

Antoine-
Chrysostôme
Quatremère de
Quincy
1755–1849

To decorate or embellish an object is nothing other than to develop sources of sensation or impression to be added to sensations and impression already produced by the object itself. [...]

Thus the taste for ornamentation relates to instinct and in this regard it is universal.

As for what we call good taste in ornamentation, this relates not to mechanical and superficial imitation but to considered study and the science of nature itself...

[...] It is absolutely certain that the concept of ornamentation or decoration in the creations of nature is no more than a metaphor. [...]

To decorate, that is to say, to introduce variety into the works of art and need according to the natural penchant of man is a thing to be seen in every place. At whatever point of civilisation we may stop and observe human industry, we see this need, always the same, always active, for the modification of marble in cities just as much as the most fragile of tools in the hands of a savage.

To decorate, that is to say, to introduce such variety, due to the principle underlying this taste and its origin, due to its relationship with the organisation of our soul and our senses, and then to deduce from those observations a system of rules founded on the laws of nature and analogous to our sensations, is the work of intelligence and genius. That work is undertaken by only a few peoples and in a small number of privileged centuries.

We have seen that there are in Architecture two types of representation or imitation, one manifest to the senses and the other abstract, one based on the models of the very first houses in each country, and the other that springs from a knowledge of the laws of nature and the impressions that our soul receives from the sight of, and the relationships between objects. [...]

The world has almost always had a false idea of what is called *order* in Architecture. Some have restricted, others have extended this idea too far, but all have fallen into error only because they have linked the existence of an order to objects that are only accessory to it, and by this I mean its decorative aspect.

There is nothing more ridiculous than all the modern attempts to invent new architectural orders. It is imagined that it is enough to design a capital in an eccentric style to produce a new order. [...]

If the existence of an order were linked to style of decoration for a capital or a column, no nation would have had more orders in Architecture than the Egyptians. Nevertheless, it is to be doubted that we can attribute to them a knowledge of what we mean by the concept of order in Architecture.

Order consists in a system of proportions of form and ornamentation, constantly related to such and such a quality that Architecture can make manifest to the senses.

Architecture is a sort of ocular music. To speak to the soul through the channel of the eyes, it needs relationships between objects made sensible and concrete by visible forms and proportions. It is the progression in those forms and proportions that is the equivalent of musical keys, and those keys are what we have termed 'orders'.

history versus antiquarianism • nature • nurture • fashion • orientalism

Thomas Jefferson (1743–1826)

Letter to the Building Committee of the Virginia State Capitol (1786)

Jefferson, the third President of the United States, was largely responsible for introducing neo-classicism in architecture to the new republic, with an emphasis not only on the 'columnar' style but also on functionality. The Virginia State Capitol, whose design he supervised, was one of the first buildings to embody this architectural philosophy (De Zurko, 1957; Fitch, 1966, 37–60).

Thomas Jefferson
1743–1826

Further reading Hamlin, 1964; Kimball, 1943–1950; Lehmann, 1947.

To the Directors of the Building Committee

Paris, 26 January, 1786

Gentlemen,

... Two methods of proceeding presented themselves to my mind. The one was to leave to some architect to draw an external according to his fancy, in which way experience shows that about once in a thousand times a pleasing form is hit upon; the other was to take some model already devised and approved by the general suffrage of the world. I had no hesitation in deciding that the latter was best, nor after the decision was there any doubt what model to take [Maison Carrée at Nimes].

... Having not had the leisure to visit it yet, I could only judge of it from drawings, and from the relation of numbers who have seen it. I determined therefore to adopt this model, and to have all its proportions justly drewed. As it was impossible for a foreign artist to know what number and sizes of apartments could suit the different corps of our government, nor how they should be connected with one another, I undertook to form that arrangement, and this being done, I committed them to an architect [M. Clerisseau] who has studied this art 20 years in Rome.... He was too well acquainted with the merit of that building to find himself restrained by my injunctions not to depart from his model. In one instance only he persuaded me to admit of this. That was to make the portico two columns deep only, instead of three as the original is. His reason was that this latter depth would too much darken the apartments. Economy might be added as a second reason. I consented to it to satisfy him, and the plans were so drawn. I knew it would still be easy to execute the building with a depth of three columns, and it is certainly what I would recommend. We know that the Maison Quaree has pleased universally for near 2,000 years. By leaving out a column, the proportions will be changed and perhaps the effects will be injured more than is expected. What is good is often spoiled by trying to make it better. . . .

classical canon • antiquity • abuses • precedent • authority • invention

Nicolas Caritat, Marquis de Condorcet (1743–1794)

Report on Hospitals (written 1786)

This unpublished manuscript (Tzonis, 1977) by the philosopher and mathematician Condorcet, one of the chief figures of the French Enlightenment, belongs to the group of studies on the problem of hospital design undertaken in the last years of the *Ancien Régime* which include the reports of Petit (1774), Leroy (1777) and Tenon (1788). The proposal for a multidisciplinary approach to design also involving the participation of the local users of the facility are among the avant-garde features of Condorcet's report (Tzonis and Lefaivre, 1984b).

Further reading Fortier *et al.*, 1975; Foucault *et al.*, 1976; Tzonis *et al.*, 1975.

Nicolas Caritat,
Marquis de
Condorcet
1743–1794

[. . .] what size should be given to a hospital in order to cure the largest number of patients at the least possible expense?

Between an establishment where each patient would have, as if he were a wealthy person, a room for himself, and a nurse only for him, and a Hôtel-Dieu, or great general hospital, where all the sick persons of a town such as Paris may be assembled, there are many degrees and it is probable that there must exist between these two extremes a middle term where the greatest possible advantage is to be found.

That middle term does not appear to me to be impossible to determine. I say this because:

1. Those who practise the art and who have studied hospitals are entirely capable of knowing how many of the sick one person may serve during a night without great fatigue and without those persons being deprived of necessary care. Once this number has been established, it will yield the number of patients that it is appropriate to assemble in a single ward, along with the number that should be gathered together in the same building.

2. The number of sick persons for which a single pharmacist, with an assistant, may prepare the necessary medicinal drugs; the number of the sick for whom a single person may prepare gruel and other beverages that are prepared in kitchens, shall also give the number of beds below which we cannot descend in any establishment without increasing the expense, almost without utility for patients.

3. I shall not speak here of the doctor and the surgeon, because, since they may see other sick persons, it would be easy to adjust their emoluments to the number of beds. But it is good that a practitioner should be within reach of patients, so that he may be awoken in extraordinary circumstances, and it is possible for those who have studied hospitals, and who have wide experience of the curative art, to know for how many patients a single man may occupy this function without the fatigue thus occasioned disturbing the service he normally provides. [. . .]

[442]

Once these numbers have been determined, not only for those parts of the service, but for all others, this will give us a form of minimum level for the number of beds. This is because we may see here that no single person is charged with the task of being the head with the task of administering, and consequently no person to apply restrictions, and with everything to lose by diminishing the size of the establishment.

Once the smallest number has been determined in this manner, it would be seen what degree of salubrity, and of comfort for the sick could be given to a hospital with this number of beds using a given initial sum of money and a given amount of annual expenditure per bed. It would then be necessary to seek to determine what could be gained, and what might be lost, by increasing the number of beds while retaining the same advantages. And in fact, I believe the method least likely to lead to error is to seek to express all things in terms of money, since where there are five, six, eight thousand patients in the same establishment, it is physically impossible to provide them with the same benefits as in a small hospice at satisfactory expense. If that expense becomes excessive, not only does it demonstrate the defects of such great establishments, but it also provides a form of scale against which they may be assessed. Since there are very many hospitals and few hospices a comparison of the mortality in these different types of establishment may shed useful light, but I believe that the method described above would be more likely to yield accurate results. It is very doubtful whether, in the Hôtel-Dieu in Paris or in the hospices sited in that town, that there are no abuses or defects independent of their size.

Nicolas Caritat, Marquis de Condorcet 1743–1794

The observation that the greater number of the sick in the Hôtel-Dieu are taken there at advanced stages in their illnesses, alters and weakens any conclusions we could draw from a comparison of mortality.

This comparison should be done according to tables in which the type of disease would be expressed, because it may be the case that the greater mortality in the Hôtel-Dieu for example relates to certain specific diseases admitted there, or to the effect of the hospital air on other sicknesses. This would alter once again the conclusions to be drawn from this observation, making them much less conclusive as proof against the large establishments. ____ has advanced the argument, as a reason for preferring large establishments to hospices, that it is easier to find a person capable of administering a large establishment than fifty persons capable of administering hospices. This opinion would appear to contradict general experience in all areas. Besides, an administrator of a vast establishment would have deputy administrators placed under him, and these would be just as difficult to find as the head administrators of small hospices. Lastly, it is almost as difficult to judge such an extensive administration as it is to administer it. The administrator placed in charge of it would have no true judges – receiving random praise or blame from the public opinion, he would in the end cease to listen to it.

If, on the contrary, there are several administrations, competition and emulation will arise between them. It is easier to judge them, both because they are smaller, and because each offers a point of comparison for the others. Public opinion becomes for each head employee a constraint that is all the more powerful for the fact that it is not an absolute judgement, but a comparative one, a preference that is more humiliating for the person placed below his colleagues by that opinion. This competition, this emulation would also arise between the superior persons of each establishment with regard to the inhabitants of the town areas where they were situated. Furthermore, the errors committed in a great establishment are almost always grave, very difficult to remedy when one is lucky enough to have detected them, and detected later in the day. Reforms are very difficult, abuses more powerfully protected. It is only with difficulty that decisions are taken to attempt a small number of improvements.

Conversely, in small establishments, enlightened one by another, and where each would profit from the experience of all, errors would be perceived earlier, corrected more swiftly and improvements made more promptly.

In the case of the very large establishments that are virtually alone, I know of no arguments that may counterbalance the advantages I have described.

Concerning the means for performance of the tasks, it seems to me that hospices situated in each parish have all the advantage. In Paris there is no parish, even the poorest, that does not have some wealthy individuals, architects, mathematicians capable of judging the drawings of an architect, doctors, surgeons, physicists, lawyers, traders, people employed or formerly employed in affairs of administration, or men who have studied the theory of the political sciences. Each parish priest should therefore gather together those men in his parish from whom he may expect the most expert knowledge and assistance. He should beg them to choose from among their number some to be charged with the task of arriving at the design of the best possible hospice for the parish. This design should be discussed, examined by the parishioners, and once written down according to their observations, presented to them, and then the hospice will become in a sense their own creation. But all questions of pride apart, if we assume that men have within them a pure love of doing good, it will be found that if that desire to do good is to lead to sacrifices, to be exercised with energy, the feeling of satisfaction at having done good must be associated with the pleasure of having worked upon it, to have dealt with it. The assistance provided will then be all the more prompt and extensive. On the other hand, the plans will, with advantage, be the product of intellects to be found throughout one of the cities where more intellect has been wasted, if ever intellect was wasted, when the matter at hand is that of very large establishments, because, in view of the great extent of the details entailed by such establishments, they cannot be dealt with without devoting oneself to them entirely.

social reform • democratisation • urbanisation of architecture • planning • environmental control and determinism

Jeremy Bentham
1748–1832

Jeremy Bentham (1748–1832)

Panopticon, or the Inspection House (1787)

Bentham was the founder of Utilitarianism, a theory in ethics which claimed that the general welfare was more important than the happiness of a few. He devised the Panopticon building as a model for all kinds of institutions in which control over humans, or animals, was important. The building was to be cylindrical and four to six storeys high. Each storey was to contain a number of cells which followed a radial plan. Each cell was to have one occupant. The doors of the cells gave onto a large covered shaft in the centre of the building, and were pierced with a crevice or a window through which a manager might peer unobserved and thus oversee the actions of the inhabitants (Evans, 1971; Foucault, 1975). Intended for use in prisons, poor houses, insane asylums and hospitals, this arrangement was a considerable improvement over the conditions which prevailed at that time, in terms of hygiene and privacy. The Panopticon is considered an early embodiment of welfare state ideals (Foucault, ibid.).

Letter I

Idea of the inspection principle Crecheff in White Russia *(1787)*

DEAR ****, I observed t'other day in one of your English papers, an advertisement relative to a HOUSE of CORRECTION therein spoken of, as intended for *******. It occurred to me, that the plan of a building, lately contrived by my brother, for purposes in some respects similar, and which, under the name of the *Inspection House*, or the *Elaboratory*, he is about erecting here, might afford some hints for the above establishment. I have accordingly obtained some drawings relative to it, which I here enclose. Indeed I look upon it as capable of applications of the most extensive nature; and that for reasons which you will soon perceive.

To say all in one word, it will be found applicable, I think, without exception, to all establishments whatsoever, in which, within a space not too large to be covered or commanded by buildings, a number of persons are meant to be kept under inspection. No matter how different, or even opposite the purpose: whether it be that of *punishing the incorrigible, guarding the insane, reforming the vicious, confining the suspected, employing the idle, maintaining the helpless, curing the sick, instructing the willing* in any branch of industry, or *training the rising race* in the path of *education*: in a word, whether it be applied to the purposes of *perpetual prisons* in the room of death, or *prisons for confinement* before trial, or *penitentiary-houses, or houses of correction, or work-houses, or manufactories, or mad-houses, or hospitals, or schools.*

It is obvious that, in all these instances, the more constantly the persons to be inspected are under the eyes of the persons who should inspect them, the more perfectly will the purpose X of the establishment have been attained. Ideal perfection, if that were the object, would require that each person should actually be in that predicament, during every instant of time. This being impossible, the next thing to be wished for is that, at every instant, seeing reason to believe as much, and not being able to satisfy himself to the contrary, he should *conceive* himself to be so. This point, you will immediately see, is most completely secured by my brother's plan; and, I think, it will appear equally manifest, that it cannot be compassed by any other, or to speak more properly, that if it be compassed by any other, it can only be in proportion as such other may approach to this.

To cut the matter as short as possible, I will consider it at once in its application to such purposes as, being most complicated, will serve to exemplify the greatest force and variety of precautionary contrivance. Such are those which have suggested the idea of *penitentiary-houses*: in which the objects of *safe custody, confinement, solitude, forced labour,* and *instruction*, were all of them to be kept in view. If all these objects can be accomplished together, of course with at least equal certainty and facility may any lesser number of them.

Jeremy Bentham
1748–1832

Letter II

Plan for a penitentiary inspection-house

Before you look at the plan, take in words the general idea of it.

The building is circular.

The apartments of the prisoners occupy the circumference. You may call them, if you please, the *cells.*

These *cells* are divided from one another, and the prisoners by that means secluded from all communication with each other, by *partitions* in the form of *radii* issuing from the circumference towards the centre, and extending as many feet as shall be thought necessary to form the largest dimension of the cell.

The apartment of the inspector occupies the centre; you may call it, if you please, the *inspector's lodge*.

It will be convenient in most, if not in all cases, to have a vacant space or *area* all round, between such centre and such circumference. You may call it, if you please, the *intermediate* or *annular* area.

About the width of a cell may be sufficient for a *passage* from the outside of the building to the lodge.

Each cell has in the outward circumference, a *window*, large enough, not only to light the cell, but, through the cell, to afford light enough to the correspondent part of the lodge.

Jeremy Bentham
1748–1832

The inner circumference of the cell is formed by an iron *grating*, so light as not to screen any part of the cell from the inspector's view.

Of this grating, a part sufficiently large opens, in form of a *door*, to admit the prisoner at his first entrance; and to give admission at any time to the inspector or any of his attendants.

To cut off from each prisoner the view of every other, the partitions are carried on a few feet beyond the grating into the intermediate area: such projecting parts I call the *protracted partitions*.

It is conceived that the light, coming in in this manner through the cells, and so across the intermediate area, will be sufficient for the inspector's lodge. But, for this purpose, both the windows in the cells, and those corresponding to them in the lodge, should be as large as the strength of the building, and what shall be deemed a necessary attention to economy, will permit.

To the windows of the lodge there are *blinds*, as high up as the eyes of the prisoners in their cells can, by any means they can employ, be made to reach.

To prevent *through light*, whereby, notwithstanding the blinds, the prisoners would see from the cells whether or not any person was in the lodge, that apartment is divided into quarters, by *partitions* formed by two diameters to the circle, crossing each other at right angles. For these partitions the thinnest materials might serve; and they might be made removable at pleasure; their height, sufficient to prevent the prisoners seeing over them from the cells. Doors to these partitions, if left open at any time, might produce the through light. To prevent this, divide each partition into two, at any part required, setting down the one-half at such distance from the other as shall be equal to the aperture of a door.

These windows of the inspector's lodge open into the intermediate area, in the form of *doors*, in as many places as shall be deemed necessary to admit of his communicating readily with any of the cells. [. . .]

To save the troublesome exertion of voice that might otherwise be necessary, and to prevent one prisoner from knowing that the inspector was occupied by another prisoner at a distance, a small *tin tube* might reach from each cell to the inspector's lodge, passing across the area, and so in at the side of the correspondent window of the lodge. By means of this implement, the slightest whisper of the one might be heard by the other, especially if he had proper notice to apply his ear to the tube.

With regard to *instruction*, in cases where it cannot be duly given without the instructor's being close to the work, or without setting his hand to it by way of example before the learner's face, the instructor must indeed here as elsewhere, shift his station as often as there is occasion to visit different workmen; unless he calls the workmen to him, which in some of the instances to which this sort of building is applicable, such as that of imprisoned felons, could not so well be. But in all cases where directions, given verbally and at a distance, are sufficient, these tubes will be found of use. They will save, on the one hand, the exertion of voice it would require, on the part of the instructor, to communicate instruction to the workmen without quitting his central station in the lodge; and, on the other, the confusion which would ensue if different instructors or persons in the lodge were calling to the cells at the same time. And, in the case of hospitals, the quiet that may be insured by this little contrivance, trifling as it may seem at first sight, affords an additional advantage.

[...] The most economical, and perhaps the most convenient, way of *warming* the cells and area, would be by flues surrounding it, upon the principle of those in hot-houses. A total want of every means of producing artificial heat might, in such weather as we sometimes have in England, be fatal to the lives of the prisoners; at any rate, it would often times be altogether incompatible with their working at any sedentary employment. The flues, however, and the fire-places belonging to them, instead of being on the outside, as in hot-houses, should be in the inside. By this means, there would be less waste of heat, and the current of air that would rush in on all sides through the cells, to supply the draught made by the fires, would answer so far the purpose of ventilation. But of this more under the head of Hospitals.

Jeremy Bentham
1748–1832

There is one subject, which, though not of the most dignified kind, nor of the most pleasant kind to expatiate upon, is of too great importance to health and safe custody to be passed over unconsidered: I mean the provision to be made for carrying off the result of necessary evacuations. A common necessary might be dangerous to security, and would be altogether incompatible with the plan of solitude. To have the filth carried off by the attendants, would be altogether as incompatible with cleanliness, since without such a degree of regularity as it would be difficult, if not ridiculous, to attempt to enforce in case of health, and altogether impossible in case of sickness, the air of each cell, and by that means the lodge itself would be liable to be kept in a state of constant contamination, in the intervals betwixt one visit and another. This being the case, I can see no other eligible means, than that of having in each cell a fixed provision made for this purpose in the construction of the building.

Betwixt every other two cells, at the end of the partition which divides them, a hollow shaft or tunnel is left in the brick-work of the exterior wall; which tunnel, if there be several storeys to the building, is carried up through all of them.

Into this tunnel is inserted, under each cell, the bottom of an EARTHEN PIPE [...]

A sight screen, which the prisoner might occasionally interpose, may perhaps not be thought superfluous. This, while it answers the purpose of decency, might be so adjusted as to prevent his concealing from the eye of the inspector any forbidden enterprise.

For each cell, the whole apparatus would not come to many shillings: a small consideration for a great degree of security. In this manner, without any relaxation of the discipline, the advantages of cleanliness, and its concomitant health, may be attained to as great a degree as in most private houses.

It would be regarded, perhaps, as a luxury too great for an establishment of this kind, were I to venture to propose the addition of a WATER-PIPE all around with a cock to it in each cell. The clear expense would, however, not be quite so great as it might seem: since by this means a considerable quantity of attendance would be saved.

[...]

Letter IV

The principle extended to uncovered areas

In my two last letters, I gave you such idea as it was in my power to give you by words, of this new plan of construction, considered in its most *simple* form. A few more with regard to what further *extensions* it may admit of.

Jeremy Bentham
1748–1832

The utmost number of persons that could be stowed in a single building of this sort, consistently with the purposes of each several institution, being ascertained, to increase the number, that of the buildings must of course be increased. Suppose two of these *rotundas* requisite: these two might, *by a covered gallery* constructed upon the same principles, be consolidated into one inspection-house. And by the help of such a covered gallery, *the field of inspection* might be dilated to any extent.

If the number of rotundas were extended to *four*, a regular uncovered area might in that way be inclosed; and being surrounded by covered galleries, would be commanded in this manner from all sides, instead of being commanded only from one.

The area thus inclosed might be either *circular* like the buildings, or *square*, or *oblong*, as one or other of those forms were best adapted to the prevailing ideas of beauty or local convenience. A chain of any length, composed of inspection-houses adapted to the same or different purposes, might in this way be carried round an area of any extent.

On such a plan, either one inspector might serve for two or more rotundas, or if there were one to each, *the inspective force*, if I may use the expression, would be greater in such a compound building, than in any of the number singly taken, of which it was composed; since each inspector might be relieved occasionally by every other.

Letter V

Essential points of the plan

It may be of use, that among all the particulars you have seen, it should be clearly understood what circumstances are, and what are not, essential to the plan. The essence of it consists, then, in the *centrality* of the inspector's situation, combined with the well-known and most effectual contrivances for *seeing without being seen*. As to the *general form* of the building, the most commodious for most purposes seems to be the circular: but this is not an absolutely essential circumstance. Of all figures, however, this, you will observe, is the only one that affords a perfect view, and the same view, of an indefinite number of apartments of the same dimensions: that affords a spot from which, without any change of situation, a man may survey, in the same perfection, the whole number, and without so much as a change of posture, the half of the whole number, at the same time: that, within a boundary of a given extent, contains the greatest quantity of room: – that places the centre at the least distance from the light: – that gives the cells most width, at the part where, on account of the light, most light may, for the purposes of work, be wanted: – and that reduces to the greatest possible shortness the path taken by the inspector, in passing from each part of the field of inspection to every other.

You will please to observe, that though perhaps it is the most important point, that the persons to be inspected should always feel themselves as if under inspection, at least as standing a great chance of being so, yet it is not by any means the *only* one. If it were, the same advantage might be given to buildings of almost any form. What is also of importance is that for the greatest proportion of time possible, each man should actually *be* under inspection. This is material in *all* cases, that the inspector may have the satisfaction of knowing, that the discipline actually has the effect which it is designed to have. [...]

A very material point is that room be allotted to the lodge, sufficient to adapt it to the purpose of a complete and constant habitation for the principal inspector or head-keeper, and his family. The more numerous also the family, the better; since, by this means, there will in fact be as many inspectors as the family consists of persons, though only one be paid for it. Neither the orders of the inspector himself, nor any interest which they may feel, or not feel, in the regular performance of his duty, would be requisite to find them motives adequate to the purpose. Secluded oftentimes, by their situation, from every other object, they will naturally, and in a manner unavoidably, give their eyes a direction conformable to that purpose, in every momentary interval of their ordinary occupations. It will supply in their instance the place of that great and constant fund of entertainment to the sedentary and vacant in towns – the looking out of the window. The scene, though a confined, would be a very various, and therefore, perhaps, not altogether an unamusing one.

Jeremy Bentham
1748–1832

Letter VI

Advantages of the plan

I flatter myself there can now be little doubt of the plan's possessing the fundamental advantages I have been attributing to it: I mean, the *apparent omnipresence* of the inspector (if divines will allow me the expression) combined with the extreme facility of his *real presence*.

A collateral advantage it possesses, and on the score of frugality a very material one, is that which respects the *number* of the inspectors requisite. If this plan required more than another, the additional number would form an objection, which, were the difference to a certain degree considerable, might rise so high as to be conclusive: so far from it, that a greater multitude than ever were yet lodged in one house might be inspected by a single person; for the trouble of inspection is diminished in no less proportion than the strictness of inspection is increased.

Another very important advantage, whatever purposes the plan may be applied to, particularly where it is applied to the severest and most coercive purposes, is that the *under* keepers or inspectors, the servants and subordinates of every kind, will be under the same irresistible control with respect to the *head* keeper or inspector, as the prisoners or other persons to be governed are with respect to *them*. On the common plans, what means, what possibility, has the prisoner of appealing to the humanity of the principal for redress against the neglect or oppression of subordinates in that rigid sphere, but the *few* opportunities which, in a crowded prison, the most conscientious keeper *can* afford – but the none at all which many a keeper *thinks* fit to give them? How different would their lot be upon this plan!

In no instance could his subordinates either perform or depart from their duty, but he must know the time and degree and manner of their doing so. It presents an answer, and that a satisfactory one, to one of the most puzzling of political questions – *quis custodiet ipsos custodes?* And, as the fulfilling of his, as well as their, duty would be rendered so much easier, than it can ever have been hitherto, so might, and so should any departure from it be punished with the more inflexible severity. It is this circumstance that renders the influence of this plan not less beneficial to what is called *liberty*, than to necessary coercion; not less powerful as a control upon subordinate power, than as a curb to delinquency; as a shield to innocence, than as a scourge to guilt.

Another advantage, still operating to the same ends, is the great load of trouble and disgust which it takes off the shoulders of those occasional inspectors of a higher order, such as *judges* and other *magistrates*, who, called down to this irksome task from the superior ranks of life, cannot but feel a proportionable repugnance to the discharge of it. Think how it is with them upon the present plans, and how it still must be upon the best plans that have been hitherto devised! The cells or apartments, however constructed, must, if there be nine hundred of them (as there were to have been upon the penitentiary-house plan) be opened to the visitors, one by one. To do their business to any purpose, they must approach near to, and come almost in contact with each inhabitant; whose situation being watched over according to no other than the loose methods of inspection at present practicable, will on that account require the more minute and troublesome investigation on the part of these occasional superintendents. By this new plan, the disgust is entirely removed, and the trouble of going into such a room as the lodge, is no more than the trouble of going into any other. [. . .]

Among the other causes of that reluctance, none at present so forcible, none so unhappily well grounded, none which affords so natural an excuse, nor so strong a reason against accepting of any excuse, as the danger of *infection* – a circumstance which carries death, in one of its most tremendous forms, from the seat of guilt to the seat of justice, involving in one common catastrophe the violator and the upholder of the laws. But in a spot so constructed, and under a course of discipline so insured, how should infection ever arise? Or how should it continue? Against every danger of this kind, what private house of the poor, one might almost say, or even of the most opulent, can be equally secure?

Nor is the disagreeableness of the task of superintendence diminished by this plan, in a much greater degree than the efficacy of it is increased. On all others, be the superintendent's visit ever so unexpected, and his motions ever so quick, time there must always be for preparations blinding the real state of things. Out of nine hundred cells, he can visit but one at a time, and, in the meanwhile, the worst of the others may be arranged, and the inhabitants threatened, and tutored how to receive him. On this plan, no sooner is the superintendent announced, than the whole scene opens instantaneously to his view.

In mentioning inspectors and superintendents who are such by office, I must not overlook that system of inspection, which, however little heeded, will not be the less useful and efficacious: I mean, the part which individuals may be disposed to take in the business, without intending, perhaps, or even without thinking of, any other effects of their visits, than the gratification of their own particular curiosity. What the inspector's or keeper's family are with respect to him, that, and more, will these spontaneous visitors be to the superintendent – assistants, deputies, in so far as he is faithful, witnesses and judges should he ever be unfaithful, to his trust. So as they are but there, what the motives were that drew them thither is perfectly immaterial; whether the relieving of their anxieties by the affecting prospect of their respective friends and relatives thus detained in durance, or merely the satisfying that general curiosity, which an establishment, on various accounts so interesting to human feelings, may naturally be expected to excite.

You see, I take for granted as a matter of course, that under the necessary regulations for preventing interruption and disturbance, the doors of these establishments will be, as, without very special reasons to the contrary, the doors of all public establishments ought to be, thrown wide open to the body of the curious at large – the great *open committee* of the tribunal of the world. And who ever objects to such publicity, where it is practicable, but those whose motives for objection afford the strongest reasons for it?

[. . .]

Letter VIII

Jeremy Bentham
1748–1832

Uses – penitentiary-houses – reformation

In my last, I endeavoured to state to you the advantages which a receptacle, upon the plan of the proposed building, seemed to promise in its application to places of *confinement*, considered merely in that view. Give me leave now to consider it as applicable to the joint purposes of *punishment, reformation,* and *pecuniary economy.*

Letter IX

Penitentiary-houses – economy – contract – plan

I am come now to the article of *pecuniary economy.*

[. . .]

I would do the whole by *contract.* I would farm out the profits, the no-profits, or if you please the losses, to him who, being in other respects unexceptionable, offered the best terms.

Letter XVIII

Manufactories

[. . .] on the application of our principle to the business of manufactories, considered as carried on by forced labour. [. . .]

The centrality of the presiding person's situation will have its use at all events; for the purpose of direction and order at least. [. . .] The concealment of his person will be of use, in as far as control may be judged useful. As to partitions, whether they would be serviceable in the way of preventing distraction, or disserviceable by impeding communication, will depend upon the particular nature of the particular manufacture. In some manufactories they will have a further use, by the convenience they may afford for ranging a greater number of tools than could otherwise be stowed within the workman's reach.

[. . .]

Letter XXI

Schools

After applying the inspection principle first to prisons, and through mad-houses bringing it down to hospitals, will the parental feeling endure my applying it at last to schools? Will the observation of its efficacy in preventing the irregular application of undue hardship even to the guilty, be sufficient to dispel the apprehension of its tendency to introduce tyranny into the abodes of innocence and youth?

Applied to these, you will find it capable of two very distinguishable degrees of extension: – It may be confined to the hours of study; or it may be made to fill the whole circle of time, including the hours of repose, and refreshment and recreation. Some of these fine queries which I have been treating you with, and finer still, Rousseau would have entertained us with; nor do I imagine he would have put his *Emilius* into an inspection-house; but I think he would have been glad of such a school for his Sophia.

Jeremy Bentham
1748–1832

Addison, the grave and moral Addison, in his *Spectator* or his *Tatler*, I forget which, suggests a contrivance for trying *virginity* by means of *lions*. You may there find many curious disquisitions concerning the measures and degrees of that species of purity; all which you will be better pleased to have from that grave author than from me. But, without plunging into any such discussions, the highest degree possible, whatsoever that may be, is no more than anybody might make sure of, only by transferring damsels at as early an age as may be thought sufficient, into a strict inspection-school. Addison's scheme was not only a penal but a bloody one: and what havoc it might have made in the population of the country, I tremble but to think of. Give thanks, then, to *Diana* and the *eleven thousand virgins*, and to whatever powers preside over virginity in either *calendar*, for so happy a discovery as this of your friend's. There you saw blood and uncertainty: here you see certainty without blood. What advantage might be made by setting up a boarding-school for young ladies upon this plan, and with what eagerness gentlemen who are curious in such matters would crowd to such a school to choose themselves wives, is too obvious to insist on.

An inspection-house, to which a set of children had been consigned from their birth, might afford experiments enough that would be rather more interesting. What say you to a *founding-hospital* upon this principle?

Neither do I mean to give any instructions to the *Turks* for applying the inspection principle to their *seraglios*: no, not though I were to go through Constantinople again twenty times, notwithstanding the great saving it would make in the article of *eunuchs*, of whom one trusty one in the inspection-lodge would be as good as half a hundred.

I hope no critic of more learning than candour will do an inspection-house so much injustice as to compare it to *Dionysius' ear*. The object of that contrivance was, to know what prisoners said without their suspecting any such thing. The object of the inspection principle is directly the reverse: it is to make them not only *suspect*, but be *assured*, that whatever they do is known, even though that should not be the case. Detection is the object of the first: *prevention*, that of the latter. In the former case the ruling person is a spy; in the latter he is a monitor. The object of the first was to pry into the secret recesses of the heart; the latter, confining its attention to *overt acts*, leaves thoughts and fancies to their proper *ordinary*, the court *above*.

When I consider the extensive variety of purposes to which this principle may be applied, and the certain efficacy which, as far as I can trust my own conceptions, it promises to them all, my wonder is, not only that this plan should never have hitherto been put in practice, but how any other should ever have been thought of.

What would you say, if by the gradual adoption and diversified application of this single principle, you should see a new scene of things spread itself over the face of civilised society? – morals reformed, health preserved, industry invigorated, instruction diffused, public burthens lightened, economy seated as it were upon a rock, the gordian knot of the poor-laws not cut but untied – all by a simple idea in architecture?

efficiency • economisation • fit • utility • mechanisation of architecture • social control • defence • social reform • democratisation • environmental control and determinism

Jeremy Bentham
1748–1832

BUILDING AND FURNITURE

FOR AN

INDUSTRY-HOUSE ESTABLISHMENT,

FOR 2000 PERSONS, OF ALL AGES.

ON THE

PANOPTICON OR CENTRAL-INSPECTION PRINCIPLE.

☞ For the Explanation of the several Figures of this PLATE, see "Outline of a Work, entitled PAUPER MANAGEMENT IMPROVED," Bentham's Works, vol. viii, p. 369 to p. 439.

The Ranges of Bed-Stages and Cribs are respectively supposed to run from End to End of the *radial* Walls, as exhibited in the GROUND PLAN: they are here represented as cut through by a Line parallel to the Side of the Polygon: in the Bed-Stages, what is represented as *one* in the Draught, is proposed to be in *two* in the Description.

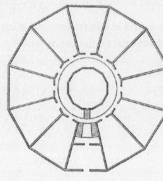

FIG. II.—SECTION

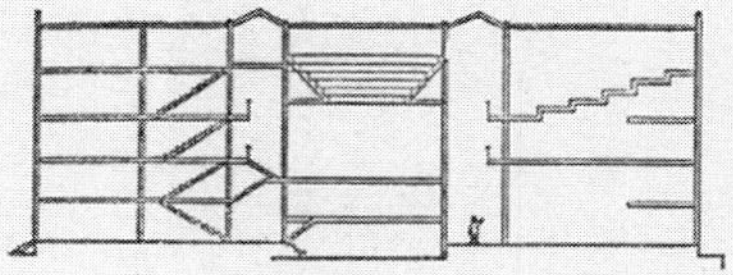

FIG. III.—GROUND PLAN.

Figure 25b

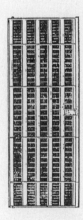

FIG. I.—ELEVATION.

Figure 25a

19 (A and B) Bentham's Panopticon,

36

129. Jeremy Bentham. *Panopticon, or the Inspection-House.* 1787. Frontispiece and prototype plan.

Jean-Louis Viel de Saint-Maux (?–1786)

Letters on the Architecture of the Ancients and Moderns (1787)

Viel was an architect, painter and lawyer (Pérouse de Montclos, 1966). Made up of fictional letters, this work contains ironic criticism of the classicists for submitting to the authority of the past. It also argues, in a novel way, that classical forms, as inventions by primitive societies meant to fill particular symbolic roles, can only be anachronistic now.

Introduction

Travellers depict some vestiges of ancient Oriental temples and the horrible ruins that accompanies them, used to house the attendants. These ruins revolt the beholder inasmuch as they make him detest the villainy that presided over such ravages. Our libraries are teeming with images of these precious vestiges in which we see that the types and symbols that decorated them were not the result of whim or arbitrary ornaments. One day things had to come to this, to a reflection worthy of these monuments. By what fate, going back almost two thousand years, did it come down to us?

Jean-Louis Viel
de Saint-Maux
?–1786

We observe an irrevocable analogy when we compare all these monuments with the liturgical fragments that the ancient peoples have left us: we see a chain in all the agricultural types that constitute the superb buildings and this chain goes from Europe to Asia, Asia to Africa, and from Africa to all that is left of religious monuments in the new world. [. . .]

The order of architecture is considered more as a poem on fecundity, as a theogonic ex-voto, than as a product of chance. One finds in it precious stones, votive altars, from which the columns and copies are derived, stones that were the mothers of the arts and sciences since they bore the first hieroglyphs or representational signs to which we owe the origin of painting and language. Let us cite examples that cannot be refuted without renouncing writing which in fact we must respect the most and nor all the authors that have been called profane.

We announced that no criticism could hold against the force of proof that we could give on existence of the symbolic types that characterise the monuments of antiquity to which we owe their elevation. However, certain persons, before knowing these proofs, claimed that in following our assertion we could say in two thousand years that our works and constructions were symbolic for us. Their imagination was unable to lend itself to this correct reflection that antiquity was unable to think or act in a modern way and that since the invention of the printing press it has become impossible to distinguish between the symbolic and the literal.

The third letter cites the people that living from agriculture like the first inhabitants of the earth, used the same emblems in their monuments. [. . .] We observe that they were the same as those in use on all the ancient monuments. This letter is finished with the analysis of travellers that believed they were contributing to our information through accounts that are cowardly and interspersed by those who keep trying to disguise the truth to us.

The fourth presents the parts that constitute the order of architecture, explains the different emblems by the analysis of the monuments and the types that were in use among the various peoples of the earth. We can plainly see that these symbols are agricultural, that they depict sowing and fecundity.

The fifth retraces the grottos or excavations dug into sheer rockbed and right into the bosom of marble and porphyre mountains, excavations often ornamented with liturgical types and that were temples. One observes in them that the chain of monuments of this type are to be found around the globe.

The sixth, comparing the architecture of the ancients to that of the moderns examines the kind of construction that they adopted in the rebirth of that art among us, a genre that they have since abandoned in order to better, they say, imitate the Greeks and the Romans.

We observe in the seventh how we have created new eras for the sciences and the arts by rejuvenating some symbolic deeds of the ancients, by taking them literally and by concealing from us the genius of the agricultural peoples. The aim of the present book is to make modern architecture better appreciate the monuments of antiquity. We also distinguish the country that has cooperated most towards giving these artists subordinate ideas. As opposed to those who only demand destruction in order to be able to rebuild, we examine antique projects in order to embellish the capital accordingly.

Jacques-René Tenon (1724–1816)

Reports on the Hospitals of Paris (1788)

In the late 1770s, the Royal Academy of Science called on a number of scientists to submit studies on the general problem of hospital reform sparked by the recent burning down of the Hôtel-Dieu in Paris. Tenon, the main surgeon at the hospital of La Salpetière and friend of Lavoisier was among these. His report influenced the architect Poyet (Fortier *et al.*, 1975; Foucault *et al.*, 1976; Rosenau, 1970).

Never was a subject worthier of holding a company of wise men's attention; every thing about it is recommendable: its object, the wishes of the Sovereign, the eagerness of the public, the merit of overcoming the countless difficulties that it presents.

No work exists on the *formation* and on the *distribution* of Hospitals, and the principles that would make it possible to judge their advantages and shortcomings have not been assembled. Thus it was necessary to collect them. That was the first difficulty.

One or more of the Houses that will replace the Hôtel-Dieu must succour poor patients without doing them harm, and at the same time, without disturbing the rest of society: these are two considerations that require us to know how the patients are to be classified and where to place Hospitals in a large city.

What method should be employed to proceed in a useful manner? After reflecting upon the matter as much as my limited knowledge enabled me to, I believed it worthwhile to share my knowledge of anatomy and pathology. 'Twas a question of man and of the sick man: his stature determines the length of the bed and the width of the rooms; his stride is shorter and less free than that of the healthy man. The height of the steps and the length of the stretcher on which he is carried determine the width of the Hospital's stairs. Furthermore, consuming a certain amount of air in a given time, depending on how frequent and how deep the breathing is, rooms of various dimensions are required; in addition, the eyes are sensitive to impressions of light during inflammations of the *dura mater* and violent ophthalmia, which requires paying attention to the position of the beds and windows.

The details are numerous; their comparison is useful, their multiplicity baffling: thus 'twas necessary to get rid of the one, and make the most of the other, by reducing every thing to general results. I took the total number of patients in each House, the number of patients by category of illness and even by room, the dimensions of each and their ratio to the number of persons inside them. I also believed that 'twas useful to collect observations on the uses, the position, the advantages and the shortcomings of the various rooms and other spaces that compose Hospitals, facilitating or increasing their usefulness, making them healthier and less expensive to operate, for 'twas necessary to study the Hospitals in the Hospitals themselves, and to understand what a long experience indicated as harmful, or marked.

I wrote a Dissertation of questions on the distribution and the usefulness of Hospitals, persuaded that a comparison of their present condition would not only guide us in their construction, but also allow us to perfect already existing Hospitals.

The Dissertation deals with the *formation* and *distribution* of the Houses intended to replace the Hôtel-Dieu. Their formation is the result of certain categories of patients in one Hospital rather than in another; their distribution is a methodical arrangement of patients, servers, jobs and departments of each Hospital.

Jacques-René Tenon 1724–1816

It is therefore a question of dividing the Hôtel-Dieu. The purpose of breaking it up is to reconcile economy in building with the advantage of the patients and the health of the City, or, which amounts to the same thing, not needlessly increasing the number of Hospitals, and the employments and departments in them; to give the poor what they need, without harming the Public and the location of the Hospitals from which contagious diseases spread: for while the poor must be given sufficient succour, at the same time the health of their benefactors must be preserved.

Thus the proposal is to divide the Hôtel-Dieu into six Houses: a supply House where the main departments would be brought together in order to not duplicate them every time a new Hospital is built. The formation of this common House shall be based on that of our Houses of Charity; this House should be built at the Rapée, considering the convenience of that place for bringing in supplies.

A Hospice should be reserved in the centre of Paris where unconscious persons found overnight in the street, injured, losing their blood, in need of first aid, will be brought.

There would be three other functions: an administrative office; an emergency room that would offer those who, without residing there, would come to ask questions, or for consultations, or for light aid, and the number of empty beds in the different Houses of the Hôtel-Dieu would be indicated there every day.

The other Hospitals, larger than the Hospice and placed at the circumference of Paris, will each have their own particular function, in addition to a general service.

In no way do I claim that this arrangement is so perfect no one can improve or even change it; I am only giving that which, after reflecting for a long while, seemed to me the best conceived plan based on the experiences we know. Furthermore, a hospital room is, so to speak, a veritable machine for treating patients, and it must be considered from this point of view. However, no machine is brought to perfection until after many attempts have been made and many experiments have been performed; and I repeat, the layout and construction of hospital rooms will only be perfected if envisaged in this manner.

I must add that for patients with contagious diseases, such as smallpox, malignant fever, scorbut and others, the rooms will be built far from those that compose the body of the hospital, and they will be located, to use a sailor's term, *downwind* from them, so that their bad air can not blow in their direction, or at least only very rarely.

efficiency • economisation • fit • utility • mechanisation of architecture • systemisation of space distribution • environmental control and determinism

Reverend William Gilpin (1724–1804)

'On Picturesque Beauty', *Three Essays* (1792)

Gilpin's descriptions of his many 'travels' through the British Isles made this amateur of the arts the most influential writer on the picturesque through the second half of the eighteenth century in England and Europe. The present work is the major exposition of his principles in relation not only to landscape but, more broadly, to painting and architecture.

Further reading Clark, 1943; Hipple, 1957; Hussey, 1967b; Monk, 1935, 223–225; O.C.A.; Wittkower, 1962, 145.

'Roughness forms the most essential point of difference between the beautiful and the picturesque; as it seems to be that particular quality, which makes objects chiefly pleasing in painting. – I use the general term roughness; but properly speaking roughness relates only to the surface of bodies: when we speak of their delineation, we use the word ruggedness. Both ideas however equally enter into the picturesque; and both are observable in the smaller, as well as in the larger parts of nature . . .'

'Having thus from a variety of examples endeavoured to show that roughness either real, or apparent, forms an essential difference between the beautiful and the picturesque; it may be expected that we should point out the reason of this difference. It is obvious enough why the painter prefers rough objects to smooth: but it is not so obvious why the quality of roughness should make an essential difference between objects of beauty, and objects suited to artificial representation.'

A fourth philosopher apprehends common sense to be our standard only in the ordinary affairs of life. The bounty of nature has furnished us with various other senses suited to the objects, among which we converse: and with regard to matters of taste, it has supplied us with what, he doubts not, we all feel within ourselves, a sense of beauty.

Pooh! says another learned inquirer, what is a sense of beauty? Sense is a vague idea, and so is beauty; and it is impossible that any thing determined can result from terms so inaccurate. But if we lay aside a sense of beauty, and adopt proportion, we shall all be right. Proportion is the great principle of taste and beauty. We admit it both in lines and colours; and indeed refer all our ideas of the elegant kind to its standard.

True, says an admirer of the antique; but this proportion must have a rule, or we gain nothing: and a rule of proportion there certainly is: but we may inquire after it in vain. The secret is lost. The ancients had it. They well knew the principles of beauty; and had that unerring rule, which in all things adjusted their taste. We see it even in their slightest vases. In their works, proportion, though varied through a thousand lines, is still the same; and if we could only discover their principles of proportion, we should have the Arcanum of this science; and might settle all our disputes about taste with great ease.

Thus, in our inquiries into first principles we go on, without end, and without satisfaction. . . . We inquire for them in vain – in physics – in metaphysics – in morals. Even in the polite arts, . . . the inquiry, we find, is equally vague. We are puzzled, and bewildered, but not informed: all is uncertainty; a strife of words; the old contest. . . .

In a word, if a cause is sufficiently understood it may suggest useful discoveries. But if it is not so . . . it will unquestionably mislead.

aesthetisation of architecture • anticlassicism • deformation • freedom • naturalism

Francesco Milizia (1725–1798)

Dictionary of the Fine Arts of Design (1797)

(See Milizia 1781)

ABUSES. Abuses in architecture are vicious practices introduced through artistic irrationality and followed by fools. Palladio devoted a chapter to them and only named four of them. Perrault calculated that there were eight. If true masters would really write about them, they could fill tomes with them. The nature of the abuses is to multiply, because the nature of rational being is to reason very little. Abuses emerge from errors, and errors from a lack of care. Attention is painful. Attentive artists avoid abuses and their correct works all together are capable of expunging them. [. . .] Most abuses arise from the mania to decorate. The slightest abuses generate the greatest vices.

ARCHITECTURE *is the art of building according to the proportions and rules determined by nature and by taste.* This definition reflects the etymology of the word *architecture*, which means *excellence of craft*. If architecture is taken to be the simple art of building according to need, it belongs to all times and to all countries, and is found among the most savage peoples. But according to the definition prescribed, the art of architecture is the preserve of certain epochs and certain privileged countries, and it can only be the fruit of the society most cultivated by civilisation, moral considerations and the concourse of all the other arts.

Audacity, or more accurately caprice, may have influenced architecture in certain isolated ways, in certain details, in certain decorations; but it cannot have produced the essential and characteristic tastes particular to each country. And here we must cast our attention back to the three primitive states of man.

The character of Egyptian architecture derives clearly from the rock-cut chambers which were the earliest dwelling-places of that country, and which are still used today. The massive, colossal character of its buildings obviously has much in common with the most ancient underground chambers and the grottoes more recently excavated and embellished by art. And although certain forms indicating the use of timber have been later grafted on to that primitive character, timber was never its primal type. The same spirit is to be found in parts of Asia, as we can particularly observe in the columns of the rock-cut shrine of Elephanta: short and squat, with their capitals and other trimmings far from suggestive of the *tree*.

In quite a contrary spirit is the architecture of China and Japan. Here the lighter woods are predominantly used in the guise of the *tent*. The earliest inhabitants of these regions would have lived in tents, and like all the Tartars and nomads they were herdsmen before they were city-dwellers. Hence their roofs, which curve in the form of pavilion-tents; their slender stanchions, which make Chinese cities look like a journeyman's encampment. The immensity of their cities is proof that their houses are too flimsy to hold many storeys.

Therefore the wooden *hut*, which is commonly taken as the universal architectural model for the peoples of the Earth, had no such function either in Egypt or in China. It did however in Greece, where art took a solid and variegated model and translated the forms of timber into stone, appropriating with happy imitation what it needed first and foremost. And what the Greek farmers needed was a *hut*.

Of these three models presented by nature to art, without doubt the finest is that of the *hut*, where art finds unity and variety. Subterranean chambers are so impressively self-contained that imitation finds nothing there to engage. Tents offer too much to imitate, and since they lack robustness the architecture that has imitated them has been similarly unable to embody that most important quality of all, so necessary in reality as well as appearance. Excessive weight and excessive lightness were the necessary outcomes of these two essays in imitation. In the first model there is nothing there to imitate. In the second, imitation can of necessity be nothing but vicious and puerile, because the distance between the material of the model and that of the copy is too great. In the underground chamber all is monotony, and monotonous too is the architecture which springs from them. Tents lend themselves to all sorts of caprice, and this caprice they cannot help but communicate to the art which imitates them, along with their bizarreness and lack of definition.

The *hut* on the other hand is sturdy and lean and is the most tractable medium for architecture. Wood is the material most suited to receive all the modifications and ornamentation which art ministers to it. Wood contains all the components necessary to usefulness and beauty. Hence the simplest of wooden *huts* contains the germ of the most magnificent palaces. At an equal remove from uniformity and caprice, art takes sound and constant principles from construction in wood, which requires calculation and reasoning for the equilibrium of forces; without which, reasoning would never have been a part of architecture. Thus the only architecture which is true and reasoned with simplicity and prudence is Greek architecture, for the Greeks only imitated the *hut*.

The first trees or posts thrust into the ground as a support for some kind of covering were the origin of the free-standing *column*, whence came the porticoes which have so enriched architecture. Trees are thicker towards the base; let columns taper in similar fashion, then. To protect posts planted unshod in the earth from damp, socles of wood were placed underneath them. Hence the *plinth* [editor's note: a plinth is a square or rectangular base for a column, pilaster or door framing] and the *base* with all its refinements. On the vertical trunks were placed horizontal beams whose purpose was to carry the roof: hence the *architrave*. To ensure that the architrave lay evenly across the heads of the columns, pieces of wood were interposed: thus the *capital* came into being. On the architrave, crossbeams were placed: hence the frieze, whose triglyphs are the ends of the crossbeams, and whose *metopes* are the intervals between them. From the laths and rafters used in forming the sloping roof, which projected outwards to throw off rain, came the *cornice* with its *modillions* and *mutules*. The sloping, ridged roof necessarily gave the form of a triangular *pediment*, which was more or less peaked according to the climate of the region. In Greece, where snow falls little and rarely, the slope of the roof was gentle; it was steeper in Rome, where the climate is less amenable; and much steeper still in the northern countries exposed to heavy snows. The sharpness of the gable is a kind of thermometer of the region it occupies.

Francesco Milizia
1725–1798

There is no part of Greek architecture, which is to say true architecture, that cannot be easily deduced from the building in wood. *Arches* and *vaults* derive from the crosspieces wedged between vertical members which are too weak, or at too great an interval the one from the other, to support the load they carry. *Pilasters* are no more than squared posts [. . .]

AUTHORITY. In all periods the arts have always borne the yoke of authority. Perhaps among them its reign was easily stabilised and only destroyed with difficulty. The sciences also established its power, but sooner or later it was weakened there and finally destroyed by truth. In contradistinction, however, time only strengthened it in the arts, and if at times it seemed to weaken, this is only because it was changing form. The despotic nature of authority grew in the arts at the same time that it was shrinking in the sciences.

Francesco Milizia
1725–1798

The causes of this difference are that the sciences tend to recognise the principles and causes of nature. The arts regard only the effects of nature, and the effects are easier to sense and the causes more difficult to adduce. That is why the first steps in the sciences were just conjecture, and the first steps in the arts were oriented towards truth. The arts made great strides, while the sciences failed to find which path to follow. But like miners who remain buried in the depths of the earth during many futile excavations, the sciences eventually found treasures. The arts were a field of, first, abundant reapings, but the sowing soon exhausted the soil and it became sterile.

From this difference there arose a difference in the type of authority that settled in. The sciences depart from an error. New discoveries keep dissipating the prejudices of authority, and make it expire. The arts start off with truth, but this precious light little by little is extinguished. What is beautiful in nature is hidden by artifice, and authority is vigorously used to this end.

Architecture, especially, that has nothing beautiful in nature to imitate is more predisposed to the changeability of fashion, all the changes of opinion, and is in general more subject to the whims of authority. Authority is a poison that mankind should never learn. If he is to learn facts of nature or of industry, these facts ought to be constant, so that they may be readily verifiable. And these do not rely on authority. As concern matters of taste, only reason counts, which can be used to observe the cause for the pleasures caused by beauty. The most beautiful monuments of the Greeks and Romans are not the stuff of authority. This is because reason demonstrates that they are endowed with beauty through the essence of architecture, and that is why we regard them as beautiful. But between so many beauties, it is still possible to find some defects. Upon which authority comes and makes us either praise or damn everything, blinding and stupefying us.

BAROQUE is the superlative of the bizarre, the excess of the ridiculous. Borromini succumbed to delirium, but Guarini, Pozzi, Marchionni in the sacristy of St Peter's etc., to *Baroque*.

The BIZARRE is preceded by caprice, is sustained by vogue and ends in delirium.

Caprice plays childish games that can nevertheless become harmful. But the *bizarre* systematically sets about destroying the order and forms which are dictated by nature and which constitute art. The greatest men, the most illustrious centuries of art, have

[461]

occasionally lapsed into caprice, but never into the *bizarre*. The *bizarre* belongs to the most corrupt of times and the most addled of minds, and it is a contagious disease.

The *bizarre* has several causes. The principal ones vary relative to the country, epoch and artist that adopt it.

1. An abundance of good things leads to satiety, and renders simple beauty insipid, and seeks to whet or deceive the tastes. Italy and Rome in particular abound in masterpieces of architecture, above all the ancient monuments of every kind. On these models for the renewal of the arts the Bramantes, Raphaels, Peruzzis, Sangallos, Palladios, Vignolas and so many others exercised their genius, not only with theory which speaks to the mind, but with practice which speaks to the eyes. Now who would not have thought that lessons and examples so potent could not promote good taste in its greatest purity, and preserve art from licence? And yet the century that followed was the century of the *bizarre*. The speedy rise of the arts accelerated their downfall. The eye grew tired of simple forms, and simplicity became monotonous, prudence became frigidity, imitation sterility, uniformity enslavement, and thus the *bizarre*, and finally delirium, was mistaken for invention. In Rome more than elsewhere can the gradual progress of modern architecture be seen. Next to well-proportioned buildings the most bizarre buildings spring up in a trice. Were the eye not accustomed to the incongruity of it, we might say that Rome was formed by peoples who were at war in their tastes. A period of ten centuries between the huts of Romulus and the meaningless luxury of Diocletian saw less disparity than a single century in modern Rome.

Francesco Milizia
1725–1798

2. But when vogue enters the manners of people, that epidemic vogue which maintains entire nations in a kind of childish thrall and with a magic spell stirs furniture, apparel, diet, opinions and language into a perpetual commotion, why should the arts remain untouched? Vogue comes from wealth, and from wealth too comes luxury. Although it was the poor relation of necessity and need, architecture has since become richer and richer, so how could it resist such a torrent of mutability? To flatter the caprice of a tyrant, architecture has turned to the *bizarre* for succour. The *bizarre* hides behind vogue; it would repel us with its deformity, if vogue did not lend it its mask; and vogue would soon consume itself, if the *bizarre* did not renew it: in their union lies their power. One takes it upon itself to invent, the other lends its vagaries to the invention. The *bizarre* cares only for excess; not for need, nor convenience, nor utility. Hence the most awkward forms, ridiculous outlines, repulsive juxtapositions, are all grist to its mill, all serve vogue excellently, on condition that today's invention differs from yesterday's. Once introduced to architecture, the *bizarre* exercises its dominion in grand style: it makes humps of straight lines, restlessly alternating straight and curved lines of regular plans, quaintness of balanced proportions, accident out of orderliness. And men prostrate themselves before the idol of vogue, and acclaim as genius and invention the monsters which the *bizarre* creates.

3. The inventors of the *bizarre* in architecture must have been glib in the extreme, with a surfeit of inventiveness and an imagination mettlesome enough to shake free from the bonds of rule. Ill-disposed towards imitation and authority, contemptible of the respect and esteem due their predecessors, and considering it cowardly and faint-hearted to follow in the footsteps of others, as if their only merit was their seniority, with this and other similar paralogisms they have aspired to the radiant glory of originality.

Unfortunately, they have succeeded. But not as before through astonishing endeavours to imitate nature in her beauty, not to seek the fairest proportions and employ them with painstaking truthfulness to produce new, yes, but also beautiful combinations. Their originality lies wholly in the *bizarre*. An envious bent of spirit has led them to flout every ancient system, and in distancing themselves more overtly from their predecessors they have even forsaken the imitation of nature. Their glory lies, therefore, in the invention of extravagant and contrived combinations, in the most incomprehensible associations, in contortion and the union of discordant parts. Thus the glorious exponents of the *bizarre*.

It is superfluous to talk of that throng of parasite artists that mediocrity and inertia always trail in the wake of the truly inventive.

It is however important to find a remedy for caprice, for the *bizarre* and the frenzy of artists and of architects in particular. This remedy might be a small catechism of the few truthful principles of imitation and invention. False ideas or the abuse of these principles are one of the principal causes of error in the reign of the *bizarre*. Architects require, therefore, a code on the essence of architecture. This would be the only specific they need. And if gifted artists took a good dose of it, instead of becoming concocters of the *bizarre* they would prove eminent and illustrious proponents of truthful beauties.

Francesco Milizia
1725–1798

BORROMINI (*Francesco*), b. Como 1599, d. 1667. Came to Rome as a young man, where he worked first as a stone-carver, and was responsible for some of the cherubs on the festoons of the small doors of St Peter's, and the relief of Attila in the same church.

The encouragement of his relative, the architect Maderno, brought him to architecture. His great talent, and great eagerness, won him many commissions, of which the principal ones are:

The Oratory of St Philip Neri. The churches of S. Agnese in Piazza Navona, S, Carlino alle Quattro Fontane, the Sapienza, the Sette Dolori. The campanile of S. Andrea delle Fratte. The façade of palazzo Doria facing the Collegio Romano, some staircases in palazzo Barberini, restorations and a scenographic colonnade in palazzo Spada, palazzo Falconieri, and the lateral façade of the Collegio di Propaganda. The restoration of the church of St John Lateran, a basilica of two rows of different marbles taken from various buildings of ancient Rome. Borromini encased the columns in broad pillars and tricked them out in ornament.

Borromini took the bizarre to the highest level of delirium. Every form he deformed: he mutilated pediments, turned volutes inside out, bevelled angles, made architraves and cornices undulate; scattered scrolls, spirals, consoles, zigzags and all sorts of pettiness everywhere. Borrominesque architecture is architecture *au rebours*. This is not architecture, it is the ravings of a mad cabinetmaker.

And what brought him to such delirium? His envy of Bernini. This envy was so furious that he finally went insane, entered a frenzy and killed himself. But he failed, in his attempt to outdo Bernini, to take the only expedient open to him, which was to do better and more correctly; the century of correctness had gone, now was the century of corruption. So he set his sights on uniqueness by trespassing every rule. Nothing is easier than irregularity: from irregularity to oddness, extravagance and frenzy the passage is inevitable.

Borromini even imbued his manner of construction with his oddness. He had a good understanding of this part of architecture, but never applied it in keeping with the material he used.

Borromini in architecture, Bernini in sculpture, Pietro da Cortona in painting, Marini in poetry, are a corruption of taste. A corruption which has infected a large number of artists. No bad comes but that we cannot take some good from it. It is good to see these works and abominate them. They serve to show what should not be done. They must be seen as delinquents, who pay for their misdemeanours with lessons in good sense.

CHARACTER, *Relative, or appropriate.* Every building has its use. The art of applying to it what most suits it makes *appropriate character* the most important and the most difficult of *characters*.

The Greeks (and we must always think of the Greeks) were admirably skilled in *characterising* their temples according to the nature of their deities, which were none other than impressions of nature. With only three orders of architecture they characterised each member of the congeries of their gods. We with five orders do not even dream of achieving *appropriate character*. With those three orders, which each have only three elements, they were able to achieve a richness of proportion giving to each temple its *appropriate character* as the nature of the idol required: majesty, elegance, haughtiness, grace, strength, pride, modesty etc.

But if the artists of Greece were to make their temples speak, the people of Greece had to understand their language. Thus if the people had not understood it, the artists would have been unable to utter it. It is an orderly and understanding people that makes the artist understandable. It is an everyday occurrence that an intelligent man among stupid men himself becomes stupid.

To give edifices their appropriate character, we must consider 1. degrees of wealth and grandeur, 2. indication of particular qualities, 3. general and particular forms, 4. manner of construction, 5. decoration and 6. attributes.

1. *Degrees of wealth and grandeur in buildings.* The most important condition of buildings is the expression of their *distinctive character.* From the humblest hut to the most sumptuous palace, how long is the series of appropriate characters for the different buildings of a city! Nothing could be clearer, and nothing is more neglected, even perverted.

Where the abuse of power and wealth gives itself the pleasure of publicly insulting what is honest and unassuming, everything becomes splendid. No more houses, but palaces. Athens had no palaces, but houses, and great public monuments. Rome, in all the centuries where restraint reigned, had nothing richer and grander than her public monuments: the orator Crassus was the first to insult his fellow citizens by placing six marble columns in his house.

If everything is sumptuous, nothing is sumptuous any longer; nothing any longer has distinction, and farewell *character.*

The artist is dragged into this vice by another, that of government. Where the *res publica* stands for nothing, or to put it better where there is no *res publica*, so too architecture stands for nothing. Every private individual is puffed up, seeks vanity, is content with appearances, with that which can only impress himself and his vile flatterers.

Architecture with *appropriate character* can only come into being where flourishes restraint, which is the offspring of good government. With this architecture the houses of the citizens are solid and comfortable, and also have beauty in the correctness of their proportions, their simplicity, modesty, plainness and in a certain elegance without luxury, and can admit of variation without wealth or ornament of any kind. With this

Francesco Milizia
1725–1798

architecture grand and wealthy public monuments will stand out, whose purpose is to delight the eye of every citizen.

The architect, then, is in chains. Public opinion prescribes *appropriate character* to him. And if he wants to break loose, all one has to do is whistle; he will promptly be brought to heel, and if he wants his designs to mean anything, he will make them express not everything that comes into his head but that which they *must* say. Buildings will then talk, and every citizen will understand their language.

2. *Indication of qualities particular to each building.* Buildings, like images in painting and sculpture, need each their own physiognomy. That a prison must inspire dread, a ballroom joviality, is clear. But it is not so clear what special physiognomy to give to other public buildings with a certain resemblance among themselves. To grasp this point of great importance, the architect has to observe the progressive use of buildings and the ideas which attach themselves to this use. This is the reckoner by which he may share out the riches of his art.

Francesco Milizia
1725–1798

Temples require a great number of columns. Columns are the principal ornament of buildings, though they should be placed not as mere ornaments but in such a way that they seem necessary.

Civil buildings rarely include columns. An arsenal should be sturdily rusticated. A cistern requires less solidity and massiveness; and it requires no windows, as it is not a dwelling. A merchant's exchange should be comfortable without pomp or elegance, but sober and unimposing. Mints, banks, pawnbrokers, should not be externally opulent, for it is inside that their wealth lies; the content of this wealth bears no relation with the appearance of the building, and so their physiognomy should be rather serious.

Buildings dedicated to the sciences and the arts require an appearance that is noble without being grave, agreeable but not voluptuous, simple but not austere: they may have porticoes, colonnades and loggie, and varying degrees of modesty and economy according to their varying uses. Schools for young girls should not look like academies of the sciences.

Granaries, hospitals etc. require only simplicity and cleanliness. Theatres on the other hand call for all the graces of architecture. City halls require a sumptuousness commensurate with the city. And law courts and *basilicas* demand solemnity, decency and austerity.

If artists inquire into the nature of each monument, they shall find how to give it its distinctive *character*, in a way that the common people understand. If the common people are insensitive to this character, they are so by fault of the artists who confound everything and express nothing.

3. *General and particular forms* bear a close relation with the nature of buildings. Ancient temples were either circular or rectangular in shape: simple forms which are apprised immediately one enters them, and from every part. Our crosses destroy unity, and the various orders destroy it more with so many cornices and so many pediments. Temples should have nothing in common with dwellings.

Tombs were always pyramids, and could have no other form than the pyramid, for they came into being from the heaping of earth upon earth, stone upon stone, above the dead person.

If an acrobat appears, immediately a semicircle of curious spectators forms around him. This is the shape indicated for theatres. No matter how much they varied in size, in proportions and in ornament, all ancient theatres were circular inside and outside. Despite reason and example none of our theatres is the shape it should be, and their exteriors are totally incongruent with their function.

Houses should only be rectangular in shape, as this is the form most comfortable for living in. Convexity is disagreeable, as it seems to repel the observer. As long as man does not change, the shapes of doorways and windows are established by nature.

All partial forms in buildings are founded on the essential and distinctive appropriateness of every thing. From the consideration and application of these relations there results *distinctive character*, the physiognomy of each edifice.

4. The *manner of construction*, that is, how materials are used, contributes greatly to how a building's *distinctive character* is expressed. The boldness with which a roof thrusts skywards, the gracefulness of the vaults, the suitability of the elevation of the ceilings, the use of contrast, give meaning to the building, and the correct meaning if correctly suited to its purpose.

Francesco Milizia
1725–1798

A general rule is that the size of materials should be proportionate to the grandeur of the building and its *character*. A large monument should be characterised by large masses. In a work dedicated to immortality, no joints should be visible, for these offer a presage of its destruction.

Rarity, richness, diverse colours, the hardness of the materials employed where appropriate, should emphasise the special physiognomy of the building. Where nature is insufficient, art shall supply by giving stones the rustic appearance they lack.

5. *Decoration* is the most effective means of impressing *distinctive character* upon buildings; and it is also the most effective means of muddling everything, and failing to give *character*, if the two following principles are lost from view.

One is to *employ appropriate decoration in keeping with the quality of the building*. Decoration is wealth; wealth represents dignity, power, grandeur, strength. Which buildings require decoration, then? And how much? And how? And where?

The other principle is that decoration should be *precise in its meaning, and clearly intelligible*. If it is incoherent, it will annoy the onlooker.

Let us apply these principles in casting our eye on the ornament, the decorative lines of architecture, of sculpture and painting, employed outside and inside buildings. Everywhere garlands, always festoons, scrolls, shells, pateras, mythological creatures, cadavers, darts, masks, mascarons, thunderbolts, sunbeams, trophies, mitres, crosiers, animals; paintings on extremely high vaults, sculptures at excessive distances etc. This kind of ornamentation clearly reveals that the artist does not know what decoration is. The people, moreover, insensitive to this profusion of idle fripperies, hold decorations, and decorators, to be frivolous.

6. *Attributes* should be treated with the same principles as decoration. And what attributes are sphinxes on fountains, lions on roof gutters, effigies of Hercules on balustrades? Attributes must have meaning, but if the building has no *distinctive character*, they shall be insipid. Inscriptions on insignificant buildings are like those legends formerly made to issue from the mouths of monsters in paintings.

If these principles are real, then real too are the inconsistencies which modern architecture has been accumulating for so long. The great disparity between the works of ancient and modern architecture is manifest, though similar elements are used in both. The lack of *character* is a creeping malaise that attacks every building. The cause of so disfiguring an illness had never previously been tracked down, let alone its remedy. Now that its cause has finally been discovered, let us hope preventive measures can be found too.

classical canon • antiquity • abuses • precedent • authority • invention • rhetoric • signification • narrative • rigorism • essentialism

James Malton (?–1803)

An Essay on British Cottage Architecture (1798)

Malton, an architect who worked mainly as a draughtsman, is the first to have applied to domestic architecture of affluent patrons the romantic aesthetic which was just gaining currency. His designs, stressing the irregularity and rusticity of vernacular buildings, aimed at replacing the classical model of the palladian villa.

Further reading Harris, 1990; Nachmani, 1968–1969; Wiebenson, 1983.

James Malton
?–1803

When mention is made of the kind of dwelling called a cottage, I figure in my imagination a small house in the country; of odd, irregular form, with various, harmonious colouring, the effect of weather, time and accident; the whole environed with smiling verdure, having a contented, cheerful, inviting aspect, and door on the latch, ready to receive the gossip neighbour, or weary, exhausted traveller. There are many indescribable somethings that must necessarily combine to give to a dwelling this distinguishing character. A porch at entrance; irregular breaks in the direction of the walls; one part higher than another; various roofing of different materials, thatch particularly, boldly projecting; fronts partly built of walls of brick, partly weather boarded, and partly brick-noggin dashed; casement window lights, are all conducive, and constitute its features ...

A peculiar regard for this description of building prevails in all ranks of people; and this regard I have often found the more fervent in those whose elevated sphere of life has excluded from the likelihood of ever tasting, but whose nice sensibility could give conception to those pleasurable sensations that are the offspring of moderate enjoyment.

The greatly affluent in sumptuous equipage, as they pass the cheerful dwelling of careless rustic or unambitious man, who prefers agrestic pleasures to the boisterous clamour of cities, involuntarily sigh as they behold the modest care-excluding mansions of the lowly contented; and often from the belief that solid comfort can be found only in retirement, forsake their noisy abodes, to unload of their oppressing inquietudes in the tranquil retreat of the rural shelter. Often has the aching brow of royalty resigned its crown, to be decked with the soothing chaplet of the shepherd swain. The human mind undergoes great revolutions: those scenes that gratified the infant heart, do not satisfy the thirsty youthful imagination; that looks beyond simple objects, and can be gratified only by stately novelty, by a something then conceived to be beyond the power of artless nature to bestow; but exhausted in the vain pursuit of happiness, amid the bustle of crowds and pageantry of courts, returns benefited by experience, and clings to pure nature again with increased delight.

The matured eye, palled with gaudy magnificence, turns disgusted from the gorgeous structure, fair sloping lawn, well turned canal, regular fence and formal rows of trees; and regards, with unspeakable delight, the simple cottage, the rugged common,

[467]

rude pond, wild hedge-rows, and irregular plantations. Happy he, who early sees that true happiness is distinct from noise, from bustle, and from ceremony; who looks for it, chiefly, in his properly discharging his domestic duties, and by early planting, with parental tenderness, the seeds of content in his rising offspring, reaps the glad harvest in autumnal age! . . .

The more modern, lofty mansions of the great excite emotions of surprise and admiration at their stately appearance and grandeur; but which soon yield place to sensations the opposite of true happiness. When considering the master as mere man, there is found no consistency between the possessor and the thing possessed: the immensity of his demands, the attentions he must necessarily exact of others, and a continual reliance upon them for the support of his dignity, more immediately renders him the dependant, rather than the lord of his servants.

. . . I cannot but lament, when I notice the devastations made by the corroding breath of time, upon those noble structures, the boast of architecture, and instance of the riches of our isle: and to observe the attractions of the metropolis, engage so long the residence, and exhaust the resources of our affluent nobility, whose exertions and whose wealth could be so nobly called into action for the good of the country at large, in promoting its manufactures and encouraging a laborious peasantry.

Though noble specimens of architecture, however applied, command admiration, yet I cannot admire the ponderous magnificence that is so often displayed in the dwellings of individuals, however high their elevation and dignity. In temples of religious worship, and in public buildings of the state, the magnificent decorations of architecture should appear, particularly in the former; no application of them can be more worthy; it would at the same time be showing the gratitude of human beings, to the fountain of their lives, and giver of all their enjoyments. "Tis shameful to observe the house of God obscurely lurking in by-lanes and alleys . . .'

As is the cottage, so is the old country church, a peculiar, beautiful and picturesque feature, in the rural scenes of England; but this, as well as the former, is fast falling away, and succeeded by others possessing not a single quality gratifying to the mind or sight; for as the gay frivolity and flat insipidity of their interiors do not inspire veneration, so neither do their exteriors call forth regard . . .

anticlassicism • deformation • freedom • naturalism • regionalism • nationalism

James Malton
?–1803

PLATE 5

130. James Malton. *An Essay on British Architecture*. 1798. Examples of country houses with regionalist attributes and no references to the canon of the classical tradition.

Etienne-Louis Boullée (1728–1799)

A Treatise on Architecture (1793–1799)

The views of Boullée, an architect and member of the Academy, about the emotional effects of architecture bear the mark of J.F. Blondel, his teacher (Kaufmann, 1952, 1955; Rosenau, 1953). Research has suggested that Burke's theories of the sublime might also have contributed to his views and unique designs (Wiebenson, 1968).

Further reading Pérouse de Montclos, 1974; Wiebenson 1982, 1993.

What is architecture? Shall I define it as Vitruvius does, as the art of building? No. There is gross error in such a definition. Vitruvius takes the effect for the cause.

One must conceive in order to realise. Our earliest ancestors only built their huts after having conceived the image thereof. It is this production of the mind, this creation that is constitutive of architecture, which we may consequently define as the art of producing and bringing to perfection edifices of all kinds. The art of building is therefore only a secondary art, which it seems to us to be appropriate to call the scientific portion of architecture. Art in the strict sense, and science, these are the notions that we believe should be marked out distinctly in architecture.

Most authors who have written on this subject have sought to discuss the scientific aspect. This can be seen to be only natural if one reflects a little. It was necessary to study the manner in which one may create a robust building before seeking to create a pleasing one. Since the scientific aspect is of first necessity, and consequently the most essential, men were naturally determined to deal with it first in a particular manner.

We cannot in fact but agree on this. Beauty in art cannot be demonstrated like the truths of mathematics, and although that beauty emanates from nature, to feel it and to employ it felicitously, it is necessary to be endowed with qualities of which nature is stinting.

What do we see in all the books devoted to architecture? The ruins of ancient temples that our learned men have unearthed in Greece. However perfect these may be, such examples are not extensive enough to replace a complete treatise on the art. [. . .]

And now, reader, I ask you, do I not have good grounds, as it were, for the argument that architecture is still in its infancy since we possess no certainties as to the basic principles of that art? I agree with all educated persons that with discernment and sensitivity it is possible to produce excellent works. I agree that without being familiar with the knowledge necessary to seek out the principles of their art among the prime causes, artists guided by that gift of nature which leads us to felicitous choices, will always be skilful.

But is it not also true that there are few authors who have considered architecture from the standpoints that are specifically those of art? I mean by this that few authors have sought to explore deeply the part of architecture that I have called art per se. While we may have a small number of precepts founded on good examples, they are very limited.

[. . .] Could we say that it would be fitting that, to follow studies of pure speculation, the architect were to abandon lucrative tasks? Alas! Which one of them would voluntarily sacrifice the fortune available to him, which may often be necessary to him? Need we add that this sacrifice must be made easy by the hope of one day being entrusted with some great monuments? But how is it possible to open oneself up to that hope? Such opportunities are so rare! [. . .]

Ah! How much to be preferred is the life of a painter or a man of letters! Free and without dependency of any kind, they may choose any subject and follow their genius where it leads. It is on themselves alone that their reputation depends. If they possess the paramount talents, no power on earth can prevent them from developing them.

And, seeking to discover in the essence of solid bodies what their properties are, and the analogy with our own organisation, I began my researches with solid bodies considered in their pure state. [. . .]

Tired with the silent and sterile image of irregular solids, I went on to an examination of regular bodies. [. . .]

All these observations lead to the conclusion that the spherical form is in all respects the image of perfection. [. . .]

Etienne-Louis
Boullée
1728–1799

Let us direct our gaze at an object! The first impression that we feel comes manifestly from the manner in which the object affects us. And I call character the effect that results from this object and causes in us an impression, whatever it may be.

To put character into a construction is to employ with good judgement all the means likely to lead us to experience other feelings than those that must result from the subject. To understand what I mean by 'character' and 'effect' imposed by the various objects, let us consider the great scenes of nature and see how we are obliged to express ourselves according to the manner in which they act upon our senses.

In our time, nature has finished its work [. . .] all things have achieved precision of form: they have dimension, they are correct and pure. Their contours are sharp and distinct; their development confers upon them noble and majestic proportions; their colours, now bright and shining, have acquired their full brilliance [. . .] the effects are sharp and brilliant. They are radiant! [. . .]

But the clement weather is eclipsed, and now is the season of dark and cold commencing. How melancholy the days! [. . .] Darkness envelops us! Ghastly winter comes to freeze our hearts! It is arriving on the wings of time! Night follows it, casting its black veils over the earth, spreading dark shadows. The brilliant crystal of the waves is already tarnished by the cruel breath of the north wind. The pleasant bowers of the woods now offer us only their bones, and funeral crepe covers all nature [. . .] all things have lost their brilliance, their colour; their shapes are collapsed in upon themselves, their contours are hard and sharply angular [. . .]

It is these extended images that I have attempted to produce in several of my designs: in that for the palace in Saint-German-en-Laye, in that of a metropolis, in that for Newton's cenotaph. I have tried to apply all those means offered me by nature and art to represent in architecture the greater scene. [. . .]

[. . .] It follows from these observations that in order to produce melancholy, sombre images, it is necessary, as I have attempted to do in funerary monuments, to present the bones of the architecture through an absolutely plain wall, to offer the image of an architecture buried in the tomb by employing only low, shrunken proportions as if the structure is buried in the earth, and lastly to form, using materials that absorb the light, the sombre picture of an architecture of shadows drawn by the effects of even blacker shadows.

This type of architecture, formed by shadows, is a discovery in the art which is mine alone. [. . .] Ornamentation, where inappropriate, does no more than aggravate the defects of which I have spoken above by making them even more visible. [. . .] ·

[471]

Why should the basilica of Saint Peter in Rome appear to be smaller than it is in reality? This intolerable defect stems from the fact that far from offering a scene commensurate with the actual space by including the number of objects that such a large space should normally contain, the architect has reduced the effect of the whole by giving colossal dimensions to the parts that compose it, believing, according to the expression of the artists, that he was *working on the large scale*, when in fact he had made his design *gigantic*.

When I pointed out that a place of worship should offer an image of that which was vast, I was not intending to speak simply of its spaciousness; I was referring to that ingenious art by virtue of which one extends, one enlarges images, which consists in the association of objects in such a manner that they are presented to us in a manner able to develop as far as possible their combination under our gaze and in an order of disposition such that in giving us the enjoyment of their multiplicity it follows that through the successive views in which they appear to us, they are constantly renewed, to the point at which we cannot count them. Such is for example the effect produced by the regular and symmetrical combination of a quincunx. If we stand outside towards one of the corners, the total mass will be offered up to our gaze in the greatest development, since we shall see two of its faces.

[...] By extending the length of the avenues in order to ensure that their termination escapes our eye, the laws of optics and the effects of perspective offer to us a scene of immensity. At each step, the visible objects, presenting themselves from new angles, renew our pleasure by creating a successive variety of scenes. Finally, through the felicitous enchantment produced by the effect of our movements, but which we attribute to the objects we see, it seems that the latter are walking along with us and that we have breathed life into them.

The reader will perhaps permit us to continue our remarks on the basilica of Saint Peter. If, for example, in lieu of the massive abutments which, through their width and their thickness, obstruct the wholeness of the temple, we imagine, as in Greek architecture, that there were light, pleasant structural elements, immense ranks of columns lining the naves and the side aisles, separating the one from the other in a manner such that the gaze can penetrate throughout the entire space and embrace that multitude of objects in the wealth of which the observer is pleased to lose himself and whose seductive effect invariably leads him to believe that he sees a greater number of such objects – who could doubt that this place of worship, whose size is reduced through the gigantic arrangement of arcades that dominates the whole, would appear infinitely greater, since the methods we have just described would (as is well known), far from diminishing the space, contribute most singularly to giving it the appearance of being greater? [...]

The image of that which is vast holds such sway over our senses that in supposing it to be awful, it invariably excites in us a feeling of admiration. A volcano spitting flame and death is an image awful in its beauty! [...]

How, I begin by saying to myself, can I succeed in conferring upon my place of worship its own intrinsic character? Are there in architecture methods specific to the art with which one may succeed in inspiring all the religious feelings appropriate to the worship of the Supreme Being?

[...] I finally obtain a glimmer of hope when I remember the sombre, mysterious effects I have observed in forests and the diverse impressions that they had led me to

Etienne-Louis
Boullée
1728–1799

experience. I began to see that if there were some means of realising the scenes which penetrated my mind, it could only be in the manner in which light would be brought into the temple. My reasoning was as follows: light is the source of such effects. Those effects cause diverse and contradictory feelings according to whether they are brilliant or dark. If I can succeed in casting throughout my place of worship magnificent effects of illumination, I shall penetrate the soul of the observer with a sentiment of happiness. I shall bring on the contrary only melancholy when the temple offers nothing but effects of darkness. If I can prevent light arriving directly and succeed in allowing it to enter without the observer being able to say from whence it comes, the resulting effects of mysterious daylight will produce incomprehensible effects, a sort of truly enchanting magic. As the master of my light, dispensing it at will, I shall be able, by diminishing the daylight, inspire in the soul a tranquil meditation, penitence, and even religious awe, especially if, during solemn ceremonies tending to excite such senti- ments, I take care to decorate the temple in a manner commensurate with this. Con- versely, during ceremonies that are to excite feelings of joy, the effects of light should be brilliant, the temple should be decked with flowers, these being the most pleasing objects in nature, and the result will be a majestic scene to instil a sentiment of delight in the soul.

Etienne-Louis
Boullée
1728–1799

[...] After having conceived the means of establishing my strengthening forces and consolidated them with the necessary abutments for the support of the dome, in order to sustain the vaults of the main nave, those of the side aisles, and those of the side chapels, I surrounded these massive elements with colonnades in all directions and it is thus that using all that is most agreeable in architecture I succeeded in removing these massive structural members from the gaze of the observer.

This disposition leads to a situation in which, as with the Gothic architects, the strengthening forces in my temple are masked and it seems to stand as if by some miracle, and indeed, in imitation of the Greek architects, it will be decorated with the richest possible architectural ornamentation. The columns occupying the foreground offer an easier means of letting in daylight in a manner redolent of mystery, since the distance by which they project into the space does not allow the observer to see how the light enters the place of worship. This latter arrangement brings with it many advantages, first among which is that of permitting the inclusion of as many windows as desired without the problem of deciding upon their shape, since they cannot be seen.

One consequence of this disposition is that the anchor points of my dome are so solidly assured that I have been able to add to the exterior of my cupola a double colon- nade and another inside. I profited from this advantage both to confer a sense of immensity on the circumference of my dome and to separate it from the temple which ornaments the inside of the dome. Since the painting on the vaulted roof is extended down to the back wall from which the columns are separated, the area of the heavens and the glory which decorate the vault and the cupola becomes apparently vast, which helps make the architectural design of this crowning element as light and airy as it could possibly be. Placed in the centre of the monument, the dome is arranged in such a manner as to strike immediately the eye of any person entering the temple, drawing his gaze by its brilliant effects, its rich ornamentation and its size. Free of those massive pillars that in our modern churches obstruct the space, impoverishing the central part, this temple offers, through the association of the colonnades in the naves with those in the dome, all the rich possibilities of architecture. Immense ranks of columns in

[473]

quincunx arrangement would multiply their apparent number to such an extent that the eye would lose itself in this wealth of riches and the effects of optics and perspective. Extending the size of the colonnades would provide, as we have noted, a scene of immensity.

This structure, intended for the use of ministers of religion, is crowned, as I have already stated, by an open temple designed to airy effect. This sort of construction has more particular need of the poetry of architecture than any other. [...]

After having said to myself that the bare bones of architecture comprise completely bare walls devoid of all ornamentation, it seemed to me that in order to provide an image of an architecture buried in the tomb, I should arrange my design in order to ensure that the construction should be satisfying in itself but at the same time should lead the observer to presume that a part of it is hidden from his gaze by the soil.

Etienne-Louis
Boullée
1728–1799

It was in the light of these reflections of general order, which seemed to me to offer the means of giving intrinsic character to my subject, that I took up my drawing pen. But how great is the distance between the conception of a design and its execution! It is doubtless the case that it is often the most difficult thing in any art to express one's thought well.

My mind continuing to be occupied by this type of architecture, after having attempted to create for the eye a buried architecture, a new idea came to me – to create an architectural design based on shadows.

The whole world is aware of the effect of a solid body placed against a source of light – as all know, the result is a shadow whose shape resembles that of the solid body concerned. It is to this effect of light that we owe the birth of the beautiful art of painting. [...]

The ordinary person contemplates without interest the effects of nature that he sees habitually and which, since they have ceased to possess the attractions of novelty for him, no longer excite his curiosity. The same is not true of the artist, who, continually finding new things to be explored, spends all his life observing the natural world.

Finding myself in the countryside one day, I passed by a wood in the moonlight. My effigy, created by the light, attracted my attention. [...] Due to my particular attitude of mind, the effect of this simulacrum seemed to me to be imbued with extreme melancholy. The trees depicted upon the ground by their shadows made the deepest possible impression upon me. This scene was made even greater by my imagination. I saw that day that which is the most sombre in nature. What did I see? The masses of objects picked out in black against the palest possible light. A nature in mourning seemed to offer itself up to me. Struck by these sentiments, I set myself in that moment the task of applying them specifically to architecture. I tried to find a design composed by the effect of shadows. [...] Such was the manner in which I proceeded when I worked to create this new genre in architecture.

[...] to confer the most appropriate character upon funerary monuments. It does not appear to me to be possible to conceive anything more melancholy than a monument formed by a plane surface, plain and unornamented, in a material that absorbs light and is absolutely devoid of all detail, whose sole decoration is the play of shadows against even blacker shadows. No, no other scene as sad as this exists, and, if we leave aside the beauty created by art, it would be impossible not to see in such a construction a melancholy picture of architecture. [...]

I have given a partial definition of architecture by saying that it is the art of creating images by the arrangement of solid bodies. The effects of solid bodies stem from their masses. Yes, it is the mass of an object that acts upon our senses, it is by the appearance of objects that we make a distinction between forms that are light and pleasant, heavy and massive, noble, majestic, or elegant and svelte. The effect of the masses of objects is the source of the art of giving character to any construction. The real talent of an architect is to present in his works the sublime charm of poetry. How can one succeed in this? Through the effects of masses – it is from them that is born the character of a construction, which leads the observer to feel no other sentiments than those genuinely appropriate to the subject.

[...]

Even the best reasoning and arguments on the fine arts will never succeed in producing artists. Why should this be? It is because reason and argument cannot lead us to feelings, and the art of expressing feelings, which comes from our sensibility, is the goal of the fine arts. The manner of study in the fine arts consists in the exercise of that sensibility, and it is in the finest productions of humankind, and above all in the creations of nature, that we must seek all means likely to develop it. [...]

Pierre Patte
1723–1814

aesthetisation of architecture • emotions • passions • sentiments • representation • truth • illusion

Pierre Patte (1723–1814)

Critical Analysis of the Construction of the Pantheon Dome (1801)

(See Patte, 1769)

The result of the examination of the bottom of the dome in question reveals that the architect had regard neither for principles nor examples in its composition: the pillars have none of the conditions required for bearing a dome on pendentives with solidity. The upper parts, instead of rising outside and being set back from the lower ones, are out of alignment and on the corbel.

Yes, assuredly, one might answer, it is always possible to do better, and to invent new means to perfect the arts or to push back their limits; but that possibility is very limited in building, and above all should not be stretched to the point of defying the laws of balance and gravity. When an architect is designing the composition of his structures, he must continuously struggle against the temptation to achieve a better ideal, and never lose sight of the principle that a continuous relationship must always exist between that which is being held up and that which is holding it up. He does not have, like the simple architectural illustrator or the painter of a theatre set, the freedom to give full rein to his genius and imagination: provided that they, by the ordering of their drawings or their paintings, create prestigious views, find interesting optical points or chiaroscuro effects whose magic is likely to produce illusions that are pleasing to the viewer's eye, naught more is asked of them, and little does it matter if their dreams cannot become reality; but, once again, the architect in charge of designing an edifice destined to go down in posterity must have numerous advantages. He is constantly obliged to obey the rules of solidity, and cannot break them with impunity. He is in the case of someone who must be sure of every step that he is taking, who must rally behind the true principles of building, and put into practice the great maxim, 'when in doubt, leave it out'.

[475]

That is what Soufflot has not paid enough attention to. Seeking to realise the pleasing whole of which he had conceived the idea by the order of his plan; convinced, it is said, above all by small-scale experiments on the resistance of stones under very heavy loads, as though full-scale conclusions can always be drawn from small-scale models in matters of building; led astray, one might add, by the lightness of certain supports observable in some Gothic edifices that can in no way be considered in the same case, he thought he could reduce the size of his pillars as much as he wanted to.

Thus convinced, instead of starting ordinarily by determining the dimensions of the design of the top or the tower in order to subjugate the bottom to them, he did the opposite and subjugated the design of the top to that which he had imagined for the bottom; and 'tis a well-known fact that the building has been under construction for almost twenty years and there is still no definitive plan for the dome.

Richard Elsam
?–1825

The Inadequacy of the Plans Proposed for the Re-establishment of the Pantheon Dome

There have been two serious plans, one proposed by the body of architects, the other by the body of civil engineers, from which none has wanted to deviate.

The architects, after having unanimously recognised the incapacity of the pillars to hold up the dome, in general agreed that the only solution was to strengthen them with sturdy dressed-stone cladding either inside or out, under the pendentives, at the risk of altering the plan of the edifice because they would project.

The engineers have put forth a plan that is exactly the opposite from that of the architects; without going any further back than they did, either to the principles or to the examples, or to the source of the problem, they believe on the contrary that the mass of the pillars must not be increased, that cladding would only mutilate the beauty of the order of this monument's interior architecture by their projections, and propose only to strengthen the pillars with flying buttresses.

As for the mathematicians who were associated with the Commission, their wisdom seems to have been tapped very little in this circumstance, because none of them is as well-versed in practice as in theory, which is very seldom encountered ...

rigorism • essentialism • scientification

Richard Elsam (?–1825)

Essay on Rural Architecture (1803)

The work was intended as a polemical response to Malton's (1789) who espoused the roughness and irregularity of the English rustic cottage in his designs for country retreats. The author, an architect who subsequently turned mainly to writing, objected to the lowly status and insalubrious effects on the mind of such buildings, preferring instead the equally nationalist but more sublime Gothic style.

Further reading Esdaile, 1917–1919; Harris, 1990; Nachmani, 1968–1969; Teyssot, 1974; Wiebenson, 1982.

The peasant's cot, and the farm-house, will therefore, for time immemorial, prove admirable subjects for the pencil of the painter, with its appropriate scenery. But they are not agreeable, to my conceptions, proper models of imitations for persons of fortune, who are desirous of building themselves rural retreats, which may be erected to convey the idea of cottages, without being subject to the imputation of grotesque, or faced with such a motley group of materials, as brick, wood, or plaster, or brick noggin, dashed to insinuate the effects of age, and the appearance of being added to at different periods: all which rather must contribute to impress the mind of the spectator with the idea of poverty, rather than with a just notion of its cheerful and independent inhabitants. Surely, no person of taste, who had the intention of building a small house in the cottage style, would, by preference, expend a sum of money to exhibit the aspect of an old house; to those, however, who are prepossessed in favour of such ruinous antiquated dwellings, are recommended to add a few extra props around them, in order to render the effect of their designs more consistent.

With the greatest veneration for the antiquity of the British cottage, as the primitive invention of our peasants, I shall leave them to devise their own plans as heretofore, satisfied they are as competent to the task, in all respects, as their forefathers. To persons of a more refined taste and discernment, the following designs of cottages are offered, not as models of perfection, but as designs from which others may be contrived to answer most of the purposes required by persons anxious to construct themselves small, comfortable, genteel cottages in the country, at a moderate expense. The peculiar characteristic, of which I have delineated in my mind, to consist in a simple uniform plan, approximating either the square or parallelogram form, with the distribution of the several out houses harmonising with the main building: the general effect low, approaching humility, seldom more than one storey high, never more than two; steep roofs, gable ends, covered with thatch or small slates, the latter preferable; large projecting eaves to shelter the walls; small dormer windows in the roof, with chimney stacks built angular ways; sash door of simple form and small dimensions, with low casement windows, but in the principal apartments sash windows down to the floor, may be introduced without grossly infringing upon its humble character.

The walls should be covered with stucco, rough cast, paretta, or flintwork; any of these having a very neat, clean and grateful aspect when surrounded by a variety of trees. These are the leading and marked features which, in my opinion, should constitute and characterise the exterior appearance of the cottage for the gentleman of fortune. To which, above all, should be considered a well digested plan, embracing all the requisite conveniences so essentially conducive to the comfort of a small family.

The greatest recommendation to the cottage itself should be its making a lively appearance, for to those persons who are desirous of partaking in a country life, as a relaxation from business, are not apt to be prepossessed in favour of a gloomy habitation: it may, therefore, not be improper to observe that windows, glazed in small compartments of hexagons, have this effect; for although they are recommended by a late author, their defects are particularly conspicuous; which are obvious to all who have seen Mr Charles Carpenter's cottage at Stockwell Green, lately converted into a house for the reception of insane persons.

How very much the study and subject of building delights mankind in general, and how deeply it is rooted in the mind, is apparent from the innumerable structures which are constantly presenting themselves over this happy isle; few persons possessing the means but what have an inclination to be building a something; many, however, without duly considering what they are about to commence, plunge into bricks and

Richard Elsam
?–1825

mortar, and flatter themselves the expense will be considerably less than what it afterwards proves. Persons, therefore, who wish to act wisely and discreetly, would do well ... obtaining an accurate detailed estimate, from some person of known skill, reputation and experience, who will faithfully discharge that duty, without leading his employer into a labyrinth of difficulties, and who will take the trouble of laying down a regular system in the execution of the work, to prevent his being hereafter imposed upon; and who will, if required, carry the same into effect for the amount thereof. It is to be lamented that gentlemen in one of the most liberal professions are not more attentive to this essential part of their duty, ... which not only tends to lessen their estimation, but to stigmatise the whole body of the profession.

Richard Elsam
?–1825

It is the prevalent opinion of most persons, who are in the practice of studying the peculiar characteristic of the Gothic style, that we cannot introduce it anywhere so advantageously as in the temples dedicated to the worship of the Deity; and it must be admitted, there is no character of building so well calculated to impress the mind with a just and awful solemnity, or with a greater religious veneration; it is therefore to be regretted, the adoption of it in our modern churches is not more frequent. The cathedral of St Paul's, the church of St Martin's in the Fields, the interior of St Stephen's, Walbrook, the exquisite chapel at Greenwich Hospital, together with many of our London churches, present to the inquisitive traveller some of the noblest magnificent examples of Roman and Grecian architecture, equal, if not surpassing, many of the renowned antiquities from whence we have gleaned the best information; but this, nevertheless, does not prove the Roman or Grecian style preferable, or equal to the Gothic or Saxon in sacred structures, with which latter no country abounds more luxuriantly than Great Britain.

It is not our intention to dispute the origin of the Gothic architecture, perceiving that we have no exact and incontrovertible data upon which to repose our opinions; ... England, perhaps, has the best founded pretensions, as well to its origin, as undoubtedly to its highest improvements, from its having been more encouraged in this island, than any other, if it is, however, employed in dwelling houses, it should possibly partake of a more cheerful character than the style usually practised in churches; it should be divided into classes of the church Gothic, castle Gothic and house Gothic; it would evidently be extremely absurd to employ the same sort of windows for a house as in a church ... Houses in this style are not very numerous; they are, nevertheless, very elegant when judiciously contrived, and are capable of being rendered, in rural scenery, more picturesque than any other class of buildings whatever.

It is a paradox not yet easy to be explained, why the architecture of foreign countries should be so well comprehended in this, so eagerly studied, and so anxiously sought after, whilst the Gothic, not less entitled to respect, the peculiarly consonant genius of our isle, lies ungratefully neglected. Would our English students, before they make the tour to Rome, bestow only a little pains to make themselves acquainted with these admirable relics, the treasure of their own country, it would certainly enable them to speak of it with pleasure abroad, and to practise it hereafter with better founded confidence at home.

anticlassicism • deformation • freedom • naturalism • regionalism • nationalism

Jean-Nicolas-Louis Durand (1760–1834)

A Precis of the Lessons in Architecture Given at the Polytechnic School (1802–1805)

Durand, a one-time student of Boullée, was the first professor of architecture appointed at the revolutionary École Polytechnique. The present work, in three abundantly illustrated volumes, is made up of the lectures he gave to his engineering students at that school. Its concern for economic, structural and functional requirements contrasts sharply with the approach which had prevailed at its predecessor institution, the Académie Royale d'Architecture, just before the revolution (Hernandez, 1969). The rationalisation of the design process which Durand advocates is also novel, stressing the importance of an explicit, systematic set of rules. The lectures influenced the development of the industrial town more than any other work at that time (Benevolo, 1961) and contain many of the notions that became widely accepted with the aesthetic functionalism of the early twentieth century.

Further reading Collins, 1965; Wiebenson 1982, 1993.

Jean-Nicolas-Louis Durand 1760–1834

Architecture is the art of designing and executing all types of public and private edifice. Of all the arts, architecture produces the most costly works. Even the smallest private buildings are expensive to construct, and the cost of the construction of public edifices is enormous, even when both these types of building are designed prudently, but if in their design the only guides are prejudice, caprice or habit, *the expense entailed will become incalculable.*

Since the importance of *architecture* is so great and so general, it would be desirable therefore for this art to be generally known, but since this is not the case, at least those who must practise it should have perfect knowledge of it.

Architects are not alone in having to build edifices; engineers of all grades, artillery officers, and so on, frequently encounter this same obligation. It might even be added that at the present time engineers have more occasion to execute great projects than do architects themselves; this is because the latter during the course of their lives often have only private houses to build, whereas the former, in addition to the latter type of edifice, with which they may also be entrusted in far-flung *départements* where architects are scarce, find themselves charged, by virtue of their condition, with the task of erecting hospitals, prisons, barracks, arsenals, magazines, bridges, ports, lighthouses, and *in fine*, a multitude of edifices of the utmost importance. For this reason, knowledge and talent in the field of architecture are at least as necessary to them as to professional architects. [...]

Thus appropriateness and economy are the means that must naturally be employed in architecture, and the sources from which it must draw its principles, the only principles that should guide us in the study and practice of that art. [...]

Once a surface area has been determined, one may observe that when it is bounded by the four sides of a square it requires a less complicated plan than when it is bounded by the sides of a parallelogram, and less still when bounded by the circumference of a circle, and that in fact the symmetry, regularity and simplicity, the shape of a square, which is superior to that of a parallelogram, is inferior to that of a circle, and it is easy to conclude that the cost of any edifice will diminish as it becomes more symmetrical, more regular and simpler. There is no need to add that if economy prescribes the greatest simplicity in all things that are necessary, it proscribes absolutely all that is superfluous. [...]

[479]

According to most architects, architecture is less the art of making useful buildings than that of decorating buildings. Its main aim is to please the eye and through that to excite in us agreeable sentiments, a goal that it can only attain, like the other arts, through imitation or representation. It must take as its model the shapes of the first huts built by men, and the proportions of the human body. [...]

But since one cannot do decorative work without money, and the more decorative work is done, the more money is spent, it is natural to ask whether architectural decoration, as conceived by architects, gives all the pleasure expected of it, or at least whether that pleasure compensates for the cost incurred. [...]

Jean-Nicolas-
Louis Durand
1760–1834

Now, if huts are certainly not natural objects, if the human body could not have been used as a model for architecture, if, supposing the contrary to be true, the orders are not imitations or representations of either of these, we must necessarily draw the conclusion that the orders are not of the essence of architecture, that the pleasure we expect of their use and the decorative effect produced are non-existent, and that, to conclude, the decorative effect is itself mere imagination, and the expense it involves, pure folly. It follows from this that if the main aim of architecture is to please, architecture must either imitate better or seek other models, or perhaps other methods of imitation. [...]

Some authors, who have argued for and developed, with all the intellectual resources imaginable, the approach based on the primitive hut, will say that until now we have been discussing buildings alone, and that from this point of view architecture is no more than a trade, and that it began to deserve to be called an art only when human societies, having reached the highest degree of opulence and luxury, sought to make agreeable the edifices erected by them. But we go back here to those authors themselves. Was it when the Romans reached the highest degree of opulence and luxury [...] that their architecture improved? The Greeks were far less opulent and is not their architecture, despite the small number of examples, to be preferred to that of the Romans? [...] In a few buildings one observes a little sculptural ornamentation, but the others, for the most part, are entirely devoid of it, and are no less esteemed for that. Is it not self-evident that this ornamentation is not essential to architecture? [...]

Whether we consult our reason, or examine the monuments themselves, it is manifest that giving pleasure could never have been the goal of architecture, and nor could architectural decoration be its object. Public and private utility, happiness and the protection of individuals and society, such is, as we saw at the beginning, the goal of architecture. [...]

We are far from thinking that architecture cannot please. What we are saying, on the contrary, is that it is impossible that it should not please, when it is practised according to its true principles. Has not nature joined pleasure to the satisfaction of our needs, and are not our most intense pleasures something more than the satisfaction of even our most imperative needs? Now, how could an art such as architecture, an art that satisfies immediately such a large number of our needs [...] fail to please us?

Doubtless the grandeur, magnificence, variety, effect and character that one observes in buildings are so many aspects of beauty, so many causes of happiness that we feel on seeing them. But what is the purpose of pursuing all those things? If one disposes an edifice in a manner such that it is appropriate for the use for which it is intended, will it not differ noticeably from another edifice destined for that same use? Will it not naturally have a character, indeed, its own specific character? If the diverse parts of that edifice, intended for diverse uses, are each arranged in the manner in which they should be arranged, will they not differ necessarily from each other? Will not that building offer a degree of variety? That same edifice, if its parts are disposed in the most economical manner, that is to say, in as simply as possible, will it not have the greatest possible grandeur and magnificence since the eye will then embrace simultaneously the greatest number of its parts? Where can therefore be the need for the pursuit of all these partial aspects of beauty?

There is more: it is that far from being necessary, it is harmful to the decorative effect itself. I say this because if, due to the fact that certain beautiful aspects of an edifice have impressed themselves on you, you wish to transfer them to another building where they are not appropriate, or if you desire to take those same beautiful aspects, present as a natural fact, to the highest point of perfection, higher than is appropriate for the building, is it not self-evident that that edifice will have an appearance, a visual aspect that is different from that which it should have, that it will have lost its specific character, that its natural beauty will fade, vanish and perhaps even be transformed into ugliness?

Jean-Nicolas-Louis Durand 1760–1834

According to what has been said above, we should not therefore attach importance to the fact that architecture should be pleasing, given that simply by seeking to attain its true goal, it is impossible for architecture not to please, and that in seeking to please it may make itself ridiculous. [. . .]

The architect must therefore address himself solely to the disposition of his building, even if he considers architectural decorativeness important, seeking only to please, since that decorative work can never be seen as beautiful, can never give rise to true pleasure, unless it springs from the most fitting and the most economical disposition.

Thus all the talent of the architect comes down to the resolution of two difficulties: 1. with a given sum of money, he must make the most fitting edifice possible, as in private buildings; 2. once what is fitting has been determined for a building, it must be built at the least possible cost, as in the case of public buildings.

It can be seen from all that has preceded that in architecture, economy, far from being, as is often believed, an obstacle to beauty, is, on the contrary, its most fertile source.

Continuation of the Introduction

Differences in mores, customs, climate, localities, materials and monetary means necessarily introduce a multitude of varieties in all types of edifice, increasing to infinity the number of designs the architect may conceive and execute.

Indeed, if, in order to learn the art of architecture it were necessary to study each in turn all the various forms of edifice in all the circumstances that may alter them, such study would, even if it were possible, certainly be of fearsome duration. It may however be thought possible to shorten that study by restricting it to a given number of designs that one might suppose to be obligatory of execution. But however great the number of the latter, that course of study would not only be quite incomplete, but would additionally be of very little profit. For it is certain that one would acquire in this way no more than some particular and isolated ideas which, far from being of mutual support, would often be mutually contradictory, creating a disorder and a confusion in the mind commensurate with their number. [. . .]

[...] since the composition of any edifice as a whole is no more than the result of the association of its constituent parts, those parts must be known before the whole can be addressed. And since those constituent parts are themselves composed of the primordial elements of all buildings, after the study of the general principles from which all particular principles must derive, those primordial elements must be the first objects of study for the architect.

Once we have become thoroughly familiar with all those diverse objects, which are to architecture what words are to discourse, or notes to music, without perfect knowledge of which it is impossible to proceed further, we shall see 1. how they can be combined, that is to say how they can be arranged each in relation to the others both horizontally and vertically, 2. how, using such combinations, it is possible to form the various parts of buildings, such as porticoes, porches, entrance halls, staircases, both exterior and interior, rooms of all kinds, courtyards, grottoes and fountains. Once these various parts are well known to us, we shall see 3. how one must combine these in their turn to compose the whole of a building.

Jean-Nicolas-Louis Durand 1760–1834

Just as it is prejudicial from all points of view to replace, in the study of architecture, with knowledge of a multitude of small aspects of appropriate design specific to each edifice, general knowledge of what is fitting in buildings, appropriate to all edifices and relevant in all times and all places, it is also advantageous, after a course of study whose nature we have just described, to review and to analyse the greatest possible number of buildings. Nothing is more conducive to the exercise of judgement, the fertilisation of the imagination, the ever deeper penetration of the true principles of the art, and their easy application.

In all teaching on architecture this art is divided into three distinct parts: decoration, disposition and construction. At first sight, this division appears simple, natural and useful. But [...] of the three concepts expressed by the terms *decoration*, *disposition* and *construction*, there is only one that is relevant to all buildings. According to the idea of *decoration* generally held, it is not appropriate to most edifices. By *disposition*, what is understood is nothing other than the art of arranging, according to our customs, the various parts that make up a residential building, for we do not talk in terms of the disposition of a place of worship, a theatre, law courts, etc. The word *construction* [...] is therefore the only one that has a meaning sufficiently general to be applicable to all edifices.

But given that architecture is not only the art of execution, but also of the design of all buildings, whether public or private, and since it is not possible to execute any building without having first designed it, the notion of construction naturally finds itself associated with another concept of general character [...]. Now, given that this general concept is not provided in any way by this method, the method is consequently tainted with error.

[...] it can provide no more than an incomplete idea of architecture, and indeed it is dangerous, for it leads to the most erroneous ideas possible of architecture: the role played by the term *decoration* suffices to makes this manifest. [...]

From this division of architecture into three arts independent each of the others, that one may, nay must, study separately, it may happen that a person wishing to become an architect finds one of the three more to his taste, and begins to give it preference, neglecting the other two, often ceasing completely to study them, consequently acquiring only part of the knowledge that he needs. This in itself is enough reason to abandon this approach totally.

Drawing is used to express one's ideas, either during the study of architecture or when designing buildings, to fix ideas in order to examine them again at leisure, and to correct them if necessary, and lastly, it is used to communicate them. [...]

Those persons who think that the essential goal of architecture is to please the eye consider, as a necessary consequence, tinted geometrical plans as being inherent to architecture. [...]

This type of drawing should be prohibited in architecture with all the more severity, since it is not only false but also extremely dangerous. [...]

Part I. Third Section. Forms and Proportions

[...] Forms and proportions may be classified in three categories: those that stem from the nature of the materials and the use of the objects in the construction of which they are employed; those of which habit has made a necessity, as it were, for us, such as the shapes and proportions that one may observe in ancient edifices; and lastly, those which, simpler and more sharply defined that others, should be preferred by us due to the ease with which we may comprehend them.

Jean-Nicolas-
Louis Durand
1760–1834

The first of these are the only ones that are essential, but they are not determined with such strictness by the nature of the things that we cannot add to or take away from them, with the result that nothing prevents the addition of the second category to them, that is, those seen in ancient edifices: [...]

[...] we are free to choose from among them those shapes and proportions which, being the simplest, are the most likely, by bringing economy to the construction of buildings, to please both eye and mind.

[...] in those public edifices that are most important, in which, at whatever price, one must neglect nothing that is appropriate to them, and where duration is a condition dictated not only by such adherence to what is appropriate, but also by economy, given that there is no economy to be had in rebuilding such edifices, and therefore the materials offering the most resistance shall be employed, and within a given space, the number of structural supports will be increased to the greatest number possible.

Part II. Third Section. The Building as a Whole

All the parts that form buildings in general are now known to us, and we have seen the manner in which the elements forming those diverse parts are to be combined. The task now is to unite those parts to form a whole.

In addressing the matter of primitive combinations of elements, we have seen that according to the general principles of architecture, walls, columns, doors and windows placed along the length or across the width of a building must be so placed along common axes. The natural consequence of this is that the rooms formed by those walls and those columns, and to which those same doors and windows provide openings, must similarly be organised along common axes. Those new axes may be combined in a thousand different fashions, and may give rise through their associations to an infinite number of different overall dispositions. [...]

To combine the various elements, to go on to address the different parts of the edifice, and to move from those parts to the building as a whole, such is the procedure that must be followed when one wishes to learn architectural design. When one is

[483]

actually practising architectural design, the contrary is true, one must begin with the whole, move on to the parts, and finish with the details.

Once the programme for a building has been defined, one must examine first whether according to its intended use all the parts composing its whole must be united or separated, or if, as a consequence, it must present in its overall plan a single mass or several; whether that mass, or those masses, must be solid, or contain empty spaces in the form of inner courtyards; whether the building, whatever its general disposition, may open out on to the public thoroughfare, or be removed from it by an enclosing wall; whether all the parts are destined for similar or for different uses, and consequently whether they must be addressed in similar or in distinct fashion. In the second of these two cases, one must look at which are the main parts and which are subordinate to them. One must determine the number in each of these categories, and what must be their necessary respective sizes and locations. Finally, one must consider whether the edifice is to have one storey or several, or a single storey in some of its parts and several in others.

Jean-Nicolas-
Louis Durand
1760–1834

When these conditions are well satisfied, one will feel that the project is well advanced, but one must also feel that in order to complete it many points remain to be addressed, and that these would be quite useless if the first were in error. Before going further, it is therefore necessary to assure oneself of their correctness. If the result of this examination is satisfactory, it is necessary to fix the ideas that have been conceived by means of a rapid sketch which, by relieving the memory of its burden, may make it possible to study those ideas again, at greater leisure and with greater exactitude, in order to go on with confidence to other points. [...]

Having indicated thus the number and location of the principal parts of the building, one must address the matter of the disposition of the subordinate parts.

Having noted that all the private meeting rooms must communicate with each other, and with the general assembly room, along new axes *cc*, etc., one should indicate the location of the communicating gallery, along with those for the private vestibules, studies, etc.

Once the general disposition of the parts has been expressed using signs and axes, one should trace out the various walls that must enclose and divide the edifice. This sketch should give a quite clear picture of this, in order to allow it to be judged soundly, before going on to more detailed points.

When the sketch has been taken to this stage, one should consider first whether the building is to have ceilings in wooden planks or vaulting [...] if columns are to be included. [...]

Once this has been done, all that remains is to determine the ratios of size which must pertain between the various parts of the building, and this can be performed by determining the number of intervals between the axes of the different parts. [...]

What extravagances can they not commit, those who, far from seeing in architecture an effective means of contributing to public and private happiness, find in it only a means of making their reputation, of acquiring a form of glory, by amusing the eye with vain images! Some, obsessed with orders and columns, reducing the vast domain that is architecture's to just those edifices in which such ornamentation is appropriate, would neglect all others; or, deigning to design such buildings, but doing so in a manner such as to satisfy their self-regard, they would transform into palaces or temples all buildings, even those intended for the most ignoble of purposes.

Conversely, others, seeking only to confer character upon buildings, and desiring to give it, by hook or by crook, to their edifices, would eschew all columns in those where they are most necessary. Finally, still others, invariably with the word genius on their lips, wishing always to invent novelty, would be in despair if their works resembled anything at all, or, through a strange paradox, they would refuse to believe they were achieving any success at all if their designs did not resemble more or less such and such an edifice built by such and such an architect, despite the fact that the edifice in question was intended for a purpose quite different from that which is at hand.

Before addressing all the points described above, it is therefore important to make efforts to determine thoroughly the nature of the building that it is proposed to erect, to determine which of all the qualities a building may have are particularly necessary in the proposed edifice: salubriousness, as in the case of a hospital, salubriousness and security at one and the same time, as in the case of a prison, cleanliness, as in the case of markets or slaughterhouses, comfort, as in that of private houses, calm and tranquillity, as in buildings intended for study, agreeableness and gaiety, in those devoted to leisure, and so on. In short, one must seek to define all things that may contribute to achieving the goal of architecture in general, and that of each edifice in particular. By making use of the approach dictated by reason, it will always be possible to design all buildings with equal ease and equal success.

Jean-Nicolas-
Louis Durand
1760–1834

design methodology • efficiency • economisation • fit • utility • representation • truth • illusion • systemisation of space distribution • professional practice • education

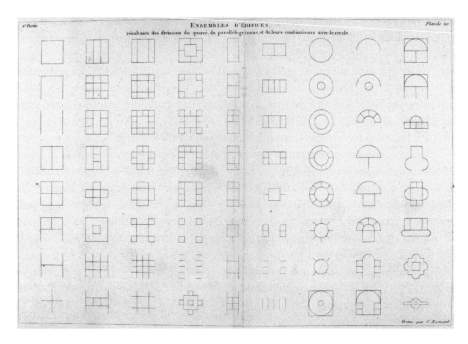

131. Jean-Nicolas-Louis Durand. *Précis des leçons d'architecture données à l'Ecole Polytechnique.* 1802. Types of building plans generated out of square, parallelogram, circle spatial elements by division and combination. Spaces are represented by their axis.

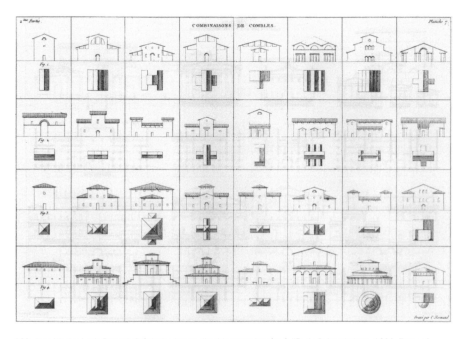

132. Jean-Nicolas-Louis Durand. *Précis des leçons d'architecture données à l'Ecole Polytechnique.* 1802. Types of building volumes and roofs generated by addition or combination of spatial elements.

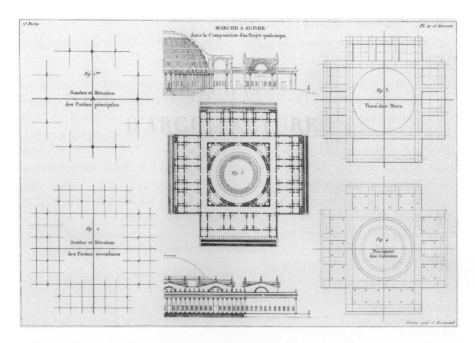

133. Jean-Nicolas-Louis Durand. *Précis des leçons d'architecture données à l'Ecole Polytechnique.* 1802. Example of the method of composition of a building plan by hierarchical embedding of space divisions and elements.

Claude-Nicolas Ledoux (1736–1806)

Concerning Architecture Seen From the Point of View of Art, of Morals and Legislation (1804)

Ledoux studied at the school of J.F. Blondel (1752) whose ideas about the expressiveness of architectural form influenced him in his departures from the classical canon (Kaufmann, 1955). He earned the position of '*Architecte du Roi*' to Louis XVI and gained the highly coveted entrance into the Academy of Architecture, measures of his highly successful career as a society architect under the *Ancien Régime*. From 1773 to 1779, he worked under royal patronage on the never completed industrial town of Chaux, whose livelihood was to depend on the lucrative exploitation of salt mines nearby in central France. While imprisoned during the French Revolution, he composed the present book describing the project in terms, ironically, of the most enthusiastic Utopian socialism.

Further reading Brion, 1937; Christ, 1961a, b; Collins, 1965; Hautecoeur, 1948–1963; Kaufmann, 1933, 1943, 1952 and 1960; Lowry, 1964; Rosenblum, 1967; Saboya, 1970; Wiebenson, 1982, 1993.

Omnia vincit amor

Introduction

In the multitude of occupations of which one may judge by the immensity of the work that I place under the gaze of the Nations, in the midst of the agitations with which my constancy has been fatigued, within the persecutions inseparable from the publication of great conceptions and passions which have exhausted themselves against my energy, almost always constrained by those narrow calculations, fearful fortunes and capricious wilfulness that stay the impetus of genius, I shall not offer to my readers that sort of project that loses itself in the vagueness of imaginary combinations, or whose awful feasibility annuls in advance the execution.

Convinced as I am that in abridging the annals of history, and gathering together the models and principles that art has deposited there, I may imprint upon time itself a creative movement that will lead it to give birth to masterpieces, and extend its domain and its glory, I have brought together, in several days' reading matter, all the riches of the centuries that have preceded us.

Before night covers over with its darkened veil the vast field in which I have placed all the forms of edifice required by social order, we shall see large factories, the mothers and daughters of industry, give birth to populous assemblies. A city shall rise to enclose and to crown them. Invigorating luxury, the fruitful companion of the arts, shall display there all the monuments that opulence cause to flourish. Its environs shall be embellished with residences devoted to rest and pleasure and shall be planted with gardens to rival celebrated Eden.

Refuges for the hard-working artisan, the villages and market towns shall enhance the beauty visible to the gaze through the contrast offered by their simplicity. The houses of the poor, through their modest exteriors, shall raise still higher the splendour of the townhouses of the rich, and of those palaces where, under the gold leaf that covers them, great personages seem to rival the brilliance of the star of the day.

We shall not deviate from the unity of reflection, nor from the lines laid down by variety of shapes, that which is fitting, correctness and economy.

Unity, the very model of the beautiful, *omnia porro pulchritudinis unitas est*, consists in the relationship between the main body and the details or ornaments, in the avoidance of interruption to lines that do not allow the eye to be distracted by prejudicial accessories.

Variety gives to any edifice the visual aspect that is appropriate to it; it multiplies and changes that aspect according to adjacent circumstances and planes that lead the eye to the horizon, and, satisfying a single desire, gives life to a thousand more.

A sense of what is fitting, which gives brilliance to wealth, and disguises its lack, shall subordinate ideas to localities, shall assemble diverse needs under relevant, inexpensive external appearances.

Correctness shall lead us to make commensurate proportions and ornamentation. It shall indicate at first glance the *raison d'être* of each construction and its allotted purpose.

Economy of material shall be more impressive to the eye than the actual expense due to that magical spell which deceives the eye through artful combination.

Symmetry must not be forgotten – taken from nature, it contributes to solidity and establishes parallels that do not exclude the picturesque, nay the bizarre, which should however be eschewed.

Claude-Nicolas
Ledoux
1736–1806

A Description of the City. Designs That May Ensure the Comfort of the Inhabitants, Extend it and Consolidate it

[...] It is world cut off from the world. This is a hard-working people, developing and bring to flower all the seeds that the earth, in its tacit contract with humankind, has promised to fertilise.

[...] when I gather together all the knowledge acquired in the salt marshes of Europe, I see nothing that justifies this difference. The entrances are made vile by the ordure that surrounds them, the walls, soiled by the vapours that envelop them, the roofs that are lost in the clouds exhale through the clay a thick smoke that hides all shapes and makes them one with the chimeras of the night.

Your reflections cause me pain. Must we entomb millions in the rags of abject poverty? Must we follow new paths that lead us astray, when the lamp of our century lights the road we should take?

General Plan of the Salt Marsh as it is Executed

One of the great motivations that bind governments to results at all times is the general disposition of a plan that brings together in an intelligently disposed centre all the parts that compose it. The eye embraces with ease the shortest route, work moves along it with a rapid step, the burden carried lightens in the hope of a rapid return. All obeys this association, which perfects the law of movement.

The shape is pure, like the curve described by the sun in its course. All is sheltered from the sleep of forgetfulness. There need be no fear of those contiguities that subject all to complete destruction by fire due to some local indiscretion. Everywhere art awakens solicitude; it commands, it is obeyed. Everywhere it controls events. That which contributes the most to impeding progress in the arts is the sentiment the artist ordinarily attaches to what belongs to him. Secretly, he harbours an initial idea which is often founded on no more than all too annoying regrets for fruitless effort. Unfortunate is he who cannot abandon thoughts that paralyse his talents, and imprison them in common habits. [. . .]

An Employee's House

On the first plots of land, intended for the construction of private houses, what do I see? Small edifices, of which most have but a single window on each face. What is their purpose? The government, wishing to provide models for that less fortunate part of humankind, had built several houses incorporating all things required for utility and solidity, and had not even neglected the disposition of each in relation to the others. In order to direct later efforts, preoccupied by that recompense which stimulates work and extends the faculties, it intended these ostensible fruits of its gratitude to go to its servants, to whom a well-deserved, but very modest, pension had been granted.

Claude-Nicolas
Ledoux
1736–1806

The nature of our errors is the identical to that which stimulates our intellect. Example, which holds man under its sway, more than any law may constrain him, will determine the neighbouring inhabitants to situate their retirement in these places of predilection. Who could doubt it?

I approach, I see porches providing protection from the intemperate equinox. I enter, I find bedrooms, to the south. One climbs to them on double staircases; these, their slopes made long and easy, cover over the woodpile. The ground floor is occupied by rooms intended for daily tasks. Small yards contain all the needs of life, and the mindful chicken gathers her family about her skirts. The stable is exposed to the winds of the west, the pantry to the north, both offering in a little space an example of the application of the great principles. In the gardens are to be found those nourishments, vegetables, aromatic herbs, and all that providential nature seems to provide in abundance in our favoured climes for the solace of man. [. . .]

A Gaming House

A gaming house? Yes, a gaming house: when a city is not sizeable enough to bear the expense of staged entertainment, one must beat the bounds of idleness in order to preserve the inhabitants from the vices that accompany it. In populous cities, gambling, which attracts the forms of corruptions on which the police keeps watch, could cleanse the public morals. It would be possible to create an establishment in which corruption would sink its ordure in order to bring relief to misery. The Architect is often obliged to follow the intentions dictated to him; it is his skill to guide erroneous conceptions, to give them definition and to bring them back to the path of correct principle.

What is needed is a building of small proportions situated in the middle of a vast field where art may unite the pleasures of a country setting, fruitful orchards and meadows on the banks of the Loue. What is needed is an area of unoccupied land, intended for the game of tennis, dance halls, chess games, backgammon, card games, restaurants, cafés, and so on, and bands. Gaming holds such sway over humankind in the provinces that it occupies a society deprived of ideas for the greater part of the day: a gaming house is perhaps more necessary than a hospice. Gambling deadens the sensitivity of men to social disorder, whereas misfortune ceases to exist when it is possible to find in work the fruits reserved for thrift. The situation of great cities in which all forms of corruption are to be found is not that of new towns: in the former, all ills are merged together in confusion, in the latter, men know and assist one another. [. . .]

A House for the Superintendents

The Architect of nature knows neither palaces nor cottages. I shall say more: the thatch of the cottage is stolen from that which should fertilise the soil. The common vault of the sky covers without distinction both wealth and poverty. And if the bronze that shines so brightly on the palaces of kings protects from the clap of thunder, he who directs it does not wish fragile wood covered with the dried hemp stalks to provoke its baleful fire, revealing the insufficiency thereof.

I agree with the principles you put forward, but in your philanthropic delirium, which seems to subordinate opulent edifices to those that are incapable of opulence, they are impossible of application.

O Gods! Do you hear him? The public treasury and interested companies can certainly seek the skills of an artist at great distances, but will indigence keep alight costly lamps to illuminate a small corner of the world unseen by any eye? What an abandonment of all principle! I see no advantage for it, and none even for the government. Indeed, what can come of such instructions concerning the isolated inhabitants of the countryside? What will come of such modest houses embellished by elevated and perhaps exaggerated concepts? What will come of these manufactories so cherished by art in its fondest dreams? [...]

Claude-Nicolas
Ledoux
1736–1806

The decorative arts that are widespread on this earth must advance in step with political economy. Do you wish to give them greater scope? Do you wish their expansion to be necessary to the greatest number? Then you must awaken common interests, and then all men will be driven to help in their progression.

Places, villages, market towns, cities shall adopt new forms exclusive of cold monotony, and shall warm the imagination. What administrators were unable to do, will be done for them. Believe me, the guarantee of this is that penetrating gaze that watches over all. It shall command the winds to ensure the salubrity of buildings. The town hall, the place of worship, the houses of the inhabitants, that the requirements of the public thoroughfare causes to be demolished or erected, shall be the preoccupation of the administration. No longer shall we see putrid sickness cause vexed regret for lack of foresight. No longer shall we see corrupted straw infect the soil or the product of digestive processes fermenting on burning roofs. New habits, dictated by example and maintained by superintendents, shall cleave body and mind to daily customs that increase strength and ensure good health. [...]

Since the time when man placed distance between himself and his basic needs, it seems that the inhabitants of the countryside have abandoned these favoured places. In vain does nature generously its accumulated creations, man disfigures the origins and prefers the deceptions of art.

It is thus that fundamental ideas hide in watery depths, and if they float to the surface above contrary influences, it is merely to reproduce impostures on a desiccated soil in which we try to restore that which has been lost to it.

Such wash-houses are placed with great pomp in our factories, they are surrounded with columns, with square pillars, ornate with decorative bosses. They are placed in our embellished farms, in our sumptuous stables, in our gardens, in our parks, where illusion replaces them at great expense.

The Director's House

[...] It is necessary to accommodáte the situation, and obtain from it the character appropriate for the subject, to the position. All those shapes that may be described with a single line drawn by a pair of compasses are allowed by good taste. The circle, the square, these are the letters of the alphabet that creators employ for the fabric of the best constructions. Epic poems, elegies are written with them; the gods are praised in song, the shepherds are celebrated; temples are erected to Value, to Strength, to Voluptuous Desire; houses are built, and those edifices that are furthest removed from the social order. In a factory, round or square pillars, columns placed on bases of mixed style, seem more fitting than any known order. Projecting portions of the structure cast curious shadows; this is a way of creating strength to stand in place of the weakness produced by distance.

Claude-Nicolas
Ledoux
1736–1806

I add this: prideful architecture would have disdained this place; elegant architecture would have been even less fitting. Such is the power of shapes that may hold sway over distance. If practical concepts cannot guarantee it against the abstractions that lead it into error, imagination surrounds itself with powers that sustain it. I hear the teacher, hemmed in by his five orders, cry that here lies abuse: he opens his manual, perplexed, leafs through it end to end, sees nothing there to justify this deviation. The rules of grammar are violated, all is lost – angular columns! Has anything so ridiculous ever been seen? Immediately the point of doctrine is attacked, the battlements are defended: in vain does he brandish his trivial manifests; he thunders throughout the place; his claps of thunder strike the insubordinate walls of the Gymnasium, and fall to the ground, leaving them intact.

The spell disappears at a stroke of the purist Architect's compasses. It reappears resplendent under the sway of ephemeral reputations. Such degenerate designs returned to favour on the plains of Palmyra: by excavating the ruins that had hidden them from view for so long, aesthetic taste was corrupted. Thus the awful winds of the north and the east rise from the summits of mountains, the trees of the forests tremble, their branches bend, break, their trunks topple, their roots wrenched from the earth. *In fine*, art, always contemporary with the world, requires a new brilliance.

[...]

The ambitious man pursues honours. The miser amasses gold, and his knowledge fails to rise above the silvery clink of the metal that pours into his maw. The lover pursues the favours of his ideal, which vanish abruptly when they are obtained. Everywhere man abases himself; in vain the Architect seeks to bind him to the laws that sustain the primordial truths; in vain, he insists upon defending the heritage of genius which, from the very beginning of the march of time, leaves to the gods of the earth and the gods of the sea the protective strength of the square to limit the possessions of empire; principle is wrapped around with the distorted designs of the sterile imitator, who disfigures it. [...]

A Collective

Sixteen families were living together in the tranquillity of the woods. Each had an entire lodging to itself. All the requirements for life in solitude – kitchen, gardens, gardens for the customary and medicinal plants, orchards, meadows, ploughed fields, other fields reserved for pasturage, vines, presses, service quarters, an assembly room, a dining room – all those accessories that ensure comfort and convenience – were united there. The heads of the families governed by trust and confidence; a deeply-felt piety and the setting of a good example, rather than schools of ethical thought, were the sources of wisdom. Religion led them to attach importance to the laws of the country; they found in consolatory religious observance a tranquil and sweet existence, hope for that which is right and fear of that which is wrong. Their worship was of the type that reason leaves to determine by our own intellect; they expressed their thanks to the Creator and lived by the accomplishment of the duties laid down by the Divine principle: surrounded as they were by all possible virtues, they had no conception of evil.

A modern philosopher, an economist appears on the scene: happiness flees, disquiet begins, all become agitated. Study of a new social system occupies their minds, ideas are exchanged, multiply with different conceptions, and like all men not yet afflicted by corruption, they are easily led into error when that which is good is presented to them under specious aspects, and they begin to reason for the sake of reasoning alone . . .

It is natural for man to wish to be happy; he finds the good he seeks only with difficulty; he is worried at what he does not have and rarely satisfied with that which he possesses: the solitary man regrets the fact that he does not have a busy life, the courtier yearns for rest, the man who has in town the modest house handed down by his ancestors destroys it to build an ostentatious palace, from which his creditors drive him before the roof can be finished.

It is well known that the disposition of the parts of a building situated in the middle of a forest must be simple and free of all those accessories that will reduce its surface areas: it is the projection of its masses, its component parts that give it its determinate character. The pyramidal form which crowns the edifice is all the more necessary for being supported by structures associated with it. It overlooks the trees and the rocks approach to complete the aesthetic design. [. . .]

It may be judged by the shadows cast upon the plain flat areas of the walls what the interplay of structural masses may achieve; it is the only effect that may be obtained from a design whose basis is the strict economy of means.

rhetoric • signification • narrative • social reform • democratisation

Claude-Nicolas
Ledoux
1736–1806

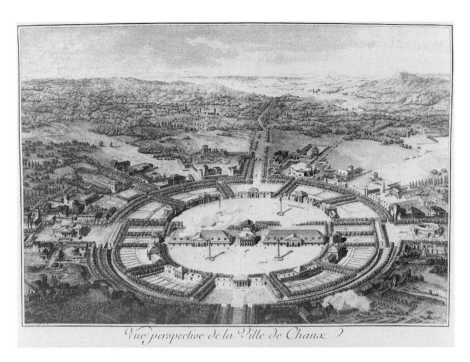

134. Claude-Nicolas Ledoux. *Architecture Considerée sous le rapport de l'art, des moeurs et de la législation.* 1804. Air view of the Royal Salt-works at Arc-et-Senans near Besançon.

135. Claude-Nicolas Ledoux. *Architecture Considerée sous le rapport de l'art, des moeurs et de la législation.* 1804.

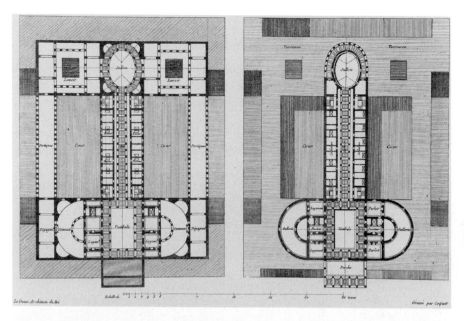

136. Claude-Nicolas Ledoux. *Architecture Considerée sous le rapport de l'art, des moeurs et de la législation.* 1804. Plans of ground and first floor of the 'Oïkima', the house of sexual instruction. The explicit phallic reference demonstrates the application of the idea of *architecture parlante*, narrative architecture even in the configuration of the plan of a building.

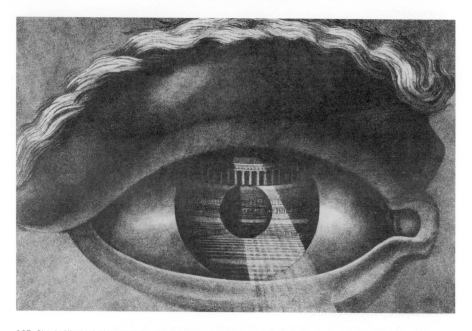

137. Claude-Nicolas Ledoux. *Architecture Considerée sous le rapport de l'art, des moeurs et de la législation.* 1804. Emblematic eye reflecting the interior of the theatre of Besançon.

Charles-François Viel (1745–1819)

On the Impotence of Mathematics to Insure the Solidity of Buildings (1805)

Viel was an architect who specialised in hospital design. The opinions in his book are part of the backlash which followed the functionalist innovations of the preceding twenty-five years which he discredited for being scientific, mathematical and foreign to the true spirit of architecture. Particularly singled out for attack as 'impotent' was Soufflot's (1741) Pantheon, earlier called Eglise Sainte Genevieve. Viel calls for architects to start drawing, stop theorising and return to the timeless principle of 'ordonnance' or 'eurythmie' in the fashion of the ancients.

Further reading Hautecoeur, 1948–1963; Herrmann, 1962, 115; Pérouse de Montclos, 1966; Rosenau, 1970; Tzonis *et al.*, 1975; Wiebenson 1982, 1993.

Charles-François
Viel
1745–1819

[...] architecture is sufficient unto itself and includes, in its most highly prized works, all the principles that belong to the art of building. Architecture does not lay down rules, it creates them.

Pleasing monuments are the source for both precept and example for the disposition of the parts and construction of the diverse buildings our needs require, because all is connected in all the parts of the same art, a principle that I have published, and one that I restate on every occasion that there is cause to make mention of it in the various related domains. This proposition is the fundamental theorem from which flow the truths that form the science of building and of which the demonstration shall prove the following: in all types of building great examples create the rule, and the art is to imitate them.

[...]

Mathematicians deprived, as I have said, of the ordinary knowledge of architecture make the science of building dependent on the theories that are their own. In this spirit, on the basis of simple, poorly formed sketches, they perform calculations to determine the quantified volumes needed for balance. We shall see the results of this systematic approach.

Such and such an edifice, before leaving their hands, begins to sag in the course of the work and retains the defects that lead to its destruction, despite the major rectifications it undergoes.

Such and such another edifice, contradicting all that is appropriate locally, is a mere assemblage of shapes displeasing to the eye of even the least knowledgeable in architecture. [...]

[...] And since the prime object in a construction is the volume and nature of the cubic forms necessary to give it solidity, it is not by mathematical calculation that they may be determined, but by those calculations based on the proportions assigned to them by the genius of architecture, which are the source of the beauty and the strength of a building, these being calculations of certain nature, guaranteed by the interconnection of all the parts of the art.

Natural mechanics were at first an inspiration of genius, and then became a science of observation well rooted in the imitation of examples in this domain, the most perfect, those that the architects of antiquity raised to the highest point of perfection.

[...]

Therefore the errors committed by men possessing deep knowledge of mathematics when judging the condition of the pillars of the dome of the Pantheon, and this despite the physical presence of the objects which they were examining, those errors prove the impotence of algebraic computations when applied to the construction of buildings. *Therefore science has not subjected all things to fixed and certain computation, and has not at the present time brought about any improvement in building.*

On the contrary, the invasion of architecture by experts during the Enlightenment has brought about disorder in the ordonnance of buildings, as is proven by the edifices of all kinds throughout France that they have been bold enough to build. This further invasion has sowed the seeds of destruction in our buildings, as I have remarked during the present chapter. [. . .]

Francesco Milizia
1725–1798

Let us pay homage here to the Government that has so well judged the difference between mathematics and architecture that it has preserved the special school in Paris for the teaching of this latter art and has restored the residential college in Rome. The Government has refrained from merging the ancient schools of painting, sculpture and architecture with those institutions where all subjects are taught together: physics, astronomy, chemistry, botany, etc. Some guardian angel has preserved the powers that be from such a mistake.

However, an unlimited love of reform and improvement never ceases to be the mania of the day. The mania for innovation has spread even to building works. Today the plan, the disposition, the nature and the type of construction, the manner of execution, all those matters that properly belong to the science of this art are ignored in far too many public edifices. [. . .]

The abandonment of those principles, caused twenty-five years ago by false economy in public building, has made them vulnerable to rapid degradation, and after having destroyed their foundations, it has been necessary to demolish them.

The fashion for reducing the prices of contracts awarded that was adopted at that time and which is returning to the fore today in building works commissioned by the State, quite apart from all the disadvantages that it brings in its wake, is a source of fatal harm to industry. [. . .]

Architecture suffices unto itself. It creates the principles that constitute it. But through a remarkable inevitability, the stagnation in which work on civil buildings now finds itself has left architects open to a febrile desire to write for publication, and we are inundated with volumes filled with the most unlikely assertions, and the most ill-conceived opinions. As a consequence of this, ideas on the essence of architecture are increasingly blurred and confused. The basic principles are poorly understood, and the ordonnance and construction of buildings is steadily degenerating. [. . .]

aesthetisation of architecture • scientification • professional practice • education

Francesco Milizia (1725–1798)

The Art of Seeing in the Fine Arts (c.1810)

(See Milizia, 1781)

p.236 We have said too often that the Greeks were a people favoured by particular circumstances. We have overestimated its climate and the beauty of its individuals. We have said too often that it was by having been exposed to so many nudes that their artists became expert at recalling and recreating beautiful forms. The truth is far from these exaggerated opinions. The maidens of Lacedemonia danced, it is true, in the public squares. But were these ever a meeting place for Greek artists? And are the Spartans, that nation of soldiers labouring under the thumb of an austere and almost monastic regime, the one that produced the great Greek artists? No. It would not be right to see in the mere exposure to the nudity of the maidens of Lacedemonia enough reason for the miracles produced by their chisels – miracles that are not necessarily properly conveyed by the enthusiastic effusions by writers like Winckelman and Mengs. . . .

The habits of the Greeks were not, from many points of view, very different from those that they are still subject to today and the Venus de Milo cannot have been modelled on their wives because their women lived in retreat-like conditions. Only their closest relatives were permitted to enter the gynaecium that they inhabited which was hardly less inaccessible than a Turkish harem . . .

Francesco Milizia
1725–1798

What accounts for the unsurpassable and supreme merit of Greek works is the ideal beauty which they bear the stamp of. This ideal beauty is no more to be found in the islands of the Archipelago than in the French regional departments. And if Greek artists found it in their imagination, their observations and their excellent taste, one should expect that modern artists could also, with taste, observations and imagination, rediscover or create it. But instead all they do is imitate Greek statues. What would happen to the fine arts if the small number of masterpieces that have been by chance saved from the sickle of time came to perish! We could no longer hope to equal Greek sculpture! This consequence is far from consoling, and appears to be so unfounded that we are tempted to suspect the existence of some great mistakes in the very subtle reasoning that has taken place up until now on the subject of ideal beauty, on the incomparable talent of the Greeks, on the impossibility of surpassing or even equalling them. And, at last, on the necessity to see in them only the one true model. Could we not tell our artists not to look at any of this, to search instead for true beauty, which is in nature; the Greeks found it without the help of any pre-existing model; do as they did; perhaps your new masterpieces will surpass those of the ancients; perhaps, better than the Greeks, you will show us that they failed to attain the sublime or the perfect in art; perhaps you will provide ideal beauty with such a character, such a consistency, that it will bring it before our eyes so that we will no longer be reduced to searching for it in a difficult theory? [. . .]

Keep us from a too superstitious cult that always smothers genius and forces us to drag ourselves along the same path as our predecessors. But let us be more moderate and more just, and tell them: study, observe nature without which we can do anything that is true, great, alive and beautiful. Study, observe the antique in order that you might be able to do justice to everything the ancient masters left us that is admirable in their masterpieces, precious results of their taste, their science, their long hours of study of nature, that will help you and will cut short the time that you would have had to spend on it. But should you not succeed as well as they, at least do your own thing; do not be a servile plagiarist. Nothing is more fatal to genius than the slavery of imitation.

p.245 Why was vandalism so harmful to the arts in France, in that glorious period when she was going through a rebirth? It is because her best artists, convinced that the existence of bad works harms the birth or regeneration of taste, said too often that it was better not to have any monuments rather than to have ones that would be misleading. That France possessed in architecture, in painting, in sculpture almost nothing that was worthy of serving as a model, that it was expedient to dismiss them all, and to destroy in order to remake everything in a new style. It is that intolerance in their critique, the enthusiasm of their declarations that any sane logic would have condemned, having got entangled with the revolutionary movement and opinions that proscribed all the monuments erected to kings or to a religious cult as capable by their mere public existence to feed and perpetuate the two superstitions, royal and Catholic, that caused them to wish to eliminate. It thus became possible for France, in the space of a very few days, to lose the work of several centuries. Of course it never occurred to these great artists that, in order to assure the triumph of taste, it was sufficient to do better than their predecessors. The comparison with them would have taught the public to see and distinguish true beauty and to put back, without destroying them, the very monuments that they thought unworthy of their esteem.

A great part of the nation had neither the taste nor the sentiment of beauty. The arts had been but the prerogative of the powerful and rich. They had been too concentrated in the capital. Where are the great artists that have lived in the provinces? The few monuments that donned them were sent there from Paris. Is it not indeed possible to cross France of immense regions, populated with several million inhabitants, without being able to find neither in the public buildings, nor in private houses, a single statue, a single painting with any value, while there exists almost no small town beyond the Alps that does not have a monument it can be proud of? It is true that one finds too often in Italy that the arts have been all too often the instruments of superstition. [...]

The arts must preach morality in their works, take up and elevate the public spirit, provide pleasure as well as usefulness. If they wander from this target, they will never reach it and they would cease to be worthy of the favour of the public. [...] The revolution has opened up to genius a new quarry, far preferable to those that mythology or the Bible offered. Let us hope our artists will have the spirit to see it, the will to enter it, the courage to follow it and that, by deviating from the path of triviality, tread by so many of their predecessors that they would have trouble getting ahead of them if they stayed on that path, they will apply themselves to making the fine arts French, national and political. And this, in spite of our customs which, although they seem ungrateful do not really present an obstacle to creativity which although it might seem unsurmountable does not really excuse them from trying to overcome it. This is how they will become the worthy followers of the new political dogmas that France has promulgated. They would not have to defend them in an army if they associated themselves with the double victories of soldiers and legislators and thus also became the benefactors of the nations. This is the new glory, more lasting that what preceded it, that awaits them. But in order to deserve these crowns, they must not, like so many young artists, dream only of Italy, so have eyes only for her. If their great achievement is to be the perfect imitation of nature, they must find her everywhere, and without doubt she is in France, as she is in their all too dear Italy. But they will object that beautiful nature is to be found here and will claim that she is only to be found there and especially in the antiquities she possesses. Well, let them go and see them, and study them. But let them look upon them with a talent that France will have given them in order to be able to acquire or perfect them. Indeed, France more than deserves their

Francesco Milizia
1725–1798

gratitude. But let them not pass over the Alps without having seen what their own country offers them in terms of excellence in the arts, without having visited the beautiful landscapes on the banks of the Seine, the Loire, the Saone, the Garonne, the picturesque sites of the Puy-du-Dome, the Pyrenees, the Alps, the Jura and Mont Blanc. They will find nothing comparable in sublimity and romanticism in the far inferior mountains of Italy. For, whatever those who have seen Italy, and refused to see France, say, they will find no equally majestuous rivers, limpid brooks, fresh fields, dark and venerable forests, rich and pleasant hillocks, prodigious summits in Italy as in France. [...]

Let the French Republic search above all to elevate to its height the genius of its artists in granting some distinction to those who will follow paths that are suitable to its institutions. Let her put much care into freeing the arts from the servility and spirit of adulation or vile interest that have always been detrimental to her. [...]

Francesco Milizia
1725–1798

It will always be difficult to comprehend why, in the formation of the national institute, they have forgotten the associate engraving to painting, which is its mother or sister. Engraving has only benefited from the art of printing. It is one of the best ways to spread good taste, by multiplying a kind of translation of good paintings that are not available to everyone. It can, when treating patriotic or moral subjects, influence opinion and public instruction almost as much as books. It can teach citizens who are less well off or more busy what it would cost them too much time to look up in books. It deserves, from this point of view, the greatest encouragement and most serious attention on the part of the legislators. The English have already managed to apply it to their history, and increase and transmit their reputation abroad. [...]

regionalism • nationalism • rigorism • essentialism • social reform • democratisation • professional practice • education

Gaspar Monge

Géometrie descriptive, 1811

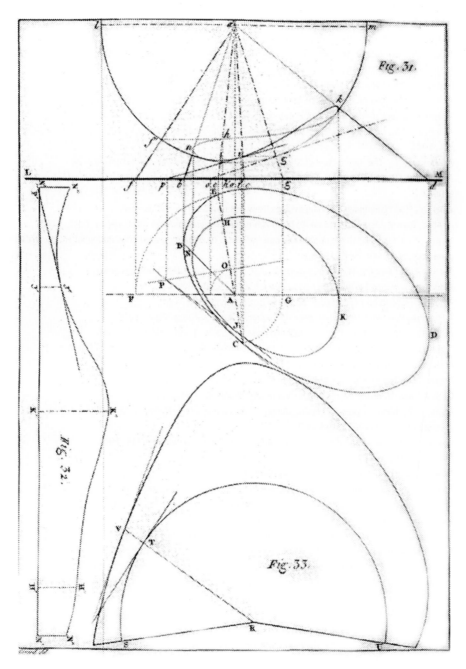

138. Gaspar Monge. *Géometrie descriptive*. 1811 (first published 1795). Intersection of sphere with cone. Monge introduced a new method for representing objects in space that led to the modern development of Computer Aided Design. He considered the problem of representation of space as critical for creative design and succeeded in making it a basic component of the revolutionary programme of the Ecole Polytechnique in Paris.

Bibliography and references

Ackerman, G.M., *The Structure of Lomazzo's Treatise on Painting*. Michigan, 1964.

Ackerman, G.M., 'Lomazzo's Treatise on Painting.' *Art Bulletin*, 69 (1967): 317ff.

Ackerman, J.S., '*Ars Sine Scientia Nihil est*. Gothic Theory of Architecture at the Cathedral of Milan.' *Art Bulletin New York*, 31 (1949): 84–116.

Ackerman, J.S., 'Architectural Practice in the Italian Renaissance.' *Journal of the Society of Architectural Historians*, 13, 3 (1954).

Ackerman, J.S., *Palladio's Villas*. Locust Valley, NY, 1967.

Ackerman, J.S., *The Architecture of Michelangelo*. New York, 1970.

Ackerman, J.S., *Palladio*. Baltimore/Harmondsworth, 1972.

Ackerman, J.S., *Distance Points: Essays in Theory and Renaissance Art and Architecture*. Cambridge, MA, 1991.

Ackerman, J.S., 'The Architecture of Rhetoric.' *Design Book Review*, 34, Fall (1994): 27–28.

Adhémar, J., 'Aretino, Artistic Advisor to Francis I.' *Journal of the Warburg and Courtault Institutes*, XVII (1954).

Adler, A., 'The "Pélerinage de Charlemagne". New Light on Saint-Denis.' *Speculum*, XXII (1947).

Al-Abed, Badi Y., *Aspecten van de Arabisch-Islamitisch architectonische verhandeling*. Delft, 1992.

Alengry, F., *Condorcet: Guide de la révolution française, théoricien du droit constitutionnel et précurseur de la science sociale*. Paris, 1904.

Annas, G. and Binding, G., 'Arcus superiores, Abt Suger von Saint-Denis und das gotische Kreuzrippengewolbe.' *Wallraf Richartz Jahrbuch*, 50 (1989): 7–24.

Antal, F., *Hogarth and his Place in European Art*. London, 1962.

Archambault de Monfort, H., *Les Idées de Condorcet sur le suffrage*. Paris, 1915.

Argan, G.C., 'Andrea Palladio e la critica neo-classica.' *L'arte*, 1, 33 (1930): 327–346.

Argan, G.C., 'Sebastiano Serlio.' *L'Arte*, 35 (1932): 183–199.

Argan, G.C., *Francesco Colonna e la critica d'arte Veneta nel quattrocento*. Turin, 1934.

Argan, G.C., 'The Architecture of Brunelleschi and the Origins of Perspective Theory in the Fifteenth Century.' *Journal of the Warburg and Courtault Institutes*, 9 (1946): 96–121.

Argan, G.C., 'Michelangiolo Architetto.' *Bollettino del Centro Internazionale di Studi d'Architettura Andrea Palladio*, 9 (1967): 198–203.

Arts, F.B., *The Development of Technical Education In France*. Cambridge, MA, 1966.

Atkinson, C.M., *Jeremy Bentham: His Life and Work*. London, 1905.

Atkinson, G., *Les nouveaux horizons de la renaissance*. Paris, 1935.

Atkinson, G., *Le sentiment de la nature et le retour à la vie simple*. Geneva, 1960.

Audiat, L., *Bernard Palissy: étude sur sa vie et ses travaux*. VII vols. Geneva, 1970.

Aurenhammer, H., *J.B. Fischer von Erlach*. London, 1973.

Babinger, F. and Heydenreich, L.H., 'Vier Bauvorschläge Leonardo da Vinci's an Sultan Bajezid II.' *Nachrichten von der Akademie der Wissenschaften in Göttingen*, 1–20, 1952.

Badinter, E. and Badinter, R., *Condorcet, 1743–1794: un intellectuel en politique*. Paris, 1988.

Bahmueller, C.F., *The National Charity Company: Jeremy Bentham's Silent Revolution*. Berkeley, 1981.

Baker, K.M., *Condorcet, From Natural Philosophy to Social Mathematics*. Chicago, 1975.

Bahktin, M., *Rabelais and his World*, trans. H. Iswolsky. Cambridge, MA, 1968.

Ballon, H., 'Constructions of the Bourbon State: Classical Architecture in Seventeenth-Century France.' *Studies in the History of Art*, 27 (1989): 136–148.

Balmas, E.H., *Un poeta del Rinascimento francese: Etienne Jodelle*. Florence, 1962.

Balmori, D., 'Architecture, Landscape and the Intermediate Structure: Eighteenth-Century Experiments in Mediation.' *Journal of the Society of Architectural Historians*, 50 (1991): 38–56.

Barbieri, F., *Vincenzo Scamozzi*. Venice, 1952.

Barbieri, F., 'Palladio e il manierismo.' *Bollettino del Centro Internazionale di Studi d'Architettura Andrea Palladio*, VI (1964): 49–63.

Barbieri, F. and Puppi, L., *L'Architettura di Michelangelo*. Milan, 1964.

Baron., H., *The Crisis of the Early Italian Renaissance*. Princeton, 1966.

Barocchi, P. (ed.), *Trattati d'arte del cinquecento, fra manierismo e controriforma*. 3 vols. Bari, 1960–1962.

Barocchi, P. (ed.), *Scritti d'arte del cinquecento*. 3 vols. Milan/Naples, 1971–1976.

Barolini, H., *Aldus and his Dream Book: An Illustrated Essay*. XXII vols. New York, 1992.

Baron, H., *The Crisis of the Early Italian Renaissance*. Princeton, 1966.

Baroni, C., 'Osservazioni su Cesare Cesariano.' *Maso Finiguerra* (1940): 83–94.

Bartlett, R., *The Making of Europe. Conquest, Colonialization and Cultural Change. 950–1350*. Harmondswoth, 1993.

Batey, M., *Alexander Pope: The Poet and the Landscape*. London, 1999.

Battisti, E., 'Riforma.' *Enciclopedia Universale dell'Arte*, 1958–1967.

Battisti, E., 'Osservazioni su due manuscritti intorno all'architettura.' *Bollettino del Centro di Studi per la Storia dell'Architettura*, 4 (1959): 28–52.

Battisti, E., *Rinascimento e Barocco*. Turin, 1960.

Battisti, E., *L'Antirinascimento*. Milan, 1962.

Battisti, E., 'Avanguardia e conservatismo nella storia del duomo di Milano.' *Il Duomo di Milano. Atti del Congresso Internazionale, Septembre 1969*, M.L. Gatti Perer (ed.), 2 vols. Milan, 1969: 43–52.

Battisti, E., 'Natura Artificiosa to Natura Artificialis.' *The Italian Garden*, D. Coffin (ed.). Dumbarton Oaks, Washington, DC, 1972.

Battisti, E., 'Il Bellori come critico.' in: G.P. Bellori, *Le vite de pittori, scultori e architetti moderni*, E. Borea (ed.). Turin, 1976.

Bauberot, J. and Lenoir, C.J., *La Tolérance ou la liberté?: Les lecons de Voltaire et de Condorcet*. Brussels, 1997.

Baudrillart, H. *Histoire du Luxe*. Paris, 1880.

Baxandall, M., *Painting and Experience in Fifteenth-Century Italy*. Oxford, 1972.

Baxandall, M., 'On Michelangelo's Mind, Review of D. Summers.' *New York Review of Books*, 8 October (1981): 42–44.

Baxmann, D., *Wissen, Kunst und Gesellschaft in der Theorie Concordets*. Stuttgart, 1999.

Becerer, R., 'The Revolutionary Look of Louis Sebastien Mercier's Tableau de Paris.' *Journal of Architectural Education*, 42 (1989): 3–14.

Bechmann, R., *Villard de Honnecourt*. Picard, 1991.

Becker, D.P., 'Piranesi: Early Architectural Fantasies, a Catalogue Raisonné of the Etchings.' *The Print Collector's Newsletter*, 18 (1987): 71–72.

Bédier, J., *Les légendes épiques. Recherches sur la formation des chansons de geste*. Paris, 1913.

Beech, G.T., 'The Eleanor of Aquitaine Vase, William IX of Aquitaine, and Muslim Spain.' *Gesta*, 32 (1993): 3–10.

Beltrami, L., 'Il Tiburio. Nuove indagini e nuovi documenti.' *La perseveranza* (15 November, 16 and 25 December 1902).

Beltrami, L., *Leonardo negli studi per il tiburio di Milano*. Milan, 1903.

Beltrami, L., *Documenti e memorie riguardanti la vita e le opere di Leonardo da Vinci*. Milan, 1919.

Beltrami, L., *Saggio di storia dell'agricoltura nella repubblica di Venezia durante l'età moderna*. Venice/Rome, 1955.

Benardi Ferrero, D. de, 'Il Conte Ivan Caramuel de Lobkowitz, . . .' *Palladio*, XV (1965): 91–110.

Benesch, O., 'A New Contribution to the Problem of Fra Luca Pacioli.' *Gazette des beaux arts* Série VI, vol. XLIV (XCVI) (1954): 203–206.

Benevolo, L., 'Considerazioni sull'architettura neoclassica.' *Saggi di storia dell'architettura in onore di V. Fasolo*. Rome, 1961: 293–298.

Benevolo, L., *Storia dell'architettura del rinascimento*. Bari, 1968.

Benhamou, R., 'Parallel Walls, Parallel Worlds: the Places of Masters and Servants in the Maisons de Plaisance of Jacques-Francois Blondel.' *Journal of Design History*, 7 (1994): 1–11.

Bennet, J.A., 'Christopher Wren: the Natural Causes of Beauty.' *Architectural History*, 15 (1972): 5–22.

Bentmann, R. and Müller, M., *Die Villa als Herrschaftsarchitektur*. Frankfurt a.M., 1970.

Berman, E.D., *Thomas Jefferson Among the Arts. An Essay in Early American Esthetics*. New York, 1947.

Bernheimer, R., *Theatrum Mundi, Art Bulletin New York*, XXXVIII (1956): 225ff.

Bettag, A., *Die Kunstpolitik Jean Baptiste Colberts: unter Berücksichtigung der Académie royale de peinture et de sculpture*. Weimar, 1998.

Betts, R.J., *The Architectural Theories of Francesco di Giorgio*. Princeton University Microfilms, 1971.

Betts, R.J., 'On the Chronology of Francesco di Giorgios Treatises.' *Journal of the Society of Architectural Historians*, XXXI (1972).

Beuchot, B., 'Avertissement.' *Voltaire, Oeuvres Complètes*. Paris, 1877.

Billanovich, M. and Menegazzo, E. 'Francesco Colonna tra Padova e Venezia.' *Italia Medievale e Umanistica*, IX (1966): 441–459.

Bilodeau, D., *Precedents and Design Thinking in an Age of Relativization. The Transformation of the Normative Discourse on the Orders between 1650 and 1793*. Delft, 1997.

Bloch, M., *The Historian's Craft*. New York, 1953.

Blomfield, R.T., *A History of French Architecture*. 2 vols. New York, 1973.

Blunt, A., 'The Hypnerotomachia Poliphili in Seventeenth-Century France.' *Journal of the Warburg Institute*, I (1937): 117–137.

Blunt, A., *Artistic Theory in Italy 1480–1600*. Oxford, 1940.

Blunt, A., *Philibert de l'Orme*. London, 1958a.

Blunt, A., 'The Palazzo Barberini: the Contributions of Maderno, Bernini and Piero da Cortona.' *Journal of the Warburg and Courtault Institutes*, XXI (1958b): 256–287.

Blunt, A., 'Struttura e forma nel trattato architettonico del Guarini.' *Guarino Guarini e l'Internazionalità del Barocco*, Atti de Convegno Internazionale promesso dall'Academia delle Scienze di Torino I, 2 vols. Turin, 1970: 451–496.

Blunt, A., 'Introduction.' *Manière de bâtir pour toutes sortes de personnes*. Richmond, 1972.

Blunt, A., *Art and Architecture in France, 1500 to 1700*. Somerset, 1973.

Blunt, A., *Borromini*. Cambridge, MA, 1979.

Blunt, A., 'Review of Serlio.' *Journal of the Society of Architectural Historians*, XXXIX (1980).

Boase, T.S.R., *Giorgio Vasari: The Man and the Book* (the A.W. Mellon Lectures in the Fine Arts, 1971, Bollingen Series, xxxv), Princeton, 1979.

Bolgar, R.R., *Classical Influences in Western Culture, AD 500–1500*. Cambridge, 1971.

Bonelli, R., ' "Nota introduttiva" in Raffaello Sanzio, "Lettera a Leone X".' *Scritti Rinascimentale d'Architettura*. Milan, 1978: 463–467.

Bonet-Correa, A.e.a., *Bibliographia de arquitectura, ingenieria y urbanismo en España (1498–1880)*. Madrid/Vaduz, 1980.

Bonet-Correa, A., *Juan Caramuel: Arquitectura Civil Recta Y Oblicua. Estudio Preliminar*. Madrid, 1984.

Borsi, F., *Per una theoria delle proporzioni*. Florence, 1967.

Borsi, F., *Leon Battista Alberti*. Milan, 1975.

Borsi, S., 'Polifilo leonardesco.' *Storia dell'Arte*, 93 (1998): 207–216.

Bottero, M., 'Panopticon.' *Abitare*, 259 Nov. (1987): 237–240.

Boudon, F., Blecon, J. and Saulnier-Pernuit, L., *Philibert de l'Orme et le château royal de Saint Léger en Yvelines*. Paris, 1985.

Boudon, F., 'Les livres d'architecture de Jacques Androuet Du Cerceau.' J. Guillaume (ed.), *Les Traités d'architecture de la renaissance*. Paris, 1988.

Bouissounouse, J., *Condorcet, le philosophe dans la Révolution*. Paris, 1962.

Braham, A., *The Architecture of the French Enlightenment*. Berkeley, 1980.

Braudel, F., *The Mediterranean and the Mediterranean World in the Age of Philip II*, trans. S. Reynolds. New York, 1972.

Briggs, M.S., *The Architect in History*. Oxford, 1927.

Brion, M., 'Un précurseur de l'architecture moderne, Claude-Nicolas Ledoux.' *Beaux-arts* (22 January 1937).

Brion-Guerry, L., *Philibert de l'Orme*. Milan, 1955.

Brion-Guerry, L., *Philibert de L'Orme*. Paris, 1955.

Brisac, C., Faucherre, N. and Coutura, J., *Vauban, réformateur: actes du colloque, Paris, Musée Guimet, 15–16–17 decembre 1983*. Paris, 1985.

Brizio, A.M., 'Il Rilievo dei monumenti antichi. Raffaello e il nascere dell'Archeologia.' *L'Arte* (June–September 1966): 20–30.

Brönner, W.D., *Blondel-Perrault: Zur Architekturtheorie des 17. Jahrhunderts in Frankreich*. Bonn, 1972.

Bruand, Y., 'Les traités d'architecture militaire francais à la fin du XVIe et au début du XVIIe siècles.' J. Guillaume (ed.), *Les Traités d'architecture de la renaissance*. Paris, 1988.

Brucker, G.A., *Florentine Politics and Society 1348–1378*. Princeton, 1962.

Brucker, G.A., *The Civil World of Early Renaissance Florence*. Princeton, 1977.

Bruschi, A., *Bramante*. Rome/Bari, 1973; London, 1977.

Bruschi, A., 'Nota introduttiva.' *Scritti Rinascimentale d'Architettura*, F. Colonna. 1978a: 145–180.

Bruschi, A., 'Nota introduttiva.' *Scritti Rinascimentale d'Architettura*, Leonardo da Vinci. 1978b: 335–347.

Bruschi, A., 'Nota introduttiva.' *Scritti Rinascimentale d'Architettura*, L. Pacioli. 1978c: 23–49.

Bruyne, E.D., *Etudes d'esthétique médiévale*. 3 vols. Brugge, 1946.

Buck, A., *Die Villa als Lebensform der italienischen Renaissance*. Stuttgart, 1992.

Buddensieg, T., 'Criticism and Praise of the Pantheon in the Middle Ages.' *Classical Influences on European Culture AD 500–1500*, R.R. Bolgar (ed.). Cambridge, 1971.

Burke, J., *Hogarth and Reynolds: A Contrast in English Art Theory*. London, 1943.

Burn, G., 'Manners and Morals: Hogarth and British Painting, 1700–1760.' *Arts Review*, 39 (1987): 708.

Burns, H., Fairbairn, L. and Boucher, B., *Andrea Palladio 1508–1580*. Exhibition catalogue, London, 1975.

Burroughs, C., 'Palladio and Fortune: Notes on the Sources and Meaning of the Villa Rotonda.' *Architectura*, 18 (1988): 59–91.

Burroughs, C., 'Grammar and Expression in Early Renaissance Architecture: Brunelleschi and Alberti.' *Res* (1998): 39–63.

Burton, N., 'Sir William Chambers.' *The Architectural Review*, 201 (1997): 97.

Butler, C., *Number Symbolism*. London, 1970.

Butler, E.M., *The Tyranny of Greece over Germany*. Boston, 1958.

Cahen, L., *Condorcet et la révolution francaise*. Paris, 1904.

Calvesi, M., *Il sogno di Polifilo prenestino*. Rome, 1980.

Calvi, I., *L'architettura militare di Leonardo da Vinci*. Milan, 1943.

Cannata, P., 'Le Placchette del Filarete.' *Studies in the History of Art*, 22 (1989): 35–53.

Caplin, E., 'Palestrina: the Temple of Fortune.' *RIBA Journal*, 96 (1989): 52–56.

Carli, E., *Pienza, la città di Pio II*. Rome, 1967.

Carpo, M., Architecture in the Age of Printing. Cambridge, MA, 2001.

Carter, B.A.R., 'Perspective.' *Oxford Companion to Art* (1975): 840–861.

Casella, M.T. and Pozzi, G., *Francesco Colonna, biografia e opere*. Padua, 1959.

Cassirer, K., *Die aesthetischen Hauptbegriffe der Französischen Architekturtheoretiker*. Dissertation, Berlin, 1909.

Castagnoli, F., 'Raffaello e le antichità di Roma.' *Raffaello, l'opere, le fonti, la fortuna*. Novara, 1968.

Cavallari-Murat, A., 'Discorso sui rapporti tra rationalità, funzionalità e composizione nelle ville dell'epoca palladiana.' *Bollettino del Centro Internazionale di Studi d'Architettura Andrea Palladio*, XI (1969).

Céard, J., 'Relire Bernard Palissy.' *Revue de l'Art*, 78 (1987): 77–83.

Cessi, R., 'Alvise Cornaro e la bonifica veneziana del secolo XVI.' *Atti dell'Academia dei Lincei, cl. sceinze morali* . . . , ser. 6, XIII (1936): 301–323.

Chanfón Olmoz, C., 'El Tratado del romano.' *Prólogo a la edición fascimilar y transcripción paleografica*. Mexico, 1977.

Chanfón Olmos, C. and Bonet-Correa, A., *Simon Garcia, Compendio de Arquitectura y Simetria de los Templos* (1681–1683), Madrid, 1979.

Chantelou, P. Fréart de, 'Bernini's journey to France.' *Fmr*, 15 (1995): 92–106.

Charageat, M., *L'Art des jardins*. Paris, 1962.

Chaslin, F., 'Les plus excellents bastiments de France par J. Androuet du Cerceau.' *L'Architecture d'Aujourd'hui*, 265 Oct. (1989): 106.

Chastel, A., *Marsile Ficin et l'art*. Geneva, 1954.

Chastel, A., *Art et humanisme à Florence au temps de Laurent le Magnifique*. Paris, 1959.

Chen, S.Y., 'The Chinese Garden in 18th Century England.' *Tien Hasia Monthly*, II, 4 (1936).

Chi, L.H., 'The Artifice of Speaking Architecture: Modernity and its Limits in Quatremere de Quincy.' *Design Book Review*, 34, Fall (1994): 64–66.

Choay, F., *La règle et le modèle*. Paris, 1981.

Christ, Y., *Projets et divagations de Claude-Nicolas Ledoux, architecte du roi: étude*. Paris, 1961a.

Christ, Y., *Projets et divagations de Claude-Nicolas Ledoux*. Paris, 1961a.

Christ, Y., *L'Oeuvre et les rêves de Claude-Nicolas Ledoux*. Paris, 1961b.

Ciapponi, L.A., 'Il "De architettura" di Vitruvio nel primo umanesimo.' *Italia Medievale e Umanistica*, III (1960): 59–99.

Ciapponi, L.A., 'Vitruvius.' *Catalogus Translationum et Commentariorum*, F.E. Cranz and P.O. Kristeller, III (eds). 3 vols. Washington, DC, 1976: 399–409.

Cicognara, L., *Catalogo ragionato dei libri d'arte e d'antichità*. Pisa, 1821.

Clark, H.F., 'Eighteenth Century Elysiums . . .' *Journal of the Warburg and Courtault Institutes*, VI (1943): 165–189.

Clark, K., 'Leonardo da Vinci. A Note on the Relation Between his Science and his Art.' *History Today*, II (1952).

Clements, R.J., *Michelangelo's Theory of Art*. London, 1963.

Clouzot, H., *Philibert de l'Orme*. Paris, 1910.

Coleman, F.X.J., *The Aesthetic Thought of the French Enlightenment*. Pittsburgh, 1971.

Collins, P., 'The Architectural Doctrine of J.F. Blondel (Silver Medal Essay).' *Journal of the Royal Institute of British Architects* (1954): 140–148.

Collins, P., *Changing Ideals in Modern Architecture*. London, 1965.

Colombier, P.D., 'Sebastiano Serlio en France.' *Etudes d'Art*, II (1946): 29–50.

Combes, F., *L'abbé Suger. Histoire de son ministère et de sa régence*. Paris, 1853.

Comito, T., 'Renaissance Gardens and the Discovery of Paradise.' *Journal of the History of Ideas*, XXXII, 4, Oct./Dec. (1971).

Comito, T., *The Idea of the Garden in the Renaissance*. New Brunswick, 1978.

Comolli, A., *Bibliografia storica-critica dell'architettura civile et arti subalterne*. Milan, 1964.

Conant, K.J., 'The Afterlife of Vitruvius in the Middle Ages.' *Journal of the Society of Architectural Historians*, XXVII (1968): 33ff.

Conner, T.P., 'The Making of Vitruvius Britannicus.' *Art History* (1977): 14–30.

Connors, J., 'Bernini's S. Andrea al Quirinale: Payments and Planning.' *Journal of the Society of Architectural Historians*, XLI, March (1982).

Connors, J., 'Francesco di Giorgio architetto.' *Journal of the Society of Architectural Historians*, 52 (1993): 487–490.

Cornford, F.M., *Plato's Cosmology*. London, 1948.

Cosenza, E., *Biographical and Bibliographical Dictionary of Italian Humanists I*. Boston, 1962: 802ff.

Costanzo, M., *Il 'gran theatro del mondo'*. Milan, 1964.

Coulton, G.G., *Life in the Middle Ages*. Cambridge, 1929.

Crepin-Leblond, T., 'Redécouvrir Bernard Palissy.' *Bulletin Monumental*, 148 (1990): 215–216.

Croce, B., *Storia dell'età barocca in Italia*. Bari, 1964.

Crosby, S., *The Royal Abbey of Saint-Denis in the Time of Abbot Suger (1122–1151)*. New York, 1981.

Curran, B.A., 'The Hypnerotomachia Poliphili and Renaissance Egyptology.' *Word and Image*, 14 (1998): 156–185.

Dagron, G., *Constantinople imaginaire*. Paris, 1984.

Dalton, G., *Economic Development and Social Change*. New York, 1971.

De Bernardi Ferrero, D., 'Il Conte I. Caramuel . . . architetto e teorico dell'architettura.' *Palladio*, XV (1965).

De Bruyne, E., *Etudes d'esthétique médiévale*. 3 vols. Ghent, 1946.

De la Croix, H., 'Military Architecture and the Radial City Plan.' *Art Bulletin New York*, XLII (1960): 263–300.

De la Croix, H., 'The Literature on Fortification in Renaissance Italy.' *Technology and Culture*, 4 (1963).

De la Croix, H., *Military Considerations in City Planning: Fortifications*. New York, 1972.

De Pagave, V., *Vita di Cesare Cesariano, architetto milanese*. Milan, 1878.

De Zurko, E.R., *Origins of Functionalist Theory*. New York, 1957.

Dechert, M.S.A., 'The Military Architecture of Francesco di Giorgio in Southern Italy.' *Journal of the Society of Architectural Historians*, 49 (1990): 161–180.

Dennett, D.C. Jr, 'Pirenne and Muhammad.' *Speculum*, XXIII (1948).

Dibner, B., *Leonardo da Vinci, Military Engineer*. New York, 1946.

Dijksterhuis, E.J., *The Mechanization of the World Picture*. Oxford, 1964.

Dinsmoor, W., 'The Literary Remains of Sebastiano Serlio.' *Art Bulletin New York*, XXIV (1942): 55–91, 115–154.

Dionisotti, C., *La letteratura Italiana nell'età del Concillo. Il concilio di Trento e la riforma tridentina*. Rome/Freiburg, 1965.

Dobai, J., 'William Hogarth and Antoine Parent.' *Journal of the Warburg and Courtault Institutes*, XXXI (1968).

Donahue, K., 'The Ingenious Bellori. A Biographical Study.' *Marsyas*, III (1946).

Donati, L., 'Polifilo a Roma. Il Mausoleo di Santa Costanza.' *La Bibliofilia*, LXX (1968): 1–38.

Donin, R.K., *Vincenzo Scamozzi*. Innsbruck, 1948.

Downes, K., 'The Publication of Shaftesbury's Letter Concerning Design.' *Architectural History*, 27 (1984): 519–523.

Duby, G., *Saint Bernard et l'art cistercien*. Paris, 1976.

Duby, G., *L'An Mile*. Paris, 1980.

Duhem, P.M.M., *Les origines de la statique*. Paris, 1905–1906.

Duhem, P.M.M., *Le Système Du Monde*. 2 vols. Paris, 1914.

Duhem, P.M.M., *To Save the Phenomena, an Essay on the Idea of Physical Theory from Plato to Galileo*. Chicago, 1969.

Dupuy, E., *Bernard Palissy, l'homme, l'artiste, le savant, l'écrivain*. Paris, 1902.

Dussinger, J.A., 'William Hogarth's translation of Watelet on Grace.' *The Burlington Magazine*, 126 (1984): 691–694.

Eck, C.V., 'The structure of *De re aedificatoria* reconsidered.' *Journal of the Society of Architectural Historians*, 57 (1998): 280–297.

Edgerton, S.Y. Jr, 'Florentine Interest in Ptolemaic Cartography as Background for Renaissance Painting, Architecture, and the Discovery of America.' *JSAH*, 33, 4, Dec. (1974).

Edgerton, S.Y., *The Renaissance Rediscovery of Linear Perspective*. New York, 1980.

Egbert, D.D., *From the Founding of the Académie Royale d'Architecture to the Revolution. The Beaux-Arts Tradition in French Architecture* . . . Princeton, 1980: 11–35.

Elam, C., ' "Lorenzo de" Medici and the Urban Development of Renaissance Florence.' *Art History*, I (1978): 43–66.

Elias, N., *Power and Civility. The Civilizing Process*. New York, 1982.

Emiliani, M.D. (ed.), *La prospettiva rinascimentale: codificazione de trasgressione*. Florence, 1980.

Eriksen, S., *Early Neo-Classicism in France*. London, 1974.

Esdaile, K.A., 'The Small House and its Amenities in the Architectural Handbooks: 1749–1847.' *Transactions of the Bibliographical Society*, XV (1917–1919): 115–132.

Evans, R., 'Bentham's Panopticon. An Incident in the Social History of Architecture.' *Architectural Association Quarterly*, III, 2, April/July (1972).

Faggin, G., 'Il mondo culturale veneto del cinquecento e Andrea Palladio.' *Bollettino del Centro Internazionale di Studi d'Architettura Andrea Palladio*, IX (1967).

Fagiolo, M., *Natura e Artificio*. Milan, 1979.

Feldhaus, F.M., 'Leonardo da Vinci als Städtebauer.' *Zentralblatt für Bauverwaltung*, XXXII (1912).

Fernie, E., 'The Royal Abbey of Saint-Denis in the Time of Abbot Suger (1122–1151).' *Art History*, 11 (1988): 289–293.

Ferrari, M.L., 'Zenale, Cesariano e Luini: un arco di classicismo lombardo.' *Paragone*, XVIII, 211 (1967): 18–38.

Fiocco, G., 'Alvise Cornaro e i suoi trattati dell'architettura.' *Atti dell'Academia Nazionale dei Lincei. Memorie*, XIII, 4 (1952).

Fiocco, G., 'La Casa di Alvise Cornaro.' *Miscellanea in onore di Roberto Cessi*. Rome, 1958.

Fiocco, G., 'La lezione di Alvise Cornaro.' *Bollettino del Centro Internazionale di Studi d'Architettura Andrea Palladio*, V (1963).

Fiore, F.P., 'La Città progressiva e il suo disegno.' *La Città come forma simbolica*, P. Marconi (ed.). Rome, 1973.

Fiore, F.P., 'Città e macchine del 400 nei disegni di Francesco di Giorgio Martini.' *Academia toscana di scienze e lettere, studi*, XLIX (1978).

Fiore, F.P., 'Funzioni e trattamenti dell'intonaco nella letteratura architettonica dal Cesariano al Valadier.' *Bollettino d'Arte*, 71 (1986): 37–46.

Fiore, F.P., 'Francesco di Giorgio Martini e l'assoluto imperfetto.' *Casabella*, 57 (1993): 30–41.

Fiore, F.P., 'Leon Battista Alberti.' *Journal of the Society of Architectural Historians*, 54 (1995): 228–232.

Firpo, L., 'La città ideale di Filarete.' *Scritti in memoria di G. Solari*. Turin, 1954: 11–59.

Firpo, L., *Leonardo, architetto e urbanista*. Turin, 1963.

Fitch, J.M., *American Building. The Historical Forces That Shaped It*. Boston, 1966.

Fleming, J., *Robert Adam and his Circle in Edinburgh and Rome*. London, 1962.

Focillon, H., *Giovanni-Battista Piranesi: essai de catalogue raisonné de son ouvre*. Paris, 1918.

Focillon, H., Calvesi, M. and Monferini, A., *Giovanni Battista Piranesi*. Bologna, 1967.

Focillon, H., *The Year 1000*. New York, 1969.

Fontaine, A., *Les doctrines d'art en France*. Paris, 1909.

Fontana, V. and Morachiello, P., *Vitruvio e Raffaello. Il 'De architectura' di Vitruvio nella traduzione inedita di Fabio Calvo Ravennate*. Rome, 1975.

Forssman, E., *Dorisch, Ionisch, Korintisch: Studien über den Gebrauch der Säulenordnung in der Architektur des 16–18. Jahrhunderts*. Stockholm, 1961.

Forssman, E., 'Palladio e Vitruvio.' *Bollettino del Centro Internazionale di Studi d'Architettura Andrea Palladio*, IV (1962): 32–42.

Forssman, E., *Palladios Lehrgebaüde*. Stockholm, 1965.

Forssman, E., 'Palladio e Daniele Barbaro.' *Bollettino del Centro Internazionale di Studi d'Architettura Andrea Palladio*, VIII (1966): 68–81.

Forssman, E., 'Goethe als Biograph und die Ursprunge der Kunstgeschichte.' *Konsthistorisk Tidskrift*, 68 (1999): 137–153.

Forster, K.W. and Locher, H., *Theorie der Praxis: Leon Battista Alberti als Humanist und Theoretiker der bildenden Kunste*. Berlin, 1999.

Förster, O.H., *Bramante*. Vienna, 1956.

Fortier, B. *et al.*, *La politique de l'espace parisien*. Paris, 1975.

Foster, P.E., *A Study of Lorenzo de Medici's Villa at Poggio a Caiano*. New York/London, 1978.

Foucault, M., *Surveiller et punir*. Paris, 1975.

Foucault, M. et al., *Les Machines à guérir. Aux origines de l'hôpital moderne*. Paris, 1976.

Fowler, L.H. and Baer, E., *The Fowler Architectural Collection of the Johns Hopkins University*. Baltimore, 1961.

Frankl, P., 'The Secret of the Medieval Masons.' *Art Bulletin New York*, XXVII (1945): 46–64.

Frankl, P., *The Gothic Literary Sources and Interpretations Through Eight Centuries*. Princeton, 1960.

Frantz, R.W., *The English Traveller and the Movement of Ideas*. Lincoln, 1934.

Fraser-Jenkins, A.D., 'Cosimo de Medici's Patronage of Architecture and the Theory of Magnificence.' *Journal of the Warburg and Courtault Institutes*, XXXIII (1970): 162–170.

Frazer, J.G., *Condorcet on the Progress of the Human Mind*. Oxford, 1933.

Frigerio, F., *Il Vitruvio del Cesariano del 1521*. Como, 1934.

Frommel, S., *Sebastiano Serlio, architetto*. Milan, 1998.

Frugoni, Ch., *Distant Cities: Images of Urban Experience in the Medieval World*, trans. W. McCuaig. Princeton, 1991.

Gadol, J., *Leon Battista Alberti, Universal Man of the Renaissance*. Chicago/London, 1969.

Gallet, M., *Claude-Nicolas Ledoux, 1736–1806*. Paris, 1980.

Gallet, M., 'Les inédits de Claude-Nicolas Ledoux: un versant ignore de son utopie.' *Gazette des Beaux Arts*, 6, 116 (1990): 9–28.

Galley, E., 'Heine und der Kolner Dom.' *Deutsche Vierfeljahrsschriftfur Literaturwissenschaft und Geistesgeschichte,* xxxv (1958): 99–110.

Gargano, M., 'Francesco di Giorgio Martini: una grande mostra.' *Domus*, 750, June (1993): 76–80.

Gargus, J., 'Guarino Guarini: Geometrical Transformations and the Invention of New Architectural Meanings.' *The Harvard Architecture Review*, 7 (1989): 116–131.

Garin, E., *La disputa delle arti nel quattrocento*. Florence, 1947.

Garin, E., 'Di G.C. Delminio.' *Giornale critica della filosofia italiana*, XXXVIII (1959).

Garin, E., *La cultura filosofica del rinascimento italiano*. Florence, 1961a.

Garin, E., *Medioevo e rinascimento*. Bari, 1961b.

Garin, E., 'Un manuale di magia: Picatrix.' *L'età nuova. Ricerche di storia della cultura dal XII al XVI secolo*. Naples, 1969.

Garin, E., *Rinascita e revoluzione: Movimenti culturali dal XiV al XVIII secolo*. Roma-Bari, 1976.

Gatti, S., 'L'Attività milanese del Cesariano dal 1512 al 1519.' *Arte Lombarda*, XVI (1971): 219–230.

Gatti-Perer, M.L., *Il mito del classicismo nel 600*. Florence, 1964.

Gatti-Perer, M.L., *Le istruzioni di San Carlo e l'ispirazione classica nell'architettura religiosa del 600 in Lombardia*. Mantua, 1970.

Gay, S.A., 'Les Considérations morales sur la destination des ouvrages de l'art de Quatremère de Quincy.' *Paragone*, 38 (1987): 50–62.

Gengaro, M.L., 'Il valore dell'architettura nella teoria settecentesca dell Padre Carlo Lódoli.' *L'Arte*, XL (1937): 313–314.

Gentili di Guiseppe, F., 'Una lettera autografa da Rafaello.' *L'Arte*, XXXVI (1933): 30–36.

Germann, G., *Gothic Revival in Europe and Britain*. Cambridge, MA, 1972.

Germann, G., *Einführung in die Geschichte der Architekturtheorie*. Darmstadt, 1980.

Geymonat, L., *Galileo Galilei*. New York, 1965.

Geymüller, H.v., 'Leonardo da Vinci als Architekt.' *The Literary Works of Leonardo da Vinci*. London, 1883: 25–104.

Geymüller, H.v., *Raffaello etudiato come architetto*. Milan, 1884.

Gibbon, E., *History of the Decline and Fall of the Roman Empire*. 6 vols., 1776–1788.

Gillot, H., *Querelle des anciens et des modernes en France*. Paris, 1914.

Gilmore, T.B., 'Introduction.' *Early Eighteenth-Century Essays on Taste*. New York, 1972.

Godwin, J., 'Poliphilo's Dream, or Alberti's?' *Design Book Review*, 41 (2000): 48–53.

Goethe, W., 'Letter to Schiller,' December 10, 1796. Quoted in Diderot, *Oeuvres*, A. Billy, (ed.). 1969: 1427.

Goldthwaite, R.A., 'The Florentine Palace as Domestic Architecture.' *American Historical Review*, 77 (1972).

Goldthwaite, R.A., *The Building of Renaissance Florence. An Economic and Social History*. Baltimore, 1980.

Gollwitzer, M., 'Francesco Milizia, Del teatro: ein Beitrag zu Ästhetik und Kulturgeschichte Italiens zwischen 1750 und 1790.' Cologne, 1969.

Gombrich, E.H., 'Icones Symbolicae.' *Journal of the Warburg and Courtault Institutes*, XI (1948).

Gombrich, E.H., 'Hypnerotomachiana.' *Journal of the Warburg and Courtault Institutes*, XIV (1951): 119–125.

Gombrich, E.H., 'The Early Medici as Patrons of Art.' *Norm and Form*. London, 1966: 81–98.

Gombrich, E.H., 'The Debate on Primitivism in Ancient Rhetoric.' *J.W.C.I.*, 129 (1966).

Gombrich, E.H., *Abby Warburg*. London, 1970.

Gombrich, E.H., *Brève Histoire du monde*, trans. A. Georges. Paris, 2000.

Gordon, D.J., 'Poet and Architect: The Intellectual Setting of the Quarrel between Ben Jonson and Inigo Jones.' *The Renaissance Imagination*, S. Orgel. (ed.). Berkeley, 1975.

Gotheim, M.L., *A History of Garden Art*. London/Toronto, 1928.

Grafton, A., *Leon Battista Alberti: Master Builder of the Italian Renaissance*. New York, 2000.

Graham, V.E. and McAllister Johnson, W., 'Introduction.' *Le recueil des Inscriptions 1558*, E. Jodelle (ed.). Toronto, 1972.

Granger, G.G., *La mathématique sociale du marquis de Condorcet*. Paris, 1989.

Grant, L., *Abbot Suger of St.-Denis: Church and State in Early Twelfth-Century France*. London/New York, 1998.

Grassi, L., *Razionalismo architettonico dal Lódoli a G. Pagano*. Milan, 1966.

Grayson, C., 'The Composition of L.B. Alberti's *Decem Libri de re aedificatoria*.' *Münchener Jahrbuch der Bildenden Kunst*, 3, XI (1960).

Greenhalgh, M., *The Classical Tradition in Art*. London, 1978.

Greenstein, J.-M., 'On Alberti's "Sign": Vision and Composition in Quattrocento Painting.' *The Art Bulletin*, 79 (1997): 669–698.

Grendler, P.F., *Critics of the Italian World (1530–1560). Anton Francesco Doni, Nicolo Franco and Ortensio Lando*. Madison, 1969.

Grene, M., 'Gerard's Essay on Taste.' *Modern Philology*, XLI (1943): 45–58.

Griggs, T., 'Promoting the Past: the *Hypnerotomachia Poliphili* as Antiquarian Enterprise.' *Word and Image*, 14 (1998): 17–39.

Griswold, W., 'Giovanni Battista Piranesi: Villa of Hadrian, Octagonal Room in the Small Baths.' *The Metropolitan Museum of Art Bulletin*, 52 (1994): 36.

Guidoni Marino, A., 'Il colonato di Piazza S. Pietro: dall'architettura obliqua di Caramuel al "classicismo" berniniano.' *Palladio*, XXIII (1973): 81–120.

Guillame, J. and de L'Orme, P., 'Un traité différent.' *Les Traités d'architecture de la renaissance*, Guillaume, J. (ed.). Paris, 1988.

Guillaume, J. (ed.), *Les Traités d'architecture de la renaissance*. Tours, 1992.

Havighurst, A.F., *The Pirenne Thesis*. Boston, 1958.

Hagelberg, L., 'Die Architektur Michelangelos in ihren Beziehungen zu Manierismus und Barock.' *Münchener Jahrbuch der Bildenden Kunst*, VIII (1931): 264–280.

Hamlin, T., *Greek Revival Architecture in America*. New York, 1964.

Harris, E., 'Burke and Chambers on the Sublime and the Beautiful.' *Essays Presented to R. Wittkower on his 65th birthday*, D. Fraser, H. Hibbard and M.J. Levine, II (eds). 2 vols. London, 1967: 207–213.

Harris, E., 'Batty Langley: a Tutor to Freemasons.' *Burlington Magazine*, CXIX, May (1977): 327–335.

Harris, E., *British Architectural Books and Writers. 1556–1785*. Cambridge, 1990.

Harris, J., *Sir William Chambers*. London, 1970a.

Harris, J., Crook, J.M. and Harris, E., *Sir William Chambers, Knight of the Polar Star*. London, 1970b.

Hart, F., *Giulio Romano*. New Haven, 1958.

Hart, V., 'The Architect as Philosopher.' *The Architectural Review*, 196 (1994): 11–13.

Hart, V., 'Decorum and the Five Orders of Architecture: Sebastiano Serlio's Military City.' *Res* (1998): 75–84.

Hart, V. and Hicks P. (eds), *Paper Palaces: The Rise of the Renaissance Architectural Treatise*. New Haven, 1998.

Hart., V. and Hicks, P., 'Introduction.' *S. Serlio on Architecture*, vol. II. New Haven, 2002.

Harvey, J.H., *The Gothic World 1100–1600. A Survey of Architecture and Art*. New York, 1969.

Harvey, J.H., *The Mediaeval Architect*. London, 1972.

Haskins, C.H., *The Renaissance of the 12th Century*. Cambridge, MA, 1927.

Hatfield, R., 'Some Unknown Descriptions of the Medici Palace in 1459.' *Art Bulletin New York*, LII (1970): 233ff.

Haus, A., 'Der Petersplatz in Rom und sein Statuenschmuck.' *Neue Beiträge*. Freiburg, 1970.

Hauser, A., *The Social History of Art*. London, 1951.

Hauser, A., *Mannerism: the Crisis of the Renaissance and the Origin of Modern Art*. London, 1965.

Hautecoeur, L., *Histoire de l'architecture classique en France*. 11 vols. Paris, 1948–1963.

Hautecoeur, L., *Les jardins des dieux et des hommes*. Paris, 1959.

Hayot, M., 'La maison d'un disciple de Soufflot.' *L'Oeil* (1985): 52–55.

Hazlehurst, F.H., *Jacques Boyceau and the French Formal Garden*. Berkeley, 1966.

Heckscher, W.S., 'Relics of Pagan Antiquity in Medieval Settings.' *Journal of the Warburg Institute*, I (1937–1938).

Heikamp, D., 'Vicende di Federigo Zuccari.' *Rivista d'arte*, XXXII (1959): 175ff.

Heikamp, D., 'Ancora su Federigo Zuccari.' *Rivista d'arte*, XXXIII (1960): 45ff.

Hellmann, G.A., 'Proportionsverfahren des Francesco di Giorgios.' *Miscellania, Bibliotheca Herziana zu Ehren von Leo Brohns*. Munich, 1961.

Hemingway, A., 'Genius, Gender and Progress: Benthamism and the Arts in the 1820s.' *Art History*, 16 (1993): 619–646.

Henrey, B., *British Botanical and Horticultural Literature*. Oxford, 1975.

Hernandez, A., 'J.N.L. Durand's Architectural Theory. A Study in the History of Rational Building Design.' *Perspecta*, 12 (1969): 153–155.

Hernandez, A., *Grunzüge einer Ideengeschichte der Französischen Architekturtheorie von 1560–1800*. Basle, 1972.

Herrmann, W., 'Antoine Desgodetz and the Académie Royale d'Architecture.' *Art Bulletin New York*, XL (1958): 23–53.

Herrmann, W., 'The Author of "Architecture Moderne" of 1728.' *Journal of the Society of Architectural Historians* (1959): 60–62.

Herrmann, W., *Laugier and Eighteenth-Century French Theory*. London, 1962.

Herrmann, W., 'Unknown Designs of the "Temple of Jerusalem" by Claude Perrault.' *Essays in the History of Architecture, Presented to R. Wittkower*, D. Fraser *et al.* (eds). London, 1967.

Herrmann, W., *The Theory of Claude Perrault*. London, 1973.

Hersey, G.L., *Pythagorean Palaces*. Ithaca, 1976.

Heydenreich, L.H., 'Pius II als Bauherr von Pienza.' *Zeitschrift für Kunstgeschichte*, VI (1937): 105–146.

Heydenreich, L.H., 'Leonardo da Vinci, Architect of Francis I.' *Burlington Magazine*, XCIV (1952).

Heydenreich, L.H., 'Leonardo.' *Encyclopedia Universale dell'Arte*, 1958–1967.

Heydenreich, L.H., *Leonardo Architetto*. Florence, 1963a.

Heydenreich, L.H., 'Strukturenprinzipen der Florentiner Frührenaissance-Architektur: Prospectiva Aedificandi.' *Studies in Western Art. Acts of the 20th International Congress of the History of Art*, II. Princeton, 1963b: 108–122.

Heydenreich, L.H., 'Leonardo and Bramante: Genius in Architecture.' *Leonardo's Legacy. International Symposium*. Berkeley/Los Angeles, 1969a.

Heydenreich, L.H., 'La villa: generi e sviluppi fino al Palladio.' *Bollettino del Centro Internazionale di Studi d'Architettura Andrea Palladio*, XI (1969b).

Heydenreich, L.H., 'Die Sakralbau-studien Leonardo da Vinci's.' Dissertation, Hamburg 1929; Munich, 1971.

Hibbard, H., *Carlo Maderno and Roman Architecture, 1580–1630*. London, 1971.

Hill, C., *Intellectual Origins of the English Revolution*. London, 1980.

Hilles, F.W. and Bloom, H. (eds), *From Sensibility to Romanticism*. Oxford, 1965.

Hind, A.M., *Giovanni Battista Piranesi: a Critical Study, With a List of his Published Works and Detailed Catalogues of the Prisons and the Views of Rome*. New York, 1922.

Hipple, W.J., *The Beautiful, the Sublime and the Picturesque in 18th-Century British Aesthetic Theory*. Carbondale, 1957.

Hirschmann, A.O., *The Passions and the Interests. Political Arguments for Capitalism before its Triumph*. Princeton, 1977.

Hofer, P., *Claude Henri Watelet. A Visit to Rome in 1764*. Cambridge, MA, 1956.

Hoffman, V., 'Brunelleschi's Architektursystem.' *Architectura, Zeitschrift für Geschichte der Baukunst*, I (1971): 54–59.

Holyoak, K. and Thagart, P., *Mental Leaps: Analogy in Creative Thought*. Cambridge, MA, 1995.

Honour, H., 'Palladio, Barbaro e le leggi della proporzione.' *Palladio, Veronese e Vittoria a Maser*. Milan, 1960: 3–24.

Honour, H., *Neo-Classicism*. Harmondsworth, 1968.

Howard, D., 'Four Centuries of Literature on Palladio.' *Journal of the Society of Architectural Historians*, XXXIX, October (1980): 224–241.

Huelsen, C., 'Letter to Schlosser.' *La letteratura artistica*, in von Schlosser (ed.). Florence, 1979.

Huizinga, J., *The Waning of the Middle Ages*, trans. F. Hopman. Harmondsworth, 1972.

Hunt, J.D., *The Figure in the Landscape*. Baltimore, 1976.

Hunt, J.D., 'Experiencing Gardens in the *Hypnerotomachia Poliphili*.' *Word and Image*, 14 (1998): 109–119.

Huper, M.S., *The Architectural Monuments of the* Hypnerotomachia Poliphili. University Microfilms, Ann Arbor, 1956.

Hussey, C., *English Gardens and Landscapes 1700–1705*. London, 1967a.

Hussey, C., *The Picturesque*. London/New York, 1927; London, 1967b.

Huxley, A., *Prisons: with the 'Carceri' etchings by G.B. Piranesi*. London, 1949.

Hyman, I., *Fifteenth-Century Florentine Studies: The Palazzo Medici and a Ledger for the Church of S. Lorenzo*. Dissertation, New York University, 1968. New York, 1978.

Ivins, W.M., *On the Rationalization of Sight: with an Examination of Three Renaissance Texts on Perspective*. New York, 1938.

Jackson, H., 'Introduction.' *The Anatomy of Melancholy*, R. Burton (ed.). New York, 1977.

Jacques, D., 'The Art and Sense of the Scribblerus Club in England 1715–1735.' *Garden History*, IV, I (1976).

Jacquot, J., *Les Fêtes de la Renaissance*. 2 vols. Paris, 1959–1960.

Jacquot, J. and Koningson, E., *Les Fêtes de la Renaissance*. vol. 3. Paris, 1972.

Jähns, M., *Geschichte der Kriegswissenschaften*. Munich, 1889.

Jannaco, C., *Il seicento*. Milan, 1966.

Jannaco, C., 'Barocco e razionalismo nel "Trattato di architettura" di Vincenzo Scamozzi.' *Studi Seicenteschi* (1961): 47–60.

Jardine, L., *Wordly Goods. A New History of the Renaissance*. London, 1996.

Jardine, L., *On a Grander Scale. The Outstanding Career of Christopher Wren*. London, 2002.

Jarzombek, M., *On Leon Baptista Alberti: His Literary and Aesthetic Theories*. Cambridge, MA, 1989.

Jencks. Ch. and Baird, G. (eds), *Meaning in Architecture*. New York, 1969.

Jestaz, B., *Le voyage en Italie de Robert Cotte*. Paris, 1966.

Jestaz, B., 'Les plus excellents bastiments de France par J. Androuet du Cerceau.' *Bulletin Monumental*, 147 (1989): 188–189.

Jestaz, B., *La Renaissance de l'architecture*, Paris, 1995.

Jones, R.F., *Ancients and Moderns: A Study of the Background*. St Louis, 1936.

Kask, T., *Symmetrie und Regelmässigkeit: Französische Architektur im Grand Siècle*. Zürich, 1971.

Kaufmann, E., *Von Ledoux bis Le Corbusier*. Vienna, 1933.

Kaufmann, E., 'Claude Nicolas Ledoux, Inaugurator of a New Architectural System.' *Journal of the Society of Architectural Historians*, III, July (1943): 12–20.

Kaufmann, E., 'At an 18th-Century Crossroads: Algarotti vs Lódoli.' *Journal of the Society of Architectural Historians*, IV (1944).

Kaufmann, E., 'The Contribution of J.F. Blondel to Mariette's Architecture Française.' *Art Bulletin New York*, XXI (1949): 58–69.

Kaufmann, E., *Three Revolutionary Architects: Boullée, Ledoux, and Lequeu*. Philadelphia, 1952.

Kaufmann, E., *Architecture in the Age of Reason*. Cambridge, MA, 1955.

Kaufmann, E., 'Piranesi, Algarotti, Lòdoli: A Controversy in 18th-Century Venice.' *Essays in Honour of Hans Tietze, 1880–1954*, E.H. Gombrich et al. (eds). New York, 1958.

Kaufmann, E., 'Memmo's Lòdoli.' *Art Bulletin New York*, XLVI (1964): 159–175.

Kaufmann, E., *Von Ledoux bis Le Corbusier: Ursprung und Entwicklung der Autonomen Architektur*. Stuttgart, 1985.

Kidson, P., 'Panofsky, Suger and St Denis.' *Journal of the Warburg and Courtauld Institutes*, 50 (1987): 1–17.

Kimball, M.G., *Jefferson*. 3 vols. New York, 1943–1950.

Kitao, T.K., 'Circle and Oval in the Square of Saint Peter's.' *Bernini's Art of Planning*. New York, 1974.

Kitao, T.K., 'Carlo Fontana Had No Part in Bernini's Planning of the Square of Saint Peter's.' *Journal of the Society of Architectural Historians*, XXXVI (1977): 85–91.

Kitzinger, E., *Early Medieval Art*. Indiana, 1964.

Klein, R., 'Les "sept gouverneurs de l'Art" selon Lomazzo.' *Arte Lombarda*, IV (1959): 277ff.

Klein, R., 'L'Urbanisme utopique de Filarete à Valentin Andreae.' *L'Utopie à la Renaissance*. Brussels, 1964.

Klein, R., *La Forme et l'intelligible*, Intr. A. Chastel. Paris, 1970.

Klein, R., 'Introduction.' *Idea del tempio della pittura*, G.P. Lomazzo (ed.), 2 vols. Florence, 1974.

Klibansky, R., *The Continuity of the Platonic Tradition During the Middle Ages*. London, 1932.

Knight, I., *The Geometric Spirit: the abbé de Condillac and the French Enlightenment*. New Haven, 1968.

Knight, I., *The Geometric Spirit of Abbé de Condillac*. Berkeley, 1968.

Knoop, D., Jones, G.P. and Hamer, D., *The Two Earliest Masonic MSS*. London, 1938.

Koehler, E., *Ideal und Wirklichkeit in der hoefischen Epik*. Tuebingen, 1956.

Korner, H. and Piel, F., 'A mon ami A. Quatremère de Quincy: Ein unbekanntes Werk Jacques-Louis Davids aus dem Jahre 1779.' *Pantheon*, 43 (1985): 89–96.

Krautheimer, R., Introduction to an 'Iconography of Mediaeval Architecture.' *Courtauld Institute*, vol. V. (1942–1943): 1–34..

Krautheimer, R., 'Alberti and Vitruvius.' *Studies in Western Art. Acts of the 20th International Congress of History of Art*. Princeton, 1963: 45–52.

Kretzulesco-Quaranta, E., *Les jardins du songe: 'Poliphile' et la mystique de la Renaissance*. Rome, 1976.

Krinsky, C.H., 'Seventy-Eight Vitruvius Manuscripts.' *Journal of the Warburg and Courtault Institutes*, XXX (1967): 36–70.

Krinsky, C.H., 'Introduction and Index.' *Di Lucio Vitruvio Pollione De Architettura Libri Decem*, C. Cesariano (ed.). Munich, 1969.

Krinsky, C.H., 'Cesariano and the Renaissance without Rome.' *Arte Lombarda*, XVI (1971): 211–218.

Kristeller, P.O., *The Philosophy of Marsilio Ficino*. New York, 1943.

Kristeller, P.O., 'Paduan Averroism and Alexandrism.' *Renaissance Thought*, II (1965).

Kruft, H.W., 'Leon Battista Alberti, l'alternativa, l'accessorio e l'essenziale.' *L'Architettura*, 34 (1988): 881.

Kruger, S.F., 'Dream Space and Masculinity.' *Word and Image*, 14 (1998): 11–16.

Kuhn, T.S., *The Structure of Scientific Revolutions*. Chicago, 1970.

Kunoth, G., *Die Historische Architektur Fischer von Erlachs*. Dusseldorf, 1956.

Kuttner, S., 'Pierre de Roissy and Robert of Flamborough.' *Traditio*, II (1944): 492–499.

Lang, S., 'The Genius of the English Garden.' *The English Garden*, D. Coffin (ed.). Washington, DC, 1972a.

Lang, S., 'Sforzinda, Filarete and Filelfo.' *Journal of the Warburg and Courtault Institutes*, XXXV (1972b): 391–397.

Lapp, J.C., *The Esthetics of Negligence*. Ann Arbor, 1971.

Lavin, S., 'In the Names of History: Quatremere de Quincy and the Literature of Egyptian Architecture.' *Journal of Architectural Education*, 44 (1991): 131–137.

Lavin, S., *Quatremére de Quincy and the Invention of a Modern Language of Architecture*. Cambridge, MA, 1992.

Lavin, S., 'Re-reading the Encyclopedia: Architectural Theory and the Formation of the Public in Late Eighteenth-Century France.' *Journal of the Society of Architectural Historians*, 53 (1994): 184–192.

Lazzaroni, M. and Munoz, A., *Filarete: scultore e architetto del secolo XV*. Rome, 1908.

Le Camus de Mezières, N., *The Genius of Architecture, or, The Analogy of That Art with Our Sensations*. Santa Monica, 1992.

Le Comte, D., *Boullée, Ledoux, Lequeu, les architectes révolutionnaires*. Paris, 1969.

Lee, R.W., 'Ut Pictora Poesis. The Humanistic Theory of Painting.' *Art Bulletin New York*, XXII (1940): 255ff.

Lee, R.W., *Ut Pictora Poesis. The Humanistic Theory of Painting*. New York, 1967.

Lefaivre, L., 'Dirty Realism. Making the Stone Stony.' *Design Book Review*, 17 (1989): 17–21.

Lefaivre, L., 'Leon Battista Alberti: Some New Facets of the Polyhedron.' *Design Book Review*, 34, Fall (1994a): 12–17.

Lefaivre, L., 'Rethinking the Western Humanist Tradition in Architecture.' *Design Book Review*, 34, (1994b): 1–3.

Lefaivre, L., *Leon Battista Alberti's* Hypnerotomachia Poliphili: *Re-Cognizing the Architectural Body in the Early Italian Renaissance*. Cambridge, MA, 1997.

Lefaivre, L. and Tzonis, A., 'La Géométrie du sentiment et le paysage thérapeutique.' *Revue du Dix-Huitième Siècle*, 9 (1977): 73–79.

Lefaivre, L. and Tzonis, A., 'Critical Realism.' *The Critical Landscape*, A. Graafland (ed.). Amsterdam: 126–147.

Lefranc, A., 'Philibert de L'Orme, Grand Architecte du Roi Mégiste.' *Revue du Seizième Siècle*, IV (1916): 148ff.

Le Goff, J., *L'Imaginaire médiéval*. Paris, 1985.

Lehmann, K., *Thomas Jefferson, American Humanist*. New York, 1947.

Lemoine, J.G., 'Brunelleschi et Ptolémé.' *Gazette des Beaux Arts*, LI, May/June (1958).

Lemonnier, H. (ed.), *Procès-verbaux de l'Académie royale d'architecture*. 10 vols. Paris, 1911–1929.

Lemonnier, H., 'Les "Variations" de l'Académie Royale d'Architecture.' *Revue de l'Art Ancien et Moderne*, LI (1927): 175ff.

Leoni, F., 'Il Cesariano e l'architettura del rinascimento in Lombardia.' *Arte Lombarda*, I (1955): 90–97.

Leroux, D., *La vie de Bernard Palissy*. Paris, 1927.

Lestringant, F., *Bernard Palissy, 1510–1590: l'écrivain, le réorme, le céeramiste: journées d'études 29 et 30 juin 1990, Saintes, Abbaye-aux-dames: actes du colloque*. Mont de Marsan, 1992.

Levit, H. and Piranesi, G., *Views of Rome, Then and Now*. New York, 1976.

Levi-Strauss, C., *Conversations with Levi-Strauss*, Charbonnier (ed.). London, 1969.

Liess, R., *Goethe vor dem Strassburger Munster: zum Wissenschaftsbild der Kunst*. Weinheim, 1985.

Linaker, A., 'Pallazzo dei Medici.' *Atti delta Socièta Colombaria di Firenze*, 1913–1914.

Little, B., *The Life and Work of James Gibbs 1682–1754*. London, 1955.

Lombard, A., *L'Abbé Dubos, un initiateur de la pensée moderne*. Paris, 1913.

Bibliography and references

Lombard, A., *Fénelon et le retour à l'antique au XVIIIe siècle*. Neuchâtel, 1954.

Lopez, R., *The Commercial Revolution of the Middle Ages, 950–1350*. Cambridge, 1976.

Lotz, W., 'Das Raumbild in der Architekturzeichnung der Italienischen Renaissance.' *Mitteilungen des Kunsthistorischen Instituts Florenz*, 7 (1956): 193–226.

Lotz, W., 'Osservazioni intorno ai disegni palladiani.' *Bollettino del Centro Internazionale di Studi d'Architettura Andrea Palladio*, IV (1962): 61–68.

Lotz, W., 'Palladio e Sansovino.' *Bollettino del Centro Internazionale di Studi d'Architettura Andrea Palladio*, IX (1967): 13–23.

Lotz, W., 'The Rendering of the Interior in Architectural Drawings of the Renaissance.' *Studies in the Italian Renaissance Architecture*, J.S. Ackerman *et al.* (eds). Cambridge, MA, 1972: 1–63.

Lovarini, E., 'Le Ville edificate da A. Cornaro.' *L'Arte*, II (1899): 191–212.

Lowry, B., 'Ledoux.' *Encyclopedia of World Art*, IX. New York, 1964: 197–198.

Lücke, H.-K., *Alberti Index*. 4 vols. Munich, 1975–1976.

Madec, P. and Boullee, E.L., *Boullee*. Paris, 1986.

Magnuson, T., *Studies in Roman Quattrocento Architecture*. Rome, 1958.

Mahon, D., *Studies in seicento Art and Theory*. London, 1947.

Majewski, H.F., *The Preromantic Imagination of L.S. Mercier*. New York, 1971.

Malaguzzi Valeri, F., *La corte di Lodovico il Moro*. Milan, 1913–1923.

Mâle, E., *L'Art religieux du XIIe au XVIIIe Siècle*. Paris, 1945.

Mâle, E., *The Gothic Image*. New York, 1958.

Malins, E.G., *English Landscape and Literature 1660–1840*. Oxford, 1966.

Maltese, C., 'Il pensiero architettonico e urbanistico di Leonardo.' *Leonardo, saggi e ricerche*. Rome, 1954.

Maltese, C., 'L'Attività di Francesco Giorgio Martini, architetto militare nelle marche attraverso il suo Trattato.' *Atti del XI Congresso di Storia dell'Architettura*, 1959.

Maltese, C., 'Introduzione.' *Trattati*, ed. F. di Giorgio. Milan, 1967.

Mandrou, R., 'Histoire sociale et histoire des mentalités.' *La Nouvelle Critique*, 49, January (1972).

Mango, C. (ed.), *Early Medieval Art 300–1150: Sources and Documents. The Art of the Byzantine Empire 312–1453*. Toronto, 1986.

Manwaring, E.M., *Italian Landscape in 18th-Century England*. New York, 1965.

Marconi, P., 'Un Progetto di Città Militare: l'VIII Libro inedito de Sebastiano Serlio.' *Controspazio*, 1 (1969): 51–59; 4/5: 52–59.

Marconi, P., *La Città come forma simbolica*. Rome, 1973.

Margiotta, R., *Le Origine italiane delle querelle* . . . Milan, 1953.

Marias, F. and Bustamante, A., *Las Ideas Esteticas de El Greco*. Madrid, 1981.

Marias, F. and Bustamante, A., 'Trattatistica teorica e vitruvianesimo nella architettura spagnola del Cinquecento.' *Les Traités d'architecture de la renaissance*, Guillaume, J. (ed.). Paris, 1988.

Martin, P.E., 'Intimations of the New Gardening: Alexander Pope's Reaction to the "Uncommon" Landscape at Sherbourne.' *Garden History*, IV, 1 (1976).

Massotti Biggiogero, G., 'Della vita e delle opere di Luca Pacioli.' In: L. Pacioli, *De Divina Proporzione*. Milan, 1956.

Mathieu, M., *Pierre Patte, sa vie et son ouvre*. Paris, 1940.

Mauclaire, P. and Vigoureux, C., *Nicolas-François de Blondel, ingenieur et Architecte du Roi*. Laon, 1938.

Mayor, A.H., *Giovanni Battista Piranesi*. New York, 1952.

Mayr, E., *What is Evolution?* New York, 2001.

McGowan, M., *Renaissance Triumphs*. Amsterdam, 1976.

McNamara, R.A., 'Hogarth and the comic muse.' *Print Quarterly*, 13 (1996): 251–258.

McTighe, S., 'Abraham Bosse and the Language of Artisans: Genre and Perspective in the Académie Royale de Peinture et de Sculpture, 1648–1670.' *Oxford Art Journal*, 21 (1998): 1–26.

Meeks, C.L.V., *Italian Architecture, 1750–1914*. New Haven/London, 1966.

Menéndez y Pelayo, M., *Historia de las ideas esteticas en España*. Madrid, 1974.

Merton Robert K. *Science, Technology and Society in Seventeenth Century England*, New York, N. Y 1970.

Michel, P.-H., *La pensée de L.B. Alberti (1404–1472)*. Paris, 1930.

Middleton, R., 'Jacques-François Blondel and the Cours d'Architecture.' *Journal of the Society of Architectural Historians*, XVIII (1959): 140–148.

Middleton, R., 'The abbé de Cordemoy and the Graeco-Gothic Ideal: A Prelude to Romantic Classicism.' *Journal of the Warburg and Courtault Institutes*, XXV (1962).

Middleton, R., 'The abbé de Cordemoy and the Graeco-Gothic Ideal.' *Journal of the Warburg and Courtault Institutes*, XXVI (1963): 90–123.

Middleton, R., 'Germain Boffrand, l'aventure d'un architecte independant.' *The Burlington Magazine*, 130 (1988a): 865–866.

Middleton, R., 'The Writing on the Walls: Ledoux.' *Casabella*, 52 (1988b): 27.

Milanesi, G., *La lettere di Michelangelo Buonarroti coi ricordi e i contratti artistici*. Florence, 1875.

Miller, N., *French Renaissance Fountains*. New York, 1977.

Miller, N., *Heavenly Caves: Reflections on the Garden Grotto*. New York, 1983.

Millon, H., 'The Architectural Theory of Francesco di Giorgio Martini.' *Art Bulletin New York*, XL, 3 (1958): 257–261.

Mirabent, F., *La estética inglesa del Siglo XVIII*. Barcelona, 1937.

Mitchell, C., 'Archeology and Romance in Renaissance Italy.' *Italian Renaissance Studies*, E.F. Jacob (ed.). London, 1960: 455–483.

Mitchell, H., 'An Unrecorded Issue of Philibert Delorme's Le Premier tome de l'architecture, Annotated by Sir Henry Wotton.' *Journal of the Society of Architectural Historians*, 53 (1994): 20–29.

Mondain-Monval, J., *Soufflot, son oeuvre, son esthétique*. Paris, 1918.

Monk, S.H., *The Sublime. A Study of Critical Theories in XVIII-Century England*. New York, 1935.

Monval, J., *Soufflot, sa vie, son oeuvre, son esthétique (1713–1780)*. Paris, 1918.

Morley, H., *Palissy the Potter. The Life of Bernard Palissy*. London, 1852.

Morrison, S., *Fra Luca Pacioli del Borgo*. New York, 1933.

Mortet, V., *Recueil de textes relatifs à l'histoire de l'architecture en France au moyen age*. Vol. I. Paris, 1911.

Mortet, V., 'Hugue de Fouilloi, Pierre le Chantre, Alexandre Neckam et les critiques dirigées au XIIe siècle contre le luxe des constructions.' *Mélanges d'histoire offerts à M. Charles Bémont*. Paris, 1914.

Mortet, V. and Deschamps, P., *Recueil de textes relatifs à l'histoire de l'architecture en France au moyen-age*. Vol. II. Paris, 1929.

Mortier, R., *Diderot et L'Allemagne*. Paris, 1955.

Muehlmann, H., *Aesthetische Theorie der Renaissance. L.B. Alberti*. Bonn, 1981.

Mueller, W., 'The Authenticity of Guarini's Stereotomy in his Architettura Civile.' *Journal of the Society of Architectural Historians*, XXVII (1968): 202–208.

Mueller Profumo, L., *El Ornamento iconico y la arquitectura 1400–1600*. Madrid, 1985.

Muelmann, H., *Ästhetische Theorie der Renaissance, Leon Battista Alberti*. Bonn, 1981.

Mumford, L., *Technics and Civilization*. New York, 1934.

Müntz, E., *Les arts à la cour des papes pendant les XVe et XVIe siècles*. Paris, 1878–1882.

Müntz, E., *Raphaël, sa vie, son oeuvre et son temps*. Paris, 1881.

Muratori, G., *La città rinascimentale. Tipi e modelli attraverso i trattati*. Milan, 1975.

Murray, P., 'Leonardo and Bramante.' *Architectural Review*, CXXXIV, 801 (1963): 346–351.

Nachmani, C.W., 'The Early English Cottage Book.' *Marsyas*, XXV (1968/1969): 67–76.

Neuman, R., 'Germain Boffrand, 1667–1754, l'aventure d'un architecte indépendant.' *Journal of the Society of Architectural Historians*, 47 (1988): 199–200.

Nicolson, M.H., *Mountain Gloom and Mountain Glory*. New York, 1963.

Nisbet, R., *Social Change and History*. New York, 1969.

Nyberg, D., 'The "Mémoires Critiques d'Architecture" by Michel de Frémin.' *Journal of the Society of Architectural Historians*, XXIV (1963): 217–224.

Bibliography and references

Nyberg, D., 'La Sainte Antiquité: Focus of an Eighteenth-Century Architectural Debate.' *Essays Presented to Rudolf Wittkower on his 65th Birthday*, D. Fraser, H. Hibbard and M.J. Levine, II (eds). 2 vols. London, 1967: 159–169.

O.C.A., *Oxford Companion to Art*. Oxford, 1970.

Oechslin, W., 'Bemerkungen zu Guarino Guarini und Juan Caramuel de Lobkowitz.' *Raggi*, II, 3 (1969).

Oechslin, W., *Bildungsgut und Antikenrezeption des fruehen Settecento in Rom. Studien zum roemischen Aufenthalt Bernardo Antonio Vittones*. Zurich, 1972.

Offerhaus, J. and Coecke, P., 'L'Introduction des traités d'architecture aux Pays-Bas.' *Les Traités d'architecture de la renaissance*, Guillaume, J. (ed.). Paris, 1988.

Ogden, H.V.S., 'Variety and Contrast in 17th-Century Aesthetics.' *Journal of the History of Ideas*, X, 10 (1949): 159–182.

Olschki, L., *Der Ideale Mittelpunkt Frankreichs im Mittelalter*. Heidelberg, 1913.

Onians, J., 'Alberti and Filarete.' *Journal of the Warburg and Courtault Institutes*, XXXIV (1971): 96–114.

Orgel, S. and Strong, S., *Inigo Jones*. London, 1973.

Pace, C., *Félibien's Life of Poussin*. London, 1981.

Painter, G.D., *The* Hypnerotomachia Poliphili *of 1499; an Introduction on the Dream, the Dreamer, the Artist, and the Printer, by George D. Painter*. London, 1963.

Paladini, G., 'Leonardo e il piano regolatore di Firenze.' *Bollettino technico del collegia ingegneri di Firenze*, X (1952): 84–85.

Palissy, B., 'Recette véritable.' *Beaux Arts Magazine*, 1996, 148, Sept. (1996): 27.

Pallucchini, R., 'Vincenzo Scamozzi e l'architettura veneta.' *L'Arte*, XXXIX (1936): 3ff.

Pallucchini, R., 'Giulio Romano e Palladio.' *Bollettino del Centro Internazionale di Studi d'Architettura Andrea Palladio*, I (1959): 38–44.

Pallucchini, R., 'Profilo di Vincenzo Scamozzi.' *Bollettino del Centro Internazionale di Studi d'Architettura Andrea Palladio*, III (1961): 89ff.

Pane, R., *Andrea Palladio*. Turin, 1961.

Panofsky, E., 'Die Perspektive als "symbolische Form".' Berlin-Leipzig, 1927.

Panofsky, E., 'Das Erste Blatt aus dem "Libro" Giorgio Vasari's.' *Städel Jahrbuch*, VI (1930): 25–72.

Panofsky, E., 'The First Two Projects of Michelangelo's Tombs of Julius II.' *Art Bulletin New York*, XIX (1937).

Panofsky, E., *Idea: Ein Beitrag zur Begriffsgeschichte der älteren Kunsttheorie*. Leipzig, 1924; Berlin, 1960.

Panofsky, E., *The Codex Huygens and Leonardo da Vinci's Art Theory*. London, 1940; Neudeln, 1968.

Panofsky, E., *Idea: A Concept in Art History*, trans. by J.J.S. Peake. New York/Evanston/San Francisco/London, 1968.

Panofsky, E., *Renaissance and Renascences in Western Art*. New York, 1969.

Panofsky, E., 'The First Page of Giorgio Vasari's "Libro".' *Meaning in the Visual Arts*, E. Panofsky (ed.). Harmondsworth, 1970.

Panofsky, E., 'Introduction.' *Abbot Suger on the Abbey Church of St. Dénis and its Treasures*. Princeton, 1979.

Papini, R., *Francesco di Giorgio, architetto*. Florence, 1946.

Parent, M. *et al.*, *Vauban*. Paris, 1971.

Paris, G., 'La Chanson du pélerinage de Charlemagne.' *Romania*, IX (1911): 1.

Paris, G., 'Sistema e giudizi nell' "Idea del Lomazzo".' *Annali della scuola normale superiore di Pisa. Lettere, storia e filosofia*, XXIII (1954): 187–196.

Parronchi, A., 'L'autore del "Poliphilo".' *La nazione*, 15 August (1963).

Parronchi, A., *Studi su la dolce prospettiva*. Milan, 1964.

Parronchi, A., 'Sulla composizione del trattati attribuiti a Francesco di Giorgio Martini.' *Atti e memorie dell'academia toscana di scienze e lettere, La colombara*, XXXVI (1971): 160–230.

Parsons, W.B., *Engineers and Engineering in the Renaissance*. Cambridge, MA, 1968.

Pastor, L.v., *History of the Popes*. London, 1955.

Patz, K., 'Zum Begriff der Historia in L.B. Albertis De Pictura.' *Zeitschrift für Kunstgeschichte*, 49 (1986): 269–287.

Pauwels, Y., 'Cesariano et Philibert de L'Orme: le piédestal dorique du Premier tome de l'architecture.' *Revue de l'Art*, 91 (1991): 39–43.

Pauwels, Y., 'Les années d'apprentissage du jeune de l'Orme: l'hôtel Bullioud à Lyon.' *Bulletin Monumental,* 153 (1995): 351–357.

Pauwels, Y., 'Les Français à la recherche d'un langage, Les ordres hétérodoxes de Philibert de L'Orme et Pierre Lescot.' *Revue de l'Art*, 112 (1996): 9–15.

Pauwels, Y., 'La méthode de Serlio dans le Quarto libro.' *Revue de l'Art*, 119 (1998): 33–42.

Payne, A.A., 'Architectural Criticism, Science and Visual Eloquence: Teofilo Gallaccini in Seventeenth-Century Siena.' *Journal of the Society of Architectural Historians*, 58 (1999): 146–169.

Pedretti, C., *A Chronology of Leonardo da Vinci's Architectural Studies after 1500*. Geneva, 1962.

Pedretti, C., 'Leonardo's Plan for the Enlargement of the City of Milan.' *Raccolta vinciana*, XIX (1962).

Pedretti, C., *Leonardo da Vinci: The Royal Palace at Romorantin*. Cambridge, MA, 1972.

Pelatti, F., 'Vitruvio nel medioevo e nel rinascimento.' *Bollettino dell'istituto di archeologia e storia dell'arte*, IV–VI (1932): 111ff.

Pelosi, O., *Cinque saggi sul Polifilo*. Naples, 1987.

Pericard-Mea, D., 'Du Songe de Poliphile à l'Astrée: les jardins d'Amour après le XVe siècle.' *Word and Image*, 14 (1998): 120–129.

Pérouse de Montclos, J.M., 'Charles François Viel, architecte de l'Hôpital Général, et Jean-Louis Viel de Saint-Maux, architecte, peintre et avocat au Parlement de Paris.' *Bulletin de la société de l'histoire de l'art français*, (1966): 257–269.

Pérouse de Montclos, J.M., *Etienne-Louis Boullée, 1728–1799, de l'architecture classique à l'architecture révolutionnaire*. Paris, 1969.

Pérouse de Montclos, J.M., *Etienne-Louis Boullée, 1728–1799. Theoretician of Revolutionary Architecture*. New York, 1974.

Pérouse de Montclos, J.M., 'Horoscope de Philibert de l'Orme.' *Revue de l'Art*, 72 (1986): 16–18.

Pérouse de Montclos, J.M., 'Les editions des traités de Philibert de L'Orme au XVIIe siècle.' *Les Traités d'architecture de la renaissance*, Guillaume, J. (ed.). Paris, 1988.

Pérouse de Montclos, J.M., *Etienne-Louis Boullée*. Paris, 1994.

Pérouse de Montclos, J.M., *Philibert de l'Orme: architecte du roi, 1514–1570*. Paris, 2000.

Perrault, C. (ed.), *Mémoires de ma vie*, A. Picon (ed.). Paris, 1993.

Perrault, C., 'Ordonnance For the Five Kinds of Columns After the Method of the Ancients.' R. Perez-Gomez (ed.), trans. I.K. McEwen. Santa Monica, 1993.

Pestilli, L., 'Shaftesbury, agente d'arte: sulla provenienza vicereale di due quadri di Salvator Rosa ed uno (scomparso?) di Claude Lorrain.' *Bollettino d'Arte*, 77 (1992): 131–140.

Pestilli, L., '*Ut pictura non poesis*: Lord Shaftesbury's Ridiculous Anticipation of Metamorphosis and the Two Versions of *Diana and Actaeon* by Paolo de Matteis.' *Artibus et Historiae*, 14 (1993): 131–139.

Petzet, M., *Soufflots Sainte-Geneviève und der französische Kirchenbau des 18. Jahrhunderts*. Berlin, 1961.

Petzet, M., 'Claude Perrault als Architekt der Pariser Observatoriums.' *Zeitschrift für Kunstgeschichte*, XXX (1967): 1ff.

Petzet, M., *Claude Perrault und die Architektur des Sonnenkonigs*. Munchen, Berlin, 2000.

Pevsner, N., 'Gegenreformation und Manierismus.' *Repertorium für Kunstwissenschaft*, 46 (1925).

Pevsner, N., *Academies of Art, Past and Present*. Cambridge, 1940.

Pevsner, N., 'The Genesis of the Picturesque.' *Architectural Review*, XCVI (1944).

Pevsner, N., 'Goethe's Von Deutscher Baukunst.' *Architectural Review*, XCVIII (1945): 155ff.

Pevsner, N., *The Picturesque Garden and its Influence Outside the British Isles*. Washington, 1974.

Pfister, F., *Kleine Texte zum Alexanderroman*. Heidelberg, 1910.

Philips, D.L., 'Paradigms and Incommensurability.' *Theory and Society*, 2, 1 (1975).

Picon, A. Claude, *Perrault ou la curiosité d'un classique*. Paris, 1988.

Pirenne, H., *Medieval Cities: Their Origins and the Revival of Trade*. Princeton, 1925.

Pirenne, H., *Mohammed and Charlemagne*. London, 1939.

Placzek, A., 'Foreword.' *Select Architecture*, R. Morris (ed.). London, 1970.

Pocock, J.G.A., *The Machiavellian Moment*. Princeton, 1975.

Polanyi, K., *The Great Transformation*. New York, 1944.

Polanyi, K. *et al.*, *Trade and Market in the Early Empires*. Chicago, 1957.

Popelin, C., *Le Songe de Poliphile*. Paris, 1883.

Poppelreuter, J., *Der anonyme Meister des Poliphilo; eine Studie zur italienischen Buchillustration und zur Antike in der Kunst des Quattrocento*. Strasbourg, 1904.

Portoghesi, P., 'Luca Pacioli e la Divine Proporzione.' *Civiltà delle Macchine*, 5/6 (1957).

Portoghesi, P., 'La Biblioteca Laurenziana e la critica michelangiolo alle tradizione classica.' *Stil und Überlieferung in der Kunst des Abendlandes. Akten des 21. Internationalen Kongress für Kunstgeschichte in Bonn*, II (1969): 3–11. 1967.

Portoghesi, P. and Wittkower, R.E., *Michelangiolo Architetto*. Turin, 1964.

Postan, M.M., *The Medieval Economy and Society*. Harmondsworth, 1972.

Pozzi, G., *Francesco Colonna e Aldo Manuzio*. Bern, 1962.

Praz, M., *On Neoclassicism*. London, 1972.

Previtali, G., 'Introduzione.' In: G.P. Bellori, *Le vite de pittori, scultori e architetti moderni*, E. Borea, (ed.). Turin, 1976.

Prevost, J., *Philibert de l'Orme*. Paris, 1948.

Promis, C., 'Prefazione biografiche.' *Trattato di architettura civile e militare di Francesco di Giorgio Martini*, C. Saluzzio (ed.). Turin, 1841.

Promis, C., *Miscellanea di storia italiana*. Rome, 1862–1874.

Prost, A., *J.F. Blondel*. Metz, 1860.

Prozillo, I., *Francesco Milizia, teorico e storico dell'architettura*. Naples, 1971.

Puppi, L., 'Vincenzo Scamozzi, trattatista nell'ambiente della problematica dell'manierismo.' *Bollettino del Centro Internazionale di Studi d'Architettura Andrea Palladio*, IX (1967): 310ff.

Puppi, L., 'Il Trattato di Palladio e la sua fortuna in Italia e all'esterno.' *Bollettino del Centro Internazionale di Studi d'Architettura Andrea Palladio*, XII (1970).

Puppi, L., *Andrea Palladio*. Milan, 1973a.

Puppi, L., *Scrittori vicentini d'architettura del secolo XVI*. Venice, 1973b.

Puppi, L., *Andrea Palladio*. Boston, 1975.

Puppi, L., *Andrea Palladio, das Gesamtwerk*. 2 vols. Stuttgart, 1977.

Quatremère de Quincy, A.C., 'On imitation.' *Architectural Design*, 58 (1988): 6–7.

Radelet-de Grave Patricia; Edoardo Bienvenuto ed. *Entre mecanique et architecture* Basel, 1995.

Ramirez, J.A., 'El Sistema de los ordenes arquitectonicos o la utopia de la razon, el sueño de la libertad.' *Arquitectura y utopia* (1981a): 209–261.

Ramirez, J.A., 'Guarino Guarini, Fray Juan Ricci and the Complete Salomonic Order.' *Art History*, 2 (1981b): 175–185.

Ramirez, J.A., *Construcciones ilusorias*. Madrid, 1983.

Reigl, A., *Die Spätromische Kunstindustrie nach den Funden in Oesterreich-Ungarn*. Vienna, 1901.

Reigl, A., *Die Entstetung der Barockkunst in Rom*. Vienna, 1907.

Restorff, J., 'Goethe und die Kunst.' *Kunstforum International*, 128, Oct./Dec. (1994): 364–366.

Richter, J.P. and Richter, I.A., *The Literary Works of Leonardo da Vinci*. 2 vols. London, 1939.

Robson-Scott, W.D., *The Literary Background of the Gothic Revival in Germany*. Oxford, 1965.

Rocchi, E., *Francesco di Giorgio nelle tradizioni dell'ingegneria militare italiana*. Siena, 1902.

Rosci, M., 'Manierismo e academismo nel pensiero critico del Cinquecento.' *Acma, annali della facoltà di filosofia e lettere dell'Università Statale di Milano*, 9 (1956): 57ff.

Rosci, M., *Il Trattato di architettura di Sebastiano Serlio*. 2 vols. Milan, 1966.

Rosci, M., I: *Il Trattato di architettura di Sebastiano Serlio*; II: *Il Sesto libro delle habitationi di tutti le gradi degli huomini*. Milan, 1967a.

Rosci, M., 'Sebastiano Serlio e il manierismo nel Veneto.' *Bollettino del Centro Internazionale di Studi d'Architettura Andrea Palladio*, IX (1967b): 330–336.

Roscoe, G., *Vita e pontificato di Leone X*. Milan, 1816.

Rosenau, H., *Boullée's Treatise*. London, 1953.

Rosenau, H., *Social Purpose in Architecture*. London, 1970.

Rosenau, H., *Boullée and Visionary Architecture: Including Boullée's Architecture, Essay on Art*. London/New York, 1976.

Rosenau, H., *Vision of the Temple*. London, 1979.

Rosenblum, R., 'Aspects of Neoclassical Architecture.' *Transformations in late 18th-century Art*. Princeton, 1967.

Rosenfeld, M.N., 'Sebastiano Serlio's Late Style in the Avery Library Version of the Sixth Book.' *Journal of the Society of Architectural Historians*, XXVIII (1969): 155–172.

Rosenfeld, M.N., 'Review of Rosci's "Il Trattato di Architettura" . . .' *Art Bulletin New York*, LII (1970): 319–322.

Rosenfeld, M.N., 'Sebastiano Serlio on Domestic Architecture.' *Sebastiano Serlio on Domestic Architecture*, M.N. Rosenfeld (ed.). Cambridge, MA, 1978.

Rosenfeld, M.N., *Serlio, On Domestic Architecture*, Cambridge, MA., 1978.

Rossi, P., 'Studi sul lullismo e sull'arte della memoria nel rinascimento. I teatri del mondo e il lullismo di Giordano Bruno.' *Rivista critica di storia della filosofia*, XIV (1959): 28ff.

Rossi, P., *Clavis Universalis*. Milan/Naples, 1960.

Rossi, P., 'Michelangelo Buonarotti, il Giovane.' *Dizionario Biografico degli Italiani*. Milan, 1968.

Røstvig, M.-S., *The Happy Man. Studies in the Metamorphoses of a Classical Ideal*. 2 vols. Oslo, 1954, 1958.

Rotondi, P., *Francesco di Giorgio nel palazzo ducale di Urbino*. Novellara, 1970.

Rouge, J., 'Goethe et l'essai sur la Peinture de Diderot.' *Etudes germaniques* (1949): 227–234.

Rowe, C., *The Mathematics of the Ideal Villa*. Cambridge, 1976.

Roy, J., *L'an mil. Formation de la légende de l'an mil: état de la France de l'an 950 à 1050*. Paris, 1885.

Rudolph, C., *Artistic Change at St-Denis: Abbot Suger's Program and the Early Twelfth-Century Controversy Over Art*. Princeton, 1990.

Rufi, E., *Le rêve laique de Louis-Sébastien Mercier: entre litterature et politique*. Oxford, 1995.

Rykwert, J., *On Adam's House in Paradise*. New York, 1972.

Rykwert, J., *The First Moderns*. Cambridge, MA, 1982.

Rykwert, J., 'Alberti.' *Connaissance des Arts*, 509, Sept. (1994): 78–85.

Rykwert, J. and Engel, A., *Leon Battista Alberti*. Milan, 1994.

Saalman, H., 'Early Renaissance Architecture and Practice in Filarete's *Trattato di Architettura*.' *Art Bulletin New York*, XLI (1959): 328–330.

Saalman, H., 'Introduction.' *Vita di Brunelleschi*, A. di T. Manetti (ed.). University Park, Pennsylvania, 1970.

Saboya, M., 'Claude-Nicolas Ledoux et son Utopie Sociale.' *L'Information d'histoire de l'art*, 1970: 136–318.

Said, E., *Orientalism, Western Conceptions of the Orient*, Harmondsworth, 1978.

Saint-Simon, L., *Mémoires*, Yves Coirault (ed.), 8 vols. Paris, 1983–1988.

Sahlins, M., *The Use and Abuse of Biology*. Ann Arbor, 1976.

Sakarovitch, Joel: *Epures d'architecture: de la coupe des pierres a la geometrie descriptive* Basel 1998.

Santinello, G., *Leon Battista Alberti: una visione estetica del mondo e della vita*. Firenze, 1962.

Santaniello, A.E., 'Introduction.' *The Five Books of Architecture*, S. Serlio (ed.). London, 1970.

Sarton, G., 'The Tradition of Zenodoros.' *Isis,* 28 (1938): 461–462.

Sartre, J., 'Germain Boffrand, 1667–1754, l'aventure d'un architecte indépendant.' *Bulletin Monumental*, 145 (1987): 240–241.

Sauer, J., *Symbolik des Kirchengebäudes*. Freiburg, 1902.

Schiavo, A., *La vita e le opere architettoniche di Michelangelo*. Rome, 1953.

Schiavo, A., 'Il Viaggio del Bernini in Francia.' *Bollettino del Centro Internazionale di Studi d'Architettura Andrea Palladio*, 10 (1956).

Schlosser, J.v., *Quellenbuch zur Kunstgeschichte des abenländischen Mittelalters*. Vienna, 1896.

Schlosser, J.v., *Kunstliteratur*. Vienna, 1924.

Schlosser, J.v., *La letteratura artistica*. Florence, 1979.

Schmidt, D., *Untersuchungen zu den Archtekturphrasen in der* Hypnerotomachia Poliphili. Frankfurt a.M., 1978.

Schneider, R., *L'esthétique classique chez Quatremère de Quincy (1805–1823)*. Paris, 1910.

Schneider, R., *Quatremère de Quincy et son intervention dans les arts (1788–1850)*. Paris, 1910.

Schneider, L., 'Leon Battista Alberti: Some Biographical Implications of the Winged Eye.' *The Art Bulletin*, 72 (1990): 261–270.

Schopenhauer, A., *The World as Will and Idea*. New York, 1958.

Schramm, P.E., *Kaiser, Rom und Renovatio*. Leipzig, 1929.

Schramm, P.E., *Der König von Frankreich*. Weimar, 1939.

Schudt, L., *Italienreisen im 17. und 18. Jahrhundert*. Munich, 1959.

Secret, F., 'Les cheminements de la kabbale à la renaissance: Le théâtre du monde de G.C. Delminio . . .' *Rivista critica di storia della filosofia*, XIV (1959): 418ff.

Secret, F., 'Un témoignage oublié de G.C. Delminio sur la renaissance en France.' *Bibliothèque d'humanisme et renaissance*, XXXIV (1972): 275ff.

Sedlmayr, H., *Johann Bernhard Fischer von Erlach*. Munich, 1956.

Sekler, E.F., *Wren and His Place in European Architecture*. London, 1956.

Semrau, M., 'Zu Nikolaus Goldmann's Leben und Schriften.' *Monatshefte für Kunstwissenschaft* (1916): 349–361, 463–473.

Sereni, E., *Storia del paesaggio agrario italiano*. Rome/Bari, 1979.

Shapiro, M., 'On the Aesthetic Attitude in Romanesque Art.' *Art and Thought: Issued in Honor of Dr. Ananda K. Coormaraswamy on the Occasion of His 70th Birthday*, K. Bharatha Iyer (ed.). London, 1937: 130–150.

Shapiro, M., 'Style,' *Anthropology Today*, A.L. Kroeber (ed.). New York, 1963.

Shearman, J., 'Maniera as an Aesthetic Ideal.' *Studies in Western Art. Acts of the 20th International Congress of the History of Art*. Princeton, 1963: 200–221.

Shearman, J., 'Raphael . . . fa il Bramante.' *Studies in Renaissance and Baroque Art, Presented to Anthony Blunt*. London, 1967: 12–17.

Shearman, J., 'Raphael as architect.' *Journal of the Royal Society of Arts*, XCVI (1968): 388–409.

Shelby, L.R., 'The "Secret" of the Medieval Mason.' *Pre-Modern Technology and Science: Studies in Honor of Lynn White Jr*, B.S. Hall and D.C West (eds). Malibu, 1976: 201–219.

Simson, O.G.v., *The Gothic Cathedral*. New York, 1962.

Sirén, O., *China and Gardens of Europe*. New York, 1950.

Smalley, B., *The Study of the Bible in the Middle Ages*. Oxford, 1952.

Smith, Ch. *Architecture and Culture in the Culture of Early Humanism: Ethics, Aesthetics and Eloquence, 1400–1470*. Oxford, 1992.

Sobotta, R., *Michelangelo und der Barockstil*. Berlin, 1933.

Sombart, W., *Luxury and the Rise of Capitalism*. Ann Arbor, 1967.

Sorbelli, A., 'Bibliografia delle edizione.' *Pier de Crescenzi (1233–1321). Studi e documenti*, T. Alfonsi *et al.* (eds). Bologna, 1933: 261–306.

Spencer, J.R., 'Filarete and his Central-Plan Architecture.' *Journal of the Society of Architectural Historians*, XVIII (1958): 10–18.

Spielmann, H., *Andrea Palladio und die Antike*. Munich, 1968.

Spina-Barelli, E., 'Il Lomazzo e il ruolo della personalità psicologiche nella estetica dell'utimo manierismo lombardo.' *Arte Lombarda* III, 2 (1958): 119–124.

Spingarn, J.E., *A History of Literary Criticism in the Renaissance*. New York/London, 1899.

Spitzer, L., 'Classical and Christian Ideas of World Harmony.' *Traditio* II (1944) and III (1945).

Stabile, G., 'Camillo, Giulio.' *Dizionario Biografico degli Italiani*, 17 (1974): 218–230.

Steigmuller, H., 'Lucas Paciuolo. Eine biographische Skizze.' *Zeitschrift für Mathematik und Physik, Historisch-Literarische Abteilung*, XXXIV (1889): 81–102.

Steinmann, E. and Wittkower, R., *Michelangelo Bibliography, 1510–1926*. Leipzig, 1927.

Stephen, L., *The English Utilitarians*. New York, 1968.

Stewering, R., 'The Relationship Between World, Landscape and Polia in the *Hypnerotomachia Poliphili.*' *Word and Image*, 14 (1998): 2–10.

Stewering, R., 'Architectural Representations in the *Hypnerotomachia Poliphili* (Aldus Manutius, 1499).' *Journal of the Society of Architectural Historians*, 59 (2000): 6–25.

Straub, H., *A History of Civil Engineering*. London, 1964.

Summers, D., 'Michelangelo on Architecture.' *Art Bulletin,* LIV (1972): 146–157.

Summers, D., *Michelangelo and the Language of Art*. Princeton, 1981.

Summerson, J.N., *Sir Christopher Wren*. London, 1953.

Summerson, J.N., *The Classical Language of Architecture*. Cambridge, MA, 1963a.

Summerson, J.N., *Architecture in Britain 1530–1830*. London, 1963b.

Szambien, W., *Jean Nicolas Louis Durand, 1760–1834: de l'imitation à la norme*. Paris, 1984.

Szepe, H.K., 'Desire in the Printed Dream of Poliphilo.' *Art History*, 19 (1996): 370–392.

Szepe, H.K., '*Hypnerotomachia Poliphili.*' *Art On Paper*, 4 (2000): 72–73.

Tadgell, C., *Ange-Jacques Gabriel*. London, 1978.

Tafuri, M., *L'Architettura del manierismo nel cinquecento europea*. Rome, 1966.

Tafuri, M., 'L'idea di architettura nella letteratura del manierismo.' *Bollettino del Centro Internazionale di Studi d'Architettura Andrea Palladio*, X (1968).

Tafuri, M., *Teorie e historia dell'Architettura*. Bari, 1968.

Tafuri, M., *Architecture and Utopia: Design and Capitalist Development.* Cambridge, MA, 1976.

Tafuri, M., 'Gli studi vitruviani.' In: C. Cesariano, *Scritti Rinascimentale d'Architettura* (1978): 389–433.

Tafuri, M., 'Ricerca dei paradigmi: progetto, verità, artificio.' *Ricerca del rinascimento.* Torino, 1992: 4–32.

Tafuri, M., *Ricerca del rinascimento*. Torino, 1992.

Tafuri, M., 'Cives esse non licere. Nicolò V e Leon Battista Alberti.' *Ricerca del rinascimento.* Torino, 1992: 33–88.

Tagliabue, G.M., 'Aristotelismo e barocco.' *Retorica e barocco*, E. Castelli (ed.). Rome, 1955: 119–195.

Tarchiani, N., 'Il palazzo mediceo.' *Emporium*, 90 (1939): 77–86.

Tatarkiewicz, W., *History of Aesthetics*, J. Harrell, C. Barrett and D. Petsch (eds). 3 vols. The Hague and Warsaw, 1970–1974.

Taton, R., *L'Enseignement et la diffusion des sciences en France au XVIII siècle*. Paris, 1964.

Tavernor, R., *Palladio and Palladianism*. London, 1991.

Tavernor, R., 'Burlington and Palladio.' *The Architectural Review*, 197 (1995): 9.

Tavernor, R., *On Alberti and the Art of Building*, New Haven, 1999.

Tavernor, R., and Schofield, R. (trans.), *Andrea Palladio: The Four Books on Architecture*. Cambridge, MA, 1997.

Taylor, J., 'El Padre Villalpando (1552–1608) e sus ideas esteticas.' *Academia, annales y boletin de la real academia de San Fernando* (1952).

Taylor, J., 'Introduction.' *Didascalicon*, Hugh of St. Victor. Chicago, 1961.

Taylor, J., 'Architecture and Magic. Consideration of the "Idea" of the Escorial.' *Essays in the History of Architecture, presented to R. Wittkower*, D. Fraser et al. (eds). London, 1967: 81–103.

Taylor, J., 'Hermeticism and Mystical Architecture in the Society of Jesus.' *Baroque Art: the Jesuit Contribution*, R. Wittkower and I.B. Jaffe (eds). New York, 1972: 63–97.

Taylor, R.E., *No Royal Road. Luca Pacioli and his Times*. Chapel Hill, 1942.

Taylor-Leduc, S., 'A New Treatise in Seventeenth-Century Garden History: André Felibien's "Description de la grotte à Versailles".' *Studies in the History of Gardens and Designed Landscapes*, 18 (1998): 35–51.

Temple, N., 'The *Hypnerotomachia Poliphili* as a possible model for topographical interpretations of Rome in the early sixteenth century.' *Word and Image*, 14 (1998): 145–155.

Teyssot, G., 'Cottages et pittoresque: les origines du logement ouvrier en Angleterre.' *Architecture, mouvement, continuité*, 34 (1974): 26–37.

Thieme, T., 'La Geometria di Piazza S. Pietro.' *Palladio*, XXIII (1973): 129–144.

Thoenes, Ch., 'La Regola delli cinque ordini del Vignola.' *Les traités d'architecture de la renaissance*, Guillaume, J. (ed.). Paris, 1988.

Thomas, K., *Religion and the Decline of Magic*. Harmondsworth, 1971.

Tiberghien, F., *Versailles, le chantier de Louis XIV 1662–1715*. Perrin, 2002.

Tigler, P., *Die Architekturtheorie des Filarete*. Berlin, 1963.

Toffanin, G., *La Fine dell'umanesimo*. Milan/Turin/Rome, 1920.

Tolnay, C.D., 'Beiträge zu dem Späten Architektonischen Projekten Michelangelos.' *Jahrbuch der preussischen Kunstsammlungen*, LI (1930): 1–48; LII (1932): 231–253.

Tolnay, C.D., *Michelangelo*. Rome, 1950.

Tolnay, C.D., 'Michelangelo architetto.' *Il Cinquecento*. Florence, 1955.

Tolnay, C.D., *Art and Thought of Michelangelo*. New York, 1964.

Tolnay, C.D., *Michelangelo*. 5 vols. Princeton, 1969–1971.

Treves, M., 'Maniera, History of the Word.' *Marsyas*, I (1941).

Trevor-Roper, H., *Princes and Artists*. Princeton, 1972.

Turner, P.V., 'Claude-Nicolas Ledoux and the *Hypnerotomachia Poliphili*.' *Word and Image*, 14 (1998): 203–214.

Tuveson, E.L., 'Space, Deity and the Natural Sublime.' *Modern Language Quarterly*, XII (1951): 20–38.

Tuveson, E.L., *The Imagination as a Means of Grace: Locke and the Aesthetics of Romanticism*. Berkeley, 1960.

Tzonis, A., *Towards a Non-Oppressive Environment*. Boston, 1972.

Tzonis, A., 'Un Mémoire sur les Hôpitaux de Condorcet.' *Revue du Dix-Huitième Siècle*, 9 (1977): 109–114.

Tzonis, A., 'Il bastione comme mentalità.' *La Città el mura*, C. de Seta and J. Le Goff (eds). Rome, 1989.

Tzonis, A. 'L'Académie Royale d'Architecture.' *El Arte las Cortes del Siglo XVIII Ancien Regime.'* Madrid, 1989.

Tzonis, A., 'From Shadow Pyramid to the Pyramid of Fire.' *Arte Lombarda*, 1993.

Tzonis, A. 'Lines of Vision, Lines of Fire. The Role of Analogy and Image Cognition in Designing the Renaissance Bastion.' *Das Bauwerk und die Stadt*, Wolfgang Boehm (ed.). Vienna, 1994.

Tzonis, A., 'Power and Representation.' *Design Book Review*, 34, Fall (1994): 32–36.

Tzonis, A. and Lefaivre, L., 'The Mechanical vs the Divine Body.' *Journal of Architectural Education*, Sept. (1975).

Tzonis, A. and Lefaivre, L., 'La Géometrie du Sentiment.' *Le Dix-Huitième Siècle*, 9 (1977): 62–73.

Tzonis, A. and Lefaivre, L., 'The Question of Autonomy in Architecture.' *Harvard Architectural Review*, 3 (1984a).

Tzonis, A. and Lefaivre, L., The Mechanization of Architecture.' *Via* (1984b).

Tzonis, A. and Lefaivre, L., 'Critical Regionalism Today.' *The Critical Landscape*, A. Graffland (ed.). Rotterdam, 1996.

Tzonis, A. *et al.*, *Systèmes conceptuels de l'architecture en France: 1650 à 1800*. Cambridge, MA, 1975.

Tzonis, A. *et al.*, *Bibliographie de langue française sur l'architecture de 1500 à 1800*. Montréal, 1982.

Ukolova, V., *The Last of the Romans*. Moscow, 1989.

Ulivi, F., 'F. Milizia scrittore.' *Paragone*, III (1942): 3–18.

Vagnetti, L., *L'Architetto nella storia di occidente*. Florence, 1973.

Vagnetti, L. and Marcuzzi, L., 'Per una coscienza Vitruviana.' *Studi e documenti di architettura*, 8 (1978): 11–184.

Van den Berghe, O., 'Le temple du Graal.' *Annales archéologiques*, XXVII (1857).

Venturi, A., *Storia dell'arte italiana*. 8 vols. Milan, 1901–1938.

Venturi, L., *History of Art Criticism*. New York, 1936.

Verga, E., *Bibliografia vinciana 1493–1930*. Milan, 1931; New York, 1970.

Vidler, A., 'Asylums of Libertinage: Sade, Fourier, Ledoux.' *Lotus International*, 44 (1984): 28–40.

Vidler, A., *Claude-Nicolas Ledoux: Architecture and Social Reform at the End of the Ancien Régime*. Cambridge, MA, 1990.

Viollet-le-Duc, M., *Dictionnaire raisonné de l'architecture française du XIe au XVIe siècle*. 10 vols. Paris, 1858–1868.

Vogel, J., 'Bramante e Raffael.' *Kunstwissenschaftlichen Studien*, IV (1910).

Vogt, A.M., *Boullées Newton-Denkmal. Sakralbau und Kugelidee*. Basle/Stuttgart, 1969.

Volkmann, H., *Giovanni Battista Piranesi. Architekt und Graphiker*. Berlin, 1965.

Waddy, P., 'Michelangelo Buonarotti the Younger, Sprezzatura and Palazzo Barberini.' *Architettura* (1975): 101–122.

Wagner, N., *Morelly, le méconnu des Lumières*. Paris, 1978.

Waldron, J., *'Nonsense Upon Stilts': Bentham, Burke, and Marx on the Rights of Man*. London, New York, 1987.

Walker, D.P., *Spiritual and Demonic Magic from Ficino to Campanella*. London, 1958.

Walpole, R.N., 'The Pélerinage de Charlemagne.' *Romance Philology*, VIII (1955).

Warburg, A., 'Der Baubeginn des Palazzo Medici.' *Gesammelte Schriften*. Leipzig/Berlin, 1932.

Watelet, C.H. and Hogarth, W. (eds), *William Hogarth's Translation of Watelet on Grace*. Chicago, 1983.

Watkins, R., *Humanism and Liberty: Writings on Freedom from Fifteenth-Century Florence*. Columbia, SC, 1978.

Weber, M., *The Protestant Ethic and the Spirit of Capitalism*. New York, 2000.

Weinberg, B., *A History of Literary Criticism in The Italian Renaissance*. Chicago, 1961.

Weiss, R., 'A New Francesco Colonna.' *Italian Studies*, XVI (1961): 78–83.

Weiss, R., *The Renaissance Discovery of Classical Antiquity*. New York, 1973.

Weller, A.S., *Francesco di Giorgio 1493–1501*. Chicago, 1943.

Westfall, C.W., *In This Most Perfect Paradise: Alberti, Nicholas V, and the Invention of Conscious Urban Planning in Rome, 1447–55*. University Park, 1974.

White, J., *The Birth and Rebirth of Pictoral Space*. London, 1967.

White Rob Lynn, JR. *Medieval Technology and Social Change,* New York, 1962.

Wiebenson, D., 'L'Architecture Terrible and the Jardin Anglo-Chinois.' *Journal of the Society of Architectural Historians*, XXVII, May (1968).

Wiebenson, D., *Sources of Greek Revival*. London, 1969.

Wiebenson, D., *The Picturesque Garden in France*. Princeton, 1978.

Wiebenson, D., 'Four Hundred Centuries of Literature on Palladio.' *Journal of the Society of Architectural Historians*, XXXIX, October (1980): 224–241.

Wiebenson, D., *Architectural Theory and Practice from Alberti to Ledoux*. Chicago, 1982.

Wiebenson, D., 'A Document of Social Change: The Small House Publication.' *English Art and Aesthetics in the 18th century*, R. Cohen (ed.). Los Angeles, 1983.

Wiebenson, D. (ed.), *The Mark J. Millard Architectural Collection, Vol. I French Books, Sixteenth through Nineteenth Centuries*. Washington and New York, 1993.

Wiebenson, D. and Baines, C., *French Books. Sixteenth through Nineteenth Centuries*. Washington, 1993.

Wilinsky, S., 'Sebastiano Serlio ai lettori dell'III e IV Libro dell'Architettura.' *Bollettino del Centro Internazionale di Studi d'Architettura Andrea Palladio*, III (1961): 57–69.

Wilinsky, S., 'Cesare Cesariano elogia la geometria architettonica della Cattedrale di Milano.' *Il Duomo di Milano. Atti del Congresso intenazionale. Septembre 1969*, M.L. Gatti Perer (ed.). Milan, 1969.

Wilkinson, K., 'Renaissance Treatises on Military Architecture and the Science of Mechanics.' *Les Traités d'architecture de la renaissance*, Guillaume, J. (ed.). Paris, 1988.

Williams, R., *The Country and the City*. London, 1975.

Wilton-Ely, J., 'Introduction.' *Giovanni Battista Piranesi. The Polemical Works*. Westmead, 1972.

Wilton-Ely, J., *The Mind and Art of Giovanni Battista Piranesi*. London, 1978.

Wind, E., *Pagan Mysteries of the Renaissance*. Harmondsworth, 1958.

Wittgenstein, L., *Philosophical Investigations,* Cambridge, 1958.

Wittkower, R., 'Piranesi's Parere sull'Architettura.' *Journal of the Warburg Institute*, II (1938): 147ff.

Wittkower, R., 'Zuccari and John Wood of Bath.' *Journal of the Warburg and Courtault Institutes*, VI (1943): 220ff.

Wittkower, R., 'Brunelleschi and Proportion in Perspective.' *Journal of the Warburg and Courtault Institutes*, XVI (1953): 257–291.

Wittkower, R., *Architectural Principles in the Age of Humanism*. London, 1962.

Wittkower, R., *Art and Architecture in Italy 1600–1750*. Harmondsworth, 1973.

Wittkower, R., *Palladio and English Palladianism*. London, 1974.

Wittkower, R., 'Pianesi's Architectural Creed.' *Studies in the Italian Baroque*. London, 1975.

Wolf, C., *Histoire de l'Observatoire de Paris de la Fondation à 1793*. Paris, 1902.

Wolf, N., *Giovanni Battista Piranesi: der Römische Circus: die Arena als Weltsymbol*. Frankfurt, 1997.

Wölfflin, H., *Renaissance and Baroque*. Ithaca, 1966.

Wolters, W., 'Sebastiano Serlio e il suo contributo alla villa veneziana prima del Palladio.' *Bollettino del Centro Internazionale di Studi d'Architettura Andrea Palladio*, XI (1969).

Wood, T.E.B., *The Word 'Sublime' and its Context, 1650–1760*. The Hague, 1972.

Woodfield, R., 'Introduction.' *The Analysis of Beauty*, W. Hogarth (ed.). London, 1971.

Worsley, G., *Classical Architecture in Britain: the Heroic Age*. New Haven, 1995.

Yates, F.A., *The French Academies of the Sixteenth Century*. London, 1947.

Yates, F.A., *The Art of Memory*. Harmondsworth, 1969.

Yates, F.A., *Theater of the World*. Chicago, 1969.

Yourcenar, M., *Carceri d'Invenzione: les prisons imaginaires de Gian Battista Piranesi*. Monaco, 1961.

Yu, Li, *Number-based Design Reasoning Systems*. Delft, 1994.

Zangheri, L., 'La Figura, l'opere, l'ambiente di Bartolommeo Vanni.' *Avvertimenti e discorsi*, B. Vanni (ed.). Florence, 1977: 9–29.

Zarncke, F., 'Der Graltempel. Vorstudie zu einer Ausgabe des Jüngeren Titurel.' *Abhandlungen der Königlichen Sächsischen Akademie der Wissenschaften*, XVII (1879): 373ff.

Zarucchi, J.M., *Perrault's Morals for Moderns*. New York, 1985.

Zaugg, R., Lukinovich, A. and Zaugg, M., *De la peinture de Leon Battista Alberti*. Geneva, 1983.

Zorzi, G., *I disegni delle antichità di Andrea Palladio*. Venice, 1958.

Zorzi, G., *Le opere pubbliche e i palazzi privati di Andrea Palladio*. Venice, 1965.

Zorzi, G., *Le chiese e i ponti di Andrea Palladio*. Venice, 1967.

Zorzi, G., *Le ville e i teatri di Andrea Palladio*. Venice, 1968.

Zoubov, V.P., 'Leon Battista Alberti et les Auteurs du Moyen Age.' *Mediaeval and Renaissance Studies*, 4 (1958).

Zoubov, V.P., 'Leon-Baptiste Alberti et Leonardo da Vinci.' *Raccolta Vinciana*, XVIII (1960): 1–14.

Zoubov, V.P., 'Vitruve et ses commentateurs du XVIe siècle.' *La Science au seizième siècle. Colloque internationale de Royaumont*. Paris, 1960: 67–91.

Index of names

Index of names

Index of names

Subject index

Index of cities

eBooks – at www.eBookstore.tandf.co.uk

A library at your fingertips!

eBooks are electronic versions of printed books. You can store them on your PC/laptop or browse them online.

They have advantages for anyone needing rapid access to a wide variety of published, copyright information.

eBooks can help your research by enabling you to bookmark chapters, annotate text and use instant searches to find specific words or phrases. Several eBook files would fit on even a small laptop or PDA.

NEW: Save money by eSubscribing: cheap, online access to any eBook for as long as you need it.

Annual subscription packages

We now offer special low-cost bulk subscriptions to packages of eBooks in certain subject areas. These are available to libraries or to individuals.

For more information please contact webmaster.ebooks@tandf.co.uk

We're continually developing the eBook concept, so keep up to date by visiting the website.

www.eBookstore.tandf.co.uk